# LEGEND AND BELIEF

# LEGEND
# AND
Dialectics of a Folklore Genre
# BELIEF

# Linda Dégh

INDIANA UNIVERSITY PRESS
BLOOMINGTON AND INDIANAPOLIS

Publication of this book is made possible in part with the assistance of a Challenge Grant from the National Endowment for the Humanities, a federal agency that supports research, education, and public programming in the humanities.

This book is a publication of

Indiana University Press
601 North Morton Street
Bloomington, IN 47404-3797 USA

http://iupress.indiana.edu

*Telephone orders*   800-842-6796
*Fax orders*   812-855-7931
*Orders by e-mail*   iuporder@indiana.edu

The paper used in this publication meets the minimum requirements of American National Standard for Information Sciences — Permanence of Paper for Printed Library Materials, ANSI Z39.48-1984.

Manufactured in the United States of America

**Library of Congress Cataloging-in-Publication Data**
Dégh, Linda.
    Legend and belief : dialectics of a folklore genre / Linda Dégh.
        p.   cm.
    Includes bibliographical references and index.
    ISBN 0-253-33929-4 (cl : alk. paper)
        1. Legends. 2. Urban folklore. 3. Belief and doubt.   I. Title.

GR78 .D44 2001
398 — dc21
                                                            00-054014

1   2   3   4   5      06   05   04   03   02   01

# CONTENTS

# ACKNOWLEDGMENTS

This book should not have taken so long to write, and I must apologize for my tardiness. My husband, Andrew Vázsonyi (theater critic, author of novels, short stories, and children's literature, doctor of jurisprudence, aestheticist, philosopher, analytical psychologist, linguist, semiotician, and self-made folklorist to whom I owe thanks for teaching me how to become a folklorist) and I made preliminary preparations to write this book through brainstorming sessions that resulted in six co-authored theoretical papers between 1969 and 1983. Our arguments were sharpened through fierce debates. Billy, our English foxhound, disappeared when he heard loud voices; to make him come back, we had to convince him that we were not fighting. Unfortunately, I could not resist temptation and strayed away to other folklore matters that required less hard thinking and less discipline. Andrew died in December 1986, leaving me with a heap of handwritten notes that I could not read, and an outline of chapters that I did not follow. In writing now I am relying on ideas he wrote in a small notebook and on our fieldwork notes and diaries. I could not have written this book without him.

I want to express my gratitude to the many people with whom I spent many long hours in discussion and without whom I could not have succeeded.

First, I thank the folk narrative specialists, my teachers, colleagues, and fellow travelers: Lutz Röhrich, Hermann Bausinger, Rudolf Schenda, Utz Jeggle, Ingeborg Weber-Kellermann, Max Lüthi, Lauri Honko, Juha Pentikäinen, Bengt af Klintberg, Carl-Herman Tillhagen, Bengt Holbek, Alan Dundes, Donald Ward, Richard M. Dorson, Jan Brunvand, Ronald Baker, Gary Alan Fine, Dan Ben-Amos, and Henry Glassie.

Second, I thank my friendly and tolerant foes, with my apologies for being so argumentative. I will be always grateful to them for their writings and criticism which made me think, and rethink: Bill Ellis, Bill Nicolaisen, and Gillian Bennett.

Third, I thank my former students who turned out to become my colleagues, and who helped me learn how to teach and keep them happy in spite of the heavy load of work I imposed on them. I am very proud of their perseverance. We experienced and explored an unknown new field together — my endeavor would not have been possible without their advice: Carl Lindahl, Joe Goodwin, Sylvia Grider, Janet Langlois, Kay Stone, Elizabeth Tucker, Christine Goldberg, Sabina Magliocco, and Linda Spetter. But why do I write Linda's name as the last when she belongs up front, right after Andrew? Because from the moment of her arrival to Bloomington, with a recommendation of her teacher, Professor Warren Walker, she has been my student. She took all my classes and soon I discovered her superior qualities and potential for becoming a true professional folklorist. Her devotion and loyalty to folklore were never shaken in the current hostile climate which threatens its survival. She became my student assistant, and my previous two books are proof of our harmonious collaboration as author and editor. Now she is a Ph.D. in folklore, and this book should be a strong statement on behalf of her application for a job in a solid folklore department — she might be among the very few who can rescue the discipline from oblivion.

Last, but not least, I thank my computer assistants Amy Goldenberg and Alex Tsow who helped me keep my sanity when my whimsical computer threatened to erase the pages it disliked.

# LEGEND AND BELIEF

# The Topic, Purpose, and Destination of This Book

1.

## A View from the Tower

As an old anecdote goes, a German tax-law professor, known for his tricky exam questions, once asked a candidate, "If you climbed up this church tower, what would you see down below?"

The quavering, puzzled answer was "Houses . . . people . . . vehicles."

"Wrong," retorted the professor, evidently a narrow-minded specialist. "You would see subjects and objects of taxation."

In the same vein, should a similarly narrow-minded folklorist ask, "What would we see from a tower overlooking contemporary Western society?" she would be most satisfied with this answer: "I see legends wherever I look. I see them in profusion, far from declining or weakening as some would believe."

The A-plus student should also add: "I see legends vigorously resisting changing times, defying the prognosis of traditional folklorists. I see them proliferating with increasing speed. They appear characteristic, indeed, determinant, of individual human thoughts, acts, and mass movements."

Exploiting the anecdote about the meticulous law scholar and inventing a new one about the scrupulous folklorist, we actually drew a parallel between a legal and a folkloristic concept. The two were brought together here by their metaphoric similarity. The legend process, meaning the life-history of the legend, and the legal process — with its lawsuits and legal actions — have many things in common. Both exhibit polarization of opinions, viewpoints, and interests. Latent or manifest dialectics is an inherent part of most legal relations as well as all legends (Dégh and Vázsonyi 1978). Like the plaintiff and the defendant in a legal process, advocates of belief and non-belief face each other in the course of the legend process. But the antagonists in the latter are much less inclined to compromise than those in the former. Why? Perhaps because

1

the debate in a court of law tackles the affairs of individuals, and is generally limited to personal problems; legends, on the other hand, treat universal concerns. They deal with the most crucial questions of the world and human life. They attack these questions: Is the order of the world really as we learned to know it? Can we expect that life will run its course as we were taught it should? Do we know all the forces that regulate the universe and our life, or are there hidden dimensions that can divert the causal, rational flow of things? And if there are unknown forces, can they be identified, changed, avoided, or exploited to our benefit?

Evidently, the legend touches upon the most sensitive areas of our existence, and its manifest forms cannot be isolated as simple and coherent stories. Rather, legends appear as products of conflicting opinions, expressed in conversation. They manifest in discussions, contradictions, additions, implementations, corrections, approvals, and disapprovals during some or all phases of their transmission, from their inception through various courses of elaboration, variation, decline, and revitalization. Anyone who has ever observed a live, naturally emerging, spontaneous legend-telling event and paid attention to the voices of all of the participants and contributors would realize what a mistake it would be to isolate the manifest texts from their situational and sociocultural environment. Text without its performance context would be as meaningless as an artist's deliberate selection of one single voice from a polyphonic musical composition, ignoring the rest.

In regard to its conversational, dialectic-polyphonic nature, the legend, more than any other folklore genre, can make sense only within the crossfire of controversies. Even if participants occasionally do not seem to be in fierce disagreement with the legend's proposition, the commonly known opposing opinion of society at large always makes its presence felt. When the teller makes his point about an extranormal condition, he argues against the known contrary opinion; he formulates his story with the anticipation that many people would argue against it if they were present. When, for example, a Pentecostal preacher translates into human language the Lord's message sent by "tongues" through one of his devotees endowed by the Holy Spirit, he is supported wholeheartedly by his congregation of believers who know very well the disbelieving nature of non-members.

The eyewitness, reporting the disappearance of the Archangel Gabriel from his car seat with seatbelt buckle unopened, after the angel had delivered a prophetic message, must be prepared for the incredulous smile of doubters. Every statement that counters notions held as rational and authentic, or beliefs that are canonized and therefore quasi-rational, embodies its own built-in dialectics. This built-in anticipation of contradiction is the main identifier of the legend, setting it apart from other folklore genres. No one in his or her right mind would stop a joke-teller and ask for the identification of the two traveling salesmen in the joke and ascertain if they really made the trip from Omaha to Lincoln. No one would expect the märchen-teller to explain how the seven-headed dragon could be domesticated into a docile husband by the golden-haired princess he had abducted. In other words, disputability is not only a feature of the legend, it is its very essence, its raison d'être, its goal. The legend demands answers — but not necessarily resolutions — to the most mysterious, critical, and least-answerable questions of life. The narrator presents a concrete case that exemplifies, illustrates, documents the crucial point for reflection and deliberation, appealing to the listeners, and inviting them to comment.

Still more similarities can be found between the practice of law and folklore. In democratic systems, rules of law approximate the performance requirements of folklore, particularly the performance of legends. These rules are in abidance with expectations of society, follow its value principles, and are conditioned upon its approval. The practical efficacy of the legend rests on the dispute. In law, as in legend, the dispute presupposes the evidence according to adequate evidentiary rules, with the testimony of witnesses as a most convincing proof. In law, "testimony" (the witness deposition) is often crucial in proving one's case, whereas in legend the corollary proofs are told in the first-person "memorate" and the third-person "fabulate."

There exists strong as well as weak and less convincing evidence both in the court of law and in the small or large community that deliberates the credibility of the legend. In both forums, comments such as "I've heard of it" or "I have been told" — typical of fabulates — are not strongly impressive. But the eyewitness confession, "I saw it with my own eyes" or "it happened to me," which is most typical in memorate-shaped legends, carries much more weight.

We also consider the "character witness" in both processes. Just as a witness in court could claim, "We were next-door neighbors and I knew him to be an honest man," a legend proponent could suggest, in front of his or her audience, "I heard it from my grandfather who was not superstitious and never told a lie." The burden of proof, a rule of the trial procedure, is valid for the law court as well as for the legend process. If the honest grandfather of the legend-teller saw the ghost with his own eyes, the teller has offered formal proof that at a certain place and at a certain time there was a ghost — and, consequently, that ghosts exist. If, on the other hand, someone with a contrary opinion refers to his own equally trustworthy grandfather who has not seen the ghost, that doesn't prove that ghosts do not exist; it only means that at another place, and at another time, there was no ghost.

Other analogies between the legend and the law process could also be made. In the court of law, some may not consider nonbelievers to be competent, dependable witnesses because they do not fear punishment in the hereafter for false testimony. The confession of skeptics not controlled by numinous threat is therefore less dependable than that of believers, particularly *in rebus fidei*, in matters of faith, with respect to supernatural subjects. It seems that ghosts and legendary encounters in general thrive under the protection of law because their extranormal statements and implications require proof and provoke the less convincing counterproof. This might be one reason why, symbolically speaking, down below the tower where more and more subjects and objects of taxation abound today, more and more legends inundate the premises.

## Legend as Power and How We Deal with It

This book is about the legends of our time. Most legends are about spirits, witches, demons, monsters, lunatics, criminals, extraterrestrials, and abilities of certain humans who are empowered with precognition and magic that can identify these evil forces and protect us from their destructive power. These legend subjects provoke people to take a stand. Thus, I suppose the reader may be curious to find out which side is taken by this book. For or against? On the side of the believers or the skeptics?

The answer is neither one nor the other. This discussion does not ask how much truth there is in any of the extranormal doctrines — be it astral projection or out-of-body experience — that, according to current occult establishments, play an increasingly important role in our daily lives. Why not? Is this stance a result of indifference? Uncertainty? Caution? The answer is, none of these. This book does not explore these occult phenomena in and of themselves but rather examines the world of the legend that surrounds them. And, for our dealings with the occult and related extraordinary legend occurrences, we will apply the more neutral and general term *extranormal*.

Widespread coffee-table parlance based on a dated and fallacious folkloristic definition identifies the legend as an objectively untrue story that is believed to be true. However, as far as legends are concerned, it is irrelevant whether they are true. Most likely, some of them are true, others are erroneous, and others are deliberate deceptions, although in most cases such distinctions cannot be made with certainty. The truth of a story neither qualifies nor disqualifies it as a legend. In keeping with our rule of neutrality, we will call extranormal stories legends, whether they are objectively true or not.

In other matters, this book will not appear completely neutral. Following the trail of the legend, we will have to enter alien territories — transient genres, where legends do not seem to be legends at all. They may be narrated as tales, anecdotes, personal stories, practical jokes, or rumors — the same story may appear in any of these forms. On our quest we will have to walk the slippery paths of other disciplines such as sociology, psychology, semiotics, theology, criminology, cultural history, literature, and what are known summarily as the occult sciences. We will also transcend traditional confines of folklore, and find that the characteristics of folklore — repetition, imitation, and patterns of dissemination — are similar to those of other social phenomena such as fashions, crazes, or "snowballing."

Folklorists have been long aware of the fact that traditional folklore genres are attractive empty formulas (Honko 1984), to be filled with meaning at will. In this fashion, throughout its history folklore has been used and abused, for both creative and destructive purposes (see, for example, Greverus 1978 and Lixfeld 1994). We must recognize what an important role the creation and dissemination of legends play in the society that created and disseminated them. Legend, as an ideology-sensitive genre par excellence, is a readily available instrument in modern society, in which it plays a leading role in the development and maintenance of a "culture of fear." The legend, even if it is not founded on reality, can create reality. The witch-hunt crazes of the sixteenth and seventeenth centuries could even be revitalized at the end of the twentieth century, destroying the lives of hundreds of innocent people (Loftus and Ketcham 1994). Thus, the legend has power, the nature of which is unknown and dangerous. And defense against this potential danger is advisable, as it can be used as a weapon in the wrong hands.

Alas, a nonproliferation treaty cannot be signed. Not even a modest "legend control" can be suggested. The product is too much in demand, and the lobby too powerful. I myself, like some of the readers, may wonder whether ghosts are desirable playmates for children and whether it is advisable to invite Dracula as a permanent guest into our homes.

For a while it seemed that modern society had condemned folklore to death, depriving it of its *Lebensraum* or natural habitat. As a matter of fact, the classic forms of oral narration for a while had disappeared from the menu of home entertainment in the Western world. No more fireside storytelling — even mothers found it more convenient to turn on the television for a Disney cartoon than to retell one of the Grimms' tales. And yet the magic of the tale, and the pseudo-reality of the legend, found its way to modern media. Television, for example, beyond programs for children, has had a leading role in disseminating tale motifs through all of its programs, including commercial advertisements. Mass media in general has helped the legend attain a never-anticipated proliferation, reaching out to unaccounted-for folk masses, gaining empowerment beyond imagination.

This extreme snowballing of the legend is symptomatic, projecting what we may identify as the irrationality explosion that characterizes our society's mindscape. This may sound somewhat enigmatic, but there is plenty of time to explain. Chapter by chapter, discussing the legend as a form of traditional folklore — as a socially transmitted text, shaped and performed by individuals for their specific audiences — we will argue and document the intensification of its authority as a means of rationalizing the irrational.

Right now, we have to clarify one thing: Why is it so important to distinguish the tale from the legend? We have no reason to go into professional details and comparative-classificatory exercises, because everyone knows the difference between the two: The tale cannot be true, the legend can be. If someone starts the tale with "once upon a time" it will be clear what follows: pure fiction. Still, or just because of that, we can identify with the hero or heroine, and we can enjoy his victory over the monster or her triumph over the greedy sisters and applaud the happy marriage at the end. This "temporary suspension of disbelief" is the key to the delight we feel when we attend an artistic tale performance. The legend, which is not performed with the intent to be artistic, tends toward the opposite direction: Its teller claims to be telling reality by reference to his or her own, or somebody else's, experience. Thus, the tale represents invention, the legend represents knowledge.

Children in the magic phase of their mental development still believe in the truth of the tale; however, quite soon, assisted by reasonable adults, they will be able to distinguish fantasy from reality. Thus, adults who still believe in the tooth fairy or who are scared of vampire attacks at a full moon need psychiatric help. But the fantastic world of the legend cannot be separated from the real world — rather, it is completely absorbed by it. The supernatural, the unexplainable, all the situations and actions that differ from the norm happen here on earth, in our everyday lives, and they furnish the topic of our legends. From literature (ranging from comics to scholarly exegeses) to television shows, movies, and the Internet, we have many uninterrupted sources that furnish us with information and evidentiary documents. The irrationality of believers is further supported, normalized, and authenticated by clubs, national and international organizations, scientific institutions, even churches. The dimensions of this condition that marks "the end of rational consensus," according to Gershon Legman, are frightening indeed.

The question arises at this point: What then is rational? Are we certain that the noises in old houses, the sights, screams, footsteps, the stopping and starting of old clocks, rocking chairs, and music boxes are not caused by restless spirits? No, we are not. Is it beyond doubt that the space aliens who visit our earth do not speak German, as one of the informants tells us? We have no such proof. Is it absolutely impossible that Mrs. Darvas's red goblet, which she received from a favorite aunt overseas, cracked in her curio cabinet at precisely the moment when she died (Dégh and Vázsonyi 1978: 253–272)? We don't know. And can we seriously doubt the news report of two twin brothers who died the same second, hit by the same stellar radiation on two different continents? Not really. Actually, we cannot even doubt authoritatively the amazing information provided by a reliable clairvoyant that my husband and I lived our first lives in ancient Greece, in good friendship with the philosopher Socrates.

How do we dare then to state that such stories are irrational? How do we dare to relegate such statements — supported by hundreds, if not thousands, of eyewitness testimonies and endorsements by respectable scholars and ancient philosophers — to the realm of legends?

My personal belief in the truth or untruth of the extranormal phenomena contained in these stories has nothing to do with their perceived irrationality. Belief — anyone's belief — does not determine the rationality of a story, or even its truth. After all, the history of knowledge and convictions is nothing else but the history of errors.

Giving public talks on Halloween has not only given me the opportunity to conduct field ethnography, but also has taught me many lessons. For example, I once was invited to an Indianapolis Methodist couple's evening. Following the relaxed spaghetti dinner, I was ready to address the audience, but before I could utter my opening words, a woman raised her hand to speak. She pointed her finger at me and asked, "Are you a witch?" and "Do you believe in the supernatural?" I had not prepared for such questions, but after a moment of panic I managed to stay composed. The answer I gave her, as honest as I could be, would become my routine response, and I have since repeated it many times. "No, I am not a witch, I am an academic professional, deeply interested in supernatural belief. So far, there is no scientific evidence of the existence of spirits, just as there is no scientific evidence of their nonexistence. This makes me tell you that I remain undecided until convincing data changes my opinion either way. But my professional goal does not include finding out the truth." Audience members, once relieved of their inhibitions in this way, rewarded me for my talks with stories they knew.

Rationality is a democratic concept, and is therefore variable, flexible. Rationality is the consensus of the majority; it is the ruling opinion, right or wrong. From the viewpoint of society, psychologically speaking, those who agree with the majority exhibit different attitudes from those who disagree. There is no value judgment in this statement, as both attitudes may be useful and honest. After all, just as it is true that the majority is not always right, it is also true that the truth is not always on the side of the minority. Social norms, by all means, are determined by the majority; thus, if our contemporary society's leading voice decides that UFOs cannot assist us in reaching the pearly gates of heaven, then those who followed Heaven's Gate evangelists Bo and

Peep to the designated site of the UFO departure acted irrationally from the viewpoint of society (see chapter 3).

But if there is an "irrationality explosion" in operation, it means that there is no social agreement in the conceptualization of what is rational. Can we speak of a socially sanctioned common opinion?

Let us imagine a choral ensemble of a hundred singers. Out of the hundred, fifty follow the baton of the conductor and sing the well-rehearsed melody of Beethoven's "Ode to Joy" in unison, while the rest, broken up into smaller groups of eight, six, two, or even single individuals tune in and join the choir singing their own diverse songs, in different rhythms, pitches, levels, and tempos. From this bizarre ensemble of unrecognizable tunes, only the "Ode to Joy" prevails. It would probably sound clear through the rumble, even if only forty or thirty people were in unison. In this fashion, the majority voice of society sounds the clearest, and the rest of the voices amount to nothing more than a cacophony of melodies that supersede, distort, cover, and confuse each other. What is common among them? Surprisingly little. What does UFOlogy have to do with Satanism? Or the evil eye with reincarnation? Or the Bermuda Triangle with dowsing? Or haunted houses with numerology, second-sight and ESP with voodoo, or astrology and palmistry with parapsychology? These are merely a random sampling from a gigantic and still growing directory of irrational establishments that initiate new Messiahs at each calendar turn. What they have in common is only that they are different from the normal, the average. They play different tunes from the "rational society," that is, the majority society that regards itself as rational. The stories of these outside-the-mainstream people present, elaborate, illustrate, and explain extranormal themes that we call legends. This does not mean that one needs to belong to such an establishment to be a bearer of legends — anyone in the mainstream may become an occasional bearer without commitment to one special area.

There were times in which people could distinguish fantasy from reality, artistic imagination from everyday life. These were "adult times," fabulous times that could cope with magic. Our time is increasingly becoming a legend-time in which reality intermingles with unreality, without the capability of discriminating one from the other. We live in a society that regards beliefs, daydreams, and hallucinations as feasible suggestions that can turn into reality. This is what we learn from legends and headline news.

They intermingle . . . but why? People do the mixing artfully and sometimes purposefully. Legman had good reason to write in 1949, "Violence in America is business . . . and everybody is in it, either as a peddler or as a consumer"; his thesis applies even more to irrationalism. But whereas violence is being fought fiercely in theory and somewhat less successfully in practice, hardly any attention has been paid to irrationalism — to my knowledge hardly anyone has proposed protection against it. Although it seems unlikely that this is the real and deepest reason of the irrationality explosion, one cannot help but ponder and reflect.

The weakening of the sense of reality is by no means caused by peddlers, just as the merchandising of drugs does not cause drug addiction. Even so, drug peddlers are responsible for much of the damage inflicted on an increasing number of consumers. Like narcotics and other means of escapism, irrationality is also disseminated by its own network of peddlers, resembling that of the operation of drug cartels. There we find drug lords, entrepreneurs, and addicted victims. And here we find the hierarchy of powerful mass media entrepreneurs as the creators and sustainers of the legend climate. There we find the diverse categories of professional, voluntary, and amateur proponent-pushers. And here we find the creative freelance tellers, who alternate in the role of narrating and listening, and whose negotiations produce and contextualize legends. These legend-tellers and legend-supporting personalities are listed in chapter 4.

## The Sources, Corpus, and Nature of This Study

This monographic study of the legend as a folklore genre is based primarily on intensive field ethnography, archive and library research, and rigorous text and context analysis. This book describes and interprets the legend as it has been, and as it currently is being, recognized in the Western world, in Europe and North America: a representative, viable traditional product of Western civilization. I am aware that these legends have been transported to other continents by Western colonizers and settlers who communicated them to the natives. I also know that, more recently, the mass media–enhanced cultural globalization of our universe has relayed massive doses of the latest crops of legends as novelties to other continents, but in this discussion I will not take them into consideration. Although the units in Thompson's *Motif-Index of Folk-Literature* prove the universality of legend episodes, the *Elementargedanken* (elementary ideas) of humankind are too vague and cannot be used for in-depth analysis of culture-specific comprehension. Cultures rooted in entirely different systems of cognition may interpret the extranormal cargo differently. Thus, to reach a feasible conclusion, I have to stay within the cultural space that generated legends originally from early European mythical-magical ideologies; these origins support a relatively homogeneous body of texts, rooted in similar sociopolitical and religio-ideological systems.

I was guided in my quest by pursuing Krohn and Aarne's folklore methodology, and probing into Erixon, Schwietering, Redfield, and Arensberg's ideas of community study. I also found useful the Boasian anthropologist's approaches, with collaborating analytical psychologist's approaches to personality study, and the Köhler and Bolte–inspired trend of German comparative philology.

Gyula Ortutay's pioneering work deserves special mention because it turned folkloristics into an important modern humanistic discipline. The classic Russian approach to the study of creative folk artists, as articulated by Asadowskij, was ingeniously transformed into a new school of folklore research by Ortutay (Dégh 1995: 7–29). Setting the foundation for a new focus on human creativity in performance, Ortutay chose to center on the spontaneous utterance of the performer, performed along the line of long-term convention and shaped by simultaneous audience reaction, resulting in the formulation of new, socially relevant messages. His ethnographic observations lifted the discipline of folklore from the narrow confines of archaic European villages and opened the way for folklorists to follow the exodus of the feudal folk into the technologically efficient industrial world. In this new world, folk groups reassemble, continue where they have left off, and multiply under diverse titles and excuses. The causes and concerns that bring folk groups together have not changed, although many forms of folklore lost their relevance and disappeared without a trace.

This, however, is not new; it has happened in the past, even if folklorists were not particularly interested in the folklore process as it is decisively governed by historical events. As my research attests, technological change, urbanization, and massive waves of migration did not eradicate folklore and did not put folklorists out of business. On the contrary, these changes helped folklore to proliferate and diversify, filling new needs of new folk groups. Folklorists of the past were not particularly interested in the folklore process; but in view of the increasing need for their expertise, modern folklorists must update their education to keep themselves competent and abreast of new developments.

The legend is among the reproduced genres that has found the most effective conduits to keep blossoming. I began collecting legends early, during my student years, when they were commonly known as "superstitious stories" or "belief stories" and were easily accessible in traditional peasant communities of Europe and geographically isolated settlements in North America. My primary interest focused on village storytellers and their magic tales, but I discovered early that the ideological foundation of these tales is identical with the magical reality base of legends. In fact, the religious worldview, which in a desacralized, objectivated form laid the foundation of magic tales, was the fuel that kept legends thriving. The two genres were linked together, like night and day, presenting two functionally contradictory views of the world: delightful fictions under the sun, tormenting nightmare during the hours of darkness. Like the didactic narratives that support an identical religious ritual and mythology, magic tales and legends teach diverse lessons by the diverse actions of identical dramatis personae. The witches, devils, monsters, fairies, dwarves, werewolves, and vampires of the folktale do not personally frighten the listener as they do when they appear in legends. The difference is that the märchen is harmless fiction, but the legend represents painful personal experience.

I became curious about these legends, but at that time no serious literature was available about supernatural encounters. Only so-called historical and etiological legends were (and still are) popular among researchers. I thought it was time to do a classification and take stock of existing texts, at least in one language area (Dégh 1963), but this kind of work did not really interest me. Wayland Hand agreed with me that identical legends may appear in the form of statements of belief, in dramatic play, and in verbal narrative, so we planned to do a joint paper showing the three ways of telling the same story. Unfortunately, we were living in different worlds. The philologist's parallel samples were only related thematically, not organically — they came from books and manuscripts of diverse locations and times. My own samples were taken from my field recordings as they manifested spontaneously and diversely to meet actual needs.

Pursuing my curiosity, I joined the International Society of Folk Narrative Research's subcommittee on the legend. The group's goal was to collaborate on a European legend study, locating materials in archives and literary sources, assessing regional resources, listings, and classifications to reach a consensus about the extent of the legend and to prepare for a new field-collecting drive that would do justice to this neglected genre. From 1962 on I participated in conferences that tried to determine the extent of the legend type as a classifiable unit. We worked to identify the legend's characteristics, its performative and intergeneric contexts, its relationships and transformative capabilities in terms of individual proponents and respondents, and the behavioral patterns of their support groups. To this end, I have visited the important European holdings in research institutions and archives of Marburg, Freiburg, Göttingen, and Rostock (Germany), Prague (Bohemia), Bratislava (Slovakia), Basel and Zurich (Switzerland), Zagreb (Croatia), Sofia (Bulgaria), Bucharest (Romania), Helsinki, and Turku (Finland), Stockholm, Lund, and Uppsala (Sweden), Oslo and Bergen (Norway), Reikjavik (Iceland), Edinburgh (Scotland), and Haifa (Israel).

To bridge the gap between my initial search in Hungary and Europe, I explored the archive holdings at diverse American universities. At Indiana University, the assemblage of a legend file within the Folklore Archives, in addition to earlier student collections and the corpus of Richard M. Dorson's Michigan material, provided important resources for a new direction in the study of contemporary American legends. And here began my second phase of research for this book. My move to America made me a participant observer of a world that is permeated by the climate of the legend — a world that lies not only beyond the city limits, in the old pockets of traditionalizing, but very much also inside the cities themselves.

Prior to World War II, the Western fieldworker approached the folk as an outsider; folklorists were like the space aliens in the popular television show *The X-Files*, viewing their subjects as inferiors, unconscious of the values they carried. Thus, we had to leave our own communities and make a trip to find the "folk." But tellers of legends may represent all social groups, and all layers and ranks of the social hierarchy — young and old, rich and poor, educated and uneducated, powerful and powerless, native, ethnic, or immigrant. After the war, we had to adopt new attitudes, enabling ourselves to join the ranks of equals who generously shared their knowledge of folklore with us. For the folklorist is also a folk, a bearer of specific kinds of inherited or acquired folklore who, *nolens volens*, disseminates that folklore in daily routine as well as through professional activities. This is true not only of the so-called public folklorists who made it their business to persuade the folk to keep on practicing their folklore events out of context, but also of any dedicated scholars who make their research public.

Most people have had some incredible experience, or have known someone who did. People have seen the reenactment of a murder committed in an old house that was a "speakeasy" during the Depression; another saw, as a picture-perfect projected vision, the funeral of a relative who would die two weeks later. According to published personal testimonies, actor Michael Landon — who had played an angel on television who helped people in distress (*Highway to Heaven*, 1984–1989) — came back to earth and saved people after his 1991 death: He cured two people of cancer, helped another quit smoking, healed a woman of her gambling addiction, stopped two robbers from shooting a driver, and pulled a child from 100-foot-deep water (*Weekly World News*, June 30, 1992, and August 20, 1991). The editor asked the public to come forward with more miraculous healings of the new angel. These people saw and heard Landon — did they hallucinate? If we do not believe them, how should we feel about the more breathtaking biblical miracles? Moses saw the Lord in the burning bush, and Jesus walked on water and fed a crowd of 5,000 with two fishes and five loaves of bread. Like Michael, he later rose from the dead and spoke to his disciples. The field ethnographer could rationalize the attitudinal patterns of fellow humans as derivatives of contemporary frames of reference. One primetime series in the mid-1990s challenged us to decide whether stories such as the one about the soldier in Vietnam whose life was saved by the voice of his mother calling to him while he was under enemy attack are "miracles or coincidences." None of us is safe from the persuasion of the legend.

I have collected legends from all kinds of people, on all kinds of occasions. I have stories from folklorists who related them during the breaks at professional meetings, from guests at banquets where I gave talks, from students in sororities and fraternities after my discussions of Halloween, from people on the street who were waiting in line to enter Halloween spookhouses, and from invalids at retirement homes where I had volunteered to entertain. Some people contacted me by telephone, and told me their strange story. I've also answered phoned-in questions on radio programs during the witching hour on Halloween nights. Nowadays the sleepless potential legend-teller can take advantage of the nightly Art Bell radio show (continued by Mike Siegel since Bell's retirement on April 27, 2000). It remains the most popular outlet of America's ghost and horror stories to entertain potential audiences.

I also had many collecting projects that made my legend corpus grow out of proportion. Most fascinating was working with students. Teaching large introductory level undergraduate folklore classes gave me an opportunity to learn more. Nothing pleased the students more than speaking about legends. They may have initially felt inhibited by the presence of an adult outsider, but what they had learned about the great cultural value of local traditions lifted their reservations and made them eager to relate their own legends to the class community, to compare notes, and to generate the legend dialectics of a genuine performance. The best stories were published in our journal *Indiana Folklore* (1968–1986) with professional annotations by myself and the editorial staff.

As classes grew, and as I graduated from teaching undergraduate courses, the graduate assistants who tutored discussion sections offered to assist me in my work. I constructed a fieldwork guide and a Halloween questionnaire to learn about people's general attitudes toward supernatural belief. This project grew into a North America–wide enterprise. With the voluntary participation of colleagues and former students, I received responses from roughly one thousand people (44 percent men, and 56 percent women), ages 8 to 75. With the generous help of social psychologist and statistician Karyl A. Kinsey, I analyzed a random sample of 300 questionnaire respondents. The result showed 60 percent total believers as well as undecided, partial believers (who positively believed in certain but not all experiential phenomena), as opposed to 28 percent unbelievers, several of whom yielded well-told, elaborate legends.

The results of my simple questionnaire were supported and validated by the increase of occult themes in the annual lists of the *Books in Print* since

A study is being conducted of the community's knowledge of stories dealing with extraordinary or supernatural ev~
We would appreciate your answering the following questions:

1. AGE _____    2. SEX Male ☐    3. OCCUPATION _____
                         Female ☐

4. EDUCATION: Grade school ☐ _____years.    High school ☐ _____years.    College ☐ _____years.

   Degree (if any)_____

5. ARE YOU FAMILIAR WITH ANY STORIES ABOUT: Ghosts? ☐    Monsters? ☐    Witches? ☐    Vampires? ☐
   murderers? ☐    Haunted places? ☐    Supernatural events? ☐    Extrasensory perception? ☐    UFOs? ☐    Other si~
   topics? ☐    Specify.

6. WHEN DID YOU LEARN THE STORY (STORIES)? Recently? ☐    Several years ago? ☐    Very long ago? ☐    (If you a~
   adult) In your childhood? ☐

7. WHAT IS THE SOURCE OF THE STORY (STORIES)? Personal experience? ☐    Friends? ☐    Schoolmates? ☐    Parents?~
   Brothers or sisters? ☐    Relatives? ☐    Teachers? ☐    Newspapers, magazines? ☐    Comics? ☐    Books (other than comics~
   Television? ☐    Movies? ☐    Other? ☐    Specify.

8. IF YOU HEARD THE STORY FROM A PERSON (FRIEND, SCHOOLMATE, ETC.), DID HE (SHE) personally experience~
   events described in the story? ☐    Learn about them from another individual who personally experienced them? ☐    Learn ab~
   them from an individual who did not personally experience them? ☐    Read about them? ☐    View them on TV? ☐
   the movies? ☐    Other? ☐    Specify.

9. DO YOU LIKE SUCH STORIES? Yes ☐
                             No ☐
                                                    Yes ☐
10. DO YOU BELIEVE IN ONE OR MORE OF THESE STORIES? Yes, with some doubt ☐
                                                    Uncertain ☐
                                                    No ☐

11. IF YOUR ANSWER WAS "YES" OR "YES WITH SOME DOUBT," <u>UNDERSCORE</u> THE SUITABLE CATEG~
    (CATEGORIES) of No. 5. above.

12. IF YOUR ANSWER WAS "YES" OR "YES, WITH SOME DOUBT," WHICH OF THE FOLLOWING BEST APPROXIMA~
    THE REASON FOR YOUR BELIEF IN THIS STORY (STORIES)? Because you have personally experienced the event descr~
    in the story? ☐    Because another party claims to have personally experienced such events? ☐    Because you accepted the fac~
    described or shown in a newspaper? ☐    Magazine? ☐    Comic? ☐    Book (other than comic)? ☐    On television? ☐
    radio? ☐    In the movies? ☐    For other reasons? ☐    Specify.

13. HAVE YOUR EVER VISITED "SCARY PLACES" (SUCH AS HAUNTED HOUSES, CEMETERIES, BRIDGES, TUNNE~
    etc.)? Yes ☐    No ☐

14. WHY? Because you believed in the story (stories) and wanted to experience the events yourself? ☐    Because you had doubts~
    wanted to find out whether the story (stories) was/were true? ☐    Because you wanted to show your courage? ☐    "For a g~
    scare"? ☐    Other? ☐    Specify.

15. DID YOUR VISIT PROVE ☐    OR DISPROVE ☐    YOUR PREVIOUS OPINION, OR LEAVE YOU UNAFFECTED? ☐

If you are willing to give further information, please give your name, address, and telephone number. If you do not want to be event~
contacted, or for any reason want to remain anonymous, leave the space below blank.

The General Legend Survey

Dr. Linda Dégh
Folklore Institute
504 N. Fess
Bloomington, IN

*01226*

A study is being conducted of the community's knowledge of stories dealing with extraordinary or supernatural events. We would appreciate your answering the following questions:

1. AGE __28__    2. SEX Male ☐ Female ☒    3. OCCUPATION **Nurse + Student**

4. EDUCATION: Grade school ☐ ____years.    High school ☐ ____years.    College ☒ __5__ years.
   Degree (if any)__**BA.**__

5. ARE YOU FAMILIAR WITH ANY STORIES ABOUT: Ghosts? ☒ Monsters? ☒ Witches? ☒ Vampires? ☐ <u>Mad murderers</u>? ☒ <u>Haunted places</u>? ☒ <u>Supernatural events</u>? ☒ <u>Extrasensory perception?</u> ☒ UFOs? ☐ Other similar topics? ☐ Specify.

6. WHEN DID YOU LEARN THE STORY (STORIES)? Recently? ☒ Several years ago? ☒ Very long ago? ☒ (If you are an adult) In your childhood? ☒ *Different stories were learned at different times*

7. WHAT IS THE SOURCE OF THE STORY (STORIES)? Personal experience? ☐ Friends? ☒ Schoolmates? ☒ Parents? ☐ Brothers or sisters? ☒ Relatives? ☐ Teachers? ☒ Newspapers, magazines? ☒ Comics? ☐ Books (other than comics)? ☐ Television? ☒ Movies? ☒ Other? ☐ Specify.

8. IF YOU HEARD THE STORY FROM A PERSON (FRIEND, SCHOOLMATE, ETC.), DID HE (SHE) personally experience the events described in the story? ☐ Learn about them from another individual who personally experienced them? ☒ Learn about them from an individual who did not personally experience them? ☒ Read about them? ☒ View them on TV? ☒ In the movies? ☒ Other? ☐ Specify.

9. DO YOU LIKE SUCH STORIES? Yes ☒ No ☐

10. DO YOU BELIEVE IN ONE OR MORE OF THESE STORIES? Yes ☒ Yes, with some doubt ☐ Uncertain ☐ No ☐

11. IF YOUR ANSWER WAS "YES" OR "YES WITH SOME DOUBT," <u>UNDERSCORE</u> THE SUITABLE CATEGORY (CATEGORIES) of No. 5. above.

12. IF YOUR ANSWER WAS "YES" OR "YES, WITH SOME DOUBT," WHICH OF THE FOLLOWING BEST APPROXIMATES THE REASON FOR YOUR BELIEF IN THIS STORY (STORIES)? Because you have personally experienced the event described in the story? ☐ Because another party claims to have personally experienced such events? ☒ Because you accepted the facts as described or shown in a newspaper? ☐ Magazine? ☐ Comic? ☐ Book (other than comic)? ☐ On television? ☐ On radio? ☐ In the movies? ☐ For other reasons? ☐ Specify.

13. HAVE YOUR EVER VISITED "SCARY PLACES" (SUCH AS HAUNTED HOUSES, CEMETERIES, BRIDGES, TUNNELS, etc.)? Yes ☒ No ☐

14. WHY? Because you believed in the story (stories) and wanted to experience the events yourself? ☐ Because you had doubts and wanted to find out whether the story (stories) was/were true? ☒ Because you wanted to show your courage? ☒ "For a good scare"? ☐ Other? ☐ Specify.

15. DID YOUR VISIT PROVE ☒ OR DISPROVE ☐ YOUR PREVIOUS OPINION, OR LEAVE YOU UNAFFECTED? ☐

If you are willing to give further information, please give your name, address, and telephone number. If you do not want to be eventually contacted, or for any reason want to remain anonymous, leave the space below blank.

A Completed Legend Survey

15

1957, the *Index of the New York Times,* and innumerable reports of professional polling agencies. All confirmed the increasing number of believers in fairies, guardian angels, Satanist conspiracies, apocalyptic prophecies, alien visitations, lurking body-snatchers who endanger the lives of children by taking their transplantable vital organs, and hauntings by earthbound spirits in our homes.

The legend repertoire in our collection is commonly known. I did not meet anyone who had not heard most of the stories, either from childhood or from recent information. For some the issue was an active concern. These simple stories tackle life's deepest, most mysterious problems. Indeed, they concern life beyond death, magic, sanity and insanity, earthly and unearthly evil and goodness, causality and blind luck. Yes, the tellers seek a resolution between reason and irrationality in their naive manner. And how do people react? The questionnaire polled many educated people, students, college graduates, and professionals. The tellers of these stories about ghosts, monsters, witches, vampires, and other legends were asked, "Do you believe in these stories?" Sixty percent of the answers were "Yes," or "Yes, with some doubt." This means that the majority of the population is not only familiar with the propaedeutics of irrationality but is also inclined to it.

The purpose of another project was to create a regional assessment of ghost

| Type of Story | Familiarity % of Total | Belief | | |
| | | % of Total | % of Those Familiar | % of Believers |
| --- | --- | --- | --- | --- |
| Ghosts | 73% | 14% | 20% | 25% |
| Monsters | 54 | 5 | 9 | 8 |
| Witches | 53 | 5 | 9 | 8 |
| Vampires | 49 | 4 | 7 | 6 |
| Mad murderers | 55 | 10 | 18 | 17 |
| Haunted places | 72 | 14 | 20 | 24 |
| Supernatural events | 62 | 16 | 27 | 28 |
| ESP | 56 | 18 | 33 | 31 |
| UFOs | 56 | 16 | 29 | 28 |
| Other | 14 | 1 | 7 | 1 |
| Number in case base | 304 | 304 | varies by question | 179 |

Stories Survey by Karyl A. Kinsey

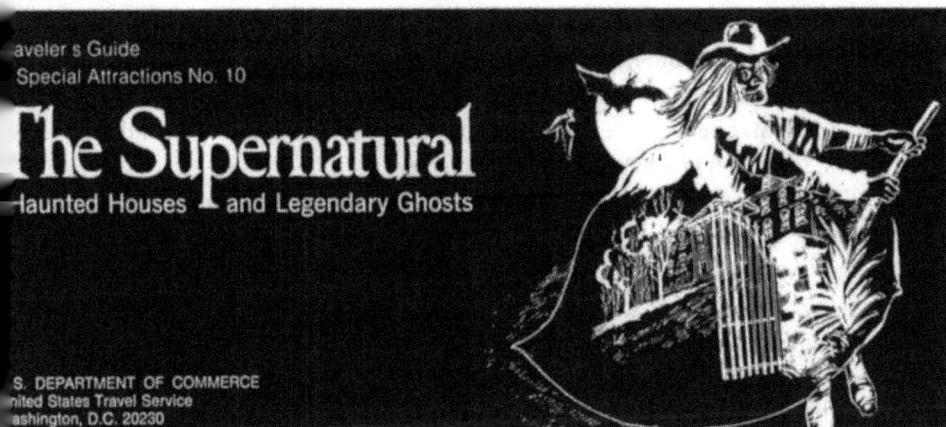

aveler s Guide
Special Attractions No. 10

The Supernatural

Haunted Houses and Legendary Ghosts

S. DEPARTMENT OF COMMERCE
nited States Travel Service
ashington, D.C. 20230

A Traveler's Guide to Haunted Places

stories, the largest category of legends. Localization is important for the legend and I was interested in seeing the variability of hauntings in close geographic proximity. The narration of legends is contextualized by a fascination
with the ritual visitation of fear-inspiring locations. At my request, the News
Bureau of Indiana University sent a news release to the editors of all Indiana
daily papers informing them about my project to record all of the haunted
locations by geographic landscape in the state. This was interesting enough
to activate editors and the newspaper-reading public. The year 1986 was the
right time for this endeavor. Countless books on the haunting of nationally
and regionally famous historic places already had appeared, published by
smart tourist agencies and ambitious local chambers of commerce seeking to
generate extra income from visitors. "Real" as well as invented haunted houses
established the haunt business. Even the U.S. Department of Commerce disseminated a national list, *The Supernatural: Haunted Houses and Legendary
Ghosts* (Traveler's Guide to Special Attractions, no. 10 of 29). Trained experts
became tour guide narrators, tabloids reported the latest ghostly encounters,
and the popular press appealed to the public to send in ghost stories for a
decent monetary reward.

Newspaper editors responded by publishing my appeals to their readers and
sending me copies of their published ghost stories. Several of them gave useful
information about unpublished, floating stories in their area that I could pursue by contacting informed individuals. Librarians, local historical society
members, schoolteachers, and businesspeople (including insurance agents,
contractors, lawyers, funeral directors, and clergy) called my attention to
"weird" places and events. By far, the most valuable help came from the believers, who wrote letters or sent tapes telling about their experiential stories

and who added personal commentaries expressing their involvement, belief, hesitation, doubt, and frustration. Whole life histories, tragic love affairs, family scandals, curses, and vendettas were revealed in these letters, often anonymously sent. I have also learned that real estate agents often know but do not reveal the secret of a haunted house marketed.

The map of Indiana haunted sites was made, but it was left incomplete, to the frustration of people who keep writing to me, asking for the list of haunted houses in their county. Those who demand that I send them my collection — whether they want to write term papers, illustrated magazine articles, or even a commercially lucrative ghost story book about indigenous ghosts — should realize that spirits, like folklore in general and legends in particular, cannot possibly be fixed on paper. They appear and disappear, multiply and vanish without warning. The survey taught me much about people's personal needs, and the meaning to them of being and staying in touch with the spirit world. Ghost legends are the most variable species of the genre in that they need to be personalized and specified to fit actual and unusual, even unique personal conditions. At the same time, because they concern uniform human experiences, basically they tell about the same things: encounters with the dead from the other world.

I was further instructed on the nature of institutional irrationality through my visitation of extranormal agencies, including fundamentalist churches, sects and communes, revivalist New Age paganist nature worshippers, agricultural Pan-worshipping communes, Satanists, UFOlogists, numerologists, Baghwam's disciples, Wicca followers, dowsers, the associations of flat- and hollow-earth believers, Ed Caycee's associates, spiritualists, and parapsychologists in New York, Berkeley, San Francisco, Los Angeles, Indianapolis, Washington (Ontario), and Freiburg, Germany. The Santeria believers in Southern California, occult bookstores everywhere but particularly in the San Francisco Bay area, Sufi dancers in New York, the many joint weekend and seasonal gatherings of diverse occult establishments in Chicago and Indianapolis, and particularly repeated visits to Camp Chesterfield in Chesterfield, Indiana, one of America's oldest spiritualist camps — all these gave me insight into the people who participate and have a leading role in the construction and maintenance of the legend climate.

Supported by a Fulbright fellowship in Germany, Austria, and Switzerland (1984–1985), I tried to connect American supernaturalism with the continental European counterpart. I knew the reluctance of European folklorists to acknowledge the new crops of modern legendry as folklore; most were engaged in rescue operations to preserve the remains of an agricultural past. Prioritizing their fieldwork in new settlements that had resulted from the negotiations of the peace treaty following the war, European scholars were focusing on cultural preservation, and the survival of archaisms during the process of accommodation, merger, mixing, and blending of population groups. Many folk narrative scholars took refuge in archives and libraries to catch up with their long overdue inventorying and classifying work, and just as many felt that the time had come to return to historic antecedents.

The Volkskunde Institut of the University of Freiburg in Breisgau, in the heart of the Black Forest, was the ideal place to begin working on my project. Its director, Professor Lutz Röhrich, one of the most prominent folk narrative scholars of our time, turned the residence and folksong archive of his predecessor, John Meier, into an important folklore training and research center, complete with library and archive, in preparation for a classification of legends. The archive, with clippings of regional and local newspapers as well as popular pamphlets provided my first clues to contemporary German legendry.

My first days in Freiburg, a university town of rare beauty founded in 1120, were spent walking in the old town around the Münster, a unique architectural gem built between 1200 and 1513. What first caught my eye were inscriptions in English: a friendly rooster in front of the Wienerwald franchise said "Welcome"; "terrific jobs" for law students were posted by an employment agency; those afflicted with "stress" were invited to try counseling by a reliable professional herbalist; and "real homemade hamburgers" made with a "Chicago recipe" were served in a Biergarten. There were so many English words — and American idioms — that I gave up on collecting evidence that Germans are being Americanized. After all, Germany, devastated and in ruins after the war, was rebuilt by America. But there were no signs of gratitude. In this hotbed of student power, where every student had a Coke can in hand and wore jeans, T-shirts, and sunglasses made in America, the university buildings were defaced by swastikas, peace signs, and hammer-and-sickle chalk marks, flanked by Uncle Sam with tiny bombs in the shape of "$$" signs in his hand. A black marker on a carved seventeenth-century gate at the main library admonished "Ronald Reagan Go Home." It is human nature to copycat the symbols of the powerful and the wealthy, as much as it is to hate those who delivered us from evil; thus, the sign language of the street displayed the political maturity of students. German youths were pacifists who scorned military service. While students served their limited tour of duty, they would use a spool of yarn to mark every evening that the day was over and that the end of their military tour was approaching. They interpreted the presence of the American army as an occupation force.

Among the several scholarly bookstores in the old town, the two largest and most versatile were centers of supernatural learning. Visitors could spend the day sitting in deep, overstuffed leather loungers, or on the carpeted floor or on the stairs, reading books from the shelves about the occult sciences, cults, sects, folk medical practices, the living dead, witchcraft, magic, shamanism, clairvoyance, and the teaching of famous gurus. Magazines, pamphlets, and fliers were also available for the interested; many directed readers to the local headquarters of practitioners, yogis, Eastern religions, healers, palmists, and card readers, and to the publications of Bauer-Verlag, Germany's foremost publisher of occult books, and the magazine *Esotera*, also published in Freiburg.

Although the Volkskunde Department kept a critical distance from its operations, the oldest and most distinguished chair of Parapsychology and Borderlines of Psychology in Germany was located at Freiburg University. Founded in 1954 by psychologist Hans Bender, it has survived controversies and still staffs an independent research institute that conducts experiments and grants stipends to international scholars who study the so-called psi phenomena, including telepathy, second-sight, spirit possession, and other mental disorders defined by parapsychologists. I had the privilege of speaking with staff members and looking into their files of case studies. Altogether, the resources in Freiburg were ideal for getting an impression of the nature of supernaturalism in Europe and its influence on modern legend formation.

Along with the autochthonous, and not necessarily frightening, stories about poor souls who return to the scene of their demise, experiential evil spirit possession accounts seemed to dominate those years. At the time of my research, satanic possession was the sensation of the day, and legends formulated around the fear of damnation covered the most popular legendary themes: extranormal violence, attack of evil spirits, seduction, transformation, and catharsis. One celebrated case, the demonic possession of pedagogy student Anneliese Michel (Goodman 1980), placed the exorcism practice of the Roman Catholic Church on public trial. I first read about Michel in a newspaper article by Ursel Kolbe, written for the *Badische Zeitung* (April 14, 1978) and preserved in the Freiburg Folklore Archive. Kolbe reported on the court trial of the two priests who had subjected the victim to twenty-three grueling exorcism ceremonies. Michel's deeply devout, conservative Catholic community was convinced that she was possessed by the devil after they had seen her hostile reaction to holy communion during pilgrimage to patron saint San Damiano in Italy. After interviewing Michel's parents, who shared responsibility for the death of the mentally sick young woman, Kolbe wrote, "None of the accused doubt the correctness of their actions."

The Michel case developed along the conduit of both secular and civic authorities and followed the traditional course of negotiations among the general population, as shown in religious, legal, educational and literary sources, the general press, television, and persistent oral tradition. It was a perfect example of legend dialectics in action. The life history of this legend — that is, this complex of legends — was greatly influenced by the showing of the American movie *The Exorcist* in 1974, despite the protests of church authorities. Possession cases continued to spread in other German-speaking countries, including Switzerland and Austria, and other contiguous countries to the east and the south.

Postwar Germany's industrial growth seemed to approximate that of the world's most technologically developed Western nation, the United States. My assumption is that the irrationality explosion, which manifests itself as a legend explosion, is somehow related to the life that humans live in the highly industrialized world of the United States. Thus, alienation and a fear of loss of identity are the causes, not some morbid fascination inherent in an Anglo-Saxon mentality. Similarly, we may attribute the growth of this phenomenon in Germany more to the country's rapid industrial growth after the war than to imitation of an American craze. Although highly publicized, sensational American horror legends reached the European public first through the popular press and electronic media and later through best-selling books of collected stories. The legends easily adjusted to local conditions and soon generated equivalents on their own turf. The Freiburg experience illustrates the contiguous emergence of American-style contemporary legends in step with industrial growth. The more peripheral areas of Europe, particularly in the satellite countries of the former Soviet Union, now continue this tendency, and show the direction of the further spread of rationalization of the irrational.

We may call the period from roughly the late 1930s to the present a transitory period. I began collecting legends for this book as soon as I realized that this genre is the most reliable barometer of human concerns in an age when fundamental changes in social relationships have been speedily, aggressively imposed by the electrification of communication technology. This age has carried over and preserved a strong body of pre-industrial legendry; some stories have been left unaltered, others have been accommodated and normalized, and yet others have been completely revised or newly invented to bridge past and present concerns. As the stories are repeated and continued, every time they are retold we discover new situations, formulations, and interpretations. We cannot yet see the end, and I cannot see myself not continuing collecting.

The legend permeates our cultural landscape, so we need to depart from the standard fieldwork guides and do a very different kind of collecting. For this book I collected legends from all possible sources. I listened to oral conversations, asked people informally whether they had heard a certain floating story, traveled to sites where legendary events had occurred to meet eyewitnesses, and routinely read the articles in daily papers, magazines, and tabloids for more legends. I recorded radio and television programs, ordered talkshow transcripts, and attended movies and theater plays to find the current versions of legends. I am fascinated by the variability of prototypes, and I keep looking.

This omnipresence of the legend makes the texts extremely diverse — showing their true nature, not the taste of the publisher who wants to compile an aesthetically pleasing collection of good stories. Originally I planned to put the texts I was using into a separate second volume, but as the book evolved, the artificiality of such a construct became clear to me. I found it a better idea to foreground the texts, illustrating and documenting the theories and methodological statements in the order of discussion. The legends in this book represent reality. They are short and long, good and bad, convincing and irritating, elaborate and fragmentary, deep and shallow, wise and silly. Some are dry and factual, others pointless and absurd, and many are fascinating and breathtaking. They vary as much as people do, and each text is precious because it characterizes the negotiation of legends in society and the need for interpretation.

# Is There a Definition for the Legend?

*2.*

## The Folk and Their Lore

As Robert Georges so circumspectly documented, ordering, classifying, and comparing is a sociobiological need of humans (Georges 1986). Instinctively we determine our place under the sun and fit ourselves smoothly and harmoniously into the order of living beings. Defining things in our environment, turning a strange, ominous landscape into a familiar one, is a part of making order and settling down. As we clean out our desks and prepare ourselves for new undertakings, we need the clarification that is definition, which may also require us to leave behind our previous ego. Yet definitions also summarize and abstract the past, that which has been completed and left behind as a safe indicator of our origin and heritage. Time-bound and place-bound, definitions from the past are useful for rethinking and recapturing when we are making a new definition that is fit for our time — even though we know that ours soon will be as dated as the previous ones. As practical devices, definitions keep us reconsidering and altering our position. And, as new knowledge dictates, we must keep trying to define our subject, because ongoing improvement of a definition is essential to a discipline so concerned with ideas that depend on continually changing human conditions: *tempora mutantur et nos mutamur in illis.*

For almost two centuries scholars have attempted, with arduous dedication, to find a definition of the legend — to capture this "elusive butterfly" (Bennett 1988: 34). This constructive exercise has paralleled the continuous attempt to define folklore within the history of our discipline. Each generation has felt it necessary to make a new start and proclaim the novelty of its views. As the goals, motivations, and ideas of the study have changed, so have the definitions. As more materials have accumulated — as better tools and more refined methods of observation, collection, and interpretation have been found — the world has also changed to accommodate the variation and expansion of what the legend as a genre is all about.

The accumulated definitions for the legend show many striking similarities, as well as diversities that are the product of the personal interests of individual definers and the particularities of legendry in their experience. Often, the definition is only a general statement: The legend is a story, a narrative, a communicative act, a social event, a performative genre, a narrative response to a stimulus, a cultural universal, an emergent form, a poetic response — all of which could be said of any other folklore form. The meaning of the legend has also been too vaguely and unspecifically characterized as elementary thought, as a human reaction to threatening conditions, as "fear and overcoming fear" (Röhrich 1988: 7), and as a psychological need. Interpretations that borrowed ideas and approaches from a number of related disciplines also attempted to explain the meaning of the legend. Scholars have defined the legend as a folk history; as naive and uncritical folk science; as folk didactics; as wisdom and philosophy; as a fantastic reflection of the real world; as religion and mythology; as a projection of the conscious and unconscious mind; as a collective response to social ambiguities; and as a specific form of narration, narrational competence, symbol system, style, form, and aesthetics. A few good descriptions have been offered with regard to the form, style, and component elements of the content of the legend, its relationship to other folklore genres, its function, and its avenues of transmission.

Taking off from too many points of departure, however, cannot lead to a definition that will satisfy all interests and serve the practical purposes of folklore research. To this end, I feel the necessity of providing an overview of definitions, and I will be empirically surveying the definitions of the legend in chronological order, as they were constructed. This type of often repetitious, tedious listing of routine definitions is necessary for pondering the state of things — for understanding the ways researchers forged ideas in the past and how we arrived where we are. In doing this, I do not promise to find a new, perfect definition, but do promise to do more than simply reuse the most often repeated definitions that were passed on, almost ritually, from generation to generation of folklorists. Certain defunct concepts may be reconsidered if we clarify their original or applied earlier meanings and their metamorphoses for continued use with modern applications. Thus, I will examine whether the definitions still fit new findings.

As I look critically at the statements of representatives of landmark trends, I will stress salient points that may be useful for further study. The criteria I am looking for are those that fit the legend and only the legend, as distinct from all other folklore genres. This task may be too ambitious, or even impossible, but its attempt will establish which facts are helpful and worth further scrutiny. Perhaps we should not look for a new definition at all, but rather seek a much broader and more flexible identification and description.

## Collecting and Archiving the Legend To Be Defined

Folklorists who do their job according to the principles of their discipline describe the personal and local variation of an item to discern the specific, meaningful construction of that variation in comparison to other regional, national, and international versions. In their routine work, folklorists collect intentional data (as intended by the teller) that constitutes the primary source for scholarly analysis. As the next step, they order, categorize, and classify their materials for whatever type of analysis and interpretation they chose to do.

Scholarly interpretation is best attempted after description and definition have been made on the basis of collected and classified materials. However, in the latter part of the twentieth century, collecting and classifying folklore went out of fashion, while interpretation gained strong acclaim. Like cult leaders, masters of interpretation were followed by worshipping scholarly factions. Alan Dundes repeatedly criticized folklorists for their "predilection" with collecting and classifying (Dundes 1966, 1969, 1980, 1996): "You see, that's the problem with folklorists. . . . They just collect, collect, collect. They classify, classify, classify. They build these big archives, and they don't *interpret* it" (Dundes 1996: 4). And yet, the same Alan Dundes who introduced American folklorists to "oral literary criticism" — the folk-evaluation of its lore — and educated hundreds of students in the importance of paying attention to performers and their audiences in the field (Narayan 1995) told two graduate students in an interview that he does not do fieldwork himself, but rather bases his interpretational work on the fieldwork of others (Dundes 1996: 4). How can the scholar interpret data without experiencing the performance *in situ*? Interpretation at all costs is not called for if the data is insufficient for a reasonable interpretation.

Like any stranger in an unfamiliar world of meanings, a folklorist should approach the practitioners to find out what they mean when their utterances are incomprehensible to the folklorist. Thus, the self-collected item is the crucial first step toward scholarly interpretation; if this first step is not dependable, the constructed meaning will collapse like a castle built on sand. How can an interpretation by an outsider that uses only texts or parts of texts, selected at random and fixed on paper, be justified? It leaves one with the uneasy feeling that the interpreter has forged a meaning on his or her own, and has subsequently selected materials to support those preconceptions.

Dundes has every reason to be critical of poor collecting and poor archiving, but it should be remembered that folkloristics is the study of the present, and modern problem-oriented collecting in itself is a deeply scientific act. What we collect today uniquely mirrors the ideas of our time: the current manifestations of many preceding versions, interpreted as unique variants from creative individuals. And the current text is also a valuable clue that allows us to conjecture past phases, the epochs of history we know nothing about. Moreover, the value of the collected data is eternal, while hypotheses, theories, and interpretations are artificial, temporal constructs that are destined to be overridden and replaced by improved theories in scholarly discourse.

Furthermore, if collecting and archiving are not done continually and systematically, we will be left with only historic materials that reveal nothing about the current meanings and functions of relevant folklore expressions rooted in the present-day social world. Archive materials, no matter how deficient they might be, represent the past and allow us to deduce the folklore process that preceded the present forms we experience in field study. Archives are precious because they store unique sources.

In the nineteenth century, inspired by the work of the Grimm brothers, Europeans enthusiastically registered all the legends they could find; soon local and regional collections grew into national treasuries. As archives were founded, classifying the materials became a practical need, to make order in the masses of manuscripts and clippings. Archivists soon came to realize that classifying legends was more problematic than that of other folklore genres. The characteristic textual inconsistency of legends kept archivists from distinguishing the narrative texts (memorates or fabulates) from the belief statements (superstitions), as the latter fallaciously appeared to be the stable motifs linking thematically variable texts. In fact, scholars were more interested in the mythological survivals represented by "superstitions" than in the miscellany of uncanny stories, and the archives contained few classifiable legend texts that were representative of what lived in oral tradition.

Not until the 1930s was the legend recognized as an autonomous, prose narrative genre worthy of serious study. However, the legend lacked a definition, so no classification could be made. This need was voiced at the first International Congress of Folk Narrative Research in 1959, where Wayland Hand suggested that a committee be formed, putting the classification of European and American folk legends on the agenda. The Legend Commission met in 1962, 1963, and 1966 (Bošković-Stulli 1966; Hand 1964, 1965; Harkort 1966; Peeters 1963a; K. Ranke 1967). All three meetings were extremely fruitful in planning regional collaborative fieldwork and elaborating an operational framework for the classification of national legendries that would eventually contribute to an international index. A question was raised: Can belief-motifs, memorates, fabulates, and everyday experience stories — texts that are formally diverse but identical in their content — be indexed together? Scholars realized that without a new, systematic collection, no legend catalogue could be made because there was not enough classifiable material available. Neither could new fieldwork and classification begin without agreement on an updated definition. Here the vicious circle closes, comprising all the preparatory work that must precede scholarly interpretation of the legend.

To be sure, the great theoretical and methodological initiatives of the short-lived Legend Commission of the International Society of Folk Narrative Research cannot be underrated. However, the Commission concerned itself with traditional legend materials in scholarly archives, as defined by the disciples of the Grimms. They didn't take stock of the monumental changes in the legend process occurring before their very eyes, as mass communication technology began to turn the world into the global village predicted by Marshall McLuhan (1964).

A couple of years later, several authors pioneered in the exploration of the "legend explosion" (a term adapted from Nat Freedland) in urban-industrial society. The 1969 American legend symposium (Hand 1971) triggered a new style of collection and revealed more formal subcategories in its findings. A new generation of scholars turned toward the legends that they found as exponents of the problems and ideologies of modern living. Groups of experts met at professional meetings and special seminars, identifying the "new" legend genre as "urban" (Brunvand 1981) or "contemporary" (Bennett and Smith 1989). Beginning in the early 1980s, American and British folklorists joined forces in dedicating themselves to collecting, archiving, and classifying these legends as they emerge, in order to reach a consensus on definition and interpretive analysis (G. A. Fine 1992: 1–42). The enterprise soon captured the interest of the lay public. Newspaper and magazine articles, horror movies, and popular scientific books educated the masses, and the term *urban legend* became a household word. The Anglo-American team's efforts also captured the attention of European folklorists, who have joined the annual gatherings of the Perspectives on Contemporary Legend Seminars since 1981, and founded the International Society for Contemporary Legend Research and its journal *Contemporary Legend*.

In the emphasis on collecting and contextualizing new data, definition is still the focus (Klintberg 1990b; Bennett and Smith 1989; Dégh 1991; Pettit, Smith, and Simpson 1995). To date, two classification attempts are notable: Bengt af Klintberg's "The Types of the Swedish Folk Legend" (1993), and Jan Brunvand's "A Type-Index of Urban Legends" (Brunvand 1993: 325–347). Klintberg accepted Tillhagen's suggestion to catalogue only fabulates (Tillhagen 1964), leaving aside the entire "legendary tradition," the too-fuzzy memorates, and other non-epic belief statements. All-inclusive classifications, wrote Klintberg, serve the practical needs of archivists such as Pirkko-Liisa Rausmaa and Lauri Simonsuuri, and contain only a minor part of "fixed legend types." By cataloguing only fixed types, Klintberg's classification was designed to provide "a tool for legend scholars." Brunvand's type index is a structured listing of the legends he published in his five anthologies (1981, 1984, 1986, 1993, 1994).

### Folklore Defined to Contextualize Legend Definitions

Beginning our survey of definitions, we may start with the more general master concept of folklore in order to reach the specific subcategory, the legend.[1] No matter what topic they cover or the level of sophistication, folklorists of all ages and regions have usually begun with a descriptive definition, including an identification of folklore-bearing communities and a list of the genres to be addressed by their handbooks, text collections, theoretical treatises, and popular picture books. Among folklorists, definitions have become an obsession during the last two decades, and "the definition game" has become a major controversy (Ben-Amos 1971: 15). Emotions have risen particularly high around certain statements about the nature of folklore (traditional, oral, artistic) and the social and educational level of the folk; the diversity of the viewpoints or orientations of folklorists has resulted in conflicting descriptions. For example, Alan Dundes's liberal definition of "the folk" as "any group of people whatsoever" — folklorists included — in his introductory folklore textbook (Dundes 1980: 6) sparked particular controversy (as noted in Oring's 1986 college reader).

Can folklore be defined at all? To be sure, folklore is the "common idea" of many people. Just how many people this includes can be expressed only in large figures like thousands and millions, even if we do not believe in cultural universals. But there is no such thing as a "common idea" because (anatomically speaking) people have not a common but rather separate brains. Their individual thoughts influence each other through time and space, flitting and resounding, mingling and ordering, diminishing and multiplying. But when these thoughts become tangible — audible, readable, affective of the subconscious — they are alive in the thought processes of one person. A choir of a hundred singers — although it is more organized than common ideas, knowledge, feelings, or memories — is nothing more than a hundred times one voice. If the whole seems definable, it means only that we can grasp and characterize the content of the loudest dominant voice, using our practically workable but imperfect capability of observation. Simultaneously, innumerable cacophonous overtones resound. And what intrudes from all the noises of the world — known as the "cocktail party phenomenon" — causes constant resoundings, and accompaniments, and sounds along the dominant idea.

The separate brain — that single brain of an individual who is a part of the folk, or the brains of many people — produces highly complicated, fluid, surging, swirling, elusive ideas. If we multiply this brain activity by an indeterminate number, we arrive at the specific means of human expression that we know as folklore. But we cannot take stock of folklore because it is camouflaged in symbols. Thus, the "common ideas" underlying folklore evolves from individual ideas through developmental processes whose complexity is impossible to deconstruct and analyze with our limited brain capacity.

Anyone who wishes to find out about sparrows can consult a technical book on birds. The curious will soon discover that the *Passer domesticus*, a nimble and prolific species, belongs to the genus "*Passers*," the class "*Aves*," and the subphylum "*vertebrata*." Furthermore, the sparrow belongs to the "*regnum animale*," to the category of "live beings," and finally to the *summum genus* of "existing things." There is perfect order in the *avifauna* — and as far as one can tell, there is nothing wrong with the house sparrow either. Beyond the zeal of ornithologists, we owe this accurate classification to the clarity of zoological criteria and the proper use of logical principles.

Unlike the scientific fields, disciplines within the realm of the humanities — if only because of the nature of their subject matters — cannot avoid ambiguities. They employ figures of speech, poetical adumbrations, and other elements that increase the appeal of definitions but at the same time weaken their explicitness. This fact is also one of the reasons why the legend — another nimble and prolific species — lacks the accurate definition accorded the house sparrow. One cannot even be sure that the "legend" — as a generic term for everything that it is commonly applied to — fits into the class of "existing things."[2] The most crucial reason for the lack of clarity is that folklore, the *proximum genus* of the legend which belongs to the immediately superior taxonomic group, also suffers from the lack of an accurate definition.

On August 22, 1846, the antiquarian William Thoms, using the self-aggrandizing pen name Ambrose Merton, created the term *folklore* to describe "what we in England designate as Popular Antiquity or Popular Literature (though by-the-by it is more a Lore than a Literature, and would be most aptly described by a good Saxon compound, Folk-Lore, the Lore of the People)."[3] Over the next century and a half, thoughtful and scholarly critics should have noticed that Thoms's term presented its own semantic difficulties and inconsistencies. Some of the listed phenomena (manners, observances) are acts of behavior; others (superstition) are certain kinds of internal psychological manifestations; and others (ballads, proverbs) are performative genres. Thoms created the generic term *folklore* by knowingly or accidentally applying three criteria: notions of antiquity, concerns over approaching demise, and the goal of salvaging. It seems obvious that these matters cannot be regarded as limited to folklore because they might be applicable as well to the narwhale, the endangered virgin forest of Alaska, or architectural monuments on the verge of collapse. The criteria are further invalidated today because few scholars believe that the manifestations of folklore are necessarily antique or approaching demise, or that, like endangered species, folklore requires protection from impending annihilation. Preservation is not necessarily the scholar's professional aim.

If this is evident, why is it that the term *folklore*, and everything belonging to the concept, is still mired in the same Thomsian disorder and confusion? As additions were made to the list of items under the rubric of folklore, these expansions greatly enriched the meaning of the word. But the steady increase of studied phenomena, up to this day, has not revealed any incontestable list of definitive features. That is to say, there is no definition that distinguishes folklore from all other things, and that can maintain its validity as being applicable to all phenomena within the total conceptual sphere of the discipline.

It seems unusual that a generic term exists without either positive identification of its constituent elements or the determination of the unifying features of these same elements. After all, any kind of classification seeks to arrange objects by selecting attributes that they all share. In spite of this lack of clarity surrounding it, the term *folklore* can be found in the vocabulary of most civilized languages, although it is not always given identical meanings — while scholars are subsequently kept busy in their attempts to define the arbitrary classification.

The confusion concerning folklore is not surprising. Thoms, like others after him, felt that, despite the logical incongruity, the component elements of the definition were somehow related to each other. Scholars after Thoms tried to find a definition, knowing that no scientific classification could afford to be constructed merely on the instinctive feeling that certain things must somehow belong together. Yet those scholars frequently glossed over the fact that no common attributes were to be found in all the constituent elements that would thereby justify uniting these elements under the same umbrella term.

It is no wonder, then, that none of the existing determinations have proved to be suggestive enough to satisfy the expectations of all or even a majority of modern academic folklorists. The most useful and multifarious definitions did not focus on any one uniform viewpoint, prevalent to all areas of knowledge. As Alver noted, there are an abundance of terms and definitions in the science of folklore, most of which are "inexact and illogical" (Alver 1967: 63). And, in the more than three decades that have passed since, the definitions have continued to make more demands and sow more confusion. If it is true that "definitions of folklore are as many and varied as the versions of a well-known tale" (Ben-Amos 1971: 3), then the critics of those definitions are nearly as many.

Utley discussed the authoritative and theoretical definitions of folklore and summarized and evaluated the twenty-one well-known statements by American scholars that were listed in the *Funk and Wagnalls Standard Dictionary of Folklore, Mythology and Legend* (Leach 1949; see also Utley 1961). Ten years later, Pentikäinen observed that these definitions, outmoded by that time but still in vogue, mention thirteen times that folklore is "oral" and that it is "tradition." On the other hand, references to "transmission," "survival," and "social" occur six times each. Pentikäinen concluded that most of the twenty-one authors could only agree that folklore is "oral tradition" (Pentikäinen 1970: 90). For some time already, though, this mostly agreed upon feature has been heavily undermined by folklore theorists (Brunold-Bigler and Bausinger 1995; Dégh 1994b; Röhrich and Lindig 1989; Schenda and ten Doornkaat 1988). The criterion "tradition" increases its ambiguous applicability in modern times (see Kvideland 1992). In general, the term has been so broadly defined that no one knows what to think anymore.

Meanwhile, a desperate attempt to restore a common ground by defining (or redefining) the keywords in the vocabulary of folklorists was displayed in a special issue of the *Journal of American Folklore* (Feintuch 1995a). Feintuch, the editor of this national journal, invited selected authors to provide their personal understandings of the most popular concepts and trends. Searching for the lacking solid foundation in the meaning of folklore as both discipline and subject, he wanted a broad discussion of "large cultural issues and consequences." He asked the rhetorical question "Why are folklorists best qualified to address such important issues?" and argues for the superior quality of our discipline. He hints at the old, unfair, and almost anecdotal accusation (made as a rule by folklorists against other folklorists) that "we have a less distinguished history of synthesizing and of theorizing" than the other humanistic fields which are more "privileged in the canons of Western academic thought." But by calling folklorists "academic outlaws and renegades" is he trying to attract "the historically and culturally canonical disciplines"? The selection of keywords in this issue is for the "Study of Expressive Culture" (Feintuch 1995a), a term used by anthropologists as a synonym for folklore, as opposed to Practical Culture (material culture or folklife). Most essays in this journal issue deviate from the canon of folkloristics, and approximate that of the "privileged" others. This attempt at reinforcement for the methods and theories of a discipline seems rather unusual. These essays might have been better placed in an introductory handbook, not the official organ of the American Folklore Society. This attempt at definition hardly turns representatives of related disciplines into folklorists, and leaves practicing folklorists unimpressed.

To return to definitional attempts by folklorists not yet confused by the keywords of other disciplines, all definitions began by explaining the word *folklore* as a unit, without adequate clarification of the separate meaning of the two elements in this compound word. The vagueness is apparent as definitions usually take the meanings of *folk* and *lore* for granted. The question of the "folk" as lore-producing entities (humans) was raised by many scholarly groups, particularly after World War II when "lore" no longer appeared to be necessarily confined to pristine peasant poetry. So what is the exact meaning of "folk" in the term *folklore*? Who qualifies as "folk"? Is it villagers? Townspeople? The uneducated? And how about the educated? Adults? Children? Does it include marginal people? Members of large communities? Members of small communities? Is "folk" a stable category? Or is it mutable, subject to the flow of history and modifications of social relationships and living conditions? Is it affected by the proliferation and acceleration of mass communication and mobility that have been caused by industrialization and urbanization? Is folklore the product of a historic group that has run its course and declined? Or is it the product of all functioning social groups, and dependent on their social and cultural needs?

The determination of "folk" is, in many respects, an ideological problem. The following examples, selected at random from the writings of influential scholars, demonstrate just how partial the definitions can be. According to most traditional folklorists, "folk" denotes a group of people inferior to them: "the simple people" (Bausinger 1958, 1961, 1967, 1968, 1985; Schenda 1992); "the common people who share a basic store of old traditions" (Hultkrantz 1960); the *"vulgus in populo"* (Hoffmann-Krayer 1902); the "lower layer," or *Unterschicht* (Naumann 1922); "the unsophisticated, unanalytic mass of mankind" (Kroeber 1948); "an old-fashioned segment within a complex civilization" or a "peasant society" (Redfield 1960); "a mental and emotional communion" (Spamer 1934); "the peculiar behavior that united people," "the mother-stratum of the nation," and the "folk within the folk" (Weiss 1946); "the usual or the typical among the people" (Erixon 1949, 1951a, 1951b). According to Marxists, the folk is "the exploited class," "the subjugated class" (Voigt 1972, 1976, 1990), and "the working class" (Sokolov 1966).

Only during the last twenty-five years has the definition become more inclusive and liberal,[4] but it has also become increasingly unspecific: "A group" or a "small group" (Ben-Amos 1971), and "any group of people whatsoever who share at least one common factor" (Dundes 1980). Additions and specifications to the modern definition have identified currently functional social units of folklore bearers, such as a "dyadic group" (Oring 1984), occupational group (M. Jones 1996; McCarl 1978, 1996), family (Zeitlin, Kotkin, and Baker 1982), women (Jordan and Kalčik 1985), men (Brandes 1980), gays and lesbians (Goodwin 1989), ethnics (Stern 1977), and the "elite" (as represented by the journal *Elite-lore*).

Thinking further, and experiencing the omnipresence of folklore in society, folklorists appear to feel uneasy about the applicability of the term *folk*. The term seems too much attached to old-fashioned "peasants" and "primitives" and is understood by the general public as the folks who professionally revive and stage performance of classic forms of folk arts and crafts. While folklorists are more concerned with their own reaction to "otherness" than ever before, they want to consider the observed performance of creativity of any individual without "prefixed" qualifiers "such as folk" (Pocius 1995: 427). Thus, a substitute qualifier, "vernacular," has also been proposed under the influence of sociolinguistic usage, which is particularly favored by students of arts, architecture, and religion. *Vernacular* can be defined simply as "personal, private," and it can also refer to arts that are "native or peculiar to a particular country or locality" (Primiano 1995: 42; Toelken 1994: 43–45).

On the other hand, what definitions do we have for *lore?* What kind of human expressions belong to this term? A disturbing lack of clarity emerges in the stated or assumed meanings: wisdom, fantasy, fancy, aesthetic expression, art, poetry, knowledge, and science. It is exceedingly difficult to tell what sort of "lore" belongs rather to the rubric of folk art, folk belief, folk medicine, folk life, folk mentality, folk idea, folk tradition, or other categories. We also find that some folklorists like to use the word *lore* in connection with diverse subjects such as plant lore, moon lore, children's lore, urban lore, drug lore, and so forth. One might feel that the specification here also depends largely on ideological differences.

To be sure, prior to World War II, the meanings of *folk* and *lore* seemed to be shared among all representatives of the discipline. However, as time passed and vistas broadened, the old definitions became obsolete and new ones had to be elaborated to fit new conditions. None of these basic concepts — "folk," "lore," or "folklore" — has a generally accepted common meaning for scholars today, nor do any of these terms provide a solid base to support other definitions, such as one for the legend.

Ben-Amos's definition of folklore, "artistic communication in small groups" (1971), was an attempt to bypass the confusion of modern folklorists. It turned away from past-oriented conceptions of the folk and its lore, and approached the ethnographic view of the present. It has become the most quoted definition — and it is the most ambiguous. It suggests a shift to the present, to the just-experienced performance of folklore; but it ignores historical antecedents and the larger society by narrowing the present to the actual communicating group's function, and denying time-depth to the emergent form. If we assume that communication is a crucial criterion for how folklore is perpetuated, then how can we limit it to small groups, particularly in the name of modernity, when the quantity of mass-mediated folklore today surpasses any imaginable number of face-to-face communicators?

The introduction of modern technology in the forms of speedy travel and mass-communicated information cannot be overlooked. Indeed, most folklorists — and legend scholars in particular — recognize that the mass media plays a dominant role in the dissemination of folklore. Television and computer narrators, for example, dispense folklore not only to small groups, but to gigantic audiences which include the inhabitants of villages, cities, countries, and continents. Thus, the elements of the Ben-Amos definition — folk, small group, orality, communication, and artistry — together do not give an idea of what constitutes folklore. It does indicate that folklore is artistic and involves people in groups, but it does not say *what* is communicated and *why*.

As long as we can uncover no common feature other than the "how" and "to whom" this thing called "folklore" is communicated, further elaboration of its criteria would be more successful if the task was left in the hands of psychics or poets than folklorists. A computer certainly could not find the definition based on the input of folklorists' skimpy data. Even so, folklorists are committed to creating a definition and to revising definitions as social conditions change. After all, it would be sheer absurdity to believe that an existing thing — like the house sparrow — cannot be defined, or, conversely, that an indefinable thing can exist.

## Stability and Variability of Legend Definitions

The subcategories of folklore suffer from taxonomic confusion as much as the definition of folklore does. Our main concern here, the legend, stimulates more definitions than most of the other genres, probably because of its inherent peculiarities. Not even its common name *legend* or the German equivalent *Sage*, a construct derived from the verb *sagen* (to tell, say, express, or pass on something),[5] remains stable and accepted without passionate dispute (Nicolaisen 1988). Pioneer American collectors such as Puckett, Hyatt, Randolph, and Brown, and generations of regional and state folklorists after them, used the term *tradition* or *superstition*. Nordic scholars, as Alver notes, who have developed one of the richest vocabularies of definition, often use such synonyms as *belief story, true story, tradition, variant, record,* and *superstition* for the legend. It is a common practice to identify the legend with Carl Wilhelm von Sydow's *fabulate* and to distinguish it from his *memorate*, concepts he defined inconsistently in his writings leaving them wide open to personal scholarly interpretations (Alver 1967: 64–65; Gwyndaf, n.d., ms; Pentikäinen 1968: 143–146; Rooth 1979). None of the numerous legend descriptions pertain to all sorts of legends in their entirety, nor do the usually cited characteristics pertain only to the legend. But in spite of the diversity of legend definitions, the essential components of the legend itself are remarkably stable, as we shall see.

At this point, a question arises: Is it at all possible to describe the legend with some accuracy by the use of existing characterizations? I must admit that some definitions catch the eye because they were written with artistic eloquence and captivating compassion, or they reflect thorough scholarly erudition, or they offer profound philosophical revelations. Several definitions come close to helping the reader guess what the legend is. At the same time, the reader gets the impression that an overwhelming and unresolvable obscurity surrounds this genre. This fuzziness, however, represents not the shortcoming but rather the inadequacy of the conception underlying the construction. The obscurity of ideas about the legend is not always immediately evident. The pertinent expressions are so current that one does not even think of questioning the lack of unanimity of their meaning.

### The Grimms' *Sagen* and the German Philological School

At the end of the eighteenth century, folklore as a term or a discipline had not yet been invented. After the great success of their work *Kinder und Hausmärchen*, the Grimm brothers published another bulky collection. The latter work, *Deutsche Sagen* (1816), contained a collection of brief, dry, chronicle-like texts that never even remotely approached the popularity of their best-selling märchen collection. Gerndt wrote that the Grimms' conception of the legend marked not a new beginning, but rather the closing of an era. Although the *Deutsche Sagen* inspired hundreds to collect and publish legends, the antiquarian, idealistic, and nationalistic prejudices of the Grimms impeded scholarly collecting for more than a century, and affected the development of an analytic approach to the legend (Gerndt 1983: 264–265). In their introduction to the *Deutsche Sagen*, the Grimms' characterization of the legend as distinct from märchen, however, proved to be useful and resourceful for generations of folk narrative scholars:

> The fairy tale is more poetic, the legend is more historical; the former exists securely almost in and of itself in its innate blossoming and consummation. The legend, by contrast, is characterized by a lesser variety of colors, yet it represents something special in that it adheres always to that which we are conscious of and know well, such as a locale or a name that has

been secured through history. Because of this local confinement, it follows that the legend cannot, like the fairy tale, find its home anywhere. Instead the legend demands certain conditions without which it either cannot exist at all, or can only exist in less perfect form.[6] (Translation by Ward 1981, vol. 1: 1)

In describing and contrasting the tale and the legend, the Grimms distinguished between two worlds — one a world of fiction and fantasy, not tied to time or location; and the other a plainer, paler place of familiar environments tied to a time-honored reality and peopled by known persons.

These differences have been asserted and elaborated upon fruitfully by others who have been interested in folk narratives as literary, behavioral, and psychological expressions. It was found that both forms share a common stock of narrative elements and building blocks, as documented by the *Motif-Index of Folk-Literature*, but the two genres use them in contrastive ways to convey their opposing, genre-specific messages. Jolles (1929) made important observations on the nature of the "simple forms" of oral narrative; since then, they have been considered as expressions of the mental attitudes and behavioral patterns that influence their conceptualizations, as seen particularly in the works of Kurt Ranke, Max Lüthi, Lutz Röhrich, and Hermann Bausinger.[7]

"*Märchen* and *Sage* are two basic contingencies of narration," wrote Lüthi, the literary folklore theorist. He added that, from their lasting coexistence, one may assume that they are both manifestations of basic needs of the human psyche (Lüthi 1961: 7). For Lüthi, the inner meaning is the essence of diversity: The märchen is "*flachenhaft*" (depthless), one-dimensional; whereas the legend is deep and multidimensional. In the legend, the experiencer is under the influence of his experience, which is the kernel of the legend event. "The subject of the legend is the altercation with the extraordinary, the entirely different, the other-worldly" (1961: 33, 43). What text analysts such as Lüthi have discovered by deep readings of variants has also been documented by fieldworkers who have observed the peculiarities of the coexistent relationship between tale and legend repertoires in live storytelling (Boratav 1966; Dégh 1989: 139–146; Gaál 1965; Lüthi 1970: 83–94).

Lüthi considered it a mistake to view belief and non-belief as principles of distinction between the two genres (1961: 24), but this was not the case with Friedrich Ranke, the first modern fieldwork-oriented legend scholar. Ranke also contrasts legend with the tale, but his definition suppresses the Grimms' localization and familiarity concept and instead stresses what he found most prominent: The legend is objectively untrue, though it purports to be true.

The legend, in essence, demands to be believed by both narrator and listener: it wants to present reality, tell about things that really took place. . . . The legend belongs according to its own awareness, to the world of reality,

it belongs to the knowledge of the folk. . . . Folk legends are popular stories
with fantastic, objectively untrue contents, told as factual event, in the form
of a simple report. (F. Ranke 1925: 14)

The idea that the main difference between the märchen and the legend
lies in their contrastive relationship to the real world had been expressed earlier by Panzer (1905: 18). It was elaborated later by Röhrich, who documented
it in a large international body of narratives (Röhrich 1974). The basis of his
distinction is an attitudinal difference toward reality. Röhrich felt that belief is
a generic trait, and he reiterated Ranke's dictum: "The legend demands from
teller and listener to believe the truth of what it tells. This is what sets it apart
from *Märchen, Schwank* and *Witz*" (Röhrich 1958: 664). It will be worthwhile
to cite Kapfhammer's definition written twenty-five years later:

Legends are worldly stories; they formulate the pessimistic view of the
world differently than the tale. Legends are not protocols of the hereafter,
and thus are not stories "to shudder" at but are reports of projections: the
dead return, documenting that the living cannot resolve the problem of
death and cannot get rid of the feeling of remorse at being unable to lay the
dead to rest. The legend—a historical document or not? The legend is
rooted in a historically authenticized or believed to be documentable event
that manifests as a specific reflection of human experience and becomes a
means for argumentation.[8] (Kapfhammer 1984: 17; my translation)

Röhrich also approached the legend from the angle of "fear." He argued
that the legend is the "cultural language of fear." People, he said, tell legends
in order to "verbalize anxieties and fears and, by explaining these away, to free
themselves from the oppressive power of their fears." He found legend-telling
to be "a kind of self-therapy" (Röhrich 1988: 8), believed that the two represented diverse models of thought. Evidently, Röhrich saw optimism and pessimism as the crucial poles of opposition in the outlooks of the märchen and
the legend. In his more recent writing, he has specified the distinctive features
with great clarity:

The Märchen, in its development, increasingly disengages itself from the
mythic while the legend absorbs the mythic world and maintains its place
also in the present. At close observation, irreconcilable differences in form,
content, world view, concept of time, credibility, involvement, the psychological basis and social perception separate the two genres from each other.
In the legend, attachment to belief and knowledge has priority over narrative composition. Most of the Märchen are multi-episodic stories, while legends are single-episodic short forms. Märchen is consciously created poetry
. . . legends are often memorates, that is, experience reports about encounters with the supernormal, the numinous. (Röhrich 1996: 2)

Fohrer agreed that the legend is a "believed story whose content is space-
and time-bound," which can be distinguished from the märchen that enter-

tains. However, the borderline between the two is blurred (Fohrer 1965: 59–60). Paul Smith contrasted the tale with the contemporary legend, saying that "irrespective of the extent of the underlying truth, it is the extent of the believability that carries the day . . . tales which are too improbable are considered to be fantasy" (1987: 195). Surveying the many differently phrased but essentially similar definitions based on contrasting views of reality in legend and tale, Gerndt found that researchers in general agree that the legend's relationship to reality differs from all other genres of folk poetry. "Legends," wrote Gerndt, "aspire to be directly or indirectly true and inform about a true past happening." He adds, "Furthermore, there is another feature that characterizes the text of the legend: A story becomes a legend only if it is presented in the twilight zone of credence and doubt" (Gerndt 1991: 139).

Others (Čistov, Bausinger, and Peuckert) also contrasted the features of tale and legend but emphasized other points. The necessity to believe appears marginal — it is recognized but not stressed — in the definitions of Peuckert, Leopold Schmidt, and Bausinger, whereas the experience/event reportage, statement of belief, documentation by reference to location and eyewitnesses, and the didactic and explanatory all become more prominent in the definitions of these scholars. Čistov stressed the difference in the way reality is presented in the tale and the legend (1967: 26). Bausinger drew a developmental scheme, interpreting the formation of three kinds of legends: (1) a subjective experience of a fearsome vision initiates supernatural legends; (2) a remarkable real happening, natural phenomenon, historical event, or murder is the basis of historical legends; and (3) the objectification of an existing phenomenon that demands explanation leads to the creation of etiological legends. From this initial core, he said, legends develop by conceptualization, interpretation, and retelling. All three steps are determined by the existent collective belief system and pertinent motif patterns. Beyschlag emphasizes that the legend functions as believable reality and is taken seriously by its bearers. It is a report of a happening that relates to the reality of the world order (Beyschlag 1941: 188).

Peuckert, in essential agreement with the above authors, pointed out the historic and explanatory nature of the legend, which he regarded as a non-aesthetic reporting of an event after it has taken place. In his words, the legend is "in essence, the expression of a truth, that reached the point of formulation, in the environment of the magical world, determined by mythical thinking." Furthermore, "the legend wants to be true, to report truth" (1965: 10) and is "a historical report describing the encounter of a mortal with the superhuman world" (1965: 80).

Mythical thinking has long been regarded as an important component of

*Legend*

△

Demonological legend

Experience
⊗

Event
⊗          ⊗
Objectification

△ Historical ←————————————————→ Aetiological △
   legend                              legend

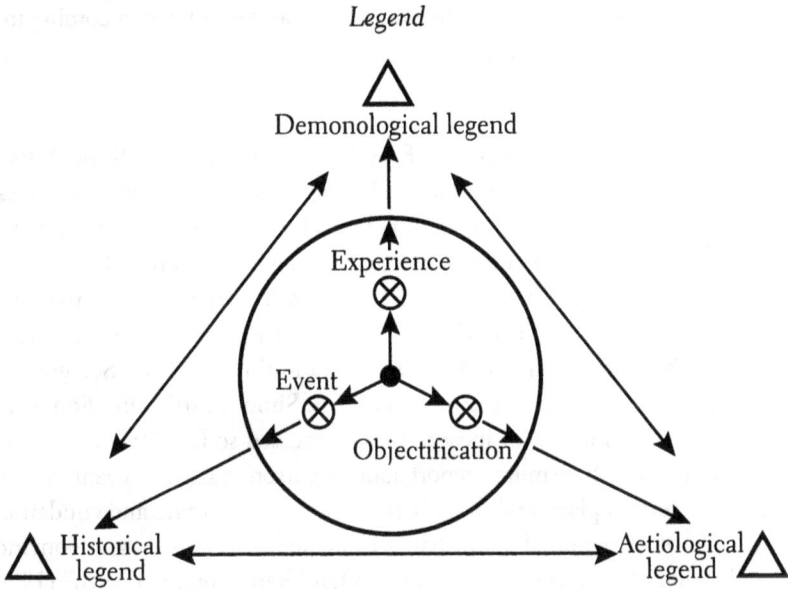

Bausinger's Developmental Scheme

legends. Early on, Laistner deduced that legends about cloudy apparitions and nightmares stem from individual perceptions of natural phenomena (1879, 1889). The juxtaposition of the real and the "entirely different" world — or "us and others" — in the legend experience was suggested first by theologian Rudolf Otto, who discussed the relationship between rational and irrational factors in the idea of the divine, the numinous, the wholly other (Otto 1958). Burkhardt saw the legend as deriving from personally experienced encounters with the "numinous." He wrote, "Legends are popular narratives with unusual contents that often stem from the break-in of the supernatural world into the world of everyday reality and factual happenings . . . [The legend] is related in the form of a simple experience-report" (Burkhardt 1951: 14). Jungian Gotthilf Isler, on the other hand, stated that "I consider each legend as a unique, and for the affected teller the best possible effort to formulate the underlying archetypal event" (1971: 32).

Although it is generally agreed by the above authors that the legend is mostly monoepisodic, nonartistic, plain, and reportive, and often relates a personal experience, little has been said about its formal features. Except for F. W. Schmidt's 1929 attempt to describe the legend as an artistic narrative, all of the authors have mentioned the formal inconsistencies of the legend text only in passing, mostly as part of a complaint about the difficulties of finding a workable body of narrative units that can be ordered according to a type and motif classification system.

## The Contribution of Nordic Folklorists

Nordic scholars contributed significantly to legend research through their industrious collection of texts. The archiving of collected materials further prompted them to describe and identify legend categories and construct classification systems. Christiansen's catalogue of migratory legends (1958), a listing of Norwegian legends that could be traced to variants in international distribution, and Simonsuuri's *Finnish Mythological Legends* (1961), a classification of the materials in the Archive of the Finnish Literature Society, represent important systematized source materials. Simonsuuri's definition of the legend is in agreement with most of those discussed so far: "The legend is a remembrance-like transmitted report about a person, a sight or event that occurred at a certain place and time. It contains clear, accurate and condensed knowledge of an assumed truth that is explained instructively and convincingly. In spite of localization, the story is often internationally known" (1964: 19). In his catalogue, Simonsuuri attempts to follow von Sydow's classification, separating "belief legend" from "memorate." This has become a practice of most Nordic folklorists, some of whom regard fabulate and memorate as two different but coexisting genres that "constantly influence each other" (Klintberg 1989: 71).

Carl Wilhelm von Sydow's legend definition, first published in 1934, dominates Nordic scholars' thinking about genre, its textual formulations, and contextual entirety. The father of the important concepts "oikotype" and "active and passive bearers of tradition," von Sydow modernized armchair speculation about an abstract and mechanistic migration of texts, and transformed the discipline into the pursuit of folklore as the product of a creative interaction of individuals. However, von Sydow himself set the guidelines for his students without being productive himself. The essence of his contribution to the field, a small volume of essays, was published in honor of his seventieth birthday. In it were his most influential writings, including his essay on the classification of categories of folklore. This brief article separated legend from tale, among other genres, and assigned names to subcategories which he identified under unifying terms. Because his classification system was not accompanied by any illustrative texts or exacting descriptions, it left room for diverse applications, creative reworkings, and redefinitions. As Bošković-Stulli pointed out in her essay "Telling about Life," "the memorate is not a suitable term for talking about reminiscences from real life, even if they were to correspond to von Sydow's insufficiently clearly stated thought on the notion of the memorate" (1988: 22).

Von Sydow's followers continue to use his definitions and classifications freely to this day (Abrahams 1992: 15; Cochrane 1987; Honko 1980b: 280–285; Palmenfelt 1993; Rooth 1979; Swahn 1955). Because his definition had such an impact on modern academic folklorists in America, I would like to quote it in full, in the German original (from which the English version had been abstracted), to avoid possible mistranslation:

> Was man jedoch gewöhnlich unter dem Worte Sage versteht, sind kurze, einepisodische Erzählungen, in deren Hintergrund allerdings Erlebnisse und Beobachtungen stehen; doch sind sie nicht unmittelbar aus diesen hervorgegangen, sondern aus einer derartigen Elementen entsprungenen Vorstellung, die sich in ihnen sozusagen kristallisierte. In der Gestalt, die sie annehmen, können sie sich nicht ereignet haben, sie wurden vielmehr von der Fabulierkunst des Volkes geformt, das den von der Sage behandelten Stoff zurechtzulegen versuchte, und zu erklären und zu bezeugen bestrebt war, wie es sich damit verhält. Ich habe sie früher Zeugensagen (vittnessägner) genannt; aber da sie in Aufbau und Verwendung so nahe mit gewissen Fabeln übereinstimmen, dürfte es richtiger sein, ihnen einen anderen Namen beizulegen. Ich schlage die Benennung Fabulat vor, was nicht nur einen guten Gegensatz zu Memorat bildet, sondern als internationaler Ausdruck auch gut für jegliche Sprache passt. (von Sydow 1934: 74; see also the version in Granberg 1969: 90–91)

The same determination of "Sagen Categories" I quote here from the English abstract, as follows:

> *Memorates* are narratives of personal happenings which may pass into the tradition of *memorial sagen* [Erinnerungssagen]. Another group which also comes under sagen is *chronical notes* [Chroniknotizen], which may deal with any subject and often combine the sagen of various kinds. Sagen properly so called are short, single-episodic tales, built, it is true, upon elements of real happenings and observations, but with this background of reality transformed by the inventive fantasy of the people. I would suggest calling these sagns *fabulates* and dividing them into the following groups: *belief fabulates* [Glaubensfabulate] are associated with popular beliefs and often with persons, objects, etc., which act as a *criterion motive* intended to confirm the truth of the story. To jocular fabulates [Scherzfabulate] I place *inter alia* some of the "Tales of the Stupid Ogre" in Aarne's *Type-Register*. Close to this are the *person fabulates* [Personenfabulate], which are connected with definite, named persons and which sometimes expand into *fabulate cycles* (e.g., Till Enlenspiegel). The large group of *aetiological sagns*, which are often fabulate in character, I divide into two groups: The "narrative" I call aetion fabulates, whereas the other, the "assertive," I call *motival ficts* [Kausal-fiktionen]. The former group is divisible into *aetiological animal fables*, to which i.a. I place The Tail Fisher (Aa. 2) and *Imitates*, which are based upon the imitation of animal voices. (von Sydow, 87)

This definition of the legend is, in essence, composed of the same elements as the others: It is a single-episode story rooted in certain (belief) conceptions, established by experience and observation. The story attempts to explain and validate its statement by evidence; but in its elaborated form, as created by the narrational art of the folk, it could not have happened. As can be seen, the observation that the legend is "told for true but is untrue" appears also in von Sydow's formulation; it is an endowment of the belief-statement with artistic polish — distanced from reality through the building of a crystallized formula.

Elaborating on von Sydow's suggestions, Pentikäinen's concise version described the legend (or fabulate) as a "report of the explicitly fabulated, composed of non-empirical, not-believable elements" (Pentikäinen 1968: 163). While planning an international classification system, Tillhagen defined the legend as a textually classifiable unit, and slightly rearranged the elements outlined by von Sydow. His definition appears in two versions:

> 1. The legend is in its form and other essentials a fixed and unified narrative built of one or more motifs communicating a belief-content. It should be available in at least two versions that have been collected from different places. (1964: 10)

> 2. A fabulate is a portrayal created and transmitted by folk fantasy and exhibits a fixed motivic pattern. Its content belongs or belonged to folk belief or has some other attachment to reality and is normally reported to prove a traditional belief concept. (1964: 10)

Tillhagen's suggestion that memorates be omitted from legend typologies met with general approval — probably for practical reasons, because of the form's textual instability. However, it is difficult to understand why variants of the same story cannot be kept under the same heading even though they are told in diverse styles.

### Anglo-American Approaches

Despite the continual interest in indigenous legendry, modern Anglo-American folklore scholarship has not displayed great originality in defining it. Scholars have been and still are exploring a new field dominated by the mass media. They are preoccupied with searching for new approaches that will enable them to have a better observation of the contemporary processes of legend formation. They are interested in describing and analyzing performance situations, and in exploring and identifying emergent subcategories. Therefore, these scholars take more interest in the specific than the general features of the legend as a genre.

The Funk and Wagnalls definition of legend emphasizes "truth" in its laconic statement: The legend is a "narrative supposedly based on fact, with an intermixture of traditional materials, told about a person, place, or incident. . . . The legend is told as true" (Leach 1949 vol. II: 612). As Jansen phrased it, the legend is a "narrative performed in the belief that it is literally or occasionally, figuratively true" (1977: xi). Hand followed the European canon with a sincere ambition to create a classification for the American folk legend (1965). But the classification never materialized because systematic collecting was never conducted. Hand's collection, deposited in the Archives of the Folklore and Mythology Center at the University of California at Los Angeles, contains only excerpts, deemed to be "popular beliefs and superstitions." Nevertheless, it has become the source for a belief and superstition encyclopedia that is still in progress.

At the symposium on the American folk legend in 1969, Dundes (1971) and Halpert (1971) reiterated the known formulas of definition. Dundes contrasted the legend to the tale and myth; Halpert noted that the legend is told as truth or is believed to be true. But no new propositions were submitted. Unsurprisingly, Georges's critical summary of the existing definitions can be read as an unintentional satire, as it highlighted the inconsistencies, contradictions, and biases: "The legend is a story or narrative," wrote Georges, "that may not be a story or narrative at all; it is set in a recent or historical past that may be conceived to be remote or antihistorical or not really past at all; it is believed to be true by some, false by others, or both or neither by most." He suggested formulating a new concept of legend instead of using the available precedents. "A concept must be sought in the nature and structure of the sets of relationships that underlie and are implicit in what we call legends and that constitute, on another level of abstraction, the least common denominators of the learning process" (Georges 1971: 18). Up to this day, many have cited this provocative article, but neither Georges nor others have taken his criticism to heart and followed his advice.

Notably, at the time of the 1969 conference, Dorson had already offered a variant on the usual definition that accommodated his concept of legendry as accompanying, marking, or characterizing epochs of American history. More than anyone else before him, Dorson emphasized the common knowledge of social groups that formulate their own body of legends:

> Because they purport to be historical and factual, they must be associated in the mind of the community with some known individual, geographic landmark, or particular episode. Many or all of the members of a given social group will have heard of the tradition and can recall it in brief or elaborated form. This is indeed one of the main tests of a legend, that it be known to a number of people united in their area or residence or occupation or nationality or faith. These groups keep alive and pass along legends of heroes and bad men, of local visitations from demons and goblins, and of miraculous interpositions in battles and plagues. (1968: 165)

The gleaning of definitions from the bulky literature on contemporary legends since the conference in 1969 proves disappointing. Here are a handful, selected at random.

According to Buchan, legends are "stories told as true which circulate by word of mouth in contemporary society and exhibit traditional variation" (1981: 1–15). McCulloch argued that "if a story is good enough it need not be true, since it ought to be true" (1987: 115). Davies wrote, "Legends are tales whose capacity to shock depends on the casual way they drop a horrid surprise into the everyday world of the audience. They are told about people who resemble those who tell and listen to the story, and their plausibility depends on yet another such person — the 'friend of a friend'" (Davies 1990: 64).

After Rodney Dale had coined the term *foaf* for the "friend of a friend" tale — an unlikely story told as true (1978) — the definition component of "eye-witness testimony" was eagerly adapted by folklorists as a principal characteristic of legends. *FOAFtale News* became the title of the Newsletter of the International Society for Contemporary Legend Research. Furthermore, Nicolaisen wrote, "The legend is (therefore) in the first place, a narrative response to a stimulus produced by accommodation of interests of both teller and listeners, by a negotiated overlap of motivations" (1984: 172).

Williams's valiant struggle with the definition of contemporary legend was self-defeating. He suggested areas where the differences between traditional and contemporary legends may be detected; however, he felt that, so far, scholars had ended up with the statement that "no definition of contemporary legend can ever be complete" (1984: 228). Thus, it is no wonder that, after considering the possible criteria for defining and classifying legends, Bennett rejected the "conventional concept" that the legend is "a story believed to be true" and concluded that "the question of the definition of the genre is . . . still wide open" (1987: 27).

The air of pessimism concerning the legend's definability may be topped by another rather eccentric (or cynical) observation by Oring. He did not say what he thought the legend was, but he did criticize folklorists for their definitions that were dependent "upon information which is either unnatural, unknowable, or unlikely." Oring charged that "legend is a function of the ideology of the folklorist" (1990: 164). But isn't this true of the definition of any existing thing?

### The Contemporary Legend

The attempts to define the "contemporary" legend have been no less problematic. In this area, the difficulty lies in the lack of a generally acceptable definition of the legend proper from which the contemporary legend should be distinguished. Gary Alan Fine's systematic, scholarly effort managed to carve out an "operational definition." He believed it would be impossible to make a definition fully acceptable but hoped at least to render it plausible:

> I propose that a "contemporary legend" is a narrative that a teller presents
> to an audience in the context of their relationship. The text is an account of

a happening in which the narrator or an immediate personal contact was not directly involved, and is presented as a proposition for belief; it is not always believed by speaker or audience, but it is presented as something that could have occurred and is told as if it happened. These occurrences are notable happenings of the kind that are allegedly "strange but true." (G. A. Fine 1992: 2)

This is an accurate description of the classic fabulate, which excludes the ego-involved memorate-style recital.

Wyckoff's definition of contemporary legend had a different emphasis. It maintained the belief-orientation but tended toward a memorate-style formulation:

Contemporary legends — those generally anonymous, apocryphal, narratable, linguistic-based rumour-stories that report on ostensibly true and relatively current events — often circulate within a community as part of an unconscious, creative, collective response to some community concern, even as they symbolically encode the social ambiguities that underlie that concern. (Wyckoff 1993: 2)

Two more succinct variants of the latest crop did not bring novelty either, but did stress other known features of the legend:

Die Sage als geglaubte, für wahr gehaltene Erlebnis-und Ereignis-geschichte. (Brednich 1990: 7)

*Legend is an account of an experience or an event considered as factual.*

In short, contemporary legends sit somewhere between mundane, everyday experiences and the extraordinary. If you like, they are about the mundane and ordinary, but with an unusual twist. And it is their mundaneness which provides them with a unique quality which sets them apart from other forms of traditional narratives. (Smith 1995: 99)

The most traditional — and almost ritually repeated, varied, expanded, and in turn condensed — definition appears in the public voice of Jan Harold Brunvand's many publications, which merchandize legends as an educational tool for the lay public: "You don't have to be afraid of these horrendous stories," is his message, "because they never happened." As an interviewer of the *Chapel Hill Newspaper* explains, "Brunvand, a folklorist at the University of Utah specializes in tracking and debunking 'urban legends'" (Sept. 26, 1990). No doubt, Brunvand's reading of legends, which he presents to the general readership, has reached and influenced new generations of academic folklorists, and has reinforced earlier notions. According to Brunvand, the goal of the legend is to "explain unusual and supernatural happenings in the natural world." Legends are "folk narratives that deal with realistic incidents set in the past. Though they are told as 'true' stories — and are often believed — legends sometimes contain supernatural and bizarre elements" (1981: 194); and "the more variations there are in a 'true tale,' the less likely it is to be true" (28–29). In his syndicated newspaper column in 1989, Brunvand wrote, "The tellers . . . are simply repeating with variations, a story they have heard. Even if there's some truth behind the stories, repetition of them in different versions, with local details inserted, all add up to a genre of modern legend." Some more recent variations of Brunvand's definition included the following: Legends are "true stories that are too good to be true" (1990: 120) and "apocryphal, anonymous, supposedly true, plotted stories, widely told in different variants over a considerable time period" (1990: 111). All these definitions seem to foreground the question of truth or falsity, as though the scholarly goal of decoding the legend depends on the determination of whether the story is true.

Is this all the legend is about? Maybe Bennett was right to confess defeat at definition attempts. She said that "only by patient work on the small print of our fascinating but oh-so-tricky chosen genre, will we be able to pin down that elusive butterfly 'legend' and begin to have the slightest idea what we're talking about" (Bennett and Rowbottom 1998: 34).

But maybe we have some more ideas to consider. I would like to conclude the parade of definitions by adding two more. Jeggle's view of the legend was an offshoot from Peuckert's and employed analytical psychology with considerable originality:

> Not all events and not all that is unexplainable together compose a legend. It is a specific connection of certain experiences and an [existing] collective explanatory model that at least in part seems to be irrational. . . . The unusual, that runs against the everyday determined by work and its enduring, posits questions. (Jeggle 1987: 38)

Rudolf Schenda's legend definition was a new summary of his lifelong experience with folk narrative tradition and mass culture over three centuries:

> The legend is a narrative produced and transmitted orally or in writing, about a single, extraordinary, supernatural or marvelous, true or fictitious, believed or slighted, often dated/localized event (experience), brought up with didactic or entertaining intent; it serves to confirm, or expand the experiential horizon of the recipient and confirm or question a momentarily valid conception of the world. (Schenda and Doornkaat 1988: 12)

Even with the addition of the last two definitions, the components seem to be crystallized and remarkably stable. The core idea remains that untruth is told for truth and that the other components are used to set up and elaborate this assumption. The place and degree of significance of these other components in particular definitions depends on the point of view of each scholar.

Anderson would have been gratified to see how his law of self-correction has manifested in a *Normalform* of definitions.

## Keywords and Concepts in the Household of the Folklorist

As we have seen, some key concepts appear frequently in past and current legend definitions. How useful are these in speculating further about the legend? Here I will mention only a few that seem to carry different meanings for different definers and therefore need clarification, which will be forthcoming in the chapters that discuss these topics. It is not my intention to take issue with the variable applications of terms and concepts in the practice of legend study nor to subject them to critical analysis. I am only taking a cursory look at the popular concepts in general circulation among folklorists to determine whether they are sufficiently clear and useful to incorporate into a summary definition.

A general uncertainty surrounds these concepts. Nevertheless, as possible definition components they may be important. It would be a mistake to believe that the legend cannot necessarily be defined because its constituent elements lack definition. And it would be nonsensical to assume — remembering the example of the sparrow — that an existing thing is indefinable. Correspondingly, it would be sheer absurdity to accept — remembering the (bird) family of Fringilladae — that a complex thing cannot be classified. If such were the case, we would indeed face a mysterious phenomenon. Although legends can be mysterious, the discipline that studies them should not be.

TRADITION     Few express doubt that folklore is "based on tradition," although some ask if all folklore is "traditional." Many folklorists have speculated about the term, seeking a distinction between "traditional" and "nontraditional" components of folklore. John Johnson, my colleague at Indiana University, has been conducting graduate seminars that invite speakers (folklorists and scholars from neighboring disciplines) to present their personal uses of the term, and the variety has been great. Nordic folklorists prefer to use "tradition-research" and "science of tradition" as synonyms of folkloristics,[9] although tradition is not only a folkloristic trait (Shils 1981). The provocative suggestion of British social historians that tradition is "constructed" or "invented" turned the interest of some folklorists away from their disciplinary focus to the larger picture of the political climate (nationalism and the politics of culture). No human act or thought lacks traditionality: Without adjustment to a socially accepted, historically developed convention in human behavior, there would be no cultural continuity.[10] But the term *tradition* deserves to be clarified when it is applied to the legend, which is regarded as a traditional story.

What is meant by the traditionality of the legend, particularly in the light of contemporary research into the legendry of the industrial world? Are we to determine the degree of traditionality in content, form, and ideological meaning of a story when it emerges from a new physical and intellectual environment? How many people should possess and share a tradition in order to constitute a legend-bearing group? A hundred? A thousand? A million? As a minimum, how many persons have to constitute the chain of transmitters so that the material passed on can be considered as "traditional"? Some folklorists require two people, others four — but why not five as the required minimum? Why not six, or ten? How old must a tradition be to qualify as traditional? Should it be timeless? A century old? A decade? A year? Less? And how much less? A day? An hour?

Instant legends abound today, when a misunderstood item of radio newscast or a convincing television drama can convert hearsay and rumor into a legend that can spread within minutes, while seasoned traditional items may fade into obscurity. Without having reached a consensus on tradition, folklorists face additional difficulties in describing the *memorate*, the personal legend based on first-hand experience.

And finally, do we consider diachronic and synchronic processes in the formulation and spread of legends? Is the legend a story that is passed from father to son, uncle to nephew, aunt to niece, from older person to younger person? If we were to follow only the legend traditions transmitted in this manner, we would have good reason to speak of legend poverty instead of legend riches.

Yet legends abound, displaying personal creativity along traditional formulaic lines. The bulk of socially-relevant legends falls more on the nontraditional side than on the traditional — if one can speak of anything at all in culture as "nontraditional."

CREATIVE FANTASY    We know that folklore — the obscure "lore" of the likewise obscure "folk" — can be considered as the product of the "creative fantasy" or "fabulating mood" of the folk who, like Goethe's mother, had *"Lust zu fabulieren"* (the pleasure to spin stories). Nevertheless, outside of the metaphorical expressions of the enraptured folklorist, how can the creative fantasy of people be considered in the sober, explicit terms of science? Can it be an independent invention or must it be the embroidery of an existing tradition? (The assumption that inherited materials are faithfully "handed down" as a result of the amazing remembering capacity of oral poets would conflict with the creative fantasy concept.) If, as seems to be the case, creative fantasy is understood as being manifested along the marked-out avenue of tradition, what should be the proportion of the resulting folklore creation? Three-quarters to one? Half and half? Less? Why so much or why so little of each? What rule regulates it?

THE EXTENT OF THE LEGEND     Everybody knows that the legend is a story. But what is the story in a legend? It is seldom a consistent epic; more often it is a kaleidoscopic conglomerate of motifs that seem to be put together by a momentary whim, often with carefree sloppiness. Short or long, the legend appears to be improvised, combining or confusing personal experiences of the past and the present. The worst of all is that variants seem to be generated by stressing one particular incident — causing great diversity simply through de-emphasizing or completely dropping the other parts of the master story (the type). Single incidents (motifs) can have an independent life, and then link up with other parts; but more often, the background — the general context — reveals their connection to a story.

For example, in 1981 the *Badische Zeitung* (March 12) featured this report: "A bearded hitchhiker . . . told about an earthquake and apocalypse to the driver before disappearing from the passenger seat. Police found no trace of the tramp and the driver, but the rumor claims that the latter is in the Tübingen hospital treated for shock in the psychiatric ward." Common knowledge of the classic "Vanishing Hitchhiker" legend provides the missing information necessary to identify this news report as a legend.

And still the question remains: What is a story? An account in which something takes place? An experience that is recounted later? But not every utterance that gives account of a happening is a story. A simple brief sentence can also state something that happened: "Uncle Bertie lost his pipe; an invisible hand grabbed it. . . ." Therefore, the legend must be longer than a brief sentence. So how much longer must it be? Should it consist of at least two sentences? Or ten? Or a hundred?

And why must a legend be a story? Where does the text of a told, read, played, or ostensibly committed legend begin and where does it end? How can it be separated from the conversation of which it seems to be a part? What is the standard of comparison or relation or opposition that we should use to determine whether a legend is a full story, or a corrupt, truncated, or fragmentary one in abstract or summary form? Many folklorists have made their own determinations concerning the completeness of legend texts, but who has the authority to decide these matters if not the performer?

TIMING     It was stated that the legend is a "historical account." Does this mean that it took place in the past? If it must be in the past, then how long ago? In the prehistoric or in the historic past? Folklorists tend to distinguish between the prehistoric, myth-producing past and the historic, legend-producing past. But how about the immediate past?

And how about the present? For example, where is the place of stories that are told about visions or hallucinations concerning "imaginary treasures" or "otherworldly beings" (Čistov 1967: 36). They exist in the present, but are based on tradition and creative fantasy. How about precognitive images, dreams, and simultaneous perceptions (Kaivola-Bregenhøj 1990; Virtanen 1990)? And where is the place of the utopias and the predictions of future legendary events?[11] These are likewise based on tradition and shaped by folk fantasy.

ORALITY    Almost all definitions state explicitly, or implicitly assume, that legends are orally told, face-to-face with an attending audience. Yet many folklorists use non-oral texts (Dégh 1994a). Why, then, is it still held that the legend is an oral genre? Should we include here also such channels of communication as the telephone, fax machine, e-mail, and the radio and television, provided they relay historical accounts, based on folk tradition and embroidered by folk fantasy, into the stream of oral transmission? Should we consider also the magnetic tape or video, which have become the vehicle of correspondence for those who dislike reading and writing? How about the letter itself? Say, for example, that a legend sender writes a legend message to a receiver, who is a member of the legend-receiving and/or transmitting audience on the Internet. In what way might this process be considered a written, emergent conversational legend session?

BELIEF    Whose belief is important? Is it the belief of the sender, or of the receiver, the community, the general public, the collector, or somebody else? Is it up to the researcher to determine belief? If so, what measure of belief is required? Should it be absolute and unconditional, or can it be with limitations, with doubt, or with hesitation?

OBJECTIVE TRUTH    Whose subjective opinion determines an objective truth? How can the raconteur, his or her audience, or anybody else involved in the legend-process possibly know in each case what is objectively true? In defining the legend, few mention a subjectively perceived truth, although this is what folklorists ought to be concerned with. For subjective beings — humans — truth that is commonly expressed cannot be objective.

BELIEF CONCEPT (*GLAUBENVORSTELLUNG*)    According to Honko, this "much used and vaguely defined term has been applied to quite different traditional items" (Honko 1965: 9; see also Simonsuuri 1964: 19–22). The belief concept is the common denominator in brief statements of belief, which usually are made upon solicitation and lack any narrative contextualization. These beliefs are kept in reserve, and have the potential to link up with legends or develop into legends.

REALITY    Interestingly, along with belief and objective truth, non-belief, objective untruth, and non-reality are the most constant components of the definition, but they are not always used in the same way.

We also could mention more nebulous terms in active circulation, such as the aforementioned "numinous," and the "totally other," which was borrowed from Otto and applied to supernatural legends and their constituents. Furthermore, "psychological needs," "attitudes toward reality," "temporary suspension of disbelief," "interstitial anxiety," and other phrases appear frequently in discussions; but they are never adequately explained or justified in *deus ex machina* interpretations.

### Persistence of Grimmian Classificatory Principles

In view of all that has been said so far, it should be noted that not only are definitions popular exercises in academe, but classifications have continued to attract interest ever since the appearance of the Grimm brothers' work. Following their guidance, folklorists have identified and keep distinguishing three kinds of legends:

1. The mythological or demonological. Accounts about ordinary people's encounters with supernatural agencies.
2. The historical. Stories about historical events, locations, and known personalities of national and social prominence.
3. The etiological, also known as *Natursagen*. Explanatory stories about the origin and nature of animate and inanimate phenomena.

This grouping of legends still prevails and can be found in basic folklore textbooks.

Saints' (religious) legends were excluded, or only marginally included, because they were regarded as literary — originating in ecclesiastic literature; however, it would be difficult to argue against the inclusion of non-canonical miracle legends and keep them separate from the category of mythological legends. The horror story, acknowledged as "modern" and "urban" but not supernatural, is listed as a separate category (Baughman 1966: Z500–599); it has not been melded into the main system, although its existence predates the industrial age and the even more urban civilization of the twentieth century (Petzoldt 1989).

The problem with the three distinctive categories — mythological, historical, and explanatory — is that they designate features that are or may be present in all three. Most legends are mythic, demonic, supernatural, or mystic; are set in human, and thus historical, time; and include an explanation or interpretation in the account. Bausinger quotes a legend about Martin Luther being tempted by the devil while he was working on his Bible translation. To get rid of the tempter, Luther hurled an inkstand at him, and the blue spot can still be seen on the wall (Bausinger 1968: 177–178). What kind of legend is this — a devil legend? A demonological, etiological, or historical legend?

Other attempts to classify legends deserve mention. One discriminates legends according to their range of dissemination: *local legends* are those known to people in one community or region because they are related to local persons and objects; *migratory legends* are those that the folklorist has experienced in other locations, so they are widespread and adjusted to other localities and people. Is this a reasonable distinction? Aren't legends both local *and* migratory? How can the folk know that their cherished repertoire pieces are by no means local and unique but rather are shared by innumerable others? How can they know that the narrated nightmare did not happen only to the local butcher — that the pale, ghostly youth who disappeared from the butcher's van has also visited many nightly motorists on highways throughout the world? The fact is that the local legend is local to the folk, no matter how far it migrates in the folklorist's experience.

Another distinction has been based on the narrative polish of the narrator. The simple, personalized rendition of a story is called *memorate* and the third-person, elaborate, more distant, and impersonal variant of the same story is called *fabulate*. Aren't these also identical with the pair called local and migratory?

## The Need and Hardships of Classification

Ordered lists of regional, local, cross-cultural, and topical legend bodies, as well as their constituent elements, comprise the majority of contributions to legend scholarship. Alver (1967: 63) speaks of the "archivist," who collects the legend material and prepares indexes for the "analyst." Dundes rightfully calls legend study "sterile and unrewarding," as it has never been able to get away from "hair splitting classification debates" (1971: 21). However, as I have already stated, I cannot condemn pioneer legend scholars for their commitment to classification. After all, the collected items have to be ordered for closer examination. Nothing can be more frustrating than a mass of good data — like Hyatt's *Hoodoo — Conjuration — Witchcraft — Rootwork* (1970) — without a structured classificatory register. The more variants we have, the better are our chances of charting the extent and variability of a type.

The largest scholarly cooperative of European and American legend scholars, launched in 1959, considered a basic legend index as its most urgent task. The communally designed and endorsed project included the determination of classifiable units, regional fieldwork, data indexing, and classification of certain legend categories. The regional diversity of materials sparked heated discussions, and criticism surrounded the preliminary reports upon their presentation (Dégh 1971, notes 7 and 8; Heilfurth and Greverus 1967). It seemed that anyone who felt dissatisfied with the existing systems constructed others according to their own principles. The situation looked chaotic, and because of the lack of clear criteria, the idea of creating a platform looked remote. Researchers grew increasingly unsure about which texts should be determined as legends, and which ones should be placed into the "transitional" (mixed) or "miscellaneous" category, which widened with suspicious rapidity (Bausinger 1968).

The orderly legend scholar had to realize that the commonly used but not always up-to-date definitions were not helpful in this endeavor. Those who experimented with classification, myself among them, began with a reverse procedure. Starting from the individual — the entities declared as legends — they moved to the more general, seeking the superior concept that would comprise the attributes of all species so that it could be considered the general determinant of the complete legend. This sounds rather cumbersome, although it is common to everyday thinking. In the specific case of the legend, this procedure was not easy because the data — the large legend corpus, preserved as a precious heirloom in national and regional archives — contained very little reliable material fit for scholarly analysis (Dégh and Vázsonyi 1971: 286–294). Modern investigators were generally critical of archival collections, calling them useless: Melville Jacobs, for example, found folklore archives "archaic" and said that there was no alternative but to rebuild them (1966: 427). The principles of collecting and publishing legends have been diverse, and this fact affected the choice of materials in many ways. But, in general, there was always one common flaw: Both recorded and published texts were truncated. This remains true of any legend material, recorded from word-of-mouth or gleaned from printed matter. In the märchen genre, the frame of the tale has been, as a rule, regarded as a constituent part, as well as a conspicuous identification mark (Petsch 1900). In contrast, the conversational frame or the situation-description that led to the recital of the legend has been most often disregarded. The reason for this negligence might be because the introductory and concluding parts of the legend are less stereotypical and less formulaic, and thus are not readily discernible. Also, the collector's interest was usually focused on publishing a smooth story, rather than one that was whimsically interrupted by comments and set in a situational context. But it is precisely these circumstances that bring legends to life, and the omission of them in legend transcripts unfortunately renders legend texts almost unrecognizable and fit only for variant documentation. In other words, in the case of the legend, interpretation from the story content itself is not enough — all of the preliminaries that lead to the story and the story's frame are also needed for analysis.

It was not enough that our forebears arbitrarily cut parts off the legend; they also made a rule out of their mistake and passed it on to our generation. "The legend has no frame" and "the legend has no form" sounded the litany. (For a detailed discussion of the formlessness of the legend, see Dégh 1991: 18–19.) Thereby the natural or any arbitrarily reconstructed shape — with its given conversational, social, or intertextual context, and meaning and socio-psychological background — fell victim to this arbitrary collecting principle.

So today it is difficult to find comparable material in the old collections. We seem to be better off with the materials deposited in archives, as well as those that were printed in older sources which displayed a harmonious rela-tionship between the legend-teller and the collector-publisher in the shaping of the stories. The publication of old Swiss legends by Schenda and ten Doorn-kaat is a good example of the latter (1988).

The material available for our analytical reading is "so immense that it touches upon the whole spectrum of folk culture" (L. Schmidt 1963: 107). The stock of legendry is exceedingly variegated, and individual legends display great dissimilarities. It was found, for example, that a principal problem of legend analysis, and indeed of legend classification generally, is that multiple agents perform a single function and that stable functions and variable *dra-matis personae* are the most difficult factors (Hand 1964; 1965: 443). Versions might unexpectedly appear any time; likewise, they may suddenly disappear, giving way to others or continuing to live in other variations. Dundes claims that the corpus of legends is unlimited: Each era adds its own contribution to legendry, whereas myths and tales are less likely to show so much vitality (1971: 25).

The continuous variability of the legend gives the impression that its classi-fication is next to impossible. Röhrich wrote that the heterogeneity of the form of the legend is not governed by epic law (Röhrich 1958: 662). "For the sys-tematizer," writes Hand, "folk legends seem endless in bulk and variety, and they are often so short and formless as to defy classification" (Hand 1965: 439). So it seems that a common denominator sufficient for all classes of legends is nowhere in sight. Folklorists seem to be skeptical of the feasibility of a com-mon basis that does not allow exceptions, hybrid subcategories, and irregulari-ties. Georges explicitly says that universals exist only "in the minds of those who insist that they must" (1971: 18).

Most of the classifiers have agreed with Stith Thompson's argument that catalogues should serve practical and not theoretical purposes; and that a simple, content-oriented retrieval system would be most useful as a guide and finder to make the otherwise inaccessible materials available for international research. Indeed, according to Tillhagen, catalogues do not need to be abso-lutely scientific (1964: 11). At the 1963 meeting of the legend commission of the International Society of Folk Narrative Research (ISFNR), a proposal was submitted to construct a unified catalogue for all narrative genres as a continuation of the *Types of the Folktale* (Peeters 1963b: 26) — this wishful thinking of archivists has yet to materialize.

## The Many Species of the Legend

Anyone who would like to find out how many kinds of legends exist just within one culture area would probably find this objective impossible. Nor would it be an easy task to ascertain how many kinds of legends are registered in the national and international scholarly classifications. Even the most general of the currently used terms engender confusion. What is the meaning of these many labels and how can they express sub-categories or coordinative relationships within the different classes of legends? Which term signifies the whole and which the part? Which term denotes a higher category, which denotes a subgroup including hybrid or transitional forms, and which is simply a synonym that reintroduces the well-known meaning in a sophisticated disguise? Which term denotes common features and which concerns only rare or unparalleled formulations? Which concerns legends of great variability and which indicates those that are long dead and gone?

The reasons for the baffling variety are numerous. One is that the legend — which has been declared as hard or impossible to define — has been subjected to many diverse definitions. Each author of definitions felt it necessary also to create custom-made terms, and this in itself inflated the international nomenclature enormously. Secondly, the plethora of rules resulted in exceptional types, which in turn spawned a proliferation of tangled word compounds in many languages. These coinages — including terms like *media narraforms* (Grider 1976) or *idionarrations* (Ward 1990a) — in turn called for new rules, and thus made for more new groupings that were in need of yet more names.

It is difficult to decide whether one should agree with Honko and regret that there are folklorists who see the legend as one homogeneous genre and forget about its categories (1965: 7–8), or whether one should think about what Hand and others say, that legends are so diverse in form and extent that they cannot be classified (Hand 1965: 440). Or should one give credit to those who state that no ordering is needed at all (L. Schmidt 1965: 74)? Naturally, all those who kept experimenting with classification were convinced that it could be done well and that there was a good reason for doing it. At any rate, prior to classifying legends, one has to familiarize oneself with the viewpoints of previous ordering attempts.

We might begin with a summary survey of the most easily accessible classes of legends, just to refresh our memory. Bødker's 1965 encyclopedic work, the last of its kind, is dependable enough and is accessible to international folklorists, although it does not contain the terms of the more productive recent years. Nevertheless, the terms listed by Bødker are impressive. Like other lexicons, its data is not ordered by any logical system or critical considerations other than the order of the alphabet. This way, the single items following each other comprise the multifarious reflections of authors from different periods over the span of 150 years. The succession of the disparate materials by itself creates a sort of unintentional humor, and the reader might find it difficult not to satirize; but the lexical organization of such useful data does not deserve mockery. In view of such wealth in legend terminology, one cannot help recalling that the Arabs have three hundred distinct terms for the camel, according to how old it is, how many offspring it has, its sex, shade, temper, and so on. Similarly, the Lapps have hundreds of words for reindeer because they attribute more significance to the distinctive features within the species than to the fact that all are basically reindeer. Similarly, the material gathered for Bødker's book seems to suggest by its proportions that folkloristics so far has been unable to create abstractions on the basis of its collections and that experts have not reached agreement on the legend and its categories (Honko 1965: 7–8).

The first entry of the Bødker dictionary is *Abendmahlslegends* (Supper Legends) because it concerns the Last Supper. This in itself makes one wonder: Even if there are Supper Legends, why do they deserve a separate category? The last entry is the *Zwergsage* (Dwarf Legend), consisting of narratives about dwarves "and other subterranean spirits" with reference to the related categories of "Demon Legend" and "Fabulate Legend." The "Demon Legend" is subdivided into four main groups, according to whether the demons live (1) in water, (2) on or in the earth, (3) in fire, and finally (4) in the air. Each of these has, of course, its subgroups, and these concern only supernatural beings, specifically spirits and revenants.

We have been dealing so far with legends under A and Z (in German), but it is worthwhile to select some choice samples from what is between the beginning and the end of the alphabet. Toward the beginning of Bødker's dictionary is the entry *Bischopssage*, that is, "Bishop Legend" (in Dutch). We rapidly turn over the pages to see whether other members of the clergy have not been bypassed, and there they are. There is an entry of *Prestasaga* or "Priest Legend" (in Icelandic); it belongs to the subclass of the humorous *Gamansaga*, and includes legends about priests of lower rank. One might ask what happens if a legend is about priests but is not humorous? No doubt, it would have been filed in a new subclass. The *Familiensage* or "Family Legend" is told about a single family. Presumably it is almost identical with the *Sippensage* or "Kinship Legend," which, according to specification, concerns "the whole family." But if the two are identical, why were separate denominations needed? And if they are not the same, what is the difference between them? Both are listed as "multi-episodic," so this raises the question of what would happen if monoepisodic legends are discovered that deal with single but whole families?

Taking a big leap toward the end of the alphabet, we find the *Verhältnissage* or "Proportion Legend," which concerns giants and compares the dimensions of their bodies and their strength to other things. Four kinds of proportion legends are split into further groups. We will look at just a few random examples:

Subgroup I. b. the nostril of the giants; d. obscene motifs; e. bathing and drinking of giants in streams in remote valleys.

Subgroup II. b. giants put men into their pockets.

Subgroup IV. b. blindness, one-eyedness, and squint of giants; c. giants have one eye on the brow; d. giants have huge fiery eyes; e. giants are pagan, foes of Christ and his church; f. giants are Christian; g. stupidity of giants.

But this is not the only classification of giant legends. Those found in the German tradition are divided into thirty-seven groups. "Pebble in the shoe of the giant" is one of the sub-categories, and it certainly sounds interesting.

This sampling will suffice, although Bødker's dictionary offers other sources for the humorist. One might agree with Dundes, who calls such systematization "antiquarian butterfly collecting" (1965: 421). Nevertheless, we should stress that these items were chosen tendentiously. I lifted these samples from their presumable contexts, instead of trying to fit them into their possible contexts. The latter would have been difficult and maybe impossible, for it is unclear which are the most characteristic attributes of a legend or legend group. We do not know which aspects are decisive in determining similarity and dissimilarity. And there are many types not registered in Bødker's dictionary.

Even if we tried to cite only the most common criteria, chosen at random, they would be disturbingly numerous. Are the sources of a legend personal experience or folk tradition? How does the teller relate it — in first or third person? Does it concern a familial, local, or a more general topic? How far has the story spread? Does it stay within a limited circle or does it tend to migrate? Is it national or international, rural or urban? What kind of belief does it express: that of the official religion or that of a particular folk religion? If it is rooted in folk religion, what is its foundation: superstition or generalized belief? Who is its hero, a human or a superhuman being? If the hero is human, is it a definite or an unnamable person? What is the story's size, and is it mono- or multi-episodic? What kind of elements comprise it? What is its function? What is the reason or the purpose of its telling — warning, admonition, edification, entertainment, disciplining, or scaring? Does it concern supernatural capabilities? Does it deal with historic topics? Which motifs of other folklore genres are intermingled with it?

We can refrain from positing further questions, even though we have not begun to exhaust all of the potential criteria. Each criterion is sensible and might have its justification. Nevertheless, some doubts arise: Do we really need all of them? Do we really have to inspect the legend from so many diverse points of view? Honko suggested the use of nine criteria for folklore analysts (some of them not included in ours): content, form, style, structure, function, frequency, distribution, age, and origin (Honko 1968: 62). Is the normal, unsquinting eye really capable of perceiving so many viewpoints?

It seems obvious that without the determination of the pertinent concepts and the clarification of ordering principles, a more profound definition of the legend would be as premature as its scientific systematization (Bausinger 1968: 171). Hence, the aim of the folk legend specialist cannot be the proposal of a new definition or a new cataloguing system. Too many suggestions have already been made, and none of them have helped much. It will be more timely to discuss the key problems that prevent the formulation of the common denominator for the species legend.

## The Memorate and Its Proper Place in the Legend Universe

Many scholars hold that the initial definition of memorate proposed by von Sydow (1934) is still valid. He asserted the need to distinguish from the legend a category of material that, although "in a way related" to the genre, exhibits neither poetical characteristics nor tradition. He decided to assign the term *memorate* to the mere productions of people's own "purely personal experiences" (close to Jolles's term *memorabile*). All later considerations and interpretations relate to this classic formulation, and most folklorists have accepted it as is, in its entirety or in its major parts. No one questioned whether this scrupulous discrimination of the memorate from other genres carried some major theoretical importance — or even whether the memorate exists at all in the form in which it was described.

Scholars seem to have followed von Sydow's advice and have made a sharp distinction between the memorate and all other narrative forms, even though the distinction actually seems impractical, if not impossible. Primarily, of course, they differentiate it from the fabulate and also from the legend (Pentikäinen 1968; Petzoldt 1989). Further, some have said that the memorate does not belong to folklore at all because it does not possess folkloristic traits. It has also been differentiated from related folklore genres such as the memory legend, the *fict*, the recently identified *Stereotyp* (Pentikäinen 1968: 161), the *Sagenbericht* (legend report), the *Erlebnisbericht* (experience report), the pseudo- and quasi-memorate, the *Sagenmemorate* (legend-memorate), the *Chroniknotiz* (chronicle note), the rumor-legend, the personal experience story, and the nontraditional personal narrative (Dolby 1989). Furthermore, according to Honko and Pentikäinen, the *Chronikat*, based on "historic facts," was sharply distinguished from the memorate, based on "supra normal" experience.

As already mentioned, Tillhagen suggested leaving memorates out of the planned legend catalogue because they do not constitute types but rather are ad hoc constructions in both form and content (1964: 13). This might be just a practical exclusion, not so much reflecting a feeling that the memorate is a *quantité negligible*, but rather that it is too volatile to stabilize for a typology. Klintberg's Swedish folk legend catalogue (in preparation) follows Tillhagen's guidance in excluding motifs and memorates and focusing on "fixed legend types" (Klintberg 1993). On the other hand, Čistov noted that the construction of a catalogue that consisted only of fabulates would be "theoretically incorrect" and would also lead to an "artificial solution." In his view, the catalogue should also contain memorates, quasi-memorates, *Sagenberichte*, and *Chroniknotizen* (Čistov 1967: 40).

A further lack of clarity is reflected in Christiansen's statement that the memorate is "almost always connected with some landmark, locality or person" (1958: 11). What about animals, inanimate objects, and natural or supernatural phenomena? Is it possible that this limitation lies in the specific nature of Norwegian materials? Or is it accounted for by the poverty of adequately ordered and statistically accessible legends? The latter supposition seems more plausible.

Honko called the memorate "a neglected traditional genre" (Honko 1965: 18). But if this was true in 1965, we cannot say it is true today. After folklorists left the narrow confines of peasant society and extended their interest to urban-industrial legendry, they came to realize that the narratives they were discovering in excess were more intimate and personal, closer to von Sydow's memorate than to his fabulate. But contemporary folklorists did not enter into the hairsplitting debate. Following academic tradition, they simply dutifully labeled their items as memorates in increasing quantity and as fabulates less often, without giving too much thought to its theoretical justification. But what should we be doing with the memorate? Is it or isn't it a genre? Is it or isn't it a legend? Should the labeling follow our instinct? If it is true that the memorate can easily be recognized and separated from related narratives, it must be true that it has recognizable attributes that are absent in the other types of stories, or that it lacks attributes present in the others. From this viewpoint, the study of the memorate should promise, among other things, better recognition of the nature of the fabulate.

In the von Sydow thesis, "personal experience" is an important ingredient of the memorate. This postulate can be interpreted only in one way: The story in question can be transmitted to another only by the person who had the experience. If the second person told the story to a third, he or she would not tell it as a personal experience but as that of the first person who had had the original experience and first reported it. The classic definition, therefore, would mean in its strict interpretation that a memorate can be known only by that single person, and respectively by as many people as heard it from him or her. This presupposes either that the second person does not retell the memorate; or that, if the second person does retell it, the narrative can no longer be called a memorate — even if it otherwise corresponds with the original telling almost to the word. In the first supposition (that only the person who had the experience can tell a memorate), the memorate is not a viable story; in the second (when the second person retells the story), it acquires a new name, the *Erinnerungssage* (memory legend) (von Sydow 1934: 73). This appears to be faithful to the idea that by assigning a new name to a phenomenon that does not fit an established rule, the rule is confirmed. Obviously, something had to be done for the memorate to save it from sinking into the swamp of terminology, for not only were single memorates in danger of being bogged down, but the general conception of the genre itself was also threatened.

Over the course of time, the postulate of a "first hand" experience became somewhat flexible. Christiansen, more liberally, found memorates to be "accounts of actual experience at either first or second hand" (Christiansen 1958: 5). Granberg even suggested that memorates can be based not only on personal experience but also on the experience of others if the story was told to the informant directly (Granberg 1969: 91). Although Isler makes a sharp distinction between the fabulate and the *Erlebnisbericht* (experience report), he does admit that the narrators seem not to take the distinction between legend categories as seriously as folklorists must in order to reach conclusions (Isler 1971: 24). Thus, "personal experience" is not an absolute requirement of the memorate, although the narrator has to know personally the people who had the experience.

Correspondingly, the story need not begin with phrases like "this happened to me," or "I saw it with my own eyes"; it also can start with such introductory comments as "I heard it from my grandfather, it happened to him" or "an old friend told me and he saw it himself." This is progress compared to the von Sydow standard, for it opens the category of memorate to a greater number of narratives. More memorates follow the "I heard it from" pattern than any other pattern. Like everyone else, I have encountered mostly such "second-hand" stories with variable contents. And everybody knows of stories beginning with statements like these: "My father told me that it happened to my grandfather" or "My friend said that a personal acquaintance . . ." In fact, most of the spontaneously told legends I have experienced began in such a way. Many of my informants began their stories by saying "I saw it in the paper" or "I heard this on the radio." Or, even more frequently, a von Sydow witness-legend is created by comments like "it was on the Sally Jessy Raphael show" or "our pastor showed us this video." This rendering makes the account a sort of third-hand tradition, because the newspapers, radio, and television take their information from someone else.

Even though the definitions of Granberg and Christiansen are permissive, they still prove to be too narrow for application as more collections from fieldwork accumulate. Pentikäinen, a most thoughtful and thorough researcher, statistically analyzed the memorate corpus of storyteller Marina Takalo and concluded that "there are at best two links in the chain (of transmission) between the one who had the supernatural experience and the one who tells it" (1970: 115). This means that a transmission chain optimally consists of four members. Pentikäinen has not found traditions communicated by a fifth person, and others might have the same finding if they subjected their material to a similar kind of analysis. Hence, by reserving our right to consider those stories learned from retellers five or more links removed as memorates, we take for granted that "normally" the communication chain of a memorate consists of four links.

But let us reflect for a while. What happened to Marina Takalo's memorates, which were heard from first-, second-, and third-person transmitters? She passed them on to Pentikäinen, the folklorist. We should remember that Pentikäinen himself is a bearer of the memorate tradition — being a folklorist does not disqualify him in this capacity. And he has an affinity for folklore and is eager to communicate his material through scholarly publications to others who might also have chosen their profession as folklorists on the basis of operotropism.[12] Experts who scrutinize and have a preference for legends should not be excluded from membership in the legend conduit in the multi-conduit system (Dégh 1975; Dégh and Vázsonyi 1975). In fact, several of my informants referred to "a book" (a volume of *Indiana Folklore*) borrowed from the bookmobile as the source of a legend that they had encountered. For example, Elsie T. from Columbus, Ohio, told me the following:

> There was this . . . ah, . . . a student did a project last fall and got fascinated with it. You know, a babysitter is tripping on LSD or sometimes they say marijuana. He collected eighteen . . . mostly from college students. One from a girl who was twelve I

believe and who had believed it. She heard it at school and is now terrified to go to babysit. She was surprised that her parents let her. His oldest informant was forty-two, a father of teenage children. But the interesting thing was that there was a paper read at the Texas Folklore Society meeting about this friend, [who] told her the story. And . . . while she was home sick, one or two weeks after he heard the paper, [he saw] a movie, that was made in Columbus, *No Deposit, No Return*, and this *legend* is in the movie. And this little girl, she got mono and missed two weeks of class I believe. . . . While she was home sick, one of her friends told her the story. And he said, "You know, this is really interesting because that story is a *legend*."

And what happens when college girls interview each other under the auspices of their professor? Carol, the collector, tells Mary, the informant, "That was — I think — my professor told it. My folklore professor told a version of it" (Ellis 1989a: 45–46). However, Takalo, Pentikäinen's verbose respondent, might also be ready to tell her memorates to others besides the folklorist. Is it probable that the person — who thus might become the fifth link in the transmission chain — considers how many hands the story has gone through when he or she chooses which memorate to reproduce? Hardly. Because this teller is not familiar with Pentikäinen's in-depth analysis (1970: 93), he or she presumably does not care. When people retell stories, they do it simply because the legend appeals to them and they feel that the next member of the transmission chain will also like it. The legend thus follows "normally" the regular and natural course of the legend process through an unlimited number of links of senders and receivers (Dégh and Vázsonyi 1971: 283–284). The memorate does not cease to exist only because it has reached the end of a sequence of four persons.

What happens to a story when it has reached fourth-hand status? "It turns into a fabulate" would be the answer of some, and as a matter of fact many memorates do turn into fabulates when first-person stories become third-person stories. But many fabulates can also be converted into memorates, because a narrator who heard an *Erinnerungssage* story in the third person may turn it into a first-person account when retelling it. This is how "pseudo-memorates" and "quasi-memorates" occur (Čistov 1967: 36). This switching was also noticed by Bausinger (1968: 174) and Woods (1959: 11), who observed that "the fabulate or ordinary legend may appear at times as a memorate." Peuckert also listed examples to illustrate how an experience that must have happened to a third party was internalized by a listener, who converted it into an "I" or an "us" story under the impact of his own narration; eventually, the subject will switch back into the "they" form (1965: 14–16). Slotkin illustrated this point convincingly by the presentation of a narrative performance in which such switching occurs. Discussing critically the use of the term *memorate*, Slotkin asked the question, "Does it help in *not* making a distinction between first- and third-person accounts of supra normal phenomena? If such accounts can move freely between various narrative voices, why do they do so? Should we distinguish between such performances and on what grounds?" (Slotkin 1988: 93).

To be sure, some legends seemingly cannot be told in any other way but in first-person singular; their formal ingredient is that of the memorate, the quasi- or the pseudo-memorate. In such cases, it is not the regular third-person legend that assumes the first-person version; rather, the first-person story maintains its *Ich Bericht* (ego-account) form throughout the entire communicative sequence. Two examples will help illuminate this point.

EXAMPLE 1.    Many years ago at an intimate family gathering like that described by Arora (1987: 91), a trustworthy, middle-aged gentleman, who happened to be my mother's brother, told us about an extraordinary experience. Once, when he came off the ferry boat that carried passengers from the Buda side to the Pest side of the Danube and back, and made his way through the crowd, he felt someone's hand in his pocket, taking his gold watch. Grabbing the hand of the man, he yelled, "Give me the watch!" The man immediately obeyed. Later, when Uncle Peter felt in his pocket, he found two gold watches therein.

Some time later, I heard the same story, also told in first-person singular, from an architect — a trustworthy middle-aged gentleman just like my uncle. He said that he had pursued the assumed thief through dark alleys and trapped him in a doorway. But he found out later, while he was undressing and emptying his pockets, that he had two watches instead of one. He rushed to the police to turn in the watch, only to discover that the second watch's owner, who had recognized him on the street, was filing a report against his assailant.

Over the years, I have come across several variants of this first-person memorate, and it was a pleasant surprise to hear it again from Paul Harvey, the noted Chicago radio commentator, during his broadcast on October 18, 1972. He told it as a "true story." There was no way for me to record it while I was driving home for lunch, but I remember the essence of his version:

On the subway during rush hour in New York, someone felt a hand in his pocket and found his wallet gone. The train had just stopped at a station, and the man saw the pickpocket getting off. "Give me the wallet," he said, grabbing the man by the neck, who handed the wallet to him without a word. On reaching his office, our man found the telephone ringing on his desk. It was his wife, informing him that he had left his wallet at home.

After hearing the old story again, I mentioned it at a party, whereupon someone noted, "This same thing happened to my uncle in Cleveland!" It seems that this decades-old migratory story had just now reached Harvey, and whoever told it to him probably said, "it happened to me," or "it happened to one of my friends."

EXAMPLE 2.    The story known as "The Stolen Grandmother" (Dégh 1968b) is a widespread and popular piece related to modern tourism. I first noticed its spread in Hungary during the early 1960s. The plot, in brief, tells that a grandmother dies in the car while on a trip with her family. When the family stops for coffee on the way home, someone steals the car with the dead body inside. Neither the thief nor the car with its contents is ever found. The Budapest version — spread by the press and by word of mouth — involved a motorcycle, a weekend trip to Lake Balaton, and a popular espresso bistro in Székesfehérvár. The informant who first told me the story had heard it from his best friend. This friend claimed it happened to someone he knew: "They live right here on the next street." Shortly thereafter, another person told me that it had happened to an acquaintance's friend's friend and that the family lived on "the next street."

Over the years, Grandma has made several appearances in Europe and in the United States and Canada. Many colleagues answered my request for variants of the legend. More than two hundred variants were piled up from New York to California and Yugoslavia to Denmark.[13] As it turned out, the dead grandmother has been a popular menace to vacationers in Spain, Italy, the Bahamas, Mexico and elsewhere, and her home base is always on "the next street." Indeed, this is one of the stories that seekers of the contemporary legend identify as a foaftale: It comes from one's own circle, not from an archaic, rural, exotic "folk."

Respondents who have heard the story will emerge unexpectedly and spontaneously with very little urging. For example, on hearing the story, a fellow folklorist at a professional meeting in Germany called out in surprise, "Is this a legend, indeed? My daughter just came back from a vacation trip in Italy and told me about it as a true event, and I believed it really happened." So did others who have read about this tourist horror in the newspaper. According to a 1968 student paper in the Berkeley Folklore Archives (published the same year my article on "The Stolen Grandmother" appeared in *Indiana Folklore*), an award-winning student film based on the story was made at the University of Southern California in 1967. About ten years later (in 1979), East European colleagues reported to me that the story was "the legend of the year," as motor cars became more accessible to them.

Here are the introductory phrases from some of the variants in my own archives:

- "Well, I heard this true story from my neighbor. . . . It happened to her friend's family."

- "It was supposed to have happened to the brother of a local doctor and his family."
- "His mother heard it at a dinner party from a lady who was involved in the event."
- "It happened to some friends."
- "She swears this story is true. She heard it from her cousin . . . [who] does not lie."

Parallel versions relate the event without reference to either a source or personal involvement:

- "The story concerns a fairly wealthy Polish couple." (Poland)
- "What you will hear now is a horrible but true story that can be found in a German newspaper of last year." (Germany)
- "A married couple in West Germany . . ." (East Germany)
- "A Slovenian family traveled by auto . . ." (Croatia)
- "Shortly after the end of the Second World War, when money for travel was tight, a young bride and bridegroom . . . " (England)
- "A young lawyer on his honeymoon went to Spain taking his mother-in-law along." (Switzerland)
- "My mother has read it in the *Corriera della Sera*." (Italy)

Indeed, the legend has appeared in the news often. The equal distribution of personal and impersonal introductions to the story shows that some respondents like to switch what they originally heard (or read) from the third person to the first. This means, generally, that some people like to fib a little. However, if we admit that the "creative fantasy" is as important an element of folklore as the faithful transmission of oral materials, we also must admit that the "folk," who apply free variation to the received material, act in the spirit of *ars poetica*. The members of the memorate-sequence are people to whom something is always happening. The memorate (*Erinnerungssage*) in question travels through the appropriate "memorate conduit."

The personal experience story of Alexander Johannes Treppenhauer, a skilled auto mechanic in the Mercedes-Benz plant in Neu-Isenburg, Germany, and scholar Max Lüthi's brother-in-law, will illustrate that the plain, personal *Bericht*, identified as memorate, should hardly be regarded as inferior to the legend or fabulate. Treppenhauer contributed to a polished narrative, typewritten by Lüthi, that retold the long story of Josef Huber, a wheelwright in the factory. According to Treppenhauer's personal introduction to the story, Huber "sat in [my] office, early Monday morning, to inform me about what his cousin, baker 'Schorsch' (George) Braun, and his family experienced as they vacationed in faraway Spain." After the introductory description of the telling situation, the narrator recounts in great detail Huber's "Stolen Grandmother" story in the third person: The dead grandma, run over by a donkey cart, was smuggled back to Germany in attractive rugs purchased originally to decorate the family living room. The narrator returns to first person only at the end: "In conclusion, I can only tell this much: I have not heard anything more about this matter from our master wheelwright, Mr. Huber" (the full German text appears in Dégh 1995b: 35–47).

I was lucky to obtain a new lead indicating where the "Stolen Grandma" story is headed, particularly in the Swiss-German culture area. Ursula Schmid-Weidmann sent me a clipping from the Swiss *Tagesanzeiger* (Dec. 9, 1999) reporting that "Ukrainian thieves removed a rug from the rack of the car of two poor Moldavians who wanted to transport their grandmother thus to her funeral. The ceremony had to be performed without the corpse." In her letter, Schmid-Weidmann, a Swiss folklorist asks, "Could it be that the story now has a political background, the disintegration of the UDSSR? Formerly under the same government, Ukraine and Moldavia are now competing countries of their own." Her brief report is a far cry from the rich story told by Treppenhauer, but she raises the question of whether there will "one day be a workman in a Moldavian factory who fills the story out and tells the flowery narrative to his friends and relatives."

By now, it might be clear why Pentikäinen could not find memorates traceable through more than four hands in the repertoire of Takalo and why no one else can find such memorates either. If witnesses in the court of justice state that "I have seen it myself," their testimonies will be formally recognized as having full value, depending only on their trustworthiness. If, however, their evidence is that "a friend said that he saw it," its probative value is significantly diminished. Moreover, testimonial that "a friend said that his friend said" can have only minimal value in the court, if any at all. Yet testimony was not invented for the codes of criminal or civil procedure; rather, it is applied in the court proceedings as a traditional and logical postulate of the human sense of justice. "Is there proof?" would be the unuttered question of the audience of every narrative labeled as "true."[14]

The audience, in the first place, must decide whether the story might be true at all. If not, the story itself—a joke, märchen, or something else—may still be of interest, but no personal testimony would be expected. Listening to an anecdote about two traveling salesmen in a train, for example, the audience would satisfy the teller by responding with laughter at the punchline, without ever asking if the pair in fact really existed and traveled together. And who would want to know where Cinderella and her sisters actually lived? The receiver of the memorate, however, does ask questions: "What is the proof?"

The more feasible the proof, the more convincing the truth of the story. Comments such as "I have seen it with my own eyes" sound perfectly convincing. And "my father told it, and he never told a lie" is still acceptable. But a statement like "my father heard it from my grandfather" leaves the door open for some doubt.

If the chain of witnesses reaches a certain limit — like the last link in Pentikäinen's four-part chain — there will be two alternatives. One is that the memorate unfolds as a story, unlikely and unprovable. The other is that the receiver-sender simplifies the situation and unwittingly — or with forgivable "forgetfulness" — bypasses one, two, or more previous members of the transmission sequence. Like other folklorists, I have also tried to track down informant statements like "I heard it on the radio" or "it was in the papers" or "I know the person it happened to" after I have heard some incredible rumor. In almost all cases, the informant did not hear the radio or read the paper personally, nor did the rumor concern his friend; rather, it was the friend of a friend whose name was omitted, perhaps to make the story more credible and less ambiguous. The day-to-day and person-to-person observation of rumors in a military labor camp during World War II proved that rumors are mostly conceived as "brand new" and "from the immediate source" — even if two hundred people have passed them on and changed them gradually over a longer period of time (Dégh and Vázsonyi 1975).

People believe their own senses first. "It happened to me," began 79-year-old Nick Mészáros in his account of how he accidentally entered the magic circle at midnight on his way home and learned the secret of eternal youth.[15] A college girl, on the other hand, began her story of snakes in Klein's Department Store with "this happened to my girlfriend's sister-in-law" (Carey 1971: 5). The immediate testimony of both narrators is convincing, but indirect testimonies, even if they are false or negative ("N. told me but I don't believe it," for instance), might represent a certain degree of evidence. The unwritten folk-law of procedure is that the further the message is from its original source of perception, the less truthful it is. The road of detachment is marked out by the fading of the personal element and the loss of the personal experience, ending at the appearance of the impersonal subject.[16] The statements that "I saw it," "a friend saw it," and "a friend of my friend saw it" carry their proof in decreasing proportion; nevertheless, they are still more convincing than such references as "many people know it" or "people talk about it." Legend introductions like "people in our village believe" or "old people say" even seem to express a grain of doubt. At the beginning of this road is the *Ich-Bericht*, the memorate, and at the end of it is the fabulate, the genre that is, according to accepted standards of folkloristics, the true expression of folk belief (Mullen 1971: 406–407).

Would this mean that folk belief is best expressed by a genre that is given the least credence by the folk? Or by the very genre that is not only the least able to prove its suggestions, but does not even try to do so? Is it that the legend-bearing folk might not totally accept the beliefs expressed in the legend and that they are not even interested in convincing anybody else to believe?

Let us assume that the folk do believe unconditionally in their own folk belief. If this is so, there must be a reason for it. Here I am not talking about the sociopsychological bases of folk belief but rather about its visible structure, its mechanism. *Homo religiosus*, the believer who gives credence to extranormal events and superstitions (Honko 1962: 120–125), thinks or assumes that the subject of his or her belief is true — that is, attestable. What kind of proof should be obtained? Above all, first-hand perception is important, especially in relation to "empirical beings" (Honko 1962: 88; 1965: 10). However, how many people could possibly have seen, for example, the ghostly hitchhiker? The newspapers widely reported accounts of this personal experience, and average people who drove to the police station to report their supernatural adventures have been made instant heroes by the press.

For example, when Briton Roy Fulton gave a vivid report to police of an encounter with a phantom hitchhiker in 1979, his report became the source of many oral and printed retellings, memorates, and fabulates (Goss 1984: 90–99). Fulton gained immediate national fame through a *Sunday Express* article, which was followed by another article in the *Dunstable Gazette* and many other news reports since. It is obvious that Fulton has retold his story orally many times to his family and friends. We also know that he was interviewed by Goss, a member of the Association for the Scientific Study of Anomalous Phenomena. Goss replayed a variant from the 1980 tape-recorded interview to "a handful of parapsychologists, and groups of schoolchildren, to friends — to anyone who cared to listen." A portion of that interview follows:

As I said, you know, I was playing in a darts match over Leighton Buzzard; I left there about twenty past nine and I was driving through Stanbridge . . . and there's a road down there called Peddar's Lane . . . about 100 yards past there the street lights finish. There was a figure I [saw] on the left-hand side, thumbing a lift down there. I pulled up in front of him, so I could see him walking back into the headlights.

He had a dark colored jumper on, dark-colored trousers, with an open white-collared shirt. He came up to the motor; he got in there and sat down — he even opened the door himself, I had nothing to do with opening the door. I asked him where he was going and he just pointed up the road — never said a word. So I assumed he was either going to Dunstable or Tottenhoe.

So I was driving up the road, I suppose I was driving for — what, four, five or six minutes, I suppose, doing a speed of about 40 minimum.

I turned round to offer him a cigarette and the bloke had disappeared.

I braked, had a quick look in the back to see if he was there. He *wasn't* and I just gripped the wheel and drove like hell. And that's all — you know . . . (Goss 1984: 90)

Goss, who seems to have kept up his interest in the story, reported that Fulton maintained three years later that his story was authentic. We have no proof, but it is highly probable that as time passes, the second-hand local and national recipients will continue Fulton's story divorced from his immediate touch.

Gaining reinforcement from other variants passed through other channels of communication, a story is shaped further. This process exemplifies how legends are molded in the branching out of first-hand perception into second-hand and further. The "Vanishing Hitchhiker" legend, a fabulate, became personalized into a memorate by Fulton; the transmitters who heard about it and who, to some degree, gave credence to it and retold it to others, are increasing in number. What is the foundation of the belief of the majority, then? What is the value of the evidence from eyewitnesses who are, presumably, not known to everyone? Every believer assumes that someone must necessarily have had first-hand information about the ghost — otherwise, how could people have knowledge about it? Someone must have seen it and reported to others this personal experience, as Fulton did in the above case. This demonstrates the decisive thesis of the definition of the memorate.

Von Sydow himself stated in a verbal communication (Peuckert 1965: 11) that the memorate often turns into a fabulate. This was also confirmed by Granberg, who spoke about the reciprocal influence between the two (Granberg 1969: 93; Honko 1962: 12), and Röhrich who called memorate "the prelude to the legend" (1969: 223). The transformation of memorates into fabulates is, of course, only a possibility, for memorates can meet diverse fates. It is a rule, though, that each fabulate — along with every other narrative that requires credence or the possibility of belief (or even the pretense of it) as a component — is based on either a truly existing or an assumed memorate, pseudo-memorate, quasi-memorate, *Ich-Bericht*, *Erinnerungssage*, or something similar. An undemonstrable legend is no legend at all. One must postulate that every fabulate is based on a memorate. This postulative memorate Andrew Vázsonyi and I termed the "proto-memorate" (Dégh and Vázsonyi 1974).

According to von Sydow's definition, the memorate has no "poetic character." Of course, "poetic character" is another of those slippery, ambiguous expressions that are seemingly unavoidable in the humanities. However, with respect to the memorate, we must assume that "poetic character" denotes some objectively recognizable feature because it appears in the definition as one of the traits that distinguishes the "nonpoetic" memorate from the "poetic creation" of the fabulate (Hand 1965: 443; Tillhagen 1964: 9). If the definition that characterizes the memorate is correct, "poetic character" is an attribute missing from the memorate but contained in the fabulate. Hence, it can be recognized, isolated, and described. If so, what exactly does "poetic" mean in relation to these two concepts?

Elucidation of the problem is impeded because aesthetic standards in folklore in general have not been sufficiently researched (Voigt 1972). Not only has the memorate been regarded as non-artistic, but the legend in its entirety was denied the poetic qualities granted to the other literary genres. Scholars seldom pondered the aesthetic value of the legend. One notable exception was F. W. Schmidt, who complained about the scarcity of authentically recorded texts and did his own fieldwork to provide materials suitable for study. Evidently, all he could find in the numerous collections were artistically embellished or radically abstracted texts edited by the collectors, under the influence of the Grimms. As is well known, terms like "from an oral source," "from folk tradition," or "people tell" referred only to legend plots, not the exact wording of individuals. Selecting the most attractive themes, folklorists and amateur enthusiasts molded variants into smooth, proportionate wholes by means of their own artistic inspiration, not that of the folk. At the same time, the stylistically unpolished, topically more earthbound and pedestrian memorates did not qualify for inclusion in the collections of texts that met the arbitrary standard of aesthetics. For a long time, memorates were not even recorded because they did not fit into any recognized category. In exceptional cases, some memorates were added to the miscellany chapters in "tale," "joke," or "tradition" collections because they were not properly identified. As a rule, however, they were published as "superstitions," "beliefs," or "customs," extracted by the collector, who — because folklorists were not interested in the verbosity and personal style of the tellers — stripped the narrative part, reducing often lengthy stories to their bare bones.

American folklore archives are loaded with collections of "popular beliefs and superstitions" in the tradition of the *Frank C. Brown Collection of North Carolina Folklore* (volumes 6 and 7, edited by Wayland D. Hand). The patient reader may find some treasures in these files and collections, but may also wonder how much precious material was mercilessly discarded or deprived of its legend identity. Here are two examples:

> Mrs. Montgomery remembered what an old servant of theirs in the fifties told her. The servant, Aunt Jenny, lived near a graveyard, and she would say that she got up so tired because the witches came out of the graveyard at night and rode her all night long. (Hand, 1961/1964, vol. 7: 115)

The brother of one of my informants is a living example of people who can see hants. One night he and a friend were walking down the road, when he looked up ahead and saw the hant of a person who recently died. He started edging over to the side of the road, telling his companion that old man Smith had to pass. His companion did not believe that Smith's hant was walking down the road. When, however, my informant's brother said that the hant was passed by, and that his companion could see him by looking over his left shoulder, the doubting person declined. Thus we miss corroborating testimony from another observer. (Browne 1958: 196)

The same style of retelling is also typical of student collections, like this one by Sherwood Wakeman (Berkeley Archive, 1968), which makes a first-person story into a third-person account:

The informant tells me he heard this story from his friends around Washington, D.C., circa 1965. This story was very widely known among Mr. Dawson's friends and was very much believed to have been true. It seems that a man was driving a 1965 Corvette Stingray around the backwoods country of West Virginia when he suffered a fatal heart attack. The car went off the road and was not found until some three months later, the body still inside, badly decomposed. The relatives of the deceased man put the car up for sale, but the body has been inside so long that they could not remove the stench of death. The person who told Mr. Dawson about the car claimed that he had a friend who knew that it was still for sale, and where it was being sold. He said that it was being sold dirt cheap (approx. $100) because the smell was driving all the prospective buyers away. (From P. Dawson, 23)

The following variant of the "Death Car" story demonstrates how legends written as class work can also undergo characteristic — even if not poetic — "internalization" by the narrator, which renders them precious for contemporary legend research:

In Seattle, in 1956, a girlfriend informed me that her brother had heard from a friend about an excellent price on a year-old Thunderbird (an automobile of the sports car variety). It was only $500 because the previous owner had committed suicide in it and his body hadn't been found until it had become quite decayed and foul smelling. The car was being sold for such cheap price because the smell could not be removed from the car. At the time, my friend and I tried to think of ways to eradicate the smell! Of course, the car never materialized. ("Myself" by Sonia Cole, Oakland, California, Berkeley Archive, 1969)

In this case, the memorate was not approached as artistic folk poesy, and it was carelessly recorded and rewritten by the collector. Through this common style of publication and collection philosophy, a vicious circle was created, from which the memorate could not escape.

Continuing the search, I read through a dozen or so reliable legend collections to discern the poetic features of the fabulate and then determine their absence from the memorates. One of the texts reads "I was a little boy at that time," and contains the experience of a neighbor. It is a memorate six lines long, with no trace of artistry in it (Simonsuuri and Rausmaa 1968, no. 173). In another text, the event is temporally placed in the vague "once," and the spatial location is not given. Its content is traditional, possessing the attributes of a fabulate. Nevertheless, it lacks artistry and exceeds the previous six-line memorate by only one line. Another text begins "the teller of this story saw some twenty years ago. . . ." Is this a memorate or a fabulate? It is neither. It is the condensed version of the collector, and as such has little aesthetic value.

There is a story about a "haunted hotel room" that begins with "one afternoon we were waiting for the school bus. . . ." This sounds like a memorate, but it is quite unusual because another person's first-person account joins it farther along in the narrative. When a janitor comes by and asks the children whether they would like to hear a scary story, the text immediately begins "Well, when I was a good deal younger . . ." (Roberts 1955, no. 92). This component confirms the memorate quality of the story. Yet, unlike the seven-line fabulate, this memorate fills three printed pages. Does it show poetic features? By virtue of its unusual and intuitive structure — which is reminiscent of oriental frame tales (a third person also tells a memorate, inserted in the frame) — it does more than one should expect from a modest memorate. There are also other elements in this story to consider: suggestive similes, dialect quotations, tasteful humor, realistic dialogues, all of which approximate the standard known as "poetic." Would it be justified, therefore, to consider this narrative a fabulate? Would it be more reasonable to infer that memorates occasionally rival fabulates in poesy?

And where should we place the many texts by student-collectors who, with the ambition of a literary author, dramatize their skimpy stories: "once upon a time . . . ," "on a dark, dark night . . . ," or "not even the leaves were trembling"?[17]

About eighteen hundred texts were published in a classic German collection that I examined, looking for any significant difference between the length of memorates and fabulates. "Poetic character" in folk prose, after all, is usually expressed by the evocative featuring of details, use of epic patterns, dialogue, and artistic verbosity that extends the core of the narrative. There were several two- and three-line memorates (Zender 1937, nos. 406 and 1083) and many fabulates of the same size or slightly longer (1041, 1048, 1113, 1124). There was no trace of poesy in either group. In a Norwegian collection, fabulates were barely an inch long. One is about church-building goblins, another is about soul transmigration in the shape of a fly, and a third tells about a changeling (Christiansen 1958, nos. 9C, 22B, and 41). These well-known, traditional, and migratory themes almost cry for poetic embroidery; neverthe-less, they remain on the level of dry reports limited to essential facts.

In the hand of inspired raconteurs, these cores or kernels can be turned into exciting adventure stories, as seen in a cycle of herdsmen memorates (Dégh 1965a: 45–46, 50), or the three-and-a-half page detailed description of how János learned magic at a crossroads, as told by a second-hand narrator (55). And, with equal skill, structured dialogues underscore the dramatic ef-fect of two revenant stories in Katharine Briggs's collection *The Dictionary of British Folktales* (1971, part B, vol. 1: 363–365).

To stress this point, and to show the unpredictability of potential formula-tion, I include the full text of a tape-recorded legend one of my undergradu-ate students, Mike Simonetto, collected and transcribed for me in 1988. His informant is Mike Blaney, 22, of Gary, Indiana. For publication I gave it to the editor of the *FOAFtale News*, who classified it as a memorate (Dégh 1990a: 2–4).

### An Experience My Mother Had

*Mike Simonetto:* Mike, you told me about some experience your mother had. Would you fill me in on that?

*Mike Blaney:* Yes, this is an experience my mother had and that was a part of . . . I actually didn't see the lady, but I went with my mother to her house. This was about . . . I guess, around seven years ago. I was home alone and my mother came home with my sister, she just got back from the grocery store, and I was helping them bringing in the groceries when all of a sudden I noticed my mother's got all these empty milk gallon jugs and a . . . she started filling them up with water, you know, and asked her, you know, what are you doing with all this water, these milk jugs and why she was filling them up with water? And she said, well, on the way back from the grocery store, when I was driving down, she says, 45th Avenue, somewhere between Grant Street and Harrison, somewhere between these streets she seen this old lady standing on the cor-ner and she said she could hardly walk. My mother said that normally she wouldn't just pick up some old lady but something told her to pick this lady up. So she pulled over. She was with my sister.

My mother asked the lady if she needed a ride. And the lady said yes, she'd like to go to the grocery store. The lady came out and couldn't even carry her packages. So my mom put the groceries in the car for her. Then the lady got in the car and my mother asked if there was any other place she'd like to go before going home. She said that, yes, she'd like to go to the bank before going home. So my mother stopped at the bank and parked her car, waiting for the lady. She said she almost left the lady at the bank because she was taking so long to come out and my mom was wondering what she could be doing that could be taking so long. But since she had her groceries in the car, she waited.

Finally the lady came out of the bank after a long while and got into the car. She opened her purse and she had all this money — a whole lot of cash — like she just withdrew a bunch of cash. So my mother asked her what she was doing with all that cash and with as much trouble as she has getting around somebody could have swiped her money. The old lady said that she didn't worry—she had lots of money and was an old person. My mother told her to be careful, and would she like to go home now? The old lady said yes. So my mom took her home which was a house between Grant and Harrison Streets, on 45th Avenue.

The lady walked up to the house with my mother, who took her groceries into the house. My mother asked her if there was anything else she could do and the old lady said that yes, she would like to have some water . . . that she didn't get water at her house and would my mother bring some over to me in milk gallon jugs . . . she specifically said milk gallon jugs. So my mom said she would bring some over tonight . . .

That was why my mom was filling the jugs with water. So she filled up about five to ten, I don't exactly remember; so I helped her bring them to the car. So we went over to this lady's house . . . my mom, my sister and me—gallon jugs and we walked up the stairs to the porch and we set them down and started pounding on the door. We drove over to this lady's house. So I got all these gallon jugs and we walked up the stairs to the porch and we set them down and started pounding on the door.

The lady did not come to the door so my mom said that she's old and maybe she's having trouble getting to the door. So she waited there about five minutes banging the door. Then I walked around to the back and banged on the door and the window curtain was halfway closed and I could see that there wasn't anyone in that room where the curtains were. So I banged on the basement window. My mom got scared and thought maybe the old lady had a heart attack or something.

So there was this house set back a little ways next door and my mom said to go over there and tell that lady, there might be something wrong with her neighbor because she has just dropped her off.

So I went over there and banged on that lady's door. She came to the door and I said that my mom just dropped off her neighbor off next door and she was pretty old and she's not coming to the door. We brought her . . . she said she wanted water. We brought it for her, left it on the porch and nobody's answering the door. We thought, maybe something might be wrong.

Then, the lady looked at me and said, "Are you talking about this house next door?" And I said, "Yes." And she said that maybe we had the wrong house because nobody's lived there for like ten years. And I just said, "Are you kidding me? This house, right here?" She said, that was right. And I walked back and said to mom, "That lady next door said there hasn't been anybody living there for ten years."

My mom just looked at me . . . you know how you turn all white and your hair gets all up on your head . . . she got all scared . . . and she got in the car and she was really scared. She said, "Mike, I know I dropped her off, that lady at that house." And my sister said the same.

*Mike S.:* So both your mother and your sister could locate that house?

*Mike B.:* Yeah, and so could I. That was wild. My mom called my grandma and my grandma's really religious and she said maybe it was somebody . . . like acting like God to see if you would help somebody out . . . That's why she had all that money to see if you'd take that right away from her because she was helpless. It was wild and I'll never forget that.

*Mike S.:* Does your mother ever talk about it?

*Mike B.:* She hadn't talked about it for a while but she remembers it . . . she'll verify the story.

*Mike S.*: Still scare you?

*Mike B.*: Yeah, when I think about it because it was like I said around seven or ten years ago . . . I was just carrying the water . . . I didn't know what to expect . . . when that lady told me that . . . wow . . . I thought maybe my mom doesn't have the right house . . . so I went up there and she was all upset. She was just sitting there saying, "This is the right house . . . this is the right house. . . ."

This deeply emotional personal experience story is a perfectly structured, and balanced legend with all the explicit features: identification of locations, people, and timing—everything that makes a legend a legend. The description of the events, characters, and their actions; the building of tension, climax, and anti-climax; and the contemplation of the meaning as a postlude proceed without hesitations that break the storyline. The narrating skill of the young informant is exceptional, as Blaney recalls his experience of seven to ten years ago. The story here is actually that of Blaney's mother, who encountered the mysterious old woman on her way to the grocery store with her daughter. He became involved in it only after they had come home. When Blaney joins the women in delivering the water jugs to the old woman's home, from here he becomes the actor: carrying the bottles to the house, trying to enter and failing, and finding out that no one lives there. Trying to make sense of the experience and negotiating its meaning does not alleviate the participants' anguish—relief is found only after consulting the grandmother, who viewed the old lady as a messenger of God testing the mother's honesty. Should we insist on calling a narrative a memorate when it has all the attributes of a fabulate except for the two principal tellers' testimony of personal involvement? The complexity of the Blaney narrative justifies this question.

This random selection from an enormous body of material has been nothing more than a spot check to determine whether it is feasible to make a standard aesthetic value distinction between the fabulate and the memorate. In all honesty, I can ascertain no distinction. The identification and acknowledgment of "poetic character" depends on personal taste and occasional frame of mind. There is no point in tracking down objective criteria through subjective approximation.

Yet I have found many irregular fabulates and memorates. In some of them, although the introductory words "once upon a time" promise a traditional tale, a *lege artis* fabulate follows the märchen invocation. In our time of literalization of folktales, the legend-telling folk is more and more often inspired to borrow tale formulas and conventions without turning the legend into a folktale (Dégh 1995a). Other items sound like perfectly regular memorates, with scrupulous reference to the three-member chain of informants, only to find a third-person story (e.g., a fabulate) of the third member in the chain following the memorate introduction. I have also read a fabulate that ended with the conclusion "I heard it from my aunt." Would this statement transform the story retroactively into a memorate? I have also encountered memorates whose tellers assign the dialogues to someone else, who tells a fabulate in the frame of a memorate. Many raconteurs began their stories with comments like "it had been said that in the cemetery of N– . . . ," and after they had finished relating the event, continued with a phrase such as "I have heard this so many times that I decided to go and see for myself." Because a legend account is verbalized in so many ways, it is difficult to situate the irregular narratives that defy classification.

As long as society needs legends, one can always discover new transitional forms and uncommon conglomerates. One could also invent new names for each. Faithful to folkloristic tradition, we might suggest the terms *memorato-fabulate* or *fabulato-memorate*, or perhaps even *pseudo-fabulate, quasi-fabulate, local fabulate,* or *migratory memorate*. But I offer these inventions with reluctance, for fear that someone might find them appealing.

Von Sydow's definition requires not only that the memorate be someone's "own experience" but also that it should be a "purely personal" (*rein persönlich*) relation of experience. Purely personal here means something that is not collective at all. Should it be understood that the experience told in the form of memorate is unique, and that no one else had a share in it? If such a legend experience did ever exist, it could not be proven. And, as it cannot be proven, it is also irrelevant. Only one factor may have significance: Is the experience regarded as "purely personal" by the memorate-teller? And, after him, the memorate-investigator (the folklorist) lived on in conscious or subconscious recollection in the narrator's mind. If it is true that folklore (and also folk belief as the vital basis of memorates) is the projection of basic polygenetic human emotions (K. Ranke 1961), then it is also true that the concretely manifested form of expression is already a social product. For example, elementary fears and desires have generated the *Elementargedanke* that "the dead haunt the living"; however, the notion that in Bloomington, Indiana, spirits of babies cry in the basement of a certain fraternity house on North Jordan every midnight because an abortionist had his office there (Lecocq 1973) is already a social product. The person who knows this story — and it has been widely reported by generations of Indiana University students and fraternity brothers who have lived in the house — obtained this information from some concrete source. The author of the presumptive proto-memorate who saw the occurrence with his own eyes (phones come off the hook, doors open by themselves, faucets, lights, and televisions turn off and on) is no exception either. It makes no difference whether we ascribe the vision to the teller's epileptic *Dämmerzustand* (semi-consciousness) (F. Ranke 1925: 18); to the recounting mood of *Homo narrans* (K. Ranke 1967a); to a hypnagogic state (Hufford 1982a: 121–123); to a "numinous scare," "sensory deprivation," "altered state of consciousness," or "supra normal encounter" (Ward 1990b); or to a kind of parapsychological phenomenon that we would have "no sufficient reason . . . to deny a priori" (Bender 1976, 1984; Isler 1971: 3). The teller must have acquired the whole vision, or at least its elements, from common social sources by way of tradition. Most scholars would more or less agree to this.

According to Honko, tradition is already present in the experience. He quoted Haavio's observation that "there are much fewer memorates composed preeminently of personal elements than those in which the memorate motifs agree with general folk tradition" (Honko 1962: 133). This agrees with my evaluation of beliefs and stories about the 1848–1849 War of Independence in Hungary that are circulating more than a hundred years later. It turned out that only those elements that conformed to traditionally available patterns had entered legend tradition. The memorate might also assume distinct traditional patterns, such as those of Dorson's sagamen (Dorson 1952: 249–272). Granberg explicitly said that "although the formulation is individual, the fabric contains mostly legend motifs" (1969: 92). Obviously, tradition is the building material of fantasy; imagination does not amount to much more than the specific function of the combinative capability of an individual human brain. Dreams, ecstatic delusions, and even lunacy are culture specific. They follow well-trodden paths, and their variations adjust to current fashions.

At the beginning of its life, almost immediately at the moment of its emergence, the memorate touches society for the second time. That is, in the words of Bausinger, "the *Erlebnisbericht* is formulated along the lines of the available collective concepts" (1968: 173). Each experience report has to face social pressure that immediately censors the anti-traditional features of the memorate. As Honko noted, "those who are more familiar with tradition correct the narrator and force him to seek the proper referential framework for his account. . . . It is clear that such a checking process has a great effect in eliminating idiosyncratic motifs from the experience report of single individuals" (Honko 1962: 12). It might easily happen that both the attempt of violation and the traditional correction are performed by the same socially controlled person, the memorate-proponent him- or herself.

Clearly, the meaning of *tradition* undergoes continual change. Tradition, in spite of the conservative implications of the word, keeps surprisingly abreast of the times. The two meanings of tradition, "culture passed on" and "the procedure of passing on culture," increasingly approximate each other. The acceleration of transportation and of information communication, as well as the continued penetration of the mass media into everyday life, have undermined the traditional meaning of tradition. Hultkrantz's definition, "culture (elements) handed down from one generation to another" (Hultkrantz 1960: 229), is applicable to our culture only with limitations. If Mrs. Kovács of East Chicago recalls a youthful personal memory of a bewitching because of a television show she has just seen, she will simply reach for the telephone. She will dial the number of her friend, Mrs. Kiss, in Gary, who is as receptive to supernatural accounts as herself, so that she can communicate the story immediately as it comes back to her. She no longer needs to keep it to herself for lack of a responsive audience; nor does she have to take the chance of it slipping from her mind while she waits to pass it "from one generation to the other" by telling it to her children (Dégh 1969d).

Moreover, the new traditions created by modern subcultures are, to a large extent, only negatively contiguous with the traditions of previous generations. These subgroups include the younger generations in the form of the multitudinous groups of teenagers and college students; and the counterculture groups and religious fanatics, who gather sometimes under the pretense of an ideology, be they radicals, drug cultists, freaks, naturalists, or anti-abortion activists. The pluralistic countercultures and fundamentalist subcultures — which display surprising dimensions of supernatural elements, as they often follow the guidance of books that describe rituals of historic cults, and listen to the acts of religious mystics mostly in the form of memorates — do not spread from parent to child. Transmission is from street corner to street corner, from high school to high school, from psychic fair to psychic fair — and the speed is not measured by the life-span of generations, but by hours. The rise and the dissemination of tradition have become almost simultaneous. "Today the action and the reaction occur almost at the same time. We actually live mythically and integrally, as it were, but we continue to think in the old, fragmented space and time patterns of the pre-electric age" (McLuhan 1964: 20).

These facts call for the revaluation of the term *tradition*. We must realize that tradition pertains not only to the distant past but also the immediate past — even so immediate as to be almost in the present. The traditional elements in a given experience, and in the accompanying experience-communicating memorate, could be recognized only by someone well-versed in both the old and the new. This would be true even if many of the new motifs are nothing more than traditional motifs disguised in blue jeans. If someone wanted to classify them, supplementary volumes to motif indexes would have to be added monthly. The supposition that the memorate is not traditional and that the experiences elaborated in it are "purely personal" has to be discarded with a sigh. The sigh is because this was the last hope for an eventual validation of the von Sydow definition. How can we tell, then, which story is a memorate and which is not?

Based on the available scholarly sources, at the end of the journey around the von Sydow memorate definition we must admit that there is no hope for validating any part of it. There is no way to avoid the direct question any longer: Is there any essential difference between the memorate and the fabulate at all? Does von Sydow's memorate really exist? Is there any scholarly need to determine which narrative is a memorate and which is a fabulate? It is obvious that all memorates might *eventually* turn into fabulates. Likewise, it is obvious that each fabulate *necessarily* presupposes a memorate — a real one (as in so many cases) or an inferential one, which can be termed *proto-memorate*. We might also add that the fabulate is preceded not only by the evidence-giving memorate, but by every utterance that seeks credibility, like folk belief itself that facilitates the formation of the legend (e.g., memorate and fabulate). "Our legends are the result of our beliefs" (Peuckert 1965: 39). And the memorate is the basis of that belief. According to Honko, "Belief . . . is founded not upon speculation, but upon concrete, personal experiences" (Honko 1965: 10). Thus, belief presupposes personal experience — the memorate, provided it is not founded on revelation. Or perhaps it is so even in the case of revelation: When Moses descended from Mount Sinai, he immediately communicated his memorate to the people.

## Definition or Delimitation of the Genre?

In his 1989 essay on folkloristic theories of genre, Honko, following his nine criteria for the formation of generic terms, constructed a system of genres in an attempt to ease the burden of definition that practicing folk narrative scholars face (Honko 1989). Streamlining the terminology, Honko distinguished global and ethnic, and primary and permanent genres and coordinated them, marking a historical-evolutionary continuum. In essence, the chart he drew summarizes what we have been reviewing (Honko 1989: 26). It deals with traditionally established categories, and hardly reflects the products of empirical legend research of the last thirty years. He mentioned his disillusionment with genre definition and suggested a practical method for the future: "If new genres are to be found or systems of folklore genres to be preserved as one method of indexing folklore, it is presumably time to permit stimuli taken from discourse analysis and text linguistics to add a new dimension to the folkloristic study of genre . . ." (1989: 27).

Wading into the immense field of linguistic narratology for new inspiration and experimenting with borrowed theories and abstractions may be an instructive excursion, or an effort to give a facelift to our further speculations about genres of folklore. But I am afraid that borrowing ideas and approaches

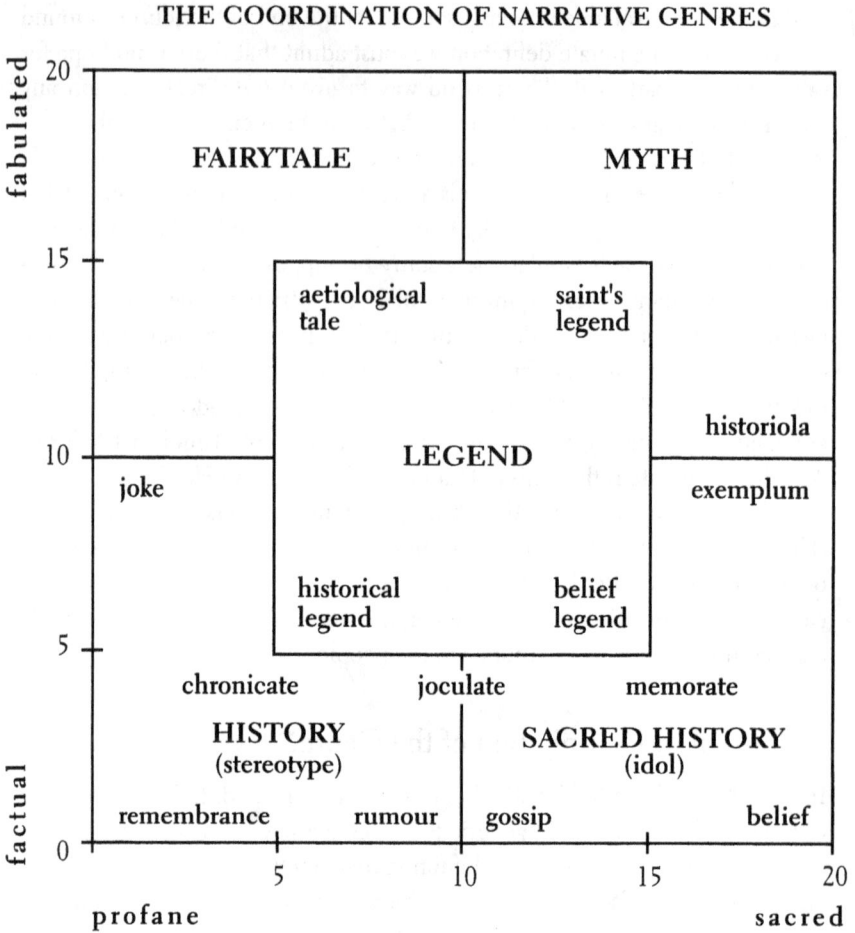

## THE COORDINATION OF NARRATIVE GENRES

| fabulated | | | |
|---|---|---|---|
| 20 | | | |
| | **FAIRYTALE** | | **MYTH** |
| 15 | | | |
| | aetiological tale | saint's legend | |
| | | | historiola |
| 10 | joke | **LEGEND** | exemplum |
| | historical legend | belief legend | |
| 5 | | | |
| | chronicate | joculate | memorate |
| | **HISTORY** (stereotype) | | **SACRED HISTORY** (idol) |
| factual | remembrance | rumour | gossip | belief |
| 0 | | | |
| | 5 | 10 | 15 | 20 |

profane                                                                 sacred

Honko's Chart

from other disciplines such as linguistics is risky, because it may lead to the abandonment of the fundamental tenets of the discipline of folklore. Besides, we have not exhausted all folkloristic approaches, old and new; they might work in dealing with the legend in its current existence, in a new era. The legend is "a part of life," Pentikäinen tells us, reminiscing about his student encounters with Tillhagen. "On one occasion," wrote Pentikäinen, "Carl-Hermann Tillhagen noted, pointing to a chair, that it is more valuable to study the person sitting in the chair than the chair itself" (1989: 176).[18] Another prominent genre theorist, Dan Ben-Amos, in a self-critical response to Honko, expressed his disappointment with the reliance on the artificial construction of ideal genre-types rather than on "the people who tell the stories, sing the songs, and cite the proverbs" (Ben-Amos 1992: 25–26). I feel discourse analysts would benefit from learning how folklore fieldworkers operate, rather than the other way around.

There is no reason to list here the many native (ethnic) and analytic (scholarly) names the legend has been assigned; they appear in many languages and local dialects, and mean the same or similar things. Native names are usually descriptive, expressing two important features that, from the viewpoint of the teller, distinguish the genre from other prose forms. For the bearer, the legend is often a "true story," meaning that it happened to known people at a known place, and a "story" (in the sense of *Geschichte*, or history), an account of something that took place involving familiar persons, in the recent past, which was observed or is remembered by witnesses. Terms coined by folklorists are more complex.

In the third part of this chapter, we discussed the historical reasons and the logic behind the formulation of the main legend categories: demonological/mythological, historical, and etiological. Most arguments supported the separation of the first two on the grounds that the underlying core of demonological legends is "to believe" (*glauben*), and that the core of the historical legends is "to know" (*wissen*) (Röhrich 1966: 49). The same idea also fuels the argument of Nordic scholars who distinguish between legends of "supranormal" subjects and down-to-earth topics (Pentikäinen 1968: 142). It is not entirely clear to me why they insist that the memorate be entirely supernatural and distinguished from the stylistically similar but fully factual chronicate. In any case, it is no simple task to differentiate between *belief*, a subjectively perceived fact, and *knowledge*, an objectively perceived fact.

Other distinguishing terms need to be clarified because they have been applied broadly and inconsistently in modern legend research over the last three decades. Now that I have taken a position concerning the status of *fabulate* and *memorate*, I feel the need to discuss some of the most popular terms in current usage and their relationship to the legend proper.

### Belief Legend and Belief Story

*Belief legend* and *belief story* as alternative terms have a long history. They hail back to the first empiricist's discovery in European villages that legends are deeply rooted in the local systems of belief, that is, in religion. Realizing that there is no way to understand living legendry without understanding the ruling system of the vernacular religion, Friedrich Ranke pioneered a concept known as *"Biologie der Volkssagen"* (1926B: 46). Reviewing four legend collections, Ranke criticized the authors, noting that their compilations more closely resembled herbariums — gatherings of single plants picked individually and separated from their mother soil, thus revealing nothing of what he

81

calls "the biology of the folk legend." "We never learn anything about the real life of the people who told and who listened to these legends; when, where and to whom were they usually told, and how strongly were they believed by their tellers and listeners" (45–48).

Collectors of village narrative repertoires explored manifestations of "belief," commonly conceptualized as "superstition." But "belief" cannot be collected because it is an invisible and inaudible cultural heritage. It lives in the minds, not on the lips, of people — it is a convention tacitly shared by a community. Everyone knows that one should not pick up a rag, a horseshoe, or a matchbox if it lies on a crossroads because it may have been placed there to confer a curse; and frogs should be avoided because they may be witch familiars and the handler might get warts by touching them. Such beliefs that are commonly understood need not be stated outright. For the folklorist, the only way to discern underlying belief is to participate in community life and look for manifest forms in everyday and holiday activities. This way, it is easy to identify belief behind elaborate acts in the performance of customs, rituals, and narratives that verbalize the belief — mainly legends and magic tales.

Traditional folklorists interested in the belief itself extracted it from custom and narrative; or, based on previous knowledge of the belief's existence, they confronted informants with questionnaires and checklists to make them do the excerpting themselves. But those who were interested in expressive forms sooner or later had to realize that these forms are integrated and held together by the indigenous system of belief. In many formats, the acted and narrated elements of belief appear in what we have identified first as legends and second as magic tales. The formation of coherent narrative contents — from the simple statement of belief through intermediate stages of completeness — had been described by many scholars, who noted the genre-relationships as well as the unpredictability of formulations. In magic tales, legends play a subordinate but important role. The incorporation of legend motifs or full legends, the transformation of tales into legends, and the transformation of legends into tales appear as an ideological measure: They connect and contrast the objectified, fictitious world of the tale with the real, supernatural realm of the everyday village (Dégh 1989).

As far as legends are concerned, they are necessarily belief stories. They are based on common knowledge about human encounters with the supernatural (or extranormal) world, concretized by personal experience (Hufford 1984). They are cases that never aspire to attain the artistic logic of the märchen, no matter how well they are rounded out with dialogues and exciting details. As I have recently stated, at the time of my first exposure to living village legendry (Dégh 1989: 298–306, 1995a: 341–357), I accepted Aurél Vajkai's term *belief story*. As I said then, "the logic in the belief story is not anchored in the composition but springs from the similarity of cases" (Dégh 1989: 133). In his superb collection and analysis of a legend cycle of herdsmen in the Bakony woods, Vajkai focused on first- or second-hand personal experience stories, which he identified as belief stories (Vajkai 1947: 55–69). He pointed out that "belief is fused into definitive narrative forms which people know intimately as a whole and in detail and faithfully repeat like a song or a Märchen. But we must not see anything accidental in the personal experience but a firm framework which forms a strong core of unity together with the belief." He was dealing with legends that were nationally widespread and treasured among the ranks of skilled narrating herdsmen (Dégh 1965a, nos. 45 and 54), legends that displayed the content stability of fabulates while maintaining the personalization of memorates. In my earlier works, the concept "belief story" or "legend" was used also to describe less stable, less coherently told variants. In fact, it included any episodes or motifs, with or without narrative elements in independent usage, that appeared in my experience as constituents of a whole, from which the analytical category of a legend type could be pieced together (Dégh 1963, 1965b, 1971).

On a broader synthesis, neither the term *belief legend* nor *folk belief story* (Blehr 1967, 1974) deserve to be retained. Such a distinction has only historic value, marking the beginnings of empirical research and fieldworkers' discovery that legends are based on and concerned with attitudes toward belief. In fact, the legends classified under this name are identical with what were earlier known as being mythological or demonological. More than twenty years after Blehr's *Fabula* article, Bennett returned to the question, "Are belief-stories legends?" and analyzed "belief related genres" on the basis of Ervin Beck's tape-recorded ghost story collection from six British teenagers. Bennett's conclusion, that belief-stories are also legends (Bennett 1989a), is in agreement with Ward's critical comments (Ward 1991) and the conclusions of my own historiographic survey of the term *belief legend* (Dégh 1996).[19]

### Rumor

*Rumor* is a term only relatively recently used by folklorists, emerging in the folklore vocabulary with the study of legends in urban-industrial life and mass communication (Bird 1979; Mullen 1970). In current usage, this sociological term covers everything that does not exhibit the standard criteria of the fabulate: grapevine, hearsay, gossip, *Glaubenvorstellung*, *Erlebnisskizze*, everyday story, personal experience story, *Sagenbericht*, and of course, memorate. In other words, it represents the unestablished, initial, emergent, and transitory but active form or forms of the legend which, after it has left the confines of a small oral or newspaper print circuit, enters the depersonalized channels of mass media. Of course, not every rumor is legendary. Only a very small contingent of what is launched carries themes with the potential of "solidifying" into legend.

Shibutani quoted authors who see legends as "conventionalized versions of accounts that were originally rumours," or "popular beliefs . . . suspected as being erroneous." Legends are "rumours that have survived" (Shibutani 1966: 155–160). But if rumors are not legends and may only become legends when they survive their initial appeal, how can we tell if a legend is a survived rumor?

Several folklorists insist that the rumor is a traditional folk narrative genre with specific formal features. According to Fine, rumor possesses a relatively limited repertoire of themes and is composed, to a large extent, of traditional materials. But he cautions us that rumor is so closely affiliated with legends, beliefs, and experience stories that "in fact, it is hard to determine where rumour ends and legend begins" (G. Fine 1985: 1102–1109). Brunvand, on the other hand, defined rumor as "a brief, anonymous, unverified report of a supposed event that circulates both by word of mouth and in the mass media. Rumors tend to be relatively short-lived and non-narrative as contrasted to legends, though rumors may contribute to legend growth and spread" (1981: 194). Klintberg defined rumor by relating it to legend: "I regard 'legend' as a narrative with fixed epic pattern, whereas a rumour might appear as a simple statement, sometimes with additional information. The term 'legend' primarily focuses upon content, while 'rumour' focuses upon the process of diffusion" (Klintberg 1985: 285).

With such conflicting and cautious descriptions of rumor, folklorists are facing a difficult problem distinguishing legends from the rumors that mushroom through all available channels of communication in their experience. They are on the alert to register all spreading accounts that have some similarity to traditional themes because they hope to capture the legend in emergence — to experience its birth. Scholars, like journalists, pursue media-spread legends or possible legends, only to discover that they do not necessarily become legends; mostly they remain liquid and ephemeral, without running a full course from inception to decline. They spread so rapidly, while competing rumor materials appear and interfere, that they have no time for total development. Before rumors can reach maturity new rumors replace them.

Often it seems legends are born and thrive through the media, and the occasionally appearing oral forms are pale epigones compared to the elaborate and diverse versions carried in the media. In fact, the media can be a springboard for rumors to become literary genres, bypassing the rocky road of oral channels. The most popular rumors of the 1980s about foodstuffs as threats to human health (McDonald's and Wendy's wormburgers, Kentucky Fried Rats, spider eggs in Bubble-Yum, spider legs in peanut butter, and mice in Coca-Cola bottles) were promoted by and blossomed in the mass media without developing a personalized narrative core to be picked up, expanded into legends, and validated by oral tellers. Likewise, the most popular horror legends appeared side by side with their rumor versions. Relating the media and oral variants in analytical depth may be difficult, if not impossible, without direct access to materials with immediate ties.

In their effort to gain a better understanding of the social problems of urban-industrial society, sociologists turned with interest to folklorists' work with the emergent horror rumors they saw as typical urban stories — legend-like projections of social ills in mass society (Best 1990; Campion-Vincent and Renard 1992; Victor 1991). Folklorists benefited from the sociologists' input as they contextualized and interpreted the texts they collected, but they also were distracted from their folkloristic research goal: identification of the legend in the industrial culture and its placement in the hierarchy of folklore genres. It was the sociological interpretation of "contemporary urban legend" (Kapferer 1990: 15, 29–32) that persuaded folklorists to accept rumor as a category of legend. It is ironic that, while memorate as a first-person experience account remains an underdeveloped legend in the view of folklorists, the haphazard rumor — hearsay and gossip without epic content — has become acknowledged as contemporary legend.

## Rumor-Legend

*Rumor-legend* is a very recent and vague term. In relationship to legend formation, Brunvand called rumors "unverified reports" (1981: 12) and "proto-legends" (175); he also mentioned "undeveloped rumours" (175), placing them at the initial stage. The first serious consideration of the "nature of the relationship between legend and rumour," however, was made by Paul Smith (1984: 210), who identified three related narrative categories: rumor, legendary rumor, and (contemporary) legend, arguing that rumor *is* in fact legend. In his elaborate analysis of a particular case, looking at processes of reversal, he observed that the legend can function as rumor and that the legend can turn into rumor. Once a unique rumor becomes a "legendary rumour," wrote Smith, it may eventually turn into legend. At the same time, Smith does not imply that "the direction of transformation is always from rumour into 'legendary rumour'" (1984: 211). Nor does he tell us what makes a rumor legendary.

Glazer also used the term *rumor-legend* in comparing Anglo and Latino versions of the "Boyfriend's Death" legend on the grounds that their telling is casual among teenagers, without a structured context (Glazer 1987: 102–103). Such a proposition is surprising for legend specialists who have always been aware of the fact that the legend does not need the planned "storytelling events" that are indispensable for märchen-telling. And encouraged by Brunvand's aforementioned terms, Boyes described the developmental stages of a "rumour legend in process." The description, including consideration of sociocultural and situational contexts, illuminated the polyphonic nature of the many interactive oral and media voices in the transmission of a "proto-legend," which the author viewed as unlikely to develop into legend (Boyes 1984). At any rate, Boyes's article contributes also to our confusion as to whether rumor proper can be regarded as an evolving contemporary legend; and it adds to our frustration for the lack of convincing, documented arguments to persuade us of the need to distinguish rumor and rumor-legend.

## Urban Legend

*Urban legend*, along with *urban belief tale, modern urban legend*, and *contemporary legend* are useful, operational terms, developed at the desk of the current generation of legend researchers, professional folklorists who are interested in the ethnography of living legendry. These names are not products of analytically tested theories, but are simple, practical terms. Unfortunately, some people take them seriously and waste time attributing highbrow meaning to them. They merely denote legend-like stories that are part of the everyday lives of people in the post–World War II urban-industrial world.

As part of informal conversation, these legends are not always clearly separable from tall tales, fables, and personal experience stories (Bennett 1985: 222–223). Nevertheless, the emphasis on "urban," "modern," and "contemporary" within the scholarly terminology is significant. It is the beginning of a new enterprise—a landmark that heralds the shift of interest from legends of "rural," "archaic," and "primitive" cultures to current legendry that lives in the context of urbanization and industrialization today. As Stewart Sanderson, a pioneer of modern legend study, pointed out,

> The modern legend constitutes . . . the most widespread, popular, and vital folklore form of the present day; and what strikes me as perhaps its most outstanding feature is the creativity, imagination, and virtuosity brought to its performance by all kinds of people, old and young, well read and barely literate, educationally privileged and educationally deprived. (1981: 14)

However, there are precedents. *Urban* legends—stories about sensational occurrences in cities, and concerning people, places, and structures known to the urban folk—have been noted and published since the mid-nineteenth century. Almost all major cities have developed their own legend repertoire that has become common knowledge to its citizens (Dégh and Vázsonyi 1978; McCulloch 1987) as well as a source of pride, with accompanying memorial displays and tourist promotions. From Prague to Berlin, from Paris to Ljubljana, Basel, and Vienna, European authors have celebrated old and new legends about revenants, curses, and miracles as well as modern incidents of witchcraft and UFOs in their cities (Golowin 1966, 1967; Gugitz 1952; Pomplun 1963; L. Schmidt 1963: 110–112).

But the newly discovered, so-called "urban" legends were allegedly different. The modern academic legend scholars who first came across these legends did not go to "the field," but rather for the first time looked at their own culture for living and emerging legends. They searched their own memories for legends they had experienced, and they asked relatives, friends, and neighbors to share their knowledge of legends with them. They reached out to their students to help confirm what they had begun to realize — that the legend is a far more important parameter of human mentality than any other folklore genre.

What they found was that the scene, the actors, and the interpersonal relationships in the narratives and in their situated contexts were contemporaneous, and that the communicative channels that spread them included the mass media. Legend events took place in the familiar pageantry of industrial living: parking lots, high-rise buildings, department stores, hotels, shopping centers, offices, college dormitories, recreational vehicles, and movie theaters. The repertoire involved modern equipment: typewriters, microwave ovens, automobiles, airplanes, televisions, computers, and cameras. And the actors and tellers could be from any walk of life. No doubt, this is the world in which we live: It reflects our life-style, our observations, our imagination, our hopes, and our frustrations. Narrators could represent the repertoire of any group, including folklorists. The contents and the form of these texts display an even greater flexibility than before, and the distinction of forms and styles has become even more difficult to discern.

All this legend activity appeared as something entirely new. It seemed to justify speaking of the urban/contemporary legend as a separate category or even as a new genre. Researchers regarded collecting these legends as their priority; they felt the need for a representative corpus before testing their contentions. As the groundwork continued, folklorists were watching for legends (or potential legendary materials) day by day as they emerged from the media and passed through diverse but often simultaneous channels that had never before been explored. Preoccupied with pursuing the data in their immediate social environments (Ellis 1990a), researchers impatiently pursued any new legend-potential without checking existing collections for antecedents with parallel contents. As Bennett and Smith explained in their important survey "The Birth of Contemporary Legend" (1989), at first they were using the presence of modern features as a defining tool. What they first considered as modern urban legends were stories of automobile disasters, dreadful contaminations, and student horrors. But as research continued, many "new" legends turned out to be makeovers of old stories, following the avenues of the normal legend process. As an overreaction to critical comments or to their own uncertainties, seekers of the "new urban" legend began to look into historical sources, and discovered similarities in materials that dated from classical antiquity and the Middle Ages to the reign of Queen Victoria. In the spirit of the comparative historic-geographic method, urban legends were traced to antecedents and originals; and historic (monogenetic) continuity and generic relationships were confirmed (Ellis 1983).

So what then is new in these "new" legends? Klintberg says the modern urban legend is not a totally new genre; its sudden burst onto the academic scene was simply a result of the folklorist's shortsightedness in having ignored everything but the stories of old peasants (Klintberg 1985: 274). Time, then, has come to repair this shortcoming. Bennett did not answer her provocative question, "What's Modern about the Modern Legend?" as the content, she suggested, is not modern because of its traditionality. But if we really want to find out, she said, we must study the performative and psychological aspects of the genre (Bennett 1985: 229).

The problem is that neither the comparative philological or performative approaches of folklore were able to deal successfully with the typologically similar, minimal, and basic legend-motifs that manifest in regional forms without necessarily being related to each other. These textual units were called "transcultural patterns" by Hufford, with the experiential base contextualized diversely among communities. His "experience-centered approach" targeted what is behind particular supernatural beliefs (Hufford 1982a: 256).

Today few people would doubt that urban legends are the current outgrowth of traditional legendry, and if they seem "entirely different," that means that their smooth accommodation to an entirely new technological world is difficult to accept by the generation that was taught that legends are mystic, metaphysical nightmares of the rural folk inspired by the natural landscape of virgin forests and tempestuous seas.

The term *urban legend* gained general popularity among lay readers through Brunvand's urban legend books. These five volumes, published between 1981 and 1993, not only disseminated commonly known scary stories but also inspired their oral and media retellings and the creation of new stories within Brunvand's network of correspondents, who yielded, and continue to yield, fresh material. As a consequence of book promotions, newspaper columns, television talk shows, and even a 1994 comic book version, Brunvand's books have inspired the adaptation (and abuse) of his popular horror and ghost legends. The movie industry in particular has taken interest. *Urban legend* became a household term and gained prestige as a folklore genre. An Internet-based "urban legend discussion group" was founded in 1992, and at the time of this writing its participants still tell and retell favorite texts, forge new texts, and conduct dialogues that advance theories about urban legends almost exclusively on the basis of Brunvand's publications. The give-and-take mechanism of Brunvand as proponent and the groups he created as recipients is something to consider as a potential continuation of legend tradition.

At the same time, the foregrounding of the urban legend issue prompted American academic folklorists to call for an open discussion: "It seems appropriate at this time for folklorists to look critically and analytically at what is going on in 'urban' or 'contemporary' legend research, both in the United States and abroad," Georges wrote to Alan Dundes and myself, inviting us to speak on the subject at the University of California in 1992.[20] He suggested the following topics for possible foci:

1. The distinction among rumor, gossip, and legend seems to have become increasingly blurred in folklorists' research and writings. Why? Should this be a matter of concern? Why or why not?

2. "Contemporary" or "urban" legend research has become a principal focus in contemporary folkloristics. Why? Is the contemporary/urban legend receiving more scholarly attention and discussion than it deserves? Why or why not? Is the preoccupation with legendry an American or an international phenomenon? Is it likely to be a short-lived or a long-term scholarly preoccupation?

3. Brunvand and others either state or imply that if a story is identifiable as an urban legend and/or as folklore, it obviously isn't true. Why do some folklorists take such a stance? How defensible is it, and why?

4. Brunvand's urban legend books attract an international readership of both scholars and the general public. Why? What kind of satisfaction/reinforcement do readers get from Brunvand's works, and what impressions of and inferences about folklore do they come away with after reading them?

5. Are folklorists who engage in urban/contemporary legend studies testing any hypotheses about, and/or developing any new insights into, the nature and function of legend and of folklore? If so, what; if not, why not?

6. Compare the accomplishments, shortcomings, and needs of legend research in the United States today with the accomplishments, shortcomings, and needs reported and assessed in papers presented at the 1969 UCLA symposium on American Folk Legend.

7. What should the objectives of folklorists' studies of rumor, gossip, and urban/contemporary legend be, and how should they be carried out? What kinds of questions or specific questions can/should folklorists' studies of rumor, gossip, and legend address, and why?

The questions speak for themselves, and will be answered in the diverse contexts of this book.

*Urban legend* was accepted as a technical term by European legend scholars. Actually, a few of them independently turned with interest toward legends in the city after World War II (just to name a few, the Austrian Leopold Schmidt [1963]; the Swiss Sergius Golowin [1964 and 1967]; the German Ingeborg Weber-Kellermann [1955]; and the Dutch Ethel Portnoy [1978]). Later on, particularly following the publication of Brunvand's first book *The Vanishing Hitchhiker* in 1981, European crops of urban legendry began to appear in academic journals. Reports about collecting urban legends and the planning of research projects (Czubala 1993; Fix 1994; Simonides 1987; Top 1990) as well as analytical studies of legends related to the concept "modern" and "urban" (Knierim 1985; Meurger 1985) soon were followed by books on the popular market.

As collaborative research developed during the same period, the original meaning of "contemporary legend" (legend of our time) became a subject of controversy. Its Anglo-American proponents could not defend it epistemologically as a separate category, distinct from the traditional legend (Klintberg 1990b; Sanderson 1981: 5). Others, including myself, have argued that legend by its nature is always contemporary at the time it is told. It addresses relevant issues and could not exist otherwise (Dégh 1991; Voigt 1990). Several others have pointed out that similar supernatural and horror stories had been noted earlier under the name of "urban myth," and some examples identified as "old contemporary legends" from the collections of Sebillot, van Gennep, and Mannhardt were brought into focus by Renard (1994, 1995). The notion that the qualifier "contemporary" suggests a crucial difference between legends today and in earlier epochs was further undermined by Simpson, who said that no matter how old legends are, they count as contemporary if their tellers present them as based on real events that recently took place (Simpson 1994: 100). This would mean that the variants of the same story belong in two categories (memorate and fabulate), depending on the presence or absence of such a presentation.

In the meantime, distinguishing features brought up by supporters of the term were too subjective and vague for serious consideration: "A contemporary legend narrates events which purportedly occurred within a temporal horizon felt as contemporary by participants in the narrative event" (Pettit et al. 1995: 97); or "contemporary legends sit somewhere between mundane, everyday experiences and the extraordinary. If you like, they are about the mundane and ordinary, but with an unusual twist" (Smith, in Pettit et al. 1995: 99). We can ask ourselves how one determines what a participant felt, or how one defines "an unusual twist." Besides, doesn't it seem that both definitions fit the legend in general?

Understandably, academic interest in current legends was motivated by the fact that they appeared as close reflections of major social problems that people were experiencing (G. Fine 1992). An entirely new, alienating urban-industrial mass society came into existence and created an entirely new system of mass information that made the legend not only more visible than other forms of folklore but also made it one of the most powerful voices of public opinion. Legends appeared as registers of people's everyday lives, beliefs, ideologies, and philosophies, expressing fears of new kinds of life-threatening dangers, representing human struggles and hopes for survival. Most importantly, these legends appear as immediate responses to the daily problems of average people; and thanks to mass media technology, they proliferate, multiply, and spread faster and farther than ever before. Mass carriers help them undergo in weeks or days the variation that oral tradition previously had afforded in the lifetime of three generations. This folklore genre, leaving the confines of marginal local groups and oral tradition, became a democratizing factor; its many repetitions resulted in many variables. Social relevance was its main lifeline. Legend created by the folk is and always has been oriented toward local groups and the present, but folklorists previously had not paid attention to social relevance. They had been interested only in the archaic folklore heritage of marginal social groups. Cultural globalization through the channels of mass communication, however, makes folklore a shared property of all, and folklorists have to move on to register the folkloric projections of the change.

Contemporary legend appears as the present manifestation of traditional legend, representative of the actual stage of an ongoing process that keeps the story meaningful and viable for all, but in diverse ways. The ethnographic present is built on historical antecedents and it cannot be understood in isolation. We must seek connections and continuity to establish the contents, the formal styles, and the intrinsic messages of the genre legend, old and new, rural and urban. Operationally, the current body of legends may be called contemporary, but the legend is destined to continue and transform into another kind in a future epoch. If we stick to the absurd idea and classify legends according to temporal frames, we may not find out how social change affects the acculturation process of this genre. The current generation of researchers have broken away from the past-oriented, *vulgus in populo*–focused conceptualization of folklore and made the transition from the old to a new social world, in which the formation of the genre legend can be pursued monographically within any community, in any permanent and occasional group of people that accommodates legends. But the rethinking of definitions and meanings must continue, as more materials are found in the steadily growing industrial society.

Those who proposed the terms *modern, urban,* and *contemporary* still question the validity of such distinctions (Bennett 1984; Brunvand 1981, 1984), while others, despite awareness of its awkwardness, feel comfortable with the term *contemporary legend* as a working term (Smith, in Pettitt et al. 1995). Others even try to distinguish "real contemporary legends" from similarly situated and performed contemporary horror stories (Ellis 1994a). It is certainly true that the currently circulating legend repertoires feature as many non-urban and non-modern plots, environments, and situations as urban and modern ones. Many take place in barns, mills, farmhouses, meadows, pastures, forests, and cemeteries, at lakesides, and on bridges, country roads, and trails. Scores of examples show the rejuvenation of old themes, transported from rural to urban environments. Critics have pondered what benefit there is in isolating legends as "contemporary" simply because they have survived. Isn't it a rule of folklore to adapt traditional themes innovatively to satisfy new needs? We can prove that legends are alive and well today, just as they were in the past (Bausinger and Brückner 1969). Those who labored with the definition of the new legend could not argue forcefully enough to find features that made it distinctive from the traditional legend.

In light of all these questions and uncertainties, it will not be a surprise to present the following definition-variant of the urban legend (contrasted against myth), in the careful wording of Brunvand:

> Urban legend belongs to the subclass of folk narratives, legends that — un-like fairy tales — are believed, or at least believable, and that — unlike myths — are set in the recent past and involve normal human beings rather than ancient gods or demigods. Legends are folk-history, or rather quasi-history. As with any folk legends, urban legends gain credibility from specific details of time and place or from references to source authorities. (1981: 3)

This does not differ from traditional definitions, including the others already quoted from Brunvand. "Ancient gods or demigods" is merely an unnecessary inclusion, as it was never a part of legend definitions. With the rest, only the emphasis has changed, so there is nothing here to justify the term *urban.* I prefer Renard's more insightful definition of what he views as urban legend:

> Anonymous recital of short forms of surprising contents, presented in multiple variants told as true and recent, taking place in a social milieu, and expressing fears and aspirations. (Renard 1999: 6)

Research and brainstorming among scholars continues. The originally small group of legend scholars (the fourteen Sheffield seminarians) has become an expanding collaboration. Their annual meetings include North American and European folklorists and volunteers from related disciplines, with the addition of writers, journalists, film makers, and amateurs. Unlike any other research team in folklore ever, we are studying a folkloric phenomenon in emergence. And never in history has folk narrative been studied with so much dedication; none of the available materials amassed by scholars over a century and a half are as dependable, genuine, and authentic, or as unselective, unbiased, and all-inclusive.

Ironically, it is precisely this approach to narrative — this openness and lack of orthodoxy — that has precipitated criticism by conservative text folklorists. For example, in his book subtitled "The History and Research of Our Folk Legends" (1989), Leander Petzoldt considered primarily legends of the past as his finished book-products. He allowed only a six-page discussion of what he called "modern legend formation and everyday narration"; he emphasized that, although these texts may be structurally similar to legends, they can be classified as memorates because they are subjective experiences. He found identical motifs in old and new narrations with reference to the collective unconscious,[21] but he admitted as a positive fact that contemporary legend researchers may be able to observe and analyze processes *ab ovo*. In essence, however, Petzoldt was pointing out that Anglo-American folklorists and pseudo-folklorists, hand in hand with the mass media, are responsible for the reinforcement and proliferation of "urban legends." While apparently meaning everyone else, he singled out Brunvand (1981) in particular as an "eager multiplicator" of legends through his popular books and his encouragement of correspondents who send him their stories. There is "no doubt," wrote Petzoldt, "that scholarly and journalistic interests of the authors direct public attention to these narratives and greatly influence their multiplication by feedback" (1989: 126). More recently, Petzoldt attributed the new popularity of legendry to globalization via tourism and foreign travel, which accelerated the spread of legends (Petzoldt, 1999: 5–12).

Indeed, Brunvand's best-selling legend books aimed at the lay readership have educated the public about "urban legends," including the legend-bearing folk he activated as contributors to his collections and syndicated column. But so have centuries of printed legend collections, schoolbooks, educational primers, folkbooks, newspapers, and other publications oriented toward the masses, as Schenda has argued. Schenda's Swiss collection proved that the legend-tellers and collectors from the sixteenth to the twentieth century have been identical (Schenda and ten Dornkaat 1988). Who can control the spread of legends in a literate society when the contributors include legend scholars, news reporters, talk show hosts, clairvoyants, parapsychologists, and other professionals — in sum, anyone who has, in any format, made a legend accessible to the folk? Petzoldt himself did so when he wrote a paper assessing the German redaction of "The Vanishing Hitchhiker" (Petzoldt 1990). Brunvand the folklorist and Brunvand the enlightener play different roles, as Mullen pointed out in his video-illustrated lecture at the 1989 meeting of the International Society of Contemporary Legend Research.

Should the legend scholar abstain from publishing legends in scholarly or popular form to avoid influencing the processes of legend transmission? For many years, it was a seasoned routine for Nordic scholars to involve the public in folkloric fieldwork. They solicited participation in collection projects through radio and television broadcasts and sent questionnaires and guides to regional correspondent collectors. In 1974, Klintberg went public with his questionnaire targeting contemporary rumors and legends. In the *NIF Newsletter*, he asked international folklorists to send him materials to complement his collection from Swedish university students; he also asked for information about data in newspapers, magazines, and scientific publications. Like Brunvand, Klintberg urged readers to send him more legends (Klintberg 1974). I myself went public by disseminating information on my "Haunted Houses in Indiana" project through the Indiana University News Bureau (see chapter 5). The news release appeared statewide in local newspapers, and, as a response, readers who lived in haunted houses or who had heard from someone who did sent their stories to me. I did not try to suggest ideas to potential respondents — my role was to encourage those who otherwise would have been too shy to come forward with their experience. But even "official" information can shed light on the depth and complexity of legends shared by the local community.

For example, Merry Barrickman, public relations officer of the East Chicago Public Library, sent me an account of local variants of the "La Llorona" legend (see George 1972), which she had written for a one-minute spot for WJOB Radio in Hammond. She summarized thirteen versions of the story of the hitchhiking ghost of Cline Avenue who vanishes when the driver tries to talk to her. The identity of the ghost varies. In one version she is a mother who drowned her child in the nearby river and out of remorse returns to look for it; in another, she is a girl killed in an auto accident on the way to her wedding and who returns to the scene every seven years; and in yet another she is a woman who was killed by her husband and his mistress, and who returns to walk the area each Halloween. These details are valuable data for starting new fieldwork. But even more valuable was the cover letter from this correspondent, which not only revealed the general popularity of revenant legends in her area but also told of her own supernatural experience, while characteristically expressing ambiguity at its feasibility:

I have one of my own which I think is developing but I can't be sure yet. I have lived in the same house in the Miller section of Gary for the past 20 years. About a year ago my husband, a copy editor for the *Post Tribune*, began smelling a freshly lit pipe in the house. Neither of us smokes and I thought it was just his imagination until I started smelling the same thing. There is no mistaking the smell of pipe tobacco. There is no other evidence of a presence, except for one or two occasions which really might have been my imagination. He is obviously a friendly ghost and I think we would miss him if he left. (May 22, 1987)

There is certainly a communication gap between armchair legend scholars, who deal with abstracts and fossils, and those who in their role as fellow travelers pursue the dynamics of narration as it unfolds, conscious of being a participant in the enterprise.

In his important synthesis, "Do the Legends of Today and Yesterday Belong to the Same Genre?" Klintberg summarized the discussions about the conception of contemporary legend:

> If we conceive legend as a scientific, ideal-typical genre, then it is my opinion that old and new legends belong to the same genre, which has continuously changed concurrently with changes in society, but which has not been documented continuously — quite the contrary. A historical perspective will help us to see which of the modern legends merely seem to be new and which are really new. (1990b: 123)

He also pointed out that in current research some areas of legendry are over-represented, while others are under-represented — specifically that the heavy interest in the macabre and sensational shows an imbalance (1990b).

This imbalance is still a problem; we do not have yet a clear idea about the distribution of legends among the diverse social groups. Gerndt considered the "modern legend" within the framework of a "*Konjunktur*" (boom) of legends over the last two hundred years. First, legend was celebrated by a romantic interest in folk poetry and concern for its preservation, Gerndt wrote. Later, legend collections were compiled to serve public education. Now the current "legend explosion," composed of city myths and legend-like (*Sagenhafte*) narratives, reaches the "consumer oriented world, as conveyed by the mass media that inundates society" (Gerndt 1991: 137).

The Anglo-American team significantly influenced the European contribution to contemporary/urban legend research. Following Brunvand's example, Europeans began collecting stories from their students and colleagues and from the popular press, discovering orally circulating American import-stories (such as "The Vanishing Hitchhiker," "The Hippie Babysitter," "The Stolen Grandmother," "The Hook," "The Murderer in the Backseat," and the like). But they also pursued the European versions of internationally spreading mass-media plots that remained mostly on the rumor level with minimal narrative development (e.g., Mickey Mouse acid, babies stolen for organ transplants, UFOs, and Satanist child abuse). Stylistically these texts are extremely dry and factual, like police reports, billboard posters, or warning flyers distributed to the public.

European legend anthologies mentioned above, like Brunvand's urban legend series, are entertaining and educational books, but they are lacking in scholarly documentation, classification, and interpretation. Like Brunvand's, the texts are not verbatim transcripts of field-recorded legends or copies of media sources but rather are retold, summarized, or abstracted versions of the originals, without professional commentaries that contextualize the performance and performers. Thus they cannot be subjected to serious folkloristic scrutiny. The illustrious authors mentioned above did not collect, transcribe, annotate, and analyze their texts according to the modern principles described in current fieldwork guides. The distinguished folk narrative specialists who edited their popular collections have yet to publish a monographic study of legends of our times. Among popular anthologies available in bookstores are the two collections of Klintberg with 100 stories in each (1986 and 1994), and Brednich's three volumes with a total of 385 texts identified cautiously and correctly as "*sagenhafte Geschichten von heute*" (legend-like stories of today; 1990, 1991, 1993). The term *sagenhaft* qualifies as cautionary because Brednich, like other European compilers, not only includes versions of the best known American and British horror and ghost stories and rumors, but also a miscellany of humorous and grotesque anecdotes, and personal experience narratives, some of them of suspect literary origin.

I believe these anthologies reveal the double standard of their compilers, who do not feel obligated to give the same scholarly attention to brief, plain, hard-to-place texts as they did to the classic peasant legends. We have to remember that European folklorists were slow to recognize that gossip, newspaper sensations, and radio and television shockers — "everyday narrations" as Bausinger described them (Bausinger 1958) — are legends in emergence, shaped by the alternative channels that air them. To note such ubiquitous trivia violated the canon that legends were circulated orally by old men in old-fashioned peasant communities who were isolated from the enlightened urban society. It was not easy to recognize folklore outside of the archaic context without the guidance of a new theory and a new method of collecting; it is still not easy to consider old and new as having equal value. More time will be needed for us to familiarize ourselves with the new situation, the new cultural landscape, and the intertextual relationship of the legend-like and related prose narratives that are appearing as much in oral as in non-oral forms.

## A Conclusion: *Legend* as an Overarching Term

At the end of our survey of terms and definitions, we have reached a point of confusingly multitudinous variation. If we accept that this genre can be divided into so many subspecies, how can we justify the use of *legend* as a common term? Hand underscored the great diversity — and thus unclassifiability — of legends, and Honko expressed regret that some folklorists see the legend as a homogeneous genre and forget about its categories. If within the categories the essential differences are greater than the similarities, it would be better to drop the term *legend* from the vocabulary of folkloristics as a misleading concept. If, on the other hand, we find that the essential similarities are greater than the differences, we do not have to eliminate the term but instead should rely on it even more.

I will use *legend* as an overarching term to include all stories, short or long, which so far have been forced into small categories based on different organizational principles. The subcategories, in ever-increasing number, usually focus on surface and not on essential features. For a more meaningful analysis, I will lump together all of the materials that contain a possible legend core, and will treat them as legend unless my analysis informs me otherwise.

Beginning with the story that is unanimously identified as legend (*Sage*, or fabulate) — because of its fullest, most elaborate, and structured form and content — I will include in my discussion throughout this book the following more or less consistently labeled categories: *Alltagsgeschichte*, anecdote, casus, *chronikate, Chroniknotiz*, contemporary legend, belief legend, belief story, *dite, Erinnerungssage, Erlebnisgeschichte, Erlebnisbericht*, entertainment legend, exemplary story, *fikt, Geschichte*, horror story, legend-like experience story, myth, personal experience story, rumor, rumor legend, *Sagenbericht, sagenhafte Erzählung*, superstition, superstitious story, true story, urban belief tale, and urban legend. I will also include more recent suggestions: media narraform (Grider 1976), retort legend, amusing legend, and admonitory legend (Pentikäinen 1989), and nasty and hostility legend (Smith 1995). Because folklorists have never been able to decide whether all of these are stories or if they belong to folklore at all, I will keep in mind all these categories and subcategories in my discussion. I hope to convince the reader that no straightjacket is needed to confine the legend, which stays the same while adjusting to new needs.

The legend is a legend once it entertains debate about belief. Short or long, complete or rudimentary, local or global, supernatural, horrible, mysterious, or grotesque, about one's own or someone else's experience, the sounding of contrary opinions is what makes a legend a legend.

# Legend as Text in Context

# 3.

## The Extent of the Text

Using *legend* as an umbrella term commits us to a problematic and difficult task. The text of the legend is the most complete form of a sequence of action — a plot — that can be found in regional, national, and international legend collections. More often than not, the texts in these collections represent analytical constructs of the types that subsume constituent elements; in reality, the elements may also live separate lives, or link up with other legend plots.

Solidified legend plots exist, without scholarly abstraction, because multiple channels are open to disseminate them and the messages they carry are important and of general appeal. These messages are also of lasting significance because they can vary or mutate to accommodate given conditions. The message each legend imparts to its bearers is also its lifeline: The message stabilizes the narrative content, keeping the form itself flexible. This means that the legend — which has often been characterized in contrast to the tale as formless, fragmentary, and incomplete[1] — has something other than formulaic constraint to hold it together.

If the folktale, acknowledged as fiction by its bearers, is the product of the imagination of skilled storytellers, then the legend can be characterized as the conveyor of information that concerns subjective human experience and answers an implicit or openly uttered question, as Peuckert and others have so convincingly documented. Each legend informs, explains, instructs, warns, or exemplifies through the telling of an extraordinary, unexplainable experience that a known person has encountered. Something in its extranormality is neither absurd nor completely impossible, which suggests that ordinary human beings may have similar experiences. In fact, sooner or later, most people are touched by a never-to-be-forgotten extranormal experience, and in it they find a message that makes them ponder or act. This message is the core, kernel, or nucleus of the legend, and because to communicate it to its audience is the main goal, the shape it takes is subordinated to the message it transmits.

The legend's incompleteness and open-endedness therefore appear as stylistic devices to underscore the significance of the legend core. The legend audience is not looking for aesthetic delight but rather to examine a problem they all share. Seeing the form and strategy of the narrative formulation in this light, it will be easy to distinguish the three possible textual units: the *belief statement*, the *experience story* (memorate), and the *legend* (fabulate), any of which may take shape when variants unfold. The three coexist but may live separate lives, and mix and merge. The legend may be short or long; it is not necessary that texts be polished or embellished with detailed descriptions of situations and dialogues — such matters depend largely on the skill of given narrators.

Attempts at classification of legends have a long history. Members of the Folklore Fellows, who have embraced the historic-geographic method of diffusional text comparison since the beginning of the century, have systematized archival data and come up with useful plot, theme, and variant lists. These have contributed to the establishment of the international *Motif-Index of Folk-Literature*; the *Motif-Index* is still a widely used reference source for legends, although it is not generally acknowledged as an integrated catalogue of regional or national motifs, and even less so as an international index of legends. As the diligent collection of legends has resulted in an enormous stock of materials, there are perhaps more legends contained in national and regional archives and in published collections than have been defined so eminently by the systems of classification. Experiments continue to be made to find common denominators and classifiable units for indexing legends, but none of the proposals has satisfied scholarly expectations.

Should the blame be put on the genre itself for defying systematization, as many folklorists have concluded? The problem has been to find classifiable, relatively stable units, taking the Aarne-Thompson tale type index as a standard. The use of the *Motif-Index* was suggested because the corresponding reference numbers of motifs already identified in tales could easily be found in annotating legend collections. At the same time, these motifs, Thompson's smallest narrative units (components of the broader tale type), cannot be identified with concrete legend texts because they are too general and unspecific; they fit large groups of related as well as unrelated legends at the same time, without characterizing them (Bošković-Stulli 1966; Harkort 1966). Experiments were also made to classify legends according to dramatis personae (Künzig 1936), but it turned out that identical stories may be told about diverse characters — revenants, witches, magicians, demons, giants, saints, fairies, lunatics, and criminals (Hand 1964: 49–54). In attempting to find a coherent unit for classification, the idea of "theme," "type," "motif" (Greverus 1965: 131–139), as well as *Glaubenvorstellung*, or statement of belief, were proposed and discussed in some detail. Regional and thematic materials were ordered and analyzed on a trial basis to see how they could be used internationally.

Classification of European and American folk legends was put on the agenda at the first congress of the International Society of Folk-Narrative Research (ISFNR) in 1959. Upon the proposal of Wayland Hand, subcommittees were formed, conferences held, and work-groups set to the task (see Peeters 1963a). Much work was accomplished between 1962 and 1967, but after a brief period of enthusiasm, the idea of a catalogue was soon put on hold. The only agreement endorsed by all was the extremely broad preliminary classificatory system shown below, created mainly to help archivists sort out their materials for a future international synthesis (see Ortutay 1964).

I. Ätiologische und eschatologische Sagen / Etiological and Eschatological Legends
II. Historische und kulturhistorische Sagen / Historical and Cultural-Historical Legends
  A) Entstehung von Kulturorten und -gütern / Origin of Cultural Sites and Properties
  B) Sagen und Lokalitäten / Legends and Localities
  C) Frühgeschichtliches / From Early History
  D) Kriege und Katastrophen / Wars and Catastrophes
  E) Aus der Gruppe herausragende Menschen / From Prominent People
  F) Verstoss gegen eine Ordnung / Revolt against an Order
III. Übernatürliche Wesen und Kräfte/Mythische Sagen / Supernatural Beings and Powers/Mythical Legends
  A) Das Schicksal / Fate
  B) Der Tod und die Toten / Death and the Dead
  C) Spukorte und -erscheinungen / Haunted Locations and Apparitions
  D) Geisterumzüge und -kämpfe / Procession and Struggle of Spirits
  E) Der Aufenhalt in der anderen Welt / Residence in the Other World
  F) Naturgeister / Spirits of Nature
  G) Geister von Kulturorten / Spirits of Cult Sites
  H) Verwandelte / The Enchanted
  I) Der Teufel / The Devil

    K) Krankheitsdämonen und Krankheiten / Diseases and Disease
       Demons
    L) Menschen mit übernatürlichen (magischen) Gaben und Kräften /
       People Endowed with Supernatural (Magic) Gifts and Powers
    M) Mythische Tiere und Pflanzen / Magical Animals and Plants
    N) Schätze / The Treasures
  IV. Legenden (Götter-und Heroenmythen) / Legends — Myths about
     Gods and Heroes

With subcategory specification, this system retains the traditional break-down of legendry into etiological, historical, supernatural, and religious legends. Scholars and archivists who have been using it to sort out incoming data in their archives found great discrepancies in the system. About eighty percent of the texts in existing legend collections belonged to the subcategories B, C, E, I, and L within category number III (Supernatural Beings and Powers/ Mythical Legends), while others remained empty or marginal to represent legend corpuses. No category was created for the rich bodies of nonsupernatural horror stories, the diverse stories of luck by magic, or the noncanonical religious legends. It is clear that the commission had historical materials in mind, not living legends cutting across cultural, ethnic, and class boundaries.

Legend specialists reached an agreement that only the legend proper (fabulate, migratory legend), divorced from its personal and local connections and carrying a fixed story attractive enough to spread through oral transmission, could be entered into a catalogue. The memorate, as someone's personal experience (Tillhagen 1964), was found to be so much a part of the informal everyday conversation of local people that, even if its coherent kernel could be captured, classifying it with the fabulate would cause confusion. The 1966 Liblice meeting of the Legend Commission was particularly revealing of the many kinds of personal experience narratives and other so-called "transitory forms" created by "*Homo narrans*" in contemporary villages (Bausinger 1969/ 1980: 225–237; see also Klímová 1996; K. Ranke 1967b). Belief statements — "nuclear beliefs" that contain minimal or no epic element — were found not to be eligible items for the catalogue.

Hand was particularly concerned with the future of the archival materials of "superstitions and popular beliefs." He had amassed a collection that he saw as a potential source from which to construct an American folk legend catalogue (1965). The symposium he organized in 1969 was meant as an appeal to scholars to follow the European example, and to push American legend studies beyond what he felt was its "infancy" (Hand 1971: vi). He called for more collecting, exploration of untapped sources, and comparative text analyses. Somewhat disappointed with the many deadlocks of the European indexing attempts, Hand still voiced a hope of working out an indexing system: "From the preliminary work trying to pattern American material after this notable European research effort, one can easily foresee, I believe, that 'The Index of American Legends' will have a special character of its own" (1971: 221).

No index materialized, but something else did. The first discussion of the American folk legend by fourteen American folklorists opened a new perspective for both American and European legend study. It called attention to the ethnography of the legend, the legend that lives in our time. The participants exchanged ideas about how to look at the legends in their own archives, the legends they directed their students to collect, and the legends they themselves had begun to collect. This landmark meeting opened the door to the discovery of new sources of legendry, leading to the new classifications, definitions, and terminologies which I mentioned earlier. The meeting was the overture to contemporary legend study in the form of annual seminars, initiated by British folklorists at the University of Sheffield (Bennett and Smith 1989).

Building on experience in the ethnography of the legend, beyond the narrow-minded fuss of setting formal categories for an index as an end-product, I believe that the legend must be seen as a plot unit regardless of the lack of formal cohesiveness of its variants. With respect to narrative sequence, ideally a legend consists of an introduction, one or more episodes, and a conclusion. The plot is sometimes clearly articulated, but more often it is quite blurred by stressing one of its parts and dropping the rest. Making up the type are variants that may range from extremely succinct statements, gestures or signs, personalized experience accounts representing diverse parts or elements of the whole, and variables of the complete story together. In other words, identifying a legend as a narrative unit and a cultural construct in its fullest extent, separated from other genres, requires us to bring together all components of its manifest forms — from the shortest statement (the one that can be considered as a narrative only by its inclusion of crucial elements of the story), to the longest, polished oral and printed versions. All forms of the legend need to be assembled and pieced together to see the extent of the type and its ramifications in the context of other narratives and folklore in general.

If a usable national or international catalogue ever materialized, it would need all the available ingredients to show the relationship between the parts and the whole, the logic of structure and meaning, the way legends are transmitted and repeated, and, above all, the identification of their constants and variables. Therefore, we need to contextualize the message that the legend contains. This means we need to observe legend-telling ethnographically, by focusing on individuals telling legends to their audiences. This is the way to find out what makes a legend a legend — to see how empty narrative formulas are turned into legend ingredients (Honko 1984).

It would exceed the purposes of this book to assemble legend corpuses for illustration, but the large number of variants of major types alerts us to the fact that monographic studies are much in need, because true understanding of variability can result only from detailed, thorough examination of corpuses. We scholars have never done such an absorbing text analysis. In fact, determination of types has resulted more from instinct than from scientific analyses, particularly if there is insufficient data at hand.[2] One should applaud the zeal of legend researchers who keep reinterpreting commonly known legends on the basis of new findings. After all, folklorists study processes in historical depth.

As data accumulates and social conditions change, new practices and meanings emerge. It is the scholar's responsibility to amplify and correct earlier assumptions based on earlier findings. However, this is easier to say than to do because it is impossible to gain access to *all* new variants of a type, from all areas of distribution, and show the variety of modifications in text, function, and interpretation. Because researchers are necessarily limited to small groups in their intensive ethnographic inquiry, they tend to generalize observations that seem valid only for that small group. For example, the conclusion, based on a small sample of texts collected by students and archived by their instructor, that "The Hook" is an "adolescent legend" — not taken seriously but rather "told for entertaining purposes," shaped as a play-like display of adolescent ambiguities, and travestied, inverted, or parodied into a joke (Ellis 1994a: 65, 71) — may hold true for certain group tellings, but as a generalization, the assumption is as speculative and biased as earlier hypotheses.

To give an idea of the potentials of motivic variation of a type, I will cite two examples of some typical variations from already assembled corpuses. The more subtle textual changes that express personal and cultural attitudes, worldview, opinions, and beliefs will be discussed later.

Example 1: The *Lidérc*

The *lidérc*, a goblin-like evil spirit in its transformational existence, connects several related international legends (about Jack O'Lantern, Fireball, Spook Light, Old Hag, Magician, Pact with the devil, treasure-hunt, malevolent revenants, and poor souls), and appears in cycles, uniquely shaped throughout the Hungarian language territory (Bihari 1980: 211–212; Dégh 1995: 45–46, 56–57; Hoppál 1969: 402–414). Thematically, the variants focus on the spirit's origin and birth, its services to and torment of its master, its shapes and travels in the air; its amorous exploits, and the methods for its expulsion. To illustrate the legend's textual variability, I will look at the constituents of one of its subvariants. In this example, the spirit flies in fiery form through the air, looking for adventure. It turns itself into a human, then torments and sexually abuses its victims.[3] Here is a succinct statement that encapsulates most of the ingredients of the total narrative complex:

> The egg of a black hen must be carried under the armpit for 3 weeks. The chicken that hatches will be the lidérc. It will bring anything the man or woman who hatched it wants. If it was a woman it will be a rooster, if it is a man it will be a hen. They live like husband and wife, they sleep together. It cannot be ridden of. To make it run away, ask it to bring flatiron. Water from the Bodrog (river) on snow, sand on a rope, light in a sack. (Hoppál 1969: 404)

Here is a selection of only a few variants:

1. Old people talked about lidérc-pressure. Uncle Joe used to sleep in the stable and the lidérc came and sat on his chest, he almost choked to death. His breasts grew big. It suckled once one, then the other at night. His soul was almost torn out. (Hoppál 1969: 405)

2. I saw it, it's like a lamp, lures people at night. I was going to the sheep herd and couldn't find the way. Like a lamp, was flickering in front of me. I was about 17–18, it was in the outskirts of Dusnok. (Hoppál 1969: 404)

3. People were talking about Mrs. K. that the lidérc dated her . . . that kind of a woman she was . . . a whore. It flew like a star and assumed the shape of a man. She got rich but died miserably. He drew her blood. (Dégh, unpublished)

4. When the Lidérc flies, it defecates sparks. It goes in the middle of the road. I went with my mother at night and she said we should not go in the middle but on the side. She didn't want to tell me why right then, only at home that the lidérc flies in the middle as high as people. (Hoppál 1969: 406)

5. In Gajcsána, the village where I was born, there lived a man with his wife and daughter. It was my mother and she was no longer young. I've heard her telling about these people to some of our neighbors. Well, the man was the village bell ringer. In the evening he often saw a star coming down, just above his stable. I might as well say his barn because it had a thatched roof. And then the star came to earth exactly at his barn. When he got home, he said to his wife, "I say, wife, can you make this out? There's a light coming down right on our barn." Now their daughter always spent the night in the barn. They have put up a bed for her in the barn, and there she slept throughout the summer. "It seems to me that our daughter is getting thinner and thinner," the woman said. "And she has got sort of a dizzy look too." "Well," he said, "we'd better get to the bottom of this and find out what's the matter with her." Next day they called her in. "Well, daughter, what about you? Is there anyone who has caught your fancy?" The girl just hemmed and hawed. "Well, then, are you going out with someone?" "I am not." "So there's someone coming to see you, is there?" "Yes, there is, a young lad; he comes in the evening." "I see, he comes to you in the evening. And it's

that lad you're in love with?" "Yes, I love him." "All right, daughter." As he was anxious to find out the whole truth, the man decided to be on the lookout for the girl's lover. When he was done with the bell-ringing and returned in the evening, he again saw the same star coming down right at their barn. So he ran to the barn to see what was going on there. Shitting fire, the star came down from the sky. As soon as it touched the earth it took on human form and went into the barn. Next day, the man called on his daughter again. "Well, daughter, tonight we'll change places. You'll come in and sleep in the house, and I'll stay for the night in the barn." "Oh no, father, that won't do." And she kept on protesting and protesting. But her father said, "You'll do just as I tell you. Here, you stay in the house, and I'll go out and sleep in your bed." And he went out, and no sooner had he stretched out in her bed than the visitor came. Of course, the father had dressed himself in his daughter's garments before he lay down in her bed. And when the visitor came, he thought it was the girl lying there in the bed and he lay down beside him. And then, the girl's father ran his hand along the fellow's leg and discovered that one of his legs was a goose leg. He jumped from the bed and ran out of the barn. The other went in pursuit. But the father ran into the house and locked the door from the inside. Next evening they made up a dummy woman of straw and dressed her in the garment of the girl. They took the dummy into the barn and laid it on the bed. Then they soiled the dummy's clothes with all sorts of filthy stuff. That night the lidérc came again. But when it saw that the girl wasn't there, it started shitting in such a fury that the whole barn was covered with a rain of sparks. Three or four nights the lidérc came back to the barn. But since the girl now slept in the house, he never again got to her. That was the only way of keeping the girl safe from the lidérc. Otherwise they couldn't have gotten rid of him. So, that's what I've heard my mother telling her cronies. (Dégh 1965a: 285–287)

## Example 2: The Hook, The Boyfriend's Death, The Roommate's Death

"The Hook" and related legends seem to be among the most popular and durable legends in the United States and have been recorded by folklorists and their students mostly from young people since the early sixties (Brunvand 1981: 5–10, 48–52, 57–62). In subsequent years these legends have never lost their attraction, and any number of new variants could be recorded and added to the existing collections. At the present, they constitute standard pieces of the repertoire of diverse age-groups from pre-teens to adults, and are told at slumber parties, Boy Scout and Girl Scout camps, dormitory parties, in vehicles while driving to popular legend sites, as well as during work breaks and at any other formal and casual gatherings of young adults.

"The Hook," "The Boyfriend's Death," and "The Roommate's Death" — three related horror stories about sex and murder — are situated in modern industrial mass society. Their world differs radically from the traditional world of supernatural beings who lurk beyond the boundaries of the familiar world of humans. This world, in which real-life criminals commit violent acts, is clearly dangerous and is commonly learned about by the general public from factual police reports printed in newspapers, sensationalized renderings by the popular press, and the fictionalized crime stories of television, radio, theater plays, movies, and novels.

The three plots are well-balanced, integral wholes with remarkable consistency. In spite of their broad geographic distribution, the majority of texts show very little content variation, only elaboration or omission of dramatic details. What variation we can observe, however, is a result of their longevity: During the thirty-odd years of their vigorous life, these three legends have been linked (in a process of contextualization) to contemporaneous, real-life criminal acts.

The three legends, nevertheless, share certain key elements that are conducive to merging and mixing. "The Hook" and "The Boyfriend's Death" are close relatives, if not diverse ramifications of an identical Ur-text, and they allow alternation between happy or tragic outcomes. In both stories, a couple's lovemaking in the privacy of a nature-adorned hideout is interrupted by a murderous intruder. In the first, a hook-armed lunatic's attempt backfires, and he is the one who is injured.[4] In the second, the parked couple tries to escape with disastrous results. The girl is locked inside for protection while the boy seeking rescue is murdered outside. She is traumatized by the spooky "swish-swish" sound caused by his shoes hitting the car top as the wind swings his lifeless body, which is hanging from a tree above. In both legends, the connecting link is the sober (nonlegendary) warning of law enforcement conveyed through the car radio, interrupting the pleasant music that has been a prelude to a sexual adventure. The news of the lunatic killer's escape from a nearby asylum comes as a turning point that changes the tone of the story. Having violated community norms and left the safety of their hometown, the dating couple must face life-threatening conditions in the isolation of the nocturnal forest.[5]

The warning delivered to the murderer's target serves as a further link to the more distant third legend, "The Roommate's Death." Here the radio alert about a deranged killer (a hatchet man or hook-man) on the loose precedes the victimization of two female roommates, one inside and the other outside of the locked door. The sounds ("scratch-scratch," "swish-swish," "drip-drip," "thump-thump," or "tap-tap") that torment the safe girl inside, who believes that the murderer is trying to unlock the door, turn out to be the attempted escape and dying sounds of the girl trapped outside.

"The Roommate's Death" is a more refined scary story than the previous two. As with "The Boyfriend's Death," the girl inside suffers only mental anguish, while the partying girl is brutally murdered outside. And the policeman, who represents the public opinion of the adult world, is more sympathetic to the survivor than the victim. As he discovers the outside girl with a hatchet in her head and her nails torn by the frantic scratching of the door, he thinks of the insider and escorts her to safety, kindly warning her not to look at the body of her friend. The story implies that the victim's life-style was the cause of her misfortune. Both the horrific noises of the bloody murder and the warning (the radio, the police) are essential dramatic devices of the legends about the boyfriend and the roommate's death. The car and the dorm room symbolize safe havens, temporary substitutes for the hometown or secure parental home.

Early on, folklorists viewed these legends as typically female stories and interpreted them from the girl's vantage point, even though they do not deal with the ordeal of women exclusively. As we have seen, both girls and boys are victims of criminal assault resulting from disobeying parental rules of conduct. The common message of the three legends is that whoever leaves the safety of the home, rejecting its moral principles, will suffer. From the functional point of view, they are not female stories either. There is only a slight difference between the number of male and female tellers; that might be attributed to the fact that the narrators (and/or collectors) were mainly college students, and the majority of enrollees in folklore classes are women. The topic of "forbidden fruit" (illegitimate sex at a secret hideout) and the double transgression of parental rules appeals equally to both boys and girls. Notably, there is a gender-specific difference between telling and the strategy of using the stories in the dating relationship, as the sample texts illustrate. In essence, the three legends are crime stories that exemplify consequences of deviance from behavioral rules sanctioned by adult society.

The affinal relationship of the three legends must have developed functionally. One informant/student, after telling "The Boyfriend's Death," wrote, "This is very similar to the 'Hook' legend found localized throughout the United States" (Jeffrey Tuttle, Berkeley Archive, 1971). In fact, the three legends are often told in sequence by young people of dating age. The local topography of these legends includes "lovers' lanes" at secluded, often spooky places located at cemeteries, bridges, and other entries from the other world. Here legend-telling functions not only to "scare the girl to make her draw closer,"[6] but also as proof of the intellectual worth of the seducer, who uses his entertaining skill, wit, and knowledge to enhance his sex appeal.

In one of his syndicated writings Brunvand, argued that "'The Hook' has become better as it has been repeated again and again. Tellers will drop details that don't fit the plot. . . . Or, they'll adapt the legend to fit local conditions. 'The Hook,' for instance would have made [the] lovebirds parked on Memory Grove, the local lover's lane" (UPI 1989). However, my opinion is that the repetition and proliferation did not make "The Hook" any better. While the number of variants greatly increased, the rate of "good," "mediocre," and "poor" telling remains about the same, following the natural process of transmission, depending not only on individual talent but on the telling situation.

"Poor" (fragmentary) versions are as attractive as the better ones to a group who knows the story because these stories are recalled for particular occasions. Besides, there is no documentable proof of the existence of a general, nonlocalized formulaic story that individuals consciously adapt to local conditions.

Separate and blended versions of the three cognates are open to the interpretive study of folklorists; however, at this time we want to concentrate on the mechanics of sequencing and textual blendings. In sequential legend tellings, "The Hook" and "The Boyfriend's Death" follow each other, as shown in this conversation situation, recorded by student Neal Raisman, in Amherst, Maine, in 1974. The informants are Terry, 20, a secretary, and Chip, 20, a carpenter.

*Neal:* . . . about a girl and a guy parking?

*Terry:* Parking?

*Chip:* Yuh, a guy with a hook, remember? The story about uhh . . .

*Terry:* Ohhh okay. There's this place, uh, I'm not sure where. Isn't it up uh, Old Stagecoach Road?

*Chip:* Well, over way back when they had stagecoaches. It's out Southampton-Westhampton area.

*Terry:* It's a place where you go parking. [giggle] Okay? I heard it through . . . I'm not sure if it's Ed or my uncle or who it was from but . . . There's this scraping, on the car door. Well, you know, hey, it's windy out, sands blowing around and uh. You know, they were going at it and afterwards when they got back . . . They heard all these reports about this guy on the radio news that had escaped from the state hospital. And they got home and he drops her off. And this guy got one arm and the other arm got a hook on it and he was like really wacked out. And he's got a hook on one hand. And they get home and like the hook was like, into the door.

*Neal:* This is . . .

*Terry:* This is a true story. This is really true.

*Chip:* I don't remember who I heard it from either.

*Neal:* You say the guy and the girl were in there . . .

*Terry:* In the car, doin' . . . going at it.

*Neal:* Getting involved . . . physically.

*Terry:* Sexually!

*Chip:* Sexually! That's the word, yuh. [Terry laughs]

*Terry:* If you wanna just come out and ask . . . they were fucking around. [laughs] Well, you know, on a windy night, if you're on a place where there's a lot of sand, when the wind comes along the sand's gonna hit the car and it makes noise. Even if you are driving down the road and there's heavy winds like there are tonight and if the ground is dry, and the sand is, you hear it hit the car. So, they're hearing the sound, think nothing at it. [pause] You wanna hear a good one? [laughs]

*Neal:* Yuh.

*Terry:* All right. I heard this one quite a while ago. There's this place. I don't know where it is. There used to be a covered bridge. This guy and this girl went parking and they had . . . They did the whole thing. They're out parking and he went to start the car up to leave and they ran out of gas. He's gonna truck on down and get some gas and supposedly there was a covered bridge one time at this place. And uh, so he leaves to go get gas and she's sitting in the car, waiting and waiting. The doors are locked and it was another windy night and it was a lot of trees around. She hears a scraping noise, on the top of the car. It's the tree branches supposedly. And uh, all of a sudden, there was a knock on the window. And she looks up and it's a cop. And a long, long ago when the covered bridge was there some guy was hung from the rafters of the bridge. But she didn't know this. So the cop's knocking on the window and he says to her, "get out of the car and don't look up." Well, this guy that she was with that went out to get gas was hung from the tree branch by the neck above the car. And the scraping sound was his feet. [pause]. Wanna hear another one? . . .

The same sequencing comes from a recollection of graduate folklore student Jacky Day in 1974. She heard both stories in high school (in Amherst, Maine) during an outing with "carload of friends, male and female, to an isolated road where we would park our car and drink. The story was always told as true . . . told by males and intended to frighten females."

The couple was out parking one night. As they sat in the car with the radio on, they heard a news bulletin that said a lunatic had escaped from a nearby mental institution and was presumed to be in the neighborhood where they were parking. He could be recognized, said the newscaster, by his hooked hand, and was very dangerous. The girl was frightened by this and wanted to go home but her boyfriend wanted to stay and neck. She kept thinking she heard noises outside the car but her boyfriend made fun of her and said she was just imagining it. Finally her fear got the better of her and she begged him to take her home. Angered that a well planned evening was ruined, her boyfriend started the car, threw it into reverse, and spun out of the parking place. When they arrived at her home he got out of the car without a word and went around to open her door. There, stuck on the handle of the door, was the hook.

The other story was told to Jacky by her boyfriend:

The two of us were parked in a small wooded drive where the wind made the tree branches brush against the hood of the car. Frank was one of the same crowd mentioned in association with the legend of the Hookman so I was not inclined to believe him. Nonetheless he frightened me with this legend that he told it much more convincingly when there were no other boys there to exchange sideways glances with over my gullibility.

One night a girl and a boy were out driving on an isolated back road when the car began to sputter and slow. Realizing that he was running out of gas, the boy pulled over to the side of the road beneath some overhanging trees. Getting out of the car, he began to walk to the gas station a couple of miles down the road. For some time the girl waited patiently. But as time rolled on and her boyfriend didn't return she began to get nervous. Just to be on the safe side, she locked all of the car doors. After a while she dozed off. The next thing she knew it was morning and the car was surrounded by police. She unlocked the door. A policeman helped her out of the car, saying he would take her home but that she mustn't look back at the car. She walked a few paces with him, but not understanding what all the big to-do was all about, she turned to see. There, hanging from the tree limbs over the car, was the body of her boyfriend.

Among the sixteen variants of "The Hook" in Joel Rudinger's collection, variability is well illustrated (1976: 62–67). But the two following variants will show something of the affinity between the three legends. In the first, Marla Chudy, 19, answers a direct question:

Yeah, this boy and a girl were in a car and they were parking. And they ran out of gas so they parked a while. And then he went to get help because he couldn't get the car started. And he told her to stay in the car, something about, yes, stay in the car—oh, that's a different one; that's about him, dangling. He told her to stay in the car with the doors locked. She had the doors locked but the windows down. And she was getting cold and she was going to go to sleep for the night and she rolled up the window, and she didn't think anything of it. And she went to sleep and her boyfriend never came back. And then in the morning when she woke up, the hook was in the window. He was just reaching in, evidently, to get her, when she rolled up the window, and she rolled up the hook in the window. (Rudinger 1976: 62)

Valerie Doerner, 10, neatly combines "The Hook" with the roommate legend:

There were two girls who lived together in the country. One night one girl wanted to go out with her boyfriend and the other wanted to stay home because she was tired. So one girl went out and the other was watching TV. While she was watching, there was a special broadcast telling you were supposed to lock your doors and windows because a man who had a hook arm was loose. So she was kind of scared from that and she made sure everything was locked up. It was about one o'clock and she was real tired and she decided to go to bed. She was a little worried because her girlfriend wasn't back yet. She woke later on during the night and it was then about three o'clock. She heard scratching on the back door on the screen. She got up and bolted the door and rechecked everything again. Her girlfriend was still not back, so she went back to bed. The next morning she got up and unbolted the door and opened it up and saw her girlfriend laying on the ground with her fingernail on the screen and a hook in her back. (Rudinger 1976: 66)

There may be a further link to make. Our last example illustrates an adaptation of the core motif of "The Murderer Upstairs" legend in this rendition by 19-year-old Patti Hirst of Madison, Wisconsin, who told it to collector Roger Mitchell in 1974:

A group of girls were walking home from a dance. All the girls lived close by, except one girl had to walk through a woods. There had been stories of a wild man living in the woods and the girls didn't want her walk back home alone. The girl finally convinced the others that she would be all right and she would call them when she got safely home. She was walking through the woods and she heard strange noises. She started running. She got home and locked all the doors. She went upstairs and picked up the phone and dialed a number. A voice came over the phone: "Sorry, wrong number." He was on the extension downstairs.

Thanks to general education, and the marketing potential of legends, some stories have acquired relative stability. Books for children and adults have popularized classic stories like "The Pied Piper of Hamelin," "The Seven Sleepers," "The Golden Arm," and "The Ghost of Sleepy Hollow." Movies and television shows have exploited many old and new legends about vampires, werewolves, witches, mad scientists, sex maniacs, monsters, UFOs, and other modern mysteries and horrors. But in reality, the living conditions of the legend do not allow formal solidification. This is probably what prompted the Grimms and their followers to blend "imperfect" variants and create complete wholes. Their editorial policy misled posterity; nevertheless, the fluidity of the legend must have been known to most field collectors — Friedrich Ranke expressed his dissatisfaction with his contemporaries' practice of "falsification of legend texts by collectors who pick and separate them, like flowers from their breeding soil" (F. Ranke 1926: 45).[7] The collections of Brinkmann, Henssen, Haiding, Zender, Peuckert, Simonsuuri and others contain more conversations about experiences and straight experience stories than depersonalized "migratory legends."

It is time we realize that an "ideal form" may be the rare product of the creative fantasy of exceptional storytellers, or that it exists in the imagination of folklorists. It is a mistake to regard the brief and simple texts encountered by contemporary folklorists as corrupted and unfinished: The living legend often appears in bits and pieces by its very nature. Themes of common knowledge and concern do not have to be told in great detail; often, a sketchy reminder will suffice.

## Collecting Legends Today

At this point we should also remember that when we speak of the "text," we are referring not only to a product of direct oral exchange but also to a more stabilized merchandise communicated through other-than-oral means to a much larger audience. People with access to technological devices may use telephones, video and tape recorders, e-mail, and fax machines. They may write letters or make photocopies.

Anyone may create an Internet Web site for a conversational genre like a legend, and people may join the Internet and become bearers, tellers, and receivers of stories in a voiceless, faceless, imaginary face-to-face narrative conduit that invents, learns, circulates, discusses, and recycles legends from oral and printed materials. Leslie Stahl, of the documentary television program *60 Minutes,* noted that "cyberspace became a dangerous place" where anyone can pretend to be whatever he or she wants to be and send false rumors. "Rumors never die on the Internet," she continued. "One false report spreads instantaneously; twenty people tell it to twenty million" (March 2, 1997).

The poly-vocality of the mass media has helped legends achieve unprecedented proliferation. The messages have continued to raise the same existential questions, but the legends have "actualized" — that is, they have become more visible and trivial through professional, consumer-oriented formulation. People contact their local newspaper hotline like the person signed "D.T." did to find out whether John Lennon's ghost came back to paint the word "Imagine" on a water tower on Tunnel Road and another on North Indiana 37: "We live on a long and winding road (allusion to McCartney's song, 'The Long and Winding Road') between the two towers and are curious about what it means" (*Herald-Times,* December 18, 1991). Readers write to the "Ann Landers" or "Dear Abby" columns about more threatening rumors such as invasion of space aliens or the import of venomous reptiles in knitwear from Hong Kong. The mass media also revive and put old legends into circulation again. Archbishop O'Connor had a large audience when he lashed out against rock music as satanic seduction. Indeed, the "formless" legend text blossoms in new formats — reports on ghosts in family homes have become daily news items, and classified ads sell voodoo dolls for use in killing unfaithful husbands by black magic.

Folklore depends on remembrance to survive in tradition, whereas literature can be forgotten, as Schenda notes. Yet, when stored in archives or old books, printed literature can be retrieved any time, in any place, and put to work. And technical reproductivity via print, radio, and television contributes to the spread of lasting messages as well as to the maintenance of tradition and the creation of new folklore (Schenda 1992).

By now, I hope it is clear that we cannot speak of the text of the legend as a polished, purely oral form that is easily separable from other informal everyday talk. We must describe the text in context as we can observe it *in situ,* based on our own field experience. Leopold Schmidt, thirty years ago, argued that the legend is so much imbedded in everyday life that it cannot be separated from it (Schmidt 1965). One might add only that since Schmidt's time the contemporary urban-industrial society has produced more legend-telling opportunities than ever. The commodification and consumer orientation of mass media have opened the door to more everyday occasions for transmitting legends through alternating vehicles of communication: oral, written, printed, broadcast, theatrical, or ostensive. Individually and together, all these create their own contexts in interaction. No legend can be described fully without the context. Contexts differ as they accommodate diverse kinds of texts and occasions; that is, the legend itself is flexible, while retaining its essential ingredients and basic goal.

Before talking about the content of the text in relationship to its context, the inevitable question arises as to how we should approach the data that arrives to us through so many communicating vehicles, in so many shapes and in such a large quantity. We must keep in mind that folkloristics is a discipline that builds its theories on empirical data, observed and registered with the utmost care, while minimizing the observer's influence on subjective (intentional) expressions as much as possible. We know that legends in historic and current collections are not fully reliable because they were shaped by their collectors who were guided by diverse principles. Nevertheless, we cannot afford to disregard even poorly collected and documented texts from the past, because even small fragments may give us a glimpse of materials from times and places we know nothing of, and they may fill gaps in seemingly unrelated scraps of information. This kind of posterior contextualization requires establishing a degree of interaction between the source and the publisher, and situating texts in their social and historical setting.

Although modern legend specialists discern their materials primarily from non-oral sources, they maintain the illusion that the legend is an oral folklore genre, and they attempt to capture occasions of live performance. It may be that they are right and that the natural state of legend transmission is an interpersonal oral exchange. We may also surmise that in the overwhelming hubbub of the multivocal mass media, oral retelling is a necessity that functions more as a bridge and relay station between non-oral channels. But at this time we lack sufficient data that would support such a hypothesis.

The fact is that we cannot determine for sure how legends and legend complexes or cycles popular in our midst have emerged from oral tradition. We notice them when they appear in the press and recognize them only after they have received a tremendous boost from the media and found their way back to oral tradition, broken into chunks in the form of gossip, rumor, eyewitness report, memorate, and possibly fabulate. Over the last fifty years following World War II, we could trace the chronology of the emergence, spread, blossoming, and decline of principal legendary themes under the impact of technological advancement. Several examples come to mind: the cyclic conglomerates of Bigfoot and other anomalous creatures; the stories inspired by religion, mythology, and science fiction about aliens and their flying machines (UFOs); the modern versions of Christian legends about Satan and his attempt to corrupt God's creatures; and the new chapter of the body-snatcher legend, a by-product of early demonization of medical experimentation that

thrives today in the popular press applied to innovative organ transplant proce-
dures (for example, see *People*, April 25, 1994: 78–80, and the *Sun*, February
20, 1996: 23) (Campion-Vincent 1997: 1–38). Traditional legends in modern
garb include narratives inspired by fundamentalist religious belief and those
influenced by the powerful establishment of Spiritualism, concentrating on
the contact between the living and the dead and related topics. Other examples of older beliefs in current circulation include near-death and out-of-
body experiences, ghosts and hauntings in homes and at accident sites; encounters with guardian angels, fairies, and other protective spirit-guides, as
well as telepathic visions (often referred to as "second-sight").

Like big trees, these themes branch into twigs and leaves, representing numerous stories and sub-stories that are familiar, authenticated, reshaped, and
varied to scare, comfort, and entertain the average reader and television
viewer. Seeking a satisfying explanation for mortals about the unknowable,
these major themes address the unknown and grapple with the topic of the
hereafter in the two main domains of trust — religion and technology —
applying and mixing the languages of both rational and irrational philosophies.

But there are concerns about "Folklore in a Box" — that is, television.
Lance Morrow tells us that stories are precious, indispensable, and that everyone must have his story or her narrative. However, what is occurring today is
a war of American myths, a struggle of contending stories. Pop culture, most
often in the form of television, is the arena where it is being fought. Furthermore, Morrow suggests that America needs to restock its repertoire of folklore
by cutting back the dominance of commercially committed television; "there
are better ways to tell a story," he feels (*Time*, September 21, 1992: 50–51).

### Legends and the Internet

How can Internet discussion groups, which often specialize in disseminating folklore, religion, legend, urban legend, rumor, and related topics, creatively influence the current legend repertoire? The communities of discussion groups are similar to folklore communicating groups in that their
membership is voluntary; individual participation is spontaneous; and participants share a common knowledge of and interest in current legendry. On the
other hand, these groups are composed of people physically isolated from
each other by potentially large distances. They have never seen each other,
may not identify themselves by real name and address, and sometimes have
no knowledge of each other's true cultural environment. In their acts of performance, participants on the Web tell, discuss, and debate legends just as
people in normative legend conduits do. However, like lighthouse operators,
they are isolated from their human contacts; they sit alone in front of the

computer, and, in lieu of live performance and the development of a natural face-to-face dialogue, they have only interactive writing on the screen.

Is this strange and unnatural new virtual community capable of replacing real human communities and maintaining old legends or creating and varying new legends? Can we expect human nature to change so radically as to develop perfect electronic, science-fiction–style storytelling centers that can fill social and cultural needs in splendid autonomous isolation? And what are the dynamics of the legend process when it lacks a dynamic social base?

New electronic communication practices seem to be on the verge of replacing real human communities with virtual ones. Perhaps we can assume that the legend conduit of the World Wide Web is capable of attracting individuals of similar cultural background, interests, and mentality. However, it is impossible to predict how long the present status of computer technology will remain stable and allow the formation of a performance etiquette before further refinements dictate new mechanisms. "We are more than ever before information-gathering machines. The whole non-atmosphere of cyberspace is filled with information, some of it vital and fascinating, some of it trivial, some of it troubling and disruptive," writes Roger Rosenblatt. "By giving our minds over to computers' minds, we delimit our imaginative capacity severely" (1997: 32). If the speed of change accelerates further, it's not clear how long human nature can endure and keep pace with the whirlwind technology, and keep moving the messages that impact folklore. With regard to the Internet's influence on folkloric production, scholars must decide how they can make a useful contribution to research when the medium is so new, unsettled, and elusive. It is in continuous transformation with regard to its influence on folkloric production.[8]

Typing into a computer for an unknown audience is an entirely different folkloric act than speaking to an assembly of familiar people. Many loners, too shy to develop real human contacts, may liberate themselves from their inhibitions under a pseudonym, maintaining total anonymity or assuming an imagined identity. Musing over the endless and still-expanding variables of Web sites in this computer-literate world, we may speculate on whether chat-group members will eventually come to the point of leaving the safety of their homes and entering real relationships on the basis of establishing common grounds. As we know, it may happen that, after a while, individuals exchange their phone numbers and decide to meet face-to-face. From there, out in the real world, real emotional bonds might develop.

The users of the Internet do not lack creativity, and consequences of their inventiveness become unpredictable as huge numbers of individuals and interest groups compose and link their Web sites, home pages, and chat rooms, and incorporate folklore, particularly legends, into their messages. In this arena where hobbyists and interest groups come together on the screen to interact, exchange ideas, and trade their merchandise for monetary and/or ideological profit, religion has become a best seller. Sects and cults composed of believers and nonbelievers in anything and everything turn their Web sites into outreach programs to teach their missions. Using the Internet, promoters and recruiters of any New Age religion can articulate convincingly the doctrines, forged from traditional legend elements, of charismatic leaders to a greater audience than ever before.

Particularly troubling in this respect is the increase of legend-based doctrines of self-destruction, such as those that were advocated by monomaniacs David Koresh and Jim Jones; these groups often attract the troubled, the misfits, the marginalized, and the most vulnerable searchers of transcendental solutions. As with all charismatic religions, sects, and cults, the rhetoric appeals to emotions and becomes an important tool for luring soulmates. Ecstatic sectarian ideologies can forge a close-knit folk group of individuals who have nothing in common except their commonly created canon, which they then propagate and perpetuate through the Internet and subsidiary electronic devices (including video and cassette tapes, photography, and the press).

We have seen in the past with groups such as the Shakers that religious belief can generate rituals and cultic behaviors that come to identify and characterize worshippers. Exemplary narratives, which we call legends, are a means of educating both insiders and outsiders in the meaning of these beliefs. I will describe the life history of an extreme religious community built on traditional Christian ideology that used modern technological devices to communicate its message. With the use of the Internet, the Heaven's Gate cult formulated its legends and evolved in full public view.

Heaven's Gate

The Heaven's Gate story first began to unfold for the nation in 1997 when a Federal Express parcel led a recently resigned former cult member, Rio Di-Angelo (formerly Richard Ford), and his employer Nick Matzorkis, owner of InterAct Entertainment, to the elegant residence in the wealthy neighborhood of Rancho Santa Fe, California, where the cult group lived and maintained their Web site development business, The Higher Source. The parcel contained an invitation to a mass wake, instructions for posterity, and videotaped farewells to friends and relatives that showed cheerful folks in the backyard, flanked by spectacular flowering trees and bushes. These twenty-one women and eighteen men believed that celestial events were messages from heaven, guidance for the deserving on how to rescue themselves from the impending apocalypse. Thus, the tape indicated, they were about to shed their "containers" and were eagerly anticipating entering the "higher evolutionary level" for which they had prepared themselves over the last twenty or so years.[9]

What the two men found when they entered the only unlocked door was the deafening stillness of death and the putrid smell of decomposing corpses. The bodies were laid out on bunk beds, displaying the neat orderliness that was characteristic of the cult. They wore uniform black outfits, with matching brand-new black Nike running shoes on their feet; as if honoring the Holy Week, their heads were covered with purple cloths. They had cash and small change in their pockets,[10] and suitcases packed with their belongings, ready for boarding. The cultists also equipped their bodies with proper information for the police about their identities, and the recipe for the suicide cocktail that killed them. According to the medical examiner, they had died in a regimented fashion, in shifts: The first fifteen were assisted by the next fifteen, seven were in the third turn, until finally the last one left was the leader, Do. The man who had orchestrated the dance macabre died alone in the master bedroom.

The cultists died as they had lived, quietly and undramatically, keeping to themselves but fired with the zeal of missionaries. Their earthly remains represented their last effort at recruiting people to their cause.[11]

But the story of the Heaven's Gate cultists had begun much earlier. On October 7, 1975, the news media first informed the American public of the mysterious disappearance of twenty people from their Oregon homes (Dégh 1977b). Responsible adults, family men and women, had left their jobs, children, homes, and earthly possessions to join a cult (a new sect called HIM — Human Individual Metamorphosis), led by "extraterrestrial" evangelists, that promised a spaceship ride to paradise. During the following weeks, as the press kept track of the events, others from across the United States also quit their jobs and abandoned their families and worldly possessions in preparation for a physical entry to a "higher level." As the local press revealed more information, the story came to resemble the Savior legend pattern, in which the ordeal of a new prophet is likened to that of Christ. "The Two," a male and a female evangelist (resembling dual deities), claimed they had come from the same "kingdom" as Jesus Christ, who had left earth "in a cloud of light (what humans refer to as UFOs) and would move and return in the same manner. . . . There are two individuals here now who have also come from the next kingdom, incarnate as humans . . . And will soon demonstrate the same proof of overcoming death." The Two expected that they would be assassinated sometime soon, and would then rise from the dead after 3½ days and leave for home on a UFO. The faithful could come along — provided they had completed an "overcoming process! — stripping away of all earthly possessions and desires" (*Time*, October 20, 1975: 25–26).

The Two were identified as Marshall Herff Applewhite, the son of a Presbyterian minister, who had been a college music teacher, singer, and stage actor, and Bonnie Lu Trusdale Nettles, a nurse. The meeting of these two people

117

was fateful. Sharing a strong religious background and a fascination with the occult, they together forged a New Age death-and-resurrection myth that combined biblical mystery with the teachings of astrology and UFOlogy. They predicted a cataclysmic destruction of the earth, within which a higher level of existence (heaven) was possible with the help of extraterrestrials (aliens, Jesus) who would run a rescue mission and send a UFO to transport the faithful. But in this myth, The Two took the place of Jesus, sacrificing themselves. In fact, they were "aliens from a higher level of reality" (Gardner 1997).

Nickell used Wilson and Barber's fourteen characteristics of the biographies of famous mystics, psychics, and mediums to analyze the personality type of Applewhite and Nettles — who had also gone by the names Bo and Peep, the Pied Pipers of Space, Winnie and Pooh, Chip and Dale, He and She, Guinea and Pig, B. P. Morgenstern and B. P. Shepard, and finally Do and Ti. He concluded that the "combined biography of the two 'UFO missionaries' manifested a similar 'fantasy-prone syndrome'" (Nickell 1997; Wilson and Barber 1983). From Oregon, the twenty cultists who had been recruited wandered across the country like pilgrims, searching for the location where the UFO would land to pick them up and take them to "the next Kingdom." The Two led their recruits on journeys that presumably paralleled those of the Prophets, the biblical leaders of Israel, and Christ. Do, says one former disciple, thought he was "Elijah, Moses, Enoch, Jesus and Abraham" (Lynn Simtoss, "Keeping Tabs on Bo, Peep and Flock, *Los Angeles Times*, December 22, 1975: 3–4). The Two also preached in public places and churches and accepted donations for the group, which was short of provisions. The papers mentioned these "recruitment meetings" of the "UFO pied pipers" and gave accounts of the fluctuating number of joiners and the great number of dropouts. The core group would always remain small (about 100 to 1,000 at its peak).

During their travels, the leaders and the recruits of the cults continuously changed their names (they went only by first names) and the names of their organization. First they called themselves HIM, then "Total Overcomers Anonymous," and later "Kingdom Level Above Human." The charismatic leaders Applewhite and Nettles introduced themselves as "extraterrestrial representatives," but their style and doctrine also changed over time (Dégh 1977b: 245–246).[12]

After the death of Nettles in 1985, the group disappeared from the public eye. The wait had been too long, nothing had happened, and bored reporters looked for more newsworthy happenings. Tired of wandering, the group settled for a while in Texas and Colorado. Do bought land in New Mexico for a "monastery" with money he had inherited, but the enterprise failed and the group moved on. In 1993 the cultists resurfaced under the name Total

Overcomers Anonymous and advertised their religious philosophy in newspapers and on the Internet. By this time, their doctrine had evolved further, and the members appeared to be eagerly waiting for the heavenly sign of the comet to lead the UFO. When they reemerged, twenty-two years after they had first surfaced, their doctrine had reached its ultimate articulation.

The group eventually settled in an elite neighborhood in San Diego, renting a mansion for $7,000 a month with the proceeds of a Web site development business that they called The Higher Source. Here they developed a much more effective recruitment strategy through the establishment of The Higher Source Web site, "Heaven's Gate," which made the headlines March 25, 1997. The Heaven's Gate site was set up to attract new converts from numerous religious chat groups on the Internet, which led to the group being later characterized as an "Internet cult" or "cybercult" by the press (Bloomington *Herald-Times*, April 4, 1997). However, the people who knew or met them at local restaurants and businesses found them to be friendly, "extremely nice, gentle people" (*Life,* May 1997: 18).

After settling in the San Diego area, as the leader of the cult, Do prescribed strict discipline. Do conceived of a monastic life-style in the mansion, which he had transformed into an efficient residence. The house was painstakingly clean and plainly furnished without frills, except for the several computer terminals; it was designed to accommodate their daily routine and help them achieve the proper level of spirituality and serenity by the time of the UFO's arrival. In a television interview with Diane Sawyer (ABC, April 9, 1997), DiAngelo explained how Do prepared his followers' "vehicles" (bodies) to be controlled and made "exactly perfect" for heaven. This preparation included his followers' diets — the amount of food was strictly prescribed, and a lemonade and syrup-based health drink had to be consumed every hour. The cleanliness of nails and the use of proper deodorant and toothpaste were all specified. The cult members' monk-like appearance, including close-cropped hair for both men and women, was intentional and was meant to "liberate" them from temptation. Following the example of their leader, several of the men underwent surgical castration to "control their vehicles," so to speak; they wished to suppress normal human drives and to follow the example of superhumans in preparation for extraterrestrial life. Their daily activities, the work with computers, and learning, meditating, exercising, and leisure activities were subordinated to the goal: leaving the planet Earth to escape its destruction and entering the Higher Level of eternity.

The cultists discussed their ideological and practical conduct in a "think-tank" manner, trying to iron out disagreements, such as their views on castration. More importantly, their earlier canon did not include mass suicide preceding departure from earth. According to a former member, the suicide option came up only in August 1994 in a hotel meeting room, when "it was mentioned that we should not discount the possibility that the Next up Level is not going to pick us up and we'll have to be the ones to leave our vehicles behind" (*Time*, April 14, 1997: 45). According to DiAngelo, Do did not live with his followers at the Rancho Santa Fe mansion, but stayed ten minutes away in the posh Lake Hodges settlement, in the company of two female followers. DiAngelo thought this separation of living quarters was appropriate because Do was of a higher order and deserved respect. DiAngelo stressed also that Do was a liberal leader and that anyone could speak his mind and express disagreement or quit any time for personal reasons, as DiAngelo himself had done just two months before the planned mass suicide. Upon leaving, he was given a check of $1,000, plus $12 for a bus ticket. Like other former members who had left, he kept in touch and remained loyal to the group, and was among them when they went shopping for the Nike shoes. He became their "final messenger" and agreed to serve the cult as an "outside representative," taking care of their business after departure. "They are my heroes," he told Diane Sawyer.

From the latest press inquiries, it is clear that the death of the thirty-nine did not extinguish the cult. Do's twenty-year odyssey "may have drawn a total of 200 to 500 adherents, many of whom remain alive," and still maintain belief in some of the doctrines (Howard Chua-Eoan, "The Faithful among Us," *Time*, April 14, 1997: 44). Left behind was a fellowship of former members, sympathizers, fellow travelers, business associates, and Internet correspondents. Two identical suicides occurred soon afterward in a hotel room four miles from the rented mansion on May 6 (AP, May 11, 1997). One of the two men, the husband of one of the original thirty-nine, died; the other was resuscitated. From reports, we know that the group's farewell floppy disk was also sent to other survivors and supporters before the suicides, with practical instructions to secure continuity and keep contact. And these supporters discuss the "meaning of their adventure and the stewardship of the legacy." An early disciple believes that the "Away Team" was limited to 39 for "numerological reasons: $3 + 9 = 12$, number of Jesus' disciples" (*Time*, April 14, 1997: 44). The cultists even planned a strategy for operating the Web site and communicating from the Level Above. A woman who did business with the Heaven's Gate Web design team, said she was instructed to contact nine former disciples who were to receive messages from Do in the Level Above and be given further instructions concerning the Web site. The woman believed that the site would continue to remain active for years to come (*Time*, April 14, 1997: 44).

Do and his followers saw themselves as pioneers, the first to leave the earth and enter the first level of a higher existence, which then would be followed by higher and higher levels. From those levels, information and instructions would be sent to the followers through the Internet. The Heaven's Gate cult was unique in its orientation toward computer technology.[13] The cultists' expertise and the information they obtained through the Internet must have been a contributing factor to the formation of their legend, just as the Internet must feed the legend for other cult groups. According to a source, there are "over 10,000 cult websites!!" (Hoffman and Burke 1997: 316), and these likely reinforce each other's obsessions. We know that the dead cultists managed to communicate their doctrine to other cult groups on the Internet, and we can expect continuity and variation of this UFO legend, surrounded by new beliefs and rites.

In recounting major events of 1997, the media kept reminding us of the thirty-nine pioneer heavenly UFO travelers with the question, "have they found their destination?" The tremendous publicity attained after the suicides may have attracted new devotees and reaffirmed the belief of hesitants who had left the cult. The eclecticism of the cult and the legendary account may have also lured members of other cults who shared the World Wide Web with them. In 1998, a new "loading dock" was reported from Gary, Indiana: On the shores of Lake Michigan, "God's flying saucer" was scheduled to carry off the survivors of the apocalypse in 1999. Twenty-one adults and eleven children, members of a Taiwanese religious group with its headquarters in Garland, Texas, prayed and performed rituals at the site on January 9. "'We just followed God's instructions,' said Hon-Ming Chen, the religious leader of the God Salvation Church which combines aspects of Christianity, Buddhism and science fiction" (*Sunday Herald-Times*, January 11, 1998: C1–2).

How did the leader Do know when the long wait would end and when the redeeming space ship would arrive? Do had received the message that the planet Earth would be recycled, said DiAngelo. "He heard voices and received instructions from above." The group believed in end-of-the-world prophecies for the year 2000, despite the fact that such recurrent predictions had failed in the past (Festinger, Riecken, and Schachter 1956). The group believed that the planet Earth was doomed and that the survival of the deserving was possible only through a rescue mission by a divine spaceship. They believed that the recently identified Hale-Bopp comet, whose progress was being tracked by scientists, was followed by a UFO that would take them to a higher evolutionary level after they had freed themselves from their "containers"; their temporarily suitable bodies would be replaced by perfect ones.

According to an Associated Press article, "The Higher Source cult's belief that a UFO is trailing the Hale-Bopp comet may have been inspired by rumors spread over the Internet and late-night talk radio," which had claimed that "a mysterious 'Saturnlike object' was photographed behind the comet by an amateur astronomer who speculated that it was up to four times the size of the earth" (Bloomington *Herald-Times*, March 28, 1997). An April 12, 1997, letter that I received from the Committee of the Scientific Investigation of Claims of the Paranormal (CSICOP) corroborated my misgivings about the impact of absurd rumors on the gullible masses. The letter informed me of a seminar held for skeptics from fifteen states featuring Dr. Alan Hale, co-discoverer of the Comet Hale-Bopp. "A score of true science?" asks the letter: "Sadly, a paranormalist claim that the comet is being closely followed by a 'Saturn-like object . . . four times the mass of planet earth . . . bent on destruction' has been exploited by the tabloid press. Hale was quick to denounce this absurd claim, but it lives on in talk shows and on the Internet." No one can stop misinformation if it fits the expectations of believers, educated or uneducated, when they see an approaching doomsday in the skies and in holy scripts. As an enlightened correspondent reminds us, "34% of Americans believe the Bible to be literally true, word for word. . . . When you reflect that this belief includes walking on water, rising from the dead, angels, ghosts, demons, unclean spirits . . . Should we be truly surprised that the Heaven's Gate leaders hoodwinked their followers? The leap from biblical belief to the absurdities of this particular cult is a small one" (*Time*, April 28, 1997: 8).

The cultists were professionals, with a businessman, a lawyer, an office worker, an educator, a nurse, a postal worker, and a therapist among them. Yet they accepted science fiction fantasies as basic educational materials. The theory their leaders had forged was a combination of Christian theology and folk legend amplified by popular pseudo-scientific conceptions about extraterrestrial life and astrology, all essentially informed by science fiction in popular movies and television documentaries. "It is time to put into practice what we've learned," said one cultist on the tape (*Time*, April 7, 1997: 33).

These educated and technologically sophisticated upper-middle-class zealots of Heaven's Gate had forged a religious mythology that combined modern science fiction with ancient occultism and outer space fantasies about superior alien worlds, with alien beings as ideological guides. *Star Trek*, *ET*, and *The X-Files* all provided ideological learning (but among the carefully selected videos, sentimental movies such as *The Sound of Music* were also included). The cultists were technologically sophisticated, but they uncritically accepted utopic science fiction as a literal truth and argument that supported their religious canon.

One might question the existence of "suicide cults" and their possible connections, as cited by newspapers. Do's doctrine was not a "suicide cult," as newspaper headlines called it to sensationalize the news. Evidently, the group performed a modern version of the Christian legend of the death and resurrection of Jesus. Their suicide was meant to be only symbolic, as they were preparing for eternal life through a voyage.

Mass suicide of religious groups has been known for centuries. In recent years, the Branch Davidians of Waco, Texas, who immolated themselves, and the People's Temple colonists of Jonestown, Guyana, who poisoned themselves en masse, have been viewed as noble martyrs by some, and as victims of fanaticism and ignorance by others. They all perished in horrible murder/suicide frenzies because they saw no other way out of the chaos they had caused. Other group suicides somewhat similar to that of the Heaven's Gate cult have been reported since 1994; followers of the Order of the Solar Temple from Switzerland, France, and French Canada swallowed sedatives and burned themselves alive so that they could be blown by the flames to the star Sirius "in the constellation Canis Major, nine light-years from Québec," where they expected to reign forever "weightless, and serene"(*Time*, April 7, 1997: 45).

As with most religions both great and deviant, the Heaven's Gate cult's main goal was to lead its followers to heaven. The Heaven's Gate cult seems different from other cults that use mass murder/suicide as a last resort. Unlike other esoteric cultists, they wanted to leave the earth happily and humbly, without blaming the government or anyone else. No violence, hate, sex orgies, drugs, alcohol, or firearms were involved in their lifestyle or ideology. Do and disciples carefully choreographed a symbolic suicide that represented not the end, but the beginning of a new, happier existence as they escaped from the doomed planet Earth. Their agenda was not death but survival. Originally, suicide was not even in the charter of the cult founded by Do and Ti; the Two expected to be assassinated and resuscitated after leaving earth. The group's mass suicide, in preparation for the UFO-lift to Heaven and resurrection incorporating the reconnection of body and soul, may be regarded as a ritual *imitatio Christi*, a pseudo-ostensive attempt at transforming biblical symbolism into fact. Religious belief, ritual, and narrative — the components of the legend — constitute perfect harmony.

The consensual suicide was rationalized by profound Christian belief in the mission of mortals to follow Christ's ordeal and gain immortality. The death and resurrection legend — the universal human hope of immortality in terms of Christian belief — has been recontextualized by the modern technological environment and its scientific and pseudo-scientific images. Exploration of outer space, the search for superior life on other planets, new fascination with traditional mysticism and mythic thinking, and the recent popular interest in angels and extraterrestrial visitors have all raised the popularity of legends about visiting superior aliens. These developments have also inspired other science fiction fantasies overlying the death and resurrection legend.

Ellen Goodman points out the disparity between the new tools we create and the old mindsets they may serve ("California's Mass Suicide Had More To Do with Life than with Technology," Bloomington *Herald-Times*, April 4,

1997: A10). Specifically, she comments on the enormous distance between our technological ingenuity (the Internet), and its use for absurd or trivial purposes such as finding evidence that there are aliens and UFOs, and propagating the doctrine of eternal life for those who wish to escape this planet by hitching a UFO ride. Thus, the Internet can be a dangerous, even a deadly, web (Hoffman and Burke 1997: 286–320); its creators are like the apprentice in Goethe's ballad, *Der Zauberlehrling*, who could not control the powers of nature once he had unknowingly released them. However, these events show what folklorists have known all along, that the fear of death, discontinuity, and perishing without a trace is the eternal human concern. This fear produces legends that respond to the current state of things, and these stories always circulate via the best inventions of the day.

Urban Legends

So far, the discussion groups composed of professional and amateur "urban" legend enthusiasts and collectors on Usenet, the World Wide Web, or e-mail mailing lists have not developed into global enterprises, and their creativity has not been too impressive. Brunvand's urban legend collections seem to be a major source of their knowledge, and most of the discussions concern similar texts heard, read, or seen elsewhere. Participants propose new stories they claim to have just heard, but these often sound like pale replicas of the Brunvand schemes. These stories resemble jokes and anecdotes, comical constructs of embarrassing situations that are possibly learned from printed sources, and their plots grow progressively detached from the unmistakable identifiers of legends. Some computer-narrated and -debated legends are real shockers because they were generated by sensational rumors of the day, like the legend about the "Stolen Kidney" (Brunvand 1993, 149–154), a moralizing exemplum of what may happen to boozers who fall prey to evil money-hungry conspirators.

Subject: Fwd: UNBELIEVABLE!!!!!
Date: Mon, 6 Apr 1998 10:06:41 EDT

Rarely, almost never, do I forward any e-mail I receive from people I know. Even though some are really funny (and don't get me wrong, I appreciate hearing from you) I do not participate in the "forwarding" process. This one was/is worth repeating. Very scary.

This story came from the "Daily Texan" — the University of Texas newspaper. Apparently it occurred during Fall Premier, a UT tradition that is a celebration of the end of midterms.

"Reason Not To Party Anymore"

This guy went out last Saturday night to a party. He was having a good time, had a couple of beers and some girl seemed to like him and invited him to go to another party. He quickly agreed and decided to go along with her. She took him to a party in some apartment and they continued to drink, and even got involved with some other drugs (unknown which).

The next thing he knew, he woke up completely naked in a bathtub filled with ice. He was still feeling the effects of the drugs, but looked around to see he was alone. He looked down at his chest, which had "CALL 911 OR YOU WILL DIE" written on it in lipstick. He saw a phone was on a stand next to the tub, so he picked it up and dialed. He explained to the EMS operator what the situation was and that he didn't know where he was, what he took, or why he was really calling. She advised him to get out of the tub. He did, and she asked him to look himself over in the mirror. He did, and appeared normal, so she told him to check his back. He did, only to find two 9 inch slits on his lower back. She told him to get back in the tub immediately, and they sent a rescue team over. Apparently, after being examined, he found out more of what had happened. His kidneys were stolen.

They are worth 10,000 dollars each on the black market. (I was unaware this even existed.) Several guesses are in order: The second party was a sham, the people involved had to be at least medical students, and it was not just recreational drugs he was given. Regardless, he is currently in the hospital on life support, awaiting a spare kidney.

The University of Texas in conjunction with Baylor University Medical Center is conducting tissue research to match the sophomore student with a donor. I wish to warn you about a new crime ring that is targeting business travelers. This ring is well organized, well funded, has very skilled personnel, and is currently in most major cities and recently very active in New Orleans.

The crime begins when a business traveler goes to a lounge for a drink at the end of the work day. A person in the bar walks up as they sit alone and offers to buy them a drink. The last thing the traveler remembers until they wake up in a hotel room bath tub, their body submerged to their neck in ice, is sipping that drink. There is a note taped to the wall instructing them not to move and to call 911. A phone is on a small table next to the bathtub for them to call.

The business traveler calls 911 who have become quite familiar with this crime. The business traveler is instructed by the 911 Operator to very slowly and carefully reach behind them and feel if there is a tube protruding from their lower back. The business traveler finds the tube and answers, "Yes." The 911 operator tells them to remain still, having already sent paramedics to help. The operator knows that both of the business travelers kidneys have been harvested.

This is not a scam or out of a science fiction novel, it is real. It is documented and confirmable.

If you travel or someone close to you travels, please be careful. Sadly, this is very true. My husband is a Houston Firefighter/EMT and they have received alerts regarding this crime ring. It is to be taken very seriously. The daughter of a friend of a fellow firefighter had this happen to her. Skilled doctor's are performing these crimes! (which, by the way have been highly noted in the Las Vegas area). Additionally, the military has received alerts regarding this. This story blew me away. I really want as many people to see this as possible so please bounce this to whoever you can.

Is this not one of the scariest things you have ever heard of?

PLEASE forward this to everyone you know.

Bye for now!

But how long can the virulent rumor about criminal commodification of body parts persist? The legend seems so much based on the current rumor and its social circumstances, that in spite of its similarity to the early rumor and legend about body theft by physicians for medical experimentation, it may have difficulty entering the bloodstream of natural legend conduits. Many old legends appear in regenerated forms, but so far no continuity has captured the attention of folklorists. And without continuity and the formation of conduits, these stories succumb quickly.

### Sociological Approach to the Legend

During the 1980s, folklorists became increasingly interested in the morphology of the legend. Its traditionality was evident. On hearing one, people often reacted with comments like "this rings a bell . . . haven't I heard this before?" The legend's amazing adaptability also became evident. For example, there is the story of the vengeful Typhoid Mary. Mary Mullen was a real person, a cook in New York City who died in 1938. She moved from household to household, causing at least ten outbreaks — fifty-one cases and three deaths — before she was recognized and detained as a carrier of typhoid fever 23 years later.[14] Not unlike some infectious diseases, after a long incubation her legend was reactivated as the story of the seductress "AIDS Mary" and was applied to the most devastating new epidemic that threatens the lives of millions around the world. This mortal disease, which as yet has no known cure, remains in the headlines of newspapers. As government agencies, private charities, and popular personalities raise public consciousness of AIDS, Mary's legendary persona has translated and underscored the magnitude of a real threat into the language of legend.

Sensational real or invented fictional events concerning threats to human existence travel by word of mouth, hearsay, gossip, and rumor, and are reported as news by the media. Revitalizing and updating traditional ideas, these localized and personalized accounts cause considerable alarm. Brief and "factual" statements about horrible criminal acts, devastating natural catastrophes, alien invasions, life-threatening conspiracies against common people by powerful interest groups or governments, and victories of evil over good (Satan against God) have spread like wildfire because they mesh perfectly with the anxieties of ordinary people, who are alienated by the sober and banal reality of everyday existence in a technological age. Through the power of information, mixed with intentional or unintentional misinformation, people live in uncertainty, not knowing truth from fiction, not knowing what to believe or not to believe.

The rumor must be similar to the emergent legend in the age of mass media. Can we then accept that rumors — messages without a story — are proto-legends that can be regarded as the prelude to the legend process, accommodated by current social conditions? Rather than attempting the impossible act of determining where rumor ends and legend begins, I would like to emphasize that Shibutani's definition of rumor comes close to showing the similarities between the two in that both are dialectic and both debate conflicting interpretations. He writes that rumor is "a recurrent form of communication through which men caught together in an ambiguous situation attempt to construct a meaningful interpretation of it by pooling their intellectual resources. It might be regarded as a form of collective problem-solving" (1966: 17).

Rumor sociologists and folklorists found each other when Halloween-related legends about adults injuring or poisoning children with adulterated treats surfaced (Best and Horiuchi 1985). Seeking remedies to social problems, sociologists turned with interest toward Brunvand's "urban legends," seeing them as closely related to their conception of rumor. The 1990 and 1991 meetings of the International Society for Contemporary Legend Research (in College Station, Texas, and in Sheffield, England) were particularly focused on the study of current rumors in the media. Among the seminar participants were sociologists and social psychologists. Participants debated whether rumors originate in real urban horrors. If this is the case, the formation and function of legends cannot be understood without knowledge of the cultural, economic, political, and ideological climate of society, including its social ills. Folklorists, who were not trained in sociology but rather had concentrated on the philological and aesthetic interpretation of the content, form, and structure of the text, began to discover sociological methodologies and to look at the real life that contextualizes both rumor and legend.

This new approach was enlightening, particularly for researchers of "contemporary legend." They struggled with the definition and delimitation of their category as they began to collaborate with distinguished rumor specialists who presented case studies of current rumors. (American studies include Best 1990; G. Fine 1992; Rosnow and Fine 1976; and Victor 1989, 1991, 1993a, 1993b. French studies include Campion-Vincent 1988, 1989, 1990, 1993, 1997; Kapferer 1990; and Renard 1991.) Victor, a prolific expert of the "satanic scare" rumor, has suggested that contemporary legends are comprised of "a variety of rumour stories . . . the stories communicate shared anxieties about newly emergent, collectively perceived threats, and are conveyed using age-old recurring motifs which usually embody a moral political message" (1993b: 68).

Engaging in field study and pursuing the dissemination of specific rumors, scholars have found that alarming allegations of threats to the safety of common people and their families follow familiar paths. Although the texts develop differently from community to community under the influence of coincidental events and locally given situations, they show essential similarities in their national and international dissemination. Sociologists speak of an essentially oral story or story complex that spreads locally by word of mouth as rumor (gossip, hearsay) and as contemporary legend; but they also include non-spontaneous variants that are reported in the news, radio, and television, as well as in warning printouts, pamphlets, letters, posters, and fliers handed out by authorities to particularly vulnerable population groups. Legends cannot be described accurately on the basis of variants collected from diverse agents such as sensation-mongers, fiction writers, health professionals, educators, law enforcement officers, criminologists, theologians, fundamentalist clergymen, and eyewitnesses of alleged events or self-proclaimed victims. Among such sources, legend texts become confused or blended, and traditional expressions are influenced by professional authors.

In spite of the confusion, the dynamism of legend dialectics remains intact as true believers and skeptics confront each other in telling and retelling stories. Rumor, rumor-story, and contemporary legend differ only in the degree of completeness; the variants together contribute to individual narrative forms. We can only agree with the observation of Campion-Vincent in her thorough study of organ theft narratives:

> If one wishes to understand the contemporary belief, rumors, and narratives that comprise the organ-theft tradition, one must investigate the examples of these emblematic thoughts that inform them. In discovering that there are universal thought patterns at work in these traditions, we can gain insight into human behaviors that are centuries old, and understand that, even though the organ-theft tradition is a modern phenomenon, it rests upon ancient, universal notions. (1997: 23)

But folklorists must keep in mind that her great diversity of data does not include oral narratives from nonprofessionals. What she identifies as "dark legends," the "collectively elaborated and entertaining fictions that generate among the listener's emotional reactions to social problems" (1997: 33), are more scholarly constructs than they are legends actually produced by individual narrators.

Situating the rumor in its ideological context — specifically, attributing it to widespread social stress, economic difficulties, and the breakdown in family relations among poorly educated rural and small town dwellers on the poverty level—Victor examined the "evolution" of a satanic cult rumor in a small town of about 35,000 from October 18, 1987, to May 20, 1988. The rumor story was that "the satanic cult was planning to kidnap and sacrifice a blond, blue-eyed virgin on Friday, March thirteenth." Tracking the developmental stages of the shaping of the story under the influence of local and national events and the input of related mass media information, Victor observed that a "triggering event" precipitated both the rumors and "persistent rumor-stories," which remained in circulation long enough to gain credibility and become identical with contemporary legends (Victor 1989, 29–35; 1990: 12; 1991: 227–228).

Retrospectively, after the satanic cult and related scare stories were discredited in sensational court trials, and the innocently accused perpetrators were exonerated (Loftus and Ketcham 1994; Nathan and Snedeker 1995), the satanic cult legend complex disappeared from the headlines and was laid to rest in the eye of the educated public. Its traditional elements returned to the place where they belonged, among the canon of high church theologians, Bible scholars, fundamentalist Christians, eccentric occultists, and criminal adolescents.

However, among the marginal, rural poor these elements remain simmering under the ashes until, like before, new waves of stressful situations bring them to the surface again. We may agree with Victor's observation that the satanic cult legend plagues mostly the underprivileged rural and urban poor, particularly those under the spell of charismatic preachers, as in the "Blue House" story in Evansville, Indiana (see the conclusion to this chapter, and Dégh 1994b), and in the Rupert, Idaho, case (Siegel 1992). More importantly, this legend complex outgrew its limitation and became a major social issue. Regardless of their class, economic, and educational level, the supporting audience of this and related supernatural belief accounts was manipulated by a gigantic community of informal believers.

As is well known, health professionals supported satanic allegations, as did the police, the clergy, and educators, on the basis of shared cultural knowledge of the power of Satan. The mass media propagated the legend as true through all its conduits. Talk show hosts on national television conducted interviews with victims and expert commentators whose credentials seemed trustworthy. The transcripts of the outrageous, shocking revelations and confessions, publicized also in printouts, pamphlets, articles, and books, appeared to be authoritative and convincing.

But as scholars concentrated on the cases, the actual performers and performances, and the behavior of individuals (both the accusers and the accused) in the communication of rumors, they did not consider audience response. And the audience is immense: Prestigious polls have shown that the majority of Americans tend to believe in the supernatural. Thus, outbreaks of presumed real cases attract masses of believers, activating the passive and convincing the hesitant. Outraged by the monstrosity of cases like satanic child abuse, for example, the general audience was convinced by the evidence presented so authoritatively and aggressively, and like an infectious disease the outrage spread by contagion from the United States to Canada and further to England and France.

Nathan and Snedeker outline the life history of this rumor and point out that it did not suddenly and unexpectedly erupt from a concrete case, but rather developed slowly and broadly on the grounds of traditional beliefs. In time, the fear of ritual abuse of children evolved into mass hysteria. Belief became industrialized; that is, "institutionalized by professional societies, journals, the mass media and the federal government that energetically promoted its champion's claims . . . Advocates used these forums to develop a new logic and language that made the unbelievable sound credible" (Nathan and Snedeker 1995: 136). No wonder the audience finally accepted the allegation; if there were skeptics, they did not have the courage to speak up (Nathan and Snedeker 1995: 245). Such witch-hunt style cycles may engulf towns, counties, and nations. As Pulitzer-prize winning author Humes has shown, unproven allegations can drive the courts of justice to mishandle the law, pondering "how a town's — and, indeed, an entire nation's — fear of crime and desire to be safe has made the conviction of innocent men and women startlingly common" (Humes 1999: 5).

During the peak years of the satanic scare many people asked me as a folklorist about Satanism; none expected me to say what I said, that the factualism of these stories and allegations were suspect. A colleague's friend from a college town in Ohio came for a visit and told me a variant of the Evansville story as a real happening in the local grade school. She had no doubt that it was true, and she wanted my advice. The mother of the victimized child was her best friend and the family was deeply depressed, not knowing what to do. When I told her that this is a migratory legend known across the country, she was relieved.

Researchers of modern legends have benefited greatly from the case study approach of rumor taken by sociologists and social psychologists. Among the best monographic essays by folklorists are those written by Ellis (1990b, 1991a, 1993, 1996) and Simpson (1994). They describe the life history and anatomy of local rumor-development and the regional spread of facts and beliefs, thus satisfying our demand for the analysis of the social base and situational context of legends, which is generally missing from legend studies. These essays demonstrate why the study of folklore in our time is a difficult, complex enterprise. They make us realize that folklore is more prominent than it ever was because it plays a more important role in shaping society and people's sense of reality and fantasy than ever before.

It is almost impossible to deconstruct for scientific scrutiny the contributing currents that build legends into more robust constructions. But Simpson's example of Chenctonbury Ring as a place of spooky and important events shows the complexity of the simplest local "rumor-legend," incorporating old and new belief traditions that have been institutionalized by religious and para-religious sects, cults, clubs, and associations. Because human nature remains the same, none of the past beliefs have disappeared; the same beliefs continue in transparent new clothing, reinforced by modern technology.

These studies of rumor also are instructive in showing that rumors that spread horrible allegations of threats to the safety of individuals and groups penetrate the common knowledge of the civilized world, connecting traditional conceptions and "rational" thinking to create mini-narratives. The major current themes — satanic cults, UFOs, cattle mutilation, LSD-laced stamps and blotting papers packaged in boxes with popular comics characters, computer virus scares, rumors of organ sellers stealing babies — are characteristic in this respect. They represent large, horrific, fearful themes composed of an unpredictable number of statements and legends with minimal narrative elaboration. Actually, the most virulent legend types are unstructured themes rather than stories, with little epic elaboration; they break up into many conventional and improvised sub-stories and tend to expand and cross each other's boundaries.

By the late 1980s the satanic scare rumor had entered the status of "fashion" or "craze," and had blended into the aforementioned legend complexes. By that time, Satanism had become so popular that it played a leading role in creating a general legend climate. Satan and satanic ritual often are mentioned in the new variants of traditional ghost stories. For example, the Indianapolis location of the 1966 torture-murder of 16-year-old Sylvia Likens by a guardian, who was tried and sent to jail for life, became the place of spooky encounters in the 1970s; however, by the time of the woman's release on parole twenty years later, the haunted house in legends had turned into the secret gathering place of Satanists.

Learning about this kind of adaptability of facts into rumor, rumor-legend, and contemporary legend aggregates, we may ask whether we should view them as rumors, solidified rumors, or legends. Not all kinds of legends have the tendency to fuse with other powerful themes and adapt to the fear of the day, so we cannot be sure if this characterizes the so-called contemporary legend. There is another trait common to these texts: They are institutionally and authoritatively imbedded in society and made credible for the opinion-leading majority.

In the case of the LSD-laced stamps, the rumor was manipulated with the participation of the educated elite: health authorities, police, churches, schools, political interest groups; even the government entered the verifying rumor-conduit that ramified into sub-conduits (Renard 1991). But, as with rumors generally, uncertainty arose and divided the disseminators of the information into believers and debunkers, who posted fliers with positive or negative commentary. It seems that the rumors (both positive and negative) and the legend-like dialectics remained within the professional disseminators of the fliers without being picked up by the folk, who were being heavily bombarded by these papers. There seem to have been no verbalized, concretized, narratable legends about LSD-coated stamps, such as "this boy was missing from class after the break and was found unconscious in the bathroom" or "my cousin and his friend saw a kid selling the boxes and the principal's sister, who is a nurse, caught him red-handed." If the last eight to ten years have not produced legends, they might emerge later, after public attention slackens, giving way to new rumors. But there is an equal chance that they may be lost and forgotten.

Folklorists did a good service to legend scholarship by adapting sociological field methods, which helped in connecting texts with their situational and ideological environments. But what they gained by contextualization was lost by paying less attention to the text. Folklorists study creativity in the production and performance of expressive forms, not the nature, causes, and possible remedies of social problems as sociologists do. Folklorists need not deviate from their disciplinary focus; they observe the text that is produced by the actual performance — the interaction of proponent performer(s) and responding audiences, following the guidance of tradition. Folklorists have learned how to contextualize and get closer to social meanings, but they have lost sight of their folkloristic orientation. Impressed by the effects of the widespread horror allegations that forecast the destruction of moral values and the takeover of brutality and violence, folklorists slipped into the shoes of sociologists and social psychologists, shifting their interest from text variation to rumor accumulation around crucial issues. They were concerned with rumors about attacks of the Infernal against the Divine and its creatures in the shape of organized acts of anti-government conspiracy — or, conversely, the government's conspiracy against its citizens — and the resulting outbreak of mass hysteria, craze, perversion, and unnaturally violent crimes, manifested in a gigantic network of interconnected rumors warning of impending doom. Sociologists were not concerned with the nature of creativity, the workings of fantasy and worldview as manifested in the emergent rumors and legends of the day; they viewed them, rather, as documents of human behavior responding to mass terror fueled by rumors.

What was earlier called fear, crisis, mania, paranoia, or mass hysteria has been identified recently as "panic." This word has not been clearly defined by sociologists and therefore does not fit well into the vocabulary of folklorists. Speaking of "an uninterrupted 20-year sequence of moral panics" concerning child abuse in modern America as reported by Best (1990), and the scandalous satanic child molestation "panic" publicized between 1988 and 1991 in the British press (Bennett 1991b), Campion-Vincent uses this term in association with legend as "contemporary legends *and* panics," as though "panic" were a folklore genre. She also states that legends and beliefs emerge from such concerns and panics (Campion-Vincent 1993: 239). Contrarily, Kapferer writes, "Rumors do not create crises or panic. Operators seek information first when the stakes are very high. It is information that generates crises and panic" and "rumors often accompany and accentuate panics" (1990: 208).

Victor has written extensively about the panic phenomenon, noting that no standardized definition or criterion exists that can be used to identify a panic. Unlike Kapferer, he asserts that "on rare occasions, fear-provoking rumor stories give rise to panics in crowds or even in whole communities" (1991: 222). Victor refers to the much-cited panic generated by the 1939 radio drama "War of the Worlds," which enacted an imaginary invasion of Martians in New York. He calls the resulting hysteria a "rumor-panic," which he defines as "a collective reaction to rumors about immediately threatening circumstances" (1991: 222), and he uses this definition in his intensive study of satanic panic (Victor 1989, 1990, 1993a). Folklorists' adaptation of the panic focus (as in Ellis 1990b, 1991c, 1996; Wyckoff 1993: 25–27) has unnecessarily deviated from the main course of folk legend study and has not strengthened otherwise well-researched descriptions.

As we have seen, when we assemble the body of texts (narratives and pertinent data) in our approach to the legend as a folklore genre, we have to face the problem of great diversity in form, meaning, manner, production, and performance. The teller's and the listener's perceptions may differ at the time of telling, and likewise, in the way it is remembered. There is also a difference between the passive audience of print and electronic media, the distant respondents in Internet-mediated legend debates, and the actively involved, physically present speakers. All media-transmitted legends have (or have had) their oral versions. People tell others what they have just heard and what has caught their attention.

Because both the language and the background information are heavily influenced by the media, how can we be sure which had priority, the media or the oral text? Schenda observed that in the eighteenth and nineteenth centuries, oral and literary narration was an evenly balanced exchange, whereas at the end of the twentieth century the equilibrium has been upset by the electronic media (Schenda 1992). Indeed, it is difficult to follow the innumerable variants of professional peddlers who serve their customers and promote their businesses. Very convincing fabulates, memorates, and other skilled formulations in the media penetrate our daily lives, while oral versions that we record seem only pale replicas. We need more study to determine if we can still speak of the legend as an oral genre. The growing body of "urban legend" books does not contain texts collected with conventional scientific rigor.

## The Oral Text

Folklorists have developed many strategies for collecting "authentic" oral materials from informants. A typical scenario is observing at gatherings when people spontaneously exchange legends rather than perform for the collector on solicitation (Dégh 1965b, 1976, 1995a; Ellis 1987, 1989). So-called "induced" legend-telling sessions and interviews between informants and folklorists are also numerous (Bennett 1989b; Slotkin 1988). Class-assigned collections assembled by students interviewing other students, friends, and family members (Ellis 1990a) are perhaps the most numerous. Some of the tape-recorded materials by students are useful and contain valuable information, but they also have considerable limitations. Questions are narrowly focused, and what they produce is earmarked by student–teacher collaboration.

With few exceptions, the informants of students' tape-recorded or written materials are young people, whose repertoire is now over-represented in American archives (Klintberg 1990b). The flood of teenage and youth legends is a consequence of publishing by newspaper, radio, and television reporters who, along with writers and scholars, have exploited student term papers deposited in folklore archives. Youth legends have not only been popularized in the public arena, but their stabilization and continuity through feedback have also been secured. Meanwhile, legends of the adult population groups are scarcely visible.[15]

It is also a problem that the legends collected from young people by young people offer little insight into spontaneous legend telling. By asking our students to collect from their peers through direct interviewing, we teach them how to act as outsiders, as participant observers in their own communities.

The best student collections have tape-recorded legends in the context of prearranged formal interviews with fraternity brothers, school friends, dormitory roommates, family members, or neighbors; to these the students have added their own personal recollections ("from myself"). These materials are valuable for their authenticity, but it is a loss that the texts were taken out of their normal contexts. We thus are left to speculate on how to reconstruct the situation from the author's and informant's commentaries. Of course, recording the rare moments of spontaneous oral performance is worthwhile to our understanding of the legends and their bearers, but we would need much more collecting to supplement the meager data we possess. Some of my own observations about legend performance and transmission are hypothetical.

The question is, how far should, or can, we go in capturing the moment? "Verbatim" recording of the folklore text was convincingly argued by a few folklorists (Preston 1982; E. Fine 1984), who were influenced by anthropologists and ethnolinguists concerned with the problem of presenting the most accurate renditions of oral texts from foreign population groups on other continents. With limited competence in language and culture, scholars who sought to textualize oral discourse and poetic expressions struggled with technical problems like transcription, translation, and the reliability of native interpreters.

Understandably, scholars studying speech as a main instrument of communication — specialists of the ethnography of speaking and ethnopoetics — developed vocabularies of signs to help in transcribing foreign texts and to avoid misinterpretation caused by researchers' ethnic biases (Hymes 1972; Jacobs 1959; Rothenberg 1969; Tedlock 1977). At the same time, folklorists eliciting data from subcultural groups of their own country — in a language and symbol system they basically understand — have no need to construct a complicated system of signs for transcription. Neither is there a need to force a narrated text into verse-form by starting a new line when the speaker pauses, catches his breath, or ponders how to continue (see, for example, Glassie 1984; Halpert and Widdowson 1996). It is a wasted effort to apply the codes to transcribed oral texts, marking matters of little use to folklorists, while rendering them almost illegible for the reader because of the markings (see, for example, Bennett 1989a, 1989b; Ellis 1987, 1989).

The transcripts of some induced-legend conversations of students in the classroom, for example, have been structured according to Labov and Waletzky's linguistic model of informal narrative discourse; they are studded with indicators of linguistic articulation of words, voice pitch, the rhythm of the prose, the speaker's tempo, pauses, stresses, and breathing. I am sure that dialectologists, being more sensitive to the articulation of phonemes and morphemes, would benefit more from listening to the original tapes and doing their own deep transcriptions. But for us folklorists, chopping up the recorded conversation that contextualizes the legends therein seems more a handicap than a benefit because it encrypts the text. Furthermore, it overemphasizes the role of speech and distracts from the simultaneous and substitute paralingual contributions that accompany the total oral performance — the expressions of mental states, body language, proxemics, facial expression, sweating, and shedding tears. The narrative performance of an excellent raconteur who dramatizes his or her story can be incredibly rich in other-than-oral devices. They may speak and act, first representing themselves as the narrator, then changing tone when representing protagonists and antagonists, and even characterizing them by simultaneous body movement, gestures and grimaces, standing up, walking up and down, raising arms, making a fist, or bowing and dropping on the floor sobbing.

One would like to capture the emotional development of legends through the spontaneous moments of legend telling, and to work out a total drama script. But moving in heavy equipment such as cameras and spotlights would destroy even a semblance of the "natural context," the moment that we may be able to capture accidentally by simply being there. Studying legends in the lives of members of a Pentecostal assembly, I found that people instinctively resisted direct questioning. However, the same people who would never yield to a formal interview would offer me tapes of miracle testimonies for copying, would retell legends for taping that they had heard the previous night, and would invite me to attend events they felt deserved my attention. I gained more by submitting myself to their guidance.

When we collect legends, the recording of surface mechanisms may destroy the material we are seeking. Of course, this all depends on what we are looking for. The legend guides me to more ambitious goals: the study of distinctive human attitudes that the legend can reflect better than other folklore genres. Regardless of what they study, I believe that folklorists reach beyond surface description for the understanding of deep meanings, be the subject land tenure, pottery, or legend. If attitudes about cities can be understood better through legends told in urban settings, why not take the opportunity? If copycat serial killings can be stopped by studying legends told by ostension, why should we not employ our abilities? No other discipline is better equipped than folkloristics to point a finger at sensitive social problems projected in expressive forms, without losing sight of its primary goal. To me, the proper recording and contextualization of folklore texts is the folklorist's art and leads to the understanding of meanings.

Ellis, who proposed verbatim recording (1987: 33), reproached me because I am not so much interested in "fussy linguistic text transcriptions" as in "what lies behind the skull of the informant." This is true. To be fair, though, in a later article, Ellis tones down his insistence on "verbatim." This time, he presents the conversation of two young female students who are discussing a campus lunatic, and examines the diverse forms and stages of the transmitted legend text. He reaffirmed the observations that other folklorists had made earlier and finally conceded that the verbatim text is an impossible achievement, a chameleon, and that folklorists, questing like Don Quixote, are still at the heels of the elusive text and know they cannot capture it (Ellis 1989).

In the case of the oral text, verbatim recording is not enough, and fixation on visual renderings of real legend performances is too much. Instead, we need detailed descriptions of participants, of the cultural milieu, and the immediate circumstances that contribute to telling legends in general and the given legend in particular. We need to consider the context more seriously than ever before.

The legend begins much earlier than its emergence as a told story detailing an event. Conversation begins casually and can lead accidentally to a legend without any planning, at any occasion among people of similar minds; but if the legendary event has just occurred and is the sensation of the day, talk can begin with the story and continue with the discussion of facts and personal opinions. Sharing some degree of intimacy and the same cultural knowledge, acquaintances talk about events and people commonly known to them, as if gossiping; and they end up with a singular account of mutual interest: One of the group is telling a legend. The conversation itself, exploring the readiness for receiving the legend, constructs the situational context. The group might be as small as two people waiting in line at the post office or as large as a bunch of sectarian believers after a prayer meeting. This preparatory phase — contextualization to situate the story or a forthcoming chain of stories — may differ slightly from group to group but remains characteristic of the legend.

College students' dormitory parties, nocturnal trips to scary places, and teenage boys' supermarket hangout sessions seem to be more conducive to the emergence of legends than the many kinds of ad hoc, professional, recreational, social, or family gatherings of adults. The preparation of the young people and students appears in the form of first-person stories: legends about making an excursion to a dangerous place and experiencing fear, breaking tabus, and enduring consequences. These stories function as frames that encase the main stories to be narrated by both lingual and paralingual means (see Clements and Lightfoot 1972; Dégh 1972: 74–75; Hall 1973). In the case of the "adult" environment, the orientation of the gathering itself — be it entertainment, work, health, religion, or an accidental meeting — defines the preparatory conversation, likewise setting the initial situation for the legend.

Concentrating on the text, for the sake of giving an accurate description of its many varieties, we find the difference between these two types of preparatory phases — teenagers' transitory versus adults' more stable environments — is not so great when we look at the function and emotional involvement, which we will discuss later. This preparatory part of the legend, never considered by earlier researchers because it preceded the narrative, is important. Participants therein clarify the situation upon which the story rests, establishing a common platform for its comprehension. Those present have already formed a conduit, which is the condition for any narration to be viable. The information brought together, then, characterizes the actors and action. The proponent (the legend-teller or main speaker) names his or her source, identifies everyone involved in the story, and describes the place, the time, and the environmental conditions of the event. In the description phase the narrator is joined by others who confirm, expand, or correct the information.

Because participants may feel prompted by the knowledge of other versions or additional episodes and become co-proponents, the rendering of the text is a dialogic and communal performance. Eventually several legends can be linked together in a chain produced by a conduit of legend transmitters (see Dégh 1992; Dégh and Vázsonyi 1971). If we remember that, in contrast, the telling of a folktale needs a recognized authority, who has rehearsed his or her act and to whom others will listen at a prepared occasion, the difference between folktale and legend is enormous.

The situational context explains the difference between the stability, length, and objectivity of the tale and the informality, subjectivity, and communal quality of the legend. The introductory formula of the tale leads the audience away from everyday reality, whereas the sober enumeration of facts introducing the legend leads into the middle of the extranormal dimension of everyday reality upon which the legend breeds. The facts must be convincing to keep the interest of the listeners. Such meticulous preparation for the main story actually frees the proponent from the responsibility of telling an elaborate and polished narrative. Obviously, to the delight of text-oriented folklorists, there are some inspired speakers among the members of a legend conduit who attract attention with their smooth, coherent versions. But this refinement is not an absolute necessity for the legend to survive.

In essence, each legend contains general knowledge specific to one particular statement in its story that is relevant to the actual teller. It is supported by more important contextual components that are *sine qua non* for any legend to exist. These components include the global cultural tradition of Western Christian civilization, its standards of morality, and its distinction of good from evil; and it also includes the common cultural knowledge of local supernatural and extranormal beliefs that is inherited and learned formally and informally in actualized, contemporary versions sanctioned by the media. This common knowledge is built on the time-honored tradition of the Bible and apocrypha, the *Malleus Maleficarum*, the *Sixth and Seventh Book of Moses*, and other popular books about terrors ranging from man-eating werewolves and vampires to enchanting elves and fairies. Also figuring prominently are the fear of the return of the dead, of eternal damnation, and of Armageddon and Satan.

The stories need not be recited in full because both global and local legend audiences already know them. As with anecdotes about traveling salesmen, which are so familiar to many that they simply refer to them by number, the legend is so commonly known by its support groups that it can be sufficiently enjoyed in the form of mere brief summaries or simple references. The capillary vessels that have carried the ingredients — belief, belief statement, ritual, rumor, personal experience, memorate, fabulate — for centuries have maintained and actualized legends, allowing them to express new concerns.

The common knowledge of symbols and metaphors we share enables us to understand legends that are told by the simplest representation. For example, a black gown, long nails, dripping fake blood, and luminous fangs can stand for the Dracula story; in this case, the story actually does not have a narratable plot but can persist by the showing of the mask alone. "The Roommate's Death" legend can be told by a note attached to a door: "The Hatchet Man was here." Likewise, a pentagram or the number 666 (the number of the beast from Revelation 13:18) tattooed on someone's arm or printed on a bumper sticker or T-shirt may signify the latest crop of legends about satanic seduction. Conversely, a crossed-out goat head inscribed with "goat-buster" on the T-shirt of a fundamentalist zealot speaks for the legend of exorcism. Few in the Western world won't understand.

Therefore, the variants of legends in our experience remain fragmentary, or "formless," as authors quoted above have observed. This is not only true of legends in the contemporary urban scene but also in old-fashioned villages. Had folklorists cared for more accurate recordings, they would have noticed that as long as legends are alive in society, they exist in episodes, brief accounts that need not be repeated in full and at the same time are parts of a complex whole. This does not mean that the main part of the legend is not complex and loaded with meaning. It is succinct because its goal is to make the message clear, not to go into unnecessary length explaining familiar things. Within the same legend, tellers can choose how to construct their own versions.

Throughout the main narrative, two voices are present, sounding together: the voice of the story itself and the voice of the people, representing reason and contemplating the feasibility of what is being said. The two may become one, conform or conflict, or may remain obscure until the end. The concluding part picks up the starting question, repeats and reaffirms the opening testimonials, and raises the questions again without settling the argument in conversation. As I have noted already, text models documented in their complete form are only sparsely accessible to us. In the past, there was no interest in full recording; and with the spontaneous oral legend telling in the modern age of legend explosion and consequential banalization, legends have become more and more difficult to capture as separate social events. We have to be satisfied with what we can do: reconstruct the whole text from variants, each of which carries some, most, or perhaps all of these attributes.

I will try to describe the most characteristic kinds of oral legends as they function in contemporary society. My goal is not to exhaust all sources but to indicate the most conventional ones. Some illustrative materials also appear in chapter 4 in relation to legend-teller personalities.

## Legends in Conversation

Three very disparate examples of the structure of spontaneous legend telling will demonstrate the relationship between legend and the creation of context, the sounding of diverse culture-specific voices in the formulation of texts. With reference to my first publication of a legend shaped by the interaction of consenting and dissenting speakers (Dégh and Vázsonyi 1976), I am taking the opportunity to present alternative examples of the basic legend discourse, broadening the saliency of the raising of the question of belief in the process of the performance. It is not the belief of the narrator, nor any beliefs of the participants, but rather *the belief itself*, making its presence felt, that is essential to any kind of legend. Explicitly or implicitly the legend must make it clear that its message is or was believed by someone, sometime, somewhere.

All three of the examples that follow exhibit ethnographic accuracy in the description of the environment, the people, the local customs and beliefs, and show an established relationship between the speakers. True to their distinctive sociocultural position, the narrators of each of the three performances take the existence of supernatural beings for granted in different ways. The landless farm workers in the first exchange show unanimity in their belief, and piece together the confirming details of their several legends. The itinerant artisan family in the second performance scrutinizes their main haunted house experience in almost anatomic detail. The third group, a larger entity of educated urban conversationalists, reacts with more ambiguity and a mild skepticism to the stories that they obviously enjoy discussing.

Example 1: "They Led Him Astray. . . ."

This is a conversation between Mrs. Vilma Horváth, 79, and John Mák, 81, in Karkhalom, Zemplén County, Hungary, in the fall of 1979. Mrs. Horváth was making plum preserves in a large clay cauldron that had been lowered into the ground over slow-burning firewood in the orchard. Mr. Mák kept her company during the tedious work of constant stirring with a large wooden spoon, which traditionally was done for twelve hours. This is part of a longer dialogue I recorded.

*Mrs. Horváth:* I don't know whether you know where Lapuvas is, this is the name of the property. Did you know this family Fojtány?
*Mr. Mák:* Sure, the wife of Mike Horváth is a Fojtány girl.

Mrs. H.: OK, it's enough to say that as one is heading towards Lapuvas, there's a well, at the corner of the house of Joe Nagy.

Mr. M.: Sure enough, I drank from it.

Mrs. H.: OK. Old Mrs. Fojtány was very old. She went out to relieve herself and they picked her up, carried her away and threw her in the well. She couldn't crawl out only next morning.

Mr. M.: Yeah. This was because she was their partner. She had all the milk of other people's cows, now in return they wanted her soul. But there were others, mind you! The old Mrs. Ivánku, mother of uncle John also went to the village one day. She left home in the morning and never came back. The sun had set, no sight of Aunt Erzsus. Her sons, Uncle Frank, Uncle John were still young at that time, 27, 28, looked for her, asked around anyone had seen her? Oh yes, they saw her on the street. The sons found her in the well. She couldn't crawl out only next morning.

Mrs. H.: Had her soul been pure, believe me, this wouldn't have happened to her, so help me God.

Mr. M.: This is as true as that the sun rose to the sky today! Poor Aunt Erzsi.

Mrs. H.: This happened when I was a kid. We lived at the Tölgyes estate. [Her parents were share-tenants.] These folks had a daughter, with a hump, Barbara. She was a great seamstress and loved me very much. And her father had a dog. And I thought this is his dog. I wasn't late yet and the dog came to me wagging his tail. And I tell him, "Come here Milord." My God, no one was there. It wasn't a dog, it disappeared right there. This happened to me. Sometimes, if I am alone by myself, these things come back to me. Oh Lord, how much I have been through, how much I toiled!

Mr. M.: I was also spooked. I was about 16, 17. I used to work in Dombrád. It was about nine o'clock, oh, it is time to go home. There was a path along the canal and there were three or four poplars along the side. I walked at least ten times up to the poplars but I could never find my way further home. I always ended up somewhere else. I woke a man in a nearby house to help me to find the road. He showed me the path: "Just follow the dike, straight ahead." It was three o'clock in the morning when I got home. But I had no idea where I was.

Mrs. H.: And then, I heard that . . . did you know Michael Dobos? They lived on the Lobosicki farm . . . and as he walked home, a little white dog was on the Inge-Hill. That dog did not let him go anywhere. He went a-courting and the little dog didn't let him.

Mr. M.: I've heard that a sack of money is buried on the Inge-Hill. It is under curse, the coachman who transported it made the curse that only someone with blue and brown eyes and black hair should be able to take it out, no one else. [Note the similarity to the Locust Hill legend below.]

Mrs. H.: Indeed not, indeed not.

The participants in this simple, casual conversation reminisced about their own spooky encounters and those of familiar villagers. First Mrs. Horváth referred to a known ordeal of a witch who stole milk and who was thrown into a well by other competing witches. Mr. Mák then reminded her that others also had suffered the consequences of having their cows bewitched and their milk stolen. The two discussed people they knew well (Bihari 1980: 54–82). In response, Mrs. Horváth told about her being frightened by a phantom dog, which she mistook for the landlord's family dog and called by the elegant title "Milord." She should not have been out on the street late at night (Bihari 1980: 25).

Another nocturnal adventure was remembered by Mr. Mák, who was "led astray" — reference is always made to "they," since mentioning the name of the spirits is tabu (Bihari 1980: 31) — on the way home from work late one night. He had to walk all night, without finding his residence. Mrs. Horváth then mentioned another man who wanted to go courting but a little dog would not let him, enforcing a village etiquette (Dégh 1992: 108–109). Mr. Mák responded with a story he had heard about a cursed buried treasure (Bihari 1980: 207).

### Example 2: A Haunted House in Fife

This story was recorded by Hamish Henderson, August 1955, from the Andrew Stewart family.[16] Lizzie Stewart, Andrew's wife, begins the narrative:

Well, it wes a property my husband an' bought about four years *ago*. And I was never used tae living in the country before, an' I always had a dread when I wes in it alone. But I used tae think it wes my own imagination, because — I mean I was sort of nervous at any time. And through the day I used tae feel very nervous in it. But I jist put that doon tae my own imagination — I was quite happy when other people were in.

So that went on for aboot a year. I couldn't settle in the house at all. I hadnea even the notion to re-decorate it or do anything with it.

The house was in a small village in Fife, and it wes on one side of the road, all by itself. It sat by itself on this side of the road. The old name of it on the title-deeds was "King of the Muir" — it wes supposed tae be one of the best houses in the district at one time — in Peat Inn, in Fife.

So here, we came tae Blairgrowrie for a holiday at one time — my sister and her husband wes living with us. And we left them in the house. So here we were over here in Blairgowrie for a holiday, an we were intending to stay a week, we only stayed four days and went home again.

So, when we cam' intae the door, my brother-in-law met us at the door.

"Thank godness," he says, "I'm gland tae see the children again, I'm glad tae hear a noise again," he says, "this is the worst house ever I lived in."

So I laughed at'm, an' ye know, joked with'm an' said that he wesnae — that he was foolish, for a man o' his size, an' his age, to talk like that. So he says, honestly, to God, he hesnae tellin' a lie, they'd got a fight that night — him an' my sister.

So I asked him what had happened. So — they lived up the stair — he said they went tae bed up the stair, an' the dog — they'd a dog an' hit lay out in the wash-house; but here he thought it was the dog running up the wooden stair — there wes a noise. So he opened the door, an' there was no dog there, there was nobody there. But it wes more like a person's foot-steps than the dog running up. They thought it wes more like a person's foot-steps than the dog running up. They thought it was imagination, perhaps like the dog, when they heard it first.

So here he came down the stair to satisfy himself, and opened the outside door, an' called tae dog in the out-house outside. And the dog was frightened o' nothing — it wes very vicious it widnae allow anyone tae come near the house. So here the dog came out; an' they knew then it wasnae the dog, for it was still in the wash-house outside.

He got sort o' scared, then, an' he called the dog intae the house tae keep it in all night. But the dog jist went intae the livin'-room, an' it went roon' about as if it was frightened, with its tail between its legs, an' it run out again. It wouldna stay in the house.

So that made them more nervous still, because they thought there was something wrong.

But anyway, they went upstairs again, an' that night passed, an' it wes the next day that we cam' home: an' he told us whit happent.

So — uch, we didnae — we jist laughed it off an' thought no more about it.

So here — it wes a lang time after that, months an' months after that: I'd forgotten — I wes beginning tae settle in the house now. I'd got it re-conditioned inside an' begun tae sort it tae my taste. An' I wes quite settled in it by this time.

So — I used tae go out with my husband throu the day selling drapery an' that, while he wes attending tae his business wi' the farmers. An' at night when I come home, I had my house-work to do. So some nights I wesnae in bed till half-past eleven.

So this particular night — I remember the day very well, it wes the last day o' March — an' when I came home. I bath'd all the children, put them tae bed, an' I had a habit — the clothes that I took off them, I used tae wash them that night, an' hang them up in the house, because that time o' the year the weather jist wasnae too good. But this happent tae be a nice weather — frosay, ye know, an' sunny, throu the day, an' moonlight at night.

So I washt a' these clothes, an' I hung them up. But I put a big fire on before I done this, an' the fire wes jist burning up intae a nice bright glow. I remember the time — it wes half-past eleven when I went tae bed —

At this point, Andrew Stewart, her husband, interrupts her story:

Now jist a minute. When we come home wan day, an' the kids come in fae school — there was nobody in the house — they come in fae school. An' — the water was in the outside pump — it was very old fashioned in Fife, ye know — it wes an out-side pump, the handle-pump that ye pump. She took a joog — now tell them whit happent, Carol, when you went out fir a drink.

Here, Carol Stewart, their son, takes over:

Well, we took the kettle out tae fill it with water, an' when we got over tae the well I put the pump in the well, an' an' the pump startit tae pump itself; so I startit tae scream "murder," an' ran away home. I wes ten at the time, now I'm thirteen.

Andrew Stewart takes over again:

Now, I'll tell ye whit he screamed like; he screamed lik' somebody that wes gettin' murdert, or stabbed — he wes hysterical, ye see? A when I heard him screamin', I dropped everything, an' I dived oot o' the door, an' he met me. An' I had tae shake'm tae get'm out o' the fit. I says "whit's wrong wi' ye mun? Whit's wrong wi' ye?" He says, "Aw daddy, daddy," he says, "the pump pumpt itsel'!" I says "don't be stupit, man." I says, "Come wi' me an' I'll show ye now." It wes gettin' dusky-dark — ye know. I trakes him over an' try tae demonstrate — tae show'm how the pump wes fallin' down itself — ye see? But here the handle o' the pump wes stiff. It couldnae pump itsself — ye see? But here the handle o' the pump wes stiff. It couldnae pump itsel'; it wes that stiff.

But anyway, I gaes on — till anither day we came home. Well, the bar — it wes an inside bar — it wes a very old-fashiont house. An old post-office, it wes. An' when we come home — there wes an attic-winde at the end o' the gable, an' a histe come up tae the attic-windae so's ye could go down the attic-stair an' open the door from the inside. We used to look it fae the inside an' go oot the back-door an' shut the windae — ye see? So the histe come up for ab ainway, up thru the windae. An' whit happent when ye come in?

Here Carol Stewart takes over:

I climbed up the rhone an' cam' in the attic-winda. An' it wes a nice summer day, nae wund or nothing, ye know — an' I come in the door an; I opened the attic door and went tae walk downstairs, an' the attic-door slammed behin' me. An' I shoved it open an' jumped out the winda.

Andrew Stewart continues:

He done a somersault — the door shut on'm an' no wund or nothing. He opened the door an' it shut behin' him. An' nobody touched it — it wes a stiff door. An' he done a somersault head first out the attic-windae, an tum'let head owre heels an' landit lik' a cat. He got a fright. That wes two frights he got in that house.

Now you carry on — it was after this that you were doin' yir washin'. This wes whaur this thing cam' in — ye see? Now you go on aboot the washin'.

The story now returns to Lizzie Stewart:

Well, that night, I remember, when I finished the washin', an' hung it up, there wes a lovely bright fire on — the fire wes jist burning up, ye know, the flames high, lightin' up the whole house. I had the light on, it wes a very old house, there wes no light, no electricity, no gas — there wes nothing anywhere in the district lik' that, except in the hotel. So it wes Tilley lamps we burnt — ye know, wi' paraffin.

And I remember I went through to the room an' I put the one out where the children were sleepin', through in the room. I come back in again, I'd finished my washin'.

Well, we'd tae empty the water outside — there wes no sinks or anything i' the hoose — ye'd tae carry yir warer out an' in. So I went tae empty the bath — an' when I lookt at the time, it wes half-past eleven. My husband wes in bed, and the children were in bed, an' the room — this room where I wes, like, ye know, the kitchen, as ye w'd say — the rest o' the children were thru in the bed-room.

So here I liftit the bath an' went tae empty it, an' there's some sort o' fright took me. I wes frightened tae open the door. So I thought tae myself: well, I'll jist leave the bath in the lobby there, an' first thing in the mornin' I'll get up, an' I'll empty it before any o' them get up tae go tae school.

So I left the bath sittin', an' I came in, an' this fire was blowin' up nice, so I turned the Tilley lamp down low, because for the babies I always keep a light in at night. I turned the lamp down low, an' I went tae bed.

Well, it was exactly half-past eleven when I went tae bed. My husbant wes lyin' — he wes awake, an' he wes watchin' the mantle-piece — he wes lyin' lik' that wi' his eyes jist watchin' the clock on the mantlepiece — ye see? So I went intae bed — I had tae go over intae the back o' the bed, ye know, next the wall.

But here — I wes really tired when I went tae bed, an' I lay down, jist lik' that, an' I think I must a' closed my eyes fur aboot ten minutes. It wes ten minutes. An' something jist made me get up on my arm, ye know; I leant my elbow on the pillow, an' jist put my han' tae my head lik' that, an' I lookt over at my husbant, towards the door, an' I jist saw the vision.

It wes an old lady — very old-fashiont dressed — I didnae see 'er face or anything. I just saw the form there. She was neat, an' awfilly neatly dressed, an' very old-fashiont, an' 'er hair seemed tae be tight back in a bun at the back — no any waves or anything, jist stright back.

That's the impression I got, like o' the figure. I didnae see 'er, I jist saw this sort o' — like it wes a smoke. Ye know, jist a sort o; greyish smoke. So I couldnae scream, I went "uh, uh, uh, uh," two or three times, an' then I shouts: *Andra!* I screamed, ye know? An' then after I screamed, I lay down t' cover my face wi' the blankets.

Well, I stoppet there — that's the last I saw o'it. So this is whit happent tae him next.

Here, Andrew Stewart takes over:

This is whit happent tae me. She's lyin' — an' she covert hersel' up wi' the bed-clothes. — ye see? The two wee ones, they're lying at the bottom o' the bed. So I'm lyin' with my — I'd a good coal fire on, an' the flames wes dancin' aff the roof, ye know, light — it wes jist comin' in aboot Aprile, wesn't it? Last day o' March. The nights were gettin' kin' o' clear, like, ye know, an' I'm lyin' wi' my hands behin' my — in my bed lik' that, lyin' on my back, lookin' at the clock. An' here the clock — everything wes perfect quiet — an' I could hear the clock goin' "tick-tick, tick-tick," ye could hear the missin' o' a beat, ye know, the weights rowein'.

An' she shouts *Andra!* an' she covers her head up. I says: "Wh-wha-whaat!" I says — I knew she'd seen something in anither place that I — ye see.

So, I daren't move my face, I couldnae even look tae see where it wes she got the fright. I jist kep' lookin' at the mantlepiece, wi' my han's behin' my head like that, an' I'm lookin' lik' this. An' wi' my elbow bein' up lik' this I couldn't see right tae the door — but I could see a bit o' a space over the top o' my elbow — ye see whit I mean?

An' I seen the shadda, comin' fae the body, like — from the elbow, lyin' lik' that, well I c'd see something. I c'd see my han' coming lik' that, ye see? Comin' over my elbow — ye see?

That's true, I c'd take anybody up tae the hoose, an' I'll get a 'paper reporter an' fetch them wi'me.

So here — I'm lyin' I darenae shift my eyes tae look at it, I jist kep' starin' at the clock. I wes jist lik' a — hev ye seen a wheasel at a rabbit? A rabbit cannae move when a wheasel's mesmerized it — it cannae move — jist squeals. Well, that's they way I felt. I stiffent, an' I jist lookt lik' that. I wes lookin' at the clock, an' I seen the shadow wi' the tail o' my eye, comin' tae the side o' the bed. It come sailin' up the side o' the bed, lik' that, an it settlet at the side o' the bed lik' that. An' stuid lik' that.

An' when it stuid at the side o' the bed, I'm still lookin' at the clock — I couldnae look at it — I'm jist lyin' lik' that. An' it lookt doon at the fuit o'the bed where the kiddies wes — it leaned over the bed, an' it lookt down at the bairns at the bottom o' the bed — lookt intae their faces.

It got up lik' that, an' turnt roon; the carpet — lookt whaur she wes happin' her heid. It got up again beside the bed, an' turnt its heid roon' tae me, lik' that.

I turnt roon' — that's as true as God's in heaven — I widnae tell ye a lie — I turnt roon.

An' lookt at her lik' that — this auld wumman. I c'd tell ya — I e'd practically describe, like, the way she wes dressed, but I couldnae see nae face or nothing — ye know?

Well, she lookt doon at me — it wes then I shiftit my eyes, I didnae shift my head, I jist shiftit my eyes away — lik' that. Thazt's as true as God! An' I seen, as I thought, her eyes settlet on 'er lik' that, she come down lik' this wi' 'er two han's tae choke me — in the bed. She come down lik' this! This is true, Hamish! This is the wey she lookt at me! She come right doon lik' this, an' pit 'er han's tae my neck lik' that, an' there's a' the power — this is a' I c'd do! I jist had the sense tae do that, Jeannie, I took my han's offae behin' me lik' this, I says: "Noh! Noh! No-Noh! Noh! *Aw* Noh!"

I done *that* wi' my han's — that's a' I'd the streb'th tae do! An' eftir I done *that*, Hamish, I says — the thought went through my brain, lik', all at once — I says: I must puhll mysel' thegither, here. Or, I'm gonae get in a jam, here — see whit I mean?

So I pulled mysel' tegither, an' I shook my head, an' done that wi' my face, lik' that — an' I lookt expec'in' tae see it wes imagination — I still lookt an' when I lookit, it covert — it blackent the light! If there were nothing there, the fire wouldnae hev been hid! But there wes a shadow there between the bed whaur I wes lookin', an' the fire. It covert the fire up.

An' I'm lookin' lik' *that*, I'm lookin' lik; that, I'm lookin' up an' doon — at this thing stan'in' there, I couldnae make it oot, it wesd jist a dark image stand'in'. An' I'm lookin' at it — the fire's away.

Well, d'ye know whit it done? It startit shakin'-lik' a wappour — ye know, it startit shakin' lik' a wappour — lik' *this* — an it wes disappearin' fae the legs up. An' I could see the light o' the fire fae the bit that wes disappearin'. I was lyin' watchin' this a' the time.

An' it went away lik' that!

Well, ye've seen yon golliwogs in a show — ye mind the golliwogs we used tae get — lik' a wee monkey, wi' elastic — hairy golliwogs? Well, it went away lik' a thing lik' thoon, wi' a bit o' string i' the mooth o'it — it wes the skeleton o' a wee baby! A baby skeleton! It went up an' doon the roof lik' *that* — a danglin' thing lik' *that* — a skeleton o' a wee babby, up an' doon the hoose. I feel my hair risin' jist when I think on that.

So here, it disappeared. I jumps oot o' my bed, an' I rins ben, an' — I'm ben fir the lamp, the lamp we had went out fir the want o' paraffin. It wes a Tilley lamp we used, no electric, no gas in the — in Fife. I run ben fir the lamp, an' my lassie wes wakent — she heard me, Jean heard me. She says: "whit is it daddy?" I says, "go tae sleep, hen" — when I wes goin' ben fur the lamp, I put my fuit in the cauld water — I think that's whit saved me. My left foot — in the bath, goin' throu. A n' when I wes comin' back wi' the lamp, my right foot went in the bath comin' back — see whit I mean? In the cold water — I think that brought me roun', man, mair'n anything.

An' I got a wee taste o' paraffin an' pit it in the lamp, an' pit it tae the fire — I'm goin' up an' tryin' tae light this lamp, ye see, the kid's lamp —. When I liftit the kid's lamp lik' *that*' it went *oot, tae make* things worse — d'ye see? It wes em'ty — hit went oot, tae make things worse, d'ye see — an' I had tae pit the rest o' the paraffin in it, beside the fire, I pit it tae the fire, an' I got it startit up. An' I'm goin' like this — even when the lamp's lightit, I wes goin' aboot the hoose lik' that, lookin' tae see if I could see anything. An' I pit it doon, an' it wes still in the hoose — wait tae ye hear this!

I pit the lamp doon on the table, an' I gaes doon — wi' the juds bein' in the hoose I w'd 'a' went fir it if i'd seen it — ye know whit I mean? — That's how I felt. I went out the attic door, an' I'm lookin' fur't, an' I'm crying the dug, an' the dug cam' in, putt its tail between its legs an' went oot again, it widnae stey in the hoose — the big dog — this dog wes a great fightin' dog, he wes wickit — widnae stay in the house.

So I come in — I gaes over tae the bed, I lifts the bedclothes, an' I creeps intae the bedclothes lik' that, I'm lookin' roon; aboot the hoose lik' this — ye know? An' I covers the blankets — well, I never went throu an experience lik' thon in my life — if I live tae be a hundert years of age I'll never go throu an experience lik' this!

I covert the blankets in lik that, at the side o' the bed, an' I says tae her: "Lizzie!"

"Whaat?" she says.

"I think," I says, "ye're goin' tae loass yir hoose the-morra!" — ye see? I meant I wes gonae leave it — ye see?

"Whu-whu-whaat?" she says, "did you see it tae?" she says.

I says: "Ay!"

"Wa — o-ow! Andra!" she says. An' she covers hersel' up tighter intae the bed — ye see whit I mean? — I made things worse fur her — ye see?

So here — this is true — so here I'm lyin' on the bed. I says: "Lizzie?"

"W — whaat?"

"D'ye feel the icy wind?" I says. It had turnt as cold as anything. It was a lovely night, ye ken, the moon wes, ye know, at the end o' March an' that the moonlight an' clear-at-nights comin' in — stretchinthe — the nights then, the moon wes shinin'. An' I felt the icy cault wind comin' throu the blankets.

I says: "feel that caul' wind, Lizzie," 'an. I'm the blankets tae keep the cauld icy wind oot fae me. An' a big fine on.

"Noo wait tae I tell ye —!"

An' when I got up an' lookt roon' aboot whaur the dog went oot — an' a wind, there wes a wind startit — in the hoose — an' *there's*, the wey the black — the courtains went — o' the hoose. Roon an' roon' aboot lik' that — in *that* hoose. They whirlt fast in the hoose!

An' it wes then it disappeared!

I got up the next mornin' at half-past five in the mornin', an' my lassie — my eldest lassie there — come throu, an' she says "God bless us Daddy! Whit's wrong wi' ye? Ye're awfly white in the face!"

"Ay," I says, "I got a fright last night, hen," I says, "never mind — it makes me feart tae think about that."

I got the larry — it was tae cover the larry — an' I went away aboot half-pastd five in the mornin', an' knocked the people in the pub, an' peyed thirty shillin's. An' stayed in the lorry doon at the fuit o'Peat Inn.

An' that hoose — as far as I know it's been selt five times since.

But wait a minute — I'd ninety pound's worth o' scrap metal tae sell, an' I come owre here tae — I sold it, tae that man in Dundee. An' he took a lorry an' four men owre tae burn it — I met them up at Maggie's — up at my sister's place here — an' asked if they w'd come back.

The house was sold but I wesnae paid for the house yet — that was it. My father —

147

Now — it was sold Lizzie: I come over here, an' the man says, he says tae me — when I come over — my father gat inter-estit — I told my father about it.

"Now," he says, "fur goodness sake, Andra," he says, "don't tell anybody," he says, "aboot the house." Somebody wes tellin' me tae go and — tell somebody — get a paper reporter, ye'd get a lot o' money fur't.

My father says: "Don't be stupid," he says, "leave the house tae ye get yir money in yir had fur it, an' then it duisnae matter who gets telt," he says, "ye mightnae get a penny fur it."

So here when I come over I met a man wi' the scrap — I sold the scrap tae. He says tae me — I says: "Hullo, whit's yir name again, old man?" — I jis forget his name. He says:

"Hullo, Mr. Stewart," he says, "whit a'ye doin' the night?"

"I've left," I says — I didnae want tawe stay I'd selt the house. I says, "I've left."

"Ye've left yir house?" he says.

"Ay," I says, "we left it."

"Why," he says, "wes it hauntit?"

So now — this wes me no paid fur the house — I thought somebody'd putit/spirited this out. Maggie'll tell ye aboot this.

"Who told you it wes hauntit, Mister — whatever hi's name," I says.

"O, nobody," he says, "but the boys jist passed remarks about the house," he says, "bein' hauntit. It lookt like a hauntit house."

"Well," I says, "it *is* hauntit. I've sold it," I says, "I've sold the house."

This is a remarkably detailed, personal, and emotionally charged account of a family's ordeal in a haunted house. Among the traveler families, performing artistry was a communally and conventionally learned skill; Andrew Stewart was a practiced narrator, as were his ancestors, parents, and siblings. He was the youngest of the large Pertshire traveler family from whom Hamish Henderson, a folklore scholar and native of Blairgowrie, collected tales and legends. Four of Andrew's tales appeared in print (Bruford and Macdonald 1994; Douglas 1987), the rest of his repertoire was preserved in the Archives of the School of Scottish Studies, University of Edinburgh, Scotland.

For Andrew Stewart, it was a fluke to break away from his clan's urban compound and settle in an old-fashioned "small village home" in Fife, without electric power and plumbing. Sustaining their itinerant life-style — Andrew did seasonal farmwork and Lizzie sold draperies while caring for their small school-age children — was almost impossible without kinship support. So why did they make this move? Were they seeking independence, or did they have a lust for travel, or did they simply love the countryside? It is hard to tell.

From the outset, when the husband and wife bought the house in 1951 and moved in, they knew something was wrong. Once, cutting short a holiday trip, they returned to their house, where a sister and brother-in-law were also residing, to discover that, in their absence, their relatives had been exposed to strange sightings and feelings, caused by phantom footsteps. They complained about having stayed in "the worst house ever [they] lived in," but the Stewarts chose to "laugh it off" and teased the brother-in-law for being foolish in spite of his insistence that "honestly, to God, he hesnae tellin' a lie."

Still, perhaps the Stewarts were not determined to settle in the house because they waited "months and months." But finally — maybe because they wanted to prove that they could not be scared away by haunts — they tidied up the house to their taste, and moved in for good. Soon enough, however, the sights, the sounds, and the presence of fearsome apparitions became unbearable, forcing them to leave the house less than two years later. Of course, it was common knowledge that the residence was haunted and that at least five families had left it before, but few people talked about concrete incidents.

The haunted house legends in our text were narrated by three members of the family of six: the mother (Lizzie Stewart), the oldest son (Carol Stewart), and the father (Andrew Stewart). Their style of speaking was more testimonial, interpretive, and evocative than entertaining and titillating. It is interesting to note that the narrators, as they take turn in speaking, begin their accounts with "So . . . ," thus connecting with, but also separating, their say from the previous speaker.

Lizzie, addressing Hamish Henderson directly as a trusted friend, opens by setting the stage. She informs Henderson about the family's move to the countryside and describes the situation, introduces the people, and mentions their concern about living in a haunted house. Then she speaks about settling down, and her own difficulties in getting acclimated to a rough climate and a new situation, in which she is a working woman whose second-shift work ends at half past eleven, who must also take care of the children, the cooking, and the laundry without proper appliances. Once she has introduced the scenario, Lizzie marks the beginning of the main legend, the last day of March at 11:30 P.M.

Before she can continue, Andrew interrupts her. He wants more evidentiary statements to prepare for the legend to begin, and he asks their oldest son, 13-year-old Carol, to narrate his fright from the hand-pump that pumped water by itself. Andrew also assists the boy in telling about an incident when the attic-door slammed shut behind him. He then directs his wife to continue where she had left off — finishing the laundry, lighting the fire, and turning on the Tilley lamp before going to bed at 11:30.

Evidently, Andrew is the main speaker. He is the architect who constructs a frame for the legend that is pieced together from the experiential incidents or motifs that he and his wife perceived during the ghostly hour. The progression of the main event — the appearance and disappearance of an old lady in an old-fashioned dress around midnight — is narrated by both husband and wife, because they experienced it simultaneously while they were lying in bed, next to each other. The experience is told from both of their individual perspectives: seeing the sights, hearing the sounds, and feeling the rise and the drop of the temperature as the fiery hot fireplace logs in the kitchen were hit by an icy cold wind.

Lizzie begins describing her sight of the apparition before she buries her head under the blanket to escape the fearsome sights and sounds. After she saw the apparition, the sight made her unable to speak — she could only scream at her husband from under the blanket.

At this point, Andrew continues by telling what happened to him, what disposition he was in, and what he heard and saw after his wife's scream alerted him. His personal interest, and his explanation of the physical and mental attempts he made to rationalize the sights and sounds is masterful. He feels paralyzed, unable to move, but his mind draws clear images. He compares himself to a rabbit mesmerized by the stare of a weasel. He sees a shadowy figure and fears for the safety of the sleeping children, but the figure — the old woman whose face he cannot see — comes toward him and attempts to choke him.

The whole story is like a classic nightmare, which torments semiconscious slumberers into imagining an attack of inanimate household objects or natural and supernatural forces while they lie helpless in bed. Lizzie's reaction to the sight of a phantom was a scream, but Andrew's was a drama of self-torture, a projection of his guilt and desire to restore family harmony: Then and there, he realized that he had to ensure the safety of his children, by moving out, selling the house, and returning to the fold.

What Andrew experiences — his mental torture upon a physical exposure to a haunting — is incredible to him, and like any teller of a legend, he must convince his audience that he is telling a truth that he himself knows is incredible: "This is true, Hamish! This is the way she lookt at me!" and "If I live tae be a hundert years of age I'll never go throu an experience lik' this!"

Example 3: Hauntings in Vincennes

The 1986 annual meeting of the Antiquarian Society of Vincennes, Indiana, was held in an old country church. The members were taken there by a bus. After the formal program, which was my talk about Indiana folklore and an Indianapolis folksinger's ballad recital, we all convened for a fried chicken supper. At the supper, I asked the man sitting next to me if he knew about a gray lady ghost in the local library. He and the others he asked shook their heads (it turned out that I had mentioned a Fort Wayne spook), but my question triggered a legend-conversation that I was allowed to record.

This was among those rare opportunities to observe spontaneous legend telling. As a point of comparison, a year later, when I was asked to speak about ghost stories at the 1989 meeting of the Tippecanoe Historical Society, I was assured that those attending the meeting knew lots of legends, but as it turned out no one was eager to speak. Instead, the secretary mailed me a printed copy of nicely romanticized "local legends" (see chapter 5).

Fortunately, the Vincennes conversation yielded eleven legends with Richard Day, a high-school teacher, as the lead speaker. His enthusiasm for legends inspired others to join. Each legend, response, commentary, evaluation, and question characterizes the participant in this discourse, his or her relationship to those present, and his or her degree of belief, doubt, and disbelief. The conversation, which continued without interruption and switched from topic to topic, characterizes the group's general attitude toward supernaturalism. The sample from the conversation is typically Midwestern, containing the most popular themes: cases of second-sight; a haunted house; deaths on roads, bridges, and in water; revolutionary war hero memorials; and young people's new versions with ritual visits to scary places.

Mrs. G: Well, a woman told me not long ago about some boys who stayed at the Niblack place overnight and the chair begins to rock of its own accord, at certain times. And I told that . . . I forgot . . .

Mr. W.: That sounds like one of Austin's tales. Is it?

Mrs. G.: No, no, it isn't.

Mr. W.: Which Niblack place?

Mrs. G.: I could call the woman and ask her, uh. Or I might have written it in my diary. I don't know.

Mr. W.: Oh, that's Susan Louise's story. Yeah. She's two generations later than I am and, uh . . .

Mrs. G.: It's a good story anyway.

Mr. W.: Yeah, it's a good story.

Mrs. L.: It was in the newspaper,[17] a ghost story in the newspaper about the Niblack house, and all kinds of tales about it. None of which we believe, having been in that house so much, that we don't believe those things.

Mrs. G.: The person who told me was Mrs. Norry, Mrs. Frank Norry. Now her son and another boy stayed in the house. Now, I can't remember why. But she was the one who told me about it. There was supposed to be a ghost who was in the chair rocking because there was nothing to propel the chair.

Mr. F.: Who is the ghost? Who was he?

Mrs. G.: I don't know, I have no idea. It might be located through the newspaper. Mr. L., do you know when the date was?

Mr. L.: It was a while ago, three or four years. Heard of the Purple Head?

R. Day: As you know, the old Big Four Bridge, when the railroad went out of business, was made into Stangles Bridge. And it's a rickety old railroad bridge that they put some planks across and you pay a toll, and you drive across; and it's the only shortcut to get from Vincennes to Francisville since they took out the old ferry boat. And the kids around St. Francisville, and down around the other side of the bridge say that if you go out on the bridge around midnight, and you turn off all the lights in your car and stop in the middle of the bridge, and honk the horn three times, you'll see this purple head come floating up in the rearview mirror. If you drive across the bridge very carefully and very slowly, that head will follow you across the bridge. And then, on the other side of the bridge, down in this gully, there's this gravestone, just a solitary single gravestone down there, with a little bench in front of it. And this is supposed to be the ghost of this person that, uh, supplied the purple head. And in fact, if you go in the daytime, you can actually see the tombstone; that's James Johnson's grave, who was a revolutionary war . . .

Mr. P.: Just crossing the bridge will make you purple in the face.

[laughter]

Emilie M.: Well, the teenagers have made a new version of that. They say, there were people . . . a young couple who had an accident there on a prom night. If you drive across . . . this only happens to teenagers, they're the only ones who can hear and see this . . . that if you drive across, you can see their faces rise up out of the water and you can hear them cry, because they were killed on a prom night. And they've got a whole new thing, but they call it "Purple Head." That's interesting because there are two people involved in this one. But my people at R. school, when I taught there, they all had some variation on that one. I mean they told it different ways, and some of them tried to write about it for the school paper. I think, it's an excuse to go out into the dark place [laughs] in your car with a girlfriend. You're trying to scare her, I think, is what it is.[18]

Richard D.: Why then there's Ghost Hollow Creek, out at the other end of the township. It's about 4 miles north. . . .

Later in the conversation, after two other legends, Daily continues with another legend about Dark Hollow:

Richard D.: On the other side of the county, over here on Robeson Hills, there is Dark Hollow . . . and it's got a creek going through it and real steep sides, and trees hanging over it; it's just very dark. In the old days, of course before the Red Skelton bridge was built, the hollow went out onto the old river road. And the story they tell, which appears in Godspeed's history, is that there was a Frenchman who was going to church. He was going to do his Easter duty. And he was supposed to be going to church—I guess, it was Thursday night. And uh, he came by the hollow, and there were these Twai Twee Indians. The Twai Twee is what the Americans called the Miami Indians, they called them the Twai Twee. And the Twai Twee Indians grabbed this Frenchman and decapitated him and then for some reason they ran off. And a few days later these hunters came and found this headless corpse lying by the entrance of the hollow. But the head was never found. And they say that on Holy Thursday, you can go by Dark Hollow, and you can hear this rumbling sound as the head comes rolling out of the hollow [laughs]. And they say that if this occurs, it will then rain on the next Holy Thursday. . . . There's a number of haunted hollows around the county. . . .

After two more stories, this tale of second-sight was told:

*Mrs. K.:* I had a very dear friend Rush; and Rush during World War II, he was at the head, and they had tried to make a machine gunner out of him. And anyone knowing Rush, bless his heart, in the supply department or something he would have been fantastic, as a machine gunner . . . Anyway, a shell came down and landed right where he was standing. But anyway, that night I was home. I was living in Kentucky at the time. And all night long, I couldn't get to sleep. And it bothered me because my brother was a fighter pilot in the Air Corps, and I thought something was happening to Bob. And it turned out, then we found out that was the night Rush was killed. And then, one night, my brother was lost. He had loaned his maps to someone who had promised he would return them, for he had to use them that night, and they hadn't. And I happened to be at home that time, and Mom and I couldn't either one sleep that night. And she'd be up pacing, you know, and she'd stop by my bedroom door and say, "Are you asleep?" And I practically would say, "Yes Mom." [laughs] We were both up all night, and, you know. He made it in safely the next day. He wound up someplace in . . . Alabama or something, hundreds of miles away from where he was supposed to be. . . . But that happens to Mom and me every now and then. She would always laugh and say it was a good thing that we didn't live at the time of Salem, Massachusetts, or they would have happily burned the two of us long, long before as witches.

This open admission of having second-sight shows people's general ambiguity toward supernatural themes. They laugh off the things that young people tell, but without interrupting the thread of conversation, they turn to their experiences which are taken very seriously.

## The Community Legend

Legend repertoires are not evenly spread among population groups, and they have different life spans and tellability. Each community has a few deeply ingrained and very durable pieces that aren't immediately visible. Some are commonly known but seldom uttered. Others are attached to particular occasions of more or less frequency; for example, some stories are associated with Halloween or other seasonal events, initiations to group membership, anniversaries, exploratory trips to legendary locations, or age-group socialization. Or stories will come up when they are made actual and informed by the media.

Nevertheless, even the best-known community legends may have little opportunity to surface. Did these ever live a vigorous life? Perhaps they never did. Maybe they have always lived only in the consciousness of people, marginally and sporadically told, yet they were and are an important part of the cultural heritage. I have discussed elsewhere this phenomenon of common awareness coupled with a notable infrequency of telling in the cases of the legend of the "Chain Bridge of Budapest" and "The Pied Piper of Hamelin" (Dégh 1985: 71–76; Dégh and Vázsonyi 1973).

The variants of the legend of the "Headless Horseman" related to Locust Hill in Millersburg, Indiana, will show that a legend can be significant, deeply ingrained in community consciousness, while living only in rudiments without requiring an occasion for telling. I do not know the legend body of this small town, nor whether its population groups share in other narratives; however, this legend seems to be genuinely local and unique to the place.

The Headless Horseman

In 1986, Steve Satterfield, 21, a psychology major, explored this legend of Millersburg, Indiana, his hometown of 400 inhabitants, where community life centers around the Baptist Church and the beauty parlor ("gossip room"). Here is his own version which he remembered from childhood:

> Just before going to bed that night I was told that many years ago on the night of a full moon a man came riding over the Locust Hill on a white horse with a long black cape and no head!!! Being a young kid, I thought that it was just a story at the time, but my friend's mother went on to say that every — and I can't remember exactly what night — that this headless horseman would ride over the Locust Hill. They scared me to death that night and I stayed awake as long as I could, listening for horse hooves to come flying over the hill.

Setting out to explore more details, Satterfield consulted the "gossip room" attendants for guidance. Everybody knew about the headless man on the Locust Hill but nobody wanted to tell the story. "I think that the reason they would not give me more information was because of the group situation which I questioned them in," he commented. He then began with the telephone interview of 83-year-old Mary King, a "historian" of the town who said she first heard it in the 1920s:

> Well, what I always heard was that there was a girl and her boyfriend driving over the Locust Hill and they either met or passed (I don't remember which) this man with no head. Well, they went home scared to death of course. It was called the Locust Hill legend because of a black couple named Locust, who then lived at the bottom of the hill.

The next taped version comes from Pearl Fread, a Sunday School teacher who was known as a "great storyteller" (she died shortly after the recording was made):

> They always say'n that this young girl was ridin' across the hill and it was late at night and . . . ah . . . think she said that as she came across she was, you know sort of . . . she had maybe had heard it, I don't know about that, anyway, she was comin' across late at night and ah . . . this man and a horse came out and stopped her and she ah . . . looked you know and he didn't have no head, 'course she was scared to death, and he took a hold of the horse and stopped it. And ah . . . he told her that his name was car . . . Chieron Burnin'ham and told her to go dig on the hill there somewheres . . . that

there was gold buried and whenever she . . . each lick that she took, say Chieron Burnin'ham as she hit you know and she would find a pot of gold. Well, it scared her! And she . . . when she got home she was so scared that they had to help her off of the horse, help her to bed, and she died! She was so scared that she never recovered from it. And we heard [laughs] that that's why a lot of you know there's gullies and places still in there where people had dug for the gold. I don't suppose they ever found it. [laughs] But that's the story that I've heard. . . . Every time we'd go over it I'd shut my eyes 'cause I expected to see that headless horseman.

Satterfield's mother, Judy, 43, was interviewed during lunch break in the day care center where she worked:

When I was a young girl ah . . . my grandfather used to tell me about the headless horseman, 'specially at night when I was gettin' ready to cross the road from his house to ours. And on our property ah . . . there was a sink hole on both sides of the house. And there's quite a few sink holes around Locust Hill.

She did not remember the exact story, but she had heard of the gold. Satterfield observed that she remembered that the story was told to her to scare her at night when she had to cross the road on this hill. When he asked her if she believed in the horseman, she replied, "Definitely."

Flo King, 83, Satterfield's great-grandmother, reported it this way:

My husband was walkin' over the hill when he's — over the Locust Hill when he's a boy and ah . . . he heard a horse behind him and he was so scared that his hair really stood on his head. When he got home he was so scared to death.

Responding to a direct question, she said she still hears about the horseman and believes of his existence because her husband told her the "truth."

Only one version of this community legend is coherent with a solid core: the headless horseman haunts the site of the buried treasure and tries to unburden himself and lead someone to the pot of gold. As in other treasure legends, the story ends tragically. The other texts simply report of sighting and hearing the horseman, and scaring children and young people out in the woods in the forbidden hour.

The landscape and life of the settlement is well reported in these scanty accounts, and together they make up a scary story that the small community endorses. The collector believes that the legend of Locust Hill is a local version of Washington Irving's "Legend of Sleepy Hollow"; he believes the local variant "came about as a result of the mass media which has published books and presented television shows about Irving's headless horseman story and that it has diffused to this small rural community." However, none of the informants referred to the Irving story, and it would be difficult to determine if the ubiquitous international legend figure needed such a direct literary connection to lead to Millersburg, where informants have reported its existence since the 1920s. More than seventy years seems too long a period for this story to persist as a media legend found in schoolbooks and later on television.

## Localized Legends and Legend Clusters

Localized legends and legend-clusters constitute the most common, traditional category. Its typical feature is that its core fact is a visible object around which the texts oscillate. This object — a man-made structure, a natural formation, or a secluded and mysterious site — is the evidence of the legendary event that people accidentally or purposely encounter. The object or place may be known and referred to by a descriptive name such as Dead Man's Hollow, Screaming Bridge, or the Devil's Backbone, but more often the name does not reflect its legend connections.

Mysterious legend sites are traditionally located on the outskirts of communities (Peuckert 1965) or are unusual buildings, and the stories related to them may refer to facts that do not conform to reality. For example, the nocturnal juvenile pilgrims who visit a particular tombstone in the Orange County (Indiana) cemetery still relate the story of the woman buried there. According to the story, she was choked to death with a chain by her cruel husband — disregarding the fact that the young man whose name is actually engraved on the stone died of tuberculosis (Clements 1969a; Incollingo 1966). Likewise, regional residents still believe that the monument on the outskirts of the village of Bodrogkeresztúr, Hungary — which commemorates the victory of the revolutionary army of Colonel Klapka in 1849 — marks the mass grave of heroes who suffered defeat from the Austrian army.

Thus, there is no face on the stone wall on Fruitridge Avenue in Terre Haute, Indiana, to give evidence of a car crash in which a boy's face was imprinted upon impact (Baker 1969), but the truth of the legend is stronger than fact.

### The Face on the Wall

A popular local legend about a face imprinted into a wall produced lively variations in the 1968 and 1969 collections of students in introductory folklore classes. Baker's exemplary analysis of the fifty-five variants with valuable contextual information reveals not only the fluidity of the active legend in general but also the constant and changing ingredients and the limits of variability of the localized clusters (Baker 1969).

The main story is plain but complete with introductory and closing reaffirmation of the evidence: There is a certain place where a boy fell victim to an accident that left his face imprinted in the wall, and anyone who drives by can see it. But, like all active legends, it varies greatly not only in textual content but also in meaning; it absorbs traditional legend motifs, and tendentiously takes alternative moralizing, mystifying, and rationalizing tones. Baker distinguishes seven thematic subvariants: A, B, and C are real legends; D, E, F, and G have no narrative content but carry important attributes. In his notes, Baker documents considerable variation within each category. The data thus enables us to establish the extent of the main legend and its ramifications for that given period of its existence. Baker's categories are as follows:

A. Eleven variants describe the face and location, and tell the story of a boy who was playing in front of the house when a truck crushed him. His father buried him behind the wall, and his face appears magically. You can see it if you drive by.

B. Six variants have a wealthy father who gave his son a new car. The boy was drinking and smashed into the wall at a high speed. His face was imprinted onto the wall. A warning to fast drivers is also added: "If you touch it, you will die."

C. Thirty-three variants describe a son who was playing on the street and hit by a car while his father was building a wall around the house. The father went into shock and carved his son's face into the wall, and "that's how the face in the wall came about." Alternately, a sculptor was hired to carve the face, and it appears mysteriously, or it appears to his mother in the moonlight.

D. One variant describes Ben Blumberg, a prominent local citizen, on whose wall the face keeps reappearing, although he tries to cover it up. The impression looks like a fossilized skeleton.

E. One variant identifies same owner (Blumberg) and locus. The impression is said to look like a skull of a close relative who is watching the property.

F. One variant describes a portion of a cement wall that looks like a face but is an act of nature. However, this informant's mother said an accident had occurred there and the man's casket had to be closed because his nose, eyes, and lips were missing, but the informant did not believe it, saying the face is too big to be real.

G. One variant is from an informant who thinks it is "a bunch of stuff." The wall is identified as belonging to the Blumbergs, close friends of his family. There was a carving of a boy's face on a stone of a torn-down building which had been bought and built into the wall, but now it is gone because "some car hit the wall and took the section of the fence where the picture was."

Some versions indicate danger to the experiencer: If you touch the face, a light will follow you and cause your death in a crash. The legend displays belief in magic while also offering the sober rebuttal by rational explanation of evidence that simply is not there. The life-threatening danger of physical contact with an object that is an extension of the dead, a common motif in traditional legends, also appears in current stories about encounters at more remote places, such as spooky woods, highway stretches, cemeteries, and bridges.

Legends attached to locations have the tendency to cluster and diversify. Here the visit to the mysterious legend event, the voyage to the unknown, forcefully effects textual change. Our exploration of the emergence and formulation of types over the years has revealed processes that probably have always taken place but have remained unnoticed by those who did not take the trouble to analyze the making of the texts. Some classic examples show how legends emerge, how they relate to each other, and how they form clusters and cycles without solidifying or divorcing from their breeding soil. Considering the locus, the places themselves, as epicenters of legends, we have found that the stories, variants, and independent legends cluster around them in diverse ways.

Traditional stories that have national or international distribution, but are regionally or locally attached to landscapes, give a hinterland familiarity to texts. This identifiability, of course, is not surprising. Why would anyone tell a legend about remote, unknown people and places? From the foregoing it should be clear that the text of the legend speaks to us and about us, sounding our problems with agencies beyond our control. No community exists that has not known these legends in the past, and there is no community that does not know them today. We can recognize them even in edited, literary versions of old collections.

The method of approach we developed in the fifteen volumes of the journal *Indiana Folklore* (1968–1984), was dedicated to the exploration of contemporary legendry and yielded valuable information unknown before to researchers. The method was simple: monographic collection of local variants with contextual data, determination of textual and thematic variation and affinity to other types, and comparison to national and international congeners. Despite the severe limitations caused by the problematic methods of collecting, this approach led us to the discovery of text formation in progress within a short period of time and space by small groups that constituted legend conduits.

Some of the intensive studies presented in *Indiana Folklore* were pioneering and seminal. My first description in 1969 of young adults' visitations to legend sites, and their performance of magico-ritual acts and recitals of an actual legend (Dégh 1971: 63–66) was amplified and confirmed by a new team of folklorists. For example, Clements and Lightfoot (1972) analyzed the legends related to Stepp Cemetery; they brought together a large repertoire from regional residents of towns within a radius of twenty miles and traced them to a 1966 newspaper article story, which had been developed and ramified during the research period (1966 to 1972). The authors' treatment and interpretation has enabled us to follow over the past twenty years the continuing formulation of the legend through the different phases of its existence — as visit, ritual, play, oral telling, newspaper report, magazine feature story, and ostensive action (see also chapter 4).

## The Cemetery Legend in Prospect

A very different cemetery legend known to Bedford residents was first reported by Bill Clements (1969a). The element in common with the Stepp Cemetery story is the danger of touching the death-related object (the ultimate dare is to kiss it; see Hall 1973: 156); in this case, the object is the growing cross-shaped chain on the monument. But unlike the Stepp Cemetery complex, the "Chain on the Tombstone" legend has remained consistent, varying only in its explanations of the different supernatural or natural causes and origins of the chain. The motif "crime inevitably comes to light" (*Motif-Index* 270–271) itself is common in international distribution, but at the same time it remains popular among modern cemetery visitors in America. Variants over the last two decades have kept the Bedford redaction alive without connecting it to other similar local cemetery legends in Indiana; it is also visible on Halloween posters drawn by children in other towns.

This seemingly unrelated variant from a different town is remarkably coherent and shows the classic characteristics of legends, both the ambiguous attitude and belief of the teller. Debbie, a 21-year-old journalism major, narrated this model story during a Halloween night gathering of some forty students at Indiana University's Harper Hall of Residence in 1989. This extracurricular activity of dormitory residents was part of an annual routine of inviting a folklorist to talk about Halloween. We sat around in a candlelit room, relaxing, watching the logs burning in the fireplace, and sipping hot cider with oatmeal cookies after I had given a professional talk about "Devil's Night." Now it was the students' turn to tell their ghost stories. Debbie did not address her story to me or the two graduate folklore students who had accompanied me on the venture, but rather was speaking to her peers:

I was wondering, are you familiar with the story of Prospect, Indiana? A grave that's located in Prospect? Again, I don't know all the details, because I really don't pay attention to these stories [laughter] . . . but . . . well they, they tend to spook me [laughter], so I just kinda ignore them. Again, I'm not sure how many years ago this was . . . it wasn't too long ago, but this man was accused for killing his wife by strangling her with a chain. And . . . I don't believe he was actually convicted of the crime, but he died before his innocence could be proven. And on his deathbed he supposedly told someone that, in testimony to his innocence, on his tombstone, there would appear a chain in the shape of a cross that . . . would form link by link. And anyway, this chain did appear and it came . . . on the side of the tombstone and . . . where the cross you know goes like this, it would come down on the sides. So, a lot of people have been making trips to Prospect to see the tombstone.

And after a while the vandals got to it, you know, and they had to replace the tombstone entirely. And now this chain link is back on this new tombstone also. And just for grins, one time a friend of mine took me up there to see it, and I actually saw the links on the stone. Now I don't know if the, they, they even come back — he told me they do but he's been there on nights when you couldn't see it at all.

And there is also another story . . . that some professors from I.U. had gone to see this. And I'm sure this is total fabrication. But when they went to look at this tombstone to make sure that nobody had taken a chain and pounded it into the stone,[19] or to, you know, alter it in some way. And they couldn't find any evidence that this had happened. And there was one person who totally believed in this spirit coming back, and the other one thought it was just another prankster. And as they were leaving Prospect . . . it's a real windy backwoods kind of road — and as they were driving, this car came from out of nowhere behind them, and just was speeding up, and getting closer, and closer, and ran them off the road. Now, this person who did not believe, was the one who was driving the car. And when they found the car, the person who did believe in the story was totally uninjured, and the person who did not, was dead. And there was a logging chain wrapped around his neck that had come from somewhere. . . . So . . . [nervous laughter from the audience].[20]

Legend Sites to Visit

Thigpen (1972) assembled a body of seventy-five localized legends of Indiana's Brown County high school students, related to their life-style and worldview; and Gutowski (1970) demonstrated the attitudes of local residents to legends attached to two separate Devil's Hollows in the same location. The remarkable collection of Rudinger (1976) included the variants of five basic legends within the context of the Firelands area in Ohio. Hall (1973) demonstrated a spontaneous legend-telling event, in preparation of experiencing the legends at the tunnel in Tunnelton, Indiana, the spot of a well-established legend site. His work inspired Ellis to construct a "legend tripping" idiom as adolescent behavior (1982–1983). He managed to publicize his idea of an adolescent legend-trip among fellow folklorists and folklore students to the extent that the "tripping became a legend itself." Explorations led to more intensive searches for emergent legendry attached to locations. In this respect, Baker's 1970 study of the spooklight visible at a certain section of the road north of Brazil, Indiana, gives us a good indication of the variety and affinity of legends that cluster around a mysterious phenomenon. Following such works, generations of students have contributed to a rich corpus of legends about violent death by accident, murder, and natural disaster.

The Spooklight Hill legends share some of the materials related to bridge legends, which are the richest set in our experience.[21] An undergraduate class assignment in 1969 led us to a repertoire concerned with the Avon and the Plainfield railroad bridges,[22] although the interviewer and informant skipped stories too well known or already printed. Fourteen texts were collected by student Gary E. Brown, who interviewed three male and two female friends. Thirty-six others were added in the comparative notes from previous collections. The corpus included the following legends: the working man in the concrete (Dégh 1968a: 61–67); baby and mother killed on the bridge; suicide on the bridge; murder on the bridge; car, train, or buggy accident; execution of criminals; "The Boyfriend's Death"; and "The Hook." Although the common theme is haunting, such as the return of the victim of violent death, the environmental conditions also accommodate popular horror legends like "The Boyfriend's Death" and "The Hook."

We see an interesting contrast when comparing the Plainfield contingent to the repertoire related to "The Screaming Bridge," located north of Westfield, Indiana. I have many archival variants, but the more current thematic and textual variety is best indicated by the 1988 collection of student Laura Zaun, who interviewed her former high-school friends about the stories they know and their involvement in the experience. The texts, accompanied by contextual commentaries, vary not only thematically but also in the style of telling, ranging from personal experience narratives to objective stories expressing diverse attitudes such as belief, fear, aloofness, and mockery. The following twenty-two legends were told by eight girls and eleven boys in this order, and comprise a representative sample of oral legendry of recent times:

- Ku Klux Klan murder
- Unexplained scream at midnight
- Place of partying and making out
- Escaped maniac killed two pursuing cops
- Crazy father killed his family and threw them off the bridge where the bloodstain glows at night.
- Working man in concrete (2)
- Devil worshippers sacrifice animals and babies. (2)
- Civil war soldier hung himself for losing in battle.
- Escaped slave hung himself.
- Satanists buried people alive under the bridge.

- Playing screaming ghost to scare friends
- Lunatic collected money from crossers, and killed and ate those who refused to pay.
- Wife and then grieving husband committed suicide.
- Mother accidentally dropped her baby into the water.
- Glowing eyes
- Satanists sacrificed a truckload of cows.
- Ghost on a bike
- Baby dropped into water
- Glowing animal eyes in the water where butcher threw them
- Escaped lunatic who ate kids yells at midnight.

In comparing these legends about haunts to other clusters, we note a conspicuous increase in horror, cruelty, and ritual murder. We count only two accidental deaths (two variants of a baby dropped by a mother, and two of the workman falling into the cement of the bridge during its construction) and three suicides. The most common and traditional legend — the car, buggy, or train accident — is completely missing. On the other hand, we find five variants about satanic human and animal sacrifices, one racial killing, and four criminal, insane, and cannibalistic murders. This change of focus no doubt resulted from the excessive publicity of violent crimes and serial murder in the daily news.

The Blue Lights House Clusters

A final example of localized legends does not show thematic riches but rather durability and the segmentation of stories into small units that coexist in relation to particular people and locations. The legendary home described in Miclot's book *Skiles Test and the House of Blue Lights* has been a popular visitation site of high-school students of Indianapolis since the early 1940s, and the stories about it have not faded away since the house was razed in 1978. This sounds amazing because the main story, repeated in small thematic units, is not tremendously interesting, nor does it contain supernatural concerns or realistic horrors to cause personal alarm.

The luxurious life-style of an eccentric millionaire could precipitate far more colorful rumors than those that surround Skiles Test, a local businessman, entrepreneur, and farmer.[23] The most atrocious facts (and legend-potentials) that neighbors and gossip mongers could provide was that he had had a large, heated swimming pool equipped with a diving board installed on his lot next to his house, which had been built in 1923. He also loved cats and dogs, adopted stray animals, and buried his dead pets in a pet cemetery on his farmland. He was a hobbyist electrician, built a hothouse using phosphorescent fixtures, and was among the first to put blue electric bulbs on his Christmas tree. Being a frugal man, he stocked up on his household needs in large quantity. The background of historical events in Skiles Test's life and death are the frame for the episodic structure of a legend: his prominence, wealth, investment in the property, and the stylish and secluded house; his love affairs, failed marriages (his last wife survived him), and family life; and the postmortem auction that opened the concealed premises to the general public and antiques buffs.

Because he lived alone, Test surrounded his property with an iron fence and gate for protection — mostly from children, who for a dare, would enter the property at night and throw glass into the swimming pool (Dégh 1969b). This legend's formation is easy to follow — it originated not with a real mystery, but with the need for a safe yet mysterious target for youthful challenges. High school kids needed a place to explore at night, a place where they could be daring, mischievous, and destructive, and they found it within the city limits. Their explorations continued after the property was willed to the city, after the house was demolished in 1978, and after the land became a public recreation area, the Skiles Test Park (Anderson 1978).

Many variants of the "House of Blue Lights" legend exist, and many more could be added by simply talking to the current students of the local high schools, who are the latest generation of those who have ensured the legend's continuity since 1940. For example, a questionnaire was prepared by a college student in 1982 and handed out to the 15- to 18-year-old students in two high schools. In it were questions about the context: Did you visit the place? How many times? What did you do, and what did you see there? Who went with you? The answers of the 73 male and 70 female students yielded 143 new variants of the story that were fairly uniform with no additions to the known elements of the legend.

In 1969, student Edward Marcus from Indianapolis provided one of the fullest versions, in which his personal involvement is given as the context and as part of the legend:

The legend that I most vividly recall was the story of "The House of Blue Lights" in the Geist Reservoir area in Indianapolis, Indiana. I heard the story while on a camping trip in the area with fellow Boy Scouts at the age of sixteen.

After drinking a few beers that someone managed to sneak past the scoutmaster, we began to tell stories about the surrounding area. Most of us were sixteen and had recently received our driver's licences. We were therefore eager to learn of good places to park with our dates. The storytelling settled down to "serious business" when the subject of the "House of Blue Lights" was mentioned.

So the legend went, an old man in a very exclusive neighborhood near our campsite was said to have the body of his wife displayed in a glass-enclosed casket. The casket was supposed to have been surrounded by eerie blue lights that were visible from the yard of the home. Young people on dates often were asked to leave the neighborhood by security police who assured them that there was no lady in a glass coffin. The eerie mood set by the storytelling on a date was always effective in evoking the proper mood for love-making when we later [after learning the story] took our dates into the area to park.

It was disappointing to many young people in the Indianapolis area when Skiles Test died; his was the "House of Blue Lights." When the house was inspected after Mr. Test's death, it was found that there was no glass coffin surrounded by a bank of blue lights. However it was odd that there was found numerous cat graves in the yard, boxes of shoes, food, etc. The eccentric old man evidently bought everything in bulk, and did indeed exhibit some strange habits.

This dry, factual report contains most of the elements of the legend in the framework of a personal experience story. The core story, "mystery house where loving widower keeps dead wife in glass casket, surrounded by blue lights," is more or less consistent with the side-episodes concerning the eccentric behavior of the old man: hoarding goods, and keeping cats and dogs and having a burial ground for them. It also includes episodes concerning the dangers that intruders must face, namely security police.

This rather thin story often breaks up into single stories and is greatly embellished with details in the variants, de-emphasizing the core in diverse ways but without developing a coherent unity. As Magnus Mullarký notes in his assessment of the first 20 variants, "there is a strange discrepancy between the richness of descriptive detail, relative variety of motives and emphases and the lack of textual development; he gives the teenager's preoccupation with the suspenseful experience as one of the causes" (1968: 89). Indeed, variants may elaborate on the adventures of high-school kids, such as scaling the fence.

The tendency of textual variation can be illustrated by quoting formulations of main points of the legend, chosen at random from 200 texts in my personal collection:

> *Dead Wife in Glass Coffin Surrounded by Blue Lights/Romantic Love-Bond Beyond Death.* "She was afraid from being buried in the ground"; "it was her last wish"; "to keep himself from being lonely"; "he was staring at her for hours"; "she was a very beautiful woman and he was jealous to let others see her"; "he loved her very much and could not part with her"; "blue was her favorite color"; "used blue lights so she can rest peacefully"; "open casket"; "kept the casket in the tower room"; "coffin in living room"; "on the sun porch"; "on the glassed-in front porch"; "kept in the picture window"; "in the swimming pool"; "he had a greenhouse to surround her with fresh flowers every day"; "moved it into the garden in summertime"; "closed casket above the ground in the garden"; "filled with flowers"; "huge dogs guard the coffin."

*Recluse with Strange Habits.* "He is invisible, no one can see him"; "never talks to anyone"; "no contact with outside world." *Wealth:* "Became a recluse because he was cheated by the company he had invested in"; "wealthy man, had hidden money throughout the house"; "his treasure is buried under the swimming pool"; "lined in the casket." *Pets:* "He had hundreds of cats, they found 200 cat caskets"; "he buried the cats in the cellar"; "great big dog and cat cemetery"; "he kept the cats in a cathouse and the dogs in a large kennel"; "kept St. Bernards"; "German Shepherd dogs"; "Great Danes"; "Dobermans"; "Pitbulls"; "there were fifteen big bloodhounds"; "there are many big dogs that seem vicious"; "if you go on the property . . . the dogs will be sent after you." *Hoarding:* "So that he should not leave the house"; "buys things by case"; "he buys his food in large grosses"; "cases of catsup"; "unbelievable amount of catsup bottles"; "powdered milk, tomato paste, canned soup"; "buys drums of nails"; "tons of trash and garbage left after the auction"; "he bought a whole truck of catsup bottles, drained the catsup and filled the bottles with bits and pieces of her body which he chopped up."

*Threat to Invaders.* "The fence is studded with nails"; "big gate locked all the time"; "man with gun to guard the gate"; "hunchback with dog to shoot at people"; "a ditch surrounding the property with vicious dogs loose"; "several big attack dogs to keep people away"; "people disappear from the place"; "policeman was found shot"; people "who go near the place will die"; "if you try to climb the fence, blue lights would come on"; "there's a caretaker who shoots you with salt pellets if he sees you"; "the caretakers are crazy. There is or was an armory in the cellar"; "there is a tunnel leading to the spring house on the side of the hill"; "if you go . . . the dogs will be sent after you . . . and an old man or woman who is caretaker of the place will come out and fill you with buckshots. I've heard there are tunnels all over the place."

Only 5 percent of the stories contain supernatural elements. Only eight tellers mentioned that the house was haunted by the spirit of Test after his personal property was auctioned in 1964. Their comments include the following: "They had to raze it to fulfill his bequest"; "the man who rented the house saw the flickering blue light all the time"; "the children who played behind the dried-out swimming pool saw the ghost"; "my girlfriend swore up and down she saw him look out from the tower room"; and "if you go there after dark you will be swallowed up by the ground and never return."

Clearly, this is not a supernatural narrative but a place for the ritual test of courage for teenagers. Ninety-eight percent of the informants claimed to have been at the house; most of them went more than once, many several times;

one admitted having been there 20 times, and one said "uncounted" times. Here is a typical narrative of the visit, as collected by Tom Gravelle in 1980:

> His wife died and he buried her in a glass casket with blue lights. Every night at 11 o'clock, or such time, you can hear her scream. . . . When I was in high-school the big thing was to try to get back to the property to see the casket or hear the scream. I was out back once.

Although the majority of the visitors were males, there were many female informants as well, some of whom claimed that they heard their version from male classmates or friends. Despite the occasional claims that the "House of Blue Lights," like other haunted locations, is a site of the teenage mating game, it seems that this particular legend does not represent the sort of adventure they identify with and like to use for this purpose. Among the causes they gave for their visit, the boys said "to have something to do," "to kill boredom," "to mess around," or simply "for fun."

Oral legends that are attached to particular places have one unifying feature: They all consist of three distinctive parts, which are themselves discrete legends connected interdependently as legend and context. In fact, these related legends provide context to each other. The most important of the three, which I would call the target legend, is the purpose of the visit. This purpose is complex, as is the means of its recital; it involves ritual, aspects of magic and adventure, as well as social and sexual significance. The second distinct part is actually not one legend but several, told by alternating group members during the event's preparatory phase, which could be the trip to the place or a preceding party where individuals decide to make the trip. To set the mood, participants drink beer and tell horror stories of real blood-spilling terror, preparing themselves for supernatural adventure. As Hall (1973) mentions, legends are "told for their 'scare' value." The third part is a personal experience story, told in first person by a participant, framing the event. This is a hero story, reporting the narrator's bravado.

## Non-Oral Texts

These days, modern-minded folk narrative scholars do not express frustration over the lost paradise of orality. As Kvideland points out, many scholars are reconciled with the fact that the "communicative channels have changed," and that "today we are far less dependent on oral transmission than earlier generations"; many scholars have acknowledged that "we no longer depend on the fellowship between storyteller and audience." Furthermore, the folklorist also slips into the audience seat for radio, television, and print media: "as watchers, listeners or readers, we have no or only very little influence of what the mass media have to offer" (Kvideland 1990: 17). But the exclusion of non-oral materials was always artificial, a result of folklorists' myopia. Thus, we should be relieved that the proliferation of mass media has forced us to realize what we should have known before: that folk narratives have always existed in both oral and non-oral forms. A new field has opened to reexamine historic documents and prepare for a broader investigation of folklore in a new era, exploring the "relationships among reading, writing and narrating, between literacy and orality" (Röhrich 1990: 10). We might ask how these relationships change, and how mass media influences the legend process in our days. Non-oral texts, formulated by professionals for an unspecific, distant, and much larger audience than the traditional folk-group, are as variable as their oral counterparts and appear in greater quantity.

The newspaper legend *"Zeitungssage"* was already discovered by Walter Anderson (1960), who clipped stories from the weekly *Kieler Nachrichten* and other newspapers and urged his colleagues to look for these hidden gems. Some folklore journals occasionally reprinted samples of folklore from the press, and random clippings from obscure local publications have also been collected by European and American folklore archives, although systematic culling of the press cannot be undertaken. Today, we are able to harvest legends from the press on a much broader scale. We may read through the index of leading newspapers or subscribe to a clipping agency, as I did, to find certain materials,[24] or work through compendia like MacDougall's on contemporary American supernaturalism (1983), or Vanden Heuvel's *Untapped Sources* (1991). But we must be specific in our searches. We have to choose to excerpt the issues of one or a very few newspapers, focusing on certain periods and topics. This is not different from what we do by collecting in the field: We seek information from individuals within one small community or a region, fully aware that we cannot exhaust oral versions situated in a community or a region, and that what we collect also exists elsewhere.

In collecting from printed sources, not only can we amass a representative sample within a specific situational context, but we can compare and coordinate it with oral and media versions of the legend. Media legend variants are as fluid as their oral counterparts, oscillating in their thematic fixity around a stable core. They appear in the form of advice, information, experience, and story, and sometimes whimsically, not quite like oral variants. They may come as asides or "by-the-ways," and be buried or camouflaged in other messages. Even so, they display amazing stability. Oral and non-oral versions are conditioned by each other and are bound together in a lasting symbiotic relationship, as long as they have social relevance. In constructing legend type-outlines, we cannot neglect the non-oral contingent.

Surprisingly, Brunvand writes that "a literary ghost story such as Washington Irving's 'Legend of Sleepy Hollow' makes a fine schoolbook piece, but being frozen in print and remote in setting, it could never keep pace with the ghost and horror lore in oral tradition. Schoolchildren *read* Irving's story (at least when they are required to), but they do not *tell* it" (1981: 38). Even were there no evidence to the contrary (Knapp and Knapp 1976: 248), it would be difficult to believe that schoolchildren, relishing horror movies on videotape at slumber parties and exploring nearby cemeteries for a little taste of fear, would read Irving's legend only under coercion. His headless horseman story is among the few that have been adapted back from print into oral circulation. Indirectly, children may have heard retold and modified versions from adults and older siblings, but there is no question concerning its general popularity. Current local legends are often traced to a place called "Sleepy Hollow," or "Ghost Hollow,"[25] but the relationship between the literary and the oral legend may be older and deeper, as our example of the Locust Hill legend indicates.

Such separation between the "frozen" text on paper and that told by word of mouth did not exist in old-fashioned villages, so why would it exist now, in a literate society, when "canned" versions seem periodically to make a comeback? We have seen the interaction of oral and media versions of the same legend type, so why not believe the informants who often refer to books and newspapers as the source of a legend? They may not have seen it themselves, but a "friend of a friend" probably read it somewhere.

In this section, I will discuss some of the non-oral legends that we can find as we engage in this peculiar fieldwork, with scissors in our hands, ready to clip from the paperwork empire. However, it is impossible to list *all* types of legends, or even to exhaust one single category. Studying the media legend opens an untrodden path, and it would require large research teams to search through the bulk of available material. Investigating the vast number of fixed texts spreading through non-oral means may still prove to be easier than capturing the *verba volens*, yet our problem here is distinguishing legends from non-legends, recognizing the ingredients and contexts, and separating these texts from related materials.

Keeping in mind our definition of the legend, we have to identify types, motifs, and episodes and prepare for a future exploration of how variation occurs, adjusting to diverse contexts. Non-oral legends are not always easy to identify, particularly if they appear in chunks or scattered within a longer text. One has to keep abreast with current events and "the sensations of the day" to identify legends as they emerge, stagnate, swell, scatter, and decrease. Sometimes they glow under the ashes until the time comes to rekindle them for a new occasion. What a legend is and what it is not often depends on current television programs like CBS's *Ripley's Believe It or Not* (1982–1986, 1999), the now syndicated *Unsolved Mysteries* (1988–present), and syndicated shows such as *A Current Affair* (1986–1999), and *Inside Edition* (1988–1999). Such shows may feature legendary personal experiences in dramatic re-creations by professional actors as if they were happening in front of the viewer; these presentations may confirm the truth of legends in the public eye. Following the life history of even a single legend would be an enormous task for future folklorists.

When legends erupt from everyday monotony without a warning, they surface simultaneously in the press, radio, television, and other media. This means they are communicated by several mechanical mediators and they reach a great number of people. For example, the same luck legend might arrive at our doorstep in the form of a bulk mailing, such as a "discrete personal letter" from a famous astrologer, a voodoo queen, an Indian mystic, a reincarnation of Confucius, or Nostradamus's great-granddaughter Nina; and it might also appear as a classified ad; or it may be read as a complete and cyclic narrative in a tabloid.

Christian establishments often repeat the same story through multimedia channels. The 1981 miracle in Medjugorje, in which the apparition of Virgin Mary appeared to three children who continued monthly talks with her, received more media attention and precipitated more media legends in twenty years than the oral experience stories of miracle-seeking pious pilgrims had through the ages. This elaborate Macedonian repetition of the Fatima legend has reached a staggering number of people. It is advertised as a "modern-day supernatural religious event" in a pamphlet about the miracle published by Lutheran Wayne Weible in 1990 with more than 15 million copies in print. Weible not only narrates the legend, but adds his own experience and conversion story; the reader is also informed of the network of agencies that help spread the legend through organized pilgrimages, the telephone lines that transmit the monthly messages of Mary, and the books, audiotapes, and videocassettes for sale.

The number of media variants of one of the most widespread and influential Satanism legends, the devil's voice on a phonograph record played in reverse, is modest by comparison. Nevertheless, this legend remains a powerful tool in the hands of fundamental Christian sects in America, who educate their public through propagandistic video and audio cassettes in church services, revivals, and other performances for targeted audiences, as well as in newspaper coverage of these events.

When legends appear in the daily news, they reflect either a new event, a first step to an evolving legend, or a reaction to a widespread concern that may have reached cult-like dimensions. Some may ideologize a new trend, fashion, or fad to herald a new era or even contribute to a turning point in contemplating human destiny. Legends concretize important aspects of larger issues, and because information on problems expresses uncertainty and ambiguity, legends fill gaps as we grapple for answers. Life on earth will never be the same since flying saucer abductees and returnees from the dead have informed the public of their experiences, since Charles Manson ideologized and ritualized serial murders, since fact and fiction about poisoned painkillers have hit the news, and since life-saving organ transplants have been tainted with rumors of suspected child murder. Mass reaction comes in many voices, and it shapes the legend in controversial forms in the writing of professional spokespeople: believers, doubters, critics, analysts, satirists, and humorists. Although it may be true that people are suspicious of the press, it is even truer that, to the masses, the printed word and radio and television broadcasts represent well-informed authority.

Newspapers are often the first indicators of emergent legends still in the rumor stage, and they play a notable role in turning rumor into legend through the simultaneous publication of variants. "Reporters, like vampires, feed on human blood" an article in *Time* commented (January 22, 1990); "tales of tragedy, mayhem and murder are the daily stuff of front-page headlines and breathless TV newscasts. But journalists rarely restrict their accounts to the sordid, unadorned facts." Television, also a powerful and believable medium, is regarded as the primary source of news for the majority of Americans. "Docudramas," video narratives that focus on actual events and real people, often include invented dialogue, characters, and even entire scenes; they treat "speculation as fact . . . It is not clear how many viewers recognize that a network may have one standard of fidelity to fact in its 7 p.m. newscast and another an hour later in its docudrama" (*Time*, February 25, 1985). One compelling example comes to mind: On May 4, 1988, newsman Boyd Madsen of NBC's morning show *Today* showed tabloid reporters interviewing a woman who demonstrated in front of the audience that her haunted toaster burns "Satan lives" into bread slices; this story also appeared in the supermarket tabloid *Globe*.

Multimedia information on the same topic is repeated in multiple forms — as complete stories (growing into literary, dramatic scripts, religious tirades, and scientific excurses), personalized subvariants, eyewitness reports, "official" or authoritative reports — related to similar but slightly divergent accounts, references, hints, and abstracts based on second-hand information and hearsay. In this way the master text is supported and enhanced by innumerable others that appear in diverse media and serve a multitude of purposes in line with the distinctive professional goals of the involved agencies. Typical non-oral legends (or legend complexes and cycles) of this kind are told about the Bermuda Triangle, Bigfoot, UFOs, and doomsday; and a plethora of satanic conspiracies have been passed on over the last three decades. Although all of them are firmly rooted in traditional belief and can be regarded as updated variants of traditional legends (Simonides 1987), in their current shape they maintain a solid presence in the media. Oral versions — as much as we can tell from the scanty collections — seem secondary. Their life span is relatively brief and often depends on impressive plays, films, or documentaries.

The life-trajectory of other similarly popular legends in the media is less intensive but more persistent. For example, retellings of legends related to Santa Claus, Halloween, and the common beliefs in ghosts, witches, and demons and the miracles of saints are attached to special (seasonal) occasions or unpredictable criminal, mysterious, fearful, or joyous events, and they feature attractive and popular personalities. These events are more directly related to active oral legendry and continue to persist after their media actualization expires.

While performing our task of clipping variants from print, we may follow one particular but broad theme — hauntings, food poisoning, or monsters, for example — that consists of one or several legends. The press provides us with data that we can review thematically or monographically, the same way we would when we conduct field ethnography. All we have to do in this case is hire a clipping agency to send us the variants of a story.

## Legend Texts in Print: Local Newspapers

For the folklorist, the most valuable legend texts appear in local newspapers. Local columnists are almost as good as an oral narrator. They know their communities, find the sources, explore the premises, interview the best informants, and write up their data as feature articles. These articles usually summarize the legends and list the floating variants framed by the personal opinion of the author. There are many opportunities to find room for such articles. Legends are matters of local attraction, both as a part of local history or as the sensation of the day. "At the boundary of the legend is news," as Oring notes (1990: 163–177). Indeed, it is an irony that the legend, as folklorists claim, is an old story in new dressing; for its adherents, the legend is newsworthy because it is the latest reportable "news." The local paper subscribers may enjoy reading about past mysteries, but with the morning coffee they want to be informed about new shockers. However, it is not only at Halloween when a good ghost story is appealing — when the reporter joins the tour of haunted houses, or spends the night at the ghostly premises with his tape recorder on, as disc jockey Jerry Castor did at the Porticos restaurant in Bloomington, Indiana, in 1988.

Some local journalists publish their legends when they happen to learn about them, or they establish a special column to solicit stories. Even more importantly, they publish emergent localized variants of the legends of current national interest. Stories of black masses, cattle mutilations, mysterious concentric circles pressed into wheat fields, and footprints of the Sasquatch in the woods, to name a few, all have their local counterparts. Local reporters cannot afford to leave a national sensation unattended, and there is always a home-brewed equivalent.

The most popular local legends reappear periodically, sometimes with tongue-in-cheek humor. Larry Incollingo, who had previously reported the Stepp Cemetery legend in 1966 and the Chain on the Tombstone in 1969, in 1979 invites readers to send "spook stories," but "only by oral recordings handed down from older folks or passed around by younger ones"; his article, "Lovers Beware! Spooks with Hooks Hang around Those Trysting Places," summarized several legends (Bloomington *Herald-Times*, September 9, 1977). Rose McIlveen, on the other hand, provides a historical overview of the Indiana legislature's program to preserve forestry as a means of debunking the commonly known Stepp Cemetery legend: "There never were any ghosts at night in Stepp cemetery," she writes. "There are only the sounds of the night" (Bloomington *Herald-Times*, May 4, 1986). Her voice, however, is ineffective at countering the numerous testimonies of regional visitors to the site.

Many of the local newspeople are serious about the legends they research. They seem to be personally fascinated with the legends they come across and express an openness in interpretation. For example, Mike White, director of a Bloomington, Indiana, television station, has been interested in UFOs since childhood after having had a vision himself. Since 1979 he has investigated "countless stories" and "worked closely with about 20 individuals who had told stories he felt were worth pursuing" (Bloomington *Herald-Times*, June 10, 1990). In our 1988 tape-recorded conversation, White identified other journalists with the same interest, and told me about landing places and abductees he knew. In a 1977 letter to me, Robert Musial of the *Detroit Free Press* abstracted the localized version of five legends he and his colleagues had been discussing. In 1980 Jerry Birge, staff writer of the *Herald* (Jasper, Indiana) investigated the case of "The Ghost in Galoshes," a widespread legend in Dubois County, Indiana (see chapter 5).

In 1978, Marilyn French researched the "old legend around the area about Sarah's Grave." A summary of her insightful description in the November 2 issue of the *Akron-Mentone News* (Ind.) shows the complexity of two underlying oral legends:

1. *Haunted house.* Sarah left Ralph and married another man, whereupon Ralph drowned their baby, Nancy. Sarah went berserk, her gown caught fire

in the fireplace, and she jumped out of the window. Sarah cannot rest, and the fireplace had to be bricked up because she appears in the flames, turns the radio, television, and lights on and off, slams doors, and rocks the rocking chair.

2. *Sarah's grave.* Girls at slumber parties in the house go to the grave following the path that Sarah herself made to have access to the house. They jump on the grave to summon her attention. ("I must admit at night, with flashlights and a gang of kids pushing and shoving and screaming, my memories were somewhat eerie," writes French.) Returning to the house, the girls turn lights off, sit on beds upstairs, hold hands, and call on Sarah to show herself (Mary Whales and evil road ghost variant). Dogs begin to bark, the room becomes darker, and Sarah walks in through the wall. As she stands with long hair and wearing a white gown, a girl yells, "Why don't you get back with Ralph?" Sarah lunges toward them, but turning the lights on makes her disappear (Ray 1976; Langlois 1978).

In a letter written on April 22, 1986, Shirley Willard, president of the Fulton County Historical Society, brings the "Sarah's Grave" legend up to date:

High school students love to scare themselves silly by going to her grave. They run through the woods falling all over each other. My teenage son told me about the time he and some friends went. He said the hair on the back of his neck rose and he was really scared because they saw and heard the ghost. The newspaper article does not mention the Bradways who lived in the house for 10 years. Bob Bradway told me he saw sister Sarah at Christmas standing by the Christmas tree. She was a white wisp shaped like a woman in long dress. But he was not scared. He felt sorry for her. There are a number of haunted houses in Fulton County, but the people will not let me publish anything about them because it would make it hard to sell the house. People have learned to make friends with the ghosts and not be scared. If the ghost is troubled, talk to it and be sympathetic, saying: "Don't be upset, everything is OK now. Let's be friends. I won't hurt you." This calms the ghost and you can feel the presence relaxing. An Indian offered tobacco to a troublesome spirit that wouldn't let him sleep and it went home with him to his house. Later when he returned to Rochester, he brought the ghost back and said stay here, this is your real home.

A final example of local legends reported by the local news illustrates how the observation of something that parapsychologists would have called a "poltergeist phenomenon" became a case of satanic possession in the context of current cultural knowledge. The case — which involved the police — is confusing, and it is composed more or less of scattered references to separate legends than to a coherent story. Lynn Ford, staff writer for the *Indianapolis Star* (February 25, 1990), dutifully interviewed the family, three policemen, and neighbors who did not want to be identified by name. Two priests declined to comment on the actions of the accused. Here is the story in brief, broken into its dominant episodes:

1. An Indianapolis family — a father, son, daughter, and 3-year-old grandson — have a houseguest, a 14-year-old grandson from Puerto Rico.

2. The daughter is called home from work for an emergency. She summons the police and reports a burglary in progress.

3. Police do not find a "burglary," but the condition of the house is "close to vandalism." Somebody was tearing up the house. "Dishes were smashed, windows were broken, a lamp exploded, eggs lined up in the refrigerator and had exploded, a mountain-climbing boot suddenly appeared in the doorway."

4. Police said the 14-year-old Puerto Rican youth, Tony, was believed to have been involved in devil worship. One police officer said that Tony "often listened to heavy metal music, a rock genre that sometimes contains satanic references," and that "the grandfather claims Tony had told him about sacrificing animals and performing [satanic] rituals in Puerto Rico." Another police officer recalled a "warm, stuffy feeling" in Tony's bedroom, where a large, portable "boom box" tape player "that I had seen on the desk moved under the bed by itself." Police also said the family sent Tony back to Puerto Rico by plane.

5. The police officers saw frightened people "walking around with crosses around their necks," and summoned a local priest "to bless the home and its occupants." Police are at odds as to how to classify the case. Who is the suspect? A spirit?

There are many loopholes in the Indianapolis story. Only the neighbors knew what happened, but they would not speak. On March 2, columnist Mike Leonard also reported the story in the Bloomington *Herald-Times*, but by that time, the police involved in the case were declining interviews: "They haven't been able to sleep because of all the press people bothering them." Reiterating the statements of the police officers, Leonard places the event into a broader context by reference to Cardinal O'Connor's disclosure of two recent exorcisms performed in New York, and his criticism of heavy metal music containing satanic lyrics (*Time*, March 19, 1990). Leonard also notes Pope John II's increase in the number of exorcists, and underscores the dictum: "*The Exorcist* is gruesomely authentic." As legend, the variant of the "Devil in Rock Music" that seems to emerge in this story is attested by three police officers as the main believers and informants of the reporter.

Similar local legends also often appear in major daily papers. The investigating reporter usually targets one particular person or place and publishes the essence of local gossip, amounting to several legends and variants. Another format has been established by illustrated Sunday supplements and magazines, which often serialize legends (topics might include "ghost stories," "haunted house stories," "witches among us," "life after life," "healers," "channeling," "famous psychics," "miracles," "monsters," and "the occult," for example). The readership always enjoys gaining new insights into the secrets of "unknown forces."

## American Tabloids

American tabloids are the most conspicuous and deliberate publishers of legends. (The tabloids in West European circulation, particularly in England, Germany, Switzerland, and Austria, are more oriented toward sex-scandals, utter absurdity, or violent crime rumors than supernatural legendry.) Each tabloid at the supermarket checkout counter contains one to five full stories, ten to twenty memorates or belief statements, and countless smaller abstracts throughout. The most elaborate stories are summarized in headlines with attractive pictures on the front page, inviting the customer to leaf through the pages and trace the whole account.

The main text of the tabloid legend has its specific style of visual presentation. It begins with an introductory paragraph and is surrounded by shocking pictures to catch the eye of the potential buyer. The aggressive persuasion of tabloid journalism exploits printing techniques (large and bold print, captions, enclosures, exclamation marks, underscoring, and spacing) and structures the text using photos and drawings, suppressing the innate ambiguity of the legend. The stated event is reported as fact without allowing a trace of doubt. We can trust in these authors' reliability because they sign their names as the possessor of all necessary information. If the legend contains a current event, the reporter personally investigates it by going to the location and talking to reliable people. If it is an old story, the reporter cites the most dependable archives and consults with respected scholars. The repertoire of the tabloids is large and comfortably familiar — variants of classic texts, revivals of old stories, or retellings of those currently in distribution. In other words, the repertoire of tabloids is representative of living legendry.

The following cursory list of headlines and abstracts gives a sampling of predominant themes bearing traditional legend motifs:

*Widow Gets Messages from Dead Husband . . . Through His Old Typewriter.*
After six months of investigation, a panel of experts has concluded that

the mysterious messages regularly printed on a widow's antique type-writer are actually communications from her dead husband! (*Weekly World News*, November 20, 1986)

*My Husband Can't Go to Heaven with Missing Parts!* A poor grief-stricken widow is suing a hospital and two doctors for the return of the trans-planted organs that they plucked from her dead husband's body without permission! (*Weekly World News*, June 21, 1987)

*A Terrified Mom's Shocking Story: I'm Pregnant with Satan's Baby.* A priest plans a bizarre exorcism on the unborn child. "I'm carrying the devil's baby," sobbed a terrified mom-to-be, who is desperately pleading for God to save her unborn child from being sacrificed by a sinister satanic cult. (*Weekly World News*, October 11, 1988)

*UFO Crashes into Army Plane.* Two servicemen were killed and at least 35 more were injured when an army transport plane crashed after a midair collision with UFO! (*Weekly World News*, January 12, 1988)

*Hanged Man's Eerie Handprint Keeps Reappearing on Cell Wall after 97 Years.* Experts are investigating this phenomenon. (*National Enquirer*, October 10, 1975)

*Hubby's Headless Ghost Ruins Ex-Wife's Honeymoon!* Horrified newlywed Rita van Michel says her ex-husband ruined her wedding—by coming back from the dead to haunt her on her honeymoon. (*Weekly World News*, June 6, 1987)

*Videotape Shows Ghost of Woman at Her Own Funeral!* A family who vid-eotaped their mother's funeral recoiled in horror when they played back the cassette and saw the ghostly image of the dead woman standing among the mourners—in her burial dress! (*National Enquirer*, June 6, 1986)

*Pilot Enters Heaven during Devil's Triangle Flight.* A German fighter pilot says he flew into heaven when he crossed the Devil's Triangle in 1938! (*Weekly World News*, June 21, 1988)

*Virgin Girl, 11, Has Baby on Christmas Day.* An amazing 11-year-old virgin schoolgirl gave birth to a healthy, nine-pound baby boy—on Christmas day! (*National Examiner*, December 27, 1988)

*JFK's Ghost Haunts Dallas Death Car.* President Kennedy's ghost haunts the car in which he died! Even though a priest and several psychics have attempted to exorcize the spirit from a distance, those who ride in the car are still terrified by unearthly sounds that seem to come from the backseat, and these sounds won't stop until justice is served. (*The Sun,* June 18, 1988)

These titles speak for themselves representing the role of tabloid variants in the composition of a current legend repertory. A discussion of the two following examples will illustrate the recounting style of their authors, and the stories' provenances and context.

Example 1: Spirit in a Bottle

### Please Don't Condemn Us to Hell!

> The people of a tiny Swiss village are living in deadly fear that their homes will once again be ravaged by the savage ghost of a madman — when it is freed from the bottle that has held it prisoner for 150 years! (*Weekly World News,* October 21, 1986)

A draft of the text of the exorcism rite and a photo of an informant and the house to be demolished enhance the story, which is recounted in a typical journalistic manner and printed with dramatic spacing. The reporter, Margareta Pfander, makes it clear in two separate glosses on both sides of the page how rewarding it will be to read the full article. These glosses foreground the essential and terrorizing elements of the legend: "When a wrecker's ball slams into this house, a madman's ghost will be freed, say scared villagers in Switzerland" and "Demonic spirit was imprisoned in bottle by exorcist monk 150 years ago."

These abstracts are shocking enough to make people read, but that information in itself would be sufficient for a legend. The main text, as a piece of investigative journalism, presents background information and an insider setting for the story pieced together by informants and rounded out by the reporter. The frame of the report features the picture of the village Moosleerau with its concerned citizens. In the article, informant Rudolph Hunziker makes it clear that what we have here is a traditional legend:

> The legend of the ghost has been handed down from generation to generation. . . . In life, he was a servant who went insane and murdered the family he worked for. He fled into the woods, but he was hunted down and hanged on the spot. His corpse was left there to rot in the sun. But his ghost returned to the mansion.

Housewife Gertrude Zieffer tells another legend. In fact, she tells the whole legend, connecting this one to another. According to her version, there was no sight of the spirit until a teacher and his family moved in, then "terrible things began to happen that had no explanation." It was not enough that the family was abused by a noisy and malignant ghost; the villagers were also struck down on the street by furniture floating in the air. Then, "a monk was summoned from a nearby monastery," recalls Mrs. Zieffer, "to relieve the community from the ordeal." She gives a good description of the exorcism ritual which she says occurred 150 years ago. She concludes with an expression of the public's concern: If government officials proceed with the demolition of the crumbling mansion, it will release the evil spirit sealed in a wine bottle and the villagers will suffer. It seems that the legend had remained alive in the community and that people had been fearfully watching the structure "slowly crumbling and rotting away. Many villagers believe it's the work of the mad ghost trying to destroy his prison."

A comparison of this legend to another printed version will show some interesting differences. This article was written by Walter Bosiger, of the Zürich paper *Blick,* on October 5, 1986:

### Spookhouse to Be Demolished: Whole Village Fears Immured Spirit

"MOOSLEERAU — In the Aargau village Moosleerau people fear a ghost. For 150 years the spirit of an evil servant has been trapped within a bottle in the old custom house. Now the customhouse is to be demolished and the Moosleerau people fear the haunting will return to the village." [My translation from the German]

The story is horrific. The old customhouse next to the beautiful "Steinerhof" was built in the fifteenth century. The vice-bailiff of the Count of Lenzburg collected taxes from the subjects there. In the previous century a teacher and his family inhabited the historic building. One day, his son found a dusty, empty bottle on the floor, sealed with a cork. As he threw the bottle through the window to the street, it made such a bright light and a loud detonation that windows shattered. From that day the custom house was haunted. At night, closed doors and drawers opened, and hideous sounds were heard. Rudolf Schaedeli, 67, a village chronicler and farmer, said, "My parents lived in this house in the '90s. My father often told me about the spirit in the bottle. Locked therein, there should be the spirit of a once very vicious farmhand."

The villagers were so scared and intimidated that they speedily fetched a capuchin-monk by horse and wagon. He banned the restless spirit of the ungodly servant back into the bottle. A mason was summoned and he sealed the bottle into the wall. In the meantime, the roof of the haunted house has caved in, and after much ado with the officers of preservation of national monuments, it is now to be bulldozed.

The villagers, mainly the older generation, are afraid that the spook will begin its antics again. One inhabitant warned: "One should not play with such things. It would not be for the first time that the spirit of a corpse would make itself noticed." Another villager said, "I would by no means want to be near when they smash the bottle into pieces." And the owner of the haunted house, Richard Hunziker, has a problem: "We don't know if the bottle was enclosed in the main support wall or in the arch of the cellar."

The German account, published in a local paper without pictures, is much more factual and dry than the American version. The informants state frankly, but do not elaborate on, the events; missing is the story of the murder, execution, the appearance of the demonic spirit, and its original confinement within the bottle. The exorcism recalled by Schaedeli, from the story of his father who had lived in the house in the 1890s, may be the second exorcism, after the teacher's son found the bottle in the house. Although facts (the historic building, the owners, and the protection of national monuments) are given, more emphasis is laid on fear of revenant spirits in general, and the one related to this building for generations in particular. Hunziker is the only informant who appears in both texts.

Evidently, both articles reveal the presence of an underlying belief in haunted houses. The informants are indeed genuine,[26] but we might question what the journalists have added to or omitted from their original interviews. Locally there may be more talkative villagers who can give fuller accounts of this community legend.

### Example 2: War of the Witches

This example will illuminate the formation of tabloid legends in the context of the raging panic over Satanism during the eighties, fueled by the media. This wave of the satanic cult legends began sometime in the early 1960s in the United States. It subdivided and multiplied into diverse forms, paraphrasing, banalizing, and mystifying elements of traditional and canonic religious belief. The wave ran its full course and seems currently to be in stagnation — but by no means is it in decline. The episode (or legend) that I am using as a sample began with a police report in 1982.

On June 1, 1982, the local press of Indianapolis reported briefly in the police beat section that a man's body had been found under the brushes on the north side of town, with no visible signs of injury. Soon after the police investigation began, the United Press International reported a fuller version on June 3, with an eye-catching title.

#### Man May Have Taken Poisonous Cult Potion

A man who was found dead earlier this week may have consumed a poisonous potion developed in a cult of Satan worshipers, police said.

Dennis A. Brotzge, 27, whose body was found on the far north side, was involved in a Satanic cult, according to Capt. Jerome L. Hubbs, from the Marion County Sheriff's Department. There were no visible marks on the body, although there were bloodstains on the head. Hubbs said human or animal blood may have been poured on Brotzge as part of a ritual. Tests will be performed to determine if Brotzge drank a poisonous mixture, Hubbs said. "A lot of times there's a struggle to see who will be the leader of these groups," Hubbs said. "They give each other potions to try to get power over each other." Hubbs said police found a considerable amount of satanic material in Brotzge's downtown apartment. His body also had several tattoos dealing with satanic worship.

More assumptions than facts appear in this report, which is based on the belief in the existence of a satanic cult with a ritual of candidates for leadership consuming poison as a form of competition. The only facts are the man's death and the satanic symbols found in his apartment and tattooed on his body. More information emerged when authorities investigated the fast food restaurant where the dead man had worked: He apparently drank blood from defrosted hamburgers. The police sought out his 20-year-old girlfriend, the "witch" who led him on a dog leash, but her mother refused to allow police to talk to her.

At this point, three policemen came to see me to learn if any traditional folk custom loomed behind their assumptions, as they had found no evidence of crime, and the autopsy had turned up no poison in the body. One of the officers told me that he had never thought the time would come when police would need the advice of a folklorist. I tape recorded our conversation and examined the pictures taken of the satanic symbols. It seemed that the deceased had been an eccentric who was fascinated with the occult, and I did not hear anything further about this investigation.

However, as it turned out, the police went much further than consulting with a folklorist. In the July 25, 1982, issue of *The Indianapolis Star*, Scott L. Miley interviewed the deputies of the Marion County Sheriff's Department about their investigation. The reporter gave discreet details about Brotzge, referring to him as "Smith" in the article to protect his family. Fearful of possible desecration, his relatives had buried him hastily at an undisclosed site.

Captain Hubbs and his deputies did everything possible to solve the mystery of Brotzge's life, his relation to cult activities, and his death. A long list of satanic paraphernalia was found during the investigation. The information of former roommates, acquaintances, and employers revealed "Smith's" eccentricity and interest in cultic activity, without shedding new light on the possible cause of his death other than the ingestion of alcohol and drugs. The police entered an unusually "weird" world and "tossed their traditional techniques aside," seeking "first person accounts of those occult and black magic practices . . . they needed the help from hard-to-find sources: folklore experts, alleged witches and a warlock." The officers told Miley that they had talked to dignified card-carrying witches and a warlock, all of whom dissociated their belief and ritual practice from what was shown as evidence in the case. The article exhausts all that can be known about Satanism.

Despite the absolute lack of evidence of a violent cultic death, the statements of the policeman were exploited by tabloid journalism. On September 14, 1982, *National Examiner* writer Cliff Linedecker used the Brotzge story (using the victim's actual name) as a point of departure, in this article:

> **War of Witches: Satan's Disciples Killing for Power. The mysterious death of a man whose body was drenched with animal blood has ignited fears among law enforcement agencies of a nationwide power struggle by a brotherhood dedicated to the worship of Satan.**
>
> > Police fear that the dead man, whose body was mutilated with Satanic symbols, is only the first victim in a merciless war for leadership that is being fought with potions, spells and other forms of black magic.
> >
> > Discovery of the pitiful remains of 27-year-old Dennis Brotzge crumpled in high weeds near Indianapolis led authorities to issue their warning of a satanic shoutout. "He worshiped Satan," said Marion county Sheriff's Captain Jerome L. Hubbs. "A lot of times there's a struggle to see who will be the leader of these groups. They call them warlocks or witches."
> >
> > The alarmed police veteran pointed to the absence of visible signs of violence on the victim's body as evidence of the use of black magic in the death, yet he was quoted saying, "They give each other potions to try to get power over each other." Police added that potions used by the evil Satanists are often poisonous, and formulas have been passed down from generation to generation for hundreds of years. Laboratory tests are being carried out to determine if poisonous drugs or chemicals were present in the victim's body. Police said they learned Brotzge belonged to a cult of Satan worshipers after carrying subliminal messages. After the Assembly's consumer protection committee listened to a selection of backward masked records, some members insisted they heard the words, "I live for Satan." Even more alarming evidence of Brotzge's involvement in obscene Satanic rites was discovered in his home. "He has Jesus on the cross turned upside down with two candles on either side of the cross," the sheriff's captain said.
> >
> > An "authority" on religions who has extensive experience with Satanic groups and witches told the *National Examiner* that Satanism began spreading in this country after publication of *The Satanist Bible* by San Francisco Satanist Anton LeVey. "You have an awful lot of groups that have sprung up as a result of that, and they're out of control," she warned. "They're self-ordained and self-taught, and everyone wants to be the leader. They're crazies and flakeouts who think only of power, and no one can control them."

As the title and headline indicate, the story goes beyond the findings of the Brotzge case. The assumption is that he is but the first victim of a deadly national competition. In fact, the article is the overture to another, claiming that the "war" is international:

> The Devil Rides Out: Black Magic Cults Plot World Terror, Black Magic Is
> Poised to Take Over the World!

This latter article cites American, French, Swiss, and English sources.

Linedecker's *National Examiner* story is based on the information provided by police reports, but it changes the focus and emphasis. The bits and pieces are put together, combining facts and assumptions to create a fiction and a claim for a legendary warning: Satanism is on the rise. The core of this legend is the struggle for power by magic, hypothesized but not stated in the materials. The text is a good example of tabloid legend-making.

### Advertisements: Legend as Magic Merchandise

Because magic is in demand, it is merchandise of prime necessity (Dégh and Vázsonyi 1979: 79; Wagner 1981: 60–70). Business entrepreneurs do everything to satisfy — indeed to cause, stimulate, and increase — this demand through their advertising. This merchandising evidently is the key to the understanding of the exploitation of magic by profit-oriented service companies in Western industrial societies. Even if one were to give priority to several forms of magic-related advertisements by American firms, the assumption that supernaturalism is a specialty of Anglo-American culture is contradicted by the evidence of a currently booming occult market in West Germany, Austria, Switzerland, England, France, Italy, and post-socialist countries. Since the collapse of the Soviet system, occult literature and paraphernalia, formerly smuggled in illegally, now fills magazine racks and bookstores.

Legend ingredients are often adapted, forged, or popularized by advertisers for television, radio, and newspapers to market and sell products. In this case, however, we are not talking about the legend that is used to sell something, but rather we speak about the legend offered for sale in the occult market that in itself is a legend market. It is also a legend factory in which old legends are re-created, modified, and improved, and new ones are created to commodify magic. Newspaper ads exploit all features and attributes of the legend, including the situational context, intellectual atmosphere, and worldview. They use content units, motifs, episodes, whole stories, cycles, and conglomerates in developing their own stylistic conventions and formulas. Although these legends address the reading audience only in printed form, they exhibit great flexibility around stable cores to fit actual interests.

The magic ad business, eager to fill the needs of its broad base of consumers, depends on oral folklore. It acts not only as a practical mediator of oral tradition but also exerts influence on the maintenance and resurgence of traditional expressive forms. The mail-order legends sold in the market pick up and convey the ideas of a partly invisible, partly very active audience and are as variable and flexible as they appear in the spontaneous performance of old-time villagers or contemporary attendants of social gatherings.

These forms belong to a special category of miracle legends. In the labyrinth of mail-order marketing, the formulation of narrative is more or less explicit, depending on the degree of elaboration of identical components within a common frame of reference. The main message of each is that anyone can achieve happiness by magic, by buying a magic object, or by submitting to the assistance of a magically endowed person. The texts may be found in a large number of print products — leading newspapers, weeklies, illustrated magazines, promotion letters distributed by mail, and billboards. They appear most prominently in tabloids (the "rainbow press," "evening papers," or "boulevard papers" in Europe).

The most succinct micro-legends in the classified ad section are summaries, using keywords and concepts:

- "Reverend Henry solves all problems fast. Straight numbers. Removes bad luck, forever."
- Mother Doris writes, "Spells performed, good and bad. Action immediately. $15.00 Limit two. Powers unlimited."
- Papa Doc asks, "Been seeking help throughout the country? I do what others claim! I use roots, dolls, love potions, spells, incense in my work. I can help you."
- Sara Richards, gifted ESP miracle psychic, offers help in "getting any lover you want; specializes in divorce control, reunites lovers, removes bad luck, helps with problems such as skin, hair, weight, alcoholism, drugs, co-worker harassment, obtaining job, longevity, luck winning lottery numbers, helps winning lawsuit, insurance claims, etc."
- "Aya promises miracles: she is a spiritualist psychic, works with three magical keys from Biblical days."
- Sister Swanee urges callers to "Dial a miracle. Have a problem you cannot solve? You've tried all the rest, now try the best."
- "Secret witchcraft spells you can do."
- "Priscilla gives crystal ball readings."

All of these examples were chosen from 96 items on a page in the *National Examiner* (March 19, 1991: 39).

A 1984 ad, chosen at random, is signed by "Psychic moneymakers":

- "Money magic. Become rich immediately. Receive millionaire spells, money attraction potion, personal lucky numbers, candle burning

> wealth ritual, lucky charm collection, full instructions. Quick results. Never fails."

These rudimentary legends often appear in larger announcements, rounded out by narrative details that focus on selling the magic power of one single person or a magic object. The description of the gifts of Nina Nostradamus, for example, occupies a full page in the *National Examiner:* "Nina and her entire family have forecast the future for over 6 centuries . . . the death of Marie Antoinette, Lincoln's assassination, the San Francisco earthquake in 1906, Stock market crash in 1929, premature death of Elvis Presley . . ." Nina also predicted the San Francisco Earthquake of 1989, so there is good reason to believe that she will give you your lucky lottery numbers, days, and signs. She responds to a 900 phone number (March 19, 1991: 38).

The half- or full-page advertisements with pictures of magic objects in the center contain the most complete and elaborate luck legends. Magic objects — religious symbols in the form of jewelry (a pendant, charm, bracelet, or key ring) that contains gemstones, crystals, water, cloth, wood, clay, or written prayer formulas — that are worn on the seeker's body and transmit power to cause miracles conform to traditional belief in contagious magic. These remarkably and expertly crafted master legends initiate a business and at the same time launch a string of other legends. In most cases, the master story is a proponent, calling for co-proponents and supporters. The main story itself is an autobiographical account of a person who signs his or her name and address as an endorsement. These people may even strengthen their credibility by including snapshots and a notarized certificate, thus making a miracle palpable for the reader. The purpose of the legend, then, is the introduction of new merchandise.

Here are outlines of two stories of the luck-legend type selling luck-bringing objects:

Example 1: "The Incredible True Story That Changed
My Life Forever!" by Kenneth Laurens

The merchandise promoted in this "Genie in the Bottle" story is shown in the middle of the page (*Globe*, June 13, 1978, p. 21). An outline of the story follows:

1. Astrologers, fortune tellers, charms, and magic prayers fail to help a bankrupt, unlucky man.
2. He does "crazy things" out of desperation. He takes a vacation in the Caribbean on borrowed money before carrying out his plan to commit suicide.

3. While scuba diving, a shark threatens his life. His spear gun fails.

4. He finds the magic bottle accidentally while attempting escape from the shark; touching it turns the shark away.

5. The genie in the bottle instructs him what to do.

6. By repeating the chant inscribed on the bottle, he gets everything he wants: "happiness, joy, contentment," the presidency of a multimillion dollar business, a home with a heated swimming pool, and consistent winnings in bingo and the lottery.

Complementary support legends:

6a. An unemployed, unhappy friend borrows the bottle. The same miracle happens to him.

6b. Five friends make replicas of the bottle and the chant. They experience the same miracle.

7. Conclusion: The narrator proposes to do a "scientific experiment," and test the power of the bottle as a bearer of good luck. He invites the general public to buy for $5.00 the replicas he orders from a master glass blower, thus helping themselves and mankind in general.

Example 2: "An Amazing but True Experience that Changed My Entire Life" told by Robert L. McCarthy

McCarthy promotes the "Inca Sun God Amulet." A similar story appeared in the *National Enquirer* in 1982:

1. A man is out of luck, out of money, and has unrewarding employment.

2. Following surgery he must use a cane. He is sent on a business trip to Peru.

3. He experiences an unexpected turn of destiny, during a visit to Machu Picchu. Prompted by "a strong urge," he finds "an amulet of the Sun God himself" when his cane gets accidentally stuck between two rocks.

4. Miracles have taken place over the period of four years since he obtained the amulet: He takes control of a multimillion dollar business, gets a home valued at $150,000, a car worth $15,000, and vacation trips to the Caribbean and Europe. He says he works "as little or as much as I feel like, and have the time and money to go anywhere I please."

Complementary support stories:

4a. Urged by friends, he orders copies from a jeweler for gifts to relatives and friends. They experience "the same amazing luck."

4b. Friends ask for more copies to pass on to their friends. They all tell the "most fantastic stories of how their luck has improved suddenly."

"Unsolicited" stories are included on the page, attesting to the successful manipulation of the magic object. The sworn statement and the photo of the author among llamas at the scene of the miracle is also complemented by the photo of a grateful family whose desperation was "turned into happiness."

The differences between the two legends are only stylistic. The first person presents himself as a carefree bachelor, a gambler, a pleasure hunter; the second describes himself as a mature and responsible family man, an intellectual, who fills the reader in on Inca history, old belief, and mythology. The "Genie in the Bottle" raconteur is at the beginning of his marketing enterprise, whereas the "Sun God Amulet" promoter can already report success.

The sales strategy in the announcement lies in its attempt to solicit audience response first by appealing to people who need to try the object. Later on, the buyers of the treasure are invited to stay in touch and tell their success stories. In fact, the marketer suggests a clearinghouse of legends — the making of a legend-telling community — and focuses on miracle stories testing the same magic power.

**Promotion Letters**

This approach opens the door for a new strategy to expand the market by following up on further variants of the same legend in newspapers and promotion letters. For example, the type of story promoting the sale of the "Mister Lucky" symbol of the ancient Mayas, the "Mystical Ancient Japanese Good Luck Charm," "The Cross of Magnator," "King Midas' pendant," and "Rub the Buddha for money" statuette refers to a research group of scholars and their experiments as well as the testimonies of grateful recipients of miracles. The same expansion technique can be seen in the operations of clairvoyants, astrologers, and spiritual healers who establish their legends and promotion strategy by use of testimonial legends of their (alleged or real) customers.

To explore their strategy, I answered the ad of Madame Daudet in *Weekly World News* (January 12, 1988). "YES! I want to win thousands — even millions. And I want a better, happier life. At absolutely NO cost" it read, with the promise to send me my magic number. And so she did — but for a chain and a charm, lottery digits, an astrological forecast, and a numerological horoscope, she charged $19.95. I discontinued correspondence with this French lady, but I continued receiving her letters filled with testimonial mini-legends from clients.

The disclosure of my birth date for the horoscope opened the door for me to other legend business persons. I received 16 letters in a year from such authorities as "Norwell, World's No. 1 Astrologer"; "Winfried Noe, Europe's No. 1 astrologer"; Mrs. Michelle Dumont; "June Penn, World Consultant" (or the "world's foremost astrological consultant," characterizing all other astrologers as less effective); the "USA Astrological Center"; "Alan Reiss, Chairman of the National Lottery Advisory Board"; and "the Reverend Ike of the United Christian Evangelistic Association." Many letters came in February, alerting me to the miracle potentials of my birthday, March 18, which was the only token of my person that the writers acquired and used. Their promises and supporting evidence were similar in content and style.

The technical design of the announcement helps the reader grasp the essentials of the message — what the object and its legend communicate. At the same time, a complementary evocative promotional narrative surrounds the target in quite a different style, appealing more to emotions than to the practical mind. Like an auctioneer, it chants its message in rhythmic and formulaic repetitious rhetoric, listing the good things in store for the buyer. Typographically, the text is marked by large and small characters, italics, capitals, boldface, and indentation.

In more advanced stages of advertising, more and more room is given to audience response, which is aggressively solicited in a separate framed section of the full-page ad-legend, on the right or left side of the page. Legend telling is encouraged by showing a picture of a bundle of $100 bills followed by this more or less standardized text:

> We want you to report the miracle that blesses your life when you wear or carry _____. We want you to tell us about the Money you receive _____ about the healing of your body and mind experience . . . about the Happiness and Joy . . . List for us some of your many, many blessings and you will be eligible to receive $100 cash. Naturally we ask you to sign the statement that certifies that you have worn the Talisman and have truly received all the miracles you list. And we ask that you have your statement notarized so that even the most skeptical will believe it.

While offering proof of the unprovable — and presumably excluding cheaters — this ad promises distribution of money among the legend-tellers. But the lure of joining the legend-sharing community is not financial gain. It is the idea of "doing a good deed" by enlightening nonbelievers and making them also recipients of happiness.

The dialectic-polyphonic nature of the legend appears to be specifically stressed in the mail-order network of exchange. The text often includes references to eyewitnesses and the time and place of occurrence, further fleshed out in the promotional material. Because the magic is offered to promote incredible miracles, it becomes necessary also to represent the anticipated opposing voice of society at large. The narrators of the "Genie in the Bottle" and the "Inca Sun God Amulet" stories stress their general sobriety and initial commonsense point of view, and the secondary contributors do the same to make their own conversion to belief more credible. Using the rhetoric of the advertiser, they state that they were converted from skeptics to believers, thus supporting the feasibility of miracles.

After the master story is launched and has received adequate publicity, the audience response can be sorted out and used for another full-page advertisement. With reference to the magic object and the story of its origin, the follow-up announcement contains the testimonial narratives of grateful and successful recipients of happiness. These legends differ from each other in size and style: They range from short statements to detailed experience accounts. Many seem to be abstracts, summarized by the editor. A page may contain six to eight full, or twenty to thirty abbreviated legends. The whole-page announcement also appears as a flier sent with other promotional materials to the customer with the purchased magic object.

"My husband was showered with $10,000.00 in the street," reports F. A. from New York. "This is really true," claims participant B/603, "I picked out a card at Bingo and saw that the next card had my lucky number on it. I took that card instead. I won $25.00." One impersonal account informs that "one Japanese housewife said that headaches and backaches she suffered every morning for years suddenly disappeared when she began to wear magnetic energy." A more polished report was given by Mrs. Marks of Oak Park, Illinois:

> In May, 1978, I left my husband. I was lonely and afraid. In my horoscope I was advised to be patient and give someone who wronged me a second chance "that would amply make it up" to me. The next day my husband called, and expressed the desire for reconciliation. I was furious, and then remembered my horoscope. I listened to all he said and then decided to move back with him. He had been unemployed since June 1977. He had gotten a job that paid $260.00 a week and he commenced to help me pay back my overdue medical bills.

Mrs. Parker from New York relates,

> My husband was with a fishing party where some of the men spent one evening drinking. One of the men complained of a terrible headache the next morning. Nothing he took seemed to bring him relief. My husband showed him Hand Reflexology but he was not interested in trying. He got worse and worse. Finally he tried it and was amazed that his pain was gone instantly . . . no more hangover.

Testimonial legends like these easily proliferate and seem to be more spontaneous, sincere folk expressions than the master legends. From the sales' point of view, their raison d'être is to confirm the efficacy of a magic object boosted earlier by the master legend.

Characteristically, however, the follow-up testimonies do not report similar fabulous gain. None of the correspondents claim to have won millions or gained instant health, wealth, and everlasting happiness as do those who first found an object or discovered the secret formula and made it available to the rest of mankind. These supportive legends report much less spectacular miracles than one would expect after reading only the sales promise. The money won at games of chance rarely amounts to more than a few hundred dollars, rather than the millions of boundless daydreams. Health is improved, not restored. The new employment is better than the old, but still modest. The average person's fantasies are limited to the fulfillment of everyday desires. The vendors of magic are aware of that and set a relatively low limit within which they promise success to everyone.

The luck that is obtained in the magic market, packaged in legend, is modest, trivial, and often symbolic; it is optimistic in a small way, and sometimes pathetic. It seems that even these little gains are not easily won without miraculous help.

### The Chain Letter Legend

The chain letter represents another type of luck legend (Dundes and Pagter 1975: 3–6; Hoppál 1986: 62–80), but one that significantly differs from the luck sold in the marketplace. Chain letter luck is not merchandise but rather is supposed to be passed by friends to friends, connecting expanding circles of well-wishers. The text itself is remarkably stable, promising (unspecified) good luck if one continues the chain and forwards it to four friends, and bad luck if one breaks the chain. Here is the basic outline:

1. *Invocation:* The letter begins with an admonition to pray, trust the Lord, or kiss someone as an expression of love.

2. *Origins:* The letter states that it was started by a specified person (a sea captain, a doctor, a priest, a saint, or other person) in Venezuela, Argentina, Capetown, the Netherlands, Great Britain, Italy, and has gone around the world nine times . . . twenty times, bringing luck to everyone who cooperates. It must be copied four, five, nine, . . . twenty times and sent to a friend immediately.

3. *Happy story:* The letter describes one or two people who forwarded the letter and were rewarded with instant wealth and happiness.

4. *Unhappy story:* The letter describes one or two people who broke the chain and were punished (died or went bankrupt).

5. *Instruction and promise:* The recipient is told to make four, five, nine, . . . twenty copies of the letter and he or she will receive good luck shortly. (Two subvariants are to send also a picture postcard or a cuisine recipe to the first person on the list.)

---

### KISS SOMEONE YOU LOVE WHEN YOU GET
### THIS LETTER AND MAKE MAGIC

This paper has been sent to you for <u>GOOD LUCK</u>. The original is in New England. It has been sent around the world 9 times. The luck has now been sent to <u>you</u>. You will receive good luck within 4 days of receiving this letter — provided you in turn send it on.

This is no joke. You will receive good luck in the mail. Send no money. Send copies to people you think need good luck. Don't send money, as fate has no price. <u>DO NOT KEEP THIS LETTER — IT MUST LEAVE YOUR HANDS WITHIN 96 HOURS</u>.

An Airforce officer received $70,000. Joe Elliott received $40,000 and lost it because he broke the chain. While in the Phillipines, Gene Welch lost his wife 51 days after receiving the letter. He failed to circulate the letter. However, before her death, she won $50,000 in the lottery. The money was transferred to him 4 days after he decided to mail this letter.

Please send 20 copies and see what happens in 4 days. The chain comes from Venezuela and was written by Saul Anthony DeGroff, a missionary from South Africa. Since the copies must tour the world, you must make 20 copies and send them to friends and associates. After a few days, you will receive a surprise — even if you are not superstitious.

Do note the following:

Constantine Dias received the chain in 1963. He asked his secretary to make 20 copies and send them out. A few days later, he won a lottery of 2 million dollars.

Andy Dodd, an office employee, received this letter and forgot it had to leave his hands within 96 hours. He lost his job. Later, finding the letter again, he mailed 20 copies. A few days later he got a better job.

Dalon Fairchild received the letter and not believing, threw the letter away. Nine days later — he died.

---

In 1987, the letter received by a young woman in California was very faded and barely readable. She promised herself that she would retype the letter and send it on, but she put it aside to do later. She was plagued with various problems, including expensive car repairs. The letter did not leave within 96 hours. She finally typed the letter as promised and got a new car.

REMEMBER: SEND NO MONEY
DO NOT IGNORE THIS

WITH <u>LOVE</u> ALL THINGS ARE POSSIBLE

Chain Letter

Only slight variation separates the texts of chain letters. Some narrate details; others simply list the bare facts. Two warnings stress the seriousness of the letter and urge the recipient to cooperate: "do not break the chain" and "this is not a joke." The texts also offer assurance to soften the threat and to comfort the suspicious ("do not send money").

The assurances distinguish the altruistic enterprise of the chain letter from commercial ones such as the "New Age Promotional Letter," which asks for $1.00 to be sent to the address on the top. This latter kind of commercial pyramid scheme is against the law, and the two kinds of letter are often confused. On a few occasions, one newspaper hotline column (Bloomington *Herald-Times*, February 22, 1988; March 20, 1989) has confused commercial promotional letters with chain letters, and has mistakenly warned that chain letters are illegal. Brunvand also warns of his suspicion that "asking people to send money or valuables" by mail is "a federal offense" (Sunday *Herald-Times*, December 18, 1988, E2).

I have received many chain letters over the years. Judging by the four names listed above the text to whom I am to send copies, I believe that senders and receivers tend to be close acquaintances, and the letters must be making slow progress in circling around the world. Within my own social network, I have received chain letters from three groups of folklorists, two of which seemed to boomerang — traveling the same international circuit twice and then seemingly stagnating. Others came from a cousin, my sister-in-law, a childhood friend, and my dentist. One of the chain letters I received (January 17, 1991) was very brief:

This letter originated in the Netherlands, and has been passed around the world at least 20 times, bringing good luck to everyone who passed it on. The one who breaks the chain will have bad luck. DO NOT KILL THIS LETTER. Do not send money. Just have a wonderful efficient secretary make four additional copies and send it to five of your friends to whom you wish good luck. You will see that something good happens to you four days from now if the chain is not broken. This is not a joke. You will receive good luck in four days.

The most remarkable quality of this particular chain legend was that it was sent to me with the attached cover letters of 57 previous addressees, beginning October 22, 1989.[27] These revealed to me the network of senders and receivers who constituted the context of the legend. The stationary showed that the letters came from the intellectual and business elite of Washington and New York: well-known reporters, writers, publishers, editors, bureau chiefs, and correspondents, as well as lawyers, stockbrokers, financiers, insurance agents, and other business executives. The brief notes sent along with the legend expressed the senders' serious belief: The playful, lighthearted comments justified the senders' obeying the appeal not to kill the letter, concealing their belief in front of a presumed rational public. A few excerpts from these cover letters (written by prominent intellectuals whose names are too well-known to reveal) express the familiarity and general attitude toward supernatural belief held by educated, affluent Americans.

- "I've already resolved 1991 will be a better year than 1990. It already has been. And then along comes something I can do about it, foolish and silly though we may all know it to be. He who dares nothing need hope for nothing, it is said. Clearly, I dared to break the chain, but I think it may be worthwhile to dare being foolish and silly, on occasion."
- "I hope you have better luck in four days than you are having today."
- "Please, don't blame me for this. It was obviously started by the paper industry and has grown too big for me to stop. Besides, I could always use a little good fortune. Best of luck!"
- I didn't send this out when I received it yesterday, and last night I received a traffic ticket for not coming to a full stop sign. I ain't superstitious but a black cat passed my path!"
- "Go for it!"
- "Being a happily married man I wouldn't want to do anything to break this lucky chain."
- "When one is getting married in less than two months bad luck is a thing to be avoided at all costs."
- "Having received this letter on Friday the 13th, I have no choice but to dispose of it as quickly as possible."
- "I think that the curse attached to this letter is somewhat emblematic of

our last few months together. Here's hoping that you have a happy Friday the 13th."

- "Having received the attached, I am in a rather compromising position. Being somewhat embarrassed but also superstitious, I remain . . ."
- "I am too risk averse to sit on this."
- "I'm on vacation. Why tempt the fates?"
- "This isn't the dumbest thing I've ever done. I think."
- "I don't fly on Friday the 13th; I don't walk under ladders; when my favorite baseball team, the Philadelphia Phillies, are winning, I don't change my underwear (thank God they've had a string of losing seasons) and I'll be damned if I'm going to break a chain letter."
- "Unlike the rest of these fools, I believe in this stuff!"
- "Having received this letter on my 65th birthday, I have no choice but to send it on as ordered. I am getting too old to take a chance of breaking the chain." (I wish I could reveal the name of this prominent political columnist!)

Even though Dear Abby, Ann Landers, Miss Manners, Hotline, and other wise columnist advisors instruct us to break the chain, the chain continues. "Superstition supports chain letters," reads the headline of an old clipping in my file." "Present day science has not been altogether successful in convincing man that everything in the realm of nature has a natural cause. . . . With Spring's new awakening comes revived hope to the chain letter enthusiast" (Smith 1969). And since e-mail and the Internet have become an attractive and faster means to practice chain-letter writing, new items become more talkative and longer (the screen is tolerant) but do not deviate from the main guidelines. This, I hope, exempts me from including a sample of these newer variations on this commonly known non-oral formula.

### Legends in the News

We have already discussed the varieties of forms that legends or legendary rumors can take in the press, and we have shown how a newsworthy event is formulated over time by combining factual and alleged information with the personal views of the presenters. Victims, eyewitnesses, community members, rumor mongers at large, involved professionals such as police, clergy, doctors, community officials, and parapsychologists (often consulted in hard-to-solve cases like the serial killing of black children in Atlanta in 1982) together construct the legend that is retold by each columnist in a more or less different way.

Roger Mitchell wrote an exemplary study of the process of rumor formation around the character of a strange sexual sociopath, the Wisconsin farmer

Edward Gein. Mitchell showed how traditional and nontraditional oral information, along with mass-media fact and fiction, molded and integrated over
a period of twenty-one years, and how a legend conditioned by the cultural
knowledge and tradition of society emerged from rumor (Mitchell 1979).
Mitchell accepted Allport and Postman's three-step rumor process (1947), but
we may argue that the third step, assimilation, is the most important and critical in making the legend (see also Kelley 1992). At the point of assimilation,
the rumor/legend loses its everyday actuality and factualness. It retains elements of tradition, the formulaic substance, ready for new adaptation: a new
version of the same legend type.

The impact of legends in the news on the processional formation of oral
texts in emergence could be instructively illustrated by assembling the printed
versions of the story about the Procter and Gamble corporation's support of
Satan. Between 1981 and 1990 the legend underwent considerable recastings
under the impact of change of the social, economic, and ideological climate
until an administrative settlement had killed it (see chapter 4, note 32). Here
we will limit our concern to one excerpt that comprises all the known elements that in time were made into separate legends:

Legend Cycle Surrounding the Procter and Gamble Logo

> CINCINNATI — Cathy Gebing's telephone rings every few minutes, and the
> question is always the same: is the moon-and-stars design on Procter and Gam-
> ble's 70-odd products the mark of the Devil? . . . The rumors, first appearing
> about two years ago, essentially contend that Procter's 132-year-old trademark,
> which shows the Man in the Moon and 13 stars representing the original colo-
> nies, is a symbol of Satanism and Devil worship. The rumor mongering also
> urges a Christian boycott of Procter's products, which includes Pampers, Dun-
> can Hines and Folger's. . . . Procter firmly rejected suggestions that it simply
> remove the offending symbol from its packages. That, however, increases the
> suspicion of some consumers. "If it causes controversy, I don't see why they have
> to have it," said Faye Dease, a clinic supervisor . . . in Fort Bragg, N.C. Mrs
> Dease said that when a mirror is held up to the logo, the curlicues on the man's
> beard becomes 666 — the sight of the Antichrist. . . . "In the beginning, God
> made the tree," a 75-year-old woman wrote the company, "where did Satan get
> Charmin'?" Many callers reported hearing that Procter's "owner" had appeared
> on a television talk show where he admitted selling his soul to the Devil in order
> to gain the company's success. (*New York Times*, June 22, 1982; see more on
> Procter and Gamble in chapter 4, note 32)

The Microwaved Pet

In another case, a widespread legend known since 1976 (Brunvand 1981:
62–65) was reported as a criminal case (Bloomington *Herald-Times*, September 1990) from Canton, Ohio, where an 11-year-old boy was arrested in con-

# Procter&Gamble

*The Procter & Gamble Company*
*Public Affairs Division*
*P.O. Box 599, Cincinnati, Ohio 45201-0599*

Dear Friends of Procter & Gamble:

The completely ridiculous and false story that the President of The Procter & Gamble Company appeared on a talk show to discuss the Company's connection to satanism has been resurfacing in your area, so we are coming to ask your help in spreading the truth. It is a variation of the lie that was spread in 1981-82, 1984-85 and again in 1990.

None of this is true. The President of P&G has never appeared on any talk show to discuss satanism. We have successfully filed lawsuits over the years against a number of people who were intentionally spreading this lie, and will do so again if necessary.

Frankly, we thought we had the spread of these falsehoods under control after the media attention given to the problem in 1982, 1985 and again in 1990. Unfortunately, the stories have been resurfacing and taking on a new life. Calls and letters from your area have increased in recent weeks. When this happens, we believe the best way to deal with this false rumor is to ask for your help in getting the truth to those people who may be contributing unwittingly to the further spread of this outrageous lie.

Thank you, in advance, for any assistance you can provide in getting the facts out to the public. Procter & Gamble has been serving the American public for over 150 years, and nothing is more important to us than the integrity of our business and the quality of our products. If you have questions or would like more information, please call one of the toll-free 1-800 numbers listed on any of our product packages.

Sincerely,

*Ann Jenemann Smith*

Ann Jenemann Smith
Public Relations Supervisor

Procter & Gamble Letter negating any connection to satanism

nection with the microwave death of a dog owned by a Humane Society worker.

> A white Maltese owned by Marlene Stephens was put to sleep after it was found in a microwave oven Thursday. The dog was cooked for an undetermined amount of time, said a Canton police officer who asked not to be identified. Someone broke into Stephens home Thursday and placed her dog, Jo Jo, into the microwave, police said. The oven was still running when she returned home from work that afternoon, officials said. Stephens said she believed the dog killing was "a form of recreation."

To me, it seems that it was a legend told by ostension, stimulated by repeated oral telling.

Monster Sighting Investigated by Police

In November of 1974, the Columbus, Indiana, newspaper the *Republic* reported another police case: Six young women told city police that they had seen a monster twice, once in broad daylight.

> And whatever it is, the six agree, it is (1) green, (2) hairy, (3) large, about six feet tall and walking upright, and (4) has claws. Four of the women, whose names police did not list, said they saw "the thing" about 3 P.M. Friday near the paved boat ramp in the park along the White river at the west end of Fifth street. The other two said it jumped on the hood of the car, leaving scratch marks on the paint. That was about 11:54 P.M. No one was hurt, only frightened, police said. Officers searched the area on both occasions but found nothing . . . they warned other residents to take care and keep an eye out for the "monster."

Legend Considered by Planning Commission

Even official county business decisions can contain legendary material. In the following case, the legend does not appear but lingers behind the commission's deliberations. The *Ball State Daily News* (February 16, 1984) reported that the demolition of two old railroad overpasses would not be sidetracked because of stories about Italian immigrants buried in them. Seventy-four-year-old August Kraft said he was one year old when the overpasses were built "but he remembers his father George, recounting vivid stories about their construction. . . . One of the immigrants was buried in the concrete of the Bender Road overpass . . . another was buried in the Boonville-New Harmony overpass." The stories Kraft refers to give support to a legend type, "The Worker (Negro) in the Concrete," which is also associated with several local bridges (Dégh 1968a).

More Newspaper Legends

More explicit legends appear as *fillers* in the papers, inserted wherever there is space left. They seem to be used for their interesting and shocking quality; nevertheless, they are always factual, with proper validating references. Here are three widespread legends in personalized newspaper reports. The first refers to "The Stolen Grandmother," internationally known since the early 1960s (Dégh 1968b; Brunvand 1981); the second is a version of the legend about "Department Store Snakes," known in many variants since 1968 (Cord 1969); and finally "The Dead Cat in the Package," first discussed by Dorson (1959: 253–254).

THE STOLEN GRANDMOTHER     This UPI report from Munich, Germany appeared in 1977:

> If grandma dies while the family is soaking up in the sun on Spain's Costa del Sol this summer, do not stuff her in the car trunk to get her home. The West German Automobile Club says this happened several times recently, when family members had no idea where to turn for help. "It is forbidden to transport a corpse in one's own car trunk and a heavy fine results if one is caught at it," the club said. They suggested that Germans who find themselves in such a situation contact the nearest West German consulate.

Baker "Schorsch" Braun, in the version told to Max Lüthi's brother-in-law (as mentioned in chapter 2), evidently was not aware that he should have contacted the consulate either (Dégh 1995b).

DEPARTMENT STORE SNAKES     The February 18, 1977, issue of the Bloomington *Herald-Times* included this piece:

> Melvyn R. Privett, shopping in the men's clothing section of a Fountain, Colo. store Wednesday, felt something strike his leg as he walked down the aisle. He looked down and saw a three-foot diamondback rattlesnake, which had just bitten him. Firemen gave Privett first aid for the bite, and he was hospitalized briefly. Police said they had no idea how the young snake, killed by another shopper, got into the store. Diamondback rattlesnakes are not common in the area, officers said.

DEAD CAT IN THE PACKAGE     Reporter Barbara Ratts, who happens to be a good legend-teller in her own right, introduced the following story in 1983:

> Sometimes a newspaper person hears a story that is worth retelling, even if some of the details may have gone astray. Bits of this tale drifted into the newsroom from three different sources, but no eye-witnesses were to be found. This week, two people were driving in the Osco's parking lot when they accidentally

hit and killed a cat. One of the individuals felt the cat deserves a proper burial, so the two put the dead animal in a sack. They decided to have lunch at Long John Silver's, so they placed the sack on the hood of their car, rather than inside the vehicle, thinking that they would keep an eye on the package from inside the restaurant. From their table, they saw a woman pass by their car, pick up the sack and carry it inside the restaurant. Wondering what prize was inside, she peeked. Seeing a dead cat, she fainted. An ambulance was called, and she and all her "belongings" were taken to the hospital. Embarrassed to tell emergency room employees what had happened, the woman underwent the full battery of tests and x-rays. She was found to be in good health. When leaving, the woman was asked what belongings had been locked up for safekeeping. She told the nurse, "my purse." Another nurse "reminded" the woman that she had brought a paper sack to the hospital with her, and went to get it. The nurse looked inside, and said, "There's a dead cat in here!" A doctor and other nurses went to check out the situation. A policeman was called to take the dead cat to the Animal Shelter for proper disposal, which was the intention of the people who put the cat in the bag in the first place. The woman's troubles weren't over. She was handed a hospital bill and then had to hire a cab to get back to her car. (Bloomington *Herald-Times*, January 27, 1983)

### Letters to the Editor: Legends Questioned

The high publicity of current legends and legendary rumors encourage readers who fear for their safety to turn to an authority for reassurance. Legends signaling danger — monstrous and absurd while appearing in the media and in everyday talks — usually surface also on opinion pages, in letters to the editor, or in syndicated columns. People personally affected also turn to telephone hotlines, particularly those who have lost money to occult organizations. Brunvand exploits the legends told and evaluated in the popular columns of Ann Landers and Abigail VanBuren (Brunvand 1981, 1986). Not only are the variants provided, but also their contexts; these dialogues, discussions, and commentaries are valuable, framing the stories with due uncertainty. The authority sometimes fails to give the answer that is expected and is rebutted by a "better informed" reader.

Ann Landers was told by "BS Detector in Chicago" that the letter she had quoted from "West Coast Warning" about an incident of child abduction and sedation in a shopping center's restroom was in fact a legend; this reader pointed out that such scare stories are old yarns and reproached Ann for printing it without checking its veracity. "These incidents never happen to the person telling the story — it's always a friend or an aunt's next-door neighbor." Ann Landers admitted she believed the story: "It was an honest mistake," she says.

In another letter, the Chicago correspondent seems to be the legend-teller, though. He seized the opportunity to tell what he qualifies as "the newest scare story," unaware that folklorists had commented on its long history some time ago (Bausinger 1968). The magic word that it is "new" calls attention to this localized variant:

> The newest scare story is about a young matron who went to her car and found an old woman in the backseat. The old woman claimed to be sick and asked to be driven to a hospital. The young matron agreed, but said she needed to go back into Marshall Field's to pick up something. She got a security guard from the store to return to the car with her. The guard discovered that the old woman in the car was a man dressed as a woman. He had an ax. (Bloomington *Herald-Times*, February 14, 1985)

Incidentally, the shopping center as a danger zone had entered the mail circuit much earlier, containing both the snakebite and the child mutilation legend and somehow connecting the two. This is seen in the following example in which the editor of "Shull's Mailbag" (*Indianapolis News*, September 9, 1969) answers a reader's question:

> [*Question:*] I heard a story about an accident that happened at a shopping center in the city; that a woman was bitten on the arm by a poisonous snake while trying on a sweater and had to have her arm amputated. Could you tell me whether the story is true?
>
> [*Answer:*] As unfounded rumors go, that's a pretty one, although I prefer the version which went around several years ago. In that one, instead of a woman and a snake, it was a small boy and a sex maniac. The current rumor, which seems to be spreading nationally, has the woman dead in some cities.

Following Brunvand's richly documented article about the "apocryphal" AIDS Mary (Bloomington *Herald-Telephone*, March 12, 1987: C6), Ann Landers's correspondent "Sleepless Nights in Canada" gives a concise but accurate version of the legend, which was faithfully reprinted because it "delivers a message" that teens are "as susceptible to AIDS as adults" (*Herald-Telephone*, July 30, 1987: D7).

The Sunday news magazine *Parade* (May 27, 1990) is visibly irritated with this inquiry:

> [*Question:*] We've heard rumors that Liz Claiborne is giving the profits from her merchandise sale to satanic organizations. If this is true, is she a devil-worshiper? We'd really appreciate an answer. — Pam Simonson and Julie Pigott, Chipley, Fla.
>
> [*Answer:*] "There is absolutely no truth to these rumors. They're nonsense originated by foolish persons.

What an unkind retort!

Brunvand has decided to enlighten the readership of his newspaper columns and books about the falsity of legends. However, the truth or falsity is not the interest of folklorists because, as we have already stated, the legend remains a legend, whether it really happened or not. The compulsion to express opinion is what counts. After all, who knows when multimedia retellings will make the story not only told but also ostensively performed?

## Concluding Remarks

The selected texts in this chapter are representative prototypes but do not and cannot exhaust the endless variety of recurrent and emergent new legends. Each text, transmitted orally or otherwise, should be regarded only as the tip of the iceberg — evidence of a story's presence in society. But there is much more to legends than oral and printed manifestations. As we know, fixed texts are also aired audio-visually and not only as news, but also as reports, rumors, short and long dramatization, or cartoons. They also appear in book-length popular science fiction and other literary texts and in full-length films. We could hardly deny the influence of horror novels and their movie versions on legend-making since the late nineteenth century (Cawelti 1976), but their impact has been diverse, filling diverse needs. For example, images of the Frankenstein monster, Dracula, the Wolfman, and Dr. Jekyll and Mr. Hyde have been remade for changing audiences over time, along with other horrors packaged for modern Halloween moviegoers. These "classics" of film and television have contributed more to the conceptualization of the world as a fearsome place shared with monsters than they have to the creation of narratives.

The movie *Rosemary's Baby* (Paramount, 1968) was a landmark in the film industry for formulating and propagating the Catholic canon of demonic possession. In perspective, however, *The Exorcist* (Warner Brothers, 1973) was the real public educator, alerting modern urban masses on two continents to the threat of satanic lures. Box office success prompted movie producers to do serials, follow-ups, and new variants of the devil legend, such as *The Omen* (20th Century Fox, 1976), *It's Alive* (Warner Brothers, 1974), *The Shining* (Warner Brothers, 1980), *Angel Heart* (TriStar Pictures, 1987), and *The Believers* (Orion Pictures, 1987). The question has been raised concerning these films' influence on reported cases of possession (Goodman 1980; Mischo and Niemann 1983), ritual child abuse, ritual cannibalism (Best 1990; Hicks 1990), and drug-related cult killings (see, for example, the Matamoros case, in Cox 1991: 406–438), which have increased dramatically. However, the legends related to these cases remain on the level of rumor formation (Ellis 1990a). In this instance, novels, movies, semi-scientific and scientific books, newspapers, and the electronic media together contribute to an information overflow that breaks so fast that the legend-creating folk apparently cannot digest it: Before single legends can be formed, new "cases" have hit the press.

It seems that whatever folklorists can conclude today will be invalidated by events of tomorrow. For example, while I was working on the first draft of this book, a phone call from an Indiana State University anthropologist informed me that mass hysteria had broken out in Evansville, Indiana (population 200,000). Rumor had it that grade school children were being taken by school bus to a mysterious Blue House for molestation, and that babies of teenage mothers were allegedly being ritually killed and eaten there. The townspeople were divided between believers (child protection activists and churchgoers) and unbelievers (police, the prosecutor, and teachers). Seven "blue houses" were identified by residents, one of the homeowners was suing, and law enforcement authorities were investigating. The local papers (*Evansville Courier* and *Evansville Press*) were full of reports about the case, which already had been whispered about for almost a decade. When the story gained national attention through a segment on the syndicated tabloid television show *A Current Affair* (May 22, 1991), the program acted as fuel for the local fire (Dégh 1995: 358–368).

In other cases, novels and movies were created from genuine folk legends. For example, *Capricorn One* (Warner Brothers, 1978) is based on the popular hearsay that the moon flight was a fiction plotted by the government, a story that is widespread among conservative Christians who find no indication of the moonwalk in the Bible (*Omni*, 1982, 110). In 1994, Charles Johnson, president of the Flat Earth Research Society still insisted that the "lunar landing was just a lot of moonshine," and according to the Washington *Post*'s random sampling, 20 percent of Americans still believe that it never happened (*Herald-Times*, July 20, 1994). *The Amityville Horror*, a book and movie (Anson 1977; Brittle 1980) based on a local haunted house legend, was exploited by Catholic churchmen as well as parapsychologists. The movie *When a Stranger Calls* (Melvin Simons Productions, 1979), "grew out of a 20 minute short film called 'The Sitter' in 1977 which in turn was based on an incident that happened chillingly enough, in Santa Monica," (*Los Angeles Times*, September 23, 1979); it was a skillful adaptation of the teenage horror legend "The Babysitter and the Man Upstairs" (Brunvand 1981: 70–71). Furthermore, the Swiss novel *Eine Goldene Tante* (Prêtre 1963) was based on "The Stolen Grandmother" legend. As an extreme case, John Fuller's book *The Ghost of Flight 401* (1976) pursued the legends surrounding a plane crash and the return of the benign ghost of the pilot. Fuller did not confine himself to the oral variants (Poulson 1978: 63) that flight attendants furnished, but rather added the stories of mediums and his own participant observations. Entering the broader field of spiritualism and other branches of the occult, Fuller combined legend, literature, and parapsychology. Moreover, in a later book by Elizabeth Fuller (1978), the "psychic" former stewardess accounts for her own search for the phantom captain. And there's no question that readings of Jan Brunvand's syndicated column inspired the 1998 horror movie *Urban Legend* (Phoenix Pictures).

Media materials, popular horror novels, and movies are too complex to become sources for retelling. They are more influential in the creation and maintenance of the ideology of the legend — the setting of a system of belief on which legends can thrive — than they are on the formulation of types. The press reports either "facts" or stories taken from oral information, not the contents of literary works. What we have described are prototypes that can be considered belief concepts (*Glaubensvorstellung*), memorates, or fabulates within their situational and ideological contexts. They are interrelated through common cultural knowledge on multiple levels of interaction.

Thus, the messages that legends convey are supported by their contexts, resulting from the cultural knowledge of the subjects and the nature of their media of communication, as I have illustrated through examples. Any audience has a clear understanding of what is artistic, enjoyable, and entertaining and can make the distinction between witty talk, spinning a good story, joking, and singing and dancing for pleasure. The legend has no such claim. The proponents and the audience of the legend are often identical, equally involved in the claims of truth related to what has just been said, and they take turns in exchanging ideas. The basis for such an understanding between people is a cultural system they share, composed of common concerns and common understandings of tradition, educational and moral values, experiences, as well as the given social situation, the occasion, the purpose of communication, and the individuals' motivations. These cognitive components are rather restrictive, but narrators are free to make their own judgments, observing the ground rules of a common consensus. There may be disagreement in judging whether someone saw a dead pirate in the basement or just had a vision, dreamed about it, or is lying about it, but such discrepancies do not mean that there is no shared concept of what a revenant is. It may be controversial to play with the Ouija board (Ellis 1994b) — which is perceived variously as a harmless social game, an instrument of damnation, an effective tool in making supernatural connection, or a trick of fraudulent soothsayers — but all know what it looks like and who has used it.

How can we separate the legend from its contextual components, some of which may appear outside, preceding, following, surrounding, or built into the main body of its text? The formal instability, localization, and conversational (or pseudo-conversational) performances are consequences of the message-orientation that makes contextualization an essential, integral part of the legend. Any teller of a legend draws on the common cultural knowledge of the group to make sense. Lifting a variant out of its natural environment means the loss of context, and thus, a loss of meaning, reducing the text to an empty formula. The message remains, but with unknown addressers and addressees; it is left to the mercy of outside interpreters to juggle with its meanings.

Contextualizing — that is, placing the manifest legend into the cultural system that produced it — is the task of the analyst, whose cultural catalogue may differ considerably from the one the legend is based on. As John Caughey writes,

> Culture, that which makes us a stranger when we are away from home, is a learned system. . . . Cultural knowledge is highly relative. People of different subgroups and societies live in different worlds because their systems of knowledge are fundamentally different. . . . People in different societies also live in different worlds because their mental plans, or how-to-do-it recipes, differ. All plans are linked cognitively to values and conceptions of reality. (1984: 9–11)

We have good reason to be concerned with the complex we may call context, which gives meaning to any legend text. In our efforts to situate legend texts, to observe the process as they emerge, develop, change, merge, decline, reawaken, and disappear, we must attempt a life history approach that places this folklore genre into the center of (individual and communal) expressive behavior. If folklorists develop a technique in "asking the natives" and describing the context from the native's point of view instead of constructing interpretations from their own cultural base, we will come closer to answering the questions of the who, why, and when of legend telling. But the method of approach cannot be borrowed from another discipline; it must use the unique resources of folkloristics.[28]

# Legend-Tellers

4.

Who are the tellers of legends? Who are the bearers of legend tradition? What kind of people constitute a conduit of transmission? And what kind of social groups play the role of supporting a climate in which legends can thrive?[1]

Over the last three decades — the same period in which a new interest in formulating a genre theory arose, making distinctions between analytical and native concepts of genre — empirical research of narrative folklore sought new aims for its orientations (Abrahams 1976; Klintberg 1990a: 117–118; Bauman 1992a; Ben-Amos 1969, 1976, 1992; Briggs and Bauman 1992; Honko 1968, 1976, 1980a, 1980b, 1989; Voigt 1976). Earlier genre theorists such as Jolles (1929), Wesselski (1931), von Sydow (1934), Ranke (1967a), and Bausinger (1980) provided the theoretical roundtable that was useful in expanding research from its earlier comparative literary focus. They helped develop a broader sociological approach to storytelling, centering on the person who produces the text, based on tradition and controlled by the attending audience and society at large (Dégh 1977a, 1983).

More recently, however, the text's function has taken center stage in research practice. Context, communication, and performance became the key concepts in scholarly discourse. Ambiguity arose around the question of whether the text or the context is more important (Bauman 1983, 1992b: 41–49), and research concentrated on texts communicated face-to-face, in small groups. Research concentrated on the behavioral design of the "storytelling event" and individuals' interactions; that is, the focus was on linguistic competence and the situated strategies of communication to produce texts in performance — the "artful mode of communication" (Bauman 1989b: 177). Furthermore, the text was targeted as "the product of the interplay of the components of specific communicative events" (Bauman 1980: 40).

This new direction provoked critical comments concerning the particularization of research. "Genre research reached the stage," wrote Honko, "where we specifically need empirical studies of the reproduction, performance and communication contexts of genres" (Honko 1989: 20). He also argued that we should scrutinize "the process of production and adaptation of transmitted texts to new narrators and auditors in particular situations" (Honko 1980a: 43–44). Donald Ward was more direct in his criticism of American performance theorists. He claimed their "revolutionary approach" had been essentially commonplace in Europe for almost sixty years, and it was based on the romantic and naive vision of the "storytelling event" (Georges 1969) that "did not correspond to the reality of folklore in the age of science, industry and technology. In insisting that true folklore only exists in oral performance, researchers were forced to deny the very existence of the myriad modes of dissemination of narratives in the modern world" (Ward 1990a: 35–36). Results would seem to indicate that singling out the "how" (rather than the "why" and the "by whom") as one of the interdependent constituents of the storytelling process for study does not lead to deeper knowledge, nor does focusing on one unique event without its historical antecedents.

Evidently, it is the prerogative of scholars to choose their subject of study, satisfying their own curiosity, determined by their own cultural and psychological personalities. This "bias" is also a virtue, because it adds the scholar's own specific voice to the many that sounded before, broadening and enriching the horizons of knowledge. However, it is more troublesome that the new orientations in research do not grow out from earlier results in folkloristics but rather from uprooting concepts, theories, and methods from other disciplines. One can only welcome creative interdisciplinary adaptations, but too often folklorists follow short-lived fashionable trends, or play lip service to attractive new ideas from influential books by currently celebrated stars of the humanities. At the same time, the works of earlier folklorists remain unread or forgotten, and the questions they raised are left unanswered.

For example, the personality of the narrator and his role in the production of texts has been intensively studied since the late nineteenth century. From the pioneering studies of the personal artistry of epic song singers by the Russian scholars Rybnikov (1861–67) and Hilferding (1873), of the tellers of magic tales by the Scottish scholar Campbell (1860–62), of the personal art of Natalya Osipowna Winokurowa by the Russian scholar Asadowskij (1926), to the description of the supporting role of community in the performance of folklore by the German scholar Schwietering (1935), researchers improved their empirical approach. A more refined direction was the discovery of the "dialectic tension" of author/performer and audience in storytelling in the formulation of Hungarian scholar Ortutay (1940, 1958, and 1972: 136–138, 268–269). This seasoned approach remains in focus today. Yet proponents of recent scholarly currents have never subjected the findings of their predecessors to scientific scrutiny and critique for the benefit of their own work with narrators, and for testing their approaches on the grounds of a broader historiographic perspective.

Looking for an up-to-date classification of folklore narrators for assessing the character of the legend-teller, I found that Kaivola-Bregenhøj's article (1989), based on archival and empirical research in the Nordic countries, was fair but not as helpful as I had hoped. In her description and categorization, the narrator appears as an abstract and vague figure who would not stand even as a theoretical construct representing the personalities of tellers of diverse kinds of narratives. Kaivola-Bregenhøj conceptualizes folklore as a collective oral tradition from which narrators adapt stories. She considers these narrators as performers, retellers of tradition rather than authors, whose identity is forgotten in the clouds of time. Furthermore, her model applies only to oral artists, a small minority of the many transmitters of legends in the modern industrial world. In her view, only memorate-tellers can be regarded as authors because they tell about their own experiences. This conception of the memorate is inaccurate, like so many of the others that have been adapted arbitrarily by modern users who seem not to have access to von Sydow's original definition.

Narrator, audience, and tradition are equally important contributors to the telling event. The narrator of a text is as much the author of the manifest or emergent version as the copyrighted author of a literary fiction. Both are rooted in a collective tradition, using traditional figures of speech, metaphors, and stylistic formulas, and traditional beliefs, values, and norms to frame their presentation of a narrative in terms of actors, action, and scenery; otherwise, their texts would never even be intelligible, let alone accepted by their society. The narrator, as the author/teller, produces the legend in a given unique circumstance in which tradition, audience, and a chosen method of communication interact. In this balanced collaborative act, the narrators are the obvious primary agents because their personalities, their psyches, prevail. It is the narrator's voice that sounds, his or her style that shapes words and sentences into sense, and his or her conception that forges epic units into coherent meanings. In other words, the creative power of narrators spontaneously produces a unique utterance every time they tell a story.

In recent years Nordic scholars have rediscovered their archives as repositories of valuable collections from storytellers of the past, complete with useful commentaries and interpretations of scholars of the past. The "back-to-the archive" trend (Apo 1986: 182) has proved rewarding, a justifiable rebuttal to criticisms claiming that archives are useless dust-collectors (see Apo 1995; Herranen 1984; Holbek 1987; Tangherlini 1994). These archival studies are significant contributions to our knowledge of past storytelling practices, but they cannot compete with first-hand observations by the analysts themselves.

Without the narrator there would be no story, no context, and no audience to consider. It is because of the person who speaks (and to whom someone listens) that there is a creative procedure and a product — that is, a text. The folklorist, competing with other humanists in the perception and interpretation of reality, makes a unique contribution by investing his or her primary interest in human creativity, in the realms of the unofficial, informal, private enculturation and education of society.

## The Everyday Legend-Teller

My long-term exposure to legends among the old-fashioned European peasant communities during the post–World War II period convinced me that legends were told by old people, who were representatives of an archaic rural worldview. At that time, modern-minded younger people, who embraced a new agricultural technology and the ideals of urban living, openly ridiculed the "superstitious" stories that their elders recounted to the folklorist as evidence of their backwardness. There are no witches, only silly old women who pick herbs from the cemetery ditch, they insisted; and there are no ghosts, only drunks who mistake their own shadow for a specter. This opinion was shared by elite society, including the folklorists who were hunting for material in marginal villages, seeking the old, illiterate, and semi-literate custodians of memory folklore — the "still remembered" ideas of the past that would soon be eclipsed by industrialization.

The young ethnographers who invaded the villages were struck with awe and guilt at the poor living conditions they found. And they employed some tricks to make people talk to them. For example, in the company of friends in the early 1930s, Ortutay described his strategy of collecting "superstitions." To capture the attention of an old woman collecting herbs in a pasture, he recited some legends he knew from textbooks. The woman was impressed. "Are you a wizard?" she asked respectfully. "Yes," he admitted. She wanted to make sure: "Did you pass all seven grades?" "When I assured her, I had her confidence," he said (Ortutay 1966: 103–104).

Folklorists were fixed on the archaic folk and never looked around in their own circles — the groups of intellectual urbanites among whom they could have found similar "superstitions." They could have interviewed friends who had second-sight, attended spiritualist séances, found friends of friends who were healed by magic practitioners or brought back from the dead, and met pilgrims who had experienced miracles at the shrines of saints. My first inquiry into modern legendry, following up some newspaper stories and radio horrors, was met with mixed reactions from my colleagues. They all knew about whispered-around legends but would dismiss them as trivia rather than accept them as issues relevant to their cultural reality.

Contrary to this European attitude, average Americans — members of an essentially literate, technologically progressive society — never regarded supernatural encounters as evidence of extreme gullibility and backwardness. Louis Jones,[2] for example, noted that "all sorts of classes of people" were telling legends, but, in particular, "oral tradition of tales of the supernatural which often crop up during the talk after a good dinner" appear "in sophisticated circles" (Jones 1959: 161). It is certainly true that legends dealing with the extranormal — horror or the supernatural — cannot be related to a particular social class or educational level. Donald Ward and his students collected 1,300 accounts of supernormal experiences in California from people who were "not uneducated," many of them with college degrees (Ward 1990b: 230). Regarding the substantial collections in America as well as in Europe, we can agree with Simonides that the legend is at home among all social classes and educational groups (1990: 48–49).

At a lecture I presented to a college audience sometime in the early 1970s in Vincennes, Indiana, I read aloud some demonic possession stories that I had heard in East Hungary from an illiterate old shepherd. "What do you mean by 'illiterate'?" asked an indignant local librarian. "My sister is also possessed by the devil, and that's a fact." The same year, a visiting Romanian ethnomusicologist expressed her amazement over student papers about modern witchcraft cases in their hometowns. "Nobody believes in witches in Romania anymore," she told me, "not even peasants." The simple division of the population of European nations into two cultures — an uneducated, conservative, superstitious, sedentary, poor folk versus an educated, enlightened, progressive, mobile, and prosperous elite — evidently cannot be applied to the more complex stratification of American society in which affluence or education do not necessarily mean disbelief in the extranormal.

If popular authors were to be believed, American legend-tellers belong only to the young generations, between early adolescence and young adulthood. This assumption is far from accurate because legend-tellers are of all ages. However, young people are not as shy as adults about their supernatural or extranormal experiences. Legends they tell are firmly situated in and supported by the common referential framework of general social knowledge and a parareligious worldview. Their repertoire is at easy reach, so it is most rewarding for the folklorist to assign legend collection projects to introductory folklore classes.

In 1967 I first asked college students to write down the legends that they had heard from others or experienced themselves. The students did an excellent job because they enjoyed remembering scary encounters that had played an important role in their childhood and adolescent life. The assignment came as encouragement and acknowledgment of a discrete, highly ambiguous, and clandestine area of consciousness. Once students understood that there was no stigma against the tellers of these experiences, they became eager to talk about what they knew. The stories and the descriptions of the circumstances of telling came easily, almost as confessions, liberating the student collectors from the fear of ridicule. As exercises in higher education, the scary legends achieved an unexpectedly high level of esteem.

At first glimpse, I did not find much difference between these legends and those that the European village youths scoffed at. The settings in which they are situated — the village and its surroundings (farmstead, country road, cemetery, mill, bridge, pasture, meadow, forest, dunes), and the hometown/school town and its surroundings (highway, country road, parking lot, shopping center, farmhouse, forest, cemetery, bridge) — do not manifest more than the obvious differences of the expansion of space through motorized travel. These legends, in essence, are similar to what American youths call "scary" or "spooky" stories. The true difference lies in their interconnectedness with ritual behavior and their social function, not in their themes or meanings. That is, the instructions I gave the young native ethnographers who acted as both insider-informants and observers, introduced me to the operating context (the deep belief-environment and the ritual enactment) of the texts. I continued the assignment with other classes, as did generations of graduate students serving as assistant instructors. My findings, published first in 1969, related to nocturnal visits to two Indiana haunted bridges and to other daring exploits (Dégh 1969a, 1971: 64–66). These night trips, later termed "legend-tripping," were claimed to be a par excellence adolescent exploit by Ellis (1982–83: 68–69, 1991e: 279–295).

The Indiana University Folklore Archive, founded in 1956, was already filled with similar collections. So were others at other American colleges and universities where folklorists were at work.[3] As already noted, in 1968 the amazing wealth of legendry in Indiana prompted me to launch *Indiana Folklore*, the journal of the Hoosier Folklore Society, to promote legend collecting, to present a model of text and context analysis, and to encourage legend research in other states. As time passed, we learned much about the young people who tell legends, and we accumulated information about why they are told. Secondary popular publications exploiting existing student collections also contributed to the general notion that the primary arbitrators of American legendry are young people. In one way or another, we all have agreed that the transformational process of growing up and the traumatic experiences of reaching sexual maturity, leaving home, and taking on adult responsibilities all contribute to projections and responses to the critical conflict of values, which are expressed best in a certain category of legends (Dégh 1971; Dundes 1971; Ellis 1987, 1990, 1994b; Roemer 1971; Samuelson 1981: 133–139). But it is a mistake to take for granted that the repertoire we have come to know best, because of our easy access to students, constitutes the majority corpus of American legendry. Africanists made a similar mistake earlier, believing that the majority of tales that Africans tell are about animals because missionary collectors took their information from children in mission schools. It is time to consider narrators of legends other than those from the 12- to 20-year-old age group.

The profuse and ubiquitous living legendry, as we already have seen, is difficult enough to pin down and divide into neat categories or identify as the production of exclusive social groups. But even more problematic is identifying the personalities of authors and their stories. Folklorists so far have not even tried to connect legends with their tellers. Variants, as a rule, were regarded as regional mutations rather than as the products of individuals. In accordance with the scholastic tradition of the Grimm brothers, märchentellers were worthy of identification as folk poets, whereas legends — the dry, factual, chronicle-like retelling of rudiments of past history — were not seen as having artistic merit. For scholars, the worth of the legend was that it preserved documents of ancient national or local heritage, not that it was told by someone to whom others listened. Collectivity was important, not personality. The legend was to be used as raw material to be rewritten, satisfying literary and patriotic ambitions.

From the late eighteenth century to this day, printed legend collections from each European country and many American states have been routinely published as collections of literary short stories, using local tradition from oral or locally printed sources. In spite of the accessibility of scholarly guides to the principles of fieldwork, authors of most regional folk narrative collections continue to rewrite their texts. The introductions romanticize the legends and tales as a community heritage, seldom mentioning the raconteurs, or if they do, the narrator is also fictionalized.[4]

Burdened with these two currents of intellectual tradition, it is no wonder that few folklorists have been curious about legend-tellers and their repertoires, even if they succeeded in compiling valuable large text collections as natives of their regions (see, for example, Haiding 1965; Henssen 1952; Zender 1937). Regrettably, Puckett (1926), Randolph (1947), and other classic American collectors molded their abstracted legend texts into topical essays to illustrate superstitions, magic acts, and customs without reference to their informants. This model of treatment was so attractive that even Montell (1975) followed it in his valuable "deathlore" book, publishing annotated ghost narratives without information on the tellers and the telling. Among the very few exceptions, mention should be made of the collections of the Hungarians Vajkai (1947), Balassa (1963), Dobos (1971), and Gaál (1965), the German Schneidewind (1960), and the Irish Lysaght (1986), all of whom described the repertoire and personality of the legend-tellers.

More than fifty years ago, Ortutay led the way by providing posterity with insightful profiles of tale, ballad, and drama performers. Furthermore, he highlighted the "dialectic tension" that defines legend-telling far ahead of the now graying "Young Turks" who discovered the "dynamic tension between the socially given and the emergent" (Ortutay 1972: 136–138, 226–232). However, in general, modern narrative performance analysts have noted the presence of an oral teller only as an analytical construct rather than as a real individual; this teller is extrapolated from the text's personal (stylistic) inferences and asides, or from the interjections of commentators/collectors. They do not identify tellers beyond their name (pseudonym), age, and occupation, and they depend more on their analytical findings than on what the person behind the text stands for.

It is the hallmark of the legend that it is subjective, introspective, personal, and that it persuades its teller to reveal his or her feelings. During the conversational process of legend-exchange, narrators exhibit their personalities and let their emotions flow freely. It is more regrettable, then, that tape-recorded sequences of legend telling have been subjected mostly to linguistic text analysis or descriptive evaluation of the content and context of conversation (see, for example, Bennett 1989b: 198–207; Ellis 1987: 40–48; Limón 1983), disregarding the spontaneous self-revelations of the tellers. Conversations during legend-trips, as we have learned from the very few recordings available to us, are particularly revealing because they not only identify active and creative bearers but also passive participants, whose choice to join, listen, and react is integral to the legend process.

It may have been believed earlier that only adolescents and young adults go on legend-trips as part of their coming-of-age ceremony (for an American college and university example, see Bronner 1990: 166–167); but we have since learned that adults also desire the experience. This is why they passionately visit sites of spiritual gratification. Adults join pilgrimages, visit and worship at places of miracles and saintly apparitions, and engage in vacation tours to experience haunted historic monuments at home and abroad. This "wonderlust" not only turns international and national tourism into a lucrative business, but it also strengthens the personal dedication of individuals to particular legend sites. Neighborhood haunted houses are visited as soon as people read or hear about them. Media information is followed up by people who join the crowd to hunt down Sasquatch in a nearby forest, or inspect the site where a flying saucer burned a circle in the wheat field, or make the pilgrimage to the jail where the pale face of an executed innocent man appears on the anniversary. It is an adult crowd that blockades State Road 912 at East Chicago every seven years to catch sight of the hitchhiking woman in white. It is mothers who load their vans with neighborhood kids to show them the local haunted cemetery.

Local agencies lead visits to "haunted happenings," such as the flier sent to me to "view over three dozen haunted sites in town, including three haunted houses, Malabar Farms, Quaker Meeting House, the Haunted Firehouse, The Homesick Haunt, Oak Hill Cottage, and The Drive-In Ghost." Another advertisement, for Waynesville, Ohio, offered an October 29–30, 1998, motor-coach excursion; $189.00 covered two lunches, one breakfast, and a murder mystery dinner with shopping, overnight lodging, and all costs, taxes, and gratuities. The annual bus tour to Chicago's haunted places on Halloween night has prospered since 1971 (MacDougall 1983: 146–147). On a larger scale, the tourist can visit the homes of Salem's famous witches at any time of the year. For folklorists, the waiting line at the modest local Halloween spook-house offers just as much opportunity to identify legend-tellers as the occasions when young people pay nocturnal visits to haunted places for supernatural replays of a tragedy.

Considering the context of such adult legend-trips, one should remember that, with each new season of coinciding UFO cult activities, these ritualistic reassertions of belief attract new crowds and transmit the legend to a new generation of believers. In 1997, according to news reports, the 50th anniversary of the alleged UFO crash in Roswell, New Mexico, drew a crowd of an estimated 50,000 to 60,000 persons to the community, which had a normal population of 48,000. Who remembered this anniversary? Who made this obscure 1947 midsummer local event into a national memorial ritual and legend — "the latest round of alien hysteria" (Frazier 1997: 5)? Evidently, it was the mass media publicizing the Roswell incident, which "didn't emerge until the late 1970s, nearly three decades after the supposed original event, when a new generation of pro-UFO writers began writing books on the subject" (Frazier 1997: 5). Participating in this epiphany of rational and irrational minds were eyewitnesses, their descendants, UFO fans and sectarians, the Air Force, the government, and representatives of the Committee for the Scientific Investigation of Claims of the Paranormal. The creative force of memory in the processual production of new versions of UFO legends can be ascertained by comparing old and new versions from participant believers and nonbelievers. "It's a glorious myth . . . that people have told and enhanced," said physicist Charles B. Moore (Spohn 1997: 7). "Even relatively small and local events evoked or involved heightened group responses," observed *Time* (December 22, 1997: 64). "A heave of national paranoia resurfaced on the 50th anniversary of the . . . flying saucer incident. So certain was an astounding number of Americans that the saucer did indeed crash in the desert near Roswell in 1947 that the Army Air Force command in Forth Worth, Texas, issued an explanation at the time of the anniversary that the vehicle in question had been a weather balloon" (64).

The career of the latest phase of the traditional "Heavenly Messengers" legend (Bullard 1977) is phenomenal. It has snowballed into an international alien-consciousness complex over the course of half a century, creating its own institutionalized system of belief, ritual, philosophy, and mythology informed by a set of stereotypical exempla. Today, an estimated one-third to one-half of adults believe in the existence of UFOs, along with another third who are uncertain about their existence and are therefore likely to be impacted by information from sources they perceive to be credible (Sparks 1998: 8). Two recent books give the folklorist a valuable demonstration of the generic clash of the two worldviews manifest in the Roswell legend. The 1994 book by Randle and Schmitt provides an impressive recounting of the Roswell Crash legend. More than forty years after the 1947 incident, the authors update the existing data over the period of 1989 to 1993, providing the folklorist with a rare treasury of folk recall. They interview primary and secondary witnesses and document the processes of textual variation that occur over time in dialectic opposition to underlying facts. The 1997 book by anthropologists Saler, Ziegler, and Moore emphasizes the historic transformation of the traditional legend into a modern myth that blends belief and technology.

There is only one question the folklorist would like to ask: How far is folk memory honoring tradition? From 1896 to 1897, thousands of people spotted cylindrical or cigar shaped "flying machines" in the skies above twenty U.S. states; but otherwise, spaceships and aliens were only sporadically reported until 1947. The Roswell crash was sighted late at night on July 4, 1947, ten days after licensed air rescue pilot Kenneth Arnold "saw" nine disc-shaped objects flying in loose formation. (This timetable was confused by reporter Sarah McClendon, who claimed that she had covered the story "in mid-June, [when] some odd debris was found on a ranch near Roswell, New Mexico," prior to Arnold's sighting.[5]) A headline news reporter coined the phrase "flying saucers" to describe these objects, and the year 1947 opened a new era for the "Heavenly Messengers" legend recast as a UFO legend. The legend was vigorously reshaped by its newly motivated carriers. This poses an interesting question: Why was the Roswell version, one among several other local crash stories, revitalized and updated? And why did it capture national attention to the extent of visitors making the "legend-trip" fifty years later?

Most Roswell tradition bearers do not seem to be aware of the earlier UFO crashes. They claim the uniqueness of their own story, that it alone is worthy of nationwide attention and celebration. Other localized episodes of the migratory UFO legend may appear unique for communities that have the good fortune, like Roswell, to find the right moment to boost their own story — putting themselves on the map (Langlois 1985: 17–33), obscuring the versions of others, and last but not least "mak[ing] some money from UFO-related tourism" (*Time*, June 23, 1997: 62).

In Texas in the spring of 1973, curiosity seekers and special investigators were exploring the nature of a pulsating, bleeding "cancerous blob composed of matter which mysteriously oozed from the ground" in the Dallas area. The account was later enriched by new elements, as the phenomenon was linked to a spaceship that was said to have crashed and burned in 1897 in Aurora, a town 75 miles northwest of Dallas. There was a prior legend that the dead aliens, arrivals from a remote planet, had been buried in the Aurora graveyard by the townspeople. These two separate legends, like all legends, had some feasible factual base: There was a spreading fungus that bled purplish-red material, and there was a cemetery grave that had long been reputed to be that of an extraterrestrial creature. Probably under the influence of space flights and science fiction — and in spite of the considerable distance between the two — *The Austin American-Statesman* (May 29, 1973) connected the two legends with each other. Speculation began that the aliens might have become a mysterious new organic life in the shape of the pulsating blob. Thus, the alien crash legend that had bloomed at the turn of the century and cooled off decades later was reactivated in a new form.

### Exploration of Potential Legend-Tellers

Finding out about the knowledge, awareness of, and attitude toward legends is a good task for an undergraduate and graduate educator to identify, and teach others to identify, legend-tellers in the general population. Roswell was an example of such identification. This section describes how Americans *learn* — and *select* — their legend repertoires and develop attitudes, preferences, etc., and thus become members of a "legend subculture."

After I designed a project for graduate students in my legend class in 1971, I first realized that telling a legend puts people in a special disposition. I repeated this project bi-annually, whenever I offered the course. In addition to my learning about the legend that lives in society, the project also taught me that thinking of legends makes people open their hearts to the fieldworker and confess about themselves in a way that they otherwise would never do.

Before anything else, the students had to answer a questionnaire concerning their knowledge of the legend as far as they could remember, retelling all of the texts they regarded as legends prior to their folklore education. Afterwards, as they learned more about the folkloristic study of legends, they were asked to subject their repertoire to scholarly analysis. Besides obvious mistakes ("legends" were misidentified as classical and tribal mythologies, children's bedtime stories, movie plots, science fiction, or literary horror stories), the chronology of learning diverse kinds of legends could be followed in this order:

1. (a) Local and personal hometown legends, family stories about haunts, premonitions about death in the family, magic healing;

(b) place name and other origin legends;

(c) religious miracle stories (mostly from Catholics, Mormons, and Jews);

(d) patriotic (schoolbook) heroic legends (about Lincoln, Washington, Paul Bunyan, and Indian chiefs).

2. Peer stock pieces: supernatural and horror stories from the regular repertoire of grade school and high-school children.

3. Currently popular legends spread in the media about UFO encounters, the Bermuda Triangle, Satanists, and Bigfoot.

4. Exotic tourist legends learned from booklets while vacationing domestically and abroad.

The average repertoire amounted to about ten items, but a few born legend-tellers went on and on, as one story brought up another; some projects ended up with twenty-five to thirty-five or more items. Confined to typing, devoted legend-tellers not only commented on their source's condition but volunteered to speak their own minds. If they were believers, they argued for the feasibility of the "incredible" story of an informant by giving an account of a similar personal experience; if they were nonbelievers, the commentary stressed the gullibility of people; and if they were undecided, a lengthy discussion of possibilities followed. More importantly, they felt persuaded to footnote the legends recalled from their own past with revealing discreet commentaries. Brief life-history episodes contained family conflicts, love affairs, desperate acts, suicide, cheating, magic curses, and frightful encounters in the twilight zone between dream and reality. The transitions from the stories of others to the student's own stories began with phrases like "As for myself . . . ," opening a new chapter of experiences that really took place, whether

Guidelines for legend self-survey

1. Your name, place of birth, age, ethnic and sociocultural background, and the places of your school education.

2. What legends do you know? Describe all stories (about witchcraft, ghosts, miracles, dream messages, strange encounters, precognitive experiences, telepathy, UFO sightings, ESP, horrible stories about monsters, killers, lunatics, etc.). Indicate which of the stories impressed you most. Answer all following questions as they pertain to each single legend you know.

3. Which were the sources of your information? Parents, friends, classmates, newspaper, radio, television, or other?

4. When did you hear the legend? At an early age, before you were six, at grade school, or later?

5. At what occasion (slumber party, scout camp, dormitory, bull session, visit to a "spooky" place, or at a specific event, like Halloween)?

6. How many people were present?

7. What kind of people were there (male, female, old, young, of what occupation)?

8. What effect had the story on you, and the others in your company (did it stimulate fear, depression, humor, confusion, indifference, negative feelings)?

9. Did your informant believe the account or did he/she state a belief in it?

10. Did you believe the story was true?

11. How about others?

12. Indicate if you ever repeated the legend heard from others or if there are some that you like to tell.

13. Did you ever visit scenes of legend events (haunted house, cemetery, or other)? Did you go alone or in a group? How many people of same and opposite sex?

14. If you went with others, how many were you? Did you walk or drive? Describe preliminary preparations for the trip, the scene, and group reaction.

15. What was expected to happen at the time of the visit?

16. Did you, or somebody else you know, experience the expected event (appearance of a spook, strange noises, lights, etc.)? Give details of the experience.

17. Apart from all this, did you ever have a supernatural or strange experience that you could not explain?

18. If so, try to describe it and explain it. Do you or did you ever talk about it with others? Do you generally like to or dislike to remember it and discuss it?

the account ended with irrational or rational explanations or finished without an answer.

"I can relate one strange experience of my own," wrote Barbara (1982), who ended her frightening family haunt story with this: "I don't know what it was, but I know what it wasn't. It wasn't a prowler."

Joseph (1974) recalled having precognitive experiences and added, "Yes, so I believe in ESP and premonitions. . . . Another experience I've had involves a presence. . . . While I don't believe in ghosts per se, I do believe that there are some sort of forces present which we do not understand."

Anthony (1974) said that he was "convinced and most willing to talk about my belief in telepathy and ESP. It's happened to me often enough that I am sure there is something to it." He recounted several telepathic contacts with people close to him, and he also admitted to having taken legend-trips. The experience he related is identical to those heard from college kids fifteen years his junior:

A friend and I decided one nice spring evening to go on his motorcycle to Cherry Isle. We specifically chose to go around midnight so that we might run into the ghost of the old brother (a monk, known in the community as the local revenant). This happened about four years ago, and though it was a kind of joke to us, I remember being somewhat excited and scared that we would actually see or experience something. We arrived at just about midnight. The air was charged with possibility. The situation was so scary that we decided not to stick around but leave before anything could happen. We saw nothing and later attributed the failure to the presence and noisiness of the motorcycle.

"The following experiences are very difficult to distance myself from," wrote Kathleen (1980). "I feel there is a great deal of risk involved in discussing these kinds of things with people you are not close to. I have no pat explanations for any of these incidents, and usually accept the unusual with a certain kind of awe." She gave three accounts of telepathy and one of a spirit lady in her bedroom "wearing a big green hoopskirt."

As I stood on the threshold she turned her head slowly, and smiled at me. Then she vanished. At the time I was not in the least bit afraid. . . . For years I would dream about her when I was undergoing a particularly stressful period in my life. I always felt she was a kind of protectress. . . .

She also told this story at a folklore student party where she met another student who had had a similar experience of her own.

Erika (1977) told a family legend about a pirate ancestor's curse that affected three generations, including her, shattering her teenage love affair with an older married man.

From the above we may conclude that legend-tellers are dreamers or visionaries, attracted to the extranormal and easily carried away from everyday realities by the most common and trivial impulses into a subjectively perceived realm of the unknown. The legend is in their own mind, and with it they are prepared to project into the experience.

## Legend-Teller Personalities

Legend-tellers do not exist in the same sense as tale tellers, epic singers, balladeers, dancers, or musicians. There is no stage for them and no social recognition for their recital skill. The legend is not considered an art of personal inspiration to be performed for the enjoyment of an attending audience, but rather it is a specific area of knowledge that the narrator can offer information about. It is not the story that counts but the message that it conveys. The message shapes the story in a way that can make sense and attract interest.

As early as 1937, Zender made some insightful comments concerning legend-tellers, who were regarded by villagers as curious characters, as "originals." Zender noted that people who cannot narrate but are believing listeners also play an important role in the narrating performance, as bearers of beliefs. Equally important are the doubters, who have never seen anything supernatural and would deny even natural facts. Only a few could tell 50 to 200 tales, but almost everyone knew a few legends, observed Zender. The legend-tellers are sensitive, extremely serious people who re-live their experience, making it realistic and persuasive to the listener while narrating (120–121). The legend-teller may be knowledgeable and experienced; he or she may be a recognized expert in certain areas and develop a large repertoire of legends, or may also gain respect for being involved in one single but overpowering legendary event that affected or completely transformed his or her life. The narrators keep repeating, and varying, their narratives throughout their lives. They may be accidental recipients of an experience, victims or beneficiaries of circumstances, active seekers, or hereditary bearers of the message.

It often happens that the legend-teller becomes initiated into one area of extranormal knowledge through one crucial experience and remains a lifelong specialist, establishing relationships with people of similar interest. Support groups arise among those who share out-of-body experiences, life-after-life travel, UFO abductions, or multiple-personality experiences. For example, Indianapolis real estate agent Ruth Loux became an advocate of PSI Inc. through her life-changing unique encounter: She met an elderly, illiterate Tennessee mountain woman who assumed the personality of an educated 16-year-old boy every time she ate a meal (McNeil 1971).

Because of the marketability of such phenomena, some individuals step into the limelight in starring roles on television programs and in the popular press. In fact, there is no limit to the possibilities. Some inspired legend-tellers — so-called psychics — may become authorities, police consultants in difficult criminal cases (such as the Atlanta child murders), and advisors to powerful politicians during times when they have to make important decisions. Nancy Reagan's long-term reliance on heavenly signs and the advice of psychic Joan Quigley was a scandalous disclosure (Seaman 1988); however, she was merely following the time-honored tradition of other first ladies and powerful personalities throughout history. From the oracles of Zeus at Dodona and Apollo at Delphi and the haruspices of Rome, to Czar Nicholas II, Stalin, and Hitler, clairvoyants have been influential confidantes of rulers. And prophets, seers, palmists, horoscope makers, herbalists, and exorcists occupy the ranks of health professionals in modern society; they open their offices and see patients just like psychoanalysts, podiatrists, orthopedic surgeons, gynecologists, and chiropractors. Some are more prominent members of the business world than others, and may appear as magazine, newspaper, or tabloid columnists and television advisors. They are most visible at the eve of a new year when they offer sensational predictions concerning the future of famous people and lucky or unlucky turns in the next year's economic, political, and social life. No one ever checks to see whether the prophecies come through.

Likewise, investigators of ghostly disturbances have risen to prominence. They call themselves ghost hunters, ghost busters, or exorcists, depending on which occult establishment they belong to, and how they interpret the role that has given them notoriety through their services to homeowners. Books, movies, public lectures, interviews in the media highlight their experiences, lending credibility to basic haunted house legends. Ed and Lorraine Warren, the ghost hunters of the famous demon-possessed Amityville house (Brittle 1980), and Hans Holzer, the occult scientist and ghost-tracer (Holzer 1973), are among the countless exorcists who have been successful in communicating traditional legends through the mass media.

A large contingent of individuals have had legend experiences. In fact, very few people can say that they have never encountered anything extranormal, and they will divulge at least one legend when cornered by a folklorist. It is quite common that average people are familiar with one particular legend; often they keep remembering and reflecting over something odd and mysterious that they came across under strange, illogical circumstances. The majority of those who have an extranormal experience remain private and withdrawn about it; they will keep the story within the family, and otherwise stay silent. They have no way to find compassionate friends to listen to their stories. This was the case with most of the people — men and women, old, middle-aged, and young — who responded to my several appeals and inquiries concerning legendary topics.

My correspondents gave me valuable information on spooky places, buried treasures, strange encounters, hidden crimes, and mysteries that occupied their minds. However, many of them felt that they had to live with the burden of "knowing something," of being a witness to a secret that others — family members, friends, or the whole community to which they belonged — would not like to hear disclosed. Some of the letter writers who sent me clippings, manuscripts, and cassette tapes with their personal statements would not disclose their names. They feared they would embarrass their families, endanger the lives of loved ones, or expose themselves to ridicule. Other articulate narrators were eccentric, socially alienated individuals who delighted in the opportunity to go public and reveal their secret without causing harm. Many were serious about their knowledge of the "facts," discovered by their personal involvement, and felt it important to inform the public about the dangers the legends suggested to them. Some characteristic confessions of Indiana informants will appear in chapter 5.

Despite the high probability that the majority of legend-bearers may remain invisible, the visible minority is strong and sufficiently organized to influence the social consciousness of modern society and to draw attention to its propositions. Proponents of legendary subjects and beliefs tend to establish their own institutions. Groups are formed that bring together tellers and audiences. In other words, practitioners and disciples together form a bond to communicate, circulate, and perpetuate the main message of their legend. Members of the group (charismatic leaders of clubs, sects, and cults; prophets, gurus, shamans, witches, spiritualists, psychics, and their followers; and activists and representatives) establish the appropriate social context and networks, and stabilize the text while they also multiply it by continued retellings. Together they help it to achieve spectacular proliferation and variation. Occult institutions infiltrate our microcosmos and educate the general public; their terms and concepts become commonplace even among the least interested.

The legend-tellers are telling the truth. They do not confabulate and are careful not to deviate from the facts they know. They give all supporting information they can find to satisfy their audience's curiosity. They depend on the support of audience members who are also familiar with the case and who are ready to assist with additional information. Because the narrative is situated in the real world, in human time, and is about events involving common people — and because it could happen to anyone — it has practical value in warning people about the dangers of human life.

Recognized traditional storytellers who are conscious of their craft are careful to distinguish legends from tales. The legends they tell appear marginal in their repertoire, as first-hand learned true events that may be part of their life histories. They know that their audience appreciates their skill at inventing fantastic tales, but at the same time that audience would not tolerate artistic embroidery applied to true stories. It is one thing to tell a märchen and to enjoy the liberty of confabulating, and another thing to tell a legend and re-produce reality. Few of the village storytellers I knew personally told legends when people were gathered to hear their märchen.

The legend-tellers do not make the story; the story makes them who they are, and that is why these narrators are appreciated by their communities. But this may not be so with the growing guild of urban storytellers. The legends urban narrators tell are often randomly selected pieces from storybooks or from miscellaneous oral sources. When they are not a part of the culture in which the legend originated, tellers have no personal commitment to its tradi-tion and feel at liberty to re-create the item for public (stage) performance or publication. Such entertainers are guided by their own tastes, selecting from traditional and literary sources, usually recasting legends into a romantic fairy-tale format or into shockers to scare their listeners. They use clothing, objects, sound, and light effects to frame their texts.

But whether the legend-teller is dedicated and self-consciously public or hidden and private is not important. Anyone may tell a legend, without partic-ular personal interest or involvement, by simply repeating something just heard. In fact, there is hardly anyone who has never been touched by the air of the legend and felt the compulsion to tell someone about it. The "numi-nous" touch (Otto 1958), the "sublogical" disposition (Marót 1940), the *Ergriffenheit* or emotionally touched (Burkhardt 1951; Jung 1959), the physio-logical condition affecting consciousness between sleep and wakefulness (Huf-ford 1982a; Laistner 1879), or simple "déjà vu" (Virtanen 1990) are very com-mon factors that may explain the creativity of legend-tellers, even if they are only occasional translators of a single experience into a legend. Real legend-tellers, however, are believers in that they are actively attracted to the uncanny, outrageous, mystic, absurd, anomalous phenomena that erupt unexpectedly from normal everyday situations. These events tell them forcefully that things in this world may not be as they had expected. To be a believer does not mean blind belief in any extranormal statements, but rather it is a general fascina-tion with such topics and a readiness to partake in the discussion of believ-ability.

Janet Callahan, a remarkable young woman with a large repertoire of pre-cognitive experiences, told me how she was initiated into what she called "per-ception,"[6] and how she reacted to her visions. This extrasensory ability was the topic of her legends. Born and raised in a Midwestern farming community, she inherited the standard belief in the supernatural. Her part-Indian grandmother was a healer and a bloodstopper, and her mother had been "born with a veil" and was extremely sensitive to premonitions. Janet's first experience occurred at age 14 when a red light streamed toward her in the backyard without a sound. Then shortly afterward, she saw a star approaching and disappearing. Four years later, a cigar-shaped UFO flew above her while she drove home from work. Her fourth encounter with the unknown came while she was at home in bed with her two younger sisters. She was reading a book about the supernatural when the light began to flicker, and little toys fell off the shelf. She did not think much about it because her mother used to tell her about "strange things," so she believed that it was nothing extraordinary:

> At a young age, you believe in ghosts and stuff — it's exciting, you laugh, joke about it with your friends. I thought, perceptions, visions are fun, I was ambitious. I wanted to become famous as a schoolgirl. Being different from others.

Her fifth supernatural experience occurred when she gave birth to her first child: Jesus appeared to tell her that the baby had a birth defect and would go to heaven, and everything would be okay. Later on, she was exposed to both negative and positive encounters. She was haunted and tormented by evil spirits and revenants (to be discussed in more detail in chapter 5), while she also enjoyed developing her skill of precognition. "When things began to happen to me I felt, this is a gift from God. I can help by knowing what's gonna happen." Watching television game shows, she knew the answers before anybody else; at the ballgame she stopped the rival team from winning. She could mentally force a slow car to get out of her way, while her kids cheered: "Wow Mom, that's neat, you can do this. I can't believe it. Man, that's neat!"

She told herself, "Keep tryin' Jan, keep tryin'. Keep working these powers, sooner you get these powers perfected, the sooner you will be able to save someone from dying . . . a real purpose in my life . . . this is it, this is really *it*, God's given me the special gift . . . I was just overwhelmed and excited inside." But when she envisioned disasters, she found that she could not prevent them from happening and this devastated her. Like many other inspired legend-tellers, Janet struggled between what her urban-industrial environment had taught her was normal and rational, and what she perceived based on her family heritage. Torn between certainty and doubt, she feared for her own sanity. She pondered the likelihood of the accounts she heard during her daily activities or what she experienced personally in a vision or a dream; she has formulated an opinion ready for expression when the occasion arises. She also has found the burden of foreknowledge unbearable and has asked for help, in case her sightings were being caused by mental illness. But when she found no support from her Methodist pastor or her well-educated husband, a math teacher and later an insurance executive, she became desperate.

After one of her haunting encounters, she tried to reason with her husband, but he wasn't ready to listen:

"Oh, Jan, are we goin' to start this crap again? For heaven's sake, when are you going to stop?" And I said, "I am not imagining it, Bill, it was there." He said, "You're crazy, Jan, absolutely crazy, I don't want to hear it anymore." "So I tried to put it behind me, tried to forget it. Then came this one, my most chilling experience."

### A Florida Vacation

And that was then, shortly after that, we all, my husband and I, a psychologist friend that I had in Indianapolis, a graduate of IU, William King, Dr. King and his wife, we all took a trip to Florida, and had a nice vacation, a lovely, lovely time. With fishing, and boating, no problem, never had anything. Until we were going back. And we took the road back, and I was driving to St. Petersburg, and got on the St. Petersburg bridge, and the . . . on the top of the bridge . . . I froze. And I grabbed the steering wheel, and I started screaming. And across Bill, and Dr. King, and his wife were all terrified because we were on the top of this tall bridge and I am screaming, and I am driving! And they were . . . "What's wrong? *What's wrong?!*" And I finally got down to the end of the bridge, and I pulled the car over, and I was gripping at the steering wheel real tight, it was just like in a state . . . I couldn't . . . I was like in a trance . . . because I knew what was goin' on around me but couldn't do anything but scream. I was just kinda, . . . I was almost frozen. And I stopped. And I turned around to Dr. King and I said, "I wouldn't want to be on this bridge in a storm." And he said, "What?" And I said, "I'm falling off this bridge. I'm dying. I am falling off this bridge." And he said, "*Jan! OK!* What's wrong with you?!" And I swept to the side and I said, "Haaaah, I don't know. I just thought that I've seen my car falling off this bridge, and I was falling in the water, and I was goin' to die. And it was rain, and storm . . ." And he said, "Are you OK?" And I said, "Yeah." But I am shaking, my hands were shaking, my body was shaking. And my husband was saying, "I'm going to drive. Oh God, you're crazy." And he looked at me and I said, "I'm sorry. I don't know what happened, I am sorry." And everybody was goin' you know, "that's all right, don't worry" . . . And we got in the car and drove home, you know.

Ah, well, two weeks to the day, Dr. King called me from Indianapolis, and he said, "Jan, have you seen the paper?" And I said, "No, why?" And he says, "Have you got it?" And I said, "Yes." And he said, "Get the paper *now*." And I got the paper and right on the top of the St. Petersburg bridge, where I had screamed that I was falling off, it had been crushed by a freak, oh, by what they call a barge, that hit the bridge. And something, that sixty, eighty people, cars and all, have gone off that bridge where I had screamed into the water and drowned and died. And it was in the worst of the storm. And he said in the phone to me, he said, "I didn't know what to think. Oh, Jan, this is unreal. Still, don't know what to think, I just know what happened to you was a prediction of the future." And he said, "I wanted you to know that I understand." And I hung up, and the most extraordinary depression came over me. I cried, I cried, I cried, and

I cried and cried. I can't handle this, I can't handle this. People are dying, why could I not save those people, what's wrong with me *God*, why couldn't I stop them? I knew what's gonna happen, but nobody listened. I mean, what else can I do? And my depression got very bad.

It got to the point where I thought that I'm really going to die. The pressure, the weight on my chest, the depression was spreading more rapidly. . . . I said to my husband . . . to please, help me. I said, "You got to help me, I'm losing my mind. I can't handle it anymore, I don't know what to do, I'm losing my mind." And he said, "Jan, you're right, you're losing your mind . . . you are the most craziest person I met in my life." I said, "Bill, I'm not crazy, you heard the crashings, you witnessed the things that happened. . . ." He said, "Yes, you're a witch, you're crazy, you're nuts . . . you need psychological help." (Recorded 1987, from a longer narrative; Dégh 1996)

If legend-tellers can step out of isolation and find allies, they usually appear as undecided seekers, curious about proof and disproof. Feeling the urge to tell the story, they submit their position to debate. The experience is easy to view as not unique and not "unheard of." Nowadays everybody who reads the newspaper or watches television is educated in the occult and knows its terminology well enough to qualify and place a vision into the context of "scientific" terminology, different from the traditional. When incidents related to the occult occur, individuals can feel comfort in experiencing something that others did and talked about. What they saw was not a spook but an astral body, an apparition, an earthbound spirit, or a poltergeist; it was not a fireball or a spooklight, but a space alien or a UFO. And if he could not catch his breath at night, he understood that he was possessed by an earthbound spirit, not plagued by a nightmare or an old hag (Hufford 1982a).

Institutions form around legendary messages and bring together kindred souls to give them comfort in association, raising their self-awareness and dignity. At weekend psi encounters, regional conventions, solstice celebrations, and spiritualist retreats, one may meet representatives of diverse groups and take stock of the great diversity of legend-tellers united by the common context of belief. Belief in *what* is not necessarily defined. The groups are represented by separate booths at these convention grounds, where one can chat with visitors, collect pamphlets, and meet initiates. It is an interesting crowd: professionals, amateurs, members, committed supporters, novices, and unaffiliated accidental guests who are mildly curious.

At a 1987 PSI meeting I talked with three people at the local cafeteria.[7] Iris, Jerry, and Don each belonged to a different legend conduit, although they had coffee together and listened to each other's stories with interest. All three spoke with confidence, adding their interpretation to assure me that they were not amateurs. The language was professional, borrowed from readings in parapsychology and other esoteric fields. But they did not regard their gift or

# PSYCHIC FAIR

**The 2nd Annual Midwest Festival of Psychic Arts**
**presented by**

# PSI

**INC.**

**Saturday and Sunday**
**October 14-15, 1972**
**10 am to 10 pm**

**Athenaeum Turners Club**
**401 East Michigan Street**
**Indianapolis**

## REPEAT
## Finder, Keeper

**$50**— Use your ESP! Somewhere within the mile square area of Indianapolis, **$50** has been "hidden" in an accessible location. Use your ESP to determine its location and find it. Joe Pickett, WFBM personality, hid the **$50.**

**ADMISSION**

| Cash Sales | Members Only |
| --- | --- |
| $4.00 — One Day | $3.00 — One Day |
| $7.00 — Two Days | $5.00 — Two Days |

(Admission includes featured speaker and entry to all booths for personal demonstration of the various arts and afternoon lectures.)

2ND ANNUAL MIDWEST PSYCHIC FESTIVAL

PSI, Inc. Conference Pamphlet

knowledge as a profession; they viewed those in the occult business critically, because "they package their gift to fool others and make a profit out of it."

Iris M., 47, of Indianapolis, claims she has a well-developed second-sight. She was born that way. She wears sunglasses because she does not look at people but into their souls, and that scares them. When she was four years old, she knew what was inside the Christmas packages and what was going on. She had a vision when her best friend was in danger.

Machinist Jerry T., 62, of Connersville, Indiana, believes in UFOs:

*Jerry:* Most unusual thing I ever seen, was something that took place about four years ago. This thing I saw was just before dark, one summer evening, and where I live, is about a quarter of a mile from where my dad lives. And just before dark, the sun just went down and I went to my dad's house. And he was gone but my brother was there. And he was doing something with the tractor. And I just stood there in front of the house. We talked a little while. And my two sons came up on their bicycles. And we fooled around a little while, then we started to walk on home, which is quite a mile away. As we got to the house, there is a hayfield, and there was a fence on each side. The field was not perfectly leveled, kinda sloping. And at that time of the day it's usually very quiet, you know, no wind blowing at all. And it was beginning to get dark. We walked over this field. There was a little mist of smoke, six inches in diameter across the field. Now, something had to pass over the field and we never did know what it was. In other words, we missed seeing something by possibly a minute. If we had come down, got away from the house a minute sooner, we would of seen what made that smoke. It looked like exhaust. . . . You ever seen a small motorcycle when a boy takes off on it and leaves a trail of smoke behind it? That's what it looked like. Except it . . . on one side of the field, it was going perfectly horizontal, on one end of the field it is, some telephone wires, it was about ten feet over the telephone wires. But on the other end of the field was high it was down within five feet on the ground. And the trail of smoke went over, over the fence, and right between a couple of trees. Now of course, we know . . .

*Linda:* Did it smell?

*Jerry:* Yeah, it had a smell like castor oil. Do you know how castor oil smells like? We've been to some car races, I suppose smells like castor oil. That's what it smells like. We did not hear any noise at all. All was a trail and the smoke, possibly exhaust and we saw that. I mean we smelled the odor of castor oil. That's all. In other words . . .

*Linda:* What did you say to each other when you saw it?

*Jerry:* We was . . . we was discussing this trail of smoke over there, we walked over in the field where it was and by the time we walked over, the smoke started to spread out. And we walked over these trees where this thing went under it, had to be pretty small however large it was because these trees were pretty close. Went over to see it, maybe if it was a UFO, maybe some of the trees would have been burned, you know, passing through the land. We did not find any trace.

*Linda:* At that time you knew already there are UFOs?

*Jerry:* Oh yeah, yeah, a lot of other people had been seeing them. Like I said, all we saw is that smoke before dark. If the wind had blown we probably would not have seen it. I thought there must be something to it. I knew it could not be a motorcycle thing in the air. It couldn't be that. No other explanation, something had to make the smoke, something had to make the smell. We didn't know what it was. I was very disappointed. I would certainly like to see what that was.

*Linda:* Do you believe in other unexplainable things?

*Jerry:* Yeah, I'm not too much interested in ghost stories and mediums and things like that but there's many other things. ESP I'm very much interested in.

*Linda:* Did you have an experience?

*Jerry:* Yes, one, fourteen years ago . . . [another story followed]

Don W., 51, of Connersville, Indiana, the third person in the group, specializes in stories of ghosts, or "apparitions" as he calls them. His account broadens our view of the legend complex related to the ritual visit of haunted bridges by young adults. Don became interested in the ghost stories told (and experienced) by couples parked under the bridge and decided to investigate the truth behind them. Don, a plumber by profession, said, "I have this as a hobby. I am naturally curious and try to understand things. That's why I am interested in an apparition of someone. I find out who lived there, and a lot of things about life, see? I came into this hobby because these objects project light beams in the area. Lit up the whole cornfield and barn and everything . . . so I began to talk to people."

He talked to ten people who saw the ghosts, and he read newspapers about drownings that happened thirty-three years ago, seeking to identify the earthbound spirits and the connection between them. Finally, he went to see for himself.

I live near this place and I have lot of time to track it down, to find out what the truth is. It's Dublin, Indiana, on Route 44, a bridge, a very spooky place. . . . Three different couples parked at this really spooky looking place, the Screaming Bridge they call. And then, this thing came around the headlights of the car, ran across the road, and what they saw was a skirt and a blouse and a white glow, looked like hair or scarf. . . . One boy did not get to look because his girlfriend got scared and hollered, and he stepped on the gas and left. . . . I still did not believe in ghosts then really, you know, I had to see this myself. We went down there, me and my nephew one night, and we parked there under the bridge. And I seen . . . first . . . it was such a moonlit night. It was bad night to watch for ghosts because it washed out lots of the colors. . . . About a half-hour, hour later, I said to my nephew, "Jack, there's someone on the bridge." There was a figure there. Took a few steps, then, hurried off the bridge in front of us. She had a skirt and a blouse on.

After talking to local people, Don found out who the restless revenant in skirt and blouse was: a girl named Jeanie who had drowned herself after her domineering sister had "chased off her boyfriend." The second one he learned about, "Jeanie's ghost," was the apparition of a little girl who saw an angel that predicted she would die as a child. The third "earthbound spirit" was a mother who had drowned "because she lost her little girl in that car wreck at the roadside."

Don ended our conversation saying, "this is not folklore; this is fact as many can testify. I have good news for you. If Jeanie's ghost is there, I know who she is, then we all, like that, we all become spirits." Not many legend-tellers make it as clear as Don does, that ghost stories are optimistic, promising eternal life to mortals. Apparently, Don wants to be prepared for life after life. "Earthbound" spirits are seen by psychics, said Don:

Don: I am as psychic as a fencepost. . . . One lady came to my house with a problem — someone is looking from across when she is home alone at night. I found out, her husband is very jealous and she is psychic, so she picks up his thought when he is away. Once he touched her on the neck; that's when she went into hysterics. I investigated many things ever since.
Linda: How do you investigate?
Don: I take the tape recorder, talk to many people, asking a lot of questions.
Linda: Why do you do that?
Don: Look, I am fifty-one, I am not goin' to be here for long. I want to know the truth. Things that I can find out myself, not what I read in some book. That's why I've done this. I did not believe in haunts, but it fits right down there. I found out about an old haunted dresser that cracks and pops when anybody dies in that family since 1910. I believe the witness, an elderly lady that would not go tell me all this story for anything. . . . Did you read about poltergeists? You should talk to the lady who moved to seven homes, was haunted for fourteen years. She lives in Hamilton, Ohio. 'Course I can't give her address, I don't think she would be in the mood to talk to you.
. . . Some go to religion. I was in church for seventeen years. I don't think that's wrong either but I go a little further than that. . . . They stress what they want to stress, the Bible, the New Testament, but I want to know where I'm goin'.
Linda: Do you believe in UFOs?
Don: I didn't see UFOs but my wife and daughter did, and they would not lie to me. But I saw more, I was rewarded by seeing apparitions we will all be. . . .

These excerpts of a much longer conversation show three types of nonprofessional legend-tellers who are actively seeking answers to their particular experiences by going to occult meetings and by investigating stories almost as a folklorist would. They contextualize their legends with as much precision as any traditional legend-teller would. They are proponents, participants in the legend conduit in search of more understanding about the spirit world.

Once I spent a Sunday afternoon with an "occult-seeking" private circle. As I was told, the house on the west side of Indianapolis where the Psychic Holiday was held had recently been exorcised. With heated zeal, members narrated supernatural experiences. At the end, listening to many legends, beliefs, wisdoms, and philosophies, I asked the man who seemed to be the leader, "Could you please tell me what it is you believe in?" "In everything," was his answer. "You name it, and we believe it." This honest statement (which I heard repeated again and again) should caution us that there are possibly fewer "things in heaven and earth than are dreamt of" in the philosophy of a latter-day Horatio. It seems more people's minds are *omni-credens* than we had imagined. Who opts for which legend-establishment, who wanders from one to another, and who keeps allegiance to several can be discerned from personal life history and psychological personality analysis. The notion of belief is the most crucial factor. As I have stated before this, however, that does not necessarily mean that the believer believes unselectively in everything with the same intensity. The person who knows and tells legends may not believe in all of them, but may express diverse degrees of belief, half-belief, or non-belief in the stories. The legend believer may believe in general that "such things are likely to happen" while having doubt when listening to a particular case. The same legend would be true for one proponent, and untrue for another.

This composite picture of the legend-teller was drafted from direct and indirect statements and commentaries of tellers and listeners engaged in actual performances. The personality dedicated to legend is actively present in all layers of modern society, whether classified according to age, sex, kin, social, occupational, or recreational groups. This personality makes the choice to listen to and pass on legends, seeking out the appropriate conduit of people of the same mind. Although there is a distinctive repertoire carried by the conduits of diverse groups within the social networks, these repertoires are closely related and interdependent. With the aid of the mass media, the legends spread as fast as news is aired, crossing all boundaries through alternating channels of communication; the stories mix and merge as the innumerable nameless and unidentifiable legend-tellers produce more and more variants with increasing speed.

We cannot speak about legend as an oral folklore genre anymore because co-existent vehicles of communication together shape it. For example, new variants of the classic ghost legend "The Vanishing Hitchhiker" are influenced by versions that were told orally, printed as a daily paper's news item or a magazine short story, examined as a parapsychological report in a popular science publication, or featured as a headline and article in a tabloid. Preadolescent girls might listen to a form of the story as a ballad on a commercial CD, or make drawings of it as a school assignment for a Halloween exhibit, or may call up the spirit from the bathroom mirror in a séance game, or make ritual visits to her grave. The multimedia existence of this classic American legend was already recognized by Jansen:

> One would not want to enter the wild goose chase of tracing the origin and ramifications of legends anymore, but the ubiquitous existence and variability of this particular ghost story would deserve in-depth functional study. Who could trace the migrations and transformations of the Vanishing Hitchhiker through a cinema version, a television show, a country western song, several journalistic articles, and dozens of straight-faced "news" accounts, particularly when each "nontraditional" appearance may be sandwiched into the midst of authentic orally performed "traditional" appearances? (1977: xii)

Since the early forties, "The Vanishing Hitchhiker" legend has remained in the focus of American folklorists; as it spread throughout the continent, it retained its solid core, even while exhibiting a remarkable flexibility in narrative development (Brunvand 1981: 24–40). As it was the only ghost story recognized as an "urban legend" by the Sheffield seminarians, a proposal was presented at their 1988 seminar to conduct systematic research of its versions by handing out written questionnaires (see Hobbs and Cornwell 1990). The proposal seemed reasonable because the legend exhibited great popularity, due in part to the mass media which had augmented its dissemination.

Since the questionnaire appeared, several old versions have come back to life, while new ones and even fresh redactions have turned up. For example, the Swiss and German press reported and sensationalized the wavelike appearance of this so-called "road ghost legend" in specific formulations related to highways of Southwest Germany and the Swiss Alps around 1975 and then again in 1981 and 1984. This regional redaction may or may not be traced to episodes of the American prototypes. Heim appealed to the academic readership to pay attention to mysterious folk narratives about road ghosts in modern times: "Have you heard of such reports? Please then, don't miss telling us about them, noting the time and place of the apparition if possible" (Heim 1981: 5). The Sheffielders, on the other hand, continued their inquiry without taking note of the coincidence of the European road ghost's manifestations. As of yet, the sociological questionnaire approach has not really answered folkloristic questions concerning the reformulation and application of ideas of the detached offshoots of this flexible legend type.

## Legend-Telling Groups and Their Repertoires

### Children

Legend ingredients belong to the earliest experiences of childhood. Building on the images of fear experienced during the course of normal mental development, adults gradually introduce children to a culture of fear, a climate in which fragments of meanings coalesce into coherent stories like pieces in a jigsaw puzzle. Once again one cannot help remembering Anderson's hypothesis of self-correction, which posits that divergent versions of stories stabilize and form together one standard story, the *Normalform* around which variants oscillate (Anderson 1923). The repertoire of children from ages 2 to 14 is relatively rich in images and characters, yet modest in the number of well-structured, distinctive stories. These, however, are commonly known and actively circulated within peer groups. It would be difficult to separate age groups into preschool children, grade-school children, and preadolescents of both sexes according to their legend repertoires, because they differ only in nuances. In fact, most of the materials they circulate are rudiments of familiar materials that most probably originated from older siblings, parents, and other influential adults, as well as the mass media. The themes are common to all generations, and distinctions can be made only on the basis of narrational competence improving by age.

With or without the consent of adults, the consumption and reproduction of legends begins early and develops consistently as children's ability to formulate meaningful, structured narratives improves (Applebee 1978: 76). The youngest children relate components of legends by identifying threatening figures and violent acts to be elaborated on at a later age. Three-year-old Kathy met Dracula in the basement and also saw witches down there; they looked like those she had seen on television. Beth, three-and-a-half years old, talks to a witch in her bedroom every night. In a private nursery, all thirty-two children interviewed knew about ghosts and a big snake in the lake. Seven-year-old Mark made a remarkably long list of the fearsome characters he knew, in this order: witch, wizard, monster, vampire, ghost, cannibal, giant, magician, empire,[8] skeleton, mummy, cannibal, goblin, demon, ghoul, gorilla.[9]

This primitive foundation of concepts is implemented later and shaped into more complete stories. Five-year-olds can already tell simple but coherent scary or spooky stories that they have learned and traded for others on the playground, at the daycare center, at the nursery, at home, or in the neighborhood.

As psychologists tell us, the experience of fear is part of human existence (Bettelheim 1976; Riemann 1984). Several branches of analytical psychology have made it their professional task to help children master their evolving fears in the course of their mental development, and to protect them from neuroses. But these professionals were mostly concerned with the usefulness of storybook fairytales, not with legends and their function of feeding a predilection for fear, which is so prominent in American urban society. By advising parents of the proper dosage of fear to administer through fantasy tales, the professionals meant to ensure proper channeling of fantastic images and to secure a healthy shock-free coming of age, preparing a child for the real

231

threats of life. Generations of scientists and educators debated the harmful and helpful (cathartic) effects of gruesome fairytales from the collection of the Grimm brothers, Hans Christian Andersen, or Andrew Lang on children of the urban middle class. The dialogue continues without consensus or a clear-cut resolution. It is up to the discretion of the parent when, if at all, to tell the story of "Hansel and Gretel" or "Little Red Riding Hood."

In view of all these efforts to secure the mental welfare of children, it seems ironic that no child psychologist or educator has considered the more direct menace contained in legends. They have never questioned the wholesomeness of the strategy adults have developed to scare children by systematically administering to them legends and legend ingredients in the guise of real threats to their safety. It is mostly, if not exclusively, mass communication specialists who have expressed concern for the impact of aggression, violence, horror, and gore on children through stories communicated by books, television, cartoons, comics, movies, and mass merchandise. Faint voices have been sounded from time to time in protest of the mass media and marketed aggression and horror addressed to the audience of children. In 1961, Pickard called for a serious study of the horror in stories that educators and parents tell children:

> Do children need horror in stories? If so, how much and how soon? It is
> said that they will meet horror later in life and so had better be schooled to
> it. That the majority of them enjoy some horror is obvious to anyone famil-
> iar with children. But this does not prove that it is an essential factor in
> their stories; they might merely have become conditioned to expect it be-
> cause we have never told them good stories without horror; or we might be
> giving them horror because we ourselves need it. (1962: 1)

Pickard also addressed the argument that children should be conditioned to horrors: "There is no question of introducing them to horrors, because the horrors already known to them are far in excess of anything we experience, as adults" (1962: 6). The natural aggression of children need not be encouraged, but rather discouraged by early education. In his monograph *Children's Stories*, Ames noted that "violence is by far the outstanding theme . . . the majority of children at every age [are] telling such stories" (1966: 342).

Legman blamed mass media for turning children into monsters. He argued that American children born since 1930 cannot read; comic books, picture magazines, and radio and movie shows supply their education with "massive doses of sadism and violence" (Legman 1949: 27). In his criticism he targeted comics, charging that their merchants claim that "children need these aggressive outlets in fantasy against parents, teachers, policemen, and total social environment[; thus] comic books have succeeded in giving every American child a complete course in paranoid megalomania" (1949: 33). Legman spells why parents do not object:

> American parents see nothing wrong with the fictional violence of comic-books because they are themselves addicted to precisely the same violence in reality, from the daily accident or atrocity smeared over the front page of their breakfast newspaper to the nightly prize-fight or murder-play in movies, radio, and television coast-to-coast. . . . Violence in America is a business — big business — and everybody is in it, either as peddler or customer. (1949: 50)

Legman's criticism of American-style comics was followed by the strong condemnation of British legislators in 1955, when on February 22 the House of Commons put the Children and Young Persons (Harmful Publications) Bill on its agenda. Lieutenant-Colonel H. M. Hyde (Belfast North) argued that "these publications were first introduced to the country by American troops during the last war and the majority have originated in the United States of America. Today, about 100,000 copies of these objectionable magazines are printed each month in America, depicting every form of sadism, violence, horror and crime" (see *Process* 1955a: 1142). Somerville Hastings (Barking) supported the Bill, feeling that particularly delinquent children love comics because they are easy to understand without the trouble of reading — "they appeal to their primitive emotions of hate, revenge, and killing" (1955a: 1161–1162). And the objections continued: "We should do all that we can to prevent horror comics reaching children. I agree with the Bill for three reasons. First, I am convinced that hero worship and imitation are tremendous factors in children" (1162), and "another objection to these horror comics is that they tend to blunt the finer feelings. They show that there is much brutality even when good overcomes evil." And finally, "I suggest that there is a third objection, which I do not think has been sufficiently stressed in the debate tonight. That is that these horror comics are terribly frightening to children" (1163). Nevertheless, the comics business has continued to blossom and expand.

Today, adults (parents and educators) are the primary sources of the legend-equipment that children come to possess. Focusing on the calendar ritual of Halloween, American children, like no other children in the world, are given massive doses of fearful experience as "adventure," fun, and entertainment at an age when they are not yet able to distinguish nightmare from reality. During the past twenty years, the Halloween novelties market has multiplied and developed thematically. As a *Time* article in 1978 noted, "for the child who does not get enough blood and ghoul from TV or movies, new Monster Make-Up and Horror-Make-Up kits provide the wherewithal for 58 basic variations of Lon Chaney" (December 28, 1978). We have not heeded the warning of Dr. Spock, who said that "the child is scared enough of his own mental creation, they should be provided with an atmosphere of calm, including no scary stories or films" (quoted in Stearns and Hoggerty 1991: 85). After all, this is a "tradition" that was carried from generation to generation: The terrorizers enjoy causing terror and the terrorized strike back at their own children twenty years later.

Society takes for granted that horror is fun. No one asks why decomposed bodies, mutilation, pools of blood, graveyards, executioners, crazy murderers, skeletons, and ghosts are enjoyable entertainers. And parents and scholars assume that children want a good scare, without ever questioning the consequences it may have on the shaping of adult character. Brunvand mentions horror as an element of urban legends, saying simply that "people of all ages love a good scare" (Brunvand 1981: 46). Twitchell notes that people, unlike animals, are drawn to re-create their fears, and are attracted to the macabre, the misshapen, the barbarous, and the deformed (Twitchell 1985: 4; for examples see Dégh 1986: 141–152). We cannot deny that these observations seem correct; nevertheless, they should not be accepted without a thorough examination and a penetrating analysis of concrete cases: a future task for the folklorist.

The result of early exposure to horror can be illustrated in the story 9-year-old Christopher wrote for a school composition assignment:

### Little Boy in an Old Church

There was a little boy that was going to the store when he past a old church and a graveyard next to it. When he came back he loved to go in the old church he rang the door bell. But the door opened itself when he went in. Do you know what was inside?! Well, back to the story. He saw a Priest. He was surrounded by skeletons. And the Priest had a bloody knife in his hand and bugs flying around his face and his eyes were poked out. Then he came closer. But then the boy ran out of the church. He tripped over a coffin and Dracula. He was the king of all monster Priests. And the Priest he saw stabbed him. (1974)

Scaring small children with horror stories is a modern routine, but no modern novelty. Since classical times, mothers, grandmothers, maidservants, and nurses have entertained children under their care with chilling stories of fear (Bolte and Polívka 1963, vol. 4: 41–94). Inciting fear in children by telling legends has been intended traditionally as a pleasurable experience that excites them and stimulates their fantasy. Reginald Scot in his *Discoverie of Witchcraft* (1584) lists the beasts, monsters, demons, and spirits with whom "in our childhood our mother's maids have so terrified us . . . that we were afraid of our owne shadows." In his letter of 1759 to his childhood nurse,

G. W. Rabener recalls with delight the cannibalistic "Mum Mum" story that made him restless and scared in the darkened room: "I sat on your lap and put my trembling arms fearful around your neck" (in Bolte and Polívka, 1963). The didactic archetypal legend about experiencing and overcoming fear — classified as a folktale in the Grimm collection, "The Youth Who Wanted to Learn What Fear Is" (AT 326) — has been varied in multiple ways and has become the best-known and most viable and variable among the ghost stories of the modern Western world. The modern legend version ends either tragically or with a pretended jocular twist that conceals its real gruesome meaning. Clements presents a very good illustration of the modern American legend-version of the Grimm-treated folktale, appearing as an account of a visitation to a haunted house for an initiation ritual, side by side with a travesty of the same story (Clements 1969b).

Scary stories traditionally are used by adults not only to entertain but also to discipline, control, and protect children from real and supernatural dangers. Witches, devils, vampires, ghosts, anomalous humanoid beasts, and real threats such as strangers, lunatics, and criminals are central agents in these scripts that exploit early childhood fantasies of infanticide as a defense mechanism (Bloch 1978). "Figures of fear" that "embody man's fears seem to be present in every culture," and "the 'bogeyman' character can take any culture-specific shape" (Widdowson 1971: 99–115) — even neutrality or friendliness, like the cute cartoon character Casper the Friendly Ghost. But children's familiarization with the idea of a ghost residing in the family home — complete with sights and sounds such as slamming doors, faucets and appliances turning on and off, footsteps running up the staircase, flickering lights, and misplaced objects — is hardly educational. The imagination of an inquisitive child is not enhanced, but the fear of the neurotic might be worsened.

In modern American society, exposure to the legend world is enculturation. Playfully, parents and teachers introduce children to the concepts, objects, and subjects of the uncanny in diverse ways. In the form of postcards, comics, coloring books, games, toys, television cartoons, and horror movies, children become acquainted with the natural and supernatural agents and symbols of evil. They are taken to commercial haunted houses, to "real" haunted cemeteries, and to evenings of ghost story tellings on Halloween or other occasions. Sometimes, adults tell or read them ghost stories, particularly on camping trips.[10] Children's libraries offer a large selection of ghost story books for the young readers.[11] Children begin with being scared by monsters, and end up by being themselves transformed into monsters when parents dress them up in spooky costumes and take them trick-or-treating, or to the shopping mall for a parade and costume contest. Finally, their education is tested by school assignments to compete in drawing posters for Halloween.

In 1975, the PTA president of one of the Bloomington elementary schools explained to me their rationale for having "ghost houses": "as long as an experience can be a constructive one, an exciting one, it's a meaningful thing. It is frightening, not damaging, if the parents are there with the children to provide assurance." One might regard this thought as an odd or meaningless statement, but, given the social context, it really is not. The general consensus is that in a secure environment, in the presence of parents, Halloween horrors are constructive and educational experiences for children. Nobody had explained why, and the parent with a Ph.D. did not feel the need to elaborate such a commonplace idea for me.

My visit to the Indianapolis Children's Museum's Haunted House in 1978 did not provide much assurance of the constructiveness of the experience. Parents were dragging their screaming children through the dark alleys in which threatening ghosts, ghouls, vampires, werewolves, insane murderers, and monsters growled and howled, wielding a human shinbone, severed limb, broom, or knife. A nice rotund lady offered visitors a liver, which she pulled from the open cavity of a corpse.

Two witches with whom I talked — a mother and daughter, both grade-school teachers, who welcomed and guided the children through the gallery of horrors — were not sure how the welfare of the children was served by the show. "Some cry and scream and must be taken home. Until 10 most kids sort of believe they are for real, not make-believe. If they have older siblings, they get soon sophisticated. But some kids cannot sleep for weeks." Despite their witches' costumes, they tried to be cheerful and reassuring in their greeting of the tiny visitors: "Happy Halloween! How are you? Ready for trick-or-treating? What will you wear?" The response came mumbled from the little ones, like a whimper.

Does early exposure to horror desensitize children? Perhaps — this was my impression at the ghost-story evening at the safe environment of the Monroe County Library on October 30, 1976. Six- and seven-year-old children watched three witches around a cauldron. As they sharpened their knives to make a potion of newborn babies' fingers and herbs, they conversed about their skills — casting spells and enchantments, predicting who would die or be lucky, peeling an apple in one piece. And they talked about their coven, midnight church services, and evil spirit contacts. Every effort was made to emphasize the occasion as real, not fiction. There was eerie music and sounds of spirits from another room. Some kids were terrified and were taken home by their parents, but most others sat quietly for an hour and a half, listening to the stories in absolute silence. They seemed to be getting used to witches and ghosts.

Another example of youthful desensitization is this note in an Associated Press article:

"Where is the ghost?" demanded 5-year-old Carissa Rhea, accompanied by her mother, in the ninety-minute $10 ghost tour tracking the early settlers of Santa Fe. Although the operator said that "I had the hair stand up on my arms in different locations," the little girl was disappointed not to "rouse one of Santa Fe's most notorious ghosts." (AP, October 28, 1990)

What if the education philosophy of parents and educators disagrees? Brad, a second grader in Bloomington, came home from school and confronted his mother with these words: "Mummy, you lied to me last Wednesday." When she asked what he meant, Brad reminded her that she had said to him the other day that there are no ghosts. However, after his teacher read a ghost story to the children in class, he asked her the same question and she told him, "Yes, there are." Brad's parents told him that he'd probably misunderstood the teacher, and they went to see her next day. It turned out that the student teacher had told the children that this was a true story. What bothered the mother, a liberal Baptist, was that "the teacher gave an emphatic statement, she gave no choice, a chance to children that they don't have to believe." I advised the mother to insist because of the boy's genuine fear from ghosts. The teacher complied and next day Brad reported that Mrs. H. told the class not to worry about revenants in America — they exist only in Europe!

Edna Barth writes,

> From [the] 1950s onward, the fright potential of Halloween ventures was curtailed. Growing hostility to vandalism joined with a desire to protect young trick-or-treaters from unregulated scares. Community authorities in the 1950s began to regulate the hours and scope of Halloween activities. Yet the idea of restricting fear as part of [a] healthy reaction did not gain an unchallenged victory. (Barth 1981: 93)

Equipped with the total armory of legends, children develop their own age-group repertoires for scaring each other. As already noted, 2- to 5-year-olds tell about witches, monsters, ghosts, bogeymen, vampires, ghouls, giants, and ferocious animals (Meves 1983). Elementary school children indulge in accounts of violence (torture, bloodshed, dismemberment) and death and the dead (Opie and Opie 1959: 32–37). Attraction to the gruesome and fascination with the "gross" (anything morbid, macabre, disgusting, and violent) seems typical of both boys and girls around age ten. Shivering and giggling at the same time, they react to themes surrounding death, burial, and decomposition (Phillips and Robie 1987).

The same ambiguity between horror and humor is shown by a set of ghost story favorites of young children. The stories are all variants or subvariants of "The Youth Who Wanted to Learn What Fear Is" (AT 326) or "Man from the Gallows" (AT 366). They feature haunted houses and cemeteries in which ghosts chase down intruders, but the horror ends with a pun, an apparently humorous twist that in fact does not turn out to be funny at all. It comes as a liberating magic gesture that lays the ghost to rest (Clements 1969b). Preadolescent girls identified this category of stories as "funny-scary," indicating ambiguity in their meaning while giving an accurate description of their feeling, a blending of fear and the ridiculous. The catch ending "effectively neutralizes the fearfulness of the initial situation." According to Elizabeth Tucker, up to the fifth grade "these narratives are central to the early development of storytelling competence. By becoming familiar with funny-scary stories, the child absorbs the concept of 'a good scare' which prepares him to deal with the more serious traditional narratives concerning the supernatural at a later age" (Tucker 1977: 62). One might add that the dramatic style of punchline-oriented youth legends like "Bloody Fingers," "Ghost of the Black Eye," "The Walking Coffin," "The Viper," "The Golden Arm," "Who Ate My Liver?" and "It Floats, It Floats" requires acting and role-playing skill.[12] Those who argue for the wholesomeness of fear and who emphasize humor and parody, or the grotesque side of the weird, insist that no one intends real terror, but only titillation. "Funny-scary" really translates ambiguity: real fear masked as the grotesque, which children subscribe to under the influence of adults. Usually, authors refer to these legends as "shaggy dog stories" (Brunvand 1963: 42–68), despite the fact that they present situations of real entrapment of children in a haunted place.

If one accepts Caughey's argument about an imaginary social world running parallel to our real world (1984), we may say that the split between the imaginary and the real occurs when children are able to distinguish themselves from their pan-animistic universe of images, dreams, and delusions, which remain fundamental to the later fantasies of fears and desires fueled by mass media exposure. Not all imaginary scenarios are necessarily legends, but legends are about imaginary relationships between the tellers or the protagonists and real but unmet actors. Stated otherwise, real relationships are constructed by costumed ghouls, monsters, and vampires enacted by adults for the entertainment of children. A music store owner in Indianapolis moonlights as Sammy Terry, a ghoul who emerges from a casket and introduces late-night horror movies with peals of sinister laughter; but he also pays visits to children's Halloween parties with George, his spider, expanding the legend tableau into narrative.

The social life of children offers ample opportunity to develop a legend repertoire. In addition to school-related gatherings, Boy Scout and Girl Scout camps and girls' slumber parties, where children alternate in telling and acting out legends, are important for youngsters in formulating dream and fantasy images and perfecting their expressive skills. The standard camp horror stories are invented or passed on by older children or adults — camp counselors, teachers, and scout leaders — to prevent younger children from straying from their tents (Dégh 1971: 64). These stories are about moldy monsters, ferocious animals, wild people, giants, hunchbacked maniacs, ghouls, restless spirits of lunatic killers, witches, and ghosts of innocent murder victims who have returned to seek revenge; all are threatening to the lives of innocent campers (Dégh 1986: 144–145; Ellis 1982–83; Leary 1973; Warshaver 1972).

There are other legends typical of this age group's creative fantasies, expanding on experience and the normal fear of the unknown, as well as the animosity that children hold toward adults. A whole mythology emerges about strange-looking mystery houses in the neighborhood that are inhabited by mean, fearsome, reclusive, and childless old people.

The story of 7-year-old Vicky W. is typical. It contains elements of storybook witch legends as well as fear of eccentric newcomers in the neighborhood who are unresponsive to the trick-or-treater's candy raid. The general belief supported by authorities that adults poison children at Halloween (Best 1990: 132–137) has encouraged the spread of these hostile legends, suppressing the fact that two generations earlier, adults lived in fear of the destructive pranks of youthful vandals.

### An Old Witch Has a Black Cat and Poisons Kids

An old witch lives in that house and you had better stay away or she will eat you, or throw you into her kettle and make you into soup. She has a black cat with her and a beautiful woman who is her slave. A friend of mine, Mary Rennata, saw a crocodile in her garden. She is a mean old woman and you should keep away.

*Have you ever gone there on Halloween?*

No, but a lot of kids I know have and said that she locks her gate because she doesn't want anyone to bother her. If she did give candy, it probably would be poisoned. (Berkeley Archive)

A 28-year-old adult, Doug M. from San Francisco, remembered a similar experience:

The old man and woman were the only people in the area with no children and were very unsociable. So everyone was afraid of them. If children came around their house the old man came out and chased them away with a shotgun.

Young girls may "build" a haunted house at Halloween parties and cook dinner, serving visitors the eyeballs (peeled grapes), liver (jelly), and entrails (spaghetti) of the dead. This very common game of preadolescents where dead body parts are being served occurs also in commercial spookhouses, which are set up sometimes in school basements or attics. In Bloomington I witnessed a teacher in ghoul costume pulling out the heart and the liver of the corpse of a dummy, offering them to the children to touch (see also Opie and Opie 1959: 35–36). The act can be easily turned into legend.

### Adults Feed Children with Body Parts

A very wealthy couple decided to have a Halloween party at their mansion. Their little girl had invited several of her friends. Around midnight they planned to have everyone seated in the living room in the dark to pass parts of the human body which would be grapes for eyeballs and so forth. The butler was supposed to pass these things around at the party. But this butler hated this family and most of all he hated the little girl. So that evening, when the little girl was upstairs during the party, the butler murdered her and cut her up and passed the parts of her body instead of the gag parts which had been prepared. Before the parts had been passed, the little girl's parents called her back to the room, but she didn't come. Afterwards, the lights came on. When the parents saw that they had handled the parts of their own little girl, both of them went crazy. (Karen Gustafson 13, Hutchinson, Kansas; Berkeley Archive, 1962)

American Halloween rituals are traced to an ancient pagan Celtic festival, celebrating the beginning of winter and believed to be the import of late-nineteenth-century Scottish-Irish settlers. Having the opportunity to teach a course at Edinburgh University's Scottish Ethnology Department during the winter of 1995, I asked students to compare their practices with those of Americans. There was evidence of some American influence — the hard-to-carve native turnip was being replaced with candle-holding pumpkins made of plastic or pottery, and American-style postcards were sold in bookstores. Rather than costume parades or spookhouses, the door-to-door mumming known as *guising* was carried out by young people in neighborhoods. Guising was not a threatening "trick or treat" negotiation; after being quizzed by the hosts, the guisers recited poems and sang songs for sweet rewards. Kids also bobbed for apples, and struggled to bite from a suspended dripping, messy pastry after removing their masks. How could this pleasant winter entertainment be turned into a symbolic robbery of tolerant adults?

The description of an earlier Scottish Halloween as remembered by a native participant observer demonstrates a more explicit ideological difference between the American and the Scottish version. In her letter of October 12, 1983, Frances Turnbull, a native of Scotland and a long-time resident of New York City, described for me the Halloween she knew in her childhood.

### The Scottish Halloween

Now that Halloween, Halloween Eve or All Souls Night is here again, I find myself going back in time to my childhood in Scotland.

If you see two witches at midnight
With a peacock feather all of white
You may be assured there's a lover's spat
So steal the feather from off their hat
Pick a four leaf clover and your temper keep
On Hallowe'en and there'll be no cause to weep

Halloween Postcard, mailed October 30, 1913, from Terre Haute, Indiana

There were many differences. We did not trick or treat, but were guisers who went out looking for our Halloween but not without putting some effort into it and giving as good as we got, we thought. Costumes were made or adult hand-me-downs (sometimes borrowed without their knowledge). We had no store-bought false faces. We made our own masks or used a cork burned over a flame, which made an excellent charcoal. Our imagination created ogres, beasties, angels, you name it. Many a parent searched in vain for the cork from the medicine or liquor bottle. No child claimed knowledge as to where it had gone, except to blame it on the ghosts or witches flying hither that eve. Pumpkins were unheard of, except Cinderella's, so father was sculptor of the biggest turnip we could find. We had practiced our skit beforehand. We did either a dance, a song, or recited a poem. We went in groups of three or four. We visited our neighbors and we spent some time in each house.

There was no standing at doors in my home town. We were welcomed in like royalty. A wee heat by the blazing fire and for any visitors we were introduced and our genealogy explained. Usually a lone relative or stray neighbor had been invited to share the festivities, and from the youngest toddler to the oldest member of the clan were gathered around the fire. This was a night for everyone.

There was the initial stage fright, much coaxing and prodding to get the first star performing. However, the applause was intoxicating, the star had to be nudged from the spotlight by group effort. Our finale was a group highland fling.

Our reward was a piece of fruit, nuts, etc. Candy was rationed for quite some years after the War, so it was a rare treat. Suet dumplings in a cloot (cloth) was a delicious repast and if you were lucky your slice obtained a surprise, either a miniature doll or a tiny silver threepenny piece. They were well wrapped in wax paper and no one ever swallowed one.

In some houses a large wooden tub or zinc bath were filled with water and apples afloat. We would now dook for apples, either by using your mouth or spearing them with a fork. You had five chances. If you snared an apple it was yours. Next came bobbin for scones. Lengths of string were suspended from the kitchen ceiling. Treacle scones and sweet meats spread with jam were attached to the string. These danced tantalizingly above our nose, the secret was to jump, lunge forward, and bite simultaneously. It was great good-hearted fun, the applause and merriment enjoyed by all, with no one too old or too young. It spanned the generations. We were tired, happy children spilling out into the cold, crisp night air heading for home.

Once home, we would regale our family about our evening. My brother and I would sit, one at each end of the hearth, the light would be low and by the blazing fire my great-aunt who always spent the Halloween with us would tell us ghost stories while we ate pomegranates and glanced over our shoulders a lot. It was even better if my grandma was there. Then they outdid each other with stories from different parts of the country.

Before going to bed, we had our parents leave out some bread and drink for any soul who passed through. I tried to stay awake to see the ghost, but sleep always caught up with me.

When I look at children today on Halloween, with their full bags, I can't help remembering the Scottish town where I grew up. Our bags may not have been so full, but my heart and memories are.

## Occasions of Performing Preadolescent Legends

For girls, a common scary entertainment is not tied to Halloween but to the slumber (or pajama) party,[13] the favorite and most creative type of all-night weekend get-together of American preadolescent girls between the ages of 8 and 14. It is a spontaneous and secret event assembled with the support but not the interference of adults. By themselves, all night in the darkness of a family home, the girls construct rhymes, sing, and narrate and enact their total scary-funny repertoire, while consuming hamburgers, pizza, hot dogs, ice cream, popcorn, and soft drinks. It is the occasion to exchange and pool together legends and other lore that contain forbidden themes (scatological, sexual, supernatural, and criminal). Constructing a haunted house, visiting a haunted cemetery, writing each other's obituary, playing at trances and séances, and "calling back" malevolent ghosts (Tucker 1977: 409–422) are among the highlights of the fun, whether the ghost is a monster, a murderer, or the ubiquitous "Mary" who haunts the highways seeking a ride home or who appears on the bathroom mirror by divination. "We called Bloody Mary back," says a 12-year-old, who saw "her bloody face in the mirror . . . one of the girls got hit in the back and we were all sitting in the circle holding hands . . . and it was really so funny" (Wayne State Folklore Archive 1976). But this was the only text calling Mary "Bloody" (as an adjective) among the many we have encountered.

From the many texts told mostly by girls (insiders), I have chosen the complex, confusing, and confused text of a boy, 18-year-old Steve Valdez (an outsider), because it blends diverse legends combining narration and enactment. He was not a participant in the ritual performance of the mirror-witch story, but he remembered it from his grade-school days.

### Calling Back Mary Worth

She is the school witch . . . she comes after little kids . . . in the night. I think it's supposed to be because she lost a child or something and was very bitter. And so, she comes to kids in the middle of the night while they're asleep and sits in a rocking chair that is part of her apparition and sits there and watches. . . . You're supposed to tell her, you have to cross your arms over your chest in the form of an "X" and say, "I believe in Mary Worth," or else she scratches you with her long, she's got one long fingernail. That's her whole legend. She's like the child protector or the child abuser, whichever you want to look at. She sits there and knits and knits.

What kids used to do in elementary school was, like, there'd be a mirror in the room and when it was lunch time and the teacher wasn't there, they'd go in the room and turn off all the lights and supposedly you'd be able to walk up to the mirror and you'd have to say, "I believe in Mary Worth," and her picture would come in the mirror and if she believed you believed in her, nothing happened. But if she didn't she would scratch you and then you had the mark and you had to beware of her.

As the collector, folklorist Sue Samuelson, explained, Steve Valdez never heard the story again after he started high school:

> It probably was told by the older elementary students to scare the little ones into doing what they wanted them because they would threaten them with, "If you don't do this, Mary Worth will get you." Almost all of the younger children believed the legend and the lunchtime ritual was to justify this belief. Most of the kids went along with the looking in the mirror tradition because they didn't want to be left out or called a "scaredy cat."

This legend about Mary — in the form of narrative, séance magic, and ritual divination, accompanied by interpretive commentaries — is a random sample construct but is broadly representative of what is performed at social gatherings of girls and boys. The rudimentary text lists alternative episodes to paint an ambiguous image of the phantom heroine as victim, witch, mother, avenger, child abuser, and protector. She seeks compassionate children who are willing to give her a chance to show her disfigured face in the mirror; or she punishes (by disfigurement) those who do not believe in her. The key in this legend is believing and trusting. The daring diviner must repeat many times (from 10 to 1,000) the phrase "I believe in Mary Worth" to persuade the unfortunate ghost to show herself. She exists because someone believes in her.

We may consider Mary's disposition in terms of a degenerative process. She is identical to "The Vanishing Hitchhiker" — the shivering, young accident victim who stood, dressed in a ball gown, by the roadside in the rain, desperately looking for a ride home. At one time she was even Resurrection Mary, who haunted the front of Resurrection Cemetery on the fringe of Chicagoland. But now, in this later stage of spirit existence, she has changed dramatically. She did not start out as a demonic horror figure, a mean attacker of young girls; but now she is a victim of violence and rejection who has turned ugly and vengeful — the heroine of a new legend, based on the older one.

This legend, ritually acted out and narrated, shares elements with all road ghost stories about women who cannot rest because they have lost their lives to a murder or accident, or have committed suicide for their own sin of infanticide. It came to the attention of folklorists when Langlois published her collection (Langlois 1978). However, the remarkable performance she described of the mirror-ritual and the connected narrative by 12-year-old Ghia and her friends, students in a Catholic school for black children in Indianapolis, was new only to the folklorist. The legend and the mirror-divination turned out to be a nationwide practice among adolescent girls. Little attention has been paid to this form of the master legend, the disturbingly complex supernatural "The Vanishing Hitchhiker" story, which is difficult to simplify and rationalize into an urban-horror plot.

Many trance and séance games with elaborate ritual prescriptions have been noted for adolescents (Tucker 1977: 409–420), but the most common and prominent is the calling back of the itinerant female specter, independent from the hitchhiker story. Other variations on Mary Jane, Bloody Mary, or Mary Worth, Whales, or White have been reported since Janet Langlois's well-documented publication (1978). Legend collectors have often described the bathroom ritual to coerce the suffering and vengeful spirit to appear in the mirror (Knapp and Knapp 1976: 242; Rudinger 180; Ray 1976; see also "Sarah's Grave" in chapter 3). This is definitely a horror figure to provoke as a dare. The provocation may also be performed at her grave by stepping and jumping on it until blood spurts, or by attacking and damaging the marker. Some of the stories tell that she did something bad in life, and here she connects with the famous localized story of the Cline Avenue Halloween hitchhiker who killed her children (Georges 1971), a local variant of the La Llorona legend widespread in Mexico and the southwestern United States (Adams 1998).

How did the ugly, sinister mirror-witch come to be related to the story of the pale beauty who is taken home by the lone driver (in the most consistent redaction of the legend)? Is it an accidental and occasional merger of two separate legends, indicated mainly by identical or similar names such as Mary Worth and Mary Whales? Or is there a historic process of transformation in the heroine's plea, as I have suggested above? The question is timely, as Bengt af Klintberg has reported that a Swedish version of the story is popular among 9- to 13-year-old schoolchildren, both boys and girls. There is a striking similarity between the American legend and the calling of the "Black (Red, White, Creepy, Dirty, Bloody, or Fortune-Telling) Madame" to come out. According to one informant, the story was in the newspaper that "a girl called up Black Madame" and died as a result (Klintberg 1988). No such tragic outcome has been reported in our American sample. Although the Swedish legend ritual probably originated in the United States, we would need to know what print medium and what form conveyed it to explain its adaptation.

But this is not the latest assessment of the ambiguous female revenant. Reiterating his complaint about the lack of analysis and interpretation of folklore materials, Alan Dundes offers a fascinating psychoanalytical discussion of the mirror ritual: the divination of Bloody Mary based on ten selected texts he considered sufficient "to demonstrate both the traditionality and the gamut of variation of the Bloody Mary ritual" (126). The problem is that the ritual is separated from the legend, and "the menstrual interpretation" is leaning on the name "Bloody" which is adjectival, as in the "Bloody Mary's Grave" legend (see chapter 3), not a surname as in the majority of variants—Worth, Whales, White (Dundes 1999: 119–136).

In his type index of urban legends, Brunvand lists the "I Believe in Mary Worth, ritual summons mirror witch" (Brunvand 1993: 334) under "Other Horrors," with reference to his own essay (Brunvand 1986: 80–82). His treatment of this legend, like others included in his urban legend books and newspaper columns, is entertaining and enlightening for a general readership, but for the folklorist his descriptions and interpretations do not offer new insights into the nature of the legend. He does not explain the reason for the great popularity of this legend among young girls, or the motivations and the purposes of the tellers and their influence on their listeners. Responding to the question raised by a librarian in a professional newsletter concerning the real or fictitious identity of the heroine, Brunvand lists her known family names with reference to the three sources he is familiar with. He ends up telling his readership with mock regret that although it would be good to know why Mary Worth, the respectable comic-strip busybody, is moonlighting as a mirror witch (to be understood as "ugly"), the question cannot be answered because the origin of folklore motifs is impossible to trace.

From all the above, we can see a fundamental problem with the determination of the legend-body of children. The available data does not make it clear what folklorists mean by "children's legends." Is it what children invent and tell to other children, or is it what they culturally learn from adults and retell, or is it both? And can we regard both as constituents of the entire repertoire of children? Or do we have to view the two sets of legends known to children separately — one as the reflection of the normal or abnormal developmental states of mentality (in terms of biological givens such as anxieties, dreams, visions, and aggressive impulses) and the other as inherited cultural conventions and/or educational matters of conscious indoctrination? It seems the two are very distinct yet are inseparable and interactive, as both the instinctive and the educational factors are at work from the earliest point of consciousness. Evidently, education plays a leading role in suppressing the instinctive; however, the proportion and relationship of nature and culture in legends need to be studied, because these factors are key to controlling children's activity in thinking, fantasizing, ideologizing, believing, and artfully speaking the language of the legend.

Children's legends are true mirrors of society. Their actors, actions, language, mannerisms, and paraphernalia originate in everyday living. Children did not invent witches, bogeymen, vampires, werewolves, Bigfoot, or the Hookman, rather they learned about them from the media the same way they learned everything else prescribed by both private and public education. In script and in custom, the canon of legendary characters, heroes, and anti-heroes is continually rewritten and updated to stay contemporary.

Adults romanticize about the wonders of childhood, full of joyous holidays, gift giving, good spirits, fairies, goblins, Santa Claus, Jack O'Lantern, and belief in miracles and horrors. But why do adults pretend that the idyllic child-oriented family Christmas is the dream-fulfillment of the child, when they know that it is part of the culture industry, which is catered by the marketplace and performed in mammoth department stores to sell merchandise? In his famous letter, "Yes, Virginia, There Is a Santa Claus," Francis Church (1896) commented "how dreary would be the world if there were no Santa Claus . . . there would be no childlike faith, then, no poetry, romance to make tolerable existence." According to parental pedagogy, joy and fear should go hand-in-hand in child education, and children should believe the unlikely stories. Bettelheim also tells parents that the small child should be able to believe in Santa and the Tooth Fairy; so do other illustrious authors like Alden Perkins (1982), who insists that "when a person stops believing, some very sad things begin to happen."

On the other hand, in her essay "Is Santa Claus Corrupting Our Children's Morals?" Boss (1991) blames parents for lying to children about Santa being a real person. She recognizes the difference between the fantasy of children and the fantasy of adults:

> There is an enormous difference between parents telling children that
> Santa Claus is real and young children engaging in fantasy play or embel-
> lishing upon reality. In their make-believe fantasy play children are not
> strictly speaking, lying, since the intention of children's fantasies is not to
> mislead or deceive others. The intention of adults, on the other hand, is to
> deliberately mislead children about the nature of Santa Claus. (1991: 25)

We can only agree with Boss that "while many parents teach children that beings such as God, leprechauns, angels, and ghosts exist, this is almost always because they are inclined to believe themselves" (1991: 26).

This indeed confirms our position that the legend repertoire of children is basically influenced by informal home education. Parents want their own early experiences transferred to their children, to revive the funny-scary memories of their own childhoods. They were scared by their parents, so why should not their own children be? Morbid Halloween characters are adult constructs. Adults make the ghoulish costumes for their little "innocents"; adults build the mock-cemeteries in the backyard of their family homes to entertain the little ones, letting them try how it feels to emerge from the coffin dressed in the garb of a tuxedoed vampire. Further evidence is found in the 1982 collection of legends from 148 sixth-grade students by a Bloomington schoolteacher. Upon my solicitation, 264 legends were written down by 10- to 12-year-olds as a take-home exercise. The collection appears as a miscellany and repository of peer-group and trans-generational tradition. The informants appear as much reporters of their own experiences as collectors of experiences of adult legend-telling groups. In addition to media sources, oral tellers include parents (mostly mothers), older family members, siblings, neighbors, educators, and peers (Dégh 1986: 127–138).

I suggest children's legendry is a subvariant of that of adults. Scary characters such as Dracula, werewolves, witches, and crazy killers are adult inventions, as are performances of costuming and acting. The adult input is powerful and overwhelming in legend formation; in fact, it is the parents who create legends on the basis of the trauma they themselves suffered in early childhood. By romanticizing, socializing, and revising their experience, they suppress the natural fantasy products of their own childhood.

### Adolescents[14] and Young Adults

The Lure of Horror, Monsters, the Dead, and Satan

The "adolescent audience is the largest for horror art," noted Twitchell in his book on horror movies. He claims horror sequences are formulaic rituals encoded with precise social information needed by the adolescent audience, whose main concern is the transition from individual and isolated sexuality to pairing and reproductive sexuality. Hence, horror myths prepare the teenager for the anxieties of reproduction (see Twitchell 1985: 7, 68, 88; also Cawelti 1976: 66).

I think it is not necessary to emphasize that literary horror narratives in print and on film and other media are inseparably intertwined with traditional legendry. Since the heyday of the Gothic novel, elements of scary tales and legends have spread uncontrollably and have contributed to the creation of literary versions, which in turn have become powerful relay stations for further distribution of folk versions. If the repeated filming of Stoker's novel *Dracula* helped keep alive the aristocratic image of the vampire in legendry for a century, much more so did the movies inspired by traditional legends revive and authenticate latent belief in lunatic killers, monsters, cannibals, witchcraft, werewolves, and demonic possession (see chapter 3).

Haunted house or ghost stories — in which the dead return to their former residence — are so common and variable in movie, television, and magazine serials that they could be registered as entries in the *Motif-Index of Folk-Literature*. When the movie *Ghost* (Paramount, 1990) became the biggest hit of the year, a note in *Time* (November 5, 1990) asked the question, "what gives 'Ghost' its spooky staying power?" and wondered at the "cultlike devotion" of repeat moviegoers. In an interview on the ABC program *Good Morning America* (October 1990), the actors in the film *Ghost* expressed their own readiness to believe in the return of the dead, because "who knows for sure?" and "nobody has proven that they don't exist." The return of the dead is the central theme of the most generally believed legends; the film writers did not invent a ghost story but rather revived and creatively adapted the ones commonly known to fit current interests. This made it possible for an immediate audience response when the story — fiction for the scriptwriter, but real for the folk who are familiar with tradition — reverted to legend. Domestication of horror film themes comes easily because of the keen interest of the press, which keeps supernatural encounters on its agenda and blurs the distinction between fact and fiction.

Just as ghosts belong to the daily news (MacDougall 1983: 137–179), so does demonic possession. If we target the swift change of horror-fashion among adolescent audiences, we will be amazed at how fast the entertainment industry has reacted to new social ills, real or imagined. For example, the concept of possession and its ritual remedy, exorcism, became prime conversation pieces after William Peter Blatty's 1971 novel, *The Exorcist*, was made into a movie and released in January 1974. We can date the beginning and spread of satanic possession legends to the showing of films like *Rosemary's Baby, The Exorcist, The Omen, The Believers, Angel Heart,* and others in America and in Europe during subsequent years. It seems evident that they have opened a new chapter in perennial theological and scientific debates concerning the devil and exorcism.

As commanded by the Bible,[15] the Roman Catholic church codified the *Roman Ritual* in 1614 to expel demons from the bodies of humans. Ever since, the Pope has appointed in each country a chief exorcist. The practice of exorcism was followed by almost all non-Catholic Christian denominations. A resurgence of traditional belief about the attack of Satan on humanity was noticeable by the late 1960s, coinciding with a number of social, political, and economic factors. Demonic possession and exorcism were put on the agenda of both Catholic and Protestant theologians, while the doctrine of fundamental sects about Satan's tactics rose to prominence in the consciousness of the masses. However, exorcisms were only sporadically reported by the press as newsworthy events,[16] until the best-selling book and successful movie *The Exorcist* "enlightened" the masses about the immediate dangers of possession. The masses responded by bombarding churches with letters and phone calls reporting cases of possession. And the film industry and newspapers, always particularly successful in popularizing and trivializing religious belief and scattering the seeds of superstitious fear among the masses, were quick in spreading fact and folklore to millions of readers and viewers of all levels of education. "The latest excursion into the bizarre," writes Paul Kurtz, "is unsettling to many, particularly because it attracts young people and has even invaded the colleges and universities — where some sophistication is supposed to be cultivated" (1974: 4). Theologians, philosophers, physicians, psychologists, occultists, parapsychologists, and anthropologists expressed their expert opinions. For example, a special bonus issue of the tabloid the *National Tattler* on exorcism in the spring of 1974 introduced the factual background of *The Exorcist*, then interviewed the following experts: Billy Graham, a Jesuit exorcist, clairvoyant Jeane Dixon, four Roman Catholic priests, a rabbi, a Baptist minister, four fundamentalist pastors, a pagan priest, a Tibetan lama, witch Sybil Leek, psychic DeLouise, a British healer, an American Indian exorcist, two high priests of two satanic denominations, ghost hunter Ed Warren, prominent actress and amateur channeler Shirley MacLaine, and a housewife who was possessed. "Sensationalism will exaggerate and create what really isn't here," commented a modest parish priest.

The controversy about the film continued and expanded when *The Exorcist* was shown in Europe. According to the September 23 *Der Spiegel* (1974, no. 39: 98–125), the synchronized showing in forty-nine movie theaters made people exorcism-conscious in Germany. Some clergymen supported banning the film, which they saw as "ungodly," luring and misguiding the public. The article reports a number of recent, documented cases of exorcism in Germany, Austria, France, Holland, England, and the United States. As the commentaries on the film continued, cases about brutal killings of the possessed were brought up.[17]

As time wore on, and possession entered the common vocabulary of the masses, the exorcism of Anneliese Michel, the pedagogy student from Klingenberg, a small town in Bavaria, came to prominence. Her demons were exorcised by two priests in twenty-three rituals, as endorsed by the Bishop of Würzburg. From the time of her death from starvation in 1976 to the indictment of the exorcists and the parents in 1978, a saint's legend and cult began to unfold around Michel, on the basis of local folk belief. The sensational press coverage, and the crucial questions over the "fatal exorcism," only deepened the controversy between the church and the state over two years following Michel's death.[18] From here the ramifications of saints, sinners, and possession legends via mass media can be followed without difficulty.

Legendry about the devil appears on all levels, too complex for our present concern. A single local case will suffice, however, to give an idea of instant legend formation as response to a new movie. Shortly after the movie *The Omen I* was shown in 1976, high school kids in Charleston, South Carolina, began to spread the rumor that a baby with huge ears and a long tail had been born in the hospital. "Everybody knows it but nobody admits it," said 15-year-old Clyde to his high school English teacher. According to him, a doctor appeared on television to say that the story was not true, and it had also been in the newspaper. But the kids who had gone to the maternity ward saw it — they said it was born to an atheist mother. She had gone to the priest, and hit him on the head with the Bible, so he cursed her and her baby was born a demon. And the demon said that if they killed it, ten others would be born; and if all ten were killed, another hundred would be born. That's all Clyde knew. "It was furry, of half-black half-white parents. The kids saw it." One may speculate about the movie and this memorate, but what is its future? And how does an instant legend like this continue?

The question concerning the influence of horror films on legend-formation among adolescents in particular remains unresolved. There is a difference between being an audience member and being a narrator — a passive recipient versus a creative performer. The passive show-watching audience absorbs attractive and familiar themes, but how much time must elapse until the merger of tradition and innovation is able to produce legend? Television violence had been related to juvenile crime as ostentative, copycat performance, although no systematic research has revealed its dimensions (Dégh and Vázsonyi 1983).

## Impact of Non-supernatural Movie Horrors

After the satanic child abuse cycle was completed, after it was reduced to aftershock waves of teenage brutality (ruthless killing of animals and people, general acknowledgment of "666" and other insignia of the devil) and harmless play with satanic symbols, the film industry found new, more realistic, non-supernatural shockers for its high school audiences. A young generation of filmmakers and actors bloodied the screen with butcher knives and other sharp tools, initiating a new wave of fashion in horror movies. The ascending career of filmmaker Kevin Williamson is a case in point: His "magic moment came . . . when millions of shrieking teens watched Drew Barrymore try to guess the original killer." His first major movie, Scream (Dimension Films, 1996), became the highest-grossing horror movie ever, and spawned a successful sequel, Scream 2 (Dimension Films, 1997) (Time, December 15, 1997). Williamson's I Know What You Did Last Summer (Columbia, 1997) was followed by The Faculty (Dimension Films, 1998) and Teaching Mrs. Tingle (Interscope, 1999). How will this massacre-minded movie fad affect the mentality of the intended teenage audience and what will be its impact on new crops of adolescent legends? The cultic performance of telling, hearing, and participating in the legend (getting the experience, transforming it into an event, and distancing it into a tellable story) may be the distinctive feature of the legend repertoire of this age group, shared largely, but not exclusively, by those between the ages 15 and 30. Roemer (1971), for example, notes that the type she identifies as "scary story legend," is told by 10- to 11-year-old schoolgirls as well as by 19- to 20-year-old female university freshmen. On the other hand, Top (1990) found that while 16- to 18-year-old students tell contemporary legends in Belgium, 21- to 22-year-olds are bored by these same stories.

It does not need much speculation to realize that these legends definitely play a role in the coming-of-age process because the tellers themselves openly speak about it. The way they contextualize their stories is revealing; it seems it is not the context that serves the purpose of the legend, it is the other way around. To be involved in the legend experience belongs to the initiation into adulthood; like other transitory steps at critical turning points in the life cycle, it is a rite of passage, appearing as a particularly fearsome strain both physiologically and psychologically. Experiencing fear appears as exposing oneself to the mysterious, unknown, dangerous world of adulthood, to challenge, dare, exhibit courage, and master it, thereby achieving maturity. This evidently means that those who seek the thrill of fright are young people, usually small groups of boys, boys and girls, girls, or couples. On the threshold of their adult life, they build on their childhood propaedeutics of fear. The legends they tell address gender-related fears of both men and women. Anxiety and curiosity about sex, conflict between social norms and liberty of conduct, and fear from violent transgression of tabus mark the avenue on the quest for a mature sexuality, an adult social identity, and a place in the metaphysical universe between the living and the dead.

Adults like to reminisce over their youthful legend excursions. Men particularly like to talk about the time when they were sitting on gravestones and sipping beer, scaring girls to make them draw closer and seek shelter in their arms. Local haunted places are well remembered as sites of dating and daring. When I published some legends surrounding the "House of Blue Lights," a local physician bought copies as Christmas gifts for his former high school friends with whom he used to pay nocturnal visits to the house; he met the girl he would later marry through one of the visits.

An unusual handwritten version of "The Hook" legend by Marty D. of Greely, Colorado (1988), illustrates the complexity of the situation behind this adolescent favorite:

### The Hatchet Lady

A group of people (four girls and four guys) went to Red Rock for a drive. Just to have a good time and be together as friends. The scene was, two couples in the back seat and two in the front. It was supposed to be a joke and ended up seriously. The joke was: have a girl (not from the group) dress up as a ghost (like the little girl), come up to the parked car and scare the couples. But not the real girl came up to the car. The two couples in the back seat were mortified. The guy on the driver's side had had his arm outside the window and the Hatchet Lady cut it off. The two couples who were in the back seat are now in mental hospital.

Another couples' car ride was reported in a 1985 paper by a participant observer, freshman Linda A. (Bloomington). Her brother Ronnie, and her boyfriend John tried to impress another girl, Lisa, by telling her of their camping adventures. Linda's comments evaluate the quality of belief in the story.

### The Witch in the Woods

Ronnie was bragging about dumb things . . . then started to talk about the weird things that used to happen in Henderson Hollow. . . . Ronnie was obviously trying to scare us. . . .

There's this lady who is thought to be a witch. I do believe it myself also. Anyway, my brother, Charles, told me that this lady does some really weird things. He was told that she gets a broom and a shotgun, and goes out into the woods in the nighttime. While she is in the woods, she collects twigs and branches. She then ties them into bundles with the twine that she brings with her. She finds a clear spot in the woods, takes the broom, and sweeps a clear spot on the ground all the way down to the dirt. Finally, she places the bundles of twigs down in a pyramid shape and burns them. While the fire is going, she dances and shouts around the flames. If anyone dared to get near her, she would take her shotgun and shoot them. . . . Lisa and I just laughed. Ronnie said that we didn't believe anything he ever said. John said, we better watch out or we would have nightmares. . . . I personally felt that Ronnie was making up the story in order to scare us. I checked to see if Ronnie was telling something that he heard, and I found out from Charles, Ronnie's brother, and other people in the community that they had heard the story of the witch also.

## Quest Stories

Most of the adolescent legends are quest stories: going to a place for an experience. The texts usually contain detailed accounts of preparation to go or to be taken to a fearsome, secluded place. The teller features the journey to the place with companions, describes physical and mental conditions, and includes the relationship between fellow seekers and their performance of ritual acts. The teller and his or her fellow travelers recite scary legends while driving to the place in order to "get into the mood," build tension, and prepare for the anticipated legend in action. But at the end, the legend in its natural environment appears in a sketchy form, or remains untold, as if at the arrival to the scene, the terror had passed the level of tolerance beyond which there is nowhere to go but back home to domestic familiarity. This category of legends includes supernatural and extranormal horror stories, all localized to appear as an immediate threat to individual safety.

If not related to the ritual visit of dangerous places for experience, they may be told at important, age-group related activities. In this case, on-campus buildings and dormitories for college students, particularly for freshmen across America (Bronner 1990: 144–164), are just as fearsome places, detached from the home environment, much like the abandoned rural cemetery. Legend-telling is a part of socialization for college or other school freshmen by already established residents, and it is common as well to indulge in the exchange of scary stories by roommates or friends in residence halls at night by candlelight (Grider 1973). New stories may start as the fall semester opens, and vary and spread over the year or longer, until the class graduates.

Legend-telling nights include Halloween while watching the flames in the fireplace, anticipating a good scare. In 1988, Terri Pugh (Teter Quadrangle, Indiana University) told me the following story.

### Bride Killed in Car Wreck Appears in Backseat

Tonight some other girls came over to talk to us and we started relating stories we had heard. My roommate had a few. One of them was about a couple who were to be married on Halloween. They were driving down this winding road and they hit some loose gravel and wrecked. The girl was killed but the man survived. This happened the week before their wedding. Rumor says if you drive down that road on the night she was killed she will appear in your backseat.

This curious combination of "The Haunted Bridge" and "The Vanishing Hitchhiker" legends indicates experience-orientation, referring to routine visits to haunted spots at Halloween.

The mechanism of new and rapid legend formation processes is hard to predict or follow. For example, in the fall of the 1990/91 school year, a traditional ghost legend emerged from a relatively new practice: the communal watching of movies on video. The sighting of the ghost of a young boy standing on the set of the movie *Three Men and a Baby* (Touchstone, 1987) was reported by young people across the United States, manifesting in several versions of the standard revenant legend. The viewers assumed the role of eyewitnesses, and elaborated on the story, adding what they saw of the dark-haired boy and how he was killed. "I saw it with my whole fifth floor," said freshman Charlisa H. in a 1990 interview:

When he came across, all you heard was "Ahhh! It's a ghost! It's a ghost!" Everybody was screaming, and fast forwarding and rewinding and fast forwarding. People taped it, and we watched it over and over. The little boy's got black hair, a white T-shirt, and a pair of black jeans, and you can't see his feet. (Kelley 1991: 12)

Legend-telling appears also as part of the initiation ceremony for pledges to gain entry into sororities and fraternities. Among other things, established fraternity brothers communicate secret stories to the novices as a shock treatment that nevertheless means also "becoming one of us" — gaining admission and being incorporated into the group. The legend-teller in this case is the self-conscious bearer of tradition about resident ghosts, and his role is to maintain continuity. As Donald O. told me: "These are widely known stories in the Greek system. Sigma Phi Epsilons learn the story during their pledgeship. It is passed down from pledge class to pledge class." Donald said that John, the man from whom he had heard the legends he told me, learned these stories just that way. Male and female resident ghosts alternate and give the necessary excitement. "Meet Suzie the sorority ghost," writes Allison Smrekar (*The Red and Black* [Athens: University of Georgia, March 15, 1989]: 6); *The Muncie Evening Press* reports a residence hall spirit in Elliott Hall (October 17, 1986); and Lecoq (1973) cites the hauntings in the former Phi Kappa Tau fraternity house on the Bloomington campus.

Military schools have also been noted for their revenants. Phil Lewis reports a story he had learned in 1978 while he was at Howe Military School, in Howe, Indiana.

### Boy Scorned by His Father

The story had been passed down from one cadet crew to another. It was the story of a young rebellious boy that was scorned by his father. After being beaten by his father, this young boy ran across the field to Lima school, an old school that sits on a hill and is painted dark gray. It looks much like the house in Psycho. He cursed his father as he climbed to the top of the belfry. Once there, he hanged himself with the rope of the bell. As his body swung, the bell tolled and tolled. The bell seemed to draw the father to school. The father was so sorry for what he had done to the boy that he went out looking for him. As the father approached the school, the bell stopped ringing, so he went inside to look around. Once inside, he climbed the stairs to the belfry. As he entered the belfry and saw his son hanging, he smelled the smoke of the old, wooden school as it began to burn. The ghost of the son had set fire to the building in order to avenge his own suicide by killing his father.

This story was obviously contrived, as Lima School still stands, but the story of the boy hanged might be true. Nobody actually knew. Cadet Mitchell told this story on December 2, 1989. It is essentially the same story that I had heard. The only difference is that when I heard it, the boiler room door was swung open and flames could be seen through the window of the school. It was late night and our imaginations were young and wild. Mitchell lives in Company B.

Also see the "Phantom at the Point" in chapter 5 (discussed in Dégh and Vázsonyi 1973).

An 18-year-old gave me his written report of visits to his hometown's Main Street graveyard. The author of this representative summarization of legend-trip ingredients in the local repertoire of young people (a characteristic mixture of themes from horror movies, mystery novels, and comics, with traditional legend elements) quotes the statements of unnamed others, and uses the word "supposedly" and question marks in parentheses to express his own disbelief in his story, except for what he states: The place is for dating and scaring.

### Visits to Main Street Graveyard

Probably the most famous legend in Madison County is the one that concerns the Main Street Graveyard. The seldom-used graveyard is located on Main Street Road, approximately eight miles southwest of Anderson. The graveyard is an excellent location for playing romantic games, thus giving pranksters and practical jokers many opportunities to practice.

Many people have agreed that the graveyard possesses weird people and happenings. Some people say that there is an old, hollow tree in the center. Supposedly, the roots have been cleared out and an underground shelter was built. Several people admitted to have seen a hunchbacked man climb up from the ground. In contradiction to this observation, others claim there is no tree that is hollow and in the center of the graveyard.

One fact (?) that almost everyone agrees on is the presence of a watchman. He is supposedly a little under seven feet tall. People say that he is either a ghoul or a maniac. He carries a shotgun and has a German shepherd at his side. Although he is supposedly always there, no one has ever come in contact with him.

In addition to human forms, forms of ghosts and animals have been sighted. One person reported that he saw a wolf and heard it howl. Several people have seen (?) And heard (?) ghosts. Five boys witnessed the appearance of a ghost. Prior to the ghost, one of the boys was hit on the head with a bottle after he touched a tombstone. Two people said that they saw the same hunchback mentioned previously; this time he was uncovering a grave.

Probably the weirdest happening of all was the "disappearing couple." As the story goes, two young people were seeking rapport alongside their car. A thick mist engulfed them, leaving only the car. And, of course they were never found.

The legend of the Main Street Graveyard is indeed a classic in Anderson. It is one of the most flexible tales that I have ever heard. Anyone who knows anything about it has something different to add.

Generally the graveyard is a good place to "make out." The legends were invented in order to scare young people. The Main Street Graveyard is a good location for terrifying obstacles (witches, warlocks, ghosts, ghouls, werewolves, and vampires), because it is secluded and seldom used. (Mike Stone, student, 1969)

The adolescent and young adult legend repertoire is quite large, including also a set of localized ghost stories, and stories that feature realistic threats to women (although women are not their exclusive narrators). As we have already seen, the most common among these legends that have remained popular during the last thirty years are "The Hook," "The Roommate's Death," and "The Boyfriend's Death." Less developed versions of these three have been noted as the children's cautionary tales "Drip-drip" and "Scratch-scratch" by Knapp and Knapp (1976: 243). Other legends include "The Killer in the

Backseat," "The Poisoned Dress," "Drugged and Seduced," "The Snake in the Sweater," and "The Kentucky Fried Rat" and other disgusting food contaminants (Brunvand 1993: 334).

The consistency of this repertoire is remarkable: It is not infiltrated by occult themes that permeate current everyday life through the mass media. Preoccupied with its own personal problems of adjustment, this age group exhibits a different attitude toward media-communicated supernatural legends or legendary rumors which comes as a new awareness, with a new terminology of the occult. UFOs, out-of-body experiences, second-sight, premonition, and possession infiltrate the repertoire; young people like to play séance, and use candles, incense, the Bible, and the Ouija board in their rituals to make contact with the dead (Ellis 1994b). Not earlier than the 1970s, elements of satanic cult activity and drug-related crimes began to inspire new versions of old stories, indicating teenagers' awareness of the general social anxieties voiced through school authorities, religious leaders, law enforcement agencies, and the media (Hicks 1990: 3, 4; Guinee 1987).

We saw already in chapter 3 how variants of haunt legends can absorb elements of Satanism. For example, a 1989 variant of the Stepp Cemetery legend mentions smoking pot and sacrificing a dog to Satan at the Warlock Seat. According to the earliest version reported by columnist Larry Incollingo in the Bloomington *Daily Herald-Telephone* (August 30, 1966), teenagers were tried in juvenile court for hanging a German shepherd dog, an act that they blamed on a black lady, who guards the grave of her child and causes the intruder to die in a car crash while escaping from the scene. Many variants have been recorded over the last two decades, but the satanic element seems to be a recent addition. Reporter Mike White provided one in 1986:

> Yeah, actually, I've been out at Stepp. There's a friend of mine who did some writing on that, back when he was in school. There's a long stump, I guess, if you sit on it you'll die sometime within a year, things like that. He also says it's an area that in terms of Satanic stuff apparently is . . . he says that it's one of those areas where rituals are performed. . . .

In 1988, Kathy R., 23, heard that someone was hiking in "The Forestry" (Stepp) and "had seen many mutilated animals . . . they have been killed in Devil worship ceremonies." Many people she was working with in the MCL cafeteria "reported seeing figures robed in dark clothing, and have seen animals strangled or butchered in strange ways." Another friend, Leandra R., 17, also heard from a friend who saw dark-robed figures, and there was "animal blood splattered all over the place."

Mystery houses and haunted houses also are inclined to be updated by Satanist components. Fresh from the popular press, symbols such as goat heads, pentagrams, black masses, red robes, and human and animal sacrifices have entered the world of traditional ghost stories but remain on the surface. Debra M., 19, has heard that "as the story goes, in Lafayette, this lady was a Satanist and if you look into her living room through the window, a Satanist pentagram will appear on the wall. It was big thing around our high school to go there at night" (1989). Haunted bridges have been given new Satanic twists (chapter 3). Even the "House of Blue Lights" legend has been affected: In Emily W.'s version (1989), the eccentric owner "killed cats and dogs for satanic ritual purposes and he buried the parts." These references are quite different from the more developed adult legends about Satanists which express concerns about the safety of children. Manifest in the form of didactic legends by fundamentalist believers, they are only marginally listed in Brunvand's Type Index of Urban Legends (1993: 334).

### Adults

Family Tradition

The attitude of adult legend communicators has already been discussed in general terms in regards to characterizing the personality of legend-tellers. In what follows, I will focus on tellers and telling, and the influence of the renewed and growing popular interest in the occult over the last three or so decades. I will identify a few prominent personalities.

Unlike the repertoire of children and young adults, the adult legend repertoire is far too complex and diffuse to let itself be characterized by clear-cut unifying features. Although it contains many of the materials that young people tell, most of that part of knowledge remains latent and is reactivated only when needed; adults remember the stories of their childhood and young adulthood and occasionally pass them on to the current young generations for educational and entertaining purposes. At the same time, adults have their own circles to pass on legends.

Characterizing mature legend-tellers, Jones notes that ghost stories "are usually told by persons of some education," and "by people who do not, generally speaking, accept the supernatural" (1959: 162). Legends of adults very much lean on tradition inherited within the family circuit. What was dismissed with a shoulder-shrug as old people's fancy has now gained new significance and respect: With the rising interest in the secrets of the metaphysical world, never-heeded family stories come alive once again. Grandparents or great-grandparents who were born with a caul or veil, or the seventh daughters of the seventh sons are remembered; relatives are recalled for their amazing healing, fire-blowing, and bloodstopping powers, or their visions of dead relatives, foreknowledge of forthcoming events, or simultaneous perception of tragic events in progress. Family stories, polished by frequent repetition at informal family gatherings, are often biographical; and the magical, mysterious powers and knowledge of the previous generation act as encouragement and a validating factor for those who currently experience premonitions, second-sight, and revenant visitations.

In fact, this body of legendry constitutes the hard core of family tradition to validate new experiences. Legends are often told at big holiday breakfasts in American homes when three generations of the family gather in the kitchen. This is the earliest legend material that children, prior to leaving home, learn and hear again at homecomings. Several of my students called their relatives and had them retell the stories over the telephone for their class assignment. Young people learn legends and attitudes toward legends from adults; a 34-year-old law student from Elyria, Ohio, confirmed this with her statement on the back of a class questionnaire distributed in an American folklore course:

Most of the supernatural stories told by my grade school teachers — nuns close to retirement age — had a moral tinge or tag. . . . My grandmother's usually were framed by the explanation that someone — her aunt, her grandmother, or some other long-dead woman — had told her the story when she was a child. . . . The professor and librarian from my undergraduate days were well-known on campus as good story-tellers. I was invited a few times to parties at the house on campus where a number of older women faculty members lived, after tea, cocoa and cookies, we would sit around the fireplace with most of the other lights off while one or the other of the women told ghost stories. They could make them very real and they always prefaced a story by explaining that someone else had told it to them. The other teller might have experienced it herself or might have heard it from still another person, but there was always the assumption of reality. The librarian . . . seemed to specialize in stories of demonic possession and haunted castles and country houses. . . .

The following two examples, which come from people of extremely different backgrounds, will show how family legends influenced the life of their bearers.

In 1978, Leopold Szondi, a famous psychologist and geneticist who held that people's fate is determined by their genes, narrated to us the following story at his Zürich residence:

### A Family Curse

My grandfather on my mother's side was a butcher in his native village. A woman used to buy meat from him for which she paid with coins. When she left the store, the money turned into fish-scales. This happened several times. My grandfather was angered by this so much — he was a quick-tempered man — and once when it happened again, he grabbed the meat-chopper, and hit the hand of the woman so hard, that he had cut it off. Thereupon the woman spelled a curse upon him, his family and all his progeny. The curse was on water. If any member of the family goes near water, something will pull them down. My mother took this curse very seriously and forbade all her family, her nine sons included, to learn how to swim. And they obeyed. I myself did not learn either, never went to the pool or the beach. But when I got married, quite late, above forty, my wife made me forget this nonsense, as she put it. One of my cousins though, forgot the curse and made a dive into the river and drowned. I don't remember how it was, maybe he was in the military, but they brought him back into the village on a gun-carriage, water flew from his mouth. My mother had said that the curse took effect.[19]

Another example concerns a dream experience (see Kaivola-Bregenhoj 1990; Virtanen 1990: 30) of Betty Johnson, 59, a working-class woman from Shelburn, Indiana:

### Precognitive Vision

I've seen Grampa Johnson, him laying in a casket. And I saw the roses on the top, and my uncles Don and Dick. I saw all their suits on. This is 'bout see, a month before he died. And their suits they had on I described to my sister, I described the whole funeral to her. And it did bother me. And I felt like I had to tell to somebody. So naturally, that time Charlene, I had to tell someone, so I told her and described the whole to her what I was dreaming. And on, when he did die, a month later . . . And my sister, it made her nervous that she almost passed out. Because when we were all at Bond's funeral home, there was the casket, like I described. There was Don and Dick, standin' right there, where I said they be standin'. They had suits on. The funny part, the suits I have described, they haven't even bought them yet. I mean, you know they haven't bought them 'til the funeral. But when I told them about the dream, they hadn't bought the suits yet. When we went to the funeral then they had the suits on like I had described. Everything I described was identical that I told her. And in my dream. It got her real nervous, and she told Mom, "I'll never doubt her again," she said, "I never will. It was just exactly as she described." I don't know what makes me have dreams like that.

This and similar precognitive stories of Betty Johnson were recorded by her daughter, Janice, 37, in 1987. Betty Johnson is the middle link in a three-generation chain of women who have a rich repertoire of legends about revenants, precognition, and miraculous healing. Her grandmother's stories of her visions and healings are very traditional, and are passed on strictly within the family without exposure to occultism. The precognitive dreams or second-sight experiences of Betty are also mainly for family telling, although she believed that consultation with fortune tellers was helpful. Janice, on the other hand, is a modern searcher and consults occult literature, although she finds the doctrines disappointing and the practitioners to be fraudulent money-makers. Nevertheless, in her legends she uses the language, terminology, and interpretations of occult factions.

The supernatural family legend does not play an active role in the making of the adolescent repertoire. Appreciation begins at later age, particularly with people who develop sensitivity toward legendary topics.

Caught between Science and Religion

In order to describe the adult repertoire on a broader scale, it will be necessary to consider its origins and historic antecedents. It is not my purpose to offer a historiographical survey of folk religion and the emergence of mystic sects, cults, and occult establishments, and the existence of extensive scholarly literature on the subject exempts me from having to do so. However, because current legendry exhibits traits of the religion, science, and philosophy of earlier epochs in a great diversity of configurations, and because the institutions and factions continue to influence, contextualize, and compartmentalize legends of today, a brief sketch of major trends may be appropriate.

The search for truth and to understand the nature of things — ourselves and the world around us — is an elementary part of coping and surviving. To find answers and to interpret experience, humans reach out in two directions, following their natural subjective-emotional drives as well as satisfying their instinctive curiosity to find objectively provable reasons. The first path leads to spirituality: belief in the guardianship of a supreme creator and the acceptance of the subjective reality of religion, with resignation, humility, and submission to authority. The second path leads to an insatiable thirst for factual knowledge of reality, which demands independence and self-reliance through engagement in scientific exploration. The truth of religion is unknowable, whereas the truth of science is knowable.[20] Yet as *Homo sapiens* and *Homo religiosus* we live with both. To believe and to know are different behavioral patterns and project different cognitive mental maps. Religion makes us believe things unconditionally, without seeking confirmation; science appeals to our intellect, to contemplating the evidence before acceptance.

Folklorists during the 1960s distinguished between historical and extranormal legends because they regarded them as either knowable or believable: a historical event can be deduced, as facts can be found, whereas a supernatural experience must be believed. Nowadays it would not be possible to separate the two types on the basis of people's belief or knowledge, or the stories' imaginary or factual basis, or our scholarly judgment thereof. Even the seemingly rational horror stories contain irrational, supernatural references; and the so-called historical legends have no valid historical sources and become even more anachronistic and mythical when lifted from their historical contexts and relocated into the environment of the present. Nevertheless, the juxtaposition of belief and knowledge, religion and science, has turned out to be productive in dealing with the growing body of legendry in the technological age.

During the last decades, the world has been inundated by a staggering body of mass-media legendry based on supernatural or extranormal belief that is claimed to be cleared and authenticated by scientific research and knowledge. Spokespersons of pseudo-scientific and scientific establishments have gained tremendous popularity after daily appearances on television, the Internet, radio, and in the print media, and they have contributed to a never-before seen boom of traditional religious belief. For example, when prestigious authorities such as Harvard psychiatry professor John E. Mack become serious about UFO aliens ("I Lost It in the Saucer. Strange but True," *New Yorker*, July 31, 1995: 75–78; "Ph.D.s Get Serious about U.F.O.s" by James Wolcott, *Time*, January 1996: 82), they are actually joining theologians in the endorsement of the popular spiritualist belief in guardian angels among us, and are lending a hand to the evolution of a new complex of age-old traditional legendry. Likewise, the conspiracy legend of satanic child abuse in the 1980s, which almost reached the magnitude of the seventeenth- and eighteenth-century witch persecutions, was consistent with Christian church doctrines and was supported by theologians as much as it was by learned health professionals, psychiatrists, and psychologists. In 1997 two medical school conferences discussed spirituality and its effect on healing, pushing "faith healing a step closer to inclusion in mainstream medical school education." It was argued that "distant prayer, faith healing, and curative 'subtle energies' play a vital role in the treatment of patients afflicted with cancer, AIDS, and other diseases," and "psychiatrist Scott Walker was awarded $30,000 from the National Institute of Health Office of Alternative Medicine for the study" (Furlow 1997: 49).

On consideration of the scientification of religious belief through the institutionalization of legends by the occult or borderline sciences as well as by religious establishments and cults focusing on the practice and spread of various kinds of belief-phenomena, it becomes necessary to deal with the semblance of dichotomy between religion and science in the thinking and behavior of people when they tell, listen, and react to legends, and as they form groups and develop ritualized practices. As religion and science are intimately related, often inseparably intertwined, confused, and conflicted with each other, belief—of any degree between positive and negative extremes—becomes the lifeline of legend communication. Controversy between two worldviews is the trademark of the legend that emerges from the normative uncertainty about the nature of things which both science and religion try to resolve. The polling of one thousand American scientists in 1916 and in 1997 showed an unchanged 40 percent of believers (Genoni 1997: 13), so not much progress in enlightenment can be expected.

Western folk religion as a belief system is the informal doppelgänger of mainstream Christian philosophy based on the Bible and its testimonial interpretations. Over the centuries, this belief system has permeated people's way of thinking, irrespective of their religious affiliations and degrees of devotion. It has affected fundamental cultural knowledge and social values, regulated human relationships, established distinctions between right and wrong, good and evil, human and superhuman, and mortal and immortal. More generally, it molded humans as humble and powerless beings, struggling for survival, dependent on the mercy of positive and negative forces that reward and punish deviation from the mainstream. Belief is manifested in ritual acts of great variety: from individual prayer, blessing and cursing, divination, conjuration, black and white magic, to organized public forms of worship as ceremonial and ritual dramas. On the other hand, effective or failed ritual enactment of belief is articulated in narrative forms that are informative and illustrative of underlying belief. These narratives are the legends that constitute the repertoire of contemporary society, hailing back to historic and even prehistoric antecedents.

From the early Middle Ages, theological, historical, scientific, legal, medical, didactic, and literary writings have communicated legends to their intended audiences. Sermons, exempla collections, vitas of saints and martyrs, chronicles, diaries, and travelogues, demonologies, and mystic, cabbalistic, and astrological books have contemporalized and complemented living and remembered folklore materials to make their points (Daxelmüller 1979). For example, among the many early works drawing on scholastic literature on Satanism and demonic possession are the accounts (legends) in Institoris and Sprenger's *Malleus Maleficarum* (1484), a guidebook for the prosecution of witches, and Reginald Scot's *Discoverie of Witchcraft* (1584). These works give a good review of their contemporaneous legendry. The highlighted cases appear similar to legends told in confessions and testimonies contained in European witch trial protocols and in modern village legends about witchcraft, despite official decriminalization of witches. The popular magic book, *The Sixth and Seventh Book of Moses* (first printed in 1797), remains a standard source for magic action, divination, and curative practices exemplified by legends. Chapbooks, folk books, broadsides, and newspapers from the seventeenth to the late nineteenth centuries effectively helped to spread, maintain, and confirm the popularity of sensational supernatural and horror legends about witches, demonic possession, vampires, werewolves, haunts, buried treasure, monsters, tragic disasters, visions, miracles, and crazy killers (Schenda 1970), to codify underlying belief and stabilize the traditional legend corpus for the modern age.

In the middle of the nineteenth century, as a result of an intellectual search for the unknown, the quest for the secrets of life and death became institutionalized. Based on their previous interests, natural scientists, philosophers, psychologists, literary scholars, and theologians, often at odds with each other, began to investigate phenomena such as apparitions and possession to legitimate spirit belief. Modern occultism began with the participation of scholars dedicated to scientific inquiry who examined people's claims to have had encounters with supernatural and extranormal beings. In the search for rational causes of the accounts that had always functioned as legends in traditional communities, scholars conducted experiments with legend-tellers. They turned with particular interest to practitioners, the seers, fortune tellers, palmists, and mediums whose personal legends of clairvoyance, precognition, telepathy, spirit possession, and materialization were attributed to what would become known as extrasensory perception (ESP). Their stories and performances were stimulated and reproduced in laboratory situations for scientific observation and scrutiny.

To connect the rational and the irrational — the world of the living as we know it, and the world of the spirits we cannot know — in itself creates an irreconcilable conflict between the *Homo sapiens* and the *Homo religiosus*. But the frame was kept generously broad to accommodate both and to conceal the conflict. To justify belief, the language of science was borrowed; and the scientification of traditional legendry opened the door for social acceptability and thus for the proliferation of legends attesting supernatural connections. In the mid-nineteenth century, the scientific exploration of the spirit rappings of the three Fox sisters (Moore 1977) led into two directions. One was the foundation of spiritualism, a religion that focused on ritual communication with the spirits of the dead through mediums; the other was the foundation of parapsychology, an empirical scientific study of the "paranormal" that examined mediums and messengers from the beyond in search of explanations for phenomena that were unexplainable by common standards of rationality (Bauer and von Lucadou 1983; Rhine 1937). And the two opposing directions — religion and science — continue their interdependence.

Spiritualism as a Christian religion has been growing in esteem, in spite of fraudulent mediums and magicians, hallucinating exorcists and clairvoyants, naive and gullible scientists, and those who experience supernormal encounters under their influence or the influence of the socially established common frame of reference. Spiritualist practitioners are given credence by the masses, even though from the outset their scientific evaluation became an embarrassment to scientists — the Fox sisters admitted to cheating. No matter what, medium-centered spiritualism became an established religious organization with an ever-increasing body of practitioners and followers whose stories conform to traditional ghost legend patterns.

By the end of the nineteenth century, faddish cults experienced a renaissance and appeared as carriers of bold new ideas, attracting the interest of the educated urban middle class. Among the public, anthroposophy and theosophy became household words, and spiritualist precursors were as welcome as the pioneers of modern analytical psychology. Lecture halls were filled when famous mystics, prophets, healers, clairvoyants, horoscopists, and palmists spoke. These sophisticated speakers attracted attention because they promised what every human being hopes: that one is capable of changing one's fate and can achieve eternal life, health, and wealth. Seminars were run and associations were founded. Local leaders emerged and formed their clubs and circles. Clusters of followers in Europe and America attended lectures and practiced table levitation, horoscope and tarot card readings, and Ouija board (or cup) communication. Following this fashion, urban housewives enhanced their ESP capabilities and made their homes the sanctuary of spirit communication.

By the early 1900s, these practices had reached village audiences on the road to modernization. Spiritualism as a religion was introduced by the village intellectuals; table levitation and clairvoyance as separate practices influenced traditional divination methods and were molded into traditional culture. For example, in 1960 I heard an old woman medium in deep trance speak in the voice of a dead ancestor in a mountain village of North Bohemia. In the mid-1970s I encountered spiritualism as religion among Hungarian wheat farmers in Kipling, Saskatchewan, where a Calvinist missionary brought the ideas of spiritualism to the community in 1908. This minister had conducted séances with an enthusiastic group of recruits until suspicion rose against his competence as a clergyman. He was recalled, but to this day mediums continue to conduct séances in a "rotund church" without corners where the devil can hide.

Leading clairvoyants have become authorities to be consulted by the police, and they contact the victim in the other world for the courts of law in hard-to-solve criminal cases. Of course, these practices have precipitated rumors that have solidified into legends — with positive or negative commentaries, showing that amateur practitioners are a curious group divided between belief and doubt. As I have already noted, there is hardly anyone who cannot cite a personal or an acquaintance's supernatural or extranormal experience.

At the same time, parapsychology — the study of the margins of psychology and mental hygiene — continues to enjoy popular acclaim, despite its failure to prove any of the "paranormal" claims of its subjects, as well as the growing number of skeptical scientists who question its right to existence. Parapsychology appears as the study of professional legend tellers whose stories address existential but unresolved questions in the hope of resolution. However, scientists have endeavored to bring respectability to the investigation of the paranormal. Biologist Joseph Banks Rhine and his wife Louisa conducted laboratory studies of ESP in the Psychology Department of Duke University from

1928 to 1965. On Rhine's retirement, Duke discontinued research into parapsychology; but German psychologist Hans Bender succeeded not only in establishing a Chair for Parapsychology and Borderline Sciences at the University of Freiburg in 1954, but also an independent research institute and a journal, *Zeitschrift für Parapsychologie und Grenzgebiete der Psychologie* (1957–present). Bender's disciples and followers have continued his work since his retirement in 1977.

Anthropologist Margaret Mead was instrumental in the acceptance of the Parapsychological Association to membership in the American Association for the Advancement of Science in 1969, which was an epoch-making boost to modern supernatural legendry. This scientific upgrading of ghost stories opened the door to academic acceptance. Thousands of colleges and universities offer courses today in parapsychology or present some aspects of occultism in relationship to fields such as medieval studies, literature, religion, history, philosophy, psychology, folklore, anthropology, and popular culture. Thus, universities introduce cult figures to their students who are not always ready to make mature evaluations.

The recognition of "borderline sciences" was encouraging to the hesitants and helped considerably those who made parapsychology and the occult sciences their means of living. The acceptance of parapsychology gave prestige to other fields of occultism, evoking latent ancient beliefs just as rain induces seeds to sprout (Assion 1976: 152), and building bridges between claims of separate factions.

The scientification of the legend has resulted in a gigantic scientific look-alike apparatus that claims that the mysterious powers and phenomena of the legend are manifestations of material energies that are not yet fully understood. The occult sciences do not refute but endow the legend with rational or rational-sounding reinforcement. Psi, astrology, or research in scientific anomalies (Sasquatch, the Loch Ness Monster, UFOs), investigations of the prestigious Hollow Earth Society and its contender, the Flat Earth Society, are just examples of an extensive directory. Without questioning the scientific value and dependability of their activities and results, we must consider their impact on the launching of countless new legends, along with pertinent fabricated theories and explanations aimed at rationalization. One single legend theme complex can provoke the birth of many newer, more personal and detailed legends. For example, stories about the existence, origin, and causes of the Bermuda Triangle are numerous. New stories, such as the one about the yacht that disappeared and then was rescued by dolphins, cluster in great number around the master legend, like grapes in a bunch. UFO-legends combine motifs of reincarnation, resurrection, spirit-guide, and satanic animal mutilation legends and are rooted in at least three unrelated cults with strong potentials to breed new cults.

Occult books and supplies stores exploit this situation and help assure the seekers in their hope. Crystal balls, meditation pillows, incense, voodoo dolls, dream books, manuals of witchcraft, divination rods, and Ouija boards are sold along with the works of Jung, Freud, Einstein, and Heisenberg. Other influential texts include the works of classic occultists Madame Blavatsky (1831–91) and theosophist Rudolph Steiner (1861–1925); the works of British anthropologist Margaret Murray (1921), whose book *The Witch Cult in Western Europe* contributed to the foundation of the modern witches' covens popularized by the media; and the works of Aleister Crowley (1929) and Gerald Gardner (1954, 1959), promoters of modern Satanism and witchcraft. With such massive persuasion it cannot come as a surprise that the seeker finds the suitable legends with accommodating context to internalize and pass on.

A growing group of scientists and humanists have raised their voice against the "seduction of the innocents" (Wertham 1954), the "occult explosion" (Freedland 1973), the "new nonsense," and the "end of the rational consensus" (Fair 1974) in modern society. A counter-sect of debunker scientists, the International Committee for the Scientific Investigation of Claims of the Paranormal, makes heroic efforts to enlighten the public, but their voice is weak in countering the globalization of irrationality.

Philosopher Paul Kurtz's report on the growth of anti-science and its heavy attacks on scientific approach points out that the mass media promotes the irrational and sensational in the areas of the paranormal:

> The paranormal imagination soars; science fiction has no bounds. This is the age of space travel and it includes abductions by extraterrestrial beings and unidentified flying objects from other worlds. The emergence of the paranormal worldview competes with the scientific worldview . . . the pseudosciences provide alternative explanations that compete in the public mind with genuine science. (1994: 258)

Kurtz points to people's genuine fears of scientific discoveries and experiments that may destroy the environment and endanger life on earth as the breeding ground of anti-science, in the form of alternative medicine, Asian mysticism, and the revival of fundamentalist religions. Krauthammer writes of "a flight toward irrationality, a retreat to pre-scientific primitivism in an age that otherwise preens with scientific pride," and remarks on how irrationalism has gained official sanction: "In 1992, Congress ordered the National Institutes of Health . . . to establish the Office of Alternative Medicine. It now directs $14 million of public monies to study, as it were, the effect of potion on prostrates" (1996: 82).

The ambiguity between science and religion at present illustrates that seeking a connection between the living and the dead is a natural response to the awareness of human destiny. Scholars and laymen find their own answers, expressed in legends that are ambiguous, dialectic, and, in fact, hesitant between science and religion. They cannot be anything else because they address the personal, subjective question of individual mortality. Spiritual belief and psi research together are a true breeding ground for the legend: The questions must be raised, but the answers remain open and controversial.

## Research in Modern Supernaturalism

The folklorist undertaking research in modern supernaturalism has to refrain from looking elsewhere before exploring his or her own peer group. During the lifetime of the last three generations (we have no direct access to earlier times when people were no more or less irrational than they are now), epidemics, economic collapse, ethnic-racial and political persecution, and crime, appear as causes of irrational activities almost everywhere.

Rural or urban, people are seeking irrational solutions to rationally unsolvable problems. People may turn to spiritualism when experiencing tragedy, as Sir Arthur Conan Doyle did when his son was killed in World War I. "My great-grandfather turned from Quaker to spiritualist when his son died of disease while in the Civil War," wrote Sarah Koehler (from Markle, Indiana, 1986). "During a seance, my grandfather wrote the answer to this question on a slate, upside down and backwards, as he hadn't learned to write." Childish scrawling was also produced by the medium who volunteered to make contact with the little children whose spooky presence in the loft of Bloomington's elegant Porticos restaurant was advertised on the back page of the menu.[21]

The periodic reappearance of end-of-war prophecies, doomsday predictions, heavenly signs, and rumors of the return of national heroes from the dead were obvious results of helplessness, but occult-trained Europeans knew how to read the signs. For example, during World War II, people desperately hiding in air raid shelters passed time by reading tea leaves, tarot cards, palms, and casting lead — without being particularly gullible. Who can tell the true believer from the agnostic in a perilous situation?

Curiously enough, the coincidence of several seemingly unrelated media-inflated events in 1997 precipitated such a global reaction. Like early stargazers who interpreted unusual signs in the sky as foretelling floods, droughts, epidemics, and wars, opinion-leading agencies and authors were quick to interpret certain news events — and particularly the emotional reaction of global masses to them — as precursors of change, as the advent of a new apocalyptic era beginning in 2000 A.D. The main concerns that year were the mass suicide of the Heaven's Gate cultists and other UFO-related events and acts of vio-

# HISTORY OF THE PORTICOS

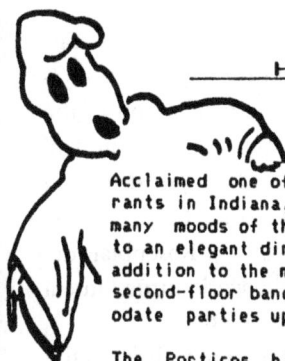

Acclaimed one of the finest restaurants in Indiana, the Porticos embraces many moods of the past to lend charm to an elegant dining experience. In addition to the main-level restaurant, second-floor banquet facilities accommodate parties up to 50 persons.

The Porticos history began in 1890 with construction by First National Bank president, Philip Kearny Buskirk. The supporting walls are of locally-hewn limestone, approximately 18 inches thick. Multiple fireplaces were necessary to heat the building despite the superior insulating qualities of the massive limestone. Approximately two-thirds of the nearly 12,000 square feet of usable space is utilized for the restaurant and banquet rooms. Slate shingles cap the hand-carved limestone exterior.

Eventually the home was sold to William Graham (who built the Graham Hotel), and later, to William Showers (Showers Furniture Factory).

The Showers family renovated the imposing 1890's interior. German craftsmen installed leaded glass (entry and main dining room), hand-carved wood (doorways and ceilings), hardwood floors (entry), solid wood walls (cherry room), and terracotta relief decorations (entry). In 1915 the local newspaper recognized this home as "the most beautiful in Bloomington."

In the late 1940's Phi Kappa Tau fraternity purchased the property. As time passed, "the most beautiful" building became host to Toad Hall (furniture store), The Whimple's of Walnut Street (restaurant), and finally, in 1980, Dr. and Mrs. Steven Lewallen purchased the home for the Porticos. Some novelties of the Porticos include a prohibition-era liquor cabinet concealed behind a false wall panel (cherry room), a wall safe hidden behind a mirror (banquet room), a number of anti-ques, and more than its share of ghost stories!

. articles mysteriously move from one location to another, even during business hours

. a few years ago the Bloomington fire department was summoned to a smoke-filled second story -- there was no fire and the source of the smoke was never determined

. while occupied by Whimple's-- place settings for a banquet were completely set up one evening. When the manager returned the following morning, piles of glass shards had replaced the precise location of each wine glass on every banquet table. Nothing else had been touched

. a friend of an employee was facing a mirror when she noticed a cloud of smoke behind her. It was gone of course when she turned to face it

. using audio monitors, a Bloomington security company has overheard children bouncing a ball in the second floor hallway while calling out "Mommy, come and play with us!"

. invited to a banquet, a woman (who just happened to be a self-proclaimed medium) refused to climb the staircase to the banquet room because "the children sitting on the staircase have their arms locked and will not let me pass."

. water was heard running between the walls. The plumber arrived, opened the wall, and discovered only dryness. All water lines had been capped off years before. The sound of running water stopped

The stories go on and on. Mrs. Lewallen is continually collecting facts and legends about the Porticos and its former occupants with a commitment to preserve the feeling, as well as the structure, of this beautiful landmark.

Back of The Porticos menu

lence, the Roswell pilgrimage, the "Diana effect," the demonstration of mass grief over the death of Mother Theresa, the angry outbursts to court verdicts concerning the au-pair babysitter Louise Woodward, the celebration of the birth of the McCaughey septuplets in Des Moines, Iowa, and the birth of Dolly, the first cloned sheep, in Scotland. The year was rich in turbulent events that caused panics and manifested in monstrous sadistic legends of the type Elaine Showalter identifies as "tales of hysteria" (1997). Rosenblatt declared it to be "The Year Emotions Ruled," in which "the world turned into a global village where it was no longer cool to be cool" (1997: 64).

Interestingly, Rosenblatt's vision of an emotional warmup of feelings in the universe had been argued more forcefully three months earlier by Mathias Schreiber in a *Der Spiegel* feature article that examined the global mass mourning of Princess Diana's tragic accidental death. Surveying the epochal controversy between reason and emotion, and economy and poetry, he pointed out that the advancement of technology has weakened the intensity of feelings, and that the victory march of science and the computer industry have blurred tradition and religion. Nevertheless, ice cold modern media machines can produce myths and tales that appeal to the real feelings concealed behind mass production; and Princess Diana's death awakened real sentiments, perhaps as an elementary resistance to the devaluation of humans through more and more globalized revaluation mechanisms. "The bereavement of Diana has shown how fast the world of millions compacted into a global village can grow into a community of soul kinship. . . . But is the global outpour of sentiments a warning sign heralding a new irrationalism?" (Schreiber 1997: 244). Maybe so.

From the folkloristic point of view something can be learned from the Princess Diana story, which not quite two years after it ran its course virtually disappeared from the limelight. When the fatal crash occurred, the media reached a new peak in inflating and orchestrating the monumental ritual epiphany of Britain's national grief. Within hours the eager information machinery had turned national tear-shedding into a global requiem. The shock was profound for the manufacturers as well as the audiences of the media princess.

Diana originally had been modeled by the media and its audience after the proverbial Cinderella as a modest, virginal kindergarten teacher who married the Prince. But her story did not work out as the projected fairytale, and the Princess did not live happily ever after with the Prince. Thus, a new heroine Princess was invented, and her story became a novella: an adventure with intrigue and sexual overtones that floated from scandal to scandal. Gossip columns, tabloid journalism, and television talk shows drafted a super-modern heroine prototype — a fin-de-siècle role model, who was a cross between a fun-loving, fabulously wealthy socialite and a forsaken, abused wife. She was depicted as a devoted mother, and secular patron saint of the poor and the sick, hugging and kissing AIDS babies and leprosy sufferers. But this story, played out in weekly installments like the better soap operas to keep the public in suspense for the next episode, also ended abruptly, unceremoniously, and untraditionally.

No one could have anticipated such a brutal end, which caused the concerted emotional outpour of the global village. The final, third act of the story-development played out in much bad taste. Any woman, one way or other, could identify with Diana, as was amply demonstrated by countless reports of the international press (see, for example, "Tribute to Princess Diana" in the commemorative issue of *Time*, September 15, 1997: 30–77). In the end, the dead Diana had turned into a legend heroine, and her story on the whole became a legend. But it turned out to be an ephemeral story, as it was eclipsed soon after she was laid to rest and the flowers faded on her grave. It had no more driving force after the tears had dried and the hysterical moaning stopped. Maybe old school folklorists were correct to insist that the formation of folklore genres needs time to undergo the process of transformation from fact to fiction, a process of being repeated and passed on from person to person. So far, writings about the "Diana effect" are limited to the collection of media reports and interviews of individual eyewitnesses with little theoretical benefit (Bennett and Rowbottom 1998).

Thus equipped with the doctrines of religious establishments and the learnings of scientific and pseudo-scientific theories, irrationality can explode and take a new, modern action: It rationalizes irrationality. A pseudo-scientific establishment uses a new language to bridge the gap and connect science and religion. The terminology of "alternative reality" has become household words, and may cover everything from quackery and faith healing to holistic health.

## Poltergeists in the Painter's Studio and Elsewhere

An emphatic unbeliever, Claire Sz., 65, widow of a prominent literary historian and novelist, and sister of a distinguished painter, is a closet clairvoyant. She distinguishes herself from her mother, a Christian and a charter member of the Anthroposophic Society, whose practices she does not condone. However, like other members of her generation of intellectuals, Claire has been educated in spiritualism and knows many stories. In 1945 she attended a table levitation session with distinguished intellectuals who were attempting to contact friends who were killed in the war. The Spanish painter Don Francisco Goya responded to them and said, "It was Greco who saw oblique [not straightforward], not me." No one knew that, but it turned out to be correct when they checked. During a conversation with her at her home in Budapest,

Hungary, in 1978, Claire mentioned two "first-hand" poltergeist accounts that she had heard from her brother shortly after the war.

You know, Andy and a group of other artists moved into this empty house after the town was freed from German occupation. They got a huge studio, bedroom, bathroom, everything. One bright day, the ghost showed up. It knocked on the glass of the pictures they hung up. No footsteps, cracking stairs, it knocked on the pictures. Then, it walked up and down in the large studio. This went on for a long time. It was not hallucination, they both heard it. They sat up in bed, scared. It roamed around, knocked on the wall but usually knocked on the pictures. This went on for a long time. For so long that Andy was unable to leave the studio because if he did, he could not go back to sleep and that exhausted him completely. They had to move out.

And another, really authentic, also a first-hand story. A couple, friends of my mother — I don't know them, but as true as Andy is my brother, that is no fairytale. But this was painful. The ghost played the trick, threw out the hangers from the closet. When they came home, all hangers were thrown out and the clothes were all thrown to the bottom. I don't know why. I can't go into details, because this couple, they are believers, I think they were spiritists, I am not sure . . . there was some exorcism, something happened. But this is a first-hand story, absolute reliable. They are not hysterical people but have a different philosophy. This really happened. It could not have been a burglar, no explanation, no logic. I know how they suffered. They kept coming home, finding the hangers criss-cross on the floor and all the garments on top of each other.

As an afterthought, Claire lightly mentioned also that she is a "witch," or that she is "nuts." She explained that she is able to sense what is going to happen. Once, on a business trip with her husband in another town, she felt the urge to go home. Hurrying back, she found her best friend dying. When she worked as a nurse in a hospital it happened several times that she went in early by instinct and prepared for surgery; half an hour later they would bring in an accident victim. Seeing the patients, she also knew who would live and who would die. She heard her mother-in-law crying the moment she died in the nursing home — they could not call because of power failure, but she knew — "just like Uncle Ernest who heard a gunshot when his son killed himself in Paris."

When I expressed amazement that I never knew she had this gift, she shrugged. "I don't believe in anything, I have no idea what it is or why I see these things and I do not want to try to find out. It's simply there, I can't help it. I never talk about it."

## Ouija Board Exorcism of Revenant

Bob P. came to my office to tell his story so that I could record it on tape, May 2, 1986. His mother who died in 1954 has talked to him twice since then, but these were not the incidents that truly convinced him to believe. In 1978, over a period of two months, strange things happened in the Bloomington fire department where Bob works, and his subsequent investigations into the phenomena convinced him that there is a spirit existence. This experience made him tell his story to many people, one of whom gave me his address. When I called, he was eager to come to my office and speak to my tape recorder.

The staff at Bob's station had experienced the usual unexplained occurrences associated with hauntings, such as footsteps, the television turning on and off, and the lights going on and off. Bob talked about it to his wife who had a Ouija board.[22] She played with it just for fun; she never meddled with the dead, and did not believe in spirits. Their daughter, who lived in Fort Worth, Texas, trusted the Ouija board more: She never started any business without consulting it. It even told her whether a newborn baby would be a boy or a girl.

Bob convinced his wife to come in and do a test. Six of the department's staff sat down one evening with the board to find out who the spirit was.

One of the men said, "It will not work for us if you don't believe in spirits!" But it did. It worked. He said who he was. It was the spirit of Jim MacHenry, the former fire chief who died in a car crash when on his way to a fire. One man asked, "In God's name, who are you?"

My God! he told us his name. I never believed in these things but there were several eyewitnesses. He was a very nice man, who knows why he came back, maybe to educate us about spirits. Certainly not to hurt you. I don't believe in the little green man, I believe that they're people on other planets that is intelligent but not more than we on earth. If we are capable of sending people to the moon, they, on other planets are just as capable of sending somebody down here.[23] I don't believe in anything until somebody shows me enough evidence. That's my philosophy.

Bob is not educated in spiritualism, yet his experience exhibits a curious blend of the traditional conjuration of revenants and the occult conception of the beyond.

### Bell, Book, and Candle Ritual

The case of Val, a 19-year-old pre-law student, shows how much personal affinity can play a role in a person's becoming a bearer of legendry (interview by J. Miller, 1988). Haunted by a "presence," she tells how she disposed of him:

I decided to get rid of him 'cause I just couldn't deal with his presence anymore. And a friend told me of an exorcism rite she had heard of which is called Bell, Book and Candle, and it's where you take the candle, the Bible and a bell and you open the Bible to any page and you read the passage and you ring the bell. And after I did that I never saw the shades anymore, I never heard footsteps, my room got warmer. And, about a minute or two ago I used a Ouija board for the first time with a couple of my friends and I wanted to contact the ghost that had haunted my room . . . and I did. And I found out his name's Haroldyn. Um, he was sacrificed when he was six years old and that was, um, I think it was like a thousand and ten years ago or something like that.

### Adult Classes in Reincarnation

Caroline W., a college instructor, was persuaded by two friends to take an adult class entitled "Increase Your Psychic Ability." It was "just for fun and [she] learned something about reincarnation by practicing. . . . They were into it with a joking attitude but quickly changed their minds when strange things kept happening" (in the account of her daughter, 1980). The teacher was a housewife who had learned from occult books and from a man who taught her how to analyze her dreams and see people in their past lives and their reincarnation. At every meeting the group "read" the past life of one participant. "They came up with some pretty amazing things," said the daughter who attended a meeting. "They all told her about some traumas and ways she died in other lives and explained why she has phobias now. They brought up problems with she and my father and how they have been carried over through other lives. It was amazing how close they were in everything they said."

To tell stories about past lives resulted in the creation of life histories from the past: "A Kansas farm girl of the 1800s, killed by Indians, house burned to the ground," and "A monk in Medieval England, killed by the French." The group had been meeting together for two years, and they had all became entwined in each other's lives. They felt they had all been brought together to help each other in this life, after being together in past lives. The class, which had started out as a four-month "fun" thing, "turned into a two-year therapy session." It also enhanced the members' ability to tell stories.

## Exorcist BarBara Lee and Her Network

Like any social act, legend-telling is based on innumerable past and present relationships between individuals, concepts, ideologies, and formulaic texts. The processes and confluence of ideas in this act is hard, if not impossible, to fathom. Fashion and innovation versus canon and tradition proceed in a continuous historical flow while the language changes, and the cause, purpose, and meaning persist. How can the impact of ideas be weighed as they spread to myriad interest groups, each with their own ideas, who make singular changes, each in different ways? I will not try the impossible task of disentangling past tellings and their compacted essence at the base of current tellings, but I will show one single example: an episode that is limited to the narration of a story and its ramifications over the course of three years. This example may suggest how an average legend-teller with a huge repertoire inspires others, creating a network of recipients who inspire still more new tellers.

BarBara Lee (a pseudonym; her real name was never revealed) is a narrator who specializes in traditional ghost stories in the frame of spiritualism, the religion that she practices as a professional and that she creatively applies to faith healing. I first saw BarBara Lee's name in the Bloomington newspaper in April 1975. In an interview, she was featured as an "exorcist," understood here as a person who helps "earthbound spirits" (the dead who think they are alive and cause distress to the living by inhabiting their bodies) to find their way to heaven, their eternal home. The reporter welcomed the exorcist, who said (as it was also printed on her business card): "In God's Name I Come." She said that she was originally from Cleveland, Ohio, where she had left her family — a husband, and four grown-up children — in response to a divine call. She then moved to Gosport, an Indianapolis bedroom community. Photographer Larry Crewell's double-image photo of BarBara and her spirit guide with outstretched hands, blessing the world, was included in the article and verified by an affidavit signed by a notary public (Judy Davis, "Exorcist: Gosport Woman Claims to Drive Out Unwanted Spirits," *Herald-Telephone*, April 15, 1975: 13). Shortly thereafter, she was interviewed by a Bloomington radio reporter and appeared on the radio show "Cross-Talk" (May 14, 1975), where she answered questions called in by telephone. Later in the year (September 16), the *Indianapolis News* staff writer Bill Roberts interviewed her in Gosport ("Don't Stand Ghost of a Chance": 1, 8); and on October 20, her story and double-image came to national attention through publication in the tabloid

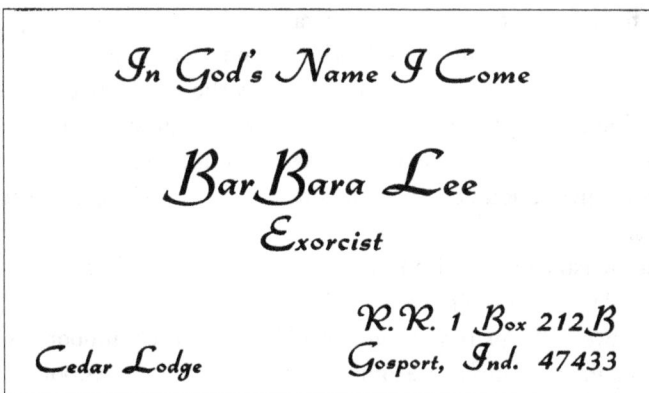

---

*In God's Name I Come*

*BarBara Lee*
*Exorcist*

*Cedar Lodge*

*R. R. 1 Box 212 B*
*Gosport, Ind. 47433*

---

Exorcist BarBara Lee's Business Card

*Midnight* (Harry Altshuler, "Woman Who Makes Miracles Tells 'How I Became an Exorcist,'" October 20, 1975: 3).

I called BarBara after reading about her in May. She sounded very eager to meet me. She said that she had heard about me, and she suggested that I come over to see her at Cedar Lodge, the cottage where she had settled by invitation of Mary Wampler, a fellow spiritualist and the owner of the local nursing home whom she had befriended at the Camp Chesterfield retreat.

Our first meeting on May 14, 1975, was followed by many others over the years. Her move to Gosport was as mysterious as her sudden return to Cleveland would be later when she was "called by God" to minister to a spiritualist congregation. My husband and I interviewed BarBara several times at her home, and she also came to visit us. We often talked in the company of others, such as my students and her fellow spiritualists and friends. She introduced us to Camp Chesterfield, in Chesterfield, Indiana, the oldest spiritualist retreat and learning center in the United States, now called a Spiritual Center of Light, founded in 1886. As a former spiritualist minister, BarBara helped my husband and me establish contact with key figures at the retreat; with her help, we were able to participate in séances and other activities, and to meet ministers, mediums, and the director of the museum exhibiting paintings and sculptures done by spirits. Also, mingling with visitors at the cafeteria and the flea market helped contextualize BarBara's cultural, spiritual, and ideological identity.

One night, when the three of us returned from Chesterfield in dense fog, the road conditions convinced her not to continue her way to Gosport, and she accepted our invitation to spend the night in our home in Bloomington. Examining our books on folk religion, she felt that we were more spiritual and knowledgeable in her trade than she. BarBara knew we were not potential converts, but that we were interested in the spiritualist sect and its negotiations between the living and the dead in general, and her belief and interpretations in particular. She took our interest seriously and spoke to us with sincere enthusiasm, even if it did not concern the cases she experienced or heard of (legends) but rather pertained to salient ideological questions she wasn't prepared for. In her letters she addressed me as "Soul Sister," and expanded on our earlier conversations, clarifying her ideas and interpreting my reactions to the issues.

Besides persuading the dead to leave the bodies of their beloved relatives or friends, BarBara also offered a helping hand to disoriented, lost souls who hovered between the planes; she also would force or trick stubborn evil spirits into leaving their victims alone and going to the retraining school on the second plane so that they would become admissible to heaven.

In order to understand her religious beliefs, theories, and practice, I

**FRIDAY JULY 14 (cont'd)**

3:00 p.m.    **Art Gallery Lecture - AGE**
        **Special Guest:** Joey Korn
        Dowsing/Healing & The Power of Prayer

        **(No Seance Starts Before 9:30 p.m.)**

**SATURDAY, JULY 15**

3 - NOON  **Art Gallery Workshop - AGE**
1 - 5 p.m.  **Joey Korn:** "Working With The Light"
        (send for information)
1:00 p.m.  **Chapel Healing Service:** Suzanne Greer
2:30 p.m.  **Cathedral Worship Service**
        **Sermon:** A. Win Srogi
        **Billets:** Shirley Srogi
6:30 p.m.  **Cathedral All Message Service**
        **Clairvoyance:** Lynda Richey
        **Flame Messages:** Rena Caddell
        **Blindfold Billets:** Louise E. Irvine

**SUNDAY, JULY 16**

9:30 a.m.  **Chapel Worship Service:** Julie Fioresi
11:00 a.m.  **Tree of Life - Book Signing:** Joey Korn
1:00 p.m.  **Chapel Healing Service:** Barbara Loft
2:30 p.m.  **Cathedral Worship Service**
        **Sermon:** Barbara Loft
        **Clairvoyance:** Terrance Ryan
        **Billets:** Suzanne Greer
6:30 p.m.  **Chapel Vespers**
        **Sermon:** Glenda Masiuk
        **Clairvoyance:** John Hein
        **Billets:** Patricia Kennedy

**MONDAY, JULY 17**

6:30 p.m.  **Art Gallery Workshop - AGE:** Susan Hill
        History of Spiritualist Religion,
        Women's Rights and Emma Britten's Parrot

        18

**TUESDAY, JULY 18**

1:00 p.m.  **Chapel Healing Service:** Rena Caddell
6:30 p.m.  **Chapel Vespers**
        **Sermon:** Angela "FoxSong" Ohlmann
        **Clairvoyance:** Pamela Bueche
        **Blindfold Billets:** Louise E. Irvine

**WEDNESDAY, JULY 19**

1:00 p.m.  **Chapel Healing Service:** Harolyn Temple
6:30 p.m.  **Chapel All Message Service**
        **Clairvoyance:** Rena Caddell
        **Flame Messages:** Nancy Joseph
        **Billets:** Judith M. Davis

**THURSDAY, JULY 20**

1:00 p.m.  **Chapel Healing Service:** Lynda Richey
2:30 p.m.  **Chapel Worship Service**
        **Sermon:** Louise E. Irvine
        **Clairvoyance:** Lynda Richey
        **Blindfold Billets:** Louise E. Irvine
6:30 p.m.  **Chapel Vespers**
        **Sermon:** Nancy Pledger
        **Clairvoyance:** Candace Smith
        **Blindfold Billets:** Hoyt Robinette

**FRIDAY, JULY 21**

1:00 p.m.  **Chapel Healing Service:** Julie Fioresi
2:30 p.m.  **Chapel Worship Service**
        **Sermon:** Harolyn Temple
        **Clairvoyance:** Dr. Marilyn Rossner
        **Billets:** Evelyn Reigle
6:30 p.m.  **Chapel Vespers**
        **Sermon:** Rena Caddell
        **Clairvoyance:** Glenda Masiuk
        **Blindfold Billets:** Evelyn Carr

        19

From the Program of the Chesterfield Annual Convocation, 2000

needed to experience her method of exorcism, not just listen to her legends and interpretations. I told her about Stepp Cemetery in the Morgan-Monroe State Forest (commonly known to local people as "the Forestry") with its "Lady in Black" and "Warlock Seat," and showed her the article Incollingo (1966) and Clements and Lightfoot (1972) had written about it. I asked her if it would be possible for her to find out what kind of spirits caused the disturbances there and would she be willing to do an exorcism ceremony. She said yes, but added that she was scared to go to such a place at night, and asked if we could go sometime around noon (an equivalent of midnight, the ghostly hour).

On May 17 (shortly after the vernal equinox), a group of us from the Folklore Institute[24] accompanied BarBara Lee, who was dressed in her long white exorcist habit with a large silver cross on a velvet strap, to the small cemetery plot. She walked from grave to grave, and ended her performance by daringly sitting down on the deadly Warlock Seat. While performing this exorcism, BarBara not only followed her standard practice, but also tried to do more. She had never exorcised an entire cemetery community of spirits before.

Not only did BarBara explore the ordeal of the Lady in Black on the Warlock Seat, who watches over her baby in the grave, but she also looked for other erring spirits around the monuments in the cemetery. We followed BarBara and listened while she talked to the spirits and made intermittent supplications to God. She talked to those she saw, and turned to us to explain what their conversation was, because only she could hear their voices. However, her responses made it clear to us, her audience, what the spirits were saying, what they looked like, and how they behaved. These often argumentative conversations were about finding out the identity of the spirits and the reason why they were earthbound. Each time, BarBara finished her performance by urging the spirit to leave the graveyard and go to heaven or seek the right way to gain entry to heaven. Then she would conclude with a prayer to God asking Him to accept the straying spirit.

The transcribed text[25] of this exorcism was the basis of the follow-up conversations that led us to the discovery of the ideological background, religious belief, and cultural and personal meanings that characterized her technique of ritual performance and amazingly rich legend repertoire. Here, BarBara performed an exorcism of the grave of a little girl and the lightning-struck tree stump known as the "Warlock Seat." She stopped in front of the monument and began to speak:

*BarBara:* What is the matter, darling? Tell me, what's wrong? [To us:] Is this a family tombstone?

*Us:* I think so.

*BarBara:* Because — somebody said it was a family tombstone. Well, darling, I don't see you, but you — you say you are lonely. [listens] What do you mean, cast out? — No, I don't fear you. No, I don't see you, either. But you don't have to be lonely anymore. Do you have a baby? — No, come back, come back here. It's all right. Do you have a baby? — Well honey, that baby's all right and you can be all right too. You haven't got to be in this graveyard. You haven't got to be — carrying the baby around. You are both ready for heaven. — Well, would you like to go to heaven? And your baby can go with you. What? — All I can tell *all* of you is somebody comes and somebody *does* cry here. Somebody cries with *all* their heart, around here.

[Explains to us:] And she said something — now I don't remember what I'm what I'm saying — I try to say, to give the idea, people around me the idea what the spirit's saying to me, because I do *not remember* what they've said. When the sentence goes through me, it's not part of me, it — goes through me. And, uh, all I remember is that it was a family tombstone. She said she's lonely, she's lonely. I said, where's your baby? and she ran that way.

[BarBara prays:] Uh — Dear heavenly Father, I ask you please to bring them both *back*. Are they vagabond? — Well, bring them back now, please. In God's name, bring them back.

BarBara Lee at a Stepp Cemetery grave with
author recording in background

BarBara Lee sitting on the Warlock Seat

[To the spirit:] Would you like to go to your heavenly home. Honey? Don't be afraid. — Somebody's hiding behind a big tombstone, but I thought it was closer to me than that. There are more than — there are more than one. — Uh-huh. And — uh — what do you mean you're in the grave? No one has to be in the grave! No one has to — be in this cemetery! Because you've lost your physical body! You've just lost it! And you don't *need* to stay here honey, you don't *need* to be bound here!

What're you afraid of? What're you afraid of? [slowly, comfortingly] But let's put you in heaven. Let's show you the way to heaven. [prays] Dear heavenly Father, I ask you please to put this spirit into the heavenly home. [Impatiently:] Yes, I know, but what has this got — why do you want to stay at this gravesite? No, it *isn't* your home. [Softly:] I know, dear, I know that, but it doesn't *have* to be your home. But it doesn't have to be your home. Don't you want to go to heaven? — [sadly] Is there more than one child buried here? — family gravesite! Now that could be because there are a lot of earthbound spirits in this family. . . . [prays] Dear angels of love, I ask you please to bring them all right here, and let's get them all to heaven. [Raises voice:] That's right. You can be there too. — Well, a part of God. My beloved, you *are* a part of God. But — uh, you see, you're afraid! You don't know what's ahead of you, do you? You're *afraid* to go to heaven! You're only — you feel safe *here*, because you don't know what's heaven's like, do you? Well-well, I . . . and, uh, but you know what, God loves you now.

[Confidingly, as if to a small child:] And there are a lot of real, real good people, honey. And they can't believe in God. But as long as they're good, they have a right to go to heaven. Have you found God? [slowly] In the trees? In the sky. A lark. [Prays slowly:] Oh Father, God, I ask you please. C'mon, c'mon. [sighs] Dear angels, I ask you please to take this spirit into our heavenly school so that she may progress, and let

279

them all be together. And you know honey, some day, a long time from now, a long, long time, you will be able to see God, but that takes a lot, a lot of development. And some day like you lost your physical body, you will lose this body, and then you will be able to see God. For soul will see soul. But you *know* there is a God. And some day you will see him. [Emphatically:] But I want to tell you, all your sins are behind you, because you have been in an earthbound condition so long, so long, that many times this darkness around you, this being bound to a grave site is part of the penalty, part of the suffering to get you fit to heaven. And I believe that there's nothing to hold you back . . . [Breathily:] And I believe that you can be happy in a new-found joy. [Tone change to low, sepulchral:] Somebody said something in the back of me — uh — Do you think you could get the spirits here, or should we go over there?

We agree to move to another tombstone whose inhabitant approaches BarBara. Another unhappy earthbound spirit's case is presented. But before that story can unfold, we ask her about the Warlock Seat, which she did not mention.

*BarBara:* It didn't feel like anything when I touched it . . . although when you even talk about it, I get a — We'll bless it when we go out. We'll bless it, because when you even talk about it I got a scary feeling. That always means evil. You see, when there's evil it hits me in my solar plexus, like a fear. And I don't have any fear. Except at night I do! [laughs] Yeah! It says here, died in '64.

Well, this was nothing. . . . Oh, that one was sobbing and crying. . . . That's what breaks your heart in this work, you know . . . 'cause you see 'em so unhappy, you know they've been crying for all those years . . . it just breaks your heart.

BarBara's attention shifts to another grave marker, and we followed her as a new spirit's case unfolds . . . and she continued her talk to spirits one by one in the graveyard until early afternoon.

An hour later our group gathered for a late lunch at my home and continued to discuss the spirit world and exorcism, bombarding BarBara with questions concerning her performance. She answered the questions cheerfully and laughed a lot. My husband, Andrew, asked her to describe heaven to us.

*BarBara:* Heaven is a summerland. It's flowers. It's beautiful paths, it's beautiful edifices. It's libraries, it's music halls, it's everything that we have here that is very very beautiful. And you know what? In heaven everything is done by thought.

There is no sun, and no sunset because it's always light. It's always beautiful bright light. Not too bright, just bright. Flowers . . . there is no sunshine, just light. The sun and the moon are different things.

*Andrew:* What makes the light?

*BarBara:* They say, it's all from God. They say the light in heaven is the spiritual light of God. God is light . . . No, that's not so, they can have lamps in their homes, they can have anything they want. When you have earned the right to the kind of home you want.

*John:* A house like here?

*BarBara:* Yes. It's a house like here.

*John:* Quite far from Dante.

[BarBara laughs loudly.]

*Andrew:* Is there heating and cooking?

*BarBara:* No, no, no. To a point now, there is fruit in heaven they can refresh with, and if they want to put in something like this, just to have company, they could. But they would serve fruit to eat in heaven. And there is water in heaven. I suppose, if you wanted a faucet in your kitchen, and you thinking it out, why couldn't you have a faucet? You can have the *exact* duplicate of this house, including the water in your kitchen.

*Andrew:* How is commuting? City or country?

*BarBara:* You mean, in heaven? It's different planes, Andrew. It's different, it's like a, like we, well, how can I say it, how do we have planes? It's like one on top of each other but the lower one cannot see into the higher ones. But the higher ones can see into the lower ones. But you have to wait until you are higher, in order to see what's going on in the lower realms.

*Andrew:* And can you return from heaven?

*BarBara:* Yes, yes, you can return for your loved ones, and they always do. And you know, it's interesting that any children . . . I had five miscarriages, and my children know all their brothers and sisters and they tell me what's going on. You know, on earth. When they talk to me, you know, so and so is doing that, "Mom, why is she doing that for?" They are right with us.

*Andrew:* How many children do you have?

*BarBara:* You mean living? Four. Two boys and two girls living and two boys and three girls living over there. [laughs] They're helping with my work. All of my angels are in this work that I am doing. There is not one of them who isn't. They are angels who were once on earth, like the ones living. Others have all been stillborn, just babies when they died, or miscarriages, mostly seven weeks, and they all have been brought up in heaven.

*Andrew:* How do you know how heaven is?

*BarBara:* My angels tell me a lot. But we do go to heaven at night and we are not aware of. We think, we are dreaming some time we think we saw someone who passed over. Really we are there with them. And when my children were little, I used to be real tired, I couldn't understand it. But I found out that many times I was in heaven, taking care of my children up there. I was really fatigued by the morning. And I realized why. So really, the invisible world is not much different of this. And you have beautiful halls of learning, Andrew, and music, everybody takes music, and they really enjoy that. And the kids? Like kids here. My little boy of five over there, went to visit my friend in Chesterfield. We heard this noise on top of the roof. It was a . . . my little son said, "Did you hear this playing on the roof last night?" [laughs] Sure did. Those little monkeys went over the field and tickled a horse so that it jumped up and down. They were all spirits. [laughs] So they are really mischievous too. [laughs]

BarBara drew us a picture to show the planes below heaven and their inhabitants, the spirit doctors and guardian angels and guides on the second plane where reincarnation occurs; she also discussed mediums and insects, plants, and animals who can also speak. A maple tree talked to her, once: "This bark is my skin," it said.

Summarily, with the *Motif-Index* in mind, I believe Barbara's exorcism-related stories are conventional. They would all fit into section D, or even into the Röhrich–Müller "Death and the Dead" legend catalogue (1967: 346–397). As she explained to me, just as there are ghosts in this cemetery, so are there ghosts in houses, living rooms, animals, plants, objects, chimneys, barns, roads, and churches; there are even ghosts in the bodies of people, whom they cause great pain in the joints, the limbs, the back, the head, and other parts. According to BarBara's philosophy, the dead live on in another plane and existence, so no one who was born will ever disappear without a trace. Normally, the dead progress toward the highest existence: heaven. Some, however, remain to cause trouble, staying in the world of the living for a variety of reasons (no different from the reasons listed in the *Motif-Index*). The exorcist must find the reason to make it possible to lay these ghosts to rest. BarBara's vocation is to establish the fact that a spirit is residing in and taking possession of the body of a person, causing sickness, or creating a haunting disturbance in the habitat; next, she must identify the spirit and the cause of its presence, and assist it in finding its way to Heaven.

As an experienced exorcist in constant consultation with her spirit guide and her angels (her five stillborn children who grew up in heaven) as executors of God's will, BarBara has a large repertoire of cases which she narrates happily, with gusto. These legends are variants of the same story about sending earthbound spirits to heaven. They consist of four parts:

1. Account of the disturbance
2. Identification of what causes the disturbance
3. Negotiation with the earthbound spirit (a narrative within the narrative)
4. Resolution: spirit sent to heaven, and victim's health and happiness restored.

This clear linear structure can be plain and smooth, or can be extended with complications or be fragmentary, reduced to hints and references. It also can be limited to a purely emotional supplication to God, and a compassionate monologue, urging the spirit to leave, accompanied by emotional outbursts, sighs, sobs, shouts, and weeping in response to the spirit's reactions.

The stories about innocent loving relatives who do not know they are dead are relatively simple compared to cases of multiple-spirit presences; even more complex are hauntings by strangers, previous owners of a residence, nasty spooks who were unwittingly imported to the home through the purchase of antique valuables, evil spirits, and malicious eternal wanderers such as murderers, drug addicts, drunks, prostitutes, and robbers. The latter spirits have gained no admission to heaven and are looking for a shelter or hideout.

BarBara's type of exorcism is actually people-oriented, not spirit-oriented, and belongs to the broad category of faith healing. Early in her life, when people instinctively complained to her, she began to treat them by laying her hand on the aching body part, also by using an anointed cloth. Beginning as early as 1958, she was chosen, because the angels sent people to her. Her parents warned her that it is dangerous to deal with such things, but she was determined to follow God's will. A soul-search made her realize that sickness is caused by no other but earthbound spirits, and that healing sick people meant exorcising these spirits from the ailing body. BarBara does such exorcisms routinely all the time, on an informal basis whenever someone in her company complains of feeling faint, having an upset stomach or heartburn, a head cold or a headache; she did this for me and some of my students during our visit with her.

On May 22, 1976, BarBara invited us to a dinner with Mary Wampler. Later Marilyn Williams, another exorcist, joined us, and we learned more about the spirit world, angels, God's messengers, our guardians, and the trouble with earthbound spirits. Mary spoke of a séance that she had attended in Seattle.

*Mary:* A man came in while we worked on the Ouija board, and said he patrolled the western coast — he spoke through a medium — he was three thousand, six hundred years old. The angels liked him, protected America.

She saw another angel in downtown Seattle, a little wrinkle-faced man:

*Mary:* We looked at each other — he was only four feet high. He never said anything, but I wondered if he wasn't one of them. Yellowish complexion, no suntan either, just different.

BarBara felt relaxed in the presence of a supporting friend and began to narrate when we asked her to tell us about some of her exorcisms. As a perfect hostess, she participated in the general conversation while she laid the table, checked the oven in the kitchen, and brought the roasted chicken dish in. As we ate, she recounted cases, like episodes of her life history. She appeared well prepared in spiritualist theology and placed her ghost legends with ease into their frame.

Compassionate with the victims and understanding with the disoriented spirits, she treats them all tenderly, like a mother would treat a disturbed child — with love, lots of tact, and a great deal of good humor. She reproduces conversations, remarks on the silly and awkward behavior of people, and laughs frequently even at her own mistakes. The spirits in her stories often come from earlier historic epochs, and she features them as being out of place, describing their looks and mimicking their speech and demeanor. As a well-mannered hostess, she interrupts her stories by offering second helpings to her guests without losing her thread. In the following cases of healing, the complexity of spirit activity behind illness is well illustrated.

### The Brother Who Hung Himself

Two women came here with horrific pains in their . . . in their head and she had pains since February. And one went to the hospital and they gave her the strongest pill they could give her and the pain didn't stop. So, she came here. She heard the broadcast on the air. Bob J. called me up and made the interview. Next day, she had examination and X-rays and they couldn't find anything. So when she heard that, she came to me. And her brother had committed suicide five years before. But he wandered around, and then was lost, but finally he found her. February, like I said. "I was about four and a half years before he died." And when she came here, there was a closeness. I never heard a spirit — you see, they always talk to me — and I never heard a spirit talk about anybody with so much love. And I said, "Who are you?" And he said, "I'm her buddy." And he was her brother. And so, I talked to him some more, and I found out, he didn't know he was dead. No, they don't. They can go hundreds of years and they don't know they are dead. . . . He had hung himself and where he hung himself, his neck broke, snapped. That's where her trouble, pain was.

### The Mother-in-law Who Hung Herself

The same week, another girl, a few days later another girl with the same name, but it wasn't in her head like that, it was in the neck, and she had just pain in the neck. She said, "BarBara, I know, it's my mother-in-law." And she said, "My husband won't believe it, but I know, it's my mother-in-law." And so it *was*. And her mother-in-law hung herself, I think, a year before. And she'd been in that girl since she'd done. And she was causing fights between the two of them. She never liked her daughter-in-law, and so she was causing fights between the two of them, they were very, very unhappy. That was two of them.

This recollection reminded her of her own troublesome mother-in-law and she continued.

*BarBara:* You want to hear something crazy that happened to me, Andy?
*Andrew:* Sure.

### The Blue Stone

*BarBara:* It is unbelievable. At least, I find it unbelievable. My mother-in-law was always a little sore at me. And when she died, she was earthbound. Well, for lot of reasons. Not that reason only, but anyway, she was earthbound. So, my husband said, "We ought to have a stone for mother's grave, like they say." She was Swedish, and she liked blue. And so, we saw a Swedish blue stone. So I said, "Well, well, let's get it." She was Swedish and she liked blue; "I know she'll like it."

So we went to this guy and Walt said, "Well." Salesman said, "You won't be wanting a small, you know, that gets close to the ground. Or you want a big one?" "Say," my husband said, "It's awful lots of money, let's go home and talk it over and decide." I was going down the stairs, and my mother-in-law said, "I'll turn it over." [laughs] So I said to my husband, I said, "Walt, I don't think your mother likes that stone, she does not like that. So we shouldn't get this big stone if she really doesn't like that." Then they call up and ask us, which one? And we said, "We take the small one." [laughs]

It wasn't long before we got the bill for the stone. And we went out there, you know, oh boy, we got to see the stone. We got out there, and there wasn't any stone. *On the grave.* Says, go back the next day, and we said, I remember she said to me "I turn it over," you know, and so, next day we go out and no *stone!* So we called up the people, and she said, "I know, we delivered it, because I know, I sent out there yesterday, it was delivered a month ago or something." That's what she said. But anyway she said, "I know because it was *delivered.*"

Anyway, we let it go, we get another bill. So, I said, "Let's go and see your mother's stone." We got out, there's *no stone.* And so, the man at the cemetery was to call some men at the city hall. The city hall got on to it, the cemetery got on to it, the people who made the stone got in on it, for a *year this went on.* A bill goes out and no stone.

So finally I went out, and my brother-in-law in the spirit world takes care of lots of souls. So I said, "Carl, I had enough of this," I said, "you can help your mother. I want you to take her to heaven," I said. "I want that stone," you know. And so I said, "Don't worry, it will turn up." So [laughs] we soon got out to the cemetery. Then the people who made the stone came in, and here they were at work, he said, he left it, and here it was *upside-down.*

*Mary:* Oh my heavens!

*BarBara:* And I have had them make it with gold on light blue and when it turned up, it was mud on all that gold, it looked terrible. And I said to my husband, I said, "Oh gee, that doesn't look so nice." And my mother-in-law said, "Well, it's your taste." [big laughter] But they put, you know, this stone in the cemetery (ha-ha), and we paid for it (ha-ha-ha). Can you *imagine* that?

*Mary:* But they straightened it out, so they reset it.

*BarBara:* It never was set on, that grave.

[General laughter while everybody ate.]

While we were still eating, BarBara delivered her most complex and horrific legend, which reveals an even broader spectrum of earthbound spirit belief. It was Mary's reference to a certain doll she does not like that recalled the account to BarBara's mind, and my question "what doll?" triggered its performance.

### The China Doll[26]

*BarBara:* Oh, some girl came here with her girlfriend . . . her girlfriend died when she started . . . oh, well, in her forties, thirtysomething. Anyway she had a start, acting like her girlfriend who has died. Her name was Laura. And Laura's husband decided to get married. And this girlfriend was very unhappy. And she said, "Why should I be unhappy," she says, "I am *glad* that Laura's children will have a mother." She said, "Why would I be unhappy?" So she got thinking about . . . read my article, and she said to her . . . close friend, she said, "I'm gonna go see BarBara," she said, "I think, something is funny."

And she came out here and we got Laura out. And Laura was in her, *making her miserable.*

And Laura — I forgot what she died with, but anyway, the girl was feeling the symptoms of what she died with, after that happened, you know. And we got Laura and she felt wonderful.

*But* she was an antique buff . . . she had lots of antiques. And she had a doll that she gone to a Chicago auction, oh . . . few years before. And she couldn't resist that doll.

*Mary:* She had to have it.

*BarBara:* She just couldn't go home without it. So, she got up to the woman who got it, and the girl came down from $150, she said, "I'll give you double." So she gave her $300 for that doll.

*Mary:* Oh my!

*BarBara:* You want some more potatoes, Andy?

*Andrew:* Yes.

*BarBara:* That's how bad she wanted it. It was a German doll, a china doll.

*Mary:* About that size. [shows size]

*BarBara:* It was . . . it is *beautiful.*

*Mary:* It had a face, it looked more like a person than any doll I ever . . . as if it were alive. Its eyes were alive. Everybody who came to the house was scared in it something . . .

*Andrew:* How tall was it?

*BarBara:* Two feet? . . . And, anyway, she got home, and she loved it, little while. She got so, she couldn't stand to touch her, and, although nobody touched it, its shoes and stockings never stayed on it. So, when I came in, she, here the shoes, one shoe was off, and one stocking and shoe were off. And anyway, I picked up the doll and I heard a voice say, "You let my dolly alone." And I put the doll down. And I got it across, well, that's the response I wanted. That's a spirit.

So I go and take the doll again, and grab it real tight: "I like that doll." She says, "If you don't put my dolly down, I'm gonna slap you." So that was it. Well, I said, "Well, I like your dolly," and I held it real tight. But she wanted it so badly that I saw her little hand materialized, and she pulled on my arm to get me put it down. And she was a beautifully dressed little girl, seven — . . . she said her name was . . . Anyway, she called the doll Rosie, that was little Rosie. And as she said, "I want my dolly," and I wouldn't give it to her, so she ran and she got the girl that everybody had seen in the house.

There was a beautiful tall young girl and . . . A lot of people staying in the house, and that's why she [the China doll] really came for, to get rid of that tall young girl. And here the little girl, that wouldn't give me the doll, turned around, and, I saw her. And she had one of those old fashioned dresses, lace, and real pretty creamy color, yeah, that was all lace. Then, she had a great big sash in the back, and she had little sleeves down to here, like in the early nineteen hundreds. So, anyway, she just like that, got to that beautiful tall girl, and she said to me, "What do you want?" And I said, I told her who I was, I am an exorcist, and "I want you to go to heaven." And she said, "You leave her doll alone, you leave her alone." And I said, "I am sorry but I can't because I can't leave until all of you go to heaven."

She turned around, just like that, and she brought in the most handsome looking older man, dressed in a black frock coat. He was so distinguished, so nice looking, and he said, "What are you doing, and what are you doing to my granddaughter?" Oh, and I asked the girl, "Who are you? Are you the girl's mother?" And she says, "I am her . . . like her mother." She was a governess. And so I said, "And who are you?" And he said, "I am her grandfather." Then, he said, "I want you to put that doll down. Leave that girl alone, get out of here." And I asked, "What year is it?" And he said, "It's 1901, maybe it's 1902." And here he was. So I called my angels, and they all left with my angels.

But I brought the doll home. Because I could not get the . . . no, I brought the doll home because I was goin' to have a lecture and she said, "If I were you, I'd want the people to see. Take the doll, BarBara, and show it to them."

I got the doll into the house. I put it on that little thing over there. I walked in the door, and I thought to myself: that doll would kill me if it could. And I didn't want to go near it. But I didn't pay attention to it. I thought, you know, I just . . . I just ignored it. Yeah, I ignored it. And some friends of mine came over that night, and when they were going to leave, they said, "I won't [weren't] going to leave you with that doll. That doll was going to murder you." I said, "How can a doll murder me? Don't be silly." But anyway, the three of them left . . . that night, and the man [the grandfather] picked her up. She called him daddy. She loved her grandfather. And she was separated from him all this time. Anyway, I put the doll down and I tried to get the spirit out. But it wouldn't leave.

The last day I was there, I went back to her, the last day I had it [the doll]. I sat down with it, I said, "Now, you've got to leave. You should be going to heaven." He [the doll] told me who he was, I got checked it out. He told what had happened. He hoped he had jumped, he was a robber on a train, in which this rich man [the grandfather] was. The man's name was Fleetwood, the robber said, his name was MacDonald. And he said that those rich people didn't know what to do with their money. "But I help'm you know, and I . . ." Then, he talks a little bit further, tells me he had a gun, he shot this man, than he jumped into this doll to escape, to hide. And you know, I took that doll home with that spirit and it wouldn't leave.

*Mary:* Have you heard anything of those folks?

*BarBara:* No, I've got to, though.

*Mary:* Where is the doll?

*BarBara:* Down in Indianapolis.

*Linda:* Where?

*BarBara:* I can't tell names, you know that.

*Andrew:* Did you check on that murder?

*BarBara:* Not yet, but I got to. Want some more?

*Mary:* But people thought about her eyes . . . you didn't tell about that.

*BarBara:* No, everybody knows how those eyes would follow everybody. . . .

*Mary:* When they came in, it was incredible those eyes, they did something to ya.

*BarBara:* But it was frightening, wasn't it?

*Mary:* I have a picture somewhere of it.

*BarBara:* Don't you? But it's a frightening thing to look at it. Just looks evil.

*Linda:* Did you warn the people who have it now? It can harm.

*BarBara:* The spirit can, yes.

*Andrew:* So you didn't succeed to exorcise it?

*BarBara:* No, sir.

*Andrew:* Why not?

*BarBara:* It would not leave. I was so glad when that doll got out of here. That doll dominated that house. And I go upstairs, and that doll's eyes would follow me. First thing in the morning, that doll be looking at me coming down those stairs.

*Andrew:* Glass eyes move?

*BarBara:* It moved. I think the eyes moved. What would you like, Linda?

As we continued our conversation over coffee and dessert, BarBara recalled more cases from her practice of exorcism: healing people stricken with supernatural illnesses by prayer appealing to God, angels, and associates among the dead who had made it to heaven. BarBara and her group do not call this sickness, condition, or altered state *possession*, the much-used term among fundamental Christians (as in being possessed by the Holy Ghost or by evil spirits or Satan).

Reinforced by the arrival of Marilyn, BarBara shifted her emphasis as she briefly summarized more cases. Rather than miracles of healing, the cases she now discussed resembled the more commonly experienced ghost stories. As in ordinary ghost stories, she said that homes are inhabited by spirits for diverse reasons: Unwitting people had brought precious objects (antiques) in the house that had an evil spirit hiding inside, or had moved into a house with restless spirits who caused lasting unhappiness to their families. Old houses in particular had had many previous residents who may have stayed to trouble later generations. Topically, BarBara's cases are traditional haunted house legends, rooted in American folk religion but articulated experientially, informed by her spiritualist exorcist's learning.

### Trouble with Spirits in the House

*BarBara:* Somebody had killed somebody on the doorstep. Two men fought about who was the father of the baby, and that was the time when it was a disgrace. And one had killed the other in her house. And I got hold of the murderer who came from Tennessee.

In a fifty-year-old house, she had pains in her leg and her back. And when her husband washed dishes he felt it. And here I went over to the sink and . . . I knew when he had those pains, you know, by the sink. And I . . . standing there, and I said, I didn't know that they had pains when they stand there. Said, "Do your legs hurt you like this, when you're standing there? Mine start to hurt!" And she said: "Yes, how do you know?" I said, "well, I got it." Then, she said, her husband admitted it afterwards that he got them too. And it was a little spirit, and she was a little tiny, oh boy, she liked to fight. She was ornery, little teeny-weeny woman. Been there for years and years, and years. Staying there. But I never . . . I was so tired in that house that I actually fell asleep on the road. . . . When you do a house, it takes twice . . . you have to go . . .

*Marilyn:* [interrupts to explain] There are so many unhappy people in the world with such trouble in the house. And they don't know what's the matter with them and they don't know what to do . . . and they just go through life like this. And other people, rest of the family don't understand what's the matter with them.

*BarBara:* There are interesting cases, one lately. She knew, she had two bad spirits with her. And she knew who they were. One of them been with her for life. And she, still in her fifties, early fifties, she has been with her since she was a little girl. I tell you who it was. Her father was engaged, and the girl was killed and she didn't know she was dead. Now the girl is fifty, in her fifties. That had to be a year before that, and the spirit said, "I am her mother, me, I'm her mother." And what had happened, her mother was miserable all her married life. And anyway, here she had this girl with her, he had always predicted all the bad things that are going to happen to her, you name it. And she hated it because she knew the bad things. And she didn't know the good things. So, that's when she came to me.

*Andrew:* How did you get him out?

*BarBara:* Just like others, with prayer.

*Mary:* Were they happy?

*BarBara:* Oh, she couldn't believe it. And she brought her daughter and the daughter brought her granddaughter. And guess what: the granddaughter woke up miserably every morning, and it was her grandfather. In the child. And I couldn't believe it, you know. All of a sudden, a voice told me, "she is a hellion." And I said, "She is a beautiful seven-year-old child . . . and are you her grandfather?" He said, "Yes." And she woke up miserable every morning.

Evidently, BarBara's ghost stories, like those of other professional exorcists, ghost-tracers, or ghost-busters, are traditional revenant-legends. However, some also resemble those of any lay person reporting a presence in a house. The former are goal-oriented and factual, answering "who?" and "why?" and concluding with a more or less satisfactory resolution. However, the latter type are often incomplete, fragmentary, highly emotional, and subjective, representing the victim's sense of vulnerability.

As a professional woman, BarBara is serious and eager to help. She made many contacts in the Morgan and Monroe counties area, but she hardly made a living from the modest donations she accepted from clients. When she laid on her hands and prayed for us, suspecting some distress from our demeanors, she refused payment from the "soul sisters and brothers" that she felt we were. Maybe it was enough to give her bags of birdseed to feed wildlife; we enjoyed watching birds, raccoons, and squirrels on her porch while taping our conversations.

While she lived in Gosport, BarBara suffered from the hostility of local churchgoers and was rumored to be a witch. Yet she found patients who turned to her for help. She was very discreet, and never identified any of them to me. Those I did meet either called me on their own, or I met them by chance. I learned, for example, that students troubled by mysterious noises in a graduate residence hall at Indiana University had asked her to help, and she had exorcised the spirit of a suicide victim who had jumped from a sixteenth-floor window. I also met Mildred R., a widow with excruciating pains in her back because, according to BarBara's diagnosis, the spirit of her husband who died two years earlier was inside her.

Once I received a phone call from two university women who wanted to talk to me about BarBara. To my amazement, they were dead serious, asking my honest opinion about her effectiveness. My surprise, or rather shock over the gullibility of academics, changed to understanding when they revealed to me that both had lost adolescent sons to suicide and were desperate to find a means of contacting them. A third woman, their friend, told me that at one time Bloomington had had a teen suicide epidemic. "Something terrible is going on in that high school, " she said. "Everybody knew, but no one would talk about it. It is evil, the Devil makes them kill themselves. But it is danger-ous to talk about it."

The most interesting and characteristic clients of BarBara, however, turned out to be practitioners themselves. That is, self-styled spiritualists who had developed a suitable format for their spirit belief. A haunting experience had brought them in contact with BarBara.

### Jane, Pat, and Ann

In the summer of 1975, Ann, a Martinsville schoolteacher and the wife of a wealthy local farmer, told me about a haunted living room in a stately man-sion, which had become the theme of regional gossip. She arranged an invita-tion to the house, where she joined two other women to talk to me about the spirit presence. The two housewives — Pat, whose family had owned the house previously, and Jane whose family was now in possession of the house — are educated and prominent members of the community. All three women were old friends and searchers who were interested in the occult. They had gone to Ed Caycee readings, studied numerology and mediumship, and attended seminars of PSI, Inc. in Indianapolis.

Somehow, none of the sects had given them satisfaction or meshed with their basic Christian education, so they had created their own Bible-reading circle some six years earlier. Among the group of twelve were Ann and her husband, Pat and her husband Bill, and Jane (whose husband, Bob, stayed away). They prayed ("talk to God"), meditated ("let God talk to you"), and had fun by "playing games" with the Ouija board when they met once a week. "I am a weird person," said Jane laughingly. Then she turned serious: "We always knew something is wrong with the living room."

"It was built in 1859," added Pat. "It belonged to my uncle. And oh, for years, people didn't want to go in. They wouldn't know why, they'd walk out." Jane had a hard time having people in that room, as there was no laughter or gaiety to be had there — people froze when they came in. The group became determined to find out what caused the fearsome atmosphere of the living room, and they turned to meditation and the Ouija board. For them, this was the instrument for making contact with the spirit world, to identify the perpetrator and the reason of its presence.

Ann spoke to me about the haunted living room, and when I indicated interest in it, she started the legend-conversation that kept its dialogic, participatory rendition style to the end, just as traditional legends do. This transcript is an authentic recording of the legend in context. It contains all the details and situational information. The women told the story to me, the interested outsider, and included all the information they felt was needed to understand their ordeal and their acts in searching for answers.

### The Haunted Living Room

*Ann:* Jane, Dr. Dégh is interested in your living room and the history behind it.
*Pat:* Are you at all sensitive?
*Jane:* I'm not to spirits. And I tell you, I have hints to the very strong feeling and I'm not sensitive. I had very strong feeling that the remaining spirit in the living room left this Christmas. I just . . . you know, no proof, I have no . . .
*Linda:* Was there a spirit, and how did you find out?
*Jane:* OK, but this is Pat's story.
*Pat:* Yes, this is my great-great-grandfather's house.
*Jane:* No, he built the house, we bought it.
*Pat:* It belonged to my uncle.
*Linda:* Your uncle sold it to them? When was the house built?
*Pat:* 1859. And oh, for years, people didn't want to go to the living room. They wouldn't know why, they'd walk out. Jane had a hard time having people in that room. But no one knew.
*Jane:* I had my club meetings, it was almost like a funeral parlor. I just . . . people talked softly . . .
[Pat laughs.]
*Jane:* You know, there was no laughter, gaiety . . .
*Linda:* What meetings did you have?
*Jane:* Women's club, charity, bridge party, arts club. Just normal people. [All three women laugh.] Not the weird things we do. But you know, but just . . . there would be a pause. But they would be in other parts of the house, in very stimulated, loud conversations or laughing, but *not* in the living room. No one knew what happened but people felt that sadness over there. But they didn't know what it was, or . . . and my husband hated that . . . [phone interrupts]
*Pat:* . . . Playing the Ouija board, you know, just having fun. Games, just *games.* Just saying, am I going to Hawaii, or this or that, or what will happen to me? One night, me and my husband were working on the Ouija board, and Jane quit. And the Ouija board went on by itself. And all of a sudden . . . and I have never in my life seen my husband cry. He started sobbing, he bawled. [Jane laughs.] He *bawled.* He threw the Ouija board down, and couldn't control himself. Jane and I were absolutely in the state of shock. She's "you want coffee?" and she's "Bob, what's the matter?" He says, "I don't know, I feel like awful, saying this, I can't stand this, it comes from that room." And we talked . . .
*Jane:* But, phase part one, I got so nervous, you know, nothing I could think of but

coffee. [laughs] I went to the kitchen and put on an electric cup, and stayed back there 'til it quit perking. And I thought, maybe Pat has him under control by now. And I came back, and [laughingly] he was still sobbing and crying. And I took him . . . he was scared to death. What had happened to him? *Yeah* . . .

[Pat tries to speak but Jane continues.]

*Jane:* He felt something came from that room, that *completely* took him over. It was like a possessing.

*Pat:* And he said, "I am really not myself, cry, cry, cry," he start crying again. And he said, "I always hated that room. I felt a *terror*, I could not stay at that room very long." And so, we went home. And the next day, she [i.e., Jane] says, "Bill's not here" — her husband wasn't going along with anything — and so, "Won't you come over and work the Ouija board? Let's find out, what in the world happened?" I felt Bob was scared. I think he'll never come to your house again! You know. [laughs]

So, I went downstairs and told him. And he said, "I gotta know, because I gotta know." He was just white, all day. And we went out and . . . it took about an hour before he got the courage to do it. And it boiled down to . . . a relative of mine, my great-aunt and a . . . who was just crying all the time. And it . . . I don't know, do you remember? It's been so long . . . it did say, her last initial was H. He even went to the old family . . .

*Jane:* Graveyard.

*Pat:* Graveyard. Up the road . . . it's abandoned. And looked . . . well, my *Lord*, everybody was H. There was there was Hendricks, Hastings . . . [laughs] Which one? So we boiled it down to my . . . they called her Beth. Her name was Beth, Aunt Beth, and she had a very, very unhappy life. And my mother gave me the history of her. And her casket had been in that place where everybody felt sadness. When she died, she, one of her husbands had drowned. She'd taken up Christian Science, but not in the constructive, positive way. Um . . . her father'd been a doctor, my great-grandfather had been a doctor, and um . . . the people, who was got hold of her, had said, "You can't have anything to do with your family." She got sick, and they kept taking medicine to her. She had it under her pillow, and they found it. She'd been dead three days. They found all this medicine that could of helped her. And it been a minor . . .

*Jane:* A pneumonia, or something.

*Pat:* Yeah, something, that could of been corrected if she would take the medicine. And this is the . . . No, we have no proof other than the Ouija board, and what happened to Bob.

*Jane:* It was later . . .

*Linda:* How did you know it was her?

*Pat:* By the name. By her name.

*Jane:* And what she had said on the Ouija board.

*Pat:* That's the only thing that . . .

*Jane:* Would have been Hendricks.

*Pat:* Yeah, it would have been Hendricks.

*Jane:* But what happened later, oh, well, a year later. I was having one of the Wednesday morning meetings here, and a stranger walked in . . .

Until this point, the conversationally narrated story was about discovering and identifying the spirit that had haunted the living room. To make it complete, the spirit needed to be sent away. And here the exorcist, BarBara Lee, came to the rescue. She was the stranger who in Jane's account "just dropped in one day."

### Exorcising Beth

*Jane:* She came with a friend of a friend to the meeting because, you know, she thought she'd be interested. So, anyway, she came to the door and asked me to come to the bathroom. And I just howled, "You didn't want to go to the bathroom, you wanted to check out my living room, didn't you?"

She said, "Yes, but I didn't know whether you knew or not." And I said, "Yes, I knew." And she said, "Well, do you want it exorcised?" And I said, "Well, it depends on how you do your exorcism. Where do you send them? And, you know, if you just cut them loose and they are free to go anyplace else then leave her here." And she said, "No, I have help and they're taken to schools where they can find out that they're dead and then start from there."

So, there must have been thirteen of us here that morning. And we all go in the living room and we proceed to exorcise Beth. And you know, you stand there and pinch her and say, am I really seeing this, or do I really believe this? But, anyway, it turns out that Beth didn't want to leave, and she'd become very happy with our family, and had begun to feel part of us. And I had known nights when I went to bed that my covers were tucked around me and I had been kissed, you know, and it was Beth. She had just really gotten in with the family life and she didn't want to leave. But finally, she agreed to with the understanding that she could come back and visit us.

*Pat:* And that was another clue that it was my relative because I had never met this woman [i.e., BarBara], and she looked straight at me and said, "*It's a relative of yours!*" [laughter]

*Linda:* How could she find out, how could she come by . . .

*Jane:* She could see spirits.

*Andrew:* So, nobody sent her?

*Jane:* No.

*Linda:* Is she a professional? A psychic?

*Jane:* Yes.

*Linda:* Does she ask for money?

*Jane:* No, she does not.

*Andrew:* Why does she do it?

*Pat:* Because it's her work.

*Andrew:* How does she make a living?

*Ann:* Her husband makes the living. She just helps people. When BarBara Lee comes here we could let you know.

*Linda:* So she's coming for a visit?

*Jane:* Yes. Last time I talked to her she thought she would be here the later part of this month.

*Ann:* I took her over to my house, and my middle son and my husband didn't like the stairway. They'd run up the stairway and there was a crippled man on my stairway. And . . . I am not sensitive, I don't feel anything either, but they do. My husband and my son are . . . fairly psychic, and he never liked the stairway at all. And this man had lived in our house many, many years ago . . . it's 130-odd years old — and he was a very crippled man.

*Linda:* Had he died long ago?

*Ann:* In the house. You couldn't see anything, but two of the family could feel it. I couldn't and the staircase didn't bother me. But I bet all these old houses have something in them. Well, I always thought, that exorcists work against the devil.[27] The devil is not a good spirit like this ghost that has been here in this house.

*Jane:* No, it isn't.

*Pat:* There's no devil.

*Ann:* Don't tell her that. You know these sprits, you've heard of older guys . . .

*Jane:* She just didn't believe that God would forgive her for what she did. That she more or less took her life by not doing . . . But anyway, we call these earthboundsters. They have something that ties them to worldly things. You know, they can't break the tie. Smoking, drinking, sex, the pleasures of the world or a guilt feeling, unfinished business, meanness or extreme goodness . . .

*Ann:* So, I've heard that those people who didn't finish some business have hidden something would come back. They would haunt or spook. . . .

*Jane:* Yes, because they really don't know they're dead. They don't mean to cause anyone any trouble.

*Linda:* There are no malicious ones?

### The Ghost that Hates a Plant

*Pat:* Well, another woman in our group, from Bean Blossom had her house exorcised. She had a very old woman . . . well, I don't know, the old woman that had owned the house that they bought from the family, her husband didn't go along with any of this, but the kids would be bothered by this woman all night. They went down the hall and I guess she roamed the house and there was a plant this woman had — I can't think of the name of it, it has beautiful white blossoms — and this ghost or whatever you want to call it, hated this plant. And you could see the blossoms going off up in the air like this. And, it would never be around the husband, and he'd say: you're crazy, it just happens. And one night, he was by himself and he happened to look over, and here were the leaves going up in the air, just like they were being thrown. And that woman finally took every leaf off the plant until it was dead.

*Ann:* Was that Norma's house?

*Pat:* It was Norma's house. And the woman was an immaculate housekeeper. They had to find this out later on. And she said that every time that she would do the dishes right after dinner, there would be a rattling of dishes and her kitchen would be rattled until she went out and cleaned the kitchen. And they found out that the woman had fallen off the back porch — had had a heart attack and fallen off the back porch and, I believe broken her neck — it had been a violent death. Incidentally that is usually the earmark of earthbound spirits, that they have gone so suddenly, they don't realize that they've passed away.

### How Beth Was Sent Away by BarBara

*Jane:* To finish my living room story, the only — I think I told you, I felt my apron strings pulled, or being tucked in bed at night or being kissed, and as far as I know I'm the only one that has felt that. But since she's been gone, the curtains have stayed in place. That was the only thing that she seemed to do was that anytime anyone came in the driveway, she would look to see who was coming. She just got involved, you know.

*Andrew:* Why did she go?

*Jane:* Because, when this BarBara Lee talked with her and explained to her that she was dead and that she has nothing to feel guilty about, and these people on the other side that were waiting to help her, would take her to her parents, you know, and she could be forgiven and everything, why, she finally felt maybe that was the better way.

*Andrew:* So she sat down, this lady, and talked to somebody she didn't see?

*Jane:* She stood up and talked to her.

*Andrew:* But you heard, you heard her speaking?

*Jane:* Yes, we only heard BarBara Lee. We just heard the one-sided conversation. Yes. And it was like we weren't in the room, just the two of them were talking and there'd be a question. You know, and then you could tell by the new question what the answer had been. It was very interesting.

*Linda:* Was it a long conversation?

*Jane:* Yes. It was just like you listen to someone talking on the phone. You'd hear one side but you get the whole gist of the conversation.

*Linda:* Did she go about it without any formality, or did she do something — close the door — or was the dead there all the time?

*Jane:* No, nothing was done, and yes, she was there all the time.

*Linda:* So, she could walk in and say hello?

*Jane:* Yes. Now let me say another interesting thing. I think it's an important thing. Because I didn't give BarBara Lee permission to exorcise her 'til I found out what she would do with her. I think this is something some people overlook. Like, you cast a spirit out, where does it go? Where is "out"? It just finds another home, you know. So, you wouldn't want her exorcised until you had told her where to go.

*Pat:* Yes, and that was only a part of it. Several people had told me how to do this myself, which I wasn't about to try. If other people could do it? And I think, there is a time for everything, you know. And I think, Beth's time was the day BarBara Lee came, because she had started coming into our Wednesday's meetings. There was a girl from Shelbyville, you know, who would feel her come in. So, you see, she had been getting interested in and she had been getting back to this kind of thing. And she was ready to go. And that answers the question.

After giving credit to BarBara for her successful exorcism of Beth, the conversation developed further, as it had started around our cautious and non-suggestive questions which kept the women on track, to speaking about Bar-Bara's specific treatment of the haunted living room. By our facial indication of interest, we also encouraged the speakers to tell their experiential legends as well as to explain their knowledge of reasons and signs of spirit presence. They then continued to tell us about other haunted houses in the region.

The three Martinsville women represent a legend-telling group that specializes in belief in spirit possession, informed by an eclectic spiritualist belief system that they cultivate and attest to. Their stories are a part of the rich Midwestern repertoire, expanding on everyday experience of spirit encounters or exchanges of accounts with fellow legend-tellers. The performance was not a natural "legend-telling event" but a conversation among three friends and practitioners who were responding to the inquiry of two scholars unknown to them before. It was a laboratory situation of a kind, showing the anatomy of generating legends and resulting in a text worth scrutiny.

The speakers were social equals with the inquirers, and felt at ease when talking about their unusual religious beliefs and practices. They presented themselves lightheartedly as being "weird," and different from their peers. They spoke of praying, meditating, and playing with the Ouija board for fun as a hobby, not a vocation — speaking of it with a down-to-earth attitude, and with laughter rather than awe. They treated encounters with the dead cheerfully, not with fear, and regard death and the afterlife as the natural continuation of existence; they were looking forward to happiness in heaven. The performance of Jane's personal legend illustrates their attitudes and beliefs in healing by prayer in domestic life.

### The Healing of Sarge

*Jane:* I was working in the yard one Sunday morning when the phone rang. And it was our neighbor. And he said, "Jane, Sarge — which was a stray dog that lived here — has been hit by a car. And he is bleeding from the mouth and rectally. And would you like for us to go ahead and dispatch him?" And I said, "Oh no, no, don't go near him, leave him alone. I'll . . . Bill will come right down." So, I went to my husband and I said, "Please." He had his gun and he started down. I said, "Please, do not shoot the dog, until you touch him." I said, "Please, touch him first." And I came in, and meditated while he went down to get the dog. And he pulled out, and he got out the truck, and picked up his gun. The dog looked at him, jumped up on top of the truck. He came home with him. And there was no blood at all. He lost about this much of his tail. I gave him two aspirins.

*Ann:* You forgot to say that he touched him before. Touched him, then he jumped up.

*Jane:* And my boy came in. He had been riding the horse, and his baby sister on the horse. And the dog was with them. And he saw the dog run over from the front of the car to the back. And he was thrown, rolled, and thrown up into the driveway. And it hurt him so badly . . . because he knew that the dog was dead, and he knew it was his fault. 'Cause he was taking him with him. And he came in through the yard. And here is Sarge, and "Wuff-wuff," you know. And you know, he said, "There must be something in this meditation . . ." The touching was to make contact with the dog and I thought it was because of the meditation.

Legend-tellers and their participant support groups usually concentrate on a specific belief system with a certain goal (exorcism, in this case). They function the same way as other groups united by a common concern, be it an out-of-body experience, worship of a saint or a charismatic leader, a UFO encounter and abduction, life-after-life travel, religious conversion, or miraculous healing. A large body of legendry sprouts within deviant church solidarity groups. For example, devout Catholics may unite around a miracle story of an unauthenticated saint; believers vary and expand the story, and engage in pilgrimages and ritual performances. Innumerable local fundamentalist religious congregations across America construct their own styles of expression, using narrative performances to strengthen their own belief and confront the belief or unbelief of others. It is not only preachers who use legends to enlighten the faithful about current temptations of the devil and God's power; any member may spontaneously tell the legends testifying to personal miracle experiences. In fact, members live in the atmosphere of everyday miracles when they are blessed by being in constant touch with Jesus Christ (Dégh 1990a). Reports of frequently trivial miracles — such as obtaining a bank loan, finding relief from arthritis, getting a burned-out battery to work (Dégh 1994c), or retrieving a lost object — are so important that testifying about them may preempt the sermon.

On the other hand, the large category of rumor-like modern horror stories, anecdotal success, big-win stories, or grotesque or humorous embarrassment stories do not have the power to induce group formation. They are not conditional upon a distinctive ideology and do not require a common belief; rather, they are more dependent on hearsay — heard from a friend of a friend, or more commonly, from the mass media or the Internet. These stories do not address so much the elementary and unavoidable threats to human existence as the immediate dangers related to living in the modern technological world (Fine 1987; Turner 1987; Wachs 1990). Although everybody likes to hear shocking, dreadful, horrible, sensational, and spicy gossip, particularly when the story involves celebrities, such stories do not make specialist legend-tellers, because anyone can tell them at any opportune moment. It is important that these stories be fresh, new, and "just heard" from an eyewitness, a well-informed person, or from the morning news. They may be appealing to any group of adults, men and women, from any socioeconomic bracket.

A last question concerns the occasion of passing on legends. Social groups and repertoires cannot be easily brought together, as illustrated by the above cases: The exorcist/patient ghost stories or one particular brand of believer's repertoires were disseminated through networking. Outside of the practice of exorcists or ghost hunters, ghost stories are otherwise like any other type of story involving supernatural agencies, and appear at the social gatherings of adults if they have some immediate relevance. One new or a re-created old story may result in a conversation that will produce several legends from people who are competent in the same system of belief; their sharing of stories functions as self-assertion. In this case, individuals submit their miracle, revenant, or space alien encounters; bewitching or bereavement experiences; or

scary dreams and visions for the debate and critical commentary of an essentially consenting audience. As shown in the transcripts of the session with the
three Martinsville women, consenting participants have an important role in
the conversational performance of legends; they refresh the memory of the
main proponent, adding details and evaluations from their own points of view.

The other kinds of legends are less constraining and do not require
personal commitment and unanimity. Any sensational, juicy, crazy, spine-
chilling, up-to-date story may be told to distant acquaintances or strangers at
accidental gatherings. These "did you hear?" or "did you read?" stories might
ease waiting at the doctor's office, be exchanged outside a conference room
during coffee break, during train, plane, bus, subway travel, church ice cream
socials, in the office or workplace of professionals, at school, in clubs, and in
sports and recreational facilities.

## Media Legend-Tellers

The legend-tellers discussed so far have been considered as oral communicators, although their telling is not exclusive or free from the use of other communicative vehicles. As we have already stated, oral narration includes body
language, acting, playing, mumming, drafting, and ostension. The application
of these substitute or collaborative means are natural in the oral telling process: Any may be used to tell the same story. But beyond these natural expres-
sives, other non-natural ones made available by modern technology also facilitate legend transmission. We have experienced in our fieldwork that writing
(diaries, letters, term papers, photocopies), telephoning, photography, tape
and video recording, e-mailing, and Internet communication have become
indispensable to the maintenance of legend tradition in our time, and narrators are comfortable with these tools in telling and discussing legends. What
unites them is that they tell legends by whatever media is convenient for them,
while their performance remains a private and informal affair. Like any traditional performers of folklore, they address their small support group members
as described above, whether they have gathered to listen at a certain place or
have a story sent individually to them. The use of electronic means does not
change the essentially folkloric exchange because the addressees, no matter
where they are, remain members of the folk group, and receive the legend
from someone of the same mind.

Granting that folklore performers may use any oral or non-oral means to
communicate legends, we cannot overlook legend-tellers who perform professionally to a large, and in many cases to a mass audience. Their performance
is public, and the formulation of their stories is guided by the ground rules,
routines, techniques, and purposes of their communicative channels. No ques-

tion about it, these proponents of mass-mediated legends are trained professionals who make it their living to tell their legends in variable ways, selling them directly, or selling something else and using legends for packaging. Their formulation of traditional contents or their use of folklore to elaborate a current concern is guided by general knowledge and public expectation.

Nevertheless, there still remains room enough for creative marks of authorship in each category of professional narrators. As much as it is true that a master storyteller restricted by the crystallized plot outline and formulaic episodes of the traditional folktale still finds the way to personalize his or her version, it is also true that even reportage of the same everyday event bears the earmark of different journalists. Each professionally told variant, be it an inconspicuous news report or a literary masterpiece, bears its teller's worldview, viewpoint, education, style, imagination, and narrative competence. Although they address an anonymous, unknown mass audience, rather than familiar individuals of their own kind in small groups, their texts can be regarded as links in an ongoing chain of transmission as much as improvised oral ones in which variants of alternative channels together build a traditional text.

For centuries, legends, like folklore in general, have also been communicated through professional channels and there seems to have been a harmonious give-and-take relationship between the village/oral and the urban/literary. But from the time printing was invented, literary formulations have multiplied and been disseminated far and wide with increasing speed, exercising a profound influence on oral tradition. As Schenda has noted, there is an essential difference between twenty listeners to stories in the spinnery and twenty thousand readers exposed to reproduced texts (Schenda 1992: 4). With the advent of electronic technology in the twentieth century, more channels have been opened, increasing the speed of the folklore process. Folklore materials have become more accessible to the audience at large, usable and manipulable for a great variety of purposes. They have gained prominence in the power struggle on the ideological front, not only influencing public opinion, but promoting and marketing ideas and products for sale. Assisted by the mass media, the folklore process — transmission, repetition, variation, and stabilization of types and subtypes — has resulted in the making of more folklore than ever before.

Inventions of modern industry that dramatically transformed the world order have been acknowledged by most of the social sciences, but folklorists have been slow to recognize the need for a new demarcation of their field to facilitate the study of contemporary folklore, which is profoundly and essentially affected by the mass media. Folklorists were disillusioned by the mass reproduction of the highly valued traditional materials for the masses; the production and marketing of folklore clichés was meant to satisfy not only the refined taste of the elite but also that of the aspiring upward-moving lower classes. Instead of considering this process as a trend of democratization, and tracing and registering the steps in the transformation that has made folklore a powerful contingent of contemporary culture, folklorists stubbornly have adhered to old definitions.

Judging with an anachronistic value system, folklorists viewed most of emergent folkloric phenomena as symptomatic of erosion and the loss of national values, signaling the total devastation of folklore by urbanization. With a good deal of cultural pessimism, they have labeled media-manipulated folklore and its cultural context as fake, mass, popular, cliché, trivia, and even trash. That is to say, all folklore products that could be traced to printed originals and be mass reproduced to fill the ritual, celebratory, and narrative needs of the folk masses — the products that were instrumental to the creation of a new folklore for a new age — have been summarily dismissed as alien pollutants infesting the pure spring water of tradition, and deemed unworthy of scholarly attention. However, a 30-year study of nationalistic-chauvinistic and culture-industry–oriented *folklorismus*, the application of folklore out of its natural contexts, has resulted in the insight that the normative folklore process includes a phase of transition between literary/professional and oral/nonprofessional formulations that occurs cyclically as a consequence of changing political and economic conditions. It is our understanding that this connecting phase is a critical twilight zone of degeneration/regeneration and therefore needs to be subjected to research (Bausinger, 1969; Bendix 1989; Beutel and Greverus 1978; Kirshenblatt-Gimblett 1988; Dow and Lixfeld 1986; Moser 1962; Newall 1986; Strobach 1987: 23–38).

Mass communication is so radically different from anything that has to do with the transmission of old-style folklore, and electronic inventions have developed so speedily, that they have not allowed people time to learn and acquire competence in one medium before the next unfolds. For folklorists it has been easier to ignore than to accommodate and to keep re-learning continuously. Flight to the illiterate Third World, or to the past with historic reconstruction of pre-industrial folk cultures, has seemed easier than facing the problems of the modern, emergent industrial lore of the folk. The most critical feature we have to cope with is that a new generation is already comfortable with the "entirely different" system of communication. Mass communication, taken as a single act of operation, consists of the intentional transmission of information from a single outlet to a relatively large number of people, to whom all the same information is being transmitted by the same transmission procedure. The transmission procedure in question has to satisfy the following criteria:

1. The transmission is not to be effectuated in its whole course by direct interpersonal communication between the single information outlet (the
communicator) and the people to whom the information is being addressed (the audience); it has to be mediated (relayed) by the use of a pur-
posively organized instrumentality which may or may not involve the application of technical devices but may admit the use of direct person-to-person
communication in certain intermediate phases of the mediated (relayed)
process.

2. The instrumentality used in the transmission should provide one-way
communication only, directed from the communicator to the audience, not
in the inverse direction or crosswise between individual members of the audience — indeed, the global villagers. (Szalai 1978: 10)

The products of this kind of communication are hard to view as folklore by
traditional folklorists who insist on authenticity.

From the mid-twentieth century, professional folklorists criticized the anti-
quarianism and romantic nationalist attitudes toward folklore and excluded
non-oral materials from their investigation of folklore genres. They shifted
their attention from the artistic beauty of a communal folk poetry to the told
story they themselves or others recorded, and that information was regarded
as the exclusive, authentic source to be subjected to scholarly scrutiny. In
many cases, collecting was careful and selective, excluding suspect materials
that might have been influenced by "alien," "urban" literary sources, contami-
nating the purely oral (illiterate) folk texts. In a revolutionary innovation during the late 1930s, it became an absolute requirement to record texts word for
word; somewhat later, sociocultural context descriptions were added to the
requirements to authenticate the texts.[28] This development opened a new
world for a better understanding of folklore as a social act and the processes
of its formulations by individuals along social change.

Meanwhile, the authors of monographic village studies, aiming at the regis-
tration of total repertoires, realized that it was sheer absurdity to imagine a
soundproofed, isolated village and to disregard materials of literary origin. Exposure to popular reading materials, schoolbooks, newspapers, magazines, radio, movies, traveling theater companies, and entertainment opportunities in
nearby urban centers has resulted in a miscellany of oral and literary changes
in the narrative folklore genres of the semi-literate villagers of the twentieth
century. Still, the majority of folklorists preferred to look back and reconstruct
archaic conditions instead of looking at the present with an eye on the future:
The myth of the existence of a self-contained, authentic oral text has still not
been laid to rest. Influential schools of literary, anthropological, and linguistic
folkloristics still conceptualize folklore as an "oral art" (although not all folklore can be defined as art), and regard telling (performance) as an oral tech-

nique of illiterate composition, not mass-mediated secondary orality. For many, an item is still either folk (oral) or non-folk (literary). If the non-oral version is also considered, the goal remains to contrast it to the oral or to infer from it an original oral version.

As we have already noted, students of contemporary ("urban") legends who collect their texts mostly from media sources, still speak of some kind of face-to-face "legend-telling sessions." While busily compiling newspaper clippings and Internet printouts, they still insist on the basic orality of their materials and engage in hairsplitting debates on how to record "verbatim" legend exchanges. Is the oral bias a survival of old-time folkloristics? Fischer's interesting analysis of seven variants of the German redaction of "The Vanishing Hitchhiker" legend also shows a preference for orality without good reason. Fischer speaks of the oral as "primary" and the non-oral as "secondary" variants. To establish the oral continuity chain of a legend that emerged in the early 1980s and kept surfacing through regional newspaper publicity in a limited area over a span of six years, he lined up a narrated memorate from 1982, three newspaper reports of the same year, a letter to the editor commenting on the news report from the same year, a reprint from a magazine series from 1986, and three "*Nacherzählungen*" (retellings of the read reports) from 1982, 1983, and 1984. However, his study is unable to establish the primacy of the oral version — as most likely the German hitchhiker originates in American newspaper sources — or the direct relationship between the listed texts. The analysis only shows that the information contained in the newspaper reports attracted attention among the reading public, but did not formulate any full-fledged oral legend narratives (Fischer 1990: 136–156). As Bausinger noted in his opening address of the 1990 SIEF Congress, "folklore was, and is still defined as only oral tradition while the massive influence of written, printed and electronic media cannot be left out of consideration. Even the supposedly pure local tradition can be traced to written sources" (1992: 8). He adds, "it is still not common to localize folk culture in the twilight zone of modern technological and social development" (9). Fischer's grandiose compilation of contemporary oral narratives from the Siegraum region includes only the spoken texts of traditional villagers, the folk, understood as peasants (Fischer 1978). Thus, there seems to be a contradiction here between theory and practice, a type of double-talk among urban legend specialists.[29]

To enable ourselves to study folklore at the beginning of the twenty-first century, and to prepare to continue in the new millennia, folklorists dealing with the modern world must give up their concentration on a part of society that has traditionally been regarded as the uneducated, illiterate rural folk, who in their subjugated, deprived condition are the unconscious and nameless bearers of national tradition, naively trivialized into oral folkloric forms.

Once we throw our net wide enough to include the traditional culture of all social classes, we can look at folklore as a universal layer of culture, basic to human cognition and creativity.

Speaking of the expressive forms of folklore, we have to forget the petty efforts to determine from a distant, academic ivory tower what is authentic and genuine as opposed to what is contaminated, spurious, corrupted, or fake. It is hopeless to determine authenticity anyway. Every text that has existed in historic literary sources or folklore collections has undergone intentional or unintentional changes; they have been redefined, rewritten, diluted, elaborated, or condensed and excerpted by innumerable individuals to serve their diverse intentions, ideologies, and fantasies. No matter how fragmentary or arbitrary single texts seem, they are equally important for a serious revaluation of all neglected and omitted sources, to help us upgrade the tools of our discipline for modern usefulness.

Social conditions have changed in the past, they continue to change in our time, and they will be changing in the future. And folklore can live only as long as it can change; if it cannot, it must die like all its ancestors, which we can never know because they lost their meaning to later generations. Each existing text of folklore, oral or literary, documents its own contemporaneous conditions and defines its own folkloricity. With similar thoughts on his mind, in his plenary paper at the SIEF Congress in 1990, Rudolf Schenda proposed a working definition of folklore that skipped the terms "artistic" and "oral" as follows: Folklore consists of "spoken or written (printed), temporally and/or spatially disseminated texts (genres), speech forms and formulas that are in everyday use" (Schenda 1992: 2).

If we consider continuity in historical depth, preceding our time, mass-communicated and media-influenced folklore can be followed along the lines of industrial growth from the turn of the century. In the course of time, industrialization lifted isolation through the construction of roads, railroads, buses, cars, airplanes, cities, factories, and electric power lines, and the establishment of printing plants, newspapers, magazines, and movie theaters. Radio and television have further removed the barriers surrounding pockets of culture and have made population groups join the global village, as defined by Marshall McLuhan (1964), in which inhabitants are exposed to unified cultural information, which acts toward an international cultural homogenization and also influences national folklore traditions.

It goes without saying that it is easier to study the folks of a quaint, isolated tribe or village than the mobile, uncontainable and complex population units in gigantic industrial centers. However, after World War II, the further refinement of communication and information technology opened new opportunities for the folklorist to study continuity and tradition on all interacting levels of communication. In this new landscape, folklore is regenerated into a new force of creativity for which no other but the folklorist has the key. And since the legend-teller is the arbitrator of the messages that are most relevant to modern life, researchers of the legend must try to enter the labyrinth of the alternative communicative vehicles they use, because it is these vehicles that have made the legend so viable.

As we have seen already, the newspaper legend did not escape the attention of folklorists; its impact on oral tradition was noted almost sixty years ago (Anderson 1960; Bausinger 1958; Wesselski 1935). But the interaction of folklore and mass-media narrators was underestimated even by those who were aware of its existence. That the radio is able to stimulate instant hysterical legend-formation became general knowledge when Orson Welles presented his radio drama "War of the Worlds" shortly before the outbreak of World War II, in 1938.[30] Today it is well known that "newspapers live from legends," especially in the dull summer season (Bausinger 1967: 219; Peuckert 1965) as illustrated by the extremely popular and variable tourism-related legend "The Stolen Grandmother" (Dégh 1995b: 35–47). It is also known that erroneous or distorted reports from newspapers and radio and television broadcasts often have a great impact on the folk legend. In such cases the retold legend assumes the distortions of the mass media.

It is beyond doubt that in countless cases the newspaper, radio, or television has been instrumental in the creation of a new legend, as well as in the revitalization, modification, dissemination, and maintenance of an old legend (Weisser 1968: 401–414). The mass media is also responsible for the weakening, disintegration, and vanishing of legends by publishing disclaiming legends, or introducing a new, updated version. Following the instructions, or the misinterpretation of instructions, in mass media reports, one by one, valiant people armed with shotguns will invade vast forests or climb dangerous cliffs to save the world from ferocious monsters. Amateur scuba divers submerge themselves in seas and lakes to personally meet all sorts of giant sea creatures. Day after day, masses gather in front of miracle sightings, like that of the face of Laura Aroyo, a little girl who disappeared but whose image showed up on a gigantic screen in Los Angeles. How many times have newspapers had to revoke their well-publicized legends about snakes in imported pullovers for fear of bringing on a lawsuit by dry-goods store operators? And how many times have police been summoned to disperse traffic jams, because, according to hearsay, a local newspaper had announced a few hours earlier that friendly outer-space aliens had landed in the nearby meadow and were leaning comfortably against their spaceship and observing life on earth? And how many times have toll-road booth operators been questioned about the whereabouts of the male or female hitchhiker who disappeared from the backseat of an automobile (Fish 1976: 5–13)? In sum, there is no doubt whatsoever that the mass media has drawn heavily from folklore, as folklore has from the mass media.

Nevertheless, this conclusion does not really differ from what could have been said about literature long ago. It is certain, for example, that their being published by the Grimm brothers was decisive for the fate of the legends incorporated in the *Deutsche Sagen*. These legends, which came from earlier or contemporary publications, were absorbed again by the folk in the course of subsequent decades, so that after more decades had passed the legends could once again mount the stairs to literature, slowly but continuously following the rules of tradition. If we wanted to sketch graphically this process, we would draw a long, mildly wavy line that fluctuates slowly and comfortably between the two levels of folk tradition and literature, encompassing great epochs with each curve. But the diagram of the relationship between modern mass media and the orally transmitted folk legend would look entirely different. This chart would consist of restlessly fluttering dense and steep straight lines that converge in a sharp angle representative of the connection between the legend, which is passed on orally, and its non-oral elaboration.

Let us assume that something happens Monday morning that could become the core of a legend. As this event occurs, a reader calls the editor of the local paper and communicates the message; the afternoon edition will already carry the novelty. That same evening, everyone in town talks about it. If the novelty — which often might be considered rightfully a folk legend — is interesting enough, the local radio station might briefly mention it, and some pictures taken at the scene might also be shown on television. Indeed, there is no reason why the same day the story could not enter the national or even the international bloodstream of the legend process. By nightfall, another reporter might encounter the story, already circulating on the oral tradition level, and transmit it farther to the news desk of some other communications medium. By Tuesday morning, the public could be introduced to a new version of this legend.

This lightning-fast process of transmission cannot be perceived authentically with any kind of human sense. Who can possibly know where a legend started out, what its original form was, and what road it followed? Who knows how much the mass media contributed to it and how much oral folk tradition has influenced its variation, degeneration, and interlacing with other legends? For example, a television news anchor, a legend-teller in his or her own right, may have heard a story long ago or just a little while ago; the broadcast communicates the new folk legend verbally in a more or less improvised performance, making the news anchor not only a participant of folk tradition (like the contributors of other mass media) but also in oral folk tradition. And on the Internet, the enthusiasts of the home page community enjoy the greatest freedom and irresponsibility of all for manufacturing and manipulating legends — what they improvise in writing may multiply the global accumulation beyond imagination.

An example of the wildfire-speed of legend multiplication is offered by the media-transmitted spread of a life-threatening danger. In this case, the core story was food poisoning (G. Fine 1992: 120–137). Following the tragic deaths in Chicago from Tylenol tablets poisoned with cyanide on September 29, 1982, a nationwide mass-media warning curtailed the trick-or-treat begging ritual on Halloween night, October 31. For this occasion, the media revitalized the "Razor Blade in the Apple" legend, which had originally spread to the media via police, teachers, parents, candy merchants, and common oral rumor mongers who were inspired by a few copycats who had attempted real poisonings (Best and Horiuchi 1985: 488–499; Dégh and Vázsonyi 1983; Grider 1984). Food and medicine poisoning scares were widely publicized throughout the period and continued for a long time afterward. The mass hysteria over the fear of a Coca-Cola poisoning at a basketball game soon after the outbreak of the story sent several people to the hospital to have their stomachs pumped in California; this case turned out to be a hoax, as did the sixty other poisonings reported in the press during a short time span. In the atmosphere of the general nationwide scare, the Bloomington, Indiana, story about a 75-year-old woman hurt by a pin in a banana that her husband bought for her at a local store was widely reported in Indiana and the Midwest. According to the AP brief:

> Indiana State Police were investigating a report Tuesday of a needle found in a banana purchased in a store here.
> The report renewed interest in a similar case of "spiked" apples reported to local police late last week.
> State Police Lt. Robert Miller said the banana was purchased at a No-Frills store Saturday and was reported by a woman who lived outside Bloomington to State Police on Monday.
> He said it was not known whether the needle's appearance was an accident, a prank or something more deadly. (*Terre Haute Star*, October 27, 1982: 1)

Celie Benson, a folklore student with a background in journalism, interviewed the people involved, and analyzed their texts to try to find out what had happened, and follow the trend of legend variation. The victimized woman, her husband who bought the banana for her dog, the sales clerk who sold it to him, the emergency room doctor who treated her, not for poisoning but for constipation, and the two newsmen who reported the incident all produced different stories, mixing facts with pseudo-facts and placing them in the context of their fear and general knowledge about food poisoning. It turned out that the original teller based her story not on her personal experience but her familiarity with the legend of Halloween assaults by food tampering.

The cyanide poisoning account appeared as the first proposition that such deeds by deranged, antisocial offenders have become fashionable, repeatable, and variable. Like kidnapping, serial murder, hostage taking, and hijacking of airplanes, it followed the trail that fashion does in the short run, or folklore genres do in the long run: It moved from emergence to evolvement, full bloom, decline, transformation, and elimination.

After a period of mass hysteria, when popular painkillers, laxatives, and cold capsules were (or were assumed to be) laced with poison, next basic food stuffs were endangered by tampering. There was a moment when it seemed that only soft drinks warranted caution. However, a year or so later, news about the contamination of popular foods such as peanut butter, canned and powdered soup, pudding, salad dressing, and hamburger patties began to trickle in, and they continue to sporadically appear. On September 26, 1990, I saw a report in the Chapel Hill, North Carolina, newspaper of a telling by ostension:

> A 14-year old girl took revenge on two playmates by inviting them to a picnic and serving them peanut butter and jelly sandwiches and grape drinks laced with poison, police say. Neither youngsters were seriously hurt. The girl told friends she got the idea of putting rat poison in the sandwich from the movie "Heathers," a R-rated black comedy featuring teen-age murder. . . .

The quantity, the number of repetitions of reciprocal effects, had been transformed into quality.

The relationship between the Grimm brothers and the folk is far from being identical with that of mass media and the folk. The creation of the Grimm legends can easily be distinguished from orally transmitted legends, but the components of the relationship between mass media and the folk cannot be separated in any practical way. Theoretically, such separation is not even necessary. One could hardly find contemporary legends that had not traveled by means of the intricate labyrinths of diverse transmission media: immediate face-to-face oral communication, letter writing, telephone messages, humorous and serious newspaper reports, radio and television programs, cartoons and comics, and popular and scientific publications. It is not easy to determine which vehicle has had the dominant share in the transmission of legends: If we tried, it would sound like a man claiming to have "traveled from the Bronx to Long Island partly by subway and partly by foot" — because he had to walk a few steps when changing trains. It is not enough to acknowledge that the mass media has a role in modern legend communication. It is closer to the truth to assert that the mass media is a part of folklore — maybe the greater part. The legend makes a part of its way, presumably the lesser part, on foot and continues on the longer trail via speedy modern vehicles.

At the given speed of passing on legends, the concept of common knowledge has immensely broadened. The elementary notions of the legend — the theses of folk belief upon which certain legends were founded at a given time and place — belonged earlier to a much smaller group of people than nowadays, when the jovial demonology of the television series *Bewitched,* the vampire-ritual of Dracula as promoted by a dignified gentlemen-club in London, the conventions of lycanthropy, and the traditions of Dr. Jekyll and Mr. Hyde or Frankenstein's monster have entered the notion-inventory of those who have turned on the television or forgotten to turn it off. This condition also necessarily has caused a new division: the polarization of readers and nonreaders, the listeners and the non-listeners (Riesman 1965: 419–420). The exceptional people who are not hooked on television probably feel the world is a less violent and dangerous place to live in. But the truth is that common knowledge of the ingredients of the legend, more or less, encompass almost everyone. The essential message of the legend sounds deep, strong, and steadily in almost all of society, turning everyone into occasional legend-tellers or recipients. "The field in which we work becomes increasingly more complex and confusing while the challenge to orient ourselves further is as attractive as earlier tasks" writes Bausinger; and "never did folklore fare better as under the banner of mass culture," writes Schenda. "The folklore debate has not been yet resolved either. Its real time will come in the totally electrified year 2000."[31]

The legends of professional tellers are important to add to the variant lists that we assemble for comparative study, when we are analyzing content, style, language, and the sociocultural context. Not only the source of their versions needs to be cited, but their names, like those of any oral informant, need to be identified. In a way, media legend-tellers are more authentic; their texts reveal more of the social and political conditions of variation than the texts solicited from oral narrators. Let us see who these mediators and arbitrators of legends are, these professional communicators whose trade is providing mass-media stories to the interested public. Media narrators in their retelling of legends provide variants that enter the mainstream of tradition in variable ways. But we cannot see yet how, because we have yet to realize their importance.

My list is not complete because it cannot be complete. For example, I have not included authors of the occult subculture who address a special audience as opposed to the general public, although there is no isolating barrier between the two. However, my research has already suggested some new avenues.

1. Writers of fiction using legends in their novels, short stories, plays, film scripts, television shows, and other literary products

2. Folklorists collecting, interpreting, and publishing legends professionally

3. Scholars in a variety of fields using legends in their scholarly works

4. Theologians, who address the public in writing or in sermons, publicizing, formulating, and interpreting legends

5. Popularizers of science and borderline sciences

6. Popularizers of folklore, including folklorists and others who write for children, and for the general public's enlightenment and entertainment

7. Daily or weekly newspaper reporters, and television and radio announcers

8. Newspaper columnists

9. Television talk show hosts

10. Magazine writers (serial editors of legend topics)

11. Tabloid authors

12. Advertisers using legend to push a product

13. Professional storytellers

14. Professional fortune tellers, clairvoyants, witches, psychics

15. Copycats and other ostensive tellers of legends

16. Producers of legend-related objects, toys, magic jewelry, clothing, and ritual paraphernalia.

It would be naive to believe that we can assemble variants of media legend-texts for a Finnish School–type comparative study, although many folklorists would like to establish historical continuity and trace the origins of legends (Brunvand 1981; Sanderson 1981). Mass media's proliferation would be as impossible to follow as looking for a poppy seed in a haystack, and as impossible to trace as the prehistoric archetypes of the tale types, as Thompson realized (1955). We should remember what Jansen already noted:

> Legends, of course are not restricted to the oral tradition, a fact that zealous folklorists sometimes forget. Historians have recorded legends; professional writers, serious and comic, skilled and inept, have created some legends and recorded others. Most — all, we hopefully assume — legends have spent a major part of their existence in the oral tradition. Most are born in the oral tradition, and some of these move into a literary tradition. Others, born in the literary tradition, move easily into the oral tradition. And for a single legend the transition may happen over and over. (Musick 1977: xi–xii)

Nevertheless, immediate connections and continuity will be easier to find if we target legends in the making (Ellis 1990a), because they tend to emerge suddenly and mushroom around a core idea expressing a current concern. They may die away shortly, but they may also linger on and enter a period of latency, losing their momentary attraction only to come back again unchanged, modified, or expanded. Virulent cyclic legends of the recent past have included several Satan-related stories, such as the Procter and Gamble symbol,[32] McDonald's "worm burgers," or satanic rock music records or instruments; stories related to specific locations such as encounters with Bigfoot or cattle mutilations by outer space aliens (Ellis 1991: 39–80) may capture national attention. We need to examine all of the variants that simultaneously function and influence the public, without prejudice and value judgments.

# The Landscape
# and the Climate
# of the Legend

5.

## Belief in the Legend Climate

In the previous four chapters, much has been said about belief in relationship to the given topics. It is now time to tie it all together, foregrounding belief as the given, underlying ideological foundation of legends. From the functional point of view based on earlier research (Dégh and Vázsonyi 1971, 1973, 1978), we explored the attitude toward belief that members of the legend conduit expressed during performance. We identified believers, half-believers, hesitants, doubters, skeptics, and nonbelievers in the course of conversational narration, producing positive and negative legends as well as anti-legends. We documented that it does not necessarily change the quality of the narrative if the narrator is a nonbeliever or a defeatist who produces an anti-legend to kill the story.[1]

Gifted and motivated narrators can tell equally good stories to advocate their positive or negative beliefs. It is essential that they state the degree of their belief or disbelief because this statement is the purpose of the discourse. It is not the positive declaration of belief that makes a legend a legend but rather the debate of participants considering the legend's believability. What was born as a legend within the legend climate, what was transmitted as a legend and received as a legend, or, in other words, what traveled through the legend conduit in society, stays a legend even if its content turns out to be true.

Belief has been described and defined by folklorists as a separate, often folkloric phenomenon that exists as a shared, culturally learned knowledge that induces people in the group to behave and act in a certain way. Without special explanation, beliefs appear to manifest themselves only if there is a need to make them public, and that may happen metaphorically, as illustration.

General belief is not necessarily folklore and is understood as trust in the dependability of someone's information, "as disposition to respond in certain ways when the appropriate issue arises, like our belief in the dependability of our neighborhood cobbler" (Quine and Ullian 1970: 49). This is like our belief that someone with a calculator will come up with the sum total faster than if we do the addition of numbers scribbled on a notepad. Furthermore, in the broader frame, every notion or opinion depends on some kind of belief or knowledge; for example, the statement "he flew from London to Paris" implies knowledge of the existence of these two cities, the concept of travel, and airplanes. Yet these conceptual constructs do not seem to qualify as beliefs in support of legends:

> To believe is equivalent to taking a position on the truth of a statement and on the actuality of the matter stated. More precisely, belief means that we think a statement true and consider the stated matter real, objectively existent. . . . It is a part of the concept of belief itself that man is certain of that in which he believes. (Pieper 1963: 7, 15)

When folklorists speak of belief, they understand a mental attitude or behavioral pattern that manifests in audibly or visibly observable texts and the generic ingredients of a belief system, amounting to a local or subcultural religion. We can also relate these beliefs to pertinent legend types, but we must make it very clear that we mean religious belief ingredients that comprise the ideological foundation of legends. What we have to consider here is the *Homo religiosus*: the individual who has inherited a view of the world that helps him to cope with the problems of human destiny. In constructing answers with trust in God, he or she is the holder of the hereditary "theological belief in the existence of God, immortality of the soul and moral government of the world, and the seeker of salvation by faith, trust and obedience" (Bellah 1970: 4). Religion is related to the condition that humans live in uncertainty because they cannot fully know and comprehend the world around them. They live in social relationships that limit their natural instincts, and they are left to digest their own unanswered questions (Dux 1982: 158).

Beliefs entertained in the legend address these questions. Everyone knows the answers are unknowable, but it would be impossible not to think about them and not to seek answers to them — not from deities, but from fellow humans traveling the same trail to the same destination. People are spending sleepless nights thinking of their dead relatives and envisioning future horrors they will have to face, like their ancestors had to. People hope for relief by matching their experiences with those of close friends. But this is not enough. Fundamentalist believers need to address God directly, distinguishing between two kinds of appeal: prayer and meditation (Dégh 1994), and supplication to God and pledging sacrifice in trust of God's help.

The legend conversation transpires between people who share a common belief system and for whom extranormal experiences (encounters with supernatural and natural horrors) are equally disturbing. This question of belief makes the legend an ideology-sensitive genre — the genre that allows, indeed coerces people to think, to philosophize, to contemplate, to argue, and to debate. It also makes people be honest and humble, and express their true feelings, concerns, fears, weaknesses, and failures. The legend experience drives people to reveal and confess their deepest secrets. The legend discourse is democratic: Every participant is entitled to express his or her opinion, exposing himself or herself to the criticism or ridicule of others. But contrary opinion does not erupt in violent confrontation; villagers do not pull their knives to stab their opponents, nor do UFOlogists settle their disagreements with a shooting match after the convention. The deep emotion of participants discussing a legend topic, and the diversity of opinions, polarizes the debate, often to extremes. Nevertheless, there is much tolerance because of the common concern and the need to rely on each other's experience. Contrary opinions usually arise because the speakers have different information concerning the case, have specific knowledge of some detail, or were involved some time ago in something similar. The most lively debate usually concerns the introductory part, when the discussants establish the topic by identifying the persons, times, and places of the event and give details about their own involvement. This is an important foregrounding of the story that then may be narrated by a proponent and co-proponents. Alternative stories may be offered by supporters and opponents, and a debate of the supporting and opposing voices will conclude the story, opening the proposition for another, as long as people have time and can stay together.

This structure may be basic to natural legend performance. It fits my earliest model of 1963 in Tiszamogyorós, an archaic peasant village in northeast Hungary (Dégh 1978); it fits even the miracle legend telling of evangelists addressing vacationers in Florida, or the television talk show broadcasts of women who told of being abducted by space aliens or about being raised in a Satanist family and forced to bear babies to be sacrificed to Satan. On the talk show, these tales are told in the company of supporting and opposing voices — an expert priest, guru, parapsychologist, psychologist, doctor, friends, or accused family members. Obviously, the legend in this performance construct is also debating the truth it purports. Incredulity is the yeast of the debate. The opponents express their hesitation, doubt, and curiosity. Their attitude provokes the proponent to sharpen and clarify his or her argument and concede what Umberto Eco stated so well: "Not that the incredulous person doesn't believe in anything. It's just that he doesn't believe in everything. . . . Incredulity doesn't kill curiosity; it encourages it" (1989: xx).

I feel one should mention here the concept known as "the common frame of reference" (Newcomb 1952; Honko 1962: 96–99), the sum total of common knowledge and common belief that is necessary for people to share in comprehending and debating a legend. Honko speaks of the actualization of this frame, by way of emergence of a belief from the unconscious to the conscious mind. Evidently, this is an imaginary concept, impossible to determine; the many unknown beliefs and notions that are necessary for legend formation converge and diverge, or rather appear in combined geometrical shapes. For us, it seems not one but several *frames* of reference need to be considered. The nonexistence of certain significant "frames" will change the character of a story and may even deprive it of its legend status. The "frame of reference" does not demand belief; the only requirement is the knowledge that some people believe its statements. Thus, the statement "there are unexplainable things" or "the dead can return" does not require unconditional belief, and it should be interpreted as having diverse qualifiers: "Many people — some — everybody — believes, that there are unexplainable things." However, the statement itself, regardless of the specifications, must be commonly known; the legend must make it convincing. In other words, the special "reference" necessary to understand the legend has to fit into the frame of a higher, commonly known "reference." For example, were it not generally known that some amputees are fitted surgically with a hook as a replacement of a lost hand, "The Hook" legend could not have become the quintessential horror story of dating adolescents. Everyone receives the reference-material through separate channels, some channels such as school or church deliver the "facts," and the less reliable channels of the media and oral communication furnish the rest.

The sketches of the frames of three legends, "The Haunted House," "The Hook," and "Romeo and Juliet" are very schematic, taking only four references out of many more that are necessary to comprehend and situate them (not to prove their veracity).

The Ghost at the Point

Even a news clipping can give an idea of the legend debate structure. The following enacted legend, reported appropriately by stressing built-in controversiality (sounding the majority voice of rationality), begins with this statement:

> About the last place one would expect to find a ghost is that most earthbound of educational institutes, the U.S. Military Academy at West Point.

Now the reporter goes on to present the absurd case to the readers:

Nonetheless, several cadets swear that they have recently seen visions of a 5 ft. 3 in. soldier in full Jackson-era regimentals, complete with shako and musket. The thought of spectral shenanigans on hallowed military grounds has officials of the Point scratching their well-clipped head in perplexity.

And here is the legend-controversy:

> It all began on Oct. 21 in Room 4714 on the 47th Division barracks. One of two plebes who occupy the room said that he awoke to see a life-sized apparition of a 19th century officer emerge from a wall. The vision receded before the plebe could summon his roommate. The next night both saw the ghost. The story eventually reached the ears of Captain Keith Bakken. He and another upperclassman commandeered the room a few days later. The ghost promptly appeared before Bakken's confederate but receded into the wall again. Bakken, who is still a firm nonbeliever, admitted that the designated point of evaporation, which is normally quite warm, felt icy to the touch. Later the men who had seen the ghost identified it from a print found at the Point.

The concluding statement refers to similar events (legends) making the legend (that is, a practical joke) plausible — with a grain of doubt:

> As it happens, this is not the first astral presence to bestir West Point. The superintendent's mansion is said to be haunted by the ghost of an Irish cook named Molly. In the 1920s, moreover, a priest was summoned to a house on Professor's Row to exorcise a spirit that had sent two young servant girls screaming naked into the night.
> To outflank the new extraterrestrial presence, Bakken had declared Room 4714 off limits until Easter. Meanwhile, one upperclassman insists that the ghost has gone. How does he know? "I am a warlock," the cadet solemnly explained. (*Time*, December 4, 1972)

Our main concern is not whether legend-telling people believe that the legends they tell are true. Obviously, some they believe, others they don't. Some they fully believe, others they doubt, some they believed in the past but don't believe now, and some they didn't believe in the past and don't believe now. It all depends on the current state of religious belief that influences the intensity of the climate of the legend in which people are persuaded to change their minds. Personal belief is whimsical; it fluctuates. As we have already seen, many concerned people say that they are ready to believe in everything. Some certainly specialize in a specific area of belief, are attracted to organizations by this interest, and reject the beliefs of the others. But it is also true that many move from one esoteric, irrational faction to another. Still, legend-tellers in actual telling express their positive or negative belief.

However, personal attitudes of individuals toward belief (positive or negative) do not determine the legend. From the point of view of artistic standards (by this, I mean whether the recording folklorist finds it aesthetically enjoyable and convincing), it is irrelevant whether the legend-teller believes the legend. The only qualification for a legend-teller is a fascination with the world featured by the legend and a deep concern with its messages. As we saw in chapter 4, the legend-teller is a thinker who has experience and vision. It is not narrational skill, but rather wisdom and competence in the area of the extranormal that makes one a legend-teller.

Legend-tellers will state whether they believe, question, doubt, or reject the veracity of a legend, but their positive or negative attitude will not change the quality — and therefore the appreciation — of their stories. For example, two competing Hungarian narrators matched their skills in the small fishing community of Sára, in 1959. János Nagy, a respected old master, told about his encounter with two traveling students; both had been born with teeth, wore black capes, and carried their black books. When he intercepted them, they were vying for power, turning themselves into red and blue flames. The red flame won — the other was never seen again. His audience knew this story, was fascinated by it, and asked him to tell it again. Nagy was routinely asked, "Have you really seen them?" And he responded enigmatically with the märchen formula: "I saw them just like now." Of course, he personally did not believe it.

So why do we talk so much about belief — that is, believability, truthfulness, factuality, veracity, or credence — when we discuss the statements that legends elaborate upon? Why do folklorists still tell their readers that the legend is told as truth, even when its tellers know it is not? The mass media is to be blamed for confusing people's sense of reality. Even after the "urban legend" fad reached its zenith and became acknowledged as a form of commonplace entertainment of horror-mongers and amateur folklorists, the *Skeptical Inquirer* noted that urban legends are everywhere and do not show any sign of slowing down. According to the author, Scott Aaron Stine, the quarter-century-old urban legend "The Snuff Film," in which the star is actually killed on the screen, continues to prosper in variant forms as slasher movie, hoax, and didactic story. He feels Hollywood's appetite for graphic stagings of extreme cruelty and elaborate depictions of bloodbaths play a part, and demands that the entertainment industry inform the public that its horror shows are fictional. Stine considers it a major social concern that the average member of the radio and television audience cannot separate fact from fiction, particularly when the media voice insists that the fiction is fact.[2]

Why is the mass media telling lies when legend-tellers in good faith aren't? Why would they lie to their cohorts in such serious ideological questions related to human existence? And why blame the legend-teller, who was force-fed mass media horror as truth and cannot help but wonder and contemplate what to believe? At this late stage of folklorists' exploration of modern legend formation, Brunvand still sees the (urban) legend as he always did, as an apocryphal contemporary story, told as true: "The truth never stands in the way of a good story," he informs his lay audience of nonfolklorists (Brunvand 1999: 29). But a story is not a good story *because* it is a lie — both teller and audience also deserve to know what the narrator thinks.

Folklorists maintain an outsider category for truth in legend and make their interpretation irrespective of what the folk thinks. Some scholars still cannot descend from their elitist ivory tower of knowing objective truth. They know for sure there are no trolls playing tricks on the sailor in the fjords of Norway, no selkies robbing fishermen of their hearts in the Scottish Highlands, so accordingly there are no beautiful AIDS victims in bars who lure unsuspecting lonely drinkers into bed to take revenge for their ordeal. Some folklore textbooks tell us that the common folk is superstitious, ignoring the commonplace observation that "one folk's religion is another's superstition." Is it that folklorists know better than the folk that there is no need to draw a pessimistic picture of our destination? Or do they want to hide the truth from the tenderhearted, those frightened by the life-and-death epiphany of the *Halloween* film cycle, telling them there's nothing to fear, that this is only a funny-scary make-believe? That there are no evil people, no killers for passion or greed, no criminals run amuck, or even trigger-happy high school lunatics?

Legends are not told to deceive people — they don't lie, even if Martin Luther did speak about the lying legend ("legende-lügende"). Folklorists should see through the eyes of the folk, not maintain a double standard that defines one folklore genre for themselves, and another for the general public. Where is the folklorist's objectivity when participating in a legend-conduit that discusses the likelihood of ghosts, or ESP, or telepathy, or the possibility that babysitters are endangered by phone maniacs as in "The Murderer Upstairs" legend? Who is misleading whom?

The legend does not tolerate deliberate lies. The subjective truth, the emotional truth is what we are seeking in the humanistic discipline of folklore, and we must be particularly careful in areas where our visions, our conceptualization of reality differs from those of our informants. If one wants to understand the legend bearer's point of view, one should not rely on one's own speculation. There is no objective truth. Our truths and beliefs are biased and culture-specific, and no one's interpretation represents absolute truth. As a philosophical category, belief (truth) is subjectively perceived, and we have to accept the subjective truth of our informants. Our role is not to argue with them and convert them to our belief or heal them from delusions as the applied fields may do, but to try to read their minds, to understand what makes them think as they do. This is what folklorists are taught to be able to do.

### Understanding Belief

The articulation of culture-specific, religion-specific truth by individuals is our guide to the understanding of belief at the heart of the legend. My long-range study of miracle stories in a Pentecostal community taught me this lesson. Miracles are the lifeline of this community of 200 believers; their miracles are not spectacularly grandiose, but without them, the community would have no hope of survival until the happy entering of the heavenly gates. Miracles occur when there is a need, such as for sickness, financial breakdown, and loss of property due to accidents, fire, flood, drought, or theft; the malfunctioning of tools, cars, or families; and problems with raising children, particularly youngsters who abandon the church and become delinquents. Through daily conversation with Jesus, members are touched by miracles that they report to the community. They first testify in church, then report the miracle to friends, relatives, and neighbors. They tape-record their stories for later reinforcement in their addressing Jesus while they pray and meditate at home, at work, and in the prayer room. This intensive community accord and life with the Lord keeps "the Saints" radiant and mentally sane. Their belief is so strong, even though they are surrounded by dissent and ridicule — they joke about being called Jesus freaks, holy rollers, and crazies. They cannot accept defeat, and they can always find the way to see a miracle in seemingly lost cases.

Lisa, one of the most intelligent and articulate tellers of miracle stories, had had a long-term concern for her two sons who were addicted to drugs and alcohol. Small miracles had encouraged her to keep praying for them to come back to church. Then something happened: One of her sons' friends, Ben, came back from California with terminal cancer. She visited him and told him that she was going to pray for him. The 21-year-old Ben said, "Pray? I would, but I never knew how." "All right," she told him, "you just take care of yourself; I'm doing the praying."

The doctors had given him twenty-four hours to live, so the next night, they held a prayer meeting for him. And Jesus told Lisa that at midnight a miracle would happen. As the women prayed at the altar, the door flew open to reveal Lisa's delinquent sons and their girlfriends — crying and praying. They came to the altar, got down on their knees, and praised the Lord.

"What's going on?" Lisa asked; "What happened?" "Oh Mom," said Skip, her son, "You should have seen. Ben sat up in bed, took off the IV he was hooked to, sat on the chair next to his hospital bed, and talked to us normally. And he hadn't spoken for days."

Lisa felt *victory!* The Lord had made a miracle, and Ben was going to be healed. The next day Lisa called me on the telephone.

"Have you seen the paper?" she asked me. I told her that I hadn't. "Ben died. I misunderstood the Lord. It was not for Ben to be healed. He was doomed. But there *was* a miracle. The kids, those drug-addicted kids who left the church and lived in sin, came back and worshipped at the altar. As the Lord had said, at midnight. This was the miracle."

Some legends are more controversial and ambiguous than others, and their proponents remain uncertain and contradictory like the story of Debbie, the journalism student who told us about the chain on the gravestone in Prospect, Indiana, during a Halloween night session (see chapter 3). Throughout the telling of her three-part story, she kept contradicting herself. Only at the end, when she told us that the believer was unharmed and the rationalist unbeliever choked to death by the chain, did we learn her belief that, indeed, it was God who had meted out justice.

What happens if the legend conduit is invaded by hoaxers, pathological liars, criminals, well-meaning educators, artists, and others with a distinctive purpose? Those who plant an invented legend are harmless because they do not derail an established conduit but start one. If their story has a future, it will become a genuine legend — like the story about the crack on the abbey's floor at a Benedictine convent invented to strengthen young entrants' belief in wonders (Gilbert 1975: 61–79), or the many monster-stories manufactured by Boy Scout camp counselors to keep kids from exploring the locality and getting lost in the woods. Folklorists have shown that the so-called *Schreckmärchen*, such as the Grimms' "Hansel and Gretel" and "Little Red Riding Hood," were told for children probably at a time when homesteads were surrounded by forests and children starved to death or were devoured by wild animals if they wandered away (Rumpf 1955).

We have heard about people in Oregon and Washington who make extrabig wooden shoes to fake the indigenous Sasquatch's footprints — this does not amount to more than the construction of a negative version by a minority of debunkers. It did not stop the monster's invasion of the distant and less accommodating woods of Pennsylvania, Ohio, and the rest of the Midwest where it is reinforced by the Bigfoot gas company's huge cardboard posters of the monster.

The firmly established legends are well enough ingrained into the belief system of the industrial community to survive, or maybe to become enhanced, by the attack of negative and anti-legend makers. This seeming paradox is true not because the rationalists and the enlighteners are wrong, but because people want to live with mysteries and do not want to wake up discovering that there is nothing to worry about.

Crop Circles throughout the World

For the large and growing community of UFO believers, the book *Circular Evidence,* by retired engineer Pat Delgado and his associate Colin Andrews, provided more evidence that an extraterrestrial "superior intelligence" was invading our earth. As reported by a London correspondent to *Time* magazine, their book sold more than 50,000 copies (Jaroff 1991: 59). They had located hundreds of "mystifying and intriguing" grain field circles in southern England "that no humans could have done," which were similar to those found in other countries in lesser number.

But soon the two legend proponents, who made a career of investigating and narrating, were rebutted by two landscape painters, David Chorley, 62, and Douglas Bower, 67 (Nickell and Fischer 1992: 136–149). The two artists came forward to admit that they had fashioned as many as twenty-five or thirty new circles each growing season over the last thirteen years. Apparently their work had inspired copycats who shaped hundreds of crop circles in England and elsewhere. According to the report, "The admission brought an end to one of the most popular mysteries Britain — and the world — had witnessed in years. Flying saucers . . . were given new life. . . . Saucer enthusiasts argued that the cropland patterns marked the landing spot of UFO bearing visitors from space. Believers in the paranormal claimed the circles radiated mysterious energy forces." Now all these ideas seemed to collapse.

Meanwhile, scientists also became involved in the debate. A new scientific discipline, "cereology," was initiated by physicist Terence Meaden. His team argued that weather phenomena may be responsible for the weird damage of the crop. Furthermore, a team of Japanese physicists also looked for an explanation and suggested that "a form of ball lightning generated by microwaves in the atmosphere flattened the crops, creating croplike circular patterns both in the laboratory and on a computer programming to stimulate ball lightning" (*Time,* Sept. 21).

The scholars were trying to find scientific evidence to enlighten the believers, but was there any serious motivation behind the hoaxers? Not really, as they told Brough. The two men were sitting in a pub, reading reports about flying saucer landing sites, and were "wondering what we would do for a bit of laugh. . . ." One of their circles was spotted in 1981 and promptly attributed to extraterrestrials. "We laughed so much at that time," recalls Chorey, "we had to stop the car because Doug was in stitches so much he couldn't drive."

Of course, Delgado was not deterred. After recovering from the shock, he said that "these two gents may have hoaxed some of the circles . . . but the phenomenon is still there, and we will carry on research" (*Time*, Sept. 21). He has the moral support of untold millions, for the current legend climate, in which the subjective truth is stronger, is on his side. In fact, the debate — and the efforts to discredit the two artists — continue: "If it is some kind of practical joke, then the organization behind it outstrips the Mafia, KGB and Illuminati combined" (Nickell 1999: 54). Best-selling legend collections containing positive crop circle legends overcome opposition by virtue of sheer numbers and the readers' desire to believe without access to convincing data. Nickell's article concluded with the words of UFOlogist Joan Creighton: "We all have an inner sense that there is a mystery behind the universe. We like mysteries. It's great fun."

Yes, human beings are irrational and do not want to be enlightened. A tacit consensus has developed that risk-taking is a form of American bravado (as exemplified by the tragic outcome of acts by young members of the Kennedy family). But world history is marked by irrational acts. People, unconcerned about their own survival, have always taken unnecessary risks and been ready to sacrifice their lives for trivial pursuits, not for noble causes, not for saving the lives of their loved ones. Crusading kings to the Holy Land lost their lives and brought misery to their countries; and ever since people have killed people for religious and political differences without a real gain to anyone. Bold seafarers discovered America by error — they were after the pepper and other spices of fabulous India; they shed blood for gold and shiny stones that had no value for them. Holocausts have followed holocausts, brothers have killed brothers, and the lands of ancient and modern civilizations have been transformed into mass graveyards.

Attraction to the weird and the mysterious is a luxury of the affluent Western world. The Gothic novel, the classical literary genre of the early romantic period, was the first to entertain a new British capitalist readership. The rising bourgeoisie was fascinated by horror stories about revenants, werewolves, vampires, and mad scientists. The reconstructed medieval scenery — castles and monasteries with trapdoors, subterranean passages, winding stairs, crypts, and chapels where the specters of innocent victims loomed and moaned — endowed the reader with the spirit of traditional legendry.

As time passed, accumulation of wealth and urbanization made life even more comfortable and secure but less challenging, with too much uneventful free time and boredom. New excitement, new stories of horror and gore reactivated numb brains, bringing danger closer to home. Readers took pleasure in looking into the face of real and supernatural danger, while never leaving the safety of comfortable living. To keep up the shiver for elite society of the twentieth century, the literary repertoire expanded to include two new related genres: rational, riddle-like crime fiction, and irrational, spiritualism-inspired supernatural mystery.

When we look for the American consumers of the irrationality market, we find them in the heartland, among those who have everything that lottery tickets, sweepstakes, lucky numbers, and amulet merchants promise to the winner. These consumers have it all, but they are bored, isolated, miserable, and dysfunctional in their comfortable homes, surrounded by a new mass media world that marginalizes them. They are open prey to occult subcultures, and as we have seen, there is a large choice. Mystery is fun, horror is fun, and they save one from boredom and loneliness by activating and compensating for a lost social life.

As one can expect, middle-aged women play leading roles in occult institutions. Many gifted women, confined to the household, find their voice and a new confidence by entering the limelight of the chosen; they teach, preach, and gain respect for their leadership with their secret, extranormal knowledge. The common belief that generates the legends that answer people's needs is the leaven that ferments a new social structure, which substitutes for a lost network of old-fashioned domesticity. Like those who debated belief in the legend for centuries, people today do not want to find the definitive answer; they just want the thrill. They want to talk about possibilities.

Humans do not want to be omnipotent, omniscient, or to take responsibility for their own follies. They like to live with mysteries, and to believe in and rely on a higher power, a Father in Heaven, a Provider.

## Is There a Haunted House in Your Life?

> All houses wherein men have lived and died
> Are haunted houses. Through the open doors
> The harmless phantoms on their errands glide,
> With feet that make no sound upon the floors.
> — Henry Wadsworth Longfellow, *Haunted Houses*

Longfellow's poetic description of the home as the transitory resting place of the living and the dead tells us about an undissolvable bond between the generations that secures continuity in both temporal and spatial senses, that is, in terms of eternity. Houses are precious documents of a continuity beyond human limitations; they are the perfect embodiments of history. Longfellow's lines remind us that this notion makes houses the natural repositories of the largest, and most characteristic body of legendry. On the surface, the house is a residence; but more, it is the protective shell that surrounds the fragile human body. A house becomes the symbol of a family home. It is a mysterious, collaborative monument of each generation's accomplishments — of their artistry, pride, and intellectual, social, and economic success. Inside and outside, with its surroundings, it contains the objects and subjects that identify not only the people who live there now, but more importantly ancestors who lived there before. These artifacts tell about these people's lives, struggles, successes, and failures, about their happy and unhappy days — weddings and births, sicknesses and funerals. People's belongings, tools, clothing, toys, accessories — everything they lived with over time — become a part of them, and may become an extension, a representative of their personalities. And indeed, they become our traditions, our models for our values and guides to our future.

Here is the corner where Maggie liked to play with her dolls, imagining a whole nursery in the nook next to the fireplace. There is grandfather's rocking chair, in which he used to nap in his Sunday best with his pipe in his mouth after church, and before lunch was served; and there is the old grandfather clock that stopped when he died, and has not been fixable since then. There is Mamaw's cookbook, and there the afghan she crocheted, covering that faded sofa. There is Aunt Laura's autograph book with pressed flowers among the pages, and there is the empty cage of little Alfie's canary bird that flew away. And there are pictures, lots of pictures, of known and unknown people in funny old costumes, in uniforms, sitting on trucks, on horseback, or standing in front of an old cabriolet; photos of naked babies in the bathtub and of a kindergarten graduating class. There are letters and postcards from unidentifiable vacation places sent by thoughtful, loving relatives; here is a saber and a military cap, brought back from overseas as war souvenirs. The porch, the staircase, the attic, the basement, and the modernized old fireplace have separate stories, full of mysteries. They hide cobweb-covered old furniture, a broken-legged piano, dusty dishes, and rusting boxes and trunks. These quiet, listless objects of the past are set into motion at night, when their dead owners make their presence felt.

The faint fragrance of old perfume, tobacco, castor oil, the scent of lavender and other dried herbs fills the air when the dead return and become active. They walk or run up and down the stairs, swing on the lighting fixtures, clank chains, bounce on the beds, move the furniture, and unlock that front door that the owner of the house had locked tightly in the evening but finds open in the morning. Ghosts turn on the lights, the dishwasher, the faucets, and the television. They answer and hang up the telephone, open and close closet doors — they even manage to swing doors open where the new thick carpet makes it difficult to move. Spirits and their extensions make little noises, sighs, cracks, pops, whispers, knocks, coughs, and moans. Some are the vicious, unpleasantly loud poltergeists (Carrington and Fodor 1953), throwing

323

large and heavy objects and crashing dishes. Or they may have a fit without doing damage; with peels of nasty laughter, they signal their presence to the petrified slumberer who is unable to move or to scream until it is gone.

The spirits may stay invisible or appear as white, black, bluish, pinkish shades or as misty, transparent, wraithlike figures. Less frequently, they appear as domestic or wild animals, rocks, bottles, wheels, and other inanimate objects. But some are recognizable humans: close relatives, men and women of any age, who assume their known shapes and clothes, looking just as they appeared on their last photograph or as they are best remembered in their framed pictures as children, young brides, or eligible bachelors. Familiar faces are reflected in the mirror, or seen in the doorway, floating away toward the ceiling or slowly vanishing as on a movie screen.

The spectral visitors are not necessarily always relatives. Apparitions may be total strangers — pale maidens, highwaymen, impish little boys, Indian chiefs, preachers, or stylish ladies carrying their bonneted heads in their hands. Occasionally the haunts, ghosts, or spooks touch the residents, caressing tenderly those they like, and pushing, kicking, or even torturing to death those they don't. Longfellow's silent haunts are ambiguous beings, and their activities are as ambiguous as the legends about them.

Who are these revenants? Why are they visiting houses? What do they want? Are houses themselves what they particularly seek, and if so, why?

## The Legend Business

In our random survey of Indiana hauntings, we found that Hoosiers in general have not been reluctant to talk about haunted houses. The impact of mass media interest in haunting has convinced them that people are not regarded backward if they happen to have such an experience. Our research was always low-key, staying within the ideological realm of Midwesterners, and staying away as much as possible from business entrepreneurs and their merchandise. However, as we have seen, it is impossible to exclude the input of mass media–manipulated supernaturalism when it concerns ghosts, which are newsworthy items. So let us deal with the input of the media now.

The market for ghost story books has been booming for a long time and never seems to decline. Temporarily other extranormal themes have made a lightning-like sweep over the landscape — as illustrated by the Roswell UFO story at its fiftieth anniversary in 1997 (see chapter 4) — but this phenomenon has not affected the steady interest in ghost story books. Old classics keep being reprinted, and new national and regional collections have steady sales. It seems every important house has its resident ghosts, including the White House and the mansions of the rich and the famous. A home that bears a marker relating its historic and architectural significance also refers to its resident ghost; the same is true of many old public buildings. No ghost story compilation is too silly or fabricated that it cannot find a publisher. All that goes under the title "incredible," "unbelievable," "horror," "scary," or "grim" can be sold by vendors eager to raise the ghost-consciousness of the credulous public.

Books are only one of the networks for the commodification of spirit belief. The fast-growing guild of vernacular exorcists has prospered in the shadow of, and with the tacit consensus of, the Roman Catholic church, whose ordained priests and appointed exorcists perform the ritual as commissioned by an archbishop. For example, the sensational ghost story about the haunted house in Amityville, New York, introduced Ed and Lorraine Warren, professional ghost hunters who investigated more than 3,000 cases of hauntings.[3] The international demand for trained ghost hunters seems to have emerged around the same time; *The Ghost Hunter's Guide* by Peter Underwood, the president and chief investigator of the Ghost Club (founded in 1862), was issued simultaneously in London, New York, and Sydney in 1986. Soon exorcism became a lucrative business, practiced by many followers, including grass roots spiritualists, who are inspired by strong belief rather than financial gain (such as BarBara Lee and associates, described in chapter 4).

Recent times have also seen a considerable increase in local psi practitioners, clairvoyants, palmists, and seers. Their prestige has grown through their magazine columns, tabloid prophecies, and above all, their invited assistance of law enforcement agencies in difficult criminal investigations. Movies and television series about ghosts have remained steady favorites, and this blitz obviously directs attention to the actors who play the ghosts. Numerous interviews and gossip columns report about the actors' own houses being haunted, and describe their secret involvement with supernatural agencies and the threat to their lives by evil spirits. And, heaven forbid, if the actors die, their benevolent acts as guardian angels hit the press (see the discussion of actor Michael Landon in chapter 1). Likewise, sports heroes and political figures in the zenith of their popularity are the subjects of tabloid stories about their secret ghost encounters.

The above suppliers of haunted house legends report on haunted sites and let their audience know they are not alone with their experiences: Such things are common to all, and there is help for those in need. Like any legend-teller, the shows offer information. Those who operate within the tourist market, on the other hand, are openly businesslike. They institutionalize haunted houses and educate people under the guise of recreational travel for a considerable fee.

Even the United States government has contributed an authoritative attempt at the rationalization of irrationality. The U.S. Department of Commerce issued a Traveler's Guide to Special Attractions No. 10 entitled "The Supernatural: Haunted Houses and Legendary Ghosts," based on national

# Haunted Happenings

## October 29-30, 1998 $189.

This trip includes visits and views of over three dozen haunted sites in town, including three haunted houses, Malabar Farms, Quaker Meeting House, the Haunted Firehouse, The homesick Haunt, Oak Hill Cottage, and The Drive-In Ghost. Two lunches, one breakfast & a murder mystery dinner are included! Shopping, Carrousel Magic, The Reformatory, overnight lodging, all admission costs, taxes, gratuities, lugggage handling, and motorcoach transportation by Star of Indiana to Waynesville, OH.

Call Linda to reserve your space 331-3413

Haunted Happenings Flier sent by a Bloomington bank to members

listings and expert authentication. A representative sampling of twenty-nine locations appear on the handout, mainly from the East Coast; the states with the most listed are Louisiana (10) and Virginia (9). All of the sites are old restored buildings of historical value; some are museums, antique shops, restaurants. Some charge an admission fee, and all have limited days and hours of visitation. The choice of hauntings vary, but the stories are often sketchy reports of the presence of a ghost.

One can learn more attractive details from AAA's magazine *Home and Away* (September 1998), which offers a selection of terrifying "Heartland Haunts." The Midwest, it says, "long renowned for its neighborly spirit . . . the Midwest has its share of friendly ghosts." Dixie Franklin, the author of this article and of the book *Haunts of the Upper Great Lakes*, invites the reader to visit elegant old houses that have been converted into restaurants and hotels. With proper arrangements and trained personnel, a spooky sojourn can be strange and mysterious but not too frightening. Franklin provides a few choice stories and phone numbers to call for reservations. Evidently, the AAA Travel counselor does not want to scare off prospective customers either, offering "arrangements for your haunting visit by providing maps, TripTiks and Tour Books." Tourists are encouraged to visit the American Ghost Society's Internet site for more assistance on tracking down ghosts in one's own area: "Society members not only investigate hauntings, but also conduct tours, organize conferences and publish *Ghosts of the Prairie*, a quarterly magazine." This closes the circle of the haunted house business network, which contextualizes the living ghost legendry in our experience.

## Haunted Locations

Our past research surveys of hauntings not only gave us a representative sample of haunted houses and other locations in Indiana, but also provided a fairly complete repertoire of ghost story types.[4] We were told of the presence and activities of spirits, and of the emotions, interpretations, and related activities of humans. Identical plots appeared in several variants, from the same and from diverse locations in the state.

We did not fulfill our study's stated purpose, the mapping of the ghostly locations of Indiana, and today our map necessarily remains incomplete. Our ghost houses did not exhibit longevity but rather flexibility, because Americans are more mobile than Europeans who often live in family homes built by their ancestors centuries ago. As we came to realize, only stately mansions and homes of important people could gain prominence and official support for restoration over a long period of time. Thus, I could not locate many haunted houses because they did not exist anymore. In our times, relatively old houses have fallen victim to industrial development. The building of bridges, reservoirs, four-lane highways, new housing complexes, factories, plants, and shopping centers speedily changed the Indiana landscape during our survey. For example, numerous old homesteads, farmhouses, barns, and stables were demolished to clear the way for Lake Monroe, one of Indiana's largest and most spectacular reservoirs, which was completed in 1969 to become the haven of vacationers and the dream residency of upper middle-class escapees of urban living. Only the cemetery gravestones escaped the bulldozer, leaving the only clues to the people who had once lived there.

Only young adventure-seekers knew the secrets of the dead. It is remarkable that the young are so curious about the past, and the houses and other sites that do not exist anymore. They go on fearsome expeditions to checkpoints—broken-down railroad bridges, grave markers, chapels, tunnels. On their daring trips to the unknown spirit underground, they challenge the dead to appear and tell how they perished. They visit the place that they assume is the site they have heard stories about from others, such as Skiles Test's "House of Blue Lights" in Indianapolis, which was demolished in 1967; or they seek the Gray Lady of Fort Wayne's library, which burned down in the 1920s. Indeed, in eight distinct Indiana locations, the young call up the Civil War soldier, who survived his last battle only to be killed by a thunderstorm at a stone's throw from his parents' home.

In some cases, the informant did not want to tell us where the house or other site was. Some of my correspondents signed their name "Anonymous" or with a nickname such as "Boots" or "A secretary who saw your appeal." Many people who "knew something" about a haunting in their neighborhoods felt the urge to tell, but were embarrassed to come forward. "Boots," for example, wrote to me about the death of an old lady who lived alone in a "spooky big old house sitting way back on a lane on a hill near Terre Haute." Her letter, especially the statement at the beginning, is structured like an orally told legend.

### Baby Bones in the Basement

This is based on a true happening. It was back in the tens, twenties. [Boots outlines the situation: Two friends from down the street stayed with the lady because she was having nightmares and couldn't sleep.]

One night the plaster fell off the ceiling upstairs right above where her bed was in the room below. It hit the floor upstairs and the door and window would shake like someone was trying to get in.

They thought it to be the wind. The night she died was the worst night of all. The two friends decided they would stay up that night with her body in the next room. The doors and windows shook so bad they decided they would go outside and see who was there. Each went in opposite directions around the house. They were scared but found no one. The noise and door knobs turned etc. all night long. It only stopped when day light came. Back then they didn't have the funeral homes like they do now. After her funeral the relatives tried to rent the house but no one would stay in it at night. So they decided to tear the old place down. Several of the neighbors came to help tear it down. In the attic they found a big shoe box and in it were the bones of a tiny baby. If I could tell you the location, the old people in her community could tell you about the old haunted house and the baby bones.

This took place in southern Indiana. (It was far worse then I can tell it.)
Signed — Boots. This is how it was told to me.

Several of the narrators who actually have lived in haunted houses told me that they did not want to embarrass their families by telling about the haunts they commonly experienced. The most common cause of secrecy about a house's location was the owner's worry that, in the event of a sale, no one would buy it if it was known to be haunted (see, for example, the story of the Stewart family in chapter 3). They also fear nasty neighbors who are capable of spreading false rumors of a noisy resident ghost, who would "swear up and down" that they'd heard it. Neither did narrators want to look ridiculous; some claimed that the rest of the family would deny such things ever happened — even a brother who had moved out of the house because of the screams from the attic and windows crashing all night would pretend he moved for another reason. The returning dead can cause trouble and discord within the family, even when they are welcome.

One of the more remarkable haunting stories was one that I could not record in its entirety because the narrator was reluctant to reveal the location of the place. A student majoring in communications studies submitted a video recording and script of a legend he had collected in Bedford as his final project for my class. Later he asked if he could borrow his paper and video to show them to his family over Christmas break; although he'd promised to return the materials, I have never seen him or his project again. The video featured a fiftyish, tall, balding man, who told his story in first person. I assume that this man probably did not want to be identified, and warned my student to forget about it. A journalist in Bedford, who had sent me some legends and was interested in my project, could identify neither the narrator nor the story I told her. Without the video and the script, I have only the brief outline of the legend.

### The New Bathtub

A man wanted to buy a house somewhere south of Bedford to relocate his family from Indianapolis to a quiet, farming area — buy a nice farmhouse and a couple of horses. Screening the real estate ads in the Sunday paper, he drove to town and looked at several houses for sale. He spent the whole day in Bedford, talked to people at a diner, and saw four houses, ending with one he really liked. This house seemed fine and reasonably priced. The man called the owner a week later and made an appointment. Everything seemed in good shape for a seasoned old house — it only needed some cleaning and a paint job, which the family could do after moving in. But something strange caught his eye in the bathroom. Unlike the rest of the house, it looked new, with a modern style sunken bathtub. "What happened to the old one?" he asked. The owner smiled: "Oh, nothing, the old one was too worn and small, so we thought we would get a more comfortable one for a new owner."

Some complications in the family made the man postpone further negotiations, but half a year later he remembered the house he'd liked so much and went back to see if it was still available. It was. To refresh his memory, he looked it over again and he liked it even better than before. Yet he noticed a new bathtub in the bathroom again. "I thought I saw a brand new bathtub last time," he told the owner; "What happened?" "Oh that," laughed the owner, "my brother-in-law built a house, and his wife liked our tub so much that we let her have it in exchange for theirs." Again, some waiting period followed, and it was next spring before the man could seriously think of buying the house. When he went back again, he found yet another new bathtub. But he was determined; without asking for a new explanation, he paid cash and the family moved in a month later.

All was nice and fine, and everyone was happy; but after a couple of months of using the bathroom, the family saw bloodstains on the tub. They could not wipe it off; it came back again and again. The man later found out why from people in the neighborhood. Someone was murdered there some time ago. But the man did not give up or run away: He turned the bathroom into a porch and built another one upstairs, forcing the murder victim's spirit to rest in peace.

The haunted house stories in most of the recently collected and professionally recorded materials in our sample are from people who have personally experienced apparitions. These stories are fewer in number because earlier collectors preferred to look for impersonal accounts, and depended more on young student collectors than on professional fieldworkers. The experiential legends in our sample, however, are more relevant and valuable because they come closest to representing the true belief and involvement of individual narrators. These stories are current: They speak of hauntings in existent residencies, including homes that house a nuclear family of parents and children, with one or two grandparents; middle-aged couples with children gone; or widows who are alone. Some involvement is shown by tellers who report experiences in abandoned houses, barns, and outbuildings in good shape or in ruins, or even at sites where a certain haunted house once stood.

Hauntings may happen in any kind of house or apartment where people — particularly families — reside. Although it is common to associate revenants with old houses, a remarkably large number of ghost activities have been reported in new houses. I had several conversations with a young couple whose house was built a year before and was still not completely finished. Their eight-month-old baby would cry and kick at certain times of the day as though the child was bothered by something that others could not see. They had not believed in ghosts before, but their relatives and neighbors had been strongly urging that they talk to an "expert" — meaning a professional clairvoyant — about the disturbance. We talked about their family history and about any dead ancestors that may have been on their minds, but the couple seemed perfectly normal, with no inclination toward parapsychological interpretations. They just did not know what to think of the phenomenon.

Rented apartments also may be viewed as being haunted. A young lawyer and his family who lived in a plush Lake Shore Drive condominium in Chicago told me they were harassed by the ghost of an Indian chief whose burial ground had been desecrated by the architects of the high-rise building. In his letter to me, he stated that this experience shook him so much that he gave up his job, moved back to the area of Greenwood, Indiana, where his family farmed, and became an organic farmer. He is now happier than ever.

Another story of a haunting came from Tom Littleton, a part-time college teacher and a Ph.D. candidate in English literature. He had a keen interest in folklore; he told me that he planned "to teach a couple of years here [in Illinois], and then move to Southern Indiana . . . and working with Hoosier folklore when we move." In his letter of January 30, 1986, he gave this report about "resident ghost[s]" at his home.

### That Scared Me Half to Death

The story is a continuing one and I will swear that it is a true story. It started in October of 1976 when we first moved into this house. Connie told me that she heard a baby crying in the house in the afternoon. It wasn't an everyday thing but would happen off and on. At that time, we only had one baby in the house — our daughter Heather. Connie said it could not be Heather crying because sometimes she would be holding the baby and still hear the crying. Personally, I must admit that I never heard the baby in question. At the time I told her it must have been a cat or some logical explanation. I did ask some old timers in the area about the possibility of an infant dying in the immediate neighborhood but nothing turned up.

Sometime in 1977 we were in bed. I thought Connie was sleeping and she thought I was sleeping. Suddenly the room became quite cold and I felt a presence in the room. I began to feel very sad for no apparent reason. The sadness increased until I felt like crying. Shortly — whatever it was seemed to leave. I noticed at this point that Connie was crying. I asked her what was wrong and she said she didn't know that she just suddenly felt sad enough to cry and related basically the same experience I had just been through.

From then until 1982 things were pretty quiet. We had a couple of minor "feelings" but nothing strong until March 1983. I had been in the hospital for a hernia operation and was home recovering. I had been building a three room addition to accommodate our growing family (now five children) and only had completed the interior of one room. On this particular night I couldn't get comfortable in our extra firm bed so I went into the boys' room and climbed into the lower bunk that was much softer. I couldn't sleep. I heard Connie get up to get the baby a bottle. She went to the refrigerator, into the living room and then back into our bedroom. She no sooner got back into bed in the other room when I heard two muffled voices in the kitchen. I wondered who the heck she could be talking with at 3 A.M. At that time I heard my son, Chuck, start to talk in his sleep. Chuck was in the same room with me in his bunk across the room. I tried to tell him to be quiet but found I couldn't speak! Also I could not move. I was unable to move my arms, legs, head — and I couldn't talk. The voices then came closer to the room and I could hear the "parties" walking. When they got to the doorway they turned left, went down the new hallway and out the back door. On the way out they kicked a coffee can full of nails that I had moved out of the hallway a day before. I heard the new door open and close. As soon as the door closed I found I could move and speak. I jumped out of bed, ran into the kitchen and looked out the window. There were no tracks in the snow. Nothing to indicate the strange visit I had just experienced. I mentioned this experience to my friend and pastor Father Stanley Limanowski expecting him to laugh it off.

His explanation was that occasionally the spirit world does intersect with our living world but not to worry about it. By the way — there was no fear involved with this experience.

It was this next one that scared me half to death. I came home from work one night at 1 A.M. — as usual — and climbed to bed. Connie was sleeping as usual. I no sooner got into bed and "it" came in the room. My back was to the door but I felt it enter. It walked around the bed to my side. Dr. Dégh, this thing was furious! It was angry about something — I don't know what it could have been about. It didn't speak but emitted two oscillating tones — one high and one low. I could move my hand — though the rest of me was frozen. And I kept jabbing at Connie until she woke up. As soon as she asked me what was wrong the thing vanished. I was frightened by this one. I know a ghost can't hurt me and have never been afraid before of "ghosts" but this really got to me. I told Father Stan about it and he had no explanation for me and could offer no suggestion concerning the violent nature of my visitor.

That's about all I can tell you. No idea as to why. It doesn't happen often enough to establish any kind of pattern and it has been some time since the last one.

Continuing with the kinds of residencies where hauntings in our corpus occurred, a good number of haunted houses in the collection are school buildings, including private, denominational, and military schools, girls' and boys' schools, and colleges. Fraternities, sororities, dormitories, and graduate residences, with their histories of accidents, hazings, suicides, love-related murders, and family cruelties, seem obvious sites for poor souls to haunt their former rooms.

The rest of the haunted buildings include offices (law firms, insurance and doctors' offices, police and fire departments), churches/chapels, welfare institutions (hospitals, asylums, a poor farm), factories, and cultural institutions (theaters, museums, libraries). There are also hotels, inns, taverns, and restaurants. In spite of mass media and business pressures, mansions of famous people are at the bottom of the list. This distribution is realistic because it shows that the majority of haunted house legends give priority to traditional ghosts in people's residences, the primary secure place of their lives, including the temporary and secondary dwellings of young people away from home. Schools and offices where people do business, are cared for, get an education, or are entertained within their own community are also a priority, not sites where they are lured for extracurricular ghost hunts. This distribution suggests that even though average people may be attracted to supernatural pageantry as a diversion and may enjoy commercial ghost shows, their vested interest lies in their own lives and with their own hereditary and acquired contacts with the dead. This is the insider's, not the outsider's, natural interest and it is not completely eradicated by the mass media.

### Haunted House Legends: Narrators and Structure

The narrators of the haunted house legends in our survey were mostly, but not exclusively, middle aged and older men and women whose experiences were joyous and uplifting but also difficult and troubling. The sensation of being in touch with the other world brings with it the burden of keeping it a secret for the sake of peace in the family. If it did not concern their own home, men liked to talk about mischievous ghosts who had played tricks in the office and misplaced important papers, locked toilet doors, and hid umbrellas; but, in general, no clear age and sex division of the tellers could be ascertained.

Unfortunately, our bulky data suffers from incompleteness. More stories are fragmentary than I expected, compared to those in some representative regional European collections.

More than half of the American legends are limited to the identification and description of the ghost's appearance and the emotional reaction the experience causes; no further information is given about the main points: the reason behind the haunting and its effect on other people, and its resolution by laying the spirit to rest. As previously noted, legends by their very nature are fragmentary; they are left open for additional information to be filled in by their communicators during the telling. Fragmentation usually means that tellers relate just a part, no matter how small or inessential, of a legend that can be discerned from its variants. All of the fragments are important in the complete story; like a puzzle, the parts come together in support of a belief statement.

In many cases, the plots in the Indiana corpus describe an observed phenomenon, comment on its eeriness, and let the rest go; these abrupt stops, open endings, or limitations on information deserve further consideration. Maybe audiences at large do not expect more than a tableau-like listing of the gallery of ghosts because ghosts are so common in people's lives — so the more and the eerier, the better for a shiver. Or perhaps the thrill lies in comparing these stories to others that are known but not told. Or perhaps elaborating on the details and the outcome would prove too disturbing, particularly if addressees are not directly involved. Or perhaps people prefer to leave the secrets to linger on. Or perhaps people are afraid of malice, of rumors that may not tell the truth — why malign an innocent victim just to entertain an uncompassionate audience?

In fact, family members of the dead have found themselves angered and dismayed at the natural, liberal variation of popular legends. Local gossip surrounding unusual or tragic deaths has intermingled with traditional legends, and been applied within oral tradition. "Some people like to slander others and make fun of their grief," Ms. Lillian Pruett wrote to me, demanding an apology for the publication of the "Chain on the Tombstone" legend in *Indiana Folklore* (Clements 1969a: 90–96). The grave marker of her brother Floyd (1894–1920), which is made of pink granite stone with an odd chain on its side as part of a cross symbol, is located in the Bonds Chapel cemetery near Orangeville, Indiana; it remains an attractive mystery place for regional Halloween adventure seekers. "He was accused of having murdered his wife," complained Ms. Pruett. "But he died of tuberculosis and his wife is still alive." In such cases, should we blame the shortsightedness of collectors and publishers who did not look for contextual information behind the allegations and speculations? As we already have noted, omissions of the context are a shortcoming of most older recordings.

But despite these shortcomings, we must be satisfied with the large corpus of texts, no matter how improperly they were recorded by today's standards. Quantity can be of great value, offering the opportunity to try analytical reconstructions of the missing information from the bits and pieces, hints, allusions, and testimonies concerning belief and non-belief within the texts. Following scrutiny of available variants, new fieldwork can shed light on the temporal and spatial variation of the stories and their meanings. We may make a lucky strike of novel findings, as occurred when ongoing popular legends such as "The Hook," "The Vanishing Hitchhiker," "The Stolen Grandmother," and "The Screaming Bridge" were systematically recollected and reexamined. As long as legends keep their relevance, or make adjustments to stay relevant under changing social conditions, any old and new knowledge can contribute to the outlining of their life history. A single text may be the tip of the iceberg, and may lead to better understanding.

The aforementioned legend, "The Chain on the Tombstone," is a good example. Since 1969 (as far as we can tell), it has kept its attraction and ambiguous role for Halloween cemetery visitors. The legend's variability increased, reinforcing its core plot — the original *exemplum mirabile* — and changing its emphasis. The chain is no longer an accusation of the dead man, who supposedly used it to murder his wife; rather it appears in the sign of the cross as God's miracle, absolving an innocent man who was unjustly accused. These two contrast legends are contextualized by argumentative subplots: Negative legends stress pseudo-rational causes for the chain/cross imprint on the tombstone; other narratives stress God's judgment, rewarding the believer and punishing the unbeliever.[5]

Examples abound of the mixed quality of the Indiana corpus of legends. Following my talk at the Tippecanoe County Historical Association, in Lafayette, Indiana, I received some ghost stories from members who were advertising a collecting project, urging readers who "know of any ghosts, haunted houses or other legends" to contribute to their newsletter. The following four texts I received were late-nineteenth-century newspaper reports.

1. An 1864 article informs of a bad train wreck at an intersection. Thirty-five out of 500 Union soldiers on furlough perished and were buried locally. As the report states, the tragedy was the more eerie in that it happened on Halloween, and involved soldiers who had survived the war. Maybe the accident's potential supernatural connection is in the hearsay of "reports on subsequent Halloweens by passersby in the area of the sound of rushing trains, a terrible loud crash and the moans and cries of the injured and dying men." So it is still an open and ongoing incident.

2. Another newspaper story from 1872 reports the sighting of chief White Wolf by the editor and four other distinguished citizens, one of whom had magic knowledge, in a haunted house at the site of an abandoned brickyard. An apparition that was a monstrous combination of wolf, frog, alligator, and kangaroo turned into an Indian with a tomahawk. A part-Indian local resident also claimed to have seen and talked to the chief, but no one had seen him since. Who laid him to rest? It remains a mystery.

3. An 1877 story in the *Lafayette Leader* reports that the fate of a prosperous farmer took a tragic turn — that "his luck runs out" at the top of his career. His wife and daughter died, the latter with a look of shock frozen on her face. Then the farmer took in the family of a laborer, who would die from a shock, as seen by the expression on his dead face. The farmer's son enlisted and was killed in the Union army. Then the laborer's family was driven out of the

house by "ghostly apparitions." After another family moved in, within a week their daughter died; she too with an expression of shock on her face. For some time after that, the house stood empty, until a local man vowed to dispel its haunted reputation and moved in. With a loaded shotgun in hand, he stood vigil; when he heard footsteps he tried to fire his weapon but it backfired. He heard loud noises, but saw only the house burning—by the next morning, only smoldering ashes remained of the house. This listing of gruesome, violent deaths does not sound like a ghost story that triggers a legend-debate. What is the point? The mystery of this haunted farmhouse remains mysterious; there is not even a hint given to suggest what triggered the disaster. This would not stimulate debate among legend contenders, only the question: What is the story?

4. In 1875, the apparition of a former prostitute by the name of Baby Alice is the focus of several newspaper reports. She was sighted around the house and the yard where she had lived; she wore a flowing white gown and clutched her heart and lungs, which had been removed during her autopsy. She was also seen surrounded by a strange bluish light, flitting about the house and the yard with a pitcher in her hand. Residents tried to ward her off by use of secret potions and even a shotgun. The account that relates the anguish caused by the lady of ill repute's apparition suggests the story had a moral, not a legendary, resolution: The madam and the girls in the brothel swore to seek respectable work and vacated the house, which was never to be used for such a "questionable profession" again. But did this lay Baby Alice to rest? We don't know, as no one raised the question.

## The Concept of Ghosts behind the Narratives

Spectral visitors to houses, as well as other locations, are poor souls who cannot rest because of some unfinished business. Something has been left undone, perhaps by the dead or perhaps by a family member; unless these lifetime obligations are completed, the cycle cannot be ended and the spirit cannot depart the earth. According to Christian theology, here the dead must enter a new, liminal phase of extreme vulnerability—they are "without a status" (Pentikäinen 1968). This period of hardship and loneliness—of being nowhere and without a shelter, trying to find a solution—may have no limitation in terms of human time.

This state has been described in diverse ways by diverse denominations, sects, and New Age religions. Early Christian belief held that purgatory prepared spirits for heaven. Orthodox, evangelical, and fundamental Protestants, who view heaven as "our original home from where God sent us for a borrowed time and where we will return," reinterpreted preparation for this ascent without a purgatory. The Spiritualists' ordeal of "earthbound spirits" does not differ much from the concept of purgatory; the spirit must suffer and make original family residents suffer until exorcists, assisted by their angels (innocent stillborn babies who grew up in heaven), show them how to find their way to the eternal mansion in heaven. As we enter the second millennium, the New Age Chosen People attain heaven by UFOs, by fire, and by mass suicides; this can be seen as a version of entering heaven that is in line with the Gospel's symbolic, poetic, powerful, and mysterious prophecies, resembling the events that surrounded earlier failed prophecies about the end of the world.

In folkloric terms, the ritual and legendary negotiation between the living and the dead at the time of sickness and death belongs under the large umbrella of the motif "The Unquiet Grave" (motif E410–420, including Baughman's classification of Anglo-American narrative motifs, particularly E415). The beloved member of the family turns into something else: a stranger whose acts we cannot predict, a lifeless corpse of our blood who does not speak and does not hear. Having the dead in the house changes our lives and shows us how we shall be when our time comes. The families would mourn, but also open the window at the time of death so that the spirit could fly away. They'd cover the mirror so that the image of the dead would not stay in the house, frozen into the mirror. They'd destroy personal belongings or bury them with the dead so that they would not miss them and come back. Then they'd fix a meal and set a place at the table for the dead, but give the food to the poor.

Nor is the burial place safe: The liminal period, as we have said, is not determinable, and the dead must be kept happy if they are to stay there in their temporary home. Thus, cemeteries are beautiful gardens, preludes of heaven. The grave marker reflects the family's grief—a carving of a rocking chair symbolizes a grandfather's "vacant place." In ancient Europe a bag of linen seeds would be placed in the casket to occupy the dead, for counting out the grains would delay its return.

Yet the family makes an effort to keep the dead away by staying in touch — they pay cemetery visits, pray, mark their anniversaries and holidays, and highlight these events by writing letters to the departed. The ambiguity of people's feelings and the slow process of distancing and transforming the relationship between the dead and the living form the basis of evolving legends.

Our sample from small towns of the "Bible Belt," with its overwhelmingly Protestant, Anglo-Saxon population, clearly shows a background of strong family cohesion. Family appears to be a powerful bond that unites the living and the dead. It is the primary group in which individuals are born and die. As Lloyd Warner has written,

> During their brief lives, they are trained by those who precede them and
> learn how to train others who follow to behave in such a way, that as mortal

men, they live in and become part of an "immortal" society. The "transient" individuals, whose births, lives and deaths are momentary events in the eternal flow of the life of the species, must learn the morals, values, and beliefs communicated to them by the generations. (1953: 36)

A family that cultivates a relationship with its dead members is relatively small and mainly consists of three generations who are closely affiliated by residence. They live together, under the same roof or in the same neighborhood, town, or region, and they maintain a relative cultural homogeneity. The cemeteries are close and families visit often, in groups on Sunday afternoons or individually for meditation, a short prayer, or gifts of flowers, candies, a toy, or a card. They also print poems in the "In Memoriam" column of the newspaper, which are essentially letters sent to the dead. These poems are intimate, confidential messages in which the family negotiates its Christian ideology to keep communication lines open to the dead family members. They look forward to the joyous reunion in the "heavenly home," which these letters describe in sentimentally crafted formulaic folk-style.

Haunted house legends that feature the return of family members are based on this primary relationship. Family members who return in whatever shape will be recognized by what they do. They'll act as they did in life — they'll sit in the usual place, make familiar sounds, and make characteristic requests. They show that they have not changed: If they had strange habits in life, they will be identified when they do strange or crazy things.

In the big picture, houses conceal more than the naked eye can see, and attract more disturbing visitors than the grand-uncle who rocks a chair at midnight on the anniversary of his death. It is interesting to note that individuals, both dead and alive, are conceptualized as beings who cross singly over boundaries; they leave safe, protected places to enter unsafe spaces, until they cross another safe protective boundary. That is, one moves from one house and family, to another house and family of one's own. There is an order behind this. Houses that have passed beyond a three-generation kinship are more likely to be populated by antagonistic spirits.

Revenant legends share a cross-cultural similarity. Legends tell us that spirits do not just come and go as they please, without a particular reason; they do not descend upon anyone's household on a whim. They are not erratic but rather are goal oriented. Although the various denominations differ in defining why the grave is unquiet and the dead must return, a divine order regulates the spirits' traffic and also their destination. Some of our informants warned us that caution is warranted, because not all revenants are misguided victims: There are evil spirits among them, there is a hell they are trying to escape, and we had better prepare for horrible encounters within our homes.

Roughly our survey data can be divided into two sets of revenants:

1. *Family members:* a spirit is a current resident's well-remembered family member, ancestor, affiliated relative, friend, or household employee.

2. *Strangers:* a spirit who is a former resident of the house prior to the current family's arrival, or was brought accidentally into the house, whose actions may be strange and frightening.

### Family Visitors

Legends involving family spirits are profoundly personal and emotional. They express the pain of loss and separation as well as remorse and feelings of guilt. ("Why did my beloved child have to die? What could I have done to spare him? Now it is too late.") These stories feature the joy of return: the realization that there *is* a return, happiness at the prospect of future encounters, and the assurance of family unity being restored "sometime soon" in heaven.

Within the emotional frame of the memory of the visit, these narrators reminisce and may spin long narratives, but most of the time their stories are brief. They elaborate on the moment of shock, when the narrator was woken from a sound sleep by the appearance at night (a sound, a sight, a voice, or a figure), followed by the recovery from the shock. Then the experience is rationalized by the observer, often with impressions that were remembered later over the years, and it is improved and sharpened by countless retellings.

Experiencers are usually sensitive people, either dreamers or visionaries who had had other supernatural experiences in life, or who became inclined to turn into believers because of the tragic loss of someone near to them. Some of the narrators are loners who are too shy to share their experience with others; they tell the story to themselves again and again in moments of sadness, mostly during sleepless nights or on lonely holidays, remembering better times. Because they could not tell their secrets to anyone, these were the letter writers who expressed happiness in their letters to me that they could finally unburden themselves.

Other narrators are chatty and personable. They relate their experiences to almost anyone ready to listen — in the waiting room at the doctor's office, at church socials, anywhere they find an audience. In fact, I met one of my contacts on an overnight Greyhound bus ride and two others in the cafeteria of Camp Chesterfield. Fittingly, the latter managed to talk to their beloved son and sister through the trumpet and clear-audience of a spiritualist minister when they attended the cathedral service.

And their ghosts make themselves visible only to one person or to one family, all of whom recognize the ghost's scent, footsteps, or whistle. They recognize who is playing on the piano, or touching the strings of the violin, or rocking in the chair. Everyone knows that it couldn't be anybody else.

The following legends are samples from a large corpus of variants from Indiana. They represent diverse personalities, men and women, young and old, of diverse social and economic classes. Their stories illustrate the mental state of people who are suffering from the loss of someone close to their hearts, and show how imagination can project visions and encounters that help them ease their pain and turn their desperation to hope.

## The Token

This account is not about a returning spirit of the dead, but about a woman's premonition of the impending death of her husband. The narrator is Gerald Skinner, 64, a retired navy man from Oolitic, who sent me a tape, along with a number of written accounts of other stories he knew. As an old-timer interested in local history, Skinner has written several books, handwritten or typed and bound, and he has sold copies of his reminiscences to schools, libraries, and interested members of the community. His grandmother was known for having "the token," which parapsychologists refer to as foreknowledge.

My grandmother, she, one night she was lying in bed, just the night before my grandfather died. And he was a big man. 'Bout six foot six, and he was healthy and nothing was ever wrong with him. And the old clock that she had (later on, I got the clock), but this clock struck thirteen times. She told me this. And the next day, my grandfather had a tooth extracted in Bloomfield, and evidently back then they didn't have the facilities like they have today, and he, uh, I guess the roots was ulcerated some way. Anyway, he come home after he had the tooth extracted. He came home and he lay on his stomach across the bed, and he never did get up. The undertaker picked him up. And I guess a poison had went all through his body and killed him. And my grandmother said she had a "token." That was a token to tell her that something bad was going to happen when the clock struck thirteen times.

## Vision of a Son and the Beauty of the Other World

The next two letters were sent to me in response to the Indiana Haunted House survey. The accounts show a remarkable similarity in spite of the marked difference between their authors' ages and educational levels. Both narrators are frank, straightforward, accept their vision gracefully, and identify themselves as believers.

Mildred Finnell wrote this letter from New Harmony:

Hello. 1½ years ago a young girl stood in my sons bedroom — she had no face. A few nights later the wire coat hangers began to rattle in the closet — where there wasn't any hangers. Then a young girl sat beside my bed for a few seconds. I told her I loved her — she slapped me on knee — I saw my son leave his body and walk over the door and looks at me. He is 59 but his spirit was about 8 yrs old. I looked at my son sleeping he wasnt breathing — the spirit returned to him and he started breathing.[6] Stil have three knocks on doors about 3 to 3.30 A.M. I saw a little boy walk through a door, he was dressed like they did 500 yrs ago. When he turned he had my husbands face. — he died in 72 — I had a white dove to fly over my face — on good Friday. I look at a picture of Jesus I have in my bedroom. For a minute a beautiful bunch of flowers sat beside the picture. They are all friendly. I never slept for seven weeks when it all started — I tried to ignore them (no way) they wouldnt let me — my body would tell me they were there. I am no longer afraid. I talk to them. They dont come as often as they did — I miss them when they dont — there are other things. I wont go into this time.

Excuse writing I am 79 years old — Mildred Finnell.

Finnell included a postscript on a separate page:

One night before I went to hospital for tests — a vision appeared at my bed — it poked me on right hip — I knew than the Dr wouldnt find any thing, and he didnt. I have seen hell and glimpse of heaven — hell was awful — a great curtain started to part — you never saw such beauty —

Vision of the Ghost of a Son Floating

This letter was sent by Leona M. Mack from Pierceton on April 23, 1986:

My 31 yr. old son passed away in Dec. 29th 1985. And he was very dear to me and was kind to everyone who knew him. Anyway about 3 weeks after he died, I was lying in my bed one morning. It was about 6:39 A.M. and I had all the lights on, and there's a hallway that goes Thro my trailor + I was just lying there leaning on my elbow getting ready to get up when I saw this ghost of my son walking or rather floating thro the hall. He had on a grey suit + not shoes, I was looking straight ahead, it just looked like my son. It never spoke or made no sound and never turned its head.

My other 17 yr old son at the same time was in the kitchen + as soon as this ghost passed the door, I yelled at my 17 yr old son and ask what color shirt he was wearing, and he said "black" + I just stayed there — enough when he walked back and past my doors he was wearing a black shirt. And I noticed he was a head taller than this ghost I saw. Then I ask him if he saw anything + he said "No," so this ghost just disapeared somewhere in thin air, + my hall leads into my kitchen, cause I live in a two bedroom mobile home.

But I never seen it no more.

I did hear like a footstep later, I had a paper sack lying in the hall. Also some other strange happenings since my son died was, my son that passed away, I had his picture size 8 × 10 sitting on the stereo that used to belong to my son. Anyway one day this picture jumped up in the air + over an ashtray fell on the floor + made a clattering noise. Like he wanted to tell me something. But I never knew what, + it fell two other times, so I moved the picture + it hasn't fell since.

And before he died, I saw a bright light come down from Heaven. It must have been God telling me that he was going to die, I never saw the light no more.

And this is true, I am 55 yrs old + live with my 17 yr old son, we have lived in this mobile home for two yrs.

I wasn't scared when I saw this ghost but couldn't sleep very well after I did see it. I was always thinking it might come back. I just figured it was my son's spirit trying to tell me not to worry. So I try not to.

I did cry a lot + missed my son terribly after his death.

So I pray some day I'll see him in Heaven.

## Ghost Asks for Forgiveness

Cathy Billings, 25, an insurance agent in Wheaton, Illinois, told the following story to Robert Russo, who was collecting ghost stories for a class term paper in 1988. Russo noted that he was "keeping an open mind about this subject" in the hope that "someday we will be able to find that link that separates the dead from the living." He is referring to a rational, not a rationalized link.

*Robert:* Cathy tell me about your experience with a ghost.

*Cathy:* Well, it all started back in 1986, when my sister was going through some hard times. We, the family didn't realize how serious her problems were until it was too late. One day my mom came home from work and found my little sister Kelly, who was 20 at the time, dead in the garage. She had closed the garage door and started the engine of the car. She died of carbon monoxide poisoning. We had to make plans for her burial and wake service. My mom wanted to make arrangements quickly so we could get over it more quickly. Anyway, we went to the wake from three o'clock to nine o'clock at night. I went home directly after the wake because I was exhausted as well as upset. There were a couple of cars in the driveway so I figured somebody my other sisters I thought because it was their cars in the driveway, no one else was home. I went in the front door and heard some footsteps upstairs so I knew somebody else was home. I didn't feel like talking to anybody so I went into the kitchen to get something to eat. When I sat down I heard a woman weeping very hard from upstairs. I figured it was one of my sisters. The woman kept weeping and saying. "I am sorry I didn't mean to hurt any of you." I figured it was one of my sisters apologizing to one of her friends for maybe snapping at her. It is easy to do that when you are in such an emotional state. However, I then heard a car pull up in the driveway and in through the door came my sister and their friends. I asked them what they were doing outside since I never heard them come down the stairs. They looked at me strangely and said that they were just gettin' home from the wake. It was at this point that I realized I had been home all alone when I heard the crying. I started to explain what I had heard to my sisters when the crying started again.

My sisters and I proceeded up the stairway, there was a cold draft, and it seemed to be coming from my sister Kelly's room. It just continued to weep.

By the time we got to the door of the bedroom the sounds were fading away. The last thing we heard was: "I'm sorry." We then pushed open the door.

*Robert:* Did you see anything there?

*Cathy:* No, but the room was very cold and none of the windows had been open.

*Robert:* Have you heard any thing since then?

*Cathy:* Well, I haven't because I moved out soon after my sister had passed away. But, my mother hears it once in awhile when she is alone in the house and each time she hears it, Kelly's room becomes cold and drafty.

*Robert:* Do you think that it is your sister's ghost?

*Cathy:* I do now, but I didn't at first. I tried to deny the whole experience.
*Robert:* Why?
*Cathy:* Well, I never believed in ghosts or spirits and so the whole thing was a shock, I guess. But it did happen I swear it did and it gave me one of the most eerie feelings I have ever had.

### An Aunt Returns

A four-generation family haunt is represented in this extremely interesting account by a highly intelligent person who is familiar with the religious and parareligious background of belief in the presence of ancestor spirits. Sarah K., an Indiana University graduate of 1940 and a native of Markle, wrote this letter on June 20, 1990.

I'll try to be brief, but this is rather involved. . . .

My great grandparents turned from Quaker to Spiritualist when their son died of disease while in the Civil war. During a seance, my grandfather wrote the answer to their question on a slate, upside down and backwards, as he hadn't learned to write.

When I was a child I went along with my grandfather and aunt to a Spiritualist camp at Chesterfield, In. They attended seances, not very productive, though.

When my grandfather died Jan. 17, 1929, circumstances caused me to stay at their house the month of February. One day when I was at my Aunt's bedroom, the drapes across the closet door started shaking. I called my aunt, and said I was afraid. She told me much later it took a lot of strength to stop them, and she felt it was caused by her father.

Much earlier, when I was too small to remember, I was playing in the yard. I went in the house and asked my mother who the lady was who had gone in the house. There was none, and my mother questioned me as to what she looked like. I described a great-grandmother (deceased several years), complete with clothing who I have never seen. She had lived with my parents in a different house before I was born. I should say, I was never comfortable living in that house.

My Aunt died in 1980, and as I was next of kin, I had to dispose of her belongings. She had asked for no sale, but there was so much, even after my children and I had taken all we could, and giving much away, I decided to have the remainder taken to an auction house and not use her name in the advertising. When the people were moving it out, I was talking to one man when there was a large crash from upstairs. He asked what it was, and I replied: "one of our people." He knew where everyone was, and none were upstairs. I went up, expecting to see a picture fallen, or something similar, but there was nothing left. I assume she was showing her displeasure.

One day, I was working in the dining room, and kept hearing a voice. I discovered it was coming from the private line phone across the room. I had just heard of cases of the recently deceased communicating in that way. I attempted to lift the phone carefully, but it fell into position, and broke the connection. I expected someone to call back, but no one did.

Shortly after my Aunt's death, I started smelling perfume. It was always at unexpected times, and unlikely places. The first time, I was lying on the couch in my living room, watching TV. I don't use any scent, so I sniffed all around trying to locate the source. Another time, I was walking across my lawn. There was also the odor of camphor. One time I was talking with the farmer who farms the farm my Aunt and I owned. It occurred in her house, and was as tho she had joined us. The scents finally faded away after about a year. They would disappear immediately each time I thought "Aunt Beth."

My mother died in 1975, and my husband in 1978, and I had no manifestations. My second husband died in May, this year, and I may have had one scent occurrence.

My Aunt was a beautician, and I had two combs disappear. I searched my suitcase thoroughly, and they were gone. When I opened it to use it much later, the comb fell into it. Also I was walking across my living room with one of her long nail files. It sort of flipped out of my hand, and is gone.

I was telling some of these things at a church supper, and a woman pulled me aside, and told me some of her experiences. . . .

After reading this, it sounds like I am a real kook, but I feel I am perfectly normal. I feel there is something to such manifestations, and I hope you make some discoveries.

## Grandfather in an Old House

As we have seen, no matter what, if the ghost is a family member, he or she is always treated with respect and tolerance. Anything the spirits do can be put into the context of overall familiarity (and they usually do not do anything out of character). However, when a dead grandfather stubbornly prefers to return to the old home that his grandchildren have sold, which is being occupied now by strangers, his reception is very different. We have here a case that is slightly divergent from the previous five stories; although the current occupants recognize the spirit and know his family, they do not approve of his presence.

*Times-Mail* "ghost writer" Eleanor Himebaugh's Halloween column (October 31, 1985) reports that an old three-story house on the banks of the White River has a resident ghost who is none other than the grandfather of the previous owners, who long ago moved into town. The present owner said that his mother-in-law woke up one night and saw "a man wearing a stovepipe hat and a black suit such as an old time banker or a funeral director would wear. He was standing over her bed looking down at her." She was shaken, although he did not harm her. Another time, the owner and his wife were in the dining room and heard the wife's mother come down from her bedroom but did not see her. "Why so early?" they asked her hours later, but she said she hadn't been down — she had just woken up. Later they thought they heard her moving heavy furniture, but she had been taking a nap. Of course, securely latched doors opened, and even the dog was disturbed by an eerie presence. Finally, the owner's mother-in-law moved out because "she does not care for spooky happenings." They are considering moving, because the owner's mother refused to stay after dark, and his wife wouldn't stay by herself in the house at night. Of course, ghost's identity was kept confidential so as not to embarrass the home's previous owners, who "may not appreciate publicizing

343

the fact their grandfather's ghost walks the halls and stairways, haunting the old homestead and spooking defenseless women." I wonder how to find out if they really moved out?

### Strangers in the House

The crowd of spooks who disturb the peace of homes of people they are not related to and who had nothing to do with their deaths are variable and strange. They are of diverse social classes, occupations, and ages; they may have lived in the house prior to the time the current residents moved in, or may have been imported unwittingly by someone; they may have met their premature violent deaths in that house at any time before the present residents moved in (sometimes as far back as the mid-1800s). What many have in common is that they were residing in the house at the time of their death. In all cases, the deaths were so dreadful, unjust, and against the order of God that the spirits must return until justice is served, the innocent are laid to rest, and the villain, if there is one, is punished.

The return to the place is essential because the victim belongs there, and because the house is the holder of the evidence to be used. In cases of reenactment, this procedure follows the logic of a court trial: The decapitated lady, the dripping new blood from the ineradicable bloodstain, the crying babies in the basement, the skeleton popping out from behind the wallpaper in the closet, and the man with the hatchet would seem to be plausible and admissible evidence.

Common and natural forced ritual reenactments of legend events usually occur at settings outside residential areas. Discounting slumber party séances and the popular bathroom mirror divination (see Mary Whales, discussed in chapters 3 and 4), invocation of poor souls is unusual in homes. Alien ghosts make their own choice to be visitors or residents — the householders do not invite them or set the stage.

A happy conclusion turns moral exempla into folktales like "The Devil's Contract" (AT 756B), or makes for an uplifting episode of a television serial such as *Touched by an Angel*. Both show the saved victim ascending to heaven, perhaps in the shape of a white dove. Yet legends attached to haunted houses seldom present the full drama and they almost never resolve the case.

We also have to realize that the narrators of these legends usually do not have the details and can give only a scanty account of signs and symptoms. They may have only bits of pieces put together from tradition, hearsay, dreams, or personal experience, from which a coherent story is hard to piece together.

Cohabitation with the dead is fearsome even if a ghost appears to be harmless, as we have already noted in the case of the grandfather in the house at the banks of the White River. The narrators of legends about stranger ghosts do not identify with the spirit; rather, they view it as an ambiguous figure, a troublemaker. Some people have said that they've gotten used to the spirit on the premises, and have become comfortable with the idea. They good-naturedly smile at the sounds they cannot otherwise account for, and may even give the imagined spirit a nickname.

## Elmer, the Office Building Spook

Another Halloween piece by *Times-Mail* reporter Eleanor Himebaugh provides us with the natural ambiguities concerning benign ghosts in a business office. The comments amount to the display of legend-dialectics within a not-too-exciting story (October 31, 1984). Himebaugh informs the reader that, according to the employees, a building in Bedford is haunted. The owner of the building has lived with the ghost for more than twenty years; he does not believe in it, but he just can't explain the things that happen. He did not want to be identified because "if anyone thought I believed this stuff, they wouldn't do business with me." One of the building's workers quit his job because of the haunting; another man refused to enter the building, preferring to wait in cold rain outside until his associate came out. However, most of the employees in the building find the ghost and his antics amusing, and people laugh when they tell their stories. Why do they admit that something is happening that they cannot explain? Why do people laugh when they are afraid?

And the legend debate continues as people talk about Elmer. From talking to employees, Himebaugh learned that the first man to hear about the ghost "was a believer in ghosts." He believed the building absorbed sounds over a period of time, then apparently released them. He reportedly said he would like to meet the ghost because he had questions he would like to ask him. We're not told whether he did meet the ghost, but he certainly gave him the name "Elmer." This means that someone once established Elmer's presence in the building. Although Elmer did not display regular haunting habits over the years, and no one had heard of any tragedy that might explain his presence in the 62-year-old building, people continued to talk about his "mischief" for the next twenty years.

"There are sensible explanations for everything . . ." Himebaugh writes, "but they haven't come up with explanations for a few things." What does Elmer do? "You hear noises all day long: someone at the door, voices, footsteps, but no one there," said a woman employee. Two men mentioned hearing footsteps when no one was there, and doors opened and closed by themselves. Someone else saw the front door open and close when no one was there; when he went to the back to check, he felt "someone breathing down his back. Then he heard footsteps behind him, but there was no one behind him."

345

The "most remarkable" part of this mild poltergeist story is what the reporter saw as "unusual": the owner's family experiences. One son closed the door of the snack room at closing time and the next morning found the door impossible to open because "heavy Coke cases had been stacked against the inside of the door." The owner's other son, who kept an old car in the basement, saw "a vapor or swirling cloud at the bottom of the basement stairs," which he considered "the only sighting of the ghost known to the establishment." And his son saw the intercom light on the telephone light up; he went from office to office, but found no one was there. The owner assured the reporter that "everyone who has worked here has a story to tell. Some people won't stay because of the little things that happen."

Are the owner and his sons the true believers in Elmer's existence, following the original visionary? That the employees were said to have good laughs as they related the latest stories about Elmer's tricks was the *Times-Mail* article's assurance for the public at Halloween: Ghosts do funny tricks but no harm.

The fuzziness and incompleteness that we mentioned earlier for the family legends also characterizes the stranger set of legends. We have only a few coherent texts in our sample that have all the dramatis personae intact and a logically built structure. We might blame the nonprofessional collectors for these gaps, but this time with less certainty.

Parents, Please, Listen to Your Children!

An anonymous letter written to me from the Elkhart area related a story of ghosts in the upstairs of its author's childhood home. The haunting was particularly felt on the staircase and in the upstairs region where she and her sister had had their bedrooms as teenagers. Identifying the presence of the ghosts was easy, because they performed all of the known disturbances: turning lights on, making noise by real or simulated door slamming, throwing heavy objects, walking up and down the staircase, blowing away papers, creating cold drafts in heated rooms, pulling blankets from slumberers, and so on.

Even worse, the letter highlights a horrific event: ghosts, a man and two women, "floated in," materialized, and reenacted a scene from their past life in the speakeasy that the house used to be. The experiencer said that the man was about to kill her, but her screams remained inaudible (fitting the nightmare phenomenon — see Hufford 1982); one of the two women saved her life.

The story of the haunting of the two teenagers in this letter is framed by legend dialectics. The experiencer has a strong conviction, her father is stubborn in his unbelief, and the mother helplessly hesitates between the two views. The sisters succeeded in proving their claim that the ghosts existed, and the girls were able to leave, although their parents stayed on. The narrator overdramatizes her and her sister's ordeal. The narrator cannot forget her traumatic experience; her conflict with her father particularly occupies her thoughts, even so many years after she has moved from the house. When she drives by her parents' house at night, she still checks for the upstairs lights.

Her letter is a plea to parents who do not listen to their children when they complain of spooks. She feels it is her mission to reveal that "ghosts are not a laughing matter," to inform the public that she had lived in a haunted house, and to urge others to come forward as witnesses.

Her handwritten letter, dated April 28, 1986, came without the name and the address of its author. The nine lined pages, torn from a copybook, are densely covered with large, and uniformly neat, grammar-school script.

Dear Linda Degh,

I read the write ups in the *Elkhart Truth* about ghosts in the Elkhart area. Reading about this has made me uneasy. It has been on my mind and I lost two nights of sleep. For years I have been troubled over the experience I had in a home in Elkhart. After losing two nights of sleep after reading Jim McNeiles article about ghosts in the Elkhart area, I feel if I would tell the citizens of Elkhart, that I might get some physiological relief with this matter.

When I was young as a child I lived in new homes my father built. When I got to my young teens an old house close to 100 years old came up for sale on east US 20. My father bought the house and remodeled the house. He wanted to be close to his business.

I had one sister and we both slept upstairs. Things started happening right away up stairs as soon as we moved in. Our bed rooms had linoleum floors. My sister and I heard walking in our rooms. Something would walk to the side of our beds and it would be real cold with a bad smell. We told our parents about it, they didn't believe it. They said we dream it. I was afraid so I would cover my head up at night. Many nights I would wake up because my face was freezing and the bad smell. As soon as my eyes would open the blanket would drop back over my head. My sister and I would tell our parents that something is watching us while we were in bed. They still wouldn't believe it. They still made us sleep upstairs. My sister and I would wake up in the morning and find our things in our room moved on many occasions. Still my parents wouldn't believe us, they said maybe we misplaced things and forgot where we put them.

One night my sister left out a stack of typing papers in her room. We woke up with a heavy wind blowing the papers in both our rooms. We both started screaming in our beds for our dad. As soon as the stairway door opened the wind stoped and the papers were all over the floors. We were accused of one of us sleep walking and throwing papers around. Still we had to stay upstairs for there wasn't enough room down stairs for bedrooms for my sister and I.

I had a chair that I would sit on that squeaked the time I did my home work for school. At night my sister and I would wake up hearing that chair squeak like someone heavier than me sitting on it. My sister and I would hold onto each other crying in my room looking at the chair squeaking real loud. It was getting kicks out of scaring us.

We called on our Lord Jesus to save us from this awful presence. We both found that when we called on our Lord to help us when the chair would squeak or the blankets be pulled off us the cold in the room would leave. But it just kept coming back moving things, walking to our beds etc. The only thing we knew was it would leave when we prayed to the Lord.

When I was seventeen my sister went to college. I was alone up stairs. One night I just turned off my light and got to bed. As soon as I layed down my head I heard voices in my sisters room. I thought for a few seconds that it might be the wind. But then a man and a woman flooted in my room and another woman also flooted in and stayed at the door way. There was three of them. The woman one at the door way had long black hair and crying. The man was 6' or more tall with white hair, long nose. The woman in the middle of the room next to the man was short and curley hair, she was smiling. I could see through them. They frighten me with horror. I screamed as loud as I could that it hurt my ears and my throat. The man said over and over that no one can hear me. He said its my time to go, and that they wanted me to be with them. He said it would be easy that I would fall down the stairs and die. Than he grabed my arm. It was cold and his *one* hand on my arm was so strong, like 3 men. He jerked me off the bed. I grabed my dresser on the side of it and pulled the dresser away from the wall. I left my finger nails bending backwards, and pain in my fingers, and all the time he had one hand on me. I wouldn't let go and the dresser was slowly sliding. The black hair woman that was crying came all the way in the room pleading with him to let me go, saying that I'm a good girl and a vergin. And that it is wrong for him to take my life. As she pleaded I prayed out loud. I was too horrified to pray at first loud, I was screaming. When I did thank God they disapeared. I didn't move off my bed till I heard my mother up and around downstairs. I called my mother to watch me come down. I couldn't hardly talk from screaming. I told her everything and showed her my fingernails.

She got worried about it and let me sleep on the couch.

My sister came home from college. So we both slept up stairs while she was here. One early morning while she was here we both woke up with a loud heavey sound falling down the stairs. The sound started from the top of the stairs and the stairway door at the bottom flew opened so hard the door handle hit the plaster wall cracking it. My sister and I thought one of us fell down the stairs, we met on the landing. We knew it wasn't us. My mother was yelling at us wanting to know who ran down the stairs and pushed the door hard on the plaster wall. She was in shock to find us standing on the landing up stairs. All three of us looked around down stairs to find what fell. We couldn't find anything.

My mother knew now the house was haunted. My father was out of state on a fishing trip in Canada. She called him home.

My father said when we first complained about the up stairs he talk to a neighbor in his 80's about the house. He said it was Elkhart's Speak Easy. They made and sold liquor there. He said there was two murders and maybe more. It was a rough place.

I asked the boy at school that lived there before us, why did they move. He just came out and said it; the house had strange things going on. We feel its haunted. I told him we feel the same way.

People that knew us that would drive by said that the upstairs light is on when no ones home. We always turn off the lights before leaving. We heard alot about the upstairs light being on when no one's home. The boy at school said the light would be on when they left the house too. The boy also said that [when] they changed the furnace from coal to gas they found a dager with blood stains on it in the vent on the steps on a ledge behind the gate.

My father was playing around with his metal detector in a field next door and found a brass hand gun. They don't make them after 1920's my dad thought. We also found a Civil War sword with the owners name on the blade ingraved. I can't tell the name, for he may have family still living in Elkhart.

I got married young at 17 for I no longer was going to stay in that house. My sister got married still going to college.

My mother and father still live in the house. The stair way door is locked with two locks. My mother said she hasn't heard anymore walking upstairs for a long time. She used to think my sister and I was walking at night. But after we left, she still heard it.

My father will not move. He said no ghost is going to make him leave. My father is hard at hearing and sleeps like a log.

Still to this day, sometime when my parents are gone and I drive by their house coming home from some where the upstairs light is on. I call them later to tell them, and my mother would check it out to find out, and the light is off.

This year alone I seen it twice. I called my sister about it. We both agreed that if anything happens to our parents, we will have the house burned or torn down.

Some people in Elkhart know what house I'm talking about. But for my familys sake I can't reveal our names. But for the Elkhart residents ghosts are not a laughing matter. Be careful!.

Some are not friendly. Amen.

Thank you.

P.S. If you drive down US 20 West at night and no ones home and the light on up stairs you seen what others have seen. And parents please listen to your children. For I still have scares from it.

(The last line I wrote is for the public if you ever print this somewhere.)

The most characteristic feature of this account is the firm belief in haunting. This young woman is convinced, without the slightest hesitation or doubt, that what she experienced was not a figment of her imagination; she is giving a factual description of truth. She felt the compulsion to write the letter as a public service to save others from what she and her sister went through.

## Remembered Haunting from Childhood

It is worthwhile to compare the letter of Anonymous in Elkhart to that of Hal Parker, as both report a similar case of living in a haunted house. The Parker letter has no core story of a life-threatening reenactment of the past, but contains the same manifestations of noisy ghosts. Although Parker declares himself in general terms as a nonbeliever, he states that what happened to his family in the house is true. His ambiguity is clear from remembering after so many years, and from his intention to visit the place and explore its present condition.

Hal Parker begins his letter (postmarked April 8, 1986) by introducing himself as a 59-year-old native of Bloomington. When he wrote the letter, he had just returned home after spending thirteen years in western Canada, and was living with his sister. My inquiry had triggered his recapitulation of a childhood episode. When he was 12 years old, he lived in a haunted house for three weeks only, because the spirit disturbances forced his family to move.

... I am the type of person who doesn't believe in anything I can't see and only half of what I hear. I have never seen UFO's, ghosts, God or Satan. But, when as a kid around twelve we did live in a house for three weeks where there were unusual things going on. I'll start at the beginning and you can take it from there.

My father, mother, brother, sister and myself moved into a house about 8 to 10 miles southeast of Bloomington on Sheilds ridge. Take Smithville road from old 37 to Handyridge road and at the top of the hill before going down to Monroe Lake, you make a right and that is or was Sheilds ridge. As we were moving in, a lady (Lucas) was moving out and she told my mother that we wouldn't be living there very long because the place was haunted and my mother laughed at her. Mrs. Lucas told her that her son tried sleeping upstairs but something would keep pulling the covers off the bed during the night and that they heard different types of noise. If they were to keep the light burning, nothing happened. I don't know how much of that was true, but I do know that the following is:

One night my father heard an old rocking chair rocking near the fireplace and another night he heard a grandfather's clock tick-tacking. Yet every night he would hear a heavy person in stocking feet walking upstairs from one end of the room to the other and then it would come down the stair to the landing where the door open, there were four more steps on into the living room.

My father didn't want to tell my mother that he had heard all of this because she was pregnant and he didn't want to scare her. However, one morning my mother, sister, brother and I got our first really good scare. It happened right after my father left for work. When we moved in, my mother had put a stack of newspapers at the bottom of the stairs, just before you came out into the living room. We heard someone walking across the floor upstairs (we didn't use the upstairs) and it came down the stairs and when it got to the landing, we thought it was going to open the door and come on out, but it walked around in the newspapers and it sounded as if they or it was tearing the papers to bits.

That night, she told my father what we had heard and she thought it was somebody trying to scare us because they could climb the rock chimney and climb into the window. My father tried to calm her down by telling her it was rats or a stray cat. Late every night before twelve, that's when the walking began, or the clock or the rocking chair. But the walking was nearly all the time at night and again in the early morning before daybreak.

My father took flour and put it evenly on all the steps and he set rat traps. That night, it walked across the flour, came down the stairs and into the papers but the papers were never disturbed. The next morning, my father checked the stairs. No tracks and no traps went off. This had him worried. The next night, he loaded his double barrel shot gun and waited until the walking started. Just as it came down the stairs, he jerked open the door and let both barrels go, he slammed the door shut. The next morning, nil. No bodies, no animals all he had was a big hole in the roof. From the time we moved in until the time we moved out was three weeks. I don't know if that house is still there or not. There was an old barn about a block away from the house.

Like I say, I've never seen anything and that was the only thing in my life that I had ever heard. As a matter of fact, I think I will take a run out that way and see if the house is still there. The last time I was there, the floor was torn up, or part of it was.

As a rule, violent death — be it murder, suicide, or accident — makes revenants return to the scene of their demise, even if the circumstances have changed, and the perpetrators of the crime or the causes of the accident are no longer there, or the inhabitants of the location have changed. The haunting and/or replay of the killing terrorizes strangers.

But it is more common that victims of domestic violence perform their demise in the house where the guilty family members can still be brought to justice. Murders committed within the family are usually passionate and ruthless; their legends describe them in gory detail, with all their profuse bloodshed and dismemberment. Stories tell about love triangles, when a wife's lover kills her husband, or a husband kills his wife to marry a younger woman, or a wife kills her husband because she cannot take his philandering "any longer." Other times a woman kills both her boyfriend and illegitimate child, or a married man kills his pregnant girlfriend. There are even more extreme cases: a woman or man goes berserk because of the death of a child and the man and woman kill each other; a man butchers his whole family before killing himself; or a husband murders his wife and daughter then stabs himself. There are an endless variety of passion killings, and the stories about them contain elaborate details about the disposal of the body, all to stress the viciousness of domestic violence.

Far less grisly are the descriptions of robbery killings — killings that remove unwanted witnesses. In these cases, the threat to the thieves is the greater. In one story, when a wife is murdered by thieves, her husband swears vengeance, dies, and now haunts the house carrying a knife. In another account, a rich man is killed in bed by robbers after he'd thrown a party; now, every night at midnight music is heard from upstairs, and a pool of blood appears on the floor. Other stories in our survey featured an old maid, a brother, a banker, a mailman, a sea captain, and a rich widow, all killed for their money.

Suicide victims also return. In one story, the wife of a Civil War soldier who was killed in action kills herself. Lots of revenants show up in the house where they blew out their brains, hung themselves, or drank themselves to death. Accidental deaths are just as numerous.

Often tragedies are repeatedly replayed on a schedule, but the times may vary. In broad daylight a house burns down with screaming children inside, on the anniversary day of the original event; or the face of a retarded girl

351

trapped and starved to death is sometimes seen frozen on a screen; or a man sucked out of a house after a tornado removed the roof is seen flying around at midnight; or people fall from windows and old ladies freeze in their beds when their heater malfunctions. There is no absolute rule: Some occur daily or whenever someone goes by; others occur regularly at anniversaries, at the exact same time or always at midnight.

Any type of death reported in daily papers has the potential to reappear as a legend, in complete or rudimentary form. Curiously enough, in this sample we have more rudiments of stories than complete forms with some kind of conclusion, which is unlike the traditional ghost stories from European villages. There seems to be some ideological confusion here. BarBara Lee instructs us that spiritualist exorcists can lead earthbound spirits to Heaven, following some kind of reeducation if they are not ready. If this is so, then why do house spooks have so little chance at redemption? Their stories contain only an apparition episode, but no eventual release. If revenant legends are so prominent and permanent because they reassure mortals of the chance at immortality, why is this chance not better foregrounded? If we keep the rhetorics of religious denominations separate from the conventional body of legendary spirits, we cannot answer these questions. But we might attribute the concentration on the spook activity to loyalty to tradition.

### Friendly Ghost in an Antique Cabinet

Although our samples are poor on evil spirits, they do exist. BarBara Lee's "China Doll" story is framed by her religious ideology, but it has deep roots in the traditional belief that objects can be the hiding place of evil spirits who may harm unsuspecting homeowners. Many people mentioned strange objects they had picked up at sales, in antique shops, or at the beach; or had brought back from foreign travel or foreign wars; or that had been inherited from relatives, like the china doll, a grandfather's Japanese spear, or other conversation pieces occupying prominent places in the living room. Some women warned me against going to estate sales and picking up objects that belonged to strangers, because this might be the way to let evil in. But benign spirits can also enter homes by hiding in a gift. Darlene H., an Indiana University administrator, told us about her "friendly ghost," which inhabited a piece of furniture she had inherited from her aunt.

Five years ago a very dear aunt passed away and willed me among other things an antique three corner cabinet. Ever since I moved the cabinet in my home (living room) we have heard knocking noises from the cabinet. Several times I have looked in the cabinet and even talked to it! Not only is the ghost in the cabinet (maybe there are more than one) I can feel a presence of another person in the room with me when I am alone. It is not a frightened feeling, only someone you can't see is in the room with you. There is no pattern to the knocking or the feeling that someone is near you. Also, the ghost likes our basement. Many times I have been in the basement and the clothes line I have will swing as if someone is touching them. Again I am not frightened by this. I have wondered many times if the ghost is my aunt or the original owner of the three corner cabinet.

No matter if the spirit is benign or vengeful, people think it is risky to move into a haunted house, because a gruesome death may be repeated by contagion. The woman who pulled Sarah K. aside at a church supper after listening to her four-generation experiential family legends, rewarded her with a real shocker. The woman's family had bought a house in front of which a husband and wife had been killed in an auto accident. Their son and his four children had been killed in another accident at the same intersection a few years later. The house's new owners unwittingly suffered the consequences in the form of terrible "manifestations. At one time their children saw the dead children playing in the yard, and their son had had a lamp knocked over on him."

There is no way to tell an evil spirit from a friendly one. Some of the erring spirits are definitely malevolent revenants who hide in attractive objects to get into good homes. They are extremely enduring — ageless and timeless. They can stay in a box or drawer unnoticed, and can remain in any household object for generations. Even though these spirits may assume the shape of a benign, familiar figure, or behave like poor souls in the house, they could be criminals, escapees of damnation, or might be even the devil incarnate. Regardless of what they appear to be, their goal is torture and the destruction of people, as the following legend complex demonstrates.

### The Monk's Head

In chapter 4, I discussed the personality and the legends of Janet Callahan, a superb narrator and a specialist in what she called "perception," a psychic ability she inherited from her female lineage. I first met Callahan in 1987. At that time she was 37, a police officer trainee, and the divorced mother of three grown children. She was also an ambitious criminal justice major who was looking forward to a career in law enforcement, which she felt to be of great importance. She took my class in Indiana folklore just for fun, because of her interest in her family heritage.

Callahan saw herself as a third-generation "percipient" woman, and for her class term paper, she tape recorded her grandmother's and her mother's perceptions, amounting to some 37 legends. Then, on a third tape, she narrated her own legends. Actually her repertoire is an offshoot of Betty's, her mother.

Betty, who had been born with a veil, was an inspired legend-teller married to a factory worker. Déclassé and poor, Betty had worked in a factory until her retirement, after which she completed her interrupted education by obtaining her GED and planning to take college classes.

On her tape, Callahan spoke freely and without inhibition, and she authorized my publication of her stories. Addressing me directly by way of a lonely confession to the tape recorder, Callahan recaptured the events of her life in chronological order. She came from an initially well-to-do but later impoverished farm family in Shelburn, Indiana:

> Raised in a poor environment, I was the oldest of 5 children. Lived on a farm most of my life and watched children while parents worked. Left home when I was 18 years old and worked various jobs, as bookkeeper, secretary, cashier. Married an Indiana State University graduate in 1969. Worked together for 17 years to increase social status. I have 3 children and due to the content of the third tape I am currently divorced.

Her autobiographical narrative, which covers her life from age 14 to 33, describes her self-conscious development of her "God given gift" of telepathy and her dedication to rescuing people from deaths she foresaw. Her amazing foreknowledge failed to save lives in the cases she discussed, and her failure caused her great pain and distress, particularly because she was being punished by evil spirits for her commitment. Callahan's uplifting career story of perceptions runs parallel to, and is undercut by, depraved encounters with sinister apparitions who turned her family's homes into haunted houses. It was as if Satan led a war against God by preventing Callahan from helping His creatures.

As she lived through failed telepathic experiences and torturous hauntings, she slowly came to understand that she was being punished for her attempts to break away from her confinement as a housewife and the control of an abusive husband. But the source of the conflict ran deeper than Callahan's ambitions to fulfill her mission and to find a profession in addition to being a good homemaker and a caring mother. She realized that the hauntings were a consequence of her marriage to an upper-middle-class man, a member of a professional and intellectual elite which assisted him in curbing her ambitions to improve her education and become his equal partner in life. Her low, working-class origin was significant.

The transcript here contains only the haunted house legends as Callahan personally experienced them, without any of her other narratives on telepathy. These experiences began after she met Alice, a high school teacher, friend, and colleague of her husband. Alice had agreed to help improve her education, but in the end would betray her. The story tells of Alice's death, her curse and ghostly returns, and her other reappearance as evil spirits hiding in an exotic souvenir. Janice's desperate attempts to destroy the object continued until she was liberated by a ceremonial exorcism.

Callahan's unique legend performance actually gives account of the most critical and painful period of her life, a period that had ended five years prior to her narration. At this point she felt liberated, had put the past behind her, and now looked forward to a bright future.

### A Highly Respected Lady

My husband introduced me to this teacher. He was a math teacher, and he told me about this teacher by the name of Alice Houston, Alice was a teacher of history. A very educated, very intelligent woman, very very highly respected in the community. This was in Bedford, Indiana. And so, I got to know Alice Houston, got to talk to her, and, I was true to my promise, because being raised in a poor family, I finished high school of course, but I was very low in my class, and my English was very poor. I wanted to learn to speak properly to be able to better myself, talk to people better, I felt very ignorant . . . low class. And I wanted to know if she can help me. And she said, "Sure, I can do all kind of things to help you. I can tell you about English structures, sentences, we can talk about how to speak properly." And I was very grateful to her because she spent lots of time trying to help me.

And we worked together for two or three months, when she found out that she had cancer, breast cancer. And she was going to, had to take cobalt treatment in Bloomington, and I offered to drive her back and forth. Because she didn't drive, and . . . at that time . . . I met her husband once, but he had had a heart attack and died, and he played golf, and just died in a heart attack. And so, I didn't know her husband very well, and . . . so she was quite alone, so that's why I was taking care of her. We were basically talking about my English while I was driving her back and forth. She was telling about her teaching history in school, and what she was doing, what she liked to do.

She was a very strange lady, she always wore black, she had her hair pulled back in a bun tightly around her face and wore spike heels. And she had a rather large nose. She really looked witchy . . . her appearance was quite out of the ordinary. I remember her fireplace. [On it] was this head, this gold head, this monk's face and it had a handle on it all in gold, and was carrying a black candle. I was fascinated by it! I looked at it and said, "My, this is a very strange piece, I never seen anything like . . . what is it?" And she said, "Oh, it's just a monk's head I picked up someplace on one of our trips that Ray and I went." And she never said more about it. I looked around, there were books, novels she was reading, and most of them very, very . . . sexy novels. I was very fascinated 'cause I was not reading that stuff. And I thought, man, this is going to be interesting, this lady must be kinky on the side! And the parlor looked really strange. She took me upstairs, we was going to her room, and then, to another, a bedroom. And she said, "That's my husband's bed," she said. I said, "Oh, neat!" And I sat down on the bed, and I was sitting there comfortably. And she said, "*Get off that bed!*" And I jumped up, and said, "What's wrong?" "*That's my husband's bed, no one* will ever sit on that bed!" . . . And she said, "I keep that for him." And I thought, "OK, OK, well, that's all right. As you say, it's fine with me." You know, I am the easy type to get along with people pretty well. So I went in the other room, and she was telling me of the other things she had, and she bought, and she did, and that was about it.

Well, Alice died. To make a long story short, she, well, before she died, she went to the hospital. She was very, very seriously ill. And I went in to see her. And . . . the change, her eyes were sunken in, and her hair was white. I mean, it was black, but was so white and it was so gray all of a suddenly, and she looked like dead, laying on the bed. And I sat there and thought: OK, God, this is horrifying. And I sat on the end of her bed. And she raised her head, and she raised her finger at me, her eyes open, and she said, "*I hate you!* I hate everything you are." I said, "Alice, you don't know what you're saying, you're talking out of your head." And she says, "I come back, *I get you.* And when I die," she says, "I guarantee you, it will rain on my funeral. It will not be a happy funeral when I die." And she laid back down. And I thought, what is this lady talking about? Something is crazy with this lady. I told my husband about it, and he was telling me, "Oh, for Heaven's sake Jan, she is dying, she is out of her head, don't worry about it."

The day she died it rained so horrifying, we could hardly stand on the gravesite. I thought, she was saying it will rain and that was what had happened.

I wasn't thinking more about it. And she made my husband the executor of her estate. And he was selling out all her things. And before the auction, my mom was invited because there were some little things that wouldn't sell, and I told my mom to go ahead and take'm what she wanted of'm."[7]

### Ray's Bed

And ah, about Ray's bed. I never even thought about the bed, never even entered my mind, except that I needed a bed. We lived, my husband and I . . . by the way, I've been pregnant with my second child and have delivered the second child, and we lived in a real small crackerbox little house on 29th Street in Bedford. And it was a living room and a little kitchen, two bedrooms and a bath, that's how small it was. And we didn't have a *bed!* And so it was very practical to buy that one of the auction. We did, and took it there. And after cleaning the bed and set it up in there — it was an ordinary bed, a little high up the floor, you could roll underneath without any problem and clean. We had that bed, and I remember goin', sleeping in that bed. And every night that I tried to go to sleep, these huge, horrifying hands, arms, there was just half arms, red and green, and they had big veins, like fingers, went up only to the elbows, long fingers . . . and they would come up at me, and they would come up to my throat. And I thought, "God, what is that?" And I opened my eyes, and they would disappear. And I tried to drift off to sleep again, and they came again. And that happened night, after night, after night. And I was so exhausted that I would drift off to sleep. And I told my husband, "I can't stand these nightmares. These things are frightening me, I don't think I am asleep, because I open my eyes and it's gone, and I must be dreaming because . . . these hands, they are coming up my throat, they are going to choke me." And he says, "Jan," he said, "you're tired," he says, "you had a child, and all these problems, for Heaven's sake, they're just dreams. Take an aspirin, take a sedative." I did do this, but I thought, I don't know what's wrong, it just kept happening, and happening, and happening.

One night, when my husband was gone, he was in the insurance business, he was out for a late call. And I was gone into my bedroom, and the bed was in the middle of the room. There was a window to the right, the door to the left, toward the hall. And I remember, I was laying on the bed, I was turning to the left, looking out the window. I said, "Oh man, I hate to go asleep. I'm here all by myself, I'm going to see these stupid arms again, trying to choke me. Oh God, I just want to get rid of that." And I was laying there, and something warm, a touch came across my left side. And I just kinda pause — what was *that!* And I turned over to see what it was, and aside me lay in bed was Alice Houston's husband! What was dead! He was laying there, and I was . . . I just . . . it was like . . . "*What are you doin' here?*" And I looked to the door, and there was Alice Houston. Standing at the door, laughing at me, and . . . in this hideous laugh. And she just laughed, and laughed, and laughed. And I remember jumping out of the bed and started screaming. And she just laughed at me, both of them laughed at me, and I ran, and I ran, right through her. Absolutely through her, to my living room, out the front door of the house. And lo, and there, my husband came home. I remember screaming, screaming, screaming, screaming. And the next thing I knew was, my husband was slapping me and saying, "*Stop it, stop it, stop it Jan. What's wrong with you?*" And I came to, and he was holding onto me, and I was crying, I said, "They were here, they were in the house!" And I told him. And he said, "You flipped out, Jan. You're crazy. We are goin' to go see a psychiatrist tomorrow. We are goin' to go see a doctor. You're crazy."

And the next day I did see Dr. C. in the Bedford Medical Center. A psychiatrist. And I related the story to him. And I told him, I said, "I'm losing my mind, I'm really crazy." He looked at me and he said, "No, you are not crazy," he said, "these things happen," he said, "they happened before." And I looked at him and said, "You're kidding me." He said, "No, they happened." He said, "The only thing I can tell you to do" — and he said this is not medical advice, but this is a spiritual advice. He said, "Go home, and go to a . . . and pray to the blood of Jesus Christ. And pray every night that God take it away from you, and that he gets all the evilness that is in the house." And he said, "You do that over and over again." He said, "It will take a while, but do it again and again." So, I told my husband that I wasn't crazy. I was also relieved. I did them, and the arms disappeared. And I didn't see them anymore. And over a period of, maybe two or three weeks, maybe a month, they disappeared. They were gone.

### Papers Falling Off

Then I was working as a secretary in the Office of Special Education. Some day I was sitting in the office, and the papers that was on top of the filing cabinet that I was working, typing one-by-one, falling off. They flew up the air and then were falling down. I was looking down on the pile and said, "Alice," I say, "I know you're here. I can't see you today, but I know you're here. You don't scare me anymore. I'm praying to the blood of Christ and I know, you need to find your own way doing things," I said, "you don't bother me, or scare me, and I'm not goin' to worry about you anymore." And the funny part about it was, that my boss who was sitting in the next room, kept coming in, and kept saying, "Who are you talking to?" . . . "Oh, just talking out loud to myself." And from that time on, I did not suffer anymore from Ray or Alice Houston.

My Mom did have these visions, but I didn't have any more problem with Alice Houston.

### The Candle Holder Reincarnates

We moved to Bloomington, Indiana, Skyline Drive, my husband and I. And as we went there, I didn't have any more problems with anything else, as for visions or anything at that time. But as we have gotten to Skyline Drive, my husband brought in this Monk's Head that Alice had on her fireplace. And he said, "Oh, I brought this with us. Before Alice died, she gave me this, and said that this is something she wanted me to have. I kinda liked it, it was neat." And I said, "I really don't wanna keep this. I don't want to have any more experience with Alice." He says, "Oh, Jan, all crazy made-up, it's just imagination, it wasn't real." "Well," I said, "whether it was real or wasn't real, I experienced it and I don't want to have any more dealings with it." He said, "This is mine, we aren't going to get rid of it." "OK," I says, "OK."

Well, the house on Skyline Drive was a large ranch style type house, and had a very long hallway, when you came in the front door, goin' north, and you turn to the right, there is the living room, and there is a little desk in the corner, and on top of the desk we put the Monk's Head, fitted with the black candle. And it sat over there. And next to the room there was the kitchen and the family room and in the back part of the house, there was three bedrooms. And I ended up . . . I was pregnant with my . . . another child. And that Monk's Head, at night . . .

My husband getting into the insurance business, and was away often. I still didn't like it, the Head, but it didn't bother me. But I didn't ever have problems with it till I would go to bed. And the strange thing about it was usually when I was alone. It didn't happen when my husband was there. And I would be laying in bed, and the monk, in brown uniform, would walk from another room, down the hallway, towards my bedroom on the nights that I was alone. And he stood at my doorway. And I would say, "Oh God, please, get rid of it, I don't wanna see it, I *know* it's there, but I don't wanna see it." But it continued to be there. I tried to explain to my husband, I was pleading to get rid of it, because I couldn't deal with this image that was coming at me. It was not harming me, it never came closer than my bedroom door, but it was there. And I could see the face that was always dark, instead of being gold and holding the black candle, was dressed in a complete brown robe and all the way down, and you know it was a monk, just by the image of it—but you could visualize an actual full bodied form of a monk.

And so . . . well, trying to get rid of it, I was looking for a piece of paper . . . I was going to throw it into the trash. So I was wrapping it up in a piece of paper and took it out in the trash. I said, "This is it! The trashman comes Thursday morning and it will be gone, and I'm goin' to be rid of the monk, whether my husband likes it or not." And that was that.

After establishing herself in a comfortable home, Janet Callahan assumed the role of the perfect partner to an upward-moving businessman. Her husband Bill worked hard as an insurance agent while Janet, the caring mother of three, found her place in the social network. She worked part time as a saleswoman, secretary, office manager, and teacher; she also volunteered for welfare organizations and attended social gatherings and cultural events.

Her telepathic sensitivity was greatly supported by young people, mainly her children and her children's friends on whom she practiced her skill, and by casual acquaintances, mostly women interested in the supernatural. A new chapter was opened in her life in 1977 when the family moved from Skyline Drive "out into the country, to Tanglewood Road, a beautiful, large fourteen-room estate, and I really loved that house." She said, "It was a gorgeous house. . . . I really loved that house, and while I was living there, things began to happen to me. At that time I discovered that I was able to know what things are going to happen."

She continued to play with "testing her powers." At a birthday party she overheard two women exchange whispers and walked over to them. She knew they were talking about a dead husband who kept coming back, and told them not to worry, that he was all right. Later she met one of the two women downtown for coffee at the Trojan Horse restaurant. When they were about to leave, the woman, a visitor from Michigan, discovered that she'd forgotten where she had parked her car. Callahan directed her to the exact location. "This is eerie, Jan," the woman said, "I never met anybody like you before." Callahan was thrilled and encouraged: "Well, frankly, I don't know anybody like me." The woman gave her names and associations to contact and books to read to enhance her abilities and left her with the assurance that "great things are going to happen" to her.

### The Monster Monk at Tanglewood

I went home, and I went to my bedroom and slept that night. Well, great things didn't happen to me. . . . There was . . . across the hall from the staircase, another small room where my little girl slept sometime, and she was sleeping in this room with my son. They were very young; and there was a huge playroom that covered the whole space of the main hallway, with two large closets on both sides. . . . But I slept that night in my bedroom upstairs — not in the huge master bedroom — and I believe I shut the door that night. I know I did, I got ready for bed, and I started to turn off the light, when suddenly I noticed that someone is in the room. And it was not a very nice person. It was a male, it was a male figure, and it didn't have an odor. I couldn't see the figure but I knew it was there. I knew it was male, it was masculine, was strong and big, I could feel it . . . it was still at the doorway. And I said, "oh God, oh my God, what is *this*? What is this thing?" And I stared at the door, it was the doorway that was blind, nobody could see anything. But I stared at the door because I knew this image was there. This scripture force.

And as the night went on, it was quite late, my eyes got drowsy, and as my eyes started closing, it would come closer, and closer. And I opened my eyes real quick, but it wouldn't jump back to the door, it previously was closer. And I thought, "My God, it's going to attack me!" And I laid there very calm. I could move, but every time I would move, like I was going to get off the bed, it would move towards my bed. And I get back on my bed, and I thought, "My God, what am I going to do?" And I tried to yell to my husband but I couldn't. . . . It was like I would make any gesture, crosswise or anything, it would come closer to me, and it was frightening. Extremely frightening.

And, it was around one, two in the morning, and I could not sleep any. I was so exhausted that night, all that energy that I expelled, and I tried to drift off to sleep. And it hit the bed. And it was sitting beside me in the bed. And I jumped up, my eyes fully awake, and I stared, and it was *there*. And it wasn't cold. And I knew about evil spirits, and about demons and . . . satanic type individuals and all that you see in movies and things and all. And the room gets extremely cold, and they feel this horrifying stench, and all these things. They never happened. The room never got cold, there was nothing. No anger, except this monster monk image that was sitting on the side of my bed. And staring at me. And I moved. I knew as well as I'm sitting here tonight, that when I closed my eyes that energy is going to physically abuse me. And I was never so absolutely frightened, even beyond Alice Houston. I was not frightened so much in my life, as I laid there knowing I could not close my eyes.

When daylight appeared with the spirit, I ran to the bedroom where my husband was (the master bedroom), and I tried to wake him, and I mean, I looked like death. My eyes were so swollen, and I was almost sickly looking, I couldn't believe it. And he says, "*What* is wrong with you?" I tried to explain to him, and he says, "Oh, Jan, are we goin' to start this crap again? For heaven's sake, when are you going to stop?" And I said, "I'm not imagining it, Bill, it was there." He said, "You're crazy, Jan, absolutely crazy. I don't want to hear it anymore." So I tried to put it behind me, tried to forget it.

But haunts in the house continued. Crashings, smashing windows were heard without any noticeable damage being found. Janet Callahan's son had inherited his mother's sensitivity, and she comforted him by telling about "Mr. Nobody," a friendly ghost like Casper, the popular cartoon figure. After her great granny's funeral, knockings were heard at the front door; when her husband opened the door, no one was there. They laughed it off: "Perhaps she wanted to say goodbye."

Callahan's painful incidents of second-sight continued. When she could not prevent the death of their family doctor's wife that she had foresaw — the woman fell asleep while smoking a cigarette — Callahan again became troubled. She felt the whole world was against her; everyone thought she was delusional, including her husband, their friends, and their Episcopalian minister. But when she felt close to despair, "God sent a miracle." Her son's piano teacher led her to the Bible, and taught her about studying on a daily basis to fight the darkness of evil. The two women learned about guardian angels and the power of darkness — and how to recognize Jesus Christ as their personal savior. They studied Emmanuel "very intensely."

### Getting Rid of the Monk

As I studied the Bible, the pressure on me became more intense, intense, intense. The pressure that was in this house was absolutely felt. I would choke to death. The pressure choked me to no end. And every time I got close to the Bible to try to read God's word, it was like it was there. I felt it was goin' to stop me. It was goin' to stop me reading. I persevered, and I read, and I read, and I read. And as I always was reading, I was staying well, and I prayed to God that he give me the strength to keep this away. As long as I was praying I was well, and I prayed in the blood of Jesus Christ. And it was still there! And I didn't know what to do. And so . . . this was going on for a good year. And then it was the summer of 1983. That is '82, I'm sorry. . . .

And we had a yard sale, all over the house. I was cleaning out the house of everything we didn't need. And the crashings were still going on. And I was cleaning up the closet out down in the hallway. And goin' upstairs, I went into the left hallway, and I was goin' to . . . clean the kid's toys, and I found a piece of the Monk's Head that I tossed away when I lived in Skyline Drive. And it had a chip on it, with the head missing. But it was still holding the black candle. And I thought, *my God*, how did it get here? So, anyway, I took it, and I . . . I was cleaning up the other side of the closet, and I found the head, the *monk's head!* And it was chipped on the top. Like it had been scraped and hit on the top of it. So I took it down to my husband and I said, "Do you know where this came from?" "*Oooh*, I haven't seen those, oh my gosh, I forgot all about those!" he said, "I found those, I found those in the trash when we lived on Skyline Drive," he said, "I thought, oh gosh, I'm not goin' to throw that away, I liked Alice, she was a good person, I'm gonna keep those things. I packed them in a box." I said, "Did you pack them in two separate boxes?" And he said, "No, I packed them in a box, one box," and he said, "And when we moved I took it with us." I said, "OK." So I asked the children. I said, "Did you see this before?" They said, "No, what is it?" "Oh," I said, "Oh," I said, "it is just a statue," I said.

"Have you seen it before?" And none of the children had seen it before. But curiously, the head without the box was outside the closet, and the hand with the candle was out of the box, inside the closet. There was two doors separating the hall on each side and how they were separated I'll never know till the day I die. But I took those two pieces, and I took them outside, and I took an ax, a sledgehammer, that what it was, and I crushed those things until they could not, absolutely have anything left of them, but dust. I swept the dust up, and I threw them into the trash and I watched the trash guy take it off and I said "God with it. *Take any evil spirit that can possibly be involved in here.*" Well, it did. And there were no more crashings in the house from that time on. There was nothing, no knockings. No more strange occurrences, no more . . . seance. But what was there, Mr. Nobody. He still existed.

And one night, as I laid in bed, in my room, or no, it was next door in my office. And I was going to read my Bible again. And the most horrifying pressure came into that room, most enormous thing, pressure that I ever felt in my life. Even more, when I was sitting on my bed. And it came right at me, and it was right at my back. I was just breathless, *hhhhh!* Like . . . I can't flee. It got me. It's got me. I grabbed the Bible, and I started reading. I got the Visions [Revelations of John]. I started reading the Visions 6:10, and I started praying: "*O God, help me God,* I can't stand it, it's gonna get me now!" And I started praying, and I prayed, and for the first time ever I prayed, "Dear Lord Jesus Christ, I can't make it, I am nothing, I have no power, I am nothing but a helpless human being. I am dying, and this is in me, in my back, it is goin' to kill me. Please, dear Lord Jesus, as my personal Savior, take it away. I cannot bear it any longer! I can only live through you." And I screamed, and I read those verses, visions, I read them loud, I read them louder, until I was shouting. And I was praying in the blood, "Dear Jesus, I believe in you, only you can save me, only your power can save me." And the evil power, in that instant . . . it was gone. The pressure on my back disappeared, the shadow in the room disappeared.

This was at the end of November of 1983, and this is now February 27, 1987, and to this day, I never had a vision, any supernatural thing appearing in my life. A premonition, any form of pressure, depression, nor have I been able to witness any future event at all. And I owe that to the Lord Jesus Christ, because he took it away and he saved my life. And from that time on, I know the power of God, the power of personal salvation. I lived for 14 years with supernatural pressures, and I know what freedom is. I know how it feels to have no fear anymore, to know that all will be OK, and I'll be fine. I never sought supernatural contacts, never went see a clairvoyant, never dealt with psychics, and I never will.

## "I Lived in a Haunted House": An Autobiographical Subgenre?

As we scrutinize several of the narratives in the previous section, we find limited variation in their experiential contents even as they display such diversity in sociocultural contexts. My research indicates that most people have experienced some kind of haunting, or have sensed a "presence" in their lives. Some suppress such an experience, sensation, or feeling, and dismiss it as nonsense, a bad dream, a daytime hallucination, or a momentary mental lapse. Others take it seriously and cannot get it off their minds; they will keep thinking about it in reinterpreted forms over time. But even those whose life was radically changed by the experience might not want to verbalize the encounter; others need to seek out an audience and talk about it. These accounts strongly resemble the letters written by the anonymous Elkhart woman and Hal Parker, as seen previously. They concentrate on a particular period in the narrator's life that was dominated by a spirit disturbance. This is the background that generates this subgenre: enumerating haunting events.

Should we consider people's accounts of ghostly encounters in their own home to be a special category of folk legend? Is it reasonable to distinguish stories composed of episodes — known also separately as mono-episodic ghost legends — that are attached to the individual and/or family in residence when they are wrought together in a temporal continuum, using traditional motifs, and stereotypical stylistic gestures of speech, dialogues, crystallized statements, and opening and closing formulas?

In what follows, I will cite four texts or variants of what I call tentatively the autobiographical haunting legend. I have sifted through a large contingent of collections deposited in Indiana archives, and have chosen these samples from student term papers that I assigned and letters sent me in response to my survey queries. My informants volunteered to tell their stories. The essential elements that their stories have in common is that they are autobiographical and experiential; they project the narrator's feelings, the subjective reactions of someone struggling to arrive at some kind of explanation. These narrators believe that what they have witnessed is not unusual, that many people are victimized by spirits and suffer from keeping silent about it. Even those who wished to remain anonymous insisted that I publish what they told me and use it for educating, helping, and enlightening people, or "just for fun."

One of my students, concluding her paper on two haunted houses in her hometown of New Albany wrote, "Ghost stories are very interesting. They could be a figment of our imagination or they could be true. We will never know until we die ourselves and maybe then we still might not find out" (Theresa M. Paris, 1988). I believe that genuine curiosity was responsible for my getting so many responses to my search for haunted houses. My informants hope that someone will prove or disprove the experience that kept them poised between trust and mistrust of their senses for so long.

Almost without exception, all of my informants were fascinated by their experience. Looking back, even those who were terrorized by revenants did not want to forget their experience. Most of these people continue to wonder about the meaning, significance, reason, and purpose of the haunting. Many people asked me what I thought about their stories, clearly anxious to get an answer to their unanswered questions and settle their uncertainty. Many wished me luck in my search, assuring me that they would buy the book if I published it.

The four sample texts below use typical formulaic features. For example, true to the convention of traditional legends, the introductory part is the statement of veracity, and the clause reaffirms it even if leaving room for uncertainties. That is to say, each narrator frames the main epic by expressing his or her opinion, and by pondering the question implied by the genre. The haunting episodes are rather plain, and none are very shocking; some would be almost unnoticeable, or noticeable only to people who respond with a pan-animistic mindset and a readiness to attribute significance to any sound, motion, or draft in the house, who regard the small physical functions of their bodies and anything their five senses may experience as symptoms of the presence of supernormal agencies. These episodes are also very familiar, almost commonplace; they use a traditional definition of what makes a house haunted. In spite of the fact that most of the haunting incidents were more odd than terrifying, the narrators usually singled out one that really had shocked them.

Three of the four families of the narrators represented here spent a very brief time in the house: from three weeks to a maximum of four and a half years. Their families moved out because of the discomfort caused by the presence. But despite the brevity of the time spent living in a haunted house, occupying just a short period of these narrators' lives, they perceived the events as overwhelming enough to provide the evidentiary narrative within a potentially manifest but usually sketchy autobiographical framework. Thus, narrators mold their experiences into episodes, foregrounded and elevated to prominence, subordinating all other life history incidents to support the argument basic to legend. The autobiographic coordination of experiential haunting stories is what reaffirms their true legend quality, because it goes

363

with the needed provision of situational, social, and cultural contextualization. To make their stories feasible, the four narrators give detailed background information about themselves and the others involved in the events, and like any legend-teller would, they intersperse their narration with comments — voicing their own and others' personal opinions and feelings, raising issues, and theorizing about the meaning of what had transpired. Evidently, these narratives are experiential and personal, and fit the frame of "personal experience stories," or *Alltagsgeschichten*, while bearing the philosophical orientation and dominant purpose of the legend, overriding all other purposes: to debate and contemplate the question it raises. In all four texts the deposition of evidence in the form of eyewitness testimony plays a major part, leaving no doubt of its being rooted in the legend climate.

1. The House on Riverside Drive

Based on the stories he had heard from his grandmother, Geoffrey B. Young systematically researched the family legend he remembered from his early childhood in South Bend for his student term paper for the fall 1988 Indiana folklore course. The result is a well-researched and structured description of spirit disturbances in a historic house in which Young's parents had lived prior to his birth. To provide a historical-sociological frame for the occurrences, he talked to his relatives and many other people who "had actually experienced the happenings," then he visited the house and interviewed its current occupants. All his informants were "well educated and rational intellects." His identity — his personal, social, and cultural relationships with his informants — as well as his penetrating ethnographic research turned this researcher into a legend-teller, a participant observer with strong affinities to the subject he researched. Throughout his writing he participates in the legend dialectics as only a narrator can. And, being an insider as well as an outsider, he is persuaded by his informants to accept their arguments rationalizing their experience.

Summarizing his investigations, Young found that the evidence convinced him of the truth presented to him by his informants: "I am convinced that there does exist 'something' unexplainable in the house," he writes. "There were no deviations or variations in the accounts of legend. What happened there 35 years ago and even perhaps today has no scientific explanation. There was or still is a presence in that house, this I am very assured of."

Young begins with a brief description of a comfortable, nine-room post-Victorian style house atop a bluff overlooking the St. Joseph River in South Bend, built in 1905 by a Dr. Mitchell. The narrator-collector then continues the history with his parents, who bought the house, then in a state of disrepair, from the son of Dr. Mitchell in 1950. His father and mother had just graduated from Indiana University and returned to South Bend to help run the family's clothing store. It took them a month to renovate the house.

It was during this renovation period, while no one was currently living in the house that the first in a series of occurrences would take place. It would be through these series of events that my parents and scores of others would be convinced someone or something else was residing in the house.

One day after my father had left from work, my parents have decided to go over to the house and do some more cleaning and painting. It was about 9 o'clock, midway through their labors they heard what could only be described as harpsichord music. At first they thought it [was] perhaps music that had floated across the river from some other house. However, it was the middle of winter and the windows and doors were shut and locked tight. The sound, described as loud as the volume of a TV set on, continued for about 6 to 7 minutes and then suddenly stopped. It was not until weeks later when my grandmother, staying at the house for a visit, mentioned over breakfast that she had heard a harpsichord playing the night before. The music, she was sure was coming from downstairs in the music room. Investigating by my mother led to the startling discovery that Mrs. Mitchell, the original wife of the house, had played the Irish harp, in sound very similar to the harpsichord, in the music room. Mrs. Mitchell had died in the house more than 10 years before.

During the renovation process, one of the painters was stripping off old wallpaper from what has been Dr. Mitchell's private office. The doctor had maintained an office on the second floor of his home to see some of his patients after he had semi-retired. The painter told my mother his estimate for the work would have to be increased for the wallpaper on the wall only had been shellacked on and was extremely hard to remove. After the painter had finally removed the wall covering from the office he summoned my mother once again, he wished to show her something in the doctor's office. On one side of the office, against the entire wall were gunshot blasts leaving a surface of pock-marked plaster, which had been concealed by the shellacked wall paper. Why did these blasts cover an entire wall? How many shots would it have taken? What had happened here long ago? Was there foul play? All these questions remain unanswered today.

The house after a month of work and renovation was not ready to move in to. The time was in the winter of 1950. My mother was 23, my father was 26. Both college graduates, both from middle-class backgrounds. My father an Easterner, my mother a Southern, but both very familiar with Northern Indiana. My father had served as a pilot in the Pacific during the Second World War. They had at that time a 1-year-old daughter.

My father in the retail business worked long hours in South Bend's downtown area. My mother stayed at home during the day, worked in the house and looked after my sister. It was during this time she started to hear the "footsteps," one of the house's most frequent occurrences.

At apparently 4 o'clock in the afternoon my mother and sister were in the living room reading and playing. Then my mother heard footsteps go up the front staircase. . . . The stairs were uncarpeted, of natural, refinished oak. My mother at first just assumed my father had come home early from work, but why had she not heard the front door open? She quickly hurried to the staircase only to see absolutely nothing. Strange, she thought, but during the interview she explained that ever since she had lived in the house, especially when my father and sister were not present, she had felt another presence. She only could describe it as "I never felt alone in that house, even though there was nobody else there." She said she was not frightened, just the feeling of another presence. When relating the story of the footsteps to my father he dismissed it as nonsense, until he himself the very next day heard them. In his interview he described them as sounding as normal as someone walking up the stairs, of normal weight, perhaps a male. Every time they would hear the footsteps, they would rush to the staircase only to find nothing. These footsteps were heard by numerous friends of the family and visitors to the house. Two Notre Dame students who rented rooms on the second floor heard them and recall the exact story. Both my grandparents, an aunt and other family friends heard them and reported the same story. An interesting side note is that in all cases the footsteps *always* went *up* the staircase, never down. Sometimes the footsteps would climb the stairs and then make their way down the upstairs hallway. The footsteps would usually travel in the direction of the doctor's office. My mother theorized perhaps these were former patients coming back for a visit!

Yet another unexplainable occurrence was that of the "classical" opening and closing of doors. This occurrence had no special time and happened anytime during the day or night without routine. Perhaps the most classic example cited was that of Captain Jack Hopopian, of the United States Airforce. A college graduate from I.U. and long time friend of my father from high school and college, he has come into town for a visit. While he and my parents sat in the kitchen and had coffee the front door opened and closed loudly. The Captain asked who had just walked in? My mother by this time used to the occurrence said it was just our resident friendly ghost! Impossible, this rational man from the Airforce thought, he proceeded from the front door only to find it locked from the inside! He then called for the person who was in the house to identify himself. With no reply, he started his very extensive search of the house. He searched the house from the basement to the attic, every closet, under the beds, everywhere anyone could be hiding, but his search was in vain — no one was there! To this day, the Captain can not account for the door occurrence, he believes there is an answer for everything but he had no explanation for this happening. The opening and closing of doors throughout the house continued the rest of the time my parents would remain in the house. Despite all explanations, the "perpetrator" of these actions were never to be found and the question could never be answered.

The doors, the footsteps, the mystery music, all nonexplained, all unanswered, did not please my parents or their Notre Dame boarders. It was not until their last winter in the house in 1953 did they experience something that shocked and frightened them till this very day. In the attic of the house there were two military footlockers belonging to my father. The attic was barren except for those objects. All holes and cracks in the structure of the attic had previously been repaired and closed by my grandfather. All tree branches close to the house had been cut away. There were no rodents such as mice or even birds in this dusty sanctuary. The time was well after midnight on a frosty December night. The Notre Dame boarders were gone on Christmas Break and my sister was staying at my grandparents. My parents would on this night experience what would be the greatest phenomenon of Riverside Drive.

My mother was awakened by a loud scratching sound across the ceiling. At the same time my parents both realized what was making these sounds. The footlockers were literally being dragged from one end of the attic to the next! The lockers had been located directly above my parents bedroom. One of the lockers would drag across the attic floor, followed a few minutes later by the second! This continued for about two hours before stopping. Despite my mother's pleading and the irritating sound of this occurrence, my father refused to leave the safety of his bed. They were the only ones home, all the windows and doors had been locked. So what was making these terrible noises? The next morning, after little sleep from the previous night's activities, my father climbed the staircase to the attic, not knowing what he would find. There in the middle of the room laid the two footlockers. In the exact position they had been when placed there months before! Covered by months of dust, no fingerprints, no marks of the dragging on the dusty floor. No explanation for the previous night's occurrences! What had made them move the night before? There was no sign of human presence, everything was coated in dust as proof nothing had been up there the night before — or had something?

One afternoon while having tea and chatting with the neighbor my mother asked if she had ever heard of anything unusual happening in this house. She said it was funny she had asked her that. Her husband rents to Notre Dame students and last week they had come home to find them packing their belongings. Concerned and upset she asked their boarders what the problem was. They replied it was not her or her husband to account for their moving, but the exceptional amount of strange and eerie noises coming from the house. Although the couple had never heard any unexplained noises, the students refused to elaborate and left. The house was built only a few feet from my parents house. Were the noises coming from my parent's house? Was the whole neighborhood haunted?

It is to be noted that neither of my parents during their occupancy of the house, except for the trunks in the attic occurrence, had ever been scared by the unexplainable occurrences. Many friends had heard the noises and sounds, one even urged my mother to contact Duke University for an investigation team to check out the house! There was well over a dozen people who had experienced the house during my parent's three year stay. All were well educated, most holding college degrees, from middle-class backgrounds. All were very rational people, none could explain the occurrences at the house. The house was sold by my parents in 1953 and it was not until two years ago in 1986 did they return for a visit. It was during a real estate "open house" inviting prospective buyers to tour the house. My parents had no interest in buying it back but just wanted to visit one more time. The house itself had changed little according to my parents. It had been kept up and was in good shape. Even some of the wallpaper my parents had put up in the 50's was still there. Since my parents had sold it in 1953, it had exchanged hands several times.

I felt to conclude my research a trip to the house was the only way to experience the house personally. Located only 5 minutes from my current home, I planned a visit during Thanksgiving Break. My father being a real estate agent had tracked down the current owner's name to be a Mr. Steven Lundeen. I had passed the house many times looking at it, knowing its strange past.

In fact, attending the grade school below the hill on which the house sat, I had played in the same neighborhood as a child.

It was a rainy Saturday morning, about 11 o'clock when I approached the house. I had decided not to call ahead, fearful they would not talk to me, but just knock on the door. The house from the outside looked very kept up. As I started my journey up the long winding porch I could not help but to feel a little anxiety. Here 35 years later after my parents had left. I rang the door bell and a young, attractive woman answered the door. I explained who I was and told her I was doing research on the house. She gladly invited me in, eager to talk and find out more about the house herself. We made our way to the living room. Unfortunately, she informed me she was not the owner of the house. Mr. and Mrs. Lundeen, Notre Dame professors, were on sabbatical in California and would not be back until June. The lady in her early thirties, was from the South, her husband was also a Notre Dame professor. The couple had rented the house in the Lundeens' absence. She gave me a full tour of the house, it was really quite beautiful, with it's lead glass windows and hard wood floors. The residence was furnished in antiques and the owner, she explained, was very concerned to make the house look the way it did around the turn of the century. I started the interview asking her basic questions like her background, how her and her husband had come to rent the house . . . how does one come right out and ask if the place is haunted? I explained, my parents had bought the house 35 years ago. She was very positive and cooperative. She seemed eager to answer my questions and was very interested in the past history of the house. She explained her husband and her and their young daughter had moved into the house in September. They had been there for only three months. It is ironic, the couple and their daughter were all about the same age my parents and my sister were when they moved into the house! It was then I interjected and asked if she or her husband had heard or experienced anything out of the ordinary since moving in the house. I added, my parents had, but underscored it as not to create false testimony. Then she told me everything had been pretty normal since their arrival. However, just recently, she had been in the kitchen in the early afternoon and heard her daughter playing on the back staircase. Fearful that her daughter might injure herself, she walked to the staircase to tell her daughter to come down however she was not there. There was no one else in the house and started to look for her daughter. She went upstairs only to find her sound asleep in her bed! Perhaps the ghosts had started to use the back staircase!

In conclusion, of all the information I have gathered from the various people and all the explanations I have proposed to them, I cannot come up with a rational explanation myself to any of the happenings. All the occurrences had been traced, with no conclusion as to their origins.

There had been no variation in any of the interviews. The legend had remained the same over the years. The footsteps, the mystery music, the doors opening and closing, the moving trunks in the attic, all experienced by numerous people, all of rational mind and intellect. One can only summarize that there was indeed something in the house on Riverside Drive. It is highly debatable what this "something" was, but if we deny the testimony of those that experienced this something are we to assume these dozen or more people are crazy or insane? Of course not, it will simply go down in the annals of the "unknown."

In 1953 my parents sold the house to a Mr. Robert Biber, an officer on the South Bend police force. Years later, one of my mother's friends who experienced the occurrences at the Riverside Drive house met the police officer at a banquet they were both attending. Knowing he was the owner of the home she asked him if he had ever experienced anything out of the ordinary in the house. His reply was short and simple: "Let's just say: It's a very noisy house."

## 2. A Very Particular Experience

A handwritten letter on ten pages of a notebook, dated April 22, 1986, came from Gary Gene Gross, 24, of Mitchell.

Hello Dr. Linda Degh,

Before I relate to you my families experiences, I want to make it perfectly clear that these experiences are (were) most real, *true*, and, can be verified by, or, I should say, *confirmed* by a different family we do not know, when the woman and my mother worked at the same Nursing Home. (Mitchell Manor).

The family who lives there, now, remodeled it on the inside. We are not, nor ever was, friends with them, because we do not *know* them. Some of our families' experiences were the same, but *some* of theirs' were even *more* bizarre than ours. The only reason we know about each others experiences, is, because, this other woman did some thing, my mother never did; she talked about them at work. My mother approached her, and, told her how relieved she was that they also experienced the same things. Now, turn the page, and, I will begin to unfold for you a very particular experience.

It was the summer of 1973 when we moved into the house. We (my mother) were buying it through the F.H.A. It was the only house they would approve of. Since we are poor, we lived in the house four years, and a half before we could move.

From the first night spent in the house, until we moved, we were to experience, first hand, phenomens most people only associate with halloween.

There were three small rooms upstairs, each connected to each other by a door. They were once used as bedrooms, but, the house was in such disrepair, my mother let us kids do what we wanted up their, and, for storage. We slept in the two bedrooms downstairs. My brother, and, I in one, our two sisters, and, mother in the biggest, which the stair case was in.

We boys' room was right under the second bedroom upstairs. We would hear, at night, the voices of three, or, four men, and, one woman up there, *every* night. Bangs, that were so loud, and, shake the whole house were heard, and, felt, but the next day we would find nothing out of place. (Bare with me, I still, haven't told about the most prominent one, yet!)

Every now, and, then, our cabinet doors would open. Some times, we would close them so many times a day. They were not magnetic, but, the kind that would snap shut.

As I said, we kids would go upstairs, and, play, or, just hang out there *a lot*. But, some times, there would be an atmosphere of "evil," tangably present, then we would run down stairs as fast as our legs would take us.

We divided the upstairs rooms between us. The two youngest girls got the first room, me, the second, our brothers the third. I had to walk in our sisters' room to get to mine, and, our brother had to walk through the first to get to his. We boys are twins, and, the oldest. But, our brother has always been scared of a lot of things, so, needless to say, he shared the first room with our sisters. It takes a lot to scare me. There were many, many times I would spend time alone upstairs. Some times all night, but, not sleeping. Not to say, though, I wasn't driven out of my room by fear, ever. Plenty of times. Though there were *plenty* of other times I would stay, in spite of whatever went on. My family thought I was stupid.

There would be times we would see faint, black, shadowy figures, mostly shapeless, moving about the rooms, and, down the stair case. I would see them more often, because, I stayed in the house more than anyone, but, we all saw them.

Also, in my room, upstairs, when, we could not keep the window closed, and, when there were no wind blowing whatsoever outside, a light, gentle breeze would blow the curtains, when no other curtains in the house would be moving. And, about the window, with both the draw cords (as I call them) broke, or, severed, the window would rise by its' self, *seemingly*. No one has been able to, reasonably, explain this. We would even turn the lock, especially at night, and, find it open again, and again. All these things I am writing about not only happened at night, but, during the day light, not hiding in the dark of night.

Suffice it to say, I could go on, and, on with more details, and, a few more experiences. But, this is turning into a book of its' self. Now, let me recount what is the most strange encounter of all, and, the most baffling, as to why it happened at all!!

As I said earlier, my twin brother is afraid of a lot of things. I can't remember exactly why, unless it was because we had an argument, which happened all the time; but, he wanted to sleep in our oldest sisters bed, in our mothers' and sisters' room. Our sister slept in bed with me that night.

My brother, mother, and, sister were awake, talking, in the dark. I, and my sister were sitting up in bed with bedroom lights on, and, door open, but, hall light was out. We were looking at a large Sears Catalog.

As we were looking at it, our "brother" (so we thought) walked to our door way on his way to the bathroom, which was just outside the door in the hall. "He" *slowly* turned our way in the door way, looking at us with this cold, blank, expressionless face. He slowly turned again, entering the bath room. The stool flashed, door opened, and, light went out. "He" walked to the kitchen, turned on the light, opened the refrigerator door, and, cabinet doors. Then, we heard the kitchen doors open, "he" walked on the enclosed back porch, opened the doors, then, went outside.

My sister, and I yelled to our mother, and asked if our brother got up. They said no, that they thought it was us making all the noise. We all met in the front room, real fast. The kitchen light was still on, cabinet doors open, refrigerator door open, but, kitchen doors *closed*, and, *locked*. I unlocked them, and, my mother and I stepped on the back porch to check those doors. They were *closed*, and *locked*. Four doors. The rest of the night, we kept the lights on, and, stayed awake till morning; even though we kids had to go to school the next day.

Who was this "personage" my sister and I saw?! Why did he/she take the bodily form of our brother?! Why did it happen at all!!?? Will we ever know?
Signed: Gary Gene Gross.


The following informative comments were written on a separate page:


The house still stands. Close to our Police Station. Still being occupied (lived in) By the same family I told of earlier? I do not know. As I said, we, really do not know them. Are the strange happenings still going on? I have no idea!

I so strongly wish I had the money to buy the place, I would like to have the *Psychical Research Foundation*, or *the Committee for the Scientific Investigation of Claims of the Paranormal* (long name, ha!) to investigate the happenings of the house, they are still happening!

It is, or, would be hard to experience things such as these, and, not have them affect your beliefs. Me. And, my family have already decided, no matter what any one else says, we shall never back down, nor retract any of what we have said. Most of my family is to worldly, to go around making up some thing of this nature. And, not that imaginative. Believe what you will. We know what we know.

Thank you for your time, and, letting me share some thing my family can only speak about amongst them selves.

There is very little that this writer tells about himself except that he is poor, lives alone, does not work, and that I can call his grandparents in case I want to contact him. But he reveals much more about his childhood persona, because his relationship with his mother and his siblings, particularly his twin brother, is important in setting the stage for the culminating story, the ghostly personification of this brother.

The underlying belief and the structuring of the narrative is similar to the South Bend story; the framing introductory and concluding statements of belief also follow the same logic. In spite of the letter format and the courteous, yet easygoing, form of address directed to a stranger, the author uses all the essential ingredients in developing the legend and expressing his (and his family's) feelings about it. And in spite of his poverty — he has an air of defiant resignation to being idle, alone, and without a job — this narrator exhibits sharp intelligence, a good writing/narrating style, and education.

## 3. The Unexplainable

The letter of Becky Kinsella, dated April 8, 1986, impressed me as a sober, no-nonsense, factual and systematic enumeration of unexplainable disturbances in a house she and her family occupied for one and a half years. She tries to give all the information she has: introducing herself, her husband, and her children; itemizing the events; and detailing everyone's strategic positions and movements in the house at the time the hauntings occurred. She even drew a floor plan to provide an accurate illustration of the premises.

The events that Kinsella's family experienced are similar to those mentioned by both Gross and Young; she maintains a certain aloofness when she states that all the events she experienced were unexplainable, and that the family never succeeded in finding a reason for the unaccountable noises, voices, footsteps, openings and closings of doors, and other false alarms. She states firmly that she indeed experienced these things but was not disturbed or tormented by them like most other people. When they did not find any traces of the entity causing the hauntings, she did not seek help from others. She did not consult friends, relatives, clergymen, clairvoyants, or books on hauntings. She did not even speculate about the nature of her observations — she was not interested in the whys and whats. Without referring to supernatural agencies, haunts, spirits, or revenants, she seems to accept summarily the idea that "there are unexplainable things in the world" while staying coolly, mildly curious.

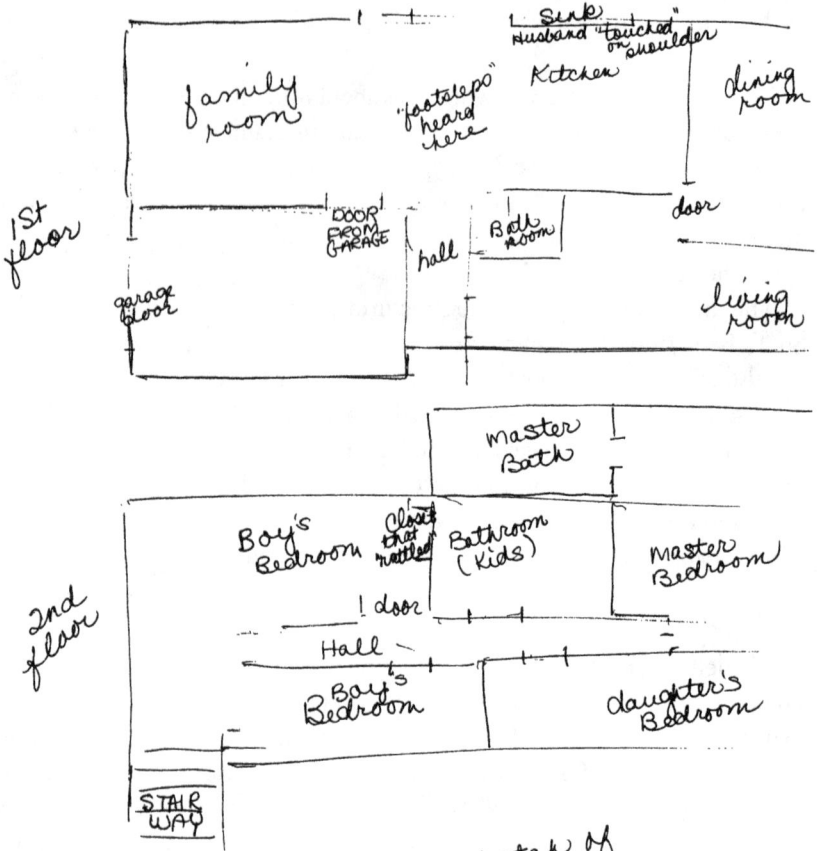

*Handwritten floor plan labels:*

**1st floor:**
family room
"footsteps" heard here
sink — Husband "touched" on shoulder
Kitchen
dining room
DOOR FROM GARAGE
hall
Bath room
door
garage floor
living room

**2nd floor:**
master Bath
Boy's Bedroom
Closet that rattled
Bathroom (Kids)
master Bedroom
! door
Hall
Boy's Bedroom
daughter's Bedroom
STAIR WAY

*This is a "rough" sketch of the floor plan, just to give you a better idea of the layout.*

Becky Kinsella's Floor Plan

She sent me her letter to help in the making of a storybook of the unexplainable. Yet even this dry report conveys the legend dialectics — the attraction to, and belief in, the unmentioned supernormal beings. Her account is similar to the last two narratives, only lacking their narrators' emotional soul-searching and commitment to believing.

Dear Dr. Degh,

I will tell you about a house our family occupied in Bluffton, Indiana. We lived there during 1978–1979 for only 1½ years.

My name is Becky Kinsella. At the time we lived in Bluffton, I was teaching at the Junior High school there. Our children were grade school and jr. "High" age. My husband is a corporate accountant and we left Bluffton for a job with a bigger company.

Our house in Bluffton was located at Sherwood Drive and was less than 10 years old.

The Wabash river ran along side us, just a block away. All the homes were newer, nicely kept ones with big yards. I never did study the history of the area, but it was near Ft. Wayne and Indians were said to have camped along the Wabash river.

Now to list the events that took place in our house:

(1). The door connecting the garage to the house didn't seem to stay locked or unlocked. For example, we'd lock the door at night, and come downstairs in the morning to find it unlocked. Or I would go to teach school in the morning, leaving that door unlocked because the kids get home before I did. I would arrive home to find them freezing outside — the door was locked! Calls to my husband at work would confirm that he had not been home or locked the door.

I should explain here that the house is a standard 2-story, 4 bedroom colonial. The connected garage had an entry door into the family room.

(2). Concerning the above mentioned door to the garage, the lights also caused a problem. I *know* I checked that door at night, even opening it and then locking it but on a few occasions in the morning we would discover the garage light had been on all night. I'm pretty thorough and would *always* turn off lights.

(3). My children heard footsteps in the kitchen after we were all upstairs and in bed, I heard my daughter calling to her brother when they were all supposed to be sleeping. I was in my bedroom and told them to be quiet. She then told me that her brother was down in the kitchen. So I went to check. Both boys were in bed. My husband went downstairs and found no one. This happened a few times.

(4). I was upstairs vacuuming in the boy's bedroom. No one else was home. When I turned the vacuum off, I heard the sliding doors of the closet rattle — exactly as if the cat was inside, trying to get out. In fact, as I walked to the closet, I said "OK. Muffin (our cat) I'll let you out." I really was surprised that the closet was empty. That rattling door was very convincing!

(5). Also, on a day when no one was home, I was in my bathroom upstairs. I clearly heard what sounded exactly like a spoon hitting a crystal glass — a clear "ping." I knew it wasn't the doorbell, but went to check anyway. By then, I think I knew I wouldn't find the answer or reason for the sound.

(6). Reading in bed one night at about 11 p.m. I smelled perfume. My husband was out of town and the kids were in bed sleeping — since about 10:00. I smelled perfume — not strong, but definitely there. It lasted for maybe a minute and a half. It wasn't shocking, but I wondered *how* it could be. Where did the smell come from?

(7). One evening, maybe 7:30–8:00 we were all in the family room watching TV. My husband walked into the adjoining kitchen to get a drink of water at the sink. As he was standing there he distinctly felt a hand touch his right shoulder. It was just for an instant, but he was sure he felt it.

I think I have covered all events that were unexplainable. At no time were any of us really scared. I hope you can use this information. If you publish a book, I'd like to buy a copy. Good luck in your endeavor!

(8). I just recalled one about 8:30 a.m. on a winter day. I wasn't working, and had just returned home from taking the children to school. I was facing the messy task of breakfast dishes when the phone rang. Glad for the distraction, I answered, ready to waste time chatting with anyone. It was my husband calling from work. As we talked, probably discussing trivial things, I suddenly heard the water go on upstairs. In a quiet house if water is turned on somewhere, you hear it running through the plumbing. I told my husband, and he knew I was scared. He even offered to come home. Then the sound stopped. I gathered my courage and said, I'd face the second floor alone. I did — to make beds, etc. Everything was normal! Another unexplained event!

The letter ends here with a "rough sketch of a floor plan, just to give you a better idea of the layout," which is as impressive and scary as the premises of a castle in a Gothic novel — updated for a nice suburban family residence. The events are so unremarkable that one is tempted to wonder what has made this accomplished woman keep them so vividly alive in her memory and view them all as "unexplainable," instead of seeking the cause of the malfunctioning locks and bolts and sounds coming from the appliances.

4. Unusual Happenings

"Anonymous" in West Baden, in a letter received April 16, 1986, provides an even more factual and complete set of legends than the Kinsella example, helping to establish the *Normalform* of our proposed legend type. This text details the hauntings experienced by the correspondent, her daughter, and her daughter-in-law, while only implying, never clearly stating or discussing, belief in the supernatural. The implication is contained in the typewritten cover letter that precedes her account of the cases she calls "unusual happenings." To establish that she is a sober and responsible adult, this author introduces herself as she would in a résumé, emphasizing that she does not use drugs or alcohol and has never suffered from mental illness. The description and history of the house and its environment as the scene of the happenings substitutes here for a direct statement of belief. This story differs from the previous three in that this family lived in the haunted house for more than forty years, and it is still in their possession.

Dear Dr. Dégh,

I read of your quest for stories about unusual happenings in *The Times Mail* newspaper and decided to share these things that have happened to our family. I am fifty five years old and have lived in Southern Indiana all my life the last fourty years near French Lick. I helped my husband on our small farm and worked in a factory. When the children grew up I went to college and earned an associate degree in business management. I have owned and operated a small business in West Baden for ten years. I do not use alcohol or drugs nor have I ever suffered from mental illness.

I do not want to make my identity known because my son who now lives in the house does not want to risk the publicity which could result. He has small children and thinks it would disturb them too much.

If you have questions about these occurances you may write to me. . . .

The house in which we lived in Martin County is a small house on a dead end road surrounded by woods and pasture on a ninety-six acre farm. The neighboring houses can not be seen from this one. I have been told that the people who built the house were very religious. They and their family lived there for many years.

We bought the house from a man whose wife had become mentally disturbed while they lived there. About 18 months after we bought the house the man committed suicide. Some time later I heard that his widow was living with a relative and was much improved.

We moved there in the fall of 1952 when our daughter was about 15 months old. I was expecting another baby in January.

The next summer I started to hear babies cry where I could see both of mine and knew it could be neither of them. Once or twice while I held my babies in the front room the crying seemed to be in the attic directly above us. It was never very loud but it was without doubt the crying of a baby or very young child in distress. Nothing unusual happened except the occasional crying of babies until we remodeled the house in the mid sixties.

Then one morning very early when I was in the kitchen alone I heard someone walk across the front room. The foot steps started near the doorway which had at one time opened to the outside but after the house had been built onto opened into the boy's bedroom. From my line of vision I could see only the legs which seemed to be wearing trousers made of dull heavy cloth. I thought one of the boys must have gotten up so I called out "Good morning whoever is up." I did not hear the front door open or close but the footsteps went toward it then there was silence. When nobody answered me I looked into their room to see who has gone out. All the children were still asleep.

On the day after John Kennedy was assassinated I was in the Kitchen in the middle of the afternoon when I glanced up and saw this same thing walk across the front room. I could not have heard footsteps that time because the TV was on. The children were all playing a board game in the bedroom. This time I told the family what I thought I had seen. My daughter told me that she had seen and heard the same thing one day when she had been in the kitchen and no one else had been home.

Many times at night when every one else was asleep or when I was at home alone during the day a very pleasant female voice that I did not recognize as having heard before would call my name.

One night when I was especially tired as I was falling asleep I felt something warm, soft and pleasant around my feet and calves. Sevaral times during that night I was aware of that pleasant warm feeling around my feet and legs.

The next morning after my husband had gone to work and the children had gone to school I went back to bed. Just as I lay down a friendly melodic voice which seemed to be right under my pillow said "Hello." I ran out of the room and closed the door. I never heard that voice again but from time to time a different female voice would call my name.

LEGEND AND BELIEF

At one time we had an almost all white cat who would slip in the front door and walk behind my husband's chair to come to the side of my chair. I would always pet her and if we were eating while we watched TV I would give her a morsel of food.

One evening I glimpsed a white shape glide around the doorway. It seemed too big to be the cat but I was engrossed in the TV program and without thinking about it reached down to pet the cat. When I felt nothing I looked down and almost fainted! Where the cat should have been was a dense white cloud about two feet long and a foot and a half wide floating about a foot and a half above the floor. As I looked it spread out and got thinner and thinner until dark holes appeared in it. The holes got bigger and bigger until they blended into each other and the whole thing disappeared.

My daughter had a somewhat similar experience. One night very late she was reading in bed because she could not sleep. She happened to glance up and saw what at first seemed to be a large white rat (although she did not notice either eyes or tail) moves slowly among the cosmetic bottles and jars on her vanity table. While she looked it changed shape spreading out like fog and flowed very slowly over the front of the vanity disappearing completely just before it reached the floor.

After we moved to town my son lived alone at the farm. I would often go out to the farm on Saturday and clean the house and do laundry. If it was late when I finished I stayed overnight and came back to town next afternoon. When I stayed overnight I slept on a Hide-A-Bed sofa which when unfolded spread across the doorway between the front room and the bedroom.

One night when I was there (my son often stayed out very late on Saturday night) I seemed to sense a presence in the house. It seemed to be very weak and to [be] floating near the ceiling of the bedroom. I could not see, feel or hear anything but I had an eerie feeling that something was there. The presence seemed to grow stronger and drift toward the doorway. About that time my dog who is my constant companion and was sleeping on the bed with me became alert. Her eyes were wide and her ears were raised. She bristled and began to growl. She then barked once and yiped. She crawled off of the bed and covered behind the arm of the sofa peeking around it with just one eye. It seemed to me that the invisible thing was tall and was standing near the foot of the bed on the left side (the side nearest the bedroom doorway) looking at me. I still could not see anything but I felt as though I were being watched. I pulled the cover over my head and lay very still.

After a few moments I felt the dog crawl back onto the bed. She lay down flat and pressed herself against me. I uncovered my head and looked around. I could no longer sense the presence. The house seemed empty and I felt that I was alone.

The next morning I folded the bed clothes and took them and the pillow into the bedroom. The dog who always follows me around the house while I work came to within three feet of the doorway and stopped then she sat down. When I talked to her she whined but she would not come into the bedroom even when I commanded her to "come."

My son and his family live in the house now. His wife Cindy says that she has heard small children running and sometimes laughing when it could not be her own children. Once she heard a baby crying when all of her children were visiting with relatives.

Cindy told me that when her daughter Sandy was little she put Sandy in the play pen while she took a shower. One afternoon while she was taking a shower Sandy got restless and started to fuss and then to cry. Just when Cindy thought she would have to get [out] of the shower and see about Sandy she heard a child's footsteps run across the front room floor and a little girl's voice talking to Sandy. Cindy thought her older daughter Tina had returned from school so she continued with her shower. Sandy stopped fussing and then laughed. Cindy called to Tina and asked her to bring something she had forgotten to take into the bathroom with her. Almost immediately Sandy began to fuss again. When Tina did not answer Cindy got out of the shower went into the front room and found that Sandy was there alone. While Cindy was trying to think where Tina could have gone the school bus stopped in front of the house and Tina got off of the bus.

## Discussion

On the basis of this small sample of autobiographical narratives about living in a haunted house, I will attempt to establish an analytical unit for a composite type outline of a legend, taking the haunting episodes or motifs from (1) Young, (2) Gross, (3) Kinsella, (4) Anonymous 2 in West Baden, and the earlier stories of (5) Anonymous 1 in Elkhart, (6) Parker, and (7) Littleton into consideration as well. This type of legend has the following common denominators:

1. It informs about spirit presence and activities in a particular house.

2. Its teller is a resident who experienced the presence and the activities of spirits in the house.

3. The teller offers his or her personal views, evaluations, and possible interpretations of the event(s), stressing authority by speaking in first-person singular.

4. The teller substantiates the legend by adding autobiographical data, and by describing the premises to help the audience visualize the narrated events.

The most dependable compendia for a general comparative survey of existing materials are in chapter E, "The Dead," of Thompson's *Motif-Index of Folk-Literature* (vol. 2, 1956: 402–517) and the comparable chapter in the revised edition of Baughman (1966: 135–202). If the usefulness of this monumental attempt to establish a systematic classification of the smallest narrative units of *Homo narrans* is problematic for some specialists, it seems a blessing for the student of legends who wants to spot the whimsical and multifarious oscillation of legend-ingredients and their agglomerations from *langue* to *parole*, back and forth, as itemized on these indexes' pages. Particularly because we still have to broaden our vistas and restore overlooked, ignored, or omitted stories, new and old, to their legend status, these source books of the miscellany of legend potentials are very precious. The *Motif-Index* is all-inclusive and provides numbers for the incidents contained also in our texts. As I am not writing down the motif numbers characteristically represented here, interested readers should let their fingers do the walking to learn about the creative flexibility of legends, and the logic of the intricacies of composing stories by linking motifs together.

The legend "I Lived in a Haunted House" describes how individuals feel when they are alone, confined between the walls of a house, isolated from the rest of the world. When they are left to their own imagination, enhanced by darkness and silence, all that is on their minds — leftovers of the day's unresolved problems — is filtered through given mental and physical dispositions. It is hard to separate natural and imaginary perceptions, and fantasy soars on the wings of cultural heritage and new learning of mass-mediated information; the two blend and homogenize on a new platform.

But the "presence" that emerges from the fear of helpless solitude in the normally protective home is an ambiguous, and often terrifying, invisible extranormal entity that precipitates the thought "I am not alone." This is often reasserted by people telling about their experience: "I never felt alone in that house" (1); "I had an eerie feeling something was there" (4); and "the room became quite cold and I felt a presence" (7). Many describe a sensation of being watched. The latter informant added that it made him feel very sad, and he started to cry. So did his wife, who could not explain why she could not stop crying in the other room. According to some people, the "presence" causes an intolerable pressure, a sense of helplessness. The approaching danger is signaled by beings who are more sensitive than humans: Plants and household pets behave abnormally. Human beings are mesmerized by the invisible, mysterious, non-human being that is on its way to invade their homes and take control of things, changing the whole environment. They know that from then on their lives in the family sanctuary will never be the same.

What the "presence" really is remains vague. It may appear to human perception as more than just a feeling, but rather in ethereal shapes — it can be seen in the shape of a white cloud, or be mistaken for a cat but be untouchable (4), or for a rat that floats over the vanity and the floor before evaporating (4), or be seen as a faint shapeless shadowy black figure bringing along the sense of an evil atmosphere (2) moving about in the rooms (5). Sometimes this indefinable "It" is visible only to a faithful, well-mannered dog who disobeys commands out of fear (4). The invisible "presence" may be perceived with a variety of senses: the smell of perfume (3); the sound of a chair squeaking (5) or objects moving (1); the sound of a spoon tapping a crystal vase (3);oscillating tones (7); the rattling of a sliding door (3); and the touch of a hand pulling blankets off the sleeper (5, 6), or patting one's back or touching one's shoulder (3). Even if the presence seems friendly — a sweet voice softly saying "hello" (4) or calling the narrator by name (4) — it never is felt as a comforting gesture. Informants speak of a tremendous feeling of relief when it is gone. The moment it leaves the house, the paralyzed can move again (7), the feeling of "something evil" (2, 5) disappears, and the pleasant atmosphere returns to the home that was temporarily turned into a place of nightmares.

In whatever form, the haunt upsets the narrator because it is a spirit, and because it infiltrates the privacy of people's residences, paying its visits at the most inconvenient times. It walks all over the place, and no locks and bolts can keep it out of the public and private places of the house; it opens the doors of rooms, refrigerators, and cabinets and leaves them ajar; it can make its presence felt while people play games, wash dishes, shower, watch television, read in bed, and go to the bathroom. The intruder often does its tricks at night, but not necessarily so — it may act at any time during the day. It may be perceived by one person, several people, or everyone in the household, at the same or diverse times. It may be noticed also by visitors and neighbors (1). The invisible presence also causes objects to move, such as an old rocking chair to rock (6); it may make sounds, such as a grandfather clock's ticking (6) or music playing (1). But no identification of this agent is given, no purpose, and no real quid pro quo.

As long as we can speak about discreet feelings, optical illusions, and temporary suspension of disbelief under the pressures of being alone in a certain situation, the haunting stories remain more the projections of the teller's point of view, than that of the "poor souls" who cannot rest until obtaining absolution. In this type of legend, the tellers themselves are the central characters, and what matters is their experience, their horrific encounter with supernatural beings who terrorize them by intruding into their home. They appeal to our compassion, as they feel threatened by the invasion and the attack of extranormals: ghosts, spooks, presences, the unexplainable as defined by our informants.

The attackers are not clearly identified in our sample texts, except in the story of Anonymous 1 (5), which is the only text that makes reference to the theological concept of evil spirits, the power of prayer, and exorcism; and in Young's paper (1), in which the revenants are assumed to be the patients of the doctor who previously lived in the house, because the footsteps are heard to climb the stairs toward his former office. In another case, a pair of trousered legs is also sighted without other parts of the body (4).

The usually faceless phantoms seem to have no identity and only one function: to enter the home — any home — and scare its inhabitants. The spirits' own identities and vital statistics remain unknown, because these really have nothing to do with their purpose. Their role is to haunt the house and terrify people, so they stay in the shadows, keeping their existence and other purposes mysterious and unknowable. They exist only in the fantasy world of the legend-tellers and fill their need of rationalizing hauntings, providing them with the raw materials from which the haunting experience can be constructed.

How can we summarize the activities of the "presence?" As we have shown, it makes noises — pretending to destroy parts of the building, crashing windows, rolling heavy objects in the attic, setting the place on fire, and even reenacting murders — and make the listening residents whimper in their beds. The next morning, after spending the night without sleep, the residents collect their courage, armed sometimes with guns and flashlights (6) and visit the suspect places in their homes; the residents will find no trace of violence, no murder victims, and no damaged property. Old treasures in the attic and the basement will remain neatly packed, without the imprint of an intruder on the dust that has gathered over decades (1). The phantom's violent acts are as symbolic as their assumed performers.

A haunt's itinerary often runs like an orderly railway timetable. From the time it enters through the front door then exits, its trail can be followed by the sound it makes: Walking is its most characteristic movement. From the entrance it walks up through the foyer and strolls throughout the house, entering the main rooms such as kitchens, bathrooms, and bedrooms. It has the greatest preference for staircases, second-floor bedrooms, and attics. It climbs up the stairs, pauses at landings, retreats, or turns; it may go only up and never come down, simply fading out in the upper regions of the house. As it walks, it particularly enjoys opening and closing doors, to the confusion and irritation of the homeowners who find entrances open in the morning that had been locked for the night. From our sample, a door that was left open for children coming home from school was found locked in the afternoon in freezing weather (1, 3). During its tour of the home, the spirit opens cabinets and appliances and leaves them open (2). It also likes to open and close windows, or make windows impossible to keep closed (2), and cause wind to blow inside on a quiet, windless day (2, 5). There is never a trace of their walk left; those who try to find footprints by putting down paper covered with flour fail to come up with the slightest evidence (6). Nor is there a sign of anything manipulating light switches, yet the lights are turned on and off during the haunting (3, 5). In two of our texts the lights were on all night after the family had left and turned them off (3, 5). The turning on of the water in the upstairs and its abrupt stoppage appears also in our sample (3).

Among the rare human voices attributed to haunts are those of babies and young children. Babies cry in the basement or in the attic; some approach disturbingly close to young mothers, and then their voices fade out (7). Children's noisemaking resounds from the attics, upstairs rooms, or the yard, as they run around, play, and laugh (4). Can we attribute the sound of youngsters to the versatile presence? As we have seen, juvenile phantoms are common in ghost stories[8]; the factual base of these stories may be the disciplinary problem of large families who need to keep children safe and out of trouble in a large country house that is close to dangerous wilderness and industrial areas. Young parents often hear crying babies while they hold their own infant (1, 4, 7).

In our sample, some worried mothers found their children sleeping in their bedrooms when they had been spotted somewhere else (3, 4). These cases of the presence turning up as the alter ego of a child are surprisingly new situations. This could be the typical projection of parental concern for children's whereabouts. In these ghost stories, children were seen playing outside, talking to someone, or babysitting, when they in fact were sleeping upstairs in their beds or just arriving home from school (1, 3, 4). The most stunning trick of the presence is certainly the impersonation of a twin brother (2), assuming his shape and his nightly routine: The phantom twin brother, "with this cold, expressionless face," continued his walk from the bedroom, to the bathroom, to the kitchen, to the back porch, then out onto the street instead of going back, while his brother and sister watched desperately. They turned off the lights and closed the doors that were left open by the phantom, but found the porch doors closed and locked — and the real brother in another room with their mother. The rhetorical question of our informant — *who* was this personage they saw, and *why* did it take the bodily form of his twin brother? — had an air of resignation, asking "will we ever know?"

Textualization of these stories was not as spontaneous as it would have been if they were uttered at a family gathering or among trusted friends at a time when "these things" came up. I spoke about my interest in class and asked my graduate students for contributions, hoping that, with fieldwork guidance, their term papers would bring some fresh materials. I was fortunate because the experiment showed me the great value of a native ethnographer who can use the insider's hereditary knowledge in the research but take the professional distance of the outsider in the evaluation of the data.

My correspondents, on the other hand, were prompted by my request to tell their haunted house narratives. Although letters cannot be as spontaneous as informal talks, interested people took the time to write down the legends they knew and found significant enough to communicate to a stranger who would publish them. These people had to make several choices before sitting down and writing. They had to decide what to tell and what not to tell, and whether to tell it exactly how it happened or change it so that others could understand the circumstances and the story. Before making public a unique experience or several experiences that only the family and close friends knew, perhaps the correspondent sought the advice of trusted friends who have heard the story repeatedly over the years. Of course, there is a good chance that had I contacted the letters' authors personally I would have received different stories and probably would have learned much more about underlying conditions. But there was no time for such an enormous project.

However, I definitely gained more by letting the narrators offer their stories to me, and letting their community advise them, than I would have had I personally sent them a questionnaire or invaded their privacy by setting up interviews. As I have noted, having students collect stories from their own peers is better than letting an unprepared stranger ask questions about such sensitive topics. Likewise, soliciting letters of information about haunted houses was a much better method of collecting than constructing private question-and-answer sessions between a researcher and narrator; this way, the informants make the personal decision and have freedom of choice, informed by tradition and negotiated by community standards.

A written legend is different from an oral legend. The writer's audience is absent and cannot exercise its right to make critical (both consenting and dissenting) comments. These writers are left alone with their memories, and must make the selections and the composition alone. Authors may need time for thinking, remembering, writing, and rewriting, until they feel ready to finalize their stories. The new version will not betray the author's peers or make a fool of the author, and it also satisfies the prospective reader. These premeditated, personalized variants from the field are important documents, because they are intended to address another world, an unknown audience. These letters intend to tell the truth, even if it is self-centered and loyal to local principles, and to defend that truth, even if it is a lie. Why would individuals be that serious about their extranormal experiences? Because their belief is uncertain, not definitive. Stating a case leaves room for many alternative and/or simultaneous truths.

## Visits to the Realm of the Dead

It should be clear by now that what the legends in our Indiana sample tell us is that for the individual, the dwelling shared by a family is the primary protective cell. But the family is in a constant state of flux; people die and enter a new phase of existence that changes relationships and responsibilities. Family members, alive and dead, belong together and are obliged to help each other through hardships in all phases of existence until they all are happily reunited in the hereafter. We know that relationships within the family are not always smooth, so why should it be different between the dead and the living members of the family? The legends show how loving relatives can become burdensome, if they come at the wrong time or keep reminding the living of their obligations to them. But this intrusion cannot cause estrangement between those who belong together — family ties are stronger than that.

Unrelated spirits are a different matter. Most of these visitors are earlier residents who suffered a violent death and have nowhere else to go to get relief from their ordeal. The more troublesome that these strangers are, even if they are benign poor souls, the more people tend to become intolerant of them. But the real trouble is with evil strangers, who are so fearsome that householders will never trust any unknown spirit intruder.

In addition to the house, the adjacent buildings — barns, stables, smokehouses, sheds, porches — and the road, bridge, or driveway that leads to the house, are also spooked by the spirits who live in the house. Some spirits will maintain regular hours at night for the activities that they had in life, such as carrying feed to the stable, turning on lights, or watering the vegetable garden. For example, the headless servant of the Moody Mansion makes a regular walk between the house and barn with his lantern.

The story of Nellie Miller, the revenant of the tiny, close-knit community of Celestine in Dubois County, is a typical local Indiana legend of a spirit who follows a regular routine. Miller, described as an odd-looking recluse, was an unmarried woman who took care of the family farm after the death of her parents. When her ancestral log cabin became inadequate for human comfort, she bought a trailer in which she lived until her death at age 78.

### The Ghost in Galoshes

Winter and summer, whether slopping hogs or going to church, Nellie always wore the same thing — a long heavy coat, galoshes, and a bandana tied under her chin. She also walked with a stooped posture, her back bent from all her years of heavy farm labor. . . .

After she had died in 1979, people began to see her; as a matter of fact, a couple saw her first on the day she was buried; they attended her funeral. They were working in their yard when they noticed her stooped figure striding up the road. "My God! It's Nellie."

. . . Just as Nellie drew even with the property line, Mrs. A. asked her, "Nellie, what is the matter? What do you want?" The figure looked at her straight in the face — and then disappeared. Mr. and Mrs. A. searched up and down the road for evidence of some kind of prank. There were no ditches, no high weeds, no fences, no place of any kind where someone could hide. . . .

A second sighting took place one Sunday morning just north of town. Mr. B. was driving home from church in his pickup truck and saw a familiar old woman walking in the same direction by the side of the road, as if she too were on her way home from church. Mr. B. knew Nellie was dead, but the figure's appearance was unmistakable. He had passed Nellie many times before and knew she preferred to walk, but occasionally when the weather was bad, or she was carrying bags of groceries, he had offered her a ride. Now, intrigued by the possibility that this figure really was Nellie, he pulled alongside her and stopped, opened the door, and said: "Nellie, what do you want?" Again, the figure looked right at him and vanished.

The third incident happened on private property, a farm at the Celestine vicinity. A woman I'll call Mrs. C. glanced out of her kitchen window one afternoon and saw a figure whom she knew looked like Nellie Miller. Again, as in the other cases, she asked Nellie what she wanted and, again, the figure disappeared.[9]

### Seeking the Dead in the Realm of Nature

The American heartland at night turns into a dangerous legend landscape. When we leave the community, town, hamlet, or homestead, we enter unprotected zones, without safe shelters, far from concerned family spirits. On moonless, rainy, hazy nights, or moonlit, freezing, windy nights, the idyllic woods, scenic drives, pleasant picnic areas, rose gardens, arboretums, parking places, river crossings, bridges, boat ramps, caves, tunnels, mills, chapels, cemeteries, and ruins of old houses change into the land of the dead — or better, the land of the dead come to life. This is an unknown and forbidden territory, far away from the world of the living. The lights and sounds that signal human interaction — people drinking in the pub, playing music on their boom-boxes, listening to the news, chatting with neighbors, riding their new motor bikes — do not penetrate the boundaries of this land. It is only stillness and tranquility, interrupted by the spooky sound of windblown trees, mystic birds, or distant dogs. Or could that be the baying of wolves? Or could that be the shriek of the Black Witch who pursues drivers who touched the grave she protects and pulls them from their cars with her long hooked arms? Or could that sound be the shovel of the Seven-Foot Crazy Humpback who digs up graves? Or could that be the bell of the chapel calling the dead to the midnight service? Or could that be the "swish-swish" of the dead boyfriend's shoes brushing against the top of the car in which his girlfriend is safely locked? No one should dare the dangerous grounds of the "entirely different," but we know that many do, and this is how we know about them.

Many folklorists since Peuckert (1965) have described the legend landscape beyond the boundaries of communities where the legend climate dominates. We know this landscape from legend-tellers' descriptions. This domain is the "entirely different," "numinous," or "liminal" territory (see chapter 2) that is not governed by human rules. Spirits, good and evil, live there, go about their errands on their own schedule, and do not like to be intercepted by mortals. Traditional European villagers knew the map of this other world that existed on the outskirts of their communities: the cliffs, caves, caverns, mounds, bays, trees, and bushes where the spirits resided; the roads, bridges, furrows, and ferries where they passed through; and the fences, mills, crossroads, mountain tops, shelters, abandoned buildings, and chapels where they rested. These places were to be avoided if possible, but people accidentally got into trouble because of the vastness of the uninhabited land. Those who wanted to learn magic sought encounters with supernatural beings, and followed their guidance to pass a hard test of courage on a crossroads. Mortals who passed the test earned supernatural power and knowledge, but lost their chance at a painless death and smooth passage to heaven. Those who did not pass the test were crippled for life.

The American legend landscape, as we have seen, is as mysterious as that of its European ancestors. In Indiana, legend seekers seldom come across Irish banshees, leprechauns, or the "little people" who remove the hump from the good man who helps improve their song and put it on the back of the bad man who spoils their song (Sweeney 1967: 176). German milk-witches who get shod by clever blacksmith boys or whose ears are cropped while they are in black cat shape are also rarities (Cockrum 1907: 338–341). In America there is a better chance of finding more indigenous ethnic victims, such as the Amish boy who was punished for reading black magic from *The Sixth and Seventh Book of Moses*. The Weeping White Woman of Mexican ancestry, La Llorona, survives perhaps because of her strong affinity with Resurrection Mary, walking the same roads of Northwest Indiana. Clearly, the revenants come from American stock, extending to Indians killed on the battlefield, and Chinese, Mexican, or black construction workers killed accidentally or lynched by the Ku Klux Klan. Historical characters — a Civil War soldier, Morgan's Raiders, lynching victims, riverboat captains, gangsters (John Dillinger and Al Capone), and underground railroad rescuees — are the least represented ghosts in our survey.

Not the heroes of past history but rather the recent victims of violent death are the focus of interest of people seeking the legend landscape. Although there are occasional mentions of mishaps from the "horse and buggy days," of pale ladies in nineteenth-century garb seeking their child who was thrown from a vehicle, recent victims are more popular. And, like the people who seek them out, the ghosts are mostly young people who engaged in dangerous or risky activities. At a time when they were full of expectations, when their life was about to take a new turn, a tragic accident cut their career short. These victims are tied to the place where they lost their lives, and knowing these locations is the way to make contact with them. Everyone knows the spirit topography, where visits to the spirits can be made at the proper time — around midnight, any day, on the anniversary of the tragic event, when weather conditions allow, on Halloween night.

But why would anyone visit the site of a tragic death of a person he or she did not know? Our survey indicates that it is exceptional for anyone between the ages of 14 and 24 not to have been a participant on a legend-trip. Some have gone only once or twice; but others, without peer pressure, have gone eight to twelve times, according to a 1986 questionnaire that polled 180 Indianapolis high school juniors and seniors who had scaled the wrought iron fence of the former House of Blue Lights.

These legend-trips need preparation and careful planning, both practically and psychologically. One needs to find others to make up a peer group eager to go — meaning anyone ready to enter and negotiate the legend climate, believer or not. The group may be composed of males and females, two to eight in a car, or even two carloads or possibly a van. The psychological preparation is based on the common frame of reference: the social information about the customs, based on family tradition and enculturation (as discussed in chapter 4).

We have to remember that a legend-trip does not mean driving to several haunted sites during the night. It means to target one particular location that is well known to the participants; they know how to get there, what to do, and what they expect to happen. Before going, they prepare themselves to think of horror and terror. To get into the mood, they remember horror stories they have heard and recite them to each other, screaming and hollering all the way to their destination. Intoxicated by the spookiness of weather conditions and an awareness of the adventure — and possibly aided by a six-pack of beer and auto-suggestion — they set the stage for the ritual invocation of the dead.

As prescribed by tradition, the living arrive with flashlights whose beams illuminate the site. They honk the horn of the car three times, or roll down the windows, or slide slowly over a stretch of road while screaming, or they yell obscenities loud enough to wake up the dead. The activities may even involve an aggressive act; for example, they jump up and down on Bloody Mary's grave to make her respond and bleed through the ground.

The experiential legends of these visitors are very emotional, endowed by the legend climate. As expected, they exhibit the mental disposition of fantasizing and hallucinating. Everyone sees the victim appear, of course; but most of the informants are not absolutely certain that it might not have been a dream or their imagination. They all saw or heard other things: white clouds that engulfed them, ferocious animals that attacked them, or a ghost that tried to strangle them in their beds. But who is really believing before, or after, the expiration of the clandestine, voluntary suspension of disbelief? The degree of belief depends on personal inclination and individual experience. Directly asking people the same question periodically would prove that the intensity of belief in this particular case or others in general is not measurable.

From the viewpoint of the legend-tellers, to participate in the performance of a life-cycle ritual is a normative behavior and does not need special explanation; this is what their parents did, as well as their older siblings — it would be more eccentric not to participate. It is a group act that is expected from young people. As many have described it, the entire experience is a coming of age ritual, a dare that proves courage and maturity. Undergoing the trip ensures that one is ready to leave the parental home and become a responsible adult who can face the real challenges of life.

The idea of entering the realm of the dead and coming back unharmed is "like a symbolic celebration of victory of life over death," I was told by my informants. Sociologists investigating the adolescent subculture may make far-reaching conclusions about the nature of these trips, but I agree with Elizabeth Bird's observation that for the performing adolescents these trips are "done for fun and excitement, not to make statements about sex, fear, and death." However, the ritual itself manifests these critical concerns of the passage from childhood to adulthood; therefore, to view it merely "as play" is a mistake (Bird 1994: 192). There is also a somewhat aggressive feature of the legend trip. The youth groups on the trip forcibly enter foreign territory. Uninvited, they intrude and force themselves on the spirits who also should have the right to their privacy. They invite danger and expect to be challenged, but with the intent to evade any real repercussions.

John Zehrings, a 22-year-old student from Bunker Hill, provided a typical account of a legend-trip to a spooky house concealed behind trees and shrubs. This haunted house narrative in which the haunt is raided by mortals is quite a reversal of the prototypical haunted house legend. His story is a very accurate recounting, with all the details of the type and the dialectic ambiguities of the legend. The main outline of this legend is "The Mystery House" (in which nasty adults lure in and scare teenagers), with some additional literary horror story/movie/comics elements.

### Visit to a Haunted House

It was early August of 1965. The time was 10:30 P.M. and four of us were on our way to Bunker Hill after watching the Babe Ruth State Tournament in Kokomo. My brother Dave was riding shotgun, two friends, Steve Erbaugh were in the backseat, and I was driving. All of a sudden, Jerry said something about a haunted house to Steve. I asked where it was, he told me and we were on our way looking for some excitement.

On the way, Jerry told us the supposed legend about the house. We all listened very intently. He said the house sets off the road about seventy-five yards and the lane is very narrow with trees and thick shrubs on both sides. The house itself, he said, is an old two story brick house with shutters that bang when the wind blows. Trees and shrub surround the house and it is very hard to see from the road, especially at night. After this brief description of the place, the rest of us were on the edge of our seats, and he hadn't even gotten to the actual legend. Jerry said he had been there before, but hadn't been inside the house. When we asked why he didn't go in and he told us, we saw his reasoning. There is supposed to be an old lady living all by herself in the house, but she is only there at night. The story goes, if anyone enters the house after dark, the door closes behind you and locks itself. The old lady is lying on the couch and at the slam of the door she gets up, and with knife in hand, stabs the intruders. We asked

Jerry why someone couldn't overpower her, being that she was an old lady. He said, according to the legend, she has the strength of many men, and after she kills the victims, she carries them down to her basement and buries them.

By this time we were all plenty scared, including Jerry. He had me turn off U.S. 31 and turn west in Indiana 218, between Peru and Bunker Hill. I drove about a mile and there it was on the right hand side on the road. His description was an accurate one. We could see the very top of the house with its white shutters. The lane looked long and trees and shrub were thick. I turned in the lane and drove slowly to the house, and believe me, that wasn't easy, because the bush and shrub seemed to enclose the drive, putting a roof on it. We finally got to the house, nobody having said a word since we turned in the lane. There stood the house, brick and two story. I hadn't noticed a strong wind that night, but there was enough to cause the shutters to bang some. I stopped the car and we were just opening our doors when Jerry and Dave yelled out that they saw an old woman looking out the window. Steve and I didn't question them, and all four of us were back in the car and heading out that lane as fast as I could possibly drive.

I have thought about this incident several times since. If Jerry was the only one who saw the old lady in the window, I would now believe that he was just putting us on. But, as I said, my brother also claimed he saw her. He would have told me by now if he and Jerry were just playing a joke on us. They both will tell you to this day that they saw the old lady. And to this day not one of us four have been back to the "haunted house" to find out if she really is there.

The nocturnal Indiana legend landscape differs from that of old Europe as much as the types of settlements — and their relationship to surrounding arable land and uninhabited natural land (including protected, national, and state forests and parks) — differ. Another difference is the availability of roads for driving cars to haunted locations. Remember, most European ghost stories tell about people who encounter spirits by accident, who unwittingly enter forbidden territories, or who are being victimized by a curse while walking home from work, from town, or from their girlfriend's home. The lonely walk in darkness may take many hours; twelve from the mining place where narrating miner József Minárcsik and fellow villagers from Kishartyán (Nógrád County), worked. Transylvanian master storyteller András Albert saw the two-headed dragon emerging from the bottomless Lake Gyilkos (Killer Lake) while he walked to the lumber camp where he was employed, up the forbidding peaks of the Hargita Mountains. His visions were blended into his life history, tales, and legends as well. "Being led away" by a spirit may mean that the person finds himself in the top of a tree or on a mountain at daybreak, or that he makes the rounds on the same road, finding his nearby home only the next day. Lonely walks in the darkness through uninhabited land can make people fantasize and see things that physically are not there, as Wilhelm Wundt and Ludwig Laistner have already taught us in their classics on folk psychology. But none of our Indiana informants walked through the darkness of the night to a dangerous spooky place, and none experienced their ghostly encounter accidentally: All of them drove there in cars, and all of them knew the dangerous forbidden land. What they encountered was expected, and if nothing happened they were disappointed; some did not even dare to confess their failure to have a shocking adventure — they lied about it, even to themselves.

Not that there were no risks involved. According to some legends, a killer or monster might have been hiding in the car's backseat, or a revenant or phantom car (or in one Indiana version, a milk truck) might have forced the driver off the road to his death. But this should not happen to a well-prepared visitor who knows the rules about how far a test of courage can go.

All of the reports were experiential accounts and indicated the locations; and several elaborated on the ritual acts and behaviors necessary to provoke the appearance of the spirit and the reenactment of the death. The spirits whose deaths were caused by a murder, suicide, or accident do not leave that site where they appear. And those who appear on command, or make sounds, or reenact their death usually are not malevolent and do not take revenge.

A random sampling will give an idea of the character of the Indiana repertoire of legend-trip related narratives. In spite of the limited number of alternatives, the legends are variable, contextualized by domestic relationships; they are personal tragedies caused by pain, madness, hate, and love. The most popular locations for death sites where the victim can be summoned are bridges: covered bridges, wooden or steel bridges, or railroad bridges/trestles. Our sample comprises legends related to thirty-eight Indiana bridges. As shown in chapter 3, these bridges usually localize not one single legend but a whole repertoire of three to twelve each, displaying trends of transmission, and typological variation and stabilization. Presentation of fully contextualized performances would distract from our goal of introducing representative stories; these brief excerpts merely show the topical variety of the best-known prototypical stories, as well as typical instructions concerning the invocation of the spirits.

1. At the Azalia Bridge in Bartholomew County, a man was cut in half in a car accident on the bridge, and now the lower half of his body appears walking across the bridge.

2. When a man once crossed the bridge over Silver Creek in New Albany in an open wagon, a hand started coming up along the side of the wagon; the man cut it off, but it was never found. Now a big hand will come into the car and grab the driver if the window is left down while crossing the bridge.

3. On the Old Steel Bridge in Matthews, "a farmer hung himself from this bridge. You can hear him scream at midnight, you park on the bridge

across from an oak tree, roll up your car window and honk your horn three times."

4. In Frankfort, a woman killed her husband, chopped him into pieces, and threw the pieces off the bridge. Lights appear on the bridge and strange noises occur; the woman's ghost scares away intruders.

5. Between Frankfort and Rossville, a girl whose boyfriend was going into the army went mad and hung herself from the bridge. Her body was found by a farmer and buried. Later the grave was found to be empty. The girl's ghost in the shape of a white shadow with red eyes chases people coming near the bridge. Dogs have been found clawed to death near the site.

6. The Amo Bridge is haunted by a stray dog who was tied to the tracks by naughty boys. Before they could come back to untie the dog, the train came and decapitated the dog, who can now be heard barking or crying after the midnight train passes on warm spring nights.

7. In Greentown, a man hung himself from a bridge. Every night at midnight he can be seen swinging over the water.

8. A covered bridge on the East Fork of the White River in Williams was the site of a horse and buggy accident that took the life of a child whose body was never found. The ghost of the mother runs through the bridge screaming "Mary!"

9. In another story related to the same bridge in Williams, a woman hung herself from the bridge after her husband left her. As she was dying, her body fell on a wagon passing through the bridge and the driver died of fright. The woman's feet dragging on the top of the car and the screams of the wagon driver can be heard by drivers passing through the bridge in cars. She can be called by going to the bridge at midnight, stopping the car, blinking the lights three times, starting the car again, and driving slowly across.

10. At Spooky Hollow Bridge in Crawfordsville, the ghost of a woman who jumped off the bridge is seen in the form of a blue light. To see the light, drivers can park on the bridge, flash the car lights, honk the horn three times, then turn off the car and the car's lights.

11. In the concrete railroad bridge of Mooresville, a fellow workman cut off the protruding arm of a trapped workman. Now the arm appears and points at midnight: "If it points at you, you will die within three days."

12. On the Screaming Bridge in Dunlapsville, a couple made love on the covered bridge, and the woman got pregnant. The woman did not want the child, so she threw it off the bridge and jumped in herself. Now, parking couples hear the mother ghost at midnight screaming for her child.

13. At the Crying Woman's bridge in Cambridge City, a mother and child died on the bridge. The mother ghost now appears crying "Where is my baby, have you seen my baby?"

14. On the middle bridge of five consecutive bridges in Churubusco, a person with green eyes was killed in an accident. The green eyes can be seen by driving all the way across the five bridges, turning around and going back to the middle bridge, and shutting the motor off. The car will not start afterward.

15. The Bloody Bridge near Earl Park has an ineradicable bloodstain that appears to come up from the floorboards if one sits quietly back on the road from the bridge when the moon is full. This is evidence that people were killed there.

16. At the Zionsville Screaming Bridge, a young girl was killed and decapitated when she and her boyfriend had a car accident on the bridge. The disembodied head comes back to search for the body on nights of the full moon.

Almost as popular as bridge legends are stories related to perils on particular sections of roads, including crossroads, intersections, stretches of highways, country roads, bends, road curves, and railroad crossings. Here are some characteristic examples:

1. In Wakarusa, a young couple was killed in a car wreck on the narrow, winding county road. The girl was killed instantly; the boy's body was never found. The ghost of the boy appears near the edge of the woods on cool, windless nights at about 12:15, and he calls the girl's name, begging forgiveness for causing the accident.

2. In Edwardsville, hoboes always rode the train and jumped off just before the tunnel. One night, the train stopped sixteen miles earlier, and they erroneously jumped over a cliff and were killed. They can be heard screaming every time a train goes over this area of tracks.

3. Outside Swayzee, the ghost of an old lady with a red neckerchief walks a section of track every night. If she takes off the neckerchief, her head will fall off.

4. On a road outside Greentown, the Ku Klux Klan hung seven black men from trees near one stretch of road, in the early 1900s. The sheriff buried the bodies beside the road, and the victims' ghosts can be seen hanging from the trees.

5. In Pleasant Ridge, Moody Lane has mysterious lights. A man killed his wife and her lover, hung the lover in the barn, then burned down the barn. He hung his wife in a tree near the house. The light is the ghost of the killer with his lantern.

6. In Merrillville's Reeder Road railroad crossing, two girls were killed accidentally. Now a ghostly train can be heard blowing its horn, and its headlights are seen at midnight.

7. Bedford's famous Devil's Backbone road was the scene of a car accident

in which the victims, a woman and her children, were killed. They are heard crying at midnight or the woman is seen walking down the road and crying.

8. The Devil's Backbone's best-known legend is about the newlywed couple who were killed when their buggy overturned in a storm or their car crashed. The story is very variable: Sometimes the girl has her accident while the wedding party is waiting at the church, or the couple never arrives.

9. On Medora Road in Bedford, a boy strangled his girlfriend and buried her. Even after stabbing her through the heart, he kept hearing her heartbeat, and he went insane. On the anniversary of her death, a heartbeat can be heard all along the road where she was killed.

10. At the junction of I-465 and I-70, a man supposedly killed his wife, chopped her up, and buried her in what was then a remote area. The roads were later built over the spot. Every year on the anniversary of her death, she can be heard screaming when drivers pass the area.

11. On the road near Koontz Lake a young boy dressed in Levi's and a T-shirt appears on the road and steps in front of cars, but no impact is ever made. No one seems to know the story behind it, but the apparition is well known in the area as "The Phantom."

The above samples should suffice to show the thematic variation of legends that are related to the visiting of death sites. Among the other natural locations, hollows, valleys, rivers, streams, creeks, ponds, and lakeshores abound. Woods (including the single "hanging trees" of victims of suicide and lynching), meadows, hills, falls, and caves also appear as settings but do not show radical deviation from the above basic pattern. Construction sites, parking lots, and boats are also favored locations. Even an abandoned bus, wrecked and left in a deserted area, is known in five story versions — if you drive by, you can hear the screams of dead black or Mexican children who were victimized by racists.

Visitors who are seeking a rite of passage are fascinated by cemeteries, as we have seen already. At many locations, cemeteries are known as the favorite hangouts for youngsters. Nearby graveyards where family members are buried and routinely visited on family timetables are not as interesting to legend seekers; rather, the most popular places of entertainment are the strange, abandoned graveyards with broken grave markers that are found off country roads, in state parks and forests, or even on the outskirts of towns.

The cemetery, as we know, is conceptualized as a city of the dead — a beautiful garden that is a temporary haven and resting place, where residents may interact socially, perhaps like the citizens of Thornton Wilder's Our Town. Mausoleums and even plain tombstones are regarded as spirit residences; according to a Shelbyville account, Hilltop Cemetery's dead residents come to life and play cards in the mausoleum. When a friend of mine who taught grade-school children in Spencer asked her class to write down what they knew about ghosts, several chose to draw pictures of cemeteries with tombstones that showed an index finger pointing up or down, indicating whether the body was in or out. Footprints were also drawn around the graves, and ghosts in sheets hovered above or sat on their headstones, or flew above the trees.

The function of cemeteries in the legend climate is considerably different from other legend locales. Cemetery visitors do not tend to be goal-oriented, ritually prepared audiences seeking reenactments. Rather, the nocturnal cemetery's general climate is what most adventure seekers hope to see and explore. Our survey data indicates that being in a graveyard around midnight in itself provides the desired spooky feeling to satisfy a visitor's expectation. These visitors want to watch the spirit activity during the witching hour at Halloween from a concealed place where they will remain unnoticed.

The dead may react in diverse ways to a curious visitor's friendly or hostile intrusions, as the legends tell us. It is more common to expect that the graveyard challenger who disturbs the slumber of the dead will be punished, as are Stepp Cemetery visitors who dare to sit down on the Warlock Seat. In his March 3, 1990, bluebook exam paper, 22-year-old student Rex Boyle remembered his youthful graveyard visits:

As a boy I visited several haunted cemeteries and found them to be very interesting and exciting. My friends and I would visit these cemeteries usually around midnight when it was pitch dark and there was a mysterious chill in the air. We always visited Bon's cemetery on Halloween night. It is located just outside of Loogootee in the Lost River Township area. The reason this cemetery was so special is because as the legend is told there is a tombstone with a naked lady carved on the front. Her arm is always extended and if you happen to be standing in the direction her hand is pointing, you will die within a years time. Another cemetery my friends and I visited regularly was Mount Pleasant cemetery. This cemetery was definitely unique. The legend of this cemetery is mysterious because it is related to organ music. While visiting this cemetery if you heard the organ playing in the church a bolt of lightning would strike and kill you. I still find these cemeteries to be very interesting and because they provide a cheap form of entertainment. That is the keyword in all of these stories and that is why they continue to be passed on from generation to generation.

As Boyle explains, cemeteries continue to be entertaining diversions. Indeed, flirting with the danger of being killed by the naked dead lady's statue or by the sound of the organ is thrilling—but who knows if this story is a boast or a real test of courage?

It is fair to say that the cemetery is a more complex place to visit than the sites haunted by individual revenants. The lengthy account of a number of

Child's Illustration

Avery night that theres a full moon the man in the grave yard with the Black Tomb stone is supposed to come out and walk around his grave and at 12:oclock you can hear him scream out. HAaaa: .. — --

Child's Story

disparate impressions and visions in Anderson's popular Main Street cemetery speaks for itself (chapter 3). Another informant provides a similarly sketchy story, that "everyone in our area knows," of the Circle Hill Cemetery of Angola, where "a male ghost lays on your car and makes weird noises. He than disappears and leave cats behind." A Palmyra cemetery visitor reports sighting mysterious lights while driving into the cemetery, but provides two disparate interpretations related to the place. In one, a set of twins was lost and their parents shot at the streaks of lights while looking for them; the lights are their souls, who still search for the children with a lantern. In the other, an old man, who was running from children who were harassing him, fell and hit his head; the light is his ghostly lantern. One of our informants from Scottsburg tells about his friend Jack's personal experience in the New Providence Graveyard: Jack had had a car wreck in which his girlfriend was killed; a year and a half later, when he took another girl to the graveyard where his girlfriend had been buried, her ghost appeared to him.

Most of the dead in cemeteries died of natural causes. As the dead in the graves are not necessarily victims of violent deaths, the cemetery is not regarded as the proper place to call on the spirits to reenact their demise in the way that hollows, roads, and bridges are. So we may speculate about where stories about the graves of victims of violence belong in our discussion. For example, visitors are supposed to stomp on Bloody Mary's grave in Tunnell Mill Cemetery in North Vernon to call her up at midnight (see chapter 3). However, the legends told about her are confusing and mixed. According to one, she was murdered by her husband one night when the moon was blood red. In another version, she was a Confederate sympathizer during the Civil War and was so harassed by the townspeople that she went berserk and killed her own child; this legend continues as the stereotypical haunted bridge story — she throws her child over the bridge and now one can hear it crying. Mary is also said to scratch or cut girls like the mirror-witch.

The cemetery is not the gathering place of revenants who individually do their own thing and replay their own tragedies. Generally, because these spirits did not die at the location, they cannot reenact their deaths here. Thus, the cemetery stories lack the evidentiary framework the legend so basically needs.

## In Conclusion

We have to note that a curious, but important series of related questions must remain unanswered. Why are most legends concerned with people who died horrible, violent deaths and less interested in those who died unspectacularly by natural causes? Why are people fascinated by detailed descriptions of the gruesome deaths of total strangers? Isn't it true that people don't care much

Child's Illustration

about the victims, but rather are far more interested in *the manner of their deaths?* We accept and understand that there is a ritual, traditional, culture-specific behavioral complex of telling and acting in this subcultural frame. So how can we explain the great enthusiasm for watching scenes of blood-curdling, morbid personal tragedy? Why is there no attempt to discover why

> At Monroe Forest there is a legend saying that in that forest a woman guards her husband's grave. And there this stump that formed like a chair she set in. They say if you ever sit in that chair a curse will be sent on you to die. Whether this is true or not I don't know. Only time will tell.

Child's Story

these scenes happen, or how they could have been prevented, or how justice could be served?

The legend-trip participants are perfect voyeurs: They are obsessed with seeing the sad sight of the pathetic victim. They want to hear the bloodshed, and see the reenactment of brutal murders, dismemberments, and decapitations. Of course, they play their part as well — they scream as an antiphonal response. Otherwise, the viewer remains calm and uninvolved, having no interest in justice, the punishment of the guilty, the reward of the innocent, or the laying to rest of the dead. Are the visitors gratified and satisfied by seeing the victim imprisoned at the location of the death scene? Do they want to keep the spirits there eternally, so that everyone, including themselves, can see the act again and again by continued visits? Do they never wonder how to stop the spirit's suffering?

As I have already mentioned, these legends — in fact, all incomplete legends in the Indiana corpus — remain incomplete and self-centered compared to their European counterparts. They show no concern with the fate of the dramatis personae; rather, it is the visitor, the voyeur, whose viewpoint is highlighted. It is the narrator's game that is played, and the narrator gets recognition for performing a daring legend-adventure, a ticket to social advancement. The visitor is the main character in the story, not the revenant that is called up. The tragic story remains just a faint and conventional video show.

Thus, in a way, the ritual invocation of the dead is like turning the crank of a jumping jack box or staging a puppet show. Or is a moral warning hidden here somewhere? Is it to be careful, and not to get involved in dangerous pursuits as did these people who lost their lives? Can we prevent death?

No, we cannot. This is why the legend is the most expressive and the most durable folklore genre. It is also the most human-friendly genre among all. Social conditions change, human relationships change, and the great inventions of the twentieth century have made human life longer, healthier, more comfortable, and more enjoyable than ever. But while the medical sciences have found remedies to many epidemics and formerly incurable diseases, others have remained as deadly as ever. New fatal bacteria and viruses continue to attack. Other mass killers — famine, political aggression, and accidents — continue to occur as well. In human experience, some people age and die after a fulfilled life; others get sick, go to war, take daredevil risks, or suffer other kinds of unnatural, premature deaths. We cannot say whether the relative mortality rate of today is significantly reduced.

There is a general — but only tacitly acknowledged — awareness that death is inevitable. In some cultures, sickness and death are tabued themes; they can only be whispered about or referred to euphemistically within the family circle, as was the case among the traditional European bourgeoisie. The children of these cultures are spared from any knowledge of why a beloved relative disappeared from their lives. In other cultures, as in Mexico, dying becomes a cause of celebration; once a year the departed members of the community return symbolically in a spectacular show of Saturnalia (Brandes 1998: 359–380). Peasants anywhere have no choice but to face reality and inform the sick that their days are numbered. Rural children, who are close to nature, are exposed and desensitized to events of death in the community, just as they see births and other natural life-cycle events. Yet folktales spare their audience from the inevitable sad curtainfall. The happy ending of every traditional folktale is the peak of life, when the swineherd becomes the king and marries the princess: "And they lived happily ever after," says the formula. But what happens thirty years later in terms of sickness and disease in the family? Nobody asks. Yet it is on everybody's mind that "Godfather Death" (AT 332) is ready to swing his scythe for a shocking and painful termination of life.

Fear of death is the mystery with which people have to live. It is the "unknowable" that makes people think, philosophize, and create religions, enhanced by arts and poetry to ensure the illusion of avoidance. Humans project their immortality in diverse religious contexts, imagining diverse deities, hierarchies, and structures that their own cultural experience can fill with meaning to make their future in "life after life" palpable. As we have seen, in a composite pedestrian vernacular religion, the living and the dead are only temporarily separated before they together enter the big, happy, and eternal life of immortality. This is what legendary horrors, and the legend's ingredients applied to calendar and life-cycle ritual performances, tell us in their seemingly morbid and frightening formats. The spirits who return are messengers, who tell of and show continuity. Ghost stories, the narratives about encounters with revenants, are the proof that death does not rob people of everything — it is not the end but the opening of a new era, for the dead can return to earth. If they can return, we also will be able to, after we die.

Some folklore genres go out of fashion because they are too attached to the particular historical and social conditions that created them; others, in order to survive, must undergo considerable adjustments and compromises to stay functional. However, I have to restate what I have already stated: the legend genre will always be in fashion, because its concerns address universal and eternal problems — the legend is the conveyor of the hope of immortality.

# Texts, Contextualized and Processed

6.

## Where Does the Legend Begin?

Usually we speak of a legend as an entity. Conversely, we also speak of its composition, traditional motifs, and episodes. More prevalent in discussions are the beliefs incorporated into and surrounded by the legend — the real and assumed knowledge as well as the fears, magic anticipations, hopes, and passions. In Klingenberg, the same devil that was ritually persuaded to leave the tormented sinner during past centuries was also coerced to leave the body of a young pedagogy student in 1978. But just as her predecessors died in Torquemada's time, Anneliese Michel also died at the hands of the pious exorcists because of medical neglect. Ancient priestesses of psi officiated at the seat of the Delphi oracle just as psychics do today; and luck-bringing talismans, crystal balls, divining rods, and magic prayers were common knowledge many centuries before they were advertised in tabloids and sold in occult bookstores. UFOs were also sighted in biblical times just as they are today. Out of these and similar examples, a remarkably limited contingent of old elements are regarded as "eternally human" ideas. The legend-forming, or more accurately, the legend-reconstructing and legend-compiling fantasy generates up-to-date variants in limitless numbers, which are always tailored to current needs. Obviously, the traditionality of motifs and the creation of countless new variants of tradition is not an exclusive characteristic of the legend: The flying carpet is akin to the supersonic aircraft, and the Tower of Babel was built of the same materials as the World Trade Center in New York.

Dictionaries tell us that "a story is an account of some incident or event." What is an *account?* "A statement of facts or events." What is a *statement?* "A recital." "What is a *recital?*" "A story," explains the dictionary,[1] leading us to a dead end. At this point, we reach the fallacy of circular definition, which dictionaries often commit, interpreting the same with the same, leaving the meaning concealed in synonyms. This time, however, the lexical synonym helps us out of the dead end. One synonym given for "recital" is *narrative*, "a relation of words or writing of the particulars of any tradition or event." By "words" I understand "by word of mouth" (orally) or in writing. This definition is either redundant or incomplete. If the story (folkloric or other) can be told *only* in words or in writing, then its inherent nature need not be emphasized. If, however, it can be told *both* in words and in writing, the exclusive mention of these two is unnecessary. But I do not suggest refinement of the dictionary, because from what it states we can infer that the legend is a story that can be told by any means of communication. This shows that the means of the oral (or other) telling does not belong to the essential elements of the legend definition and allows us to recognize this genre on the basis of its inherent attributes. So far, we learned that it is a traditional or nontraditional story that is communicated by someone to someone else in some way.

The legend, as a story, must also have content: "an incident or an event" or "facts of events," as the dictionary spells it out. The content can be told by words or other means; that is, it can be formulated into words. But this formulation is only the condition of telling or writing, whereas the legend can exist before it has been put into words. Thus, here is the question: Is the legend communicable before it is put into words, and then the content becomes text? Or, like a caterpillar wanting to fly like a butterfly, does it have to wait until it grows wings? What are the chances of telling a legend without words?

For example, in my parents' home, a big round loaf of bread was placed on the dinner table; the bottom side was flat and floury, the upper side round and crunchy brown. My mother cut thin slices for all of us children, but my father always got the first crust-covered, thick, still-warm piece. Sometimes someone would mistakenly reverse the loaf, but my mother always turned it over. She was no more superstitious than any other typical, nonsuperstitious person. She never said anything while habitually performing this act, and her facial expression did not change. The reversal of the bread was done regularly as an "indexical sign." This made it clear that what she was doing was important. If the loaf, as I came to understand, was improperly placed on the table, this violation of the rule caused or signaled grave danger: poverty or a death in the family.

I understood the warning and I also followed the rule for a while. But how did my mother know? She probably learned it from somebody, possibly from her mother, as I learned it from her. Beliefs and customs often spread through imitation. We cannot know how long this imitation continued, but it started somehow, sometime, in the far or near past. Someone, somewhere, launched the warning that the bread loaf must be placed with the flat side down. Maybe this person explained "because it brings bad luck" or "because someone will die" for violating this practice. But how did he or she know? Again, it was learned from someone. Here, again, a long or short chain of transmitters must have existed, traceable to the first link, the person who may have heard, "They say that someone put the bread on the wrong side on the table and on the following day . . . " or "I know it from my best friend that the neighbor. . . ." All in all, this never-explained habit of my mother's correction of the wrongly placed bread originated in the unknown past. It appears as a fairly complex imitation belief-legend or memorate preceded by a long chain of witness testimonies. At the time I observed the act, this background no longer had conspicuous traces. Although the observers around the dinner table were not experts in folkloristic semiotic or psychological analysis, they were necessarily aware of the fact that there was such a chain behind the ritual act. That is, my mother, with a simple movement, told an extremely abbreviated, condensed, but perfectly clear legend each time about "Our Daily Bread," which God had provided to feed us and keep us: The bread is sacred; it symbolizes family unity, and thus must be handled respectfully, with care — we kissed the dry, moldy, greenish leftover pieces before throwing them into the trash can.

No matter their length, such stories can be regarded as condensed legends, and according to their function, as *postulated legends*. Such condensed and postulated legends must exist profusely, even if they have not been recognized by their bearers or by folklorists. They are told through major and minor ritual acts and behaviors — expressed through folk medical practices, fertility rites, everyday magic manipulations, and symbolic imitative actions surrounding critical turning points of the life cycle and the calendar year. Indeed, entering the dark alleys of the unconscious mind, we can see that they are manifest in some of the compulsive actions of neurotics.

Where does a legend begin? When can we consider a kernel a legend? It is a question of quantity. Artfulness cannot be a functionally valid and characteristic requirement: A legend remains a legend even if it is incoherent, garbled, or recited by inarticulate people. Short legends, von Sydow's *dite* and *fict*, are also legends. If it contains an epic core — a comprehensive account — without the story being recounted, it is still a legend from the vantage point of individual and social psychology. Body language, a gesture, a grimace, a shoulder shrug, or any kind of signifying behavior can be substituted for the parole. An action can comprise a fabulate, a concentration of component elements: If a possessed man points in the direction where he beholds an apparition, his companions or followers will be aware of the sight, be it a spirit, an angel, or the Virgin Mary. Which of these apparitions is present will be clarified by the context. From his own viewpoint, the visionary saw a legend; if his companion mentions to others that "Jack saw something in the bush," this comment is the germ of a legend — or, in fact, *is* a legend. It is an embryonic legend — imperfect and maybe ephemeral — but functionally it is a legend.

Just from observing the daily media, we can see that miracles populate the world, and they increase by leaps and bounds. We are not even surprised by the frequency of miracle legends anymore. Long ago they left the confines of Sunday church services and the religious education of children, and now daily papers, magazines, and electronic audio-visual communications from cyberspace inform us that divine interventions multiply on the planet Earth. Marking the geographic locations of the saint apparitions that become cult sites and generate miracle-legends would be worthwhile for tracking the environmental conditions or other local causes that are behind their occurrence. Such a directory would be of interest to ethnographers who are willing to observe local legend formation in emergence. The life history of legends — from birth to decline, through death, transformation, latency, rebirth, and so on — would give us an idea of the constituencies and the total extent of the legend, as contextualized by systems of belief and unbelief, by ritual and magical acts, by social, political, and economic life, and by consumers and tourists.

I did not succeed even in the modest undertaking of mapping the haunted houses of the state of Indiana, and I lost hope that such a large, ambitious project could succeed because of the elusiveness and unpredictability of the relationship of ingredients that make the legend a legend. Here is an example to illustrate the significance of local conditions, relationships, coincidences, and seemingly trivial, minor elements within the complex of a miracle legend.

In 1979, I had the opportunity to observe a legend in the making at a new miracle site in Eisenberg an der Raab in Austria, located in the triangle of land that is bordered by Hungary and Yugoslavia. By the time of my visit, the place had become a magnet for anyone seeking consolation and help that no one else could give. Here the promise that "who seeks will find, who knocks will be asked in, will be realised" (Pinsker 1976: 3). What was it that made this small, obscure village into the Mecca of thousands of pilgrims from Germany, Austria, and Switzerland?

Sandwiched between Tito's Yugoslavia and Soviet satellite Hungary, and separated from both by a no-man's-land of barbed wire fences and minefields, Eisenberg's pious people saw their community as a symbol of peaceful tranquility, protected by the Lord from Communist invasion. Awakened often by gunshots, barking dogs, explosions, and the screams of victims who had tried to scale the fence, the people of Eisenberg knew what was going on and gave shelter to lucky escapees. On October 23, 1956, Hungarian revolutionaries briefly opened the Iron Curtain to let 200,000 people escape from the invading Soviet army into friendly Austria and farther out into the free world. It was only a short-lived victory, as the Curtain sealed again on November 4, 1956, when the Communists again seized power and restored the status quo by mass-executions, torture, and the jailing of the freedom fighters.

Forty-six days later, on the morning of December 6, 1956, Frau Aloisia Lex, a peasant woman in her seventies and mother of eleven children, encountered the bleeding, thorn-crowned, life-size Jesus Christ. Later, at 3 P.M., when she went to the garden to feed her pigs, she found a cross burned into the grass. Previously, in 1954 and 1955, Frau Lex's youngest daughter, Anne-Marie, had also had visions but had been ridiculed and called a liar by the neighbors and children in school. Now, enclosed by a wrought iron fence and surrounded by flowers, Frau Lex's scorched grass cross had become a cult site, a destination of pilgrims. In spite of some people raising eyebrows over this family's spirituality, soon pilgrims guided by prophetic dreams arrived to worship at the site of the cross, and began to experience miraculous healings. As Pope Paul VI endorsed the divine origin of many personally experienced and documented medical wonders, the Roman Catholic Church allowed the collection and the publication of testimonial stories to be sold at the cult place (Machac 1972; Maller 1971). The pilgrims sent their stories in private letters, wrote them down in the guest book, or told them orally.

Frau Lex's remodeled home became a clearing house of legends. This center of devotion and worship accommodated large crowds, and sold religious jewelry, postcards, slides, and legend collections; and the presence of the radiant holy woman in itself became the source of new miracle legends. She was somewhat nervous when I interviewed her, with my tape recorder in hand. "I don't feel well, I am too weak to talk," she apologized. But then, as she responded to questions, I was able to fill half of a ninety-minute cassette tape with her personal testimonies.

The whole village benefited from the miracle — the streets were paved and equipped with stylish candelabra lampposts, public buildings were renovated, and luxury hotels and motels were built for the affluent West European pilgrims. But while incurable diseases were being cured by prayer at the cross on Frau Lex's lawn and orally exchanged and dispensed legends were authenticated by clergymen and public notaries, the voice of the local folk provided the legend dialectics. Gathered at the local pubs, gossip mongers scorned the cheap merchandise for tourists and dismissed the miracles as lies, hallucinations, even fads.

But, I asked, who was crazy in this deeply devoted, church-attending family? A local grade-school teacher led me to the house of the saintly woman's younger sister: Two streets away from the Lex showplace, the sister's shingle-roofed, mud-walled house sat in hopeless disrepair — without a lawn, flowers, or cultivated vegetable garden, with the whitewash peeling from the wall facing the street. Of the three windows in view, one had a broken wooden frame molding, and the other two were decorated with bright red, blue, yellow, and green ornamental paint. To the right and to the left of the windows, human and animal figures that looked like drawings by children had been painted on the wall. "She is being tormented by evil spirits," my guide explained. "The poor, mentally imbalanced girl is under treatment. She believes if she imitates evil spirits trying to enter the house by illustration, the real ones will go away and leave her alone." This act of avoidance magic is a well-known practice, and appears in many forms throughout the region. People will place a broom in front of the door or put out a sign such as "Susie is not home" to send the evil away. The picture drawings on the house were the ostensive telling of a legend.

In the case of the Eisenberg legend complex, the drawings on the sister's house appear as the negative counterpoint in the legend's dialectics, a comment that would have stayed hidden had I not talked to the villagers while trying to place the miracle legend into its situational context. Distant as it is from the main statement of the legend, it appears as a part of the debate that fuels the legend and makes the cult manifested by the miracle legend prosper.

A reference that calls to mind a whole legend or even a cycle of legends can also be viewed as a legend communication. But isn't a legend a text? A reference to a legend *is* exactly the recollection of a text. The novel on the bookshelf is still a novel, even if no one reads it; Beethoven's piano concerto on a CD is a musical composition, even if the CD is not played. But these examples are not adequately tangible. Take, for example, a mention of *Le Père Goriot* in conversation; no one would remember the entire text of Balzac's bulky novel as a whole, in all its details. The mention of a well-known, simple, short legend, on the other hand, would recall the whole story immediately to the listener. Furthermore, the listener would remember not only *one* legend, but many more. All similar legends possibly would line up in memory simultaneously, or one might be recalled after the other — each one attracting the next, and the next, and the next. Personal and communal legend repertoires consist of such safe deposits: An allusion, a keyword, a *Reizwort* (a word that stimulates) from a legend can bring up many materials from memory storage. The process is not unlike the scene in Maurice Maeterlinck's allegorical fantasy *L'Oiseau Bleu* (1908) in which lifeless, subterranean shades regain their human shapes when someone remembers them.

Are these "dormant" legends? Not really. Rather, they are legends that are known but out of fashion, which are resuscitated from latency by, for instance, a tabloid report. It is quite common that a new legend or an allusion will bring one or several old legends back into circulation. Notably, among all the genres of folklore, the legend treats its text as its least important component — instead, it foregrounds the communication of its statement as most important.

Frau Lex standing in front of her house near a tree
where saints appeared

Whatever form this statement takes, it is subject to eventual alterations when individuals and groups make their choices in expressing their views about the essential meanings surrounding the text. The liberty of making choices is a *Leitfaden,* or guide, to legend communication.

## The Creative Process of Legend Transmission and the Freedom of Choice

Many years ago, Vázsonyi and I departed from the purely theoretical and entered the realm of the practical, with experimentation to explore the ways that legends are transmitted and varied. The conclusion of these studies was the

Souvenir Postcard

Frau Lex's Sister's House: The window is framed by figures
painted to deter evil spirits

"multi-conduit hypothesis" (see Dégh and Vázsonyi 1975). In this study, we chose to reexamine the best-known, most controversial folkloristic experiment ever performed, the "volkskundliches Experiment" of Walter Anderson, a tireless polemicist who had been much respected and feared among folklore scholars of his time. This old Estonian master of the Finnish school was so impressed by his experiments in the chain transmission of stories that he declared his result a "law," not a hypothesis (Anderson 1951). Our intention from the outset was not so much to repeat Anderson's experiments, but rather to scrutinize the unintended results of them, the consequential mistakes. To do this, we had to perform a penetrating analysis not only of Anderson's own allegations, but also of his critics' rebuttals. What we learned led to our conclusion that the experiment, in spite of — or perhaps because of — its spectacular layout, did not seem sufficiently convincing to prove Anderson's theses. However, we were persuaded by the evidence that his mistakes confirmed the existence of certain important regularities. After so many years, it is still worthwhile for current practitioners of the discipline of folkloristics to discuss Anderson's theses, and to continue to check their feasibility and acceptability, both practically and theoretically.

Anderson first began to consider the transmission process in his monographic study of the novella tale "The Emperor and the Abbot" (AT 922; Anderson 1923). In this work, Anderson explained that the "unbelievable stability" of this widespread popular anecdote could be attributed to the condition that each informant had heard it several times, from several people, in several versions. He believed that this repetition caused the integration and homogenization of a stable normative form of the text, a process he called the "law of self-correction." Anderson had a deep conviction of the overall validity of his "law," and wanted to prove his self-correction thesis with the same argument that he used to explain the stability of folktales (Anderson 1935). Thus, much later, in 1951, Anderson developed a systematic laboratory experiment, using three transmission chains of narrators, to discover the regularities of the creative processes of transmission of folk narratives. He had hoped that, by the use of artificially set up teams of transmitters, the performance would give an idea of the tendencies of variation and stabilization, thus providing insight into the process that, under normal conditions, would take the lifetimes of generations of narrators to observe.

We can briefly summarize Anderson's folkloristic experiment, which he designed under the influence of one of Bartlett's tests of remembering (Bartlett 1920, 1932; El-Shamy 1967: 21–26). In 1947 at the University of Kiel, where he was a professor of folklore, Anderson constructed three chains, each consisting of twelve students. He read a brief, 246-word, Pomeranian devil legend to the first three students in each chain, and had these students write the legend down the next day. They in turn read their text to the second member of their sequence, who read his version to a third student, and so on; in this fashion, the story moved from person to person until the modified text arrived at the twelfth member of each of the three chains. In accordance with his theory, Anderson designed the experiment so that the members of the experimental chain would hear the given narrative only once. Anderson observed that "step by step, the text degenerated and the three final products . . . resembled each other and the original text only in the most general way" (Anderson 1956: 3–5). He felt this proved that "the extraordinary stability of folk narratives is explained by the fact that (in the natural context) every narrator had heard the respective Märchen from his predecessor, as a rule, not once but several times"; and that "as a rule, he has heard it not from one single person but from a whole group of persons." He believed that the results demonstrated his "law": Individuals who had heard a story only once from only one individual cannot provide a sound retelling—as the story is passed on, the text degenerates and eventually disintegrates.

In response to his critics, Anderson reaffirmed his findings in 1956 and the discussion brought the complex problem of transmission and dissemination (variation and stabilization, survival and revival, tradition, innovation, and devolution) into the focus of European and American folklorists (Dundes 1969; El-Shamy 1967; Ortutay 1958). During the 1950s and 1960s, enthusiastic folklorists repeated Anderson's experiments with the participation of their students; some made slight modifications in the procedure and in their choice of special age or social groups, others simply repeated Anderson's scheme. Remarkably, in spite of its striking methodological and logical errors, this experiment has been carried out by innumerable other folklore scholars and is still performed sporadically at diverse university departments (Oring 1978; Röhrich 1969b: 131–132). And, unsurprisingly, the results of each experiment are very much the same as Anderson's, which proves little more than that identical experiments under identical conditions only can bring—again and again— identical results. In 1992, a proposition was made to apply Anderson's originally legend-oriented experiment to other types of narratives as well as to other folklore genres (Hiemäe and Krikmann 1992). Up to the present, neither Anderson's law of self-correction nor the construction of transmission chains has lost its appeal to students who are exploring the creative processes of folklore transmission. It remains basic to the approach of folklorists to folklore.

Although this folklore experiment has been valuable for making people ponder the process of transmission, it does not carry enough weight to promote an unsubstantiated supposition. For example, from the time that the legendary apple fell on the head of Sir Isaac Newton and he was inspired to establish his law of gravitation, physicists have had no scientifically acceptable reason to stretch themselves under apple trees and wait for more apples to fall, unless they were interested in the supposition that diverse apple species react diversely to the mass of the earth. A friend of Newton stated that he was an eyewitness to the fall of the apple (Stukeley 1752: 98), but Sir Isaac and his followers regarded the incident as an irrelevant anecdote, a conjecture to start a trend of thoughts. It was an exemplum to illustrate a theory, not the proof of it, so physicists have refrained from wasting their time and money on trying to study gravity by intentionally dropping scores of china soup tureens.

In the same manner, it should be clear in the case of chain transmission that an experiment carried out on the same material, under the same conditions, can bring only the same result. But even the description of the result was incorrect, as was the conclusion. How many times an individual narrator repeats a text *does* matter; however, to blame distortion on the lack of an individual's repetition is negligent, as only some transmitters — not *all* transmitters — distort it. And because each distorted text creates an entirely different condition, the experiment will consist of numerous experiments, all separate and incomparable with each other. In essence, the result is a chain of separate experiments without a common denominator. Only one thing can be ascertained with accuracy: Some necessary conditions — including repetition — are missing; and, conversely, some conditions exist that are not needed. Thus, it is not proven, and cannot be proven, that repetition is the only or the most vital aspect of transmission; so self-correction is not a "law," but rather is merely a hypothesis at best.

Anderson did not prove that *"repetitio est mater studiorum"* (Anderson 1923: 399) in a positive sense; he only illustrated that in a situation where narrators could not indulge in repetition, certain distortions were likely to happen. The deviations — the quantity and quality of the distortions — were not taken into consideration by the experimenters. As El-Shamy observed, instead of studying the positive aspect of self-correction of the transmitted text, Anderson "turned to negative aspects of the folklore process, such as forgetting and change, without ever trying to prove his original assertion that stability in folk narrative relies on repetition" (El-Shamy 1967: 26). Thus, because the methods are familiar, the results expectable, and the frequentation secured, those who imitate Anderson and repeat his test look less like scientists than like organizers of demolition derbies.

In 1975 Vázsonyi and I discussed the fallacies of this experiment in order to suggest new solutions, liberating the text of the folk from doctrinaire manipulation. Anderson and his critics never brought up the question of voluntariness and freedom of choice: "the members of the transmission sequence did not *volunteer* to narrate, and were not given the *freedom of choice*." The distinction is crucial, for "without these two features of normal tradition, tale transmission cannot materialize" (Dégh and Vázsonyi 1975: 243). To us, this observation was a simple, self-evident fact. In the natural context, the participants in a folklore event enjoy the freedom of choice; narrators decide whether to participate in the performance, and choose the material to perform. We did not think this observation needed proof; however, Oring, without being a supporter of Anderson's postulate of "self-correction," expressed his opinion that instead of freedom (or, as he mistakenly referred to our denotation, "complete freedom" or "total freedom") only "certain freedom" "should be given to participants of the experiment" (Oring 1978: 200).

The problem of "total" or "complete" freedom, along with "certain" freedom, must be clarified: How much choice does folklore transmission require and permit? First of all, I am ready to admit that participants do not have "total" or "complete" freedom of choice in either the natural or the experimental situations; the questionable and pretentious qualifiers "total" and "complete" do not come from our vocabulary — we did not use them in the past, and will not use them in the future either. Nor will I use the cautious qualifier "certain freedoms" as Oring recommended; it would not be possible to know whether the implied limitation, whose nature and extent we cannot predict, does not contradict the concept of freedom necessary to the processing of folklore. I am comfortable using the unqualified term *freedom*, without any attribute or allusion to theories borrowed from other disciplines that seek answers to their intrinsically formulated questions of how free is free, and how total is total. The freedom of people who participate in spontaneous, non-laboratory folklore communication is sufficiently well defined in terms of common sense.

Oring wrote, without revealing the reason for his doubt, that "it is more surmised than demonstrated that such complete freedom exists in the natural environment" (Oring 1978: 200). It seems safe to me to assume that, although narrators do not commit "totally free," unmotivated *actes gratuites*[2] (after all, they are acting under the influence of their sociocultural environment), they are indeed virtually free. At least, they must feel so. No immediate outside pressure forces them to take part in or abstain from a folklore activity. They make choices based on their own motivations, and they do whatever they feel is necessary in the processing of folklore. Actually, it is hard to imagine how someone could be coerced into being a communicator of folklore in its natural context. Certainly there may be exceptional situations — for example, the witty princess Shahrazad was compelled to tell tales to her sultan through 1,001 nights in order to stay alive. Nevertheless, she was free to make her choice to do so!

It is, however, not so much surmised as it is demonstrated that the lack of ("complete") freedom — or, in other words, the presence of coercion — distorts the folklore process. As I have mentioned before, we have found Anderson's chain transmission experiment *a contrario* to be extremely useful, because not only "total" freedom but even "some" freedom was denied its participants, and almost all possible coercion imaginable in relation to folklore transmission was in operation. Consequently, anyone who wants to investigate the meaning and significance of voluntariness and freedom of choice in the performance of folklore cannot do better than to begin at the beginning, and return to Anderson's experiment. Anderson's target was the transformational process of a legend, but his narrow "volkskundliches Experiment" viewpoint left crucial questions unheeded; we have to move on and explore the problem of choice in general terms, focusing on the transmission of folklore, the problem addressed by many but to the satisfaction of none.

Once, I thought of choice as a minimal folklore-act in itself, and wrote, "the freedom of choice is the selection of an item and its elements; it is not only an indispensable condition of storytelling as an act of artistry; it is also an inherent part of it" (Dégh and Vázsonyi 1975: 246). It may happen that, after concluding my current considerations, a modification will be in order: "Not only is choice an inherent part of it, but it is the very essence that folklore cannot exist without." It may also happen that I will conclude that *folklore is choice*, or even perhaps that *choice is folklore*. However, instead of contemplating whether there is or should be free choice in the folklore process, revitalization of the subject matter — the creative process of folklore transmission with particular emphasis on legend narration — is a challenging task.

Our 1975 criticism of the experiment of Anderson and his followers need not be repeated here in great detail; it is sufficient to show how his trend of thought was the result of a series of well-meant fallacies. In addition to the joy of making an argument, it is my sincere hope that revisiting the topic will open the opportunity to examine the meaning and significance of voluntariness and freedom of choice in folklore. Like before, we will consider Anderson's theorem as a very helpful contrast in the development of our multiconduit hypothesis.

## The Truth, and Nothing but the Truth

The American court oath requires that those who furnish evidence must declare that in addition to "the truth" they also will tell "the whole truth" and "nothing but the truth." Let us see if, tested against this three-step formula, Anderson's experiment and its appended reasoning satisfy our expectation of finding the true nature of the legend.

### The Truth

Is it true that "step by step, the text degenerates rapidly" ("*Stufe zu Stufe*," Anderson 1956: 5)? "Step by step" indicates moderately spaced, regularly repeated movements, divided into sections. The size and the speed of this periodically interrupted progress would be more or less even. There would be no jumps, no breaks into a run, and no sudden balking. In other words, progress would be gradual and even. Nevertheless, the interim results of the Anderson experiment indicate that "step by step" by no means characterizes the changes; the moves would be better described as "unexpected," "rhapsodic," "uneven," or "abrupt." We will see that this stylistic difference means a salient theoretical difference.

The first six participants in Anderson's experimental chain transmitted faithfully that the hero of the legend, a wealthy nobleman, had led a life of sin and seduced girls. The seventh, however, made a mistake. For some unknown reason, he had completely changed the character of the villain. He stated that the baron's "only joy was playing the flute." Thus, it is no surprise that from here on the motifs of "life of sin" and "seducing girls" were completely eliminated from the ten to twelve ensuing variants. This change also strongly altered the whole story: Rather than being a vicious womanizer, the baron now appeared as a pious music lover who was tempted by a beautiful seductress, herself a devil incarnate, to commit a sin. Under such circumstances it would be difficult to understand why the meek flutist had to repent—he did not commit any sin. This is why the sin motif was dropped by almost all of the later members of that chain; almost all new variants change "repenting" to "prayer of gratitude" for deliverance.

Who is to be blamed for the distortion of the story? We can catch the culprit: Narrator number 7 inserted the flute motif into the legend. But why did he do it? He certainly must have had a reason, something that was characteristic of his personality. Had this personal reason been absent or the sequence of transmitters different (that is, had someone different taken the place of number 7), the passionate sexual drive of the nobleman would not have been substituted by a love for playing the flute. Without this deviation, the story probably would not have undergone essential changes throughout its total course.

At this point, Anderson, the executor and interpreter of the experiment, stood very close to discovering the folk in folklore, and the individual in the folk. Instead, he blamed Bartlett's memory tests for the shortcomings of his experiment because Bartlett had failed to perform parallel comparative examinations on parallel running tradition sequences. Had he done so, according to Anderson, he would have noticed that "one and the same narrative develops diversely in diverse tradition-chains under the influence of chance factors" (1951: 5). At this point it was almost impossible to avoid the idea that diverse modifications are caused by diverse conditions, which would not be proper to attribute to mere chance without a thorough examination. Had Anderson not abstained from the consideration of individuals, and had looked into the re-

413

search results of contemporary psychologists, the necessary modifications in his experiment could have led to the clarification of a number of problems. Inadvertently, one remembers the "*se non e vero*" anecdote pertaining to a nineteenth-century event at a Paris photo laboratory. The lab director, on discovering that plates packed in light-proof conditions had turned brown in the proximity of certain sample bedrocks, simply ordered that the plates be kept elsewhere in the future. By not investigating this phenomenon further, he surrendered the discovery of radioactivity to his successor, Henri Becquerel.

Many anecdotal examples could be quoted from Anderson's study, but instead I have chosen a shorter one that is characteristic of more recent experiments. Clements examined the single-chain progress of what he called a "humorous anti-legend" (1969b). This parody of a horror story is a negative rendition of a classic haunted house legend (Baughman E538.1. Spectral coffin). In this story, a coffin appears in a house and floats up the stairs into a central room. The residents are terrorized and fall into despair until Mr. Vicks, the cough drop manufacturer, comes to the rescue: His interference, by taking a cough drop, makes the coffin (coughin') stop and float out of the room, to the relief of all present. However, the second member of this chain killed the punchline by substituting the synonymous word "casket" for "coffin"; thus, he not only killed the "anti-legend" quality of the legend, but robbed the story's victims of their miraculous rescue. Oring reported this bungling (1978: 194), noting that the third member of the transmission chain "when called upon to relate the narrative found it rather 'pointless'." The culprit was reteller number 2: Had he not destroyed the punchline, the story might have traveled through a very long chain to its end, perhaps without any degeneration, or even, as often happens with jokes, with improvements. Who knows?

We should remember the rule that a chain is only as strong as its weakest link — if that link breaks, it renders the chain useless. One single mistake in the chain of transmission can change, or indeed completely stop, the entire folklore process. In its natural context, the coffin/coughin'/casket story, for example, would have been stranded and then sunk by profound narrator disinterest, because people seldom forward stories they find pointless.[3] This brings us to the important point: In this situation, "step by step" does not apply. This experiment has proven that texts narrated from person to person — whether in a chain-like laboratory setup or possibly in a natural context — will change, deteriorate, or improve, assume new shapes, extent, and significance, and gain overt and covert meanings by no means in measured steps, but rather by leaps and bounds. This movement is clearly observable, and is not without reason. I regard this as precious evidence, more generally, of the significance of *choice* in folklore.

The Whole Truth

Clearly, Anderson and his followers would believe that no matter what causes the variation of the text, the law of self-correction, sooner or later, stops the oscillation and helps it back to the *Normalform* (Anderson 1951: 56). Is this the whole truth? Can it be true that a part of folklore products owe their "remarkable stability" to the condition that individuals have heard them not once but several times? No doubt the principle *"repetitio mater studeorum,"* cited above, is still valid. Everybody who has studied for an exam knows that reading something twice gives one a better chance of remembering the material than reading it only once. And yet there are exceptions. Bîrlea, for example, wrote that Romanian storytellers told him that they had learned almost all of their stories, long or short, after hearing them only once. He even quotes a narrator who stated explicitly that a second hearing would confuse his memory (Bîrlea 1973: 459). Thus, some outstanding folk prose narrators have a remarkable capacity of recall, especially those who know two or several hundred separate prose stories (Faragó 1971).

Late in the summer of 1998, I learned about the incredible memory storage of storytellers among the Scottish traveler clans. During my visit to his home, Duncan Williamson, doyen of his ranks, told me that he is a "collector" — he has learned tales from his peers all his life, has never forgotten anything he has learned, and he keeps learning wherever he travels. He picks what he needs from his ever-growing repertoire to satisfy the particular audience he is going to face. He is active in three roles: as a traditional storyteller in his natural environment, as a seasoned international festival performer, and as an educational entertainer of urban and rural schoolchildren. How many stories does he know? He told me he knew "a couple of thousand." We also know that epic singers such as Gopala Naika from southern Karnataka, India, can recite poems by heart over six days that are the length of Homer's *Iliad* (Honko et al. 1998). Indeed, this feat is at least as "remarkable" as the stability of their stories.

Of course, I mention outstanding, not average, performers who have an excellent capacity of remembering; however, their extraordinary memory makes it feasible that performers of folklore do not necessarily require or tolerate "self-correction." We must realize that the texts that Anderson used in his experiments were simple stories — they were only about thirty lines long, and took four or five minutes to recite. The texts deteriorated in Anderson's three transmission chains, as did the texts in other experiments set up and repeated according to the same guidelines. Anderson attributed the deterioration of the text in the course of traditionalization to the *"Einquellenprinzip"* (single source principle) in the sense that every member of the chain heard the story only once. What he means by this is that, had these individuals heard the story more than once, they would have learned it.

The statement hidden within Anderson's explanation is that the essentials of a simple story of about thirty lines cannot be memorized without several repetitions and repeated "superorganic" tutoring over twenty-four hours. This is an obvious fallacy. With reference to anyone's personal experience, within such a short amount of time, forgetting such stories is (that is, their essence, not the exact words) is more difficult than remembering them. What was revealed by the experiment then? It showed that certain people, under certain circumstances, at a certain occasion, reproduced a certain text differently from its original. This is the truth, the whole truth. The story, the people, the circumstances, and the occasion are all variables. Thus, the outcome of the narrative performance is a question with many unknown quantities—and without an unambiguous solution.

But something is missing from the whole truth. Although Anderson spoke in general about the unusual stability of folk narratives, he believed that his statements were pertinent to all kinds of folk traditions. He doesn't say that some, or even numerous, folk narratives or folk traditions are stable (which is obviously true), but that *all* are, without exception. Stable folklore? This is an absurd vision of a petrified world. Missing are the traditions we consider folklore because they vary; because they are parts of the personal and the social life of people, they accommodate to human needs. Under our very eyes they are born and shaped, float and circulate, break into pieces and reassemble, dwindle and perish, and finally come back to life in renewed, more satisfying forms. It is not only the remarkably stable, large, and attractive stars that belong to the cosmos of folklore; the planet-like, ephemeral variants do as well, including lonesome motifs, errant episodes, punchlines that have lost their connection, sayings that have detached from their original base, beliefs and traditions and shreds of remembering, shades of visions, sudden explosions of legends, rumors that erupt and decline, and anecdotes, jokes, riddles, and improvisations. All of these, and many more, appear and appeal to people in our world, as individuals and as groups.

If there is any law these forms abide by, it is certainly not an inorganic law of self-correction. If the human eye is capable of following their course at all, they seem to be remarkably unstable. And anyone who professes to tell the whole truth should not forget about them.

## Nothing but the Truth

One of the simplest rules of formal deductive reasoning is that if one of the premises in a syllogism is particular, the conclusion too will be particular. And if two propositions are particular, no useful conclusion can be drawn. We see here two facts proven on the basis of Anderson's experiment:

A. Certain people, under certain conditions, on a certain occasion, re-produced certain texts in a form that deviated from the original.

B. In the natural context, a part of folk traditions is remarkably stable.

Since both of the above propositions are particular, hardly any usable conclusion can be drawn. However, in this form the conclusion is ours. So, let us return to the theories of Anderson and try to assist his reasoning to come up with a conclusion. In essence, Anderson made these statements:

A1. During the experiment, in several cases when members of the tradition chain heard stories (legends) only once (*"Einquellenprinzip"*), the story considerably deviated from the original during the process of retelling.

B1. In normal context where the storytellers hear the story more often (*"Mehrquellenprinzip"*), such deviations do not occur.

These two points bring Anderson to the following conclusion:

C1. Folk traditions owe their stability to the condition that narrators hear them more than once (the "law of self-correction").

This is the largest fallacy of them all. The first statement, A1, obviously only pertains to a limited number of cases, because they repeated the experience only a limited number of times. It is therefore not universal but particular. To simplify this debate, we should acknowledge that it seems likely, even probable, that the same experience could have taken place in other situations as well. But possibility and probability differ from certainty.

Statement B1 also contains some underlying limitations; it does not, and cannot, state that the artificial laboratory situation only differs from real life in that narrators in a natural context hear a tradition from more than one source. Obviously this is not the only difference, but the theory does attribute considerable impact to the multiple source. Are there other undeterminable causes among which the multiple source principle is one?

Avoiding all of the fallacies, the ultimate conclusion would thus sound as follows:

C1. Folk traditions owe their stability either to the narrators hearing the text multiple times, or to other causes which may or may not include the multiple source.

Admittedly, for a "law" this seems somewhat uncertain, and is more like a hypothesis or a point of departure than it is the conclusion of an analysis. To acquire certainty, one would need to perform another identical experiment situated within the natural context. But that would not be an experiment any-more — it would be real life.

Anderson also responded to other criticisms of his position. Why did he use students in his experiment? Because they are supposed to be good at memoriz-ing and remembering. Why did he want them to write their story down instead of reciting it orally? Because he believed literacy is better than orality. How-ever, the main problem is that Anderson — and most of his critics — polem-icize about questions of *mechanisms* related to the technique of transmission. No one addresses the circumstances that facilitate or impede transmission, and there is no mention of the *content* of the material to be transmitted, or the *purpose* of its conveyance. A comparable situation would be if someone were to argue that the persistence of Goethe's *Faust* can be attributed to its author writing it on durable paper. So this is also a matter of truth, but is quite a distance from the whole truth.

The survival of folklore materials in stable or other conditions depends more on internal causes inherent in their content than it does on the mere techniques of their transmission. Doubtless, most folklore materials — the tales and legends in particular — do contain messages, whether they are stable or variable, that are important to humankind. Without denying the commitment of a logical mistake, I dare to answer this question: How can we know that these messages are important? We know it from the very fact that they have survived.

## Choice within the Multi-Conduit System

According to the multi-conduit theory that Vázsonyi and I developed in 1971, folklore messages do not ramble erratically from one person to another, but follow definite destinations in society. These lines — which we call "con-duits" — are communicative sequences of individuals who have similar per-sonality characteristics and inherent frames of reference. These frames are built from sets of social impulses, such as advertising, peer group pressure, fashion, beliefs, and fears, all of which persuade the participants to conformity in responding to information. Because they share similar attitudes toward sim-ilar messages, these individuals qualify as senders and receivers within this particular communication system.

Our experiments have clearly shown that different types of people in an audience exhibit selective attention and perception — that is, they select and interpret the contents of mass communication in widely varying ways. When a message travels through the adequate conduit — leading from a person who is willing to tell, to a person who is ready to accept the message in its original form — it remains practically unaltered. When, however, a message reaches an inappropriate person — one who refuses to listen to a text that he or she finds uninteresting or perhaps repulsive — it will discontinue; the message either comes to a dead end, or continues onward only after undergoing minor or major modifications. This is the origin of deviations from the original text — and from the original destinations. The changed message proceeds down another, fitting conduit, which leads to a person receptive to the altered message. The modification may consist merely of a change of perception, such as a narrator's joke being transformed into a legend; then the next transmitter may give the material a new twist and return to its roots, back to being a joke. Conduits that are suited to carrying major complexes of essentially similar messages (such as, for example, a märchen or a specific set of related märchen types) often divide into sub-conduits or micro-conduits that single out and convey diverse subtypes, clusters, episodes, motifs, or even disintegrated particles of the whole to individuals of adequate receptivity. The existence of the multi-conduit system — which is not only theorized but also is fairly well-documented in experimental situations — might contribute to the survival and the "remarkable stability" of folklore forms.

We are getting closer to the understanding of when and how variants are generated, and how "affinities" (Ortutay 1959) develop in certain phases of the process of aggregation of loose, single elements into new types. The conduit theory may also help us with this puzzle: How do individuals satisfy their special preferences through serviceable conduits, and how do performers become real specialists in particular species of folklore (magic tales, ghost stories, riddles, jokes, etc.) and create their personal repertoires? Marina Takalo, the Finnish folklore performer, for example, learned different genres from different specialists (Pentikäinen 1978).

Folklore as a discipline reached its maturity when it was weaned from its romantic nationalistic roots. When scholars refrained from constructing imaginary communities with imaginary communal artistic production and stopped catering to the political ambitions of nations, they began to discover real people's real creativity. But we cannot set a date when the enchantment with the superior art of the rustic folk was definitely replaced by serious scholarship, because modern booksellers and publishers continue to shun the rich authentic texts of present day people which are collected by academic authors. Instead, they still prefer to market the older classics and newer folklore collections that have been rewritten by their collectors and editors. The general readership deserves to be enlightened about the anachronistic presentation of its lore.

Field ethnography, particularly since World War II, has opened new vistas. Scholars have succeeded in accumulating well-researched, scientifically observed data. There now is plenty to transcribe and analyze, and upon this

419

material can be built methods and theories representing the social reality of modern times concerning folklore, its genres, its performers, and their performances. Our research based on field collections has shown that it is not the communal genius of "the folk" that emanates lore, but rather it is individuals, in the capacity of personal creativity, who play the important role in transmitting folklore. Addressers and addressees[4] negotiate the message that is the key to the formation of folklore conduits between senders and receivers.

The terms *sender* and *receiver* — to borrow the vocabulary of the postal service and its clientele — suggest a certain activity on the part of the "sender" as initiator, and passivity on the side of the "receiver." However, in folklore the role of the receiver might be considered to be almost as active as that of the sender. The senders select and send the messages that appeal to them in anticipation that the message will also appeal to the receivers; and the receivers obtain what they ordered. But in folklore communication, the receiver has a more important role. To continue with the postal service metaphor, the relationship of the folklore sender and receiver can best be compared to the mail chute: The conduit does not so much push as it does suck the messages along the tube. Likewise, in the conceptual conduit of folklore transmission, the main driving force is the receiver's expectation. But the receivers, who deserve to be called the addressees, have the right to refuse any message addressed to them: "Not Accepted." And they also have the right to accept but not to forward the message, thereby inactivating that branch of the conduit. The media selects its messages haphazardly, on the basis of a superficial knowledge of senders; so the major task — the fine choice — belongs to the receivers.

Thus, the folklore process is one of interaction. When viewed from the side of the person who has ordered the message, reception cannot be regarded as a simple, mechanical act but rather as signifying the fulfillment of a need.

In his book on the inner world of choice, F. G. Wickes uses a Hebrew saying as his motto: "Man was created for the sake of choice" (1963). The language of choice (or language as choice?) is one of the oldest human responses. This pertains to all behaviors because everything is equal with itself, and unequal with anything else. The human life-span consists of sets divided by subsets of choices made every minute of our life. Every action to be taken is preceded by the contemplation of alternatives as we ponder the chances before deciding which way to go. This makes choice basic to human mentality — a part of everyday life that is routine while challenging, and trivial while ambitious, leading to an equal chance of success or failure. This is why social scientists — philosophers, sociologists, psychologists, economists, and linguists — scrutinize its forms both theoretically and experimentally. In his book *On Liberty*, John Stuart Mill suggested that "free, rational choice is to a meaningful degree possible." To contextualize the folklorist's position on the matter, I will acknowledge the importance of prominent theorists of choice, such as Cassierer, Jung (who spoke of "the divine gift of choice"), Szondi, Shibutani, and Bourdieu. Linguist G. Herdan's book, *Language as Choice and Chance* (1956: 6), contains two particularly interesting statements that stress the importance of freedom in choice-of-speaking behavior:

> Within the limits of structure imposed by the community, the individual speaker makes his choices. . . . He sees his choices as free and . . . comes to ignore the limitations and move about them comfortably, so that the real choice becomes the only of the choices he sees. (W. F. Twadell quoted in Herdan)

> He who is most skilled in making his choices is most "free" and the special characteristics of those choices constitute his distinctive style. (Herdan)

With reference to the transmission of folklore according to the multi-conduit system, I see the creative process through the interaction of senders and receivers who make their moves by making their choices. Choice may be the most general characteristic of folklore, which cannot be defined as an orally communicated message but only as a message, communicated by free choice through its proper conduit. The choice made about which television channel to watch only becomes a real choice when the sender has decided and acts on the transmission of the chosen text, by not only watching but also communicating the content to others. Likewise, to clip legend items from a tabloid is not an act of choice yet — it becomes one only once the item is selected and retold through the conduit.

Creation of folklore is selection from sets and subsets.[5] The legend performer may select a whole set, a type, one or more unique pieces, a string of motifs, one motif, or may simply affirm the existence of magic without conveying any specific content. This is, of course a minimal act of folklore — an expression of a taste or a need, ranging from the tastes of an individual to the needs of a community, or perhaps even a society, at large. An act of minimal folklore is, in itself, an artistic behavior in the sense that it is not a routine function necessary for survival, but rather is a mentally projected, strategically intended, and executed act. Personal selection and combination of several motifs is not only a behavior, but is obviously a creative act. And because all motifs are traditional and well known, there is no other way of creation than to choose from what is available. A sequence of choices is suggested and supplied, from primitive to sophisticated elements, from micro-folklore to repertoire. Choice is the prelude of every folkloric act.

Over the ages, prior to the introduction of copyright law and the professionalization of authors and performing artists, ownership was not an issue, or was understood differently from modern practice. Medieval monks copied their collections of exempla from earlier editions, reformulating the texts to fit their purpose of religious education from the pulpit. They never claimed authorship for their selecting, editing, and copying work. But in the nineteenth century, village draftees into the military and labor migrants in foreign countries compiled songsters, ritual books, and storybooks as they remembered nostalgically their homelands. I have seen several of these handwritten copybooks, filled with songs, stories, autobiographical recollections, and home remedies, and each piece was signed by the copier. For example, in a collection of songs from 1914 — both folk and popular — all of the items are signed by the recruit: "written by Sándor Kiss."[6] And two of my Indiana Harbor informants, József Almásy and Jimmy Lábas, generously gave me their compilations of songs; and József Kállay gave me his own "Best Man's Guide," which he had personally copied from an older version and still used as master of ceremonies at Hungarian ethnic weddings. In these works, each song, joke, story, and ritual cadence was separately signed, as if the copiers (and users) were their authors. They are indeed convinced that the choice and the copying of the selected pieces is equivalent with authoring. In folklore, if not in modern literary practice, selection is a substantial attribute. Of course, literary authors make choices too, but only in a practical, mathematical sense; choice is not a conceptual element of their art as it is in folklore. It is through choice, following the consensual decision of both the sender and the receiver, that their material enters the conduit.

## Ostension

A conduit is not the equivalent of a channel. A conduit is like a tunnel, accommodating the passage of either trains, or cars, or pedestrians. Members of the process not only choose their conduits, they also choose their means: speech, writing, or other signs, the telephone, the media, and so on. The deaf-mute community, for example, uses sign-language in passing on the messages they may have received by mail. An orally told story can be also *acted out* dramatically, using redundant signs, gestures, and mimics, like in the case of the Irish Christmas mumming which is performed as a symbolic death-and-resurrection winter solstice game. Likewise, a spectacular annually repeated performance of a pseudo-historical event in Hamelin (Hameln), Germany, enacts a version of an oral legend about the vengeance of the Pied Piper; when he was not paid for his service of abducting rats from the city, the Pied Piper abducted 130 children with his magic pipe music (Humburg 1985). Narrators who have seen this play may restore it to narrative form if they wish, and recite it as an oral story. This is a matter of choice, evidently the result of a complicated permutation.

The theatricality, the sincerity, and the ability of the actor to enter into the spirit of the dramatic reproduction are only a question of degree. If the performer can disavow Diderot's actor's paradox[7] and identify *completely* with the figure he or she personifies, we cannot call it play anymore. This is not mumming, wearing a false face, masquerading, or assuming another's character for the sake of a temporary act, while keeping a real, lasting identity intact. Rather it is the telling of a personal story by actually doing it.

Using the plot of a legend that the conduit passed on to him or her, the performer assumes and unites several roles. Perusing the received text for repeating or retelling it later is the "copycat" mode. The recipients are the scriptwriters, editors, directors, narrators, and actors in one person, who will convert the legend — or create the legend — on the basis of what their conduits have passed on to them. The material may be a full-blown legend, a motif, a reference, a name, or any small provocative ingredient. A pocket-lighter can be used to light a single stove burner and burn down the entire house. This legend is done, realized, like underground snuff-movie plots, or, putting it another way, the narrative is turned into an act of ostension.

As I noted in the opening chapter of this book, legends can be dangerous. The text in legend reenactments is the event in which the anti-social act is committed, sometimes by children or pranksters, but recently more often by sociopaths and violent criminals. They meticulously follow the rules of folklore transmission through the multi-conduit system, taking advantage of its guidelines, and stylistic and technical devices. A characteristic of this growing category of legends is the affinity for the short-term goal, which holds together the links of this transmission chain. These narrators perform the content of their legend, doing it by pure *ostension*.

We came across two Halloween-related stories during our fieldwork in Kipling, a wheat farmer's settlement in Saskatchewan, Canada. At an evening gathering following the children's trick-or-treating, we were sipping hot apple cider and laughing as the kids told us about naughty teens who had removed the seat from the outhouse in the backyard of an old bachelor farmer, who fell into the uncovered cesspool when he came home later that night. The original incident had happened a long while ago, but old people still talked about it. However, we were told that this last Halloween "someone" in a neighbor town had really done it, and so-and-so helped to clean up the poor bastard — we could go ask him. The other legend was also about mean young pranksters, but this time they dismantled a wagon and placed it on the roof of a farmer's residence. Half of the village had to help take the pieces down and restore the wagon.

Both stories are known to folklorists in the Old and New World, but have been only scarcely reported (Siporin 1994: 47, 49; M. Smith, 1982). Registered as belonging to the "practical joke" or "prank" category, they both seem to appear as normative oral legends that imply or refer to a real ostensive performance. Without evidence we cannot tell, but it is plausible that these often repeated hilarious stories inspired Halloween enthusiasts to have fun — and to do the ostensive variant not once, but again and again — thus reinforcing the narrative legend in both memorate or fabulate form.

We can identify ostensive versions in much simpler legend sub-conduits as well. Magic healing is the most representative area of practice, alternating between narrative and ostensive variants. Most of the traditional milk witch stories mix the two; the narrative describes the whole procedure, past, present, and future, and the act of ostension shows how action and counteraction are taken. Together both relate and show what had happened: how an evil woman bewitched the cow, how the healer was found, how the healer forced the perpetrator to appear, and how the witch was punished. The legend closes by drawing a conclusion, and offering general instruction about what people should do when they have a bewitched cow.

The same structure accommodates legends about healing people who are under a curse, particularly when they are afflicted by the evil eye. For example, here is the abstract outline of the magic healing ceremony for a sick child: The procedure is performed by a wise woman who bathes the child while nine other women circle the house nine times, either in the nude or wearing their white nightgowns turned inside out, calling in a magic formula through the open window after each round. This can be considered as a legend told by ostension. What the procedure implies without words is this: "If such sickness occurs, people commonly turn to the healer who recognizes the cause of the problem and knows what to do and how to counteract it so that the sick can be healed and the witch can be punished. Others have also done it, with success." Or, in another version the act may signify: "We heard that people do it because they believe in it, and if they do it, it must work. That's why we do our best to succeed."

Here is the content of another healing legend that appears interdependently, in alternate formats:

1. *Ostension*: A ritual healing is performed on the patient by a wise woman who uses water from a holy well. She sprinkles and massages the child without uttering a sound while the mother looks on.

2. *Ostensive and postulated legend*: Why does she do it? Because she believes it helps. Why does she believe it helps? She heard that it helps from others. How was the holy well found? She tells the legend about the well, and mentions cases where the ritual helped.

3. *Memorate:* The mother testifies that the treatment helped. She saw it work. (Is this imagination, a dream, or a lie?) She tells others about it.

4. *Ostension and legend:* Another person tries it, and the treatment helps. She tells the story to others.

When I was working in peasant villages in Europe, I realized the connection between the performance of magic acts and their meticulous description in legends, but didn't think to view the often secret practices of healing, cursing, and divining as legends told by ostension. I was aware that the ritual practice of black and white magic and the legends that informed about individual cases of their effective performance represented two ways of telling the same thing, but I regarded the healing as a part of the vernacular folk religion, not as an enacted version of a legend. Because customary rituals are protected by tabus and performed in deep secrecy (their effectiveness is usually dependent on the prohibition against speaking about them), folklorists learn about them mostly from informative, exemplum-style, narrated legends.

So how did I get to the discovery of the legend as ostension — a part of the conduit that processes the narratives as acted-out legends?

During the 1970s and 1980s, Andrew Vázsonyi and I began our research into the creative process of legend formation under new conditions. We identified certain regularities in the changing relationship of performers and their audiences, all largely under the influence of technological innovations. Changing lifestyles, urbanization, and greater mobility had weakened the bonds of traditional communities, and the uprooted, alienated, and intellectually and emotionally drained masses found new associations to identify with and to believe in. As we have seen, beliefs that generate, support, and maintain legendry in our time are group-based. Legends support and reaffirm the group's ideology, be it a high, fundamental, or alternative religion, an esoteric doctrine, an idea, a hobby, a craze, a game, a trade, or a skill that can be performed, exhibited, propagated, practiced, and enjoyed in company. We should not be surprised about the great proliferation of legends thus instituted, as vehicles now are available to communicate them from the local to the global audience.

Our work started with the village folk but led us to the Internet enthusiast — and to the realization that human beings change their priorities and adapt to changing conditions easily, even beyond imagination. All the while they also hang onto their hereditary values and keep stubbornly to their traditions. People today have the same dreams, hopes, and disappointments as previous generations, and the stories people tell are not entirely different from what they ever were. The variants listed in the Aarne-Thompson *Types of the*

*Folktale*[8] and the *Motif-Index of Folk-Literature,* whose numbers are useful in legend identification, may increase by the addition of several volumes, but basically they will not need to add anything but variants of the already known ageless stories.

After discovering the conduit, which is open to accommodate myriad existing and potential legends, we were shocked to also discover ostension. We had the traumatic realization, while pursuing fieldwork and talking to practicing narrators, that the legend could be dangerous. Can a legend become a menace to the safety of people because its ostensive performers may cause an epidemic outbreak of violent, criminal acts? And can these acts become the nucleus for the formation of conduit-like chains that imitate and replay, copycat style, acts of violence and indeed murder?

When I studied supernatural legends told in relation to Halloween, I discovered that legends were acted out by people who saw in them models for their actions. Although such legends were not recognized by the traditional, oral-transmission–centered theories of folklore communication, we decided to look into ostension — and ostensive action in particular — as it seemed to gain prominence during the 1970s and the 1980s. This was before the cyclic presentation and representation of the complex of ostensive satanic child abuse legends in America (Sebold 1995), which approximated the bigotry and sadism of the Salem witch trials. It took years to exonerate the victims, who had been falsely accused of absurd crimes. The gullible, intimidated, neurotic American audience, always ready to debase itself, was the recipient in the legend conduit, communicated by all available means. Witnessed by observers in more sophisticated nations, we experienced once again a public acknowledgment of guilt for believing make-believe acts of pseudo-ostension.

As educators and police were deeply concerned with crime and violence in the cities, and social scientists issued warnings, pointing a finger at the lure of the mass media, the seriousness of the danger was still not recognized by the public. Violence has been jokingly — and alas, proudly — acknowledged as a national trait; it became a slogan: "as American as cherry pie."[9] Likewise, crime is regarded as being "as American as Jesse James" (Silberman 1978). Taking it lightly and looking the other way are still traditional responses; the public dismisses the symptoms indicating that the folklore of violence has penetrated society's cultural spheres. Keeping up the etiquette of mild criticism, sociologist Abrahamson quoted from the public lecture of Dr. Karl Menninger: "Ladies and gentlemen, we do not tolerate violence, we love it. We put it on the front pages of our newspapers. One-third or one-fourth of our television programs use it for amusement of our children. Condone! My dear friends, we love it" (Abrahamson 1970: 35). And that was more than a decade before our research began.

426

If the communication of story plots — or mere beliefs, allegations, or rumors (because we anticipate the proto-plots behind them) — can be considered folklore, and their statement represents a "real" legend-like account, then they stay folklore no matter what means was used to communicate them, including ostension or iconic action. Thereby, ostension forwards and retells the item, performing the repetition by a simultaneous presentation and representation. If we accept this trend of thought, and recognize that stories not formulated into words can be passed on by folkloristic means, then their retelling and transmission still must become subject to variation. This means that actions deviating from the originals must be regarded as variants, as much as they are in the case of textualized and retextualized oral variants. Thus, when one person tells about shooting his grandfather, and the other tells about shooting his grandmother, their texts are variants of the same plot, which used ostension instead of verbal utterance. And all of these legends need to be listed separately in a legend index.

Applying Umberto Eco's definition of ostension as "human action . . . *shown* as the expression of the class of which it is a member" (Eco 1979: 225), we examined legend-related Halloween atrocities and additionally explored a number of contemporary cases of criminal ostension (Dégh and Vázsonyi 1983: 5–34).[10] We believed that the phenomenon of legend-telling by ostension had become more frequent in our time than ever before, and we attributed this mostly to the special effect of the mass media. We claimed that television, daily papers, and tabloid journalism in particular have had an impact on less sophisticated readers and watchers, who have difficulty decoding the messages sent to them. These consumers cannot always distinguish what is clearly fiction (including commercial ads) from factual reports, particularly when the ambiguity is intentional. Fictitious actions — often with irrational, aggressive, and even criminal content — seem to be understood as real; by their frequent repetition, they can lead to inhibition reduction, banalization, and eventually to the retellings of the action by ostension. Thus, the story retold by action becomes a legend, verbalized and textualized; then, after it has been disseminated verbally, it returns to its ostensive mode, and so on.

The folklore process, as I have described it, forms conduits of diverse character that produce the variants told by diverse means. These conduits are multiplying in our time. They act and behave like legend transmission chains, focusing on one basic text, presenting eyewitness testimonies, and twisting the theme around from fact to fiction, from fiction to fact, back and forth. They erupt unexpectedly, develop and intensify, and then — as unexpectedly as they started — they drop out of sight completely. Although they may yield to another sensational story, it is only for a while, because they can return from latency and drag their earlier existence along as supporting evidence, as their birthright. Our most visible modern legends appear alternately in narrated, theatrically acted, and ostensively executed forms; they have gained independence and power, and claim separate conduits. They do not have to share the conduit with the other variants, subvariants, equivalents, and affinal forms under the umbrella of their type construct.

Because these legends are about deviants, should we view them as simply modern versions of the traditional *enfant terrible* cycle of stories? Are they legends of social heroes, "bad men," and noble robber prototypes that have been influenced by current fads of destruction and decadence? Were they propagated by the hippie revolutionaries of the 1960s, and by subsequent deviants in the aftermath, to manifest now in the current cultic pop and rock musical styles and lifestyles? Have they manifested as alternate religions? Escape from culture back to nature? To deviate from the "specifically human ability to act upon, and regulate, rather than passively move with and be moved by the givens of natural existence" (Ortner, 1974: 72)? It would be impossible to tell. The general picture, in essence, is predictable and remains the same; therefore, researching it would not be terribly helpful. Fads and crazes, on the other hand, change so rapidly that anything one would say today about them would be invalid tomorrow.

We are pursuing the relevant, spontaneously emerging legends and their spontaneous narrators — who act and tell out of necessity in an effort to make sense of the local and global universe, in accordance with the current state of affairs. We are committed to exploring the characterization of social reality and the individuals who construct, shape, and reconstruct it into a more convenient form. But we cannot know which of the many keys will lead through the maze and open the box where the heart of the monster is hidden. This metaphor, borrowed from folktales, would be a much easier task than walking the legend labyrinth. I am afraid that I cannot finish this book by handing out straight answers on a silver platter to the reader. Instead, I have laid out questions. The answers, because of the nature of things, must be left open indefinitely.

## Criminal Ostension: Legends of Our Time

In the 1980s, a case of product tampering — a horrible, tragic, and fearsome news item of national importance — led to a group of legends committed by ostension. All these legends were reported by all vehicles of the media as events, and were whispered around like rumors and gossip with accompanying commentaries. All the details were made accessible by the press: Day by day, the public was supplied with old, already known information, and new material appended that disclosed previously unknown details. The press repetitiously revised and refined its earlier statements, thus keeping people on their toes, excited, even spellbound. The public reacted as it normally would to the daily installments of a magazine pulp novel, waiting for the gratifying conclusion. These types of legends breed on sensationalism and feed on sado-masochistic thrill. All texts are focused on the legend proponent: the actual, known or unknown, ostensive teller.[11]

Tylenol Poisoning

In 1982, following a brief report in the police beat column of daily papers, the news about the late September Tylenol tampering event sent shock waves through America, traumatizing the nation. And, in the surrounding events, we discovered an interesting folkloristic process of legend retellings by ostension. The Chicago cyanide poisoning, which killed seven people and forced authorities to cancel Halloween trick-or-treating that year, was the first proposition that a deranged person who suffered from an antisocial disorder could rise to prominence by committing a fashionable, repeatable, variable, deadly act.

"Copycats Are on the Prowl — Emulators of the Tylenol Killer Made This Halloween Truly Scary," reported *Time* magazine, discussing the events of the following October (Church 1982). The acted-out legend followed the same trail as all folklore genres do in the long run, or fashion does in the short run. It progressed from emergence to evolvement; it attained full bloom, declined, and then was transformed and eliminated by the substitution of a new threat.

After a period of mass hysteria in which all popular painkillers, laxatives, and cold capsules were assumed to be laced with poison, the public's attention moved on to basic foodstuff, which was seen as endangered by tampering. Later, apparently only soft drinks, juices, and sodas warranted caution; for no rational reason other than mass hysteria and the continued fear of poisoning, one hundred and eighty people's stomachs were pumped after they had drunk Coca-Cola at a California football game.

A year or so later, reports about the contamination of popular foods — including peanut butter, canned and powdered soup, salad dressing, and hamburger patties — began to trickle into the news and continued to make sporadic appearances. As with all varieties of legend-like rumors or real legends, the reports could identify people who confirmed the "rumor" or "hoax" by claiming to be among the victims or playing with the idea by giving false confessions of guilt or lying about it in a narrative.

Diet Pepsi Tampering

The story of Diet Pepsi tampering was a small-scale case that exemplified the folkloristic nature of the poisoning conduit. It also typified the frustration of officials, who have failed to stop the poisoning conduit from remaining a constant threat to public safety. A pseudo-ostensive initiator and several copycat followers, all of whom were oriented toward diverse goals, created one, or potentially several, legend conduits. The authorities caught these legend-tellers red-handed, and thus, on the basis of five news clippings dating from June 16 to August 5, 1993, we can reconstruct both the legend and its conduit.

Between June 10, 1993, when the act — a hypodermic needle being found in a can of Diet Pepsi — was first reported, until August 5, when the case was closed, reporters and columnists presented a full and satisfying story to the public. The newspaper reader could follow the course of events like observing a stage play, as the conduit developed, ramified, became quite crowded, then came to an abrupt end. The actors and narrators performed their versions, and the authorities — Pepsi executives, government officials, the police and other law enforcement agencies, the Food and Drug Administration (FDA), lawyers, physicians, psychologists, political strategists, other experts, and the general public — played their roles, providing feedback to the allegations, gossip, rumors, educated guesses, and expert opinions. Although this case was closed, the door stands open for a repeat at some time in the future.

1. Bloomington *Herald-Times*, June 16, 1993. Journalist John Schwartz reports in the Washington *Post* the allegation that hypodermic syringes were found in cans of Diet Pepsi in Washington State the previous week, and later also were found in other soft drink cans in Indiana, Louisiana, Missouri, Oklahoma, Iowa, Ohio, Illinois, Michigan, and Wyoming. A special mention was made: "in Indiana, a woman reported Tuesday that she found a sewing needle in a can of Pepsi, Indianapolis police said." The unidentified woman said that "she felt the 2½ inch needle with her lip as she was drinking," but she wasn't cut. FDA officials found no obvious connection between the incidents and believed that "at least some of the incidents are not true cases of product tampering." The reporter emphasized the likelihood that the story was a hoax as so many similar cases had been in the past, adding that the previous night an FDA representative had said "one person had been arrested in Pennsylvania on federal charges on making false report of finding a syringe in a Pepsi can."

2. Bloomington *Herald-Times*, June 17, 1993. The Washington *Post* continued to pursue the story with an article informing the reader that "several dozen people in more than 20 states have reported finding hypodermic syringes in cans of Diet Pepsi and other soft drinks," and that "some complainants have video-taped reenactments of their syringe recoveries: some have contacted the Food and Drug Administration through their attorneys." The rest of the article concerned the response of the Pepsi-Cola Company, and their intent to fight the accusation that they were endangering the lives of Pepsi drinkers. Corporate officials appeared on the three primary networks' morning

news programs to insist on the safety of their products. Other agencies referred to experts who had experienced similar rumors earlier and claimed that the reported incidents were nothing more than repetitions of earlier hoaxes, or copycat crimes. They stressed that "tampering with products is a felony, as is falsely reporting a tampering."

The tone and composition of this article impresses on the common reader that there is a concerted attempt by the company and authority figures to reject the possibility of accidental injury of innocent consumers and that "big business" will make a counterattack to criminalize the reports of the victims, threatening them with punishment by law. In fact, before they even investigated the cans with sharp objects, on the basis of remembering earlier, unrelated cases the authorities jumped to the conclusion that those making these reports were liars.

3. Bloomington *Herald-Times*, June 18, 1993. This text provides the meatiest information on legend dialectics, featuring the negotiation of a message between individual narrators, conduits, and big business. There are two headlines: *FBI Probing Report of Pepsi Tampering* and *FDA Unable to Verify Any Pepsi Tampering*. They sound contradictory, don't they?

The first article is a brief report about the investigations of two Indiana cases by the FDA and the FBI. A Hammond resident claimed that pins were found in a can of Pepsi on Wednesday evening (not a hypodermic needle). And Mary Danielson of Indianapolis said she had found a 2½ inch sewing needle in a can of Pepsi on Tuesday. The agents were still conducting interviews and had not yet reached a conclusion.

The second article stated that the FDA could not confirm any tampering, and dismissed the allegation that there was nationwide meddling with soda cans. The commissioner noted that the rumor of a nationwide organized conspiracy was "a vicious circle." (He did not realize that this was in fact an accurate picture of the regional legend conduits.) Furthermore, the commissioner reinforced the threat of legal action: "Let me stress one point, and I am serious about this: We will prosecute false reports of tampering." He said that "in day-and-night work since the reports of possible tampering started, we have been unable to confirm even one case of tampering." On the same page, however, the reader could not have missed the listing of "reported tamperings," in seeming denial of the FDA stance. So were there or weren't there tamperings? The list of the ostensive narrators and the abstract of their expressive subvariants is worth adding to our sample texts:

> Dozens of claims have been made about objects found in soda cans since June 9, when a 82-year-old man in Tacoma, Washington, said he peered into a Pepsi can to see if he won a contest and discovered a syringe

and a needle. The second report also came in Washington state, on June 11, when a woman reported finding a syringe and needle in a Pepsi can. Similar reports have been pouring in. Many were pronounced hoaxes by authorities. At least nine people have been arrested.

A rundown on the arrests:

- A 61-year-old woman from suburban Denver was captured on a grocery store surveillance tape furtively putting a syringe-like object in a Pepsi can and then watching as a clerk poured it into a cup for her.
- A 29-year-old woman in Beach City, Ohio, was accused of faking a report that she found a sewing needle in a Pepsi can her 5-year-old daughter was drinking.
- A 28-year-old woman in Albion, Michigan, admitted to investigators that she made up a story about being pricked in the lip with a hypodermic needle while drinking a can of Pepsi.
- A 28-year-old man in New York City admitted to police that he intentionally swallowed two pins and told investigators they had come from a bottle of Pepsi.
- A 59-year-old man from Greenville, South Carolina, confessed to putting a needle in a bottle of Pepsi in a convenience store after the incident was captured on a security camera.
- A 37-year-old man in Rantout, Illinois, told police he made up a claim that his son found a syringe in a Pepsi can. He admitted he had lied when investigators mentioned contacting the FBI.
- A 25-year-old man in Williamsport, Pennsylvania, was accused of taking a diabetic relative's hypodermic needle out of the trash and claiming he found it in a Pepsi can.
- A 21-year-old man in Branson, Missouri, told investigators he made up a claim of finding a hypodermic needle in a Pepsi can. Police said he told them that the report was intended as a joke.
- A 62-year-old woman in Covina, California, planted a syringe in a Pepsi can in order to play a joke on her daughter. Her lawyer says a confession she gave was the result of the language barrier.

4. *Time* magazine, June 28, 1983. Journalist Anastasia Toufexis reported on the similar cases of product tampering. The three previous news reports were dry and factual, but this article tried to paint a whole picture of the phenomenon, interpreting America as a "fad-happy nation." The public, it implied, were enslaved by the hegemony of soft drink marketers who appear first as victimizers, and then end up as stoic victims. Touflexis re-created the initial legend that was not reported by the previous articles: Earl and Mary Triplett,

who had just returned to their home near Tacoma, Washington, from a sixty-first wedding anniversary trip to Alaska, opened a can of Diet Pepsi (like most thirsty Americans after a long trip do), and went to bed. The next morning, "Earl picked up the can, heard a rattle, and found a syringe inside. The couple called their lawyer, who called the press and local health officials, who alerted the police. And thus a frenzy was born." The author continued by noting that fifty complaints had poured in from twenty-three states within days, explaining that many of them were considered hoaxes and some were arrested for making false reports. She concluded that the whole thing was blown out of proportion, because product tampering had become a common concern after the cyanide-laced Tylenol capsules in Chicago.

In explaining the outbreak of faked complaints and scams in the Pepsi scare, Touflexis tried to rationalize and find answers. But why would people cry "Wolf!" on finding a syringe in an empty soft drink can? And why would it remind anyone of the cyanide poisonings over ten years before? Are people that neurotic? From this rapid snowballing of legends we must think so. Particularly if one has to believe that a man finding a syringe in an empty soda container destined for the trash can become the start of a nationally terrifying horror story. Why do people play pranks? Why do they love to attract attention? Why are they so greedy for monetary rewards? Why do they want to impress others, or need to gain sympathy by playing the victim? These are good questions, but they lead only to truisms that have no relevance to this episode of the multi-conduit system. More ethnographic knowledge about the ostensive performing personalities would tell us more.

5.  Bloomington *Herald-Times*, August 5, 1993. "At Least 39 Facing Pepsi Hoax Charges." After five weeks, the Associated Press evidently felt it necessary to lay the legend to rest by praising the FDA, which was on the warpath to mete out justice, prosecute the liars, and secure syringe-proof empty Diet Pepsi cans. No one, it said, would now dare to put pins, needles, or any sharp objects into the cans, or to use that tactic to play a trick on relatives and friends. Is a hoax a major crime or did the FDA overreact, shooting a fly with a submachine gun and escalating fear of violence over a non-dangerous case? "According to the FDA," said the article, "at least 39 storytellers in 20 states could be in big trouble." Storytellers (and hoaxers) are folklore performers — and their acts are folkloric behavior — are they punishable by law?

The listed ostensive legends — except for non-dangerous practical jokes and invented reports such as those about being injured or endangered by sharp objects while drinking Pepsi — are non-stories about non-events. In fact, the most prominent among the non-stories is the absurd trigger story of the couple returning from an Alaskan vacation, as it is hardly believable that the elderly couple acted as was reported. Something must be missing from the story; otherwise, the couple would have been characterized as troublemakers who craved attention or forgot what really took place. Wasn't it possible that they were perhaps cleaning their medicine cabinet and used the empty can for disposing of a used syringe, just like some of the other hoaxers under investigation must have done? Evidently, in the given cultural-political climate in which there is fear from the devaluation of human life, a syringe in an empty Pepsi container may be seen as a killer weapon, generating new versions in the legend-cycle about dangerous contaminations of food, drink, and medicine, and making lawmakers work to curb further ostensive storytelling.

Folklore-style ostensive killings — or "death by folklore"[12] — are somewhat more credible and factual, and therefore far more disturbing than the simple, pointless, and ultimately harmless soft-drink tampering stories. Let us explore something juicier. Murder legends are too many and too diverse to be discussed here in depth, no matter how central a role they play in the promotion of ostensive narration. Thus, I will limit the description of the variants to one legend, focusing on serial murder. That should shed light on other legends of homicidal maniacs, characterizing their function in the maintenance of a culture of violence.

## The Rise of a Murder Subculture

Murderers and their acts are in the center of public fascination and have held that position for a long time, thanks to the lasting popularity of crime fiction, the broad publicity of court trials, and the access to the details of real criminal cases through newspapers, magazines, and books. They have also been a subject in oral circulation since the mid-nineteenth century. The stereotypes established in the nineteenth century were standardized in the twentieth by the media, primarily by the film industry, which reworked earlier scripts and exploited real criminal cases from court records; they followed the fashions and the interest of the audience, whose taste and expectations in turn were advised and controlled by the entertainment industry. Thus, the image of murderers as culture heroes and anti-heroes was co-produced by Hollywood scriptwriters, literary agents, the fashion and beauty industries, criminology, and folklore. They modeled the image-making after traditional characters — outlaws, noble robbers, traitors, and supermen. The real criminals also invented themselves by placing their violent acts on constant display to the public. The killers, their stories, and the supporting characters were homogenized and stereotyped by the press and rumor-mills, allowing little variation to legend formation.

One of the oldest, and most infamous and mysterious, of these characters was Jack the Ripper, whose acts illuminate the role of ostension and its power in legend proliferation. Jack has been recognized as the model for modern serial killings, and we can see him as the first ostensive killer, whose serial murdering sprees were imitated by copycats. His bravado and violent, blood-curdling reputation were kept alive for a century through diverse means of communication: Everyone knows that in 1888, a murderer whose identity was never ascertained killed five prostitutes in the East End of London. At that time, violent killing was not a boring, everyday event, so it received much publicity in the newspapers, and people kept talking about his deeds. There was a great deal of speculation over the identity of the Ripper. According to gossip, he was never arrested because he was a member of the royal family or a high official in the police force. Soon the Ripper became a folk hero, whose story was written up in a novel and sung in a ballad. As so often happens, the spreading rumors solidified into legend and the legend spread farther, changed, declined, and started a new life. It has remained very much alive to this day — when a similar murder occurs anywhere else in the Western world, Jack the Ripper's name is cited.

Many mass murders have been committed since Jack the Ripper's time, and many of the killings have, like his, remained unsolved. Within the last few decades a great number of serial killers gained prominence, such as Britain's homegrown Yorkshire Ripper, who "slashed and mutilated his victims [prosti-tutes], in a style reminiscent of the original Jack the Ripper" (*Time*, April 23, 1979). Although the police did not discuss "the unique aspects of the [York-shire] Ripper's murder technique for fear of other killers imitating his meth-ods," imitation happened anyway. In America, he inspired the Boston Stran-gler, the Hillside Strangler, the Black Dahlia Murderer, the Zodiac Killer, the Atlanta Children's Killer, the Son of Sam, Ted Bundy, and, recently, the Mexican Railroad Murderer. In each case, the killer was compared to Jack the Ripper, and attention was devoted to the similarities, which were seen as overwhelmingly greater than the dissimilarities. All fitted the description of so-called "expressive crimes" (that is, not resulting from rational thought pro-cesses). Their murders signal, express, and sometimes narrate something. For over a hundred years, irrational, senseless, brutal acts have recalled the mem-ory of Jack the Ripper, and killers have taken him as their model.

As we have mentioned already, when, as in these cases, the perpetrators commit similar violent acts, police fear the possible actions of the copycat, an imitator who repeats the offense in a like fashion. There are numerous copy-cat series in American life. With murderers, they are also called serial kill-ings — in the cases previously cited, they murdered prostitutes, or pretty long-haired college students, or parked couples in lovers' lanes, or little black boys, or tourists, or train passengers in the same area, or men or women, both young and old. The very poor, such as migrant farm workers, may be targeted, or the very rich and famous, the people who have it all. In each case, the killer performed only one act of killing, but he performed it repeatedly, rhythmically. In essence, he killed the same person, with the same method, with the same cool, circumspect, neat regularity. And he continued to do so as long as he was not cornered and caught.

From the standpoint of "ostensive definition," one Ripper is very much like another. All belong to the class of perpetrators who perform irrational, ruthless, and elusive mass murders. Their main features agree, and the minor differences are insignificant. Thus, of all versions of the story, the copycat's is the most lifelike, authentic, and dramatic. It is also the most dialectic because through its deviance it stands in opposition to a frightened, doubting, astounded society. Here, the sociopath who could not conform had to use action. He killed people, thus contributing his part to the constant growth of the legend, and passing it on to those who will return it to more conventional forms and complete one cycle of the whole story. After each new Ripper has communicated the old story again by ostension, it spreads intermittently with the aid of other communication vehicles.

Meanwhile, the border traffic between ostensive and non-ostensive narration has greatly increased, due to the opening of many new mass media channels that expose the masses to more information than ever before. The press communicates the story with updated news items throughout the day in the papers, on the radio, and on television. The news forms a refrain-like repetition that creates an illusion in the mind of the reader/viewer/listener that it is not only one single murder, but several — and that it is an oft-repeated, common occurrence. Individuals exposed to excessive doses of murder and gore experience the feeling of apathy; they become used to the wildest, most bizarre violent acts. This causes an inhibition reduction, which is a dangerous symptom of mass reaction. Those who suffer from personality disorders and are capable of deviant acts are stimulated by the frequency of these cases, and may themselves be tempted to tell their legends through acts of ostension that are violent and criminal.

The long list of assaults on famous political figures begins with John Wilkes Booth, the killer of Abraham Lincoln. He initiated a conduit of people who aspired to the title of "presidential assassin," which ended (we hope) with the failed attempt of John Hinckley to kill President Reagan — or rather, with Edward Richardson, Hinkley's "copycat gunner" whose ambition was to do even more. Richardson aspired to killing several other important politicians, such as Alexander Haig and Senator Jesse Helms, and also actress Jodie Foster whom Hinckley had wanted to impress by his act.

Expert criminologists tell us that killers of famous people are usually losers and loners, whose aim is satisfying their ambition to become dominant and to enjoy the limelight of the proverbial fifteen minutes of fame. Some may keep a horde of trophies from their murderous hunting expeditions, but they also may grossly exaggerate the numbers, because they crave the recognition of being the most notorious among their kind. Many fail to carry out their serial killing plans and are caught; they may end up with one killing or may only inflict one, non-fatal injury, like the assailant of Pope John-Paul II. Sirhan Sirhan reached his goal: He was quoted as saying, "They can gas me, but I am famous . . . I have achieved in one day what it took Robert Kennedy all his life to do" (*Time*, April 13, 1981). Oswald, the killer of President John F. Kennedy, apparently had earlier also shot a right-wing fanatic, General Edward Walker. Arthur Bremer, who had first thought of killing presidential candidate George McGovern, managed only to cripple Governor George Wallace. And Mark Chapman's rage was silenced after he killed his idol, former Beatle John Lennon.

In this system, weird underground fan clubs of adoring women and religious and political extremist support groups emerge, which institutionalize and rationalize murder. A strange crowd of people of different persuasions and vocations gather, united by their dedication to saving life, and do the incredible: They make these doomed, inhuman criminals look human and convertible. Women write love letters to notorious death-row inmates, visit them with candies and flowers, plead with state officials for clemency, organize prayer groups, dramatize the ordeal of the suffering families of the convicted murderers, and organize spectacular candlelight vigils in front of the prison buildings when executions are about to take place. Even "The Candyman" Mark O'Bryan, who had slipped cyanide into the Halloween candy of his own child, had a fan, a young girl who wrote him love letters.

The whole emotionally charged process of attempted and failed rescue, climaxing with the vigil, has its roots in the traditional ritual mourning for and celebration of outlaw heroes in eighteenth- and nineteenth-century European broadside literature. Historically, heroization of criminals appears, as a rule, when tension between the establishment and the have-nots intensifies, as it has today under the impact of economic globalization and labor migration. In the eyes of the audience, social conditions are to be blamed for the guilt of the guilty. Few of the compassionate supporters of leniency shed a tear for the victims, who are soon to be forgotten, if not blamed for the circumstances that made the killer kill.

Another potential member of the ostension-conduit is the innocent person who comes forward and confesses to being the killer. According to expert psychiatrists, those who make false confessions are "psychotics and pranksters." But how many of those who show up to claim guilt are numbered among those who anxiously follow murder trials? Police say nearly every notorious case, from the Boston Strangler to Los Angeles's Skid Row Slasher, has elicited a number of would-be criminals proclaiming, "I am the one": "some 40 men and women . . . have confessed to Los Angeles' Black Dahlia murder of 1947" (*San Francisco Chronicle*, April 4, 1978). Maybe these volunteer participants are "mentally disturbed," but the folklorist cannot be satisfied with such a verdict. The transmission chain forwards a message and it is negotiated by the conduit members who have common interests but diverse positions — in the given sociological climate, they respond to and try to take positions in dealing with relevant contemporary problems. It is hard to tell reality from fiction, sane from insane; one almost could say that ruling social conditions determine what is real and what is not, and the performed folklore cannot do any better but mirror and imitate created social reality. This same pattern applies to other legends performed by ostensive acts in our time, focusing on the same act with fashion-like, cyclic regularity.

Perhaps this discussion of the ramifications and ups-and-downs of the Jack the Ripper legend prototype goes a little bit too far, but showing the general tendencies of the plot will exempt us from going into the details of other legends of the near past. From a certain distance, perhaps from that anecdotal tower I mentioned at the beginning of my "legend-trip" in chapter 1, the contours can be discerned that give an idea of the extent of folklore penetrating our everyday life. Or shall we say that everyday life has penetrated folklore? Folklore concerns imitation and repetition. The other popular legend types — no less influential or typical than the Ripper or the poisoning cycles — include animal mutilation, diverse forms of political terrorist acts (from skyjacking of planes to hostage-taking), and the hate-killings of minorities such as blacks, Jews, or any group of people who are not "us" — those who do not look like us or worship like us. These stories are legends, acted out. They start unexpectedly one day, without any warning sign; they generate copycats in broad distribution; they intensify by frequent repetition and variation; and then they expire as soon as the perpetrators get tired of them and run out of steam. Just like fashions, fads, or crazes, this species can last only as long as people do not get bored, until something newer, more attractive, and more shocking is proposed.

At the time of this writing, we are in the midst of a legend that is still accumulating an increasing number of copycats. This text is told by a series of trigger-happy schoolchildren who vent their hatred against their parents, teachers, classmates, and themselves by collecting an arsenal of weapons, and showering the premises of their schools with bullets that are meant to kill all, including themselves, if no one interferes. The press has become well informed in both criminology and in modern folklore, as one can see from the brief summary of *Time* reporter Cohen in the aftermath of the April 20, 1999, Littleton, Colorado, shooting at Columbine High School, in which thirteen students, a teacher, and the two perpetrators — who committed suicide afterward — lost their lives. "The copycat syndrome has been working overtime," he wrote, and asked, "What causes the epidemic of imitation?" His answer: "Copycats model themselves on crimes, both real and fictional, that grab a lot of attention" (*Time*, May 31, 1999). This is well said, for the criminal ostensive narrator imitates (and repeats) the story he imagined or committed, causing a fast, epidemic-style proliferation. Only three weeks after the Columbine shootings, four boys in Michigan "were charged with plotting their own copycat shootings" (*Herald-Times*, May 16, 1999). These boys, aged 12 to 14, were pupils at Holland Woods Middle School, and they were arrested after a 14-year-old classmate told police that she overheard them discussing a shootout "to kill all the school's 'preps' the popular clique of students." Supposedly, she also had heard them plan "to go on a shooting spree in a gym and detonate a bomb afterwards." Prosecutors alleged that these teenagers "planned to top the death toll at the April 20 massacre at Columbine."

Over a period of fifteen months, four similar high school mass shootings had been committed by children whose ages ranged from 11 to 18: Jonesboro, Arkansas, on March 24, 1989; Springfield, Oregon, on May 21, 1989; Littleton, Colorado, on April 20, 1999; and Conyers, Georgia, on May 20, 1999. These were only the meanest and most bloodthirsty of the many gun-related activities that were talked about, dreamed about, planned, contemplated, and initiated or committed by young children across the country. Teachers, parents, and lawmakers in every state of the union expressed their concern. New laws were suggested to take murder weapons out of children's hands — to stop them from carrying guns to school, playing with guns, or planning a career of dominating others by gun-related heroism. There were plans also to stop them from having access to action movies and aggressive video games and television shows.

If gunning down high school students and teachers, setting schools on fire, destroying educational equipment, or killing school biology laboratory animals and mascot dogs becomes a fashion trend, it follows no dictate of some central agency. It must be a voluntary act of imitation executed with the perpetrator's freedom of choice. It follows the model of folklore.

Max Weber, a pioneer of modern sociology, connected "freedom of will" ("freedom of action" or "freedom of choice") as an expression of human dignity with rationality and the concepts examined throughout this book. In his famous work on the Protestant ethic (1905), Weber associated the highest measure of empirical feeling of freedom with those actions that we are conscious of performing rationally, day by day. To act as a free person, oriented toward a goal, argued Weber, is evidenced concomitantly with rationality. The freedom to bind oneself to the pursuit of one's ultimate ends in relation to specifically given means signifies responsibility of human action. However, Weber also sees a distinctive irrationality that forms itself in the process of rationalization in modern society. Accordingly, the relationship between freedom and rationality, which was confrontational from the beginning, has developed further as an ambiguous coexistence — a split personality — while changing its original meaning. This reversal has affected modern culture, its establishments, institutions, and enterprises, and has itself become rationalized. Thus, human conduct, from which these institutions originally sprang, is forced to adjust to its own creations — which have literally escaped its control. Weber declared that it is here that the cultural problem of rationalization toward the irrational lies (Loewith 1970: 101–122).

## Concluding Remarks

Chapter by chapter, I have dealt with the key issues of legend communication in our time, as they came up and as they needed to be addressed in relation to other topics covered in this book. But it was necessary to readdress separately the question of transformation of the legend text, as it spreads under the influence of advanced electronic technology, market economy, and urbanization, and as it progresses to a not-yet-fully understood global village.

My developmental survey of the legend probed into the new theories and methods that are applicable to folkloristic interpretation. Since its earliest beginnings, the study of folklore developed around the paradox of stability and variability of the prototypical text, which is a scholarly construct composed from the available variants of potentially limitless items. Researchers have examined the trajectories of type development in historical depth and geographical breadth. They have asked how texts are generated and launched, how they get around, how far they go, and how they are revised by their bearers — both individuals and communities — to keep them abreast of cultural change. Text variables could be mapped and general developmental tendencies sketched out, but they could result only in highly speculative interpretations because the variants, once they were uprooted and isolated from their breeding soil, could not be used to document the regularities of cultural adaptation.

Folklorists must realize the need to change their tactics and go into the "field" as well-prepared observers, not as uninvolved strangers who "collect" items and do their interpretations at their desks after returning home. Legends can be collected only monographically by participating in the life of the community. Not only are legends "sensitive topics" that people do not share with strangers, but they are so much imbedded in everyday life that a short-term visitor would have difficulty recognizing them. I propose focusing on the narrator who negotiates texts with audiences, and whose understanding can lead us to the often cited "oral literary criticism" (Dundes 1966). To think with the natives is to adapt the viewpoint of narrators and listeners in their interpretations and uses of the texts. This approach — the approach I am taking in this work — follows the disciplinary tradition of folkloristics. My goal is to apply traditional knowledge and practice as far as it is possible, and try new techniques in new situations where the old tools do not work anymore. Of course, like everything new, this is a risky business, but I take responsibility for any mistakes.

In chapter 1, I made the statement that the legend is dangerous, and that defense against its potential danger is advisable. Each chapter of this book contributes hard data to prove that I was not exaggerating. And I have mentioned only a fraction of the materials that I have collected from oral and non-oral sources, a modest sampler of what I have in my files or what I could have gleaned easily from the many coexistent oral and non-oral sources within easy reach of anyone.

As an afterthought, I will offer another news clipping, providing information about yet another high school massacre to show the links, the processual development, of similar stories. We can see the transition of these stories under the influence of related or unrelated events of crime. This one is anchored in different circumstances and follows a different trend of fashion, as it is still under the influence of the declining Satanist cult canon. Presumably, there is a close connection between these two ostensive legends — the satanic ritual killing and the high school shootout. Both are linked to the folklore-inspired horror films which television and the movie industry have been mass producing to keep adolescent audiences screaming.

### Teen Says Demon Made Him Kill

PHILADELPHIA — A teenager accused of fatally stabbing his mother and gunning down two classmates testified Tuesday that he was driven by demons who told him he would be "nothing if he didn't kill."

A sobbing Luke Woodham, 17, said he remembered getting a butcher knife and seeing his mother's bloody body — all the while his head ringing with instructions from his satanic mentor, fellow teen-ager Grant Boyette.

Investigators say the 19-year-old Boyette led a cultlike group of teen-agers who plotted to kill students in Pearl High School. Several members of the group, including Boyette, face conspiracy charges.

Woodham is on trial in the slaying of his mother, Mary Woodham, who was found dead in her bedroom, October 1, the same day he is accused of killing classmates and wounding seven others in the school. (Bloomington *Herald-Times*, June 5, 1998)

As I had mentioned in chapter 1, I am not completely neutral in handling the materials in this book. Indeed, it is hard to stay neutral in the midst of so much horror and gore. But what can I do as a folklorist? How can I serve my profession and people in need? I am not a missionary, a social worker, or a policewoman, but my research can help in their work. As a folklorist, I have climbed up the symbolic tower to report what I see. I gather as much information as possible from my observer perspective, and report the facts as elaborately and insightfully as I can. I can put the facts and fiction together, and describe the situational context from strategically diverse angles. And I will certainly do my best to blow my whistle and alert those who can turn theory into practice.

My fieldwork was aimed at just such an understanding of the legend. I have gathered information about the state of things—about the truth, as people have informed me. Thus, I can represent the reality as they see it. I am convinced that what people tell me through telling legends is true, and because they use the legend to tell their truth, this make legends socially relevant. Speaking the language of concern, fear, and pain, legends reveal the desperate attempts that people make to escape—to survive on the planet Earth or beyond—by finding irrational solutions, or by rationalizing the irrational.

# NOTES

## 2. Is There a Definition for the Legend?

1. In his classic essay "Memorates and the Study of Folk Beliefs," Lauri Honko (1965) suggested just the opposite: If we define the genres one by one, we will be able to arrive at the definition of folklore.

2. For a long time, folklorists envied the perfect order in the natural sciences when they were trying to find an organizing principle for the classification of folk narratives. Lajos Katona mentioned the Linnean system of botany in the introduction of his tabulation of nineteen Hungarian folktales in 1889 (1912, vol.1: 200–201); C. W. von Sydow likewise expressed his hope that models of zoology and botany could be used in indexing texts (1948: 60, 64).

3. Leading American folklorists keep misquoting Thoms's "good Saxon compound" as "Anglo-Saxon compound" (Abrahams 1993: 9; Santino 1999: 3).

4. The milestone works that most effected the broadening of vistas include Bausinger's *Volkskultur in der technischen Welt* (1961); Richard Dorson's *American Folklore* (1959) and *Land of the Millrats* (1981); Américo Paredes and Ellen Steckert's journal volume *The Urban Experience and Folk Tradition* (1970); Jonas Frykman and Orvar Löfgren's *Culture Builders* (1987); Barbara Kirshenblatt-Gimblett's "The Urban Frontier" (1983); R. Kvideland's volume *Tradition and Modernisation* (1992); and Robert Baron and Nicholas R. Spitzer's volume *Public Folklore* (1992).

5. This is similar to the Hungarian noun *monda* from the verb *mondani* (to tell).

6. "Das Märchen ist poetischer, die Sage historischer, jenes stehet beinahe nur in sich selber fest, in seiner angeborene Blüte und Vollendung: die Sage, von einen geringeren Mannigfaltigkeit der Farbe, hat noch das besondere, dass sie an etwas Bekanntem und Bewusstem haftet, an einem Ort oder einem durch die Geschichte gesicherten Namen. Aus dieser ihrer Gebundenheit folgt, dass die nicht, gleich dem Märchen, überall zu Hause sein konne, sondern irgendeine Bedingung voraussetze, ohne welche sie bald gar nicht da, bald nur unvollkommener vorhanden sein wurde" (Grimm 1816, vol. 1: 7–9).

7. See Bausinger's compact summary in "Einfache Formen" (1985). Also see Honko 1968, 1976, 1989; and Ben-Amos 1976: ix–xv.

8. "Sagen sind welthaltige Geschichten, sie formulieren anders als das Märchen die pessimistische Weltsicht des Menschen. Sagen sind nicht Jenseitsprotokolle und damit auch nicht Geschichten 'zum gruseln,' sondern sie berichten von Projektionen — ein Toter, der wiederkommt, belegt, das die Lebenden das Problem Tod nicht lösen konnen, das ihr Schuldgefühl die Toten nicht zur Ruhe kommen lasst, das man Ungelöstes mit ihnen lösen mochte. Sage — historisches Dokument oder nicht? Nur bedingt ein historisches Dokument, sondern ein Dokument besonderer Art, ein Dokument menschlicher Welterfahrung, wobei die Reflexion von einem konkreten Anlass, einem historisch belegten odere für historisch belegbar gehaltenen Ereignis ausgeht, das dann zur Argumentationshilfe wird" (Kapfhammer 1984: 17).

9. In a thought-provoking essay, "Research Tradition in Tradition Research" (1983),

Honko suggested to participants of the 22nd Nordic Congress of Ethnology and Folk-loristics a future inventory of the "paradigms of tradition research" that are used by tradition scholars; Tamás Hofer (1984) expanded on the Scandinavian and European ethnological approaches to tradition; and Dan Ben-Amos surveyed its meanings in American folkloristics (1976: 97–134). Richard Bauman reviewed tradition as "the pro-cess of transmission of an isolable cultural element through time," and "elements transmitted in this process." He distinguished also "an emergent reorientation" toward the concept "an understanding of tradition as symbolically constituted in the present" (1989a: 178). By "reconceptualization" he does not invalidate the two meanings but adds the dimension of conscious construction or manipulation of tradition by the bear-ers themselves or others who intend to influence the bearers. The elegant rhetoric of Glassie's brief essay defining what folklorists mean by tradition revealed his commit-ment to the performance school's specific view in spite of his courtesy mention of other conceptualizations and examples from his field experiences. His conclusion that "tradition is the means for deriving the future from the past and then define tradition . . . as volitional, temporal action" and that "history, culture, and human action meet in tradition" (Glassie 1995: 409) did not add to the definitions already known.

10. Eric Hobsbawm's idea of the institutionalization of an invented tradition (Hobs-bawm and Ranger 1983) inspired many students of culture, politics and nationalism, folklorism, ethnicity, and identity. Tradition was described as something arbitrarily constructed, as suggested, reconstructed, initiated, reviewed, and applied. This branched out from the idea that culture itself appears as the figment of human imagi-nation, a masterpiece of social conspiracy (Bendix 1998; Carpenter and Vidutis 1984; Kirshenblatt-Gimblett 1998; Handler and Linnekin 1984; Wagner 1981).

11. For example, a legend complex evolved around the prediction of clairvoyant Jeane Dixon about a mass killing of dormitory coeds at colleges across America (Dégh 1969c: 70–74), and the reunification of Berlin predicted by prophetess Ursula Kardos (Weber-Kellermann 1955: 482–88). More examples of this "double prophecy" legend were examined by Klintberg (1990a). For a reappearance of this legend on Halloween of 1998, see chapter 4, note 30.

12. Operotropism relates to the process by which the vocational choice is deter-mined by the influence of latent genes (Szondi et al. 1959: 88).

13. A belated thanks to Carsten Bregenhøj who responded to my inquiry and asked amateur field workers with the Danish Archives if they knew the story. He sent me seven handwritten and tape-recorded texts.

14. The proofs, according to Peuckert (1965: 11), are the testimonies of given per-sons, the eye- and ear-witnesses of an event.

15. From my own collection in Györtelek, County Szatmár, East Hungary, 1963.

16. Jason's linear continuum shows a similar trend from personal to impersonal formulation of legends (1971: 144).

17. These are examples from my 1986 Halloween legend collection from middle-school students.

18. Tillhagen must have meant the chair as a folk art object, referring to the object-orientation of material culture in the Nordic Museum, where he was director of the Ar-chives.

19. My conclusions were presented in a paper at the San Antonio (Texas) meeting of the International Society for Contemporary Legend Research in 1994, and ex-panded into a critical essay for *Folklore*, at the request of editor Gillian Bennett.

20. This took place May 9, 1992, with two invited speakers—Alan Dundes and myself—at the campus of the University of California, Los Angeles. The well-attended session from 1:00 to 5:00 P.M. was moderated by Robert Georges.

21. Amateur adaptation of Freudian-Jungian ideas are as common in folkloristics today as those of solar mythologists were at the turn of the century.

### 3. Legend as Text in Context

1. When, in 1929, Friedrich Schmidt stated that "it is the ruling opinion that folk legend has no specific form" (1929: 21), he argued that the legend is an art form. Yet leading authorities such as Max Lüthi, Lutz Röhrich, Leopold Schmidt, and Wayland Hand saw exactly that the "relative formlessness," incompleteness, and shortness was characteristic of the genre (see my summary in Dégh 1991: 18–20). Of course, questions had been raised as to whether the legend is a narratable story. Does it have a narrative structure (Nicolaisen 1987, 1988) and an "identifiable discourse silhouette"? Bennett answers these questions: The legend is "liquid" and takes the shape of the bottle when poured (1989b: 193). This is metaphorical, of course, but who would want to "pour" legends? That is, the legend is "fixable" though never fixed because it is variable. This is in essence what researchers generally acknowledge, without the bottle metaphor.

2. The brief critical appraisal concerning contemporary legend study by Jason (1990) is well taken, particularly because it precipitated lively discussions and clarifications responding to the charges by the Sheffield seminarians (Bennett 1991a; Ellis 1991a, 1991b, and 1991c; also Pettitt, Smith, and Simpson 1995: 97, 99).

3. On the basis of ninety-two variants, I have outlined the legend of the "Incubus as Lover," showing direct links to tale type 407/B (Dégh 1965b: 83–85). For a particular function of the legend, see Dégh 1995a: 345–357.

4. More discussion of "The Hook" is found in chapter 4.

5. The performance of the dating-couple killer David Berkowitz, alias Son of Sam, is a perfect exemplification of ostensive legend-telling (Workman 1978).

6. This statement, selected at random, is representative: "The best time to tell this story . . . is when it is dark. . . . Your best audience is girls, guys tend to try to keep a masculine, strong air. . . . He once told a girlfriend when they were parked in a dark road and she got so scared she made him start the car and get the hell out of there," says Glenn Daniels, 19 (Berkeley Archive, 1969). Ellis's scrupulous statistical analysis suggests the predictable: The frequency of telling "The Hook" by young males and females is almost even (Ellis 1994a: 66) because of their interactional gender roles prescribed by society. It is more important, however, that the purpose of telling this legend by men and women, as couples or in the presence of other men and women, might be different.

7. Ranke criticizes the compilers of four legend collections for their disregard of context: "Wir erfahren nie von ihrem eigentlichen Leben im Volke, nicht wer sie erzählt, nicht wann und wo und wem sie erzählt zu werden pflegen, nicht wie stark der Glaube an sie beim Erzähler und Hörern ist" ("We almost never learn about their life among the folk, not who tells them, when, where, and to whom they are commonly told; we don't learn how strongly tellers and listeners believe in them") (1926).

8. Ingo Schneider is among the very few folklorists who have given a general overview of the culture of communication that is evolving by narrating through the Internet. Recognizing the need to explore the nature of new narrational communities

opened up by computer technology, he stresses the significance of the humanization of the equipment by the global communication of plain, everyday stories. On the other hand, Schneider does not feel entirely comfortable with the speed and unpredictability of how this technology seems to be developing. He sees cyberspace causing considerable isolation and alienation for the people of our time (1996: 26).

9. The Heaven's Gate cultists' relationship to heaven projects the same Protestant mythology as the influential Victorian novel *The Gates Ajar* (1869) by Elizabeth Stuart Phelps. This image of heaven became conventionalized among fundamentalist believers. The most enlightening historical survey of the cult of Bo and Peep is a compilation of news reports by the staff of the *New York Post*, written by Bill Hoffman and Cathy Burke (1997).

10. The cultists' pocket contents were explained on the Internet:

> What was the significance of the driver's licenses, passports, five dollar bills and quarters each cultist had in their pocket? Blame Mark Twain. The famed American humorist wrote a short story called "Extract from Captain Stormfield's Trip to Heaven" in 1907. In it the protagonist departs earth on a whimsical trip through outer space. His transportation: a comet's tail. His fare for the celestial voyage: $5.75. And, like a good American tourist, he had his passport. (Twain's life was entwined with another comet. He died in 1910, when Halley's Comet was in the sky. He was born in 1835, during Halley's previous visit to our end of the solar system.) (Heaven's Gate: The Life and Death of a UFO Cult.
> *ParaScope* Web site, http://209.207.141.249/articles/0397/hgate5.htm, accessed May 15, 2000)

11. There was a substantial early report of *Time*, April 7, 1997, by Elisabeth Gleick, "Planet Earth about to be Recycled . . ." (28–36); and Richard Lacayo, "The Lure of the Cult" (45–46); and observations by Joshua Quillner, "Life and Death on the Web" (47). The issue also summarizes earlier reports by Joseph Wambaugh (34–35), Howard Chira-Evan (40–41), and Paul Groll (41) for a background of the mass suicide.

12. My research article was based on newspapers and magazine reports between Oct. 9 and Dec. 22, 1975, as columnists and reporters followed the sensational journey of devotees of an evolving new cult "promising a spaceship ride to paradise." Louisville *Courier-Journal*, Oct. 9; *Indianapolis Star*, Oct. 11; Bloomington *Herald-Telephone*, Oct. 15, Oct. 17, and Oct. 20; *Time*, Oct. 20; Bloomington *Herald-Telephone*, Oct. 25 and Nov. 16; and finally, the *Los Angeles Times*, Dec. 22. This longer article seemed conclusive of the first phase of presentation of this "newsworthy" legend report, exhausting the interest of the public. It essentially sums up all other reports based on UPI, AP releases.

13. The Heaven's Gate site propagated the doctrine of escape from this world explaining such juicy topics as "Our Position Against Suicide," "Last Chance to Advance Beyond Human," "How a Member of the Kingdom of Heaven Might Appear," and "Last Chance to Evacuate Earth" (Hoffman and Burke 1997: 163). But isn't it a curious contradiction that the residents of the Rancho Santa Fe "had taken out a multi-million dollar insurance policy against alien abduction, alien impregnation and death by alien attack" (Hoffman and Burke 1997: 319)?

14. *Encyclopedia Britannica*, 15th ed., 1974, vol. 10: 220.

15. Notably, European collectors of modern urban legends do not exhibit a similar emphasis on youth legends, and even fewer regard them as adolescent entertainment.

Brednich and Top were greatly influenced by the Sheffield Seminar held in 1982, and Brunvand's first popular urban legend book relied heavily on the term papers of his folklore students. Top organized systematic legend collection, also engaging students in the project. Within six years, 161 Belgian students had harvested 450 stories, and 26 were received from correspondents. Top found that in Belgium "21- and 22-year-old students are past the age for this kind of narrative, which seems to circulate more often among youngsters between 16 and 18" (Top 1990: 274). Fix reported on a seminar project she initiated in former East Germany, right after the collapse of the Socialist system, to explore the specific East German features of the new crops of international urban legendry. The appeal for new legends yielded 87 items (Fix 1994: 94–109). On the other hand, Brednich did not depend entirely on student collectors. His students in the Göttingen University folklore program did contribute to his collection, but he himself added some 30 texts that he heard from friends and colleagues. The legends came from family circles, workplaces, summer jobs, recreational travel, and other informal occasions (Brednich 1990: 20–21). Klintberg does not even mention youth legends. He has been gathering materials for more than two decades from friends and colleagues, university students, and anyone throughout Sweden who responds to his radio and newspaper appeals (Klintberg 1990b: 17). As former archivist of the Nordic Museum, he clipped legends from newspapers and made a questionnaire for the perusal of collectors. Simonides, discussing modern legend formation in Poland, reported more than 100 variants of the known urban legend stock, widespread throughout the country. Simonides does not specify age or social status of the bearers of the material she presents (1987). Virtanen claims that modernization — that is, electrification — eliminated ghost and horror legends from the repertoire of young people in Finland. They visit the disco, not spooky places, she says (1992: 225–231).

16. MS SA 1955/152.A1. My grateful thanks to Dr. Henderson for permitting me to use this exquisite item from his collection among the Travelling People in the Highland of Scotland. "Hamish's Great Discovery," his pioneering collection among the "Travelling People," is one of the most important contributions to European folk narrative scholarship of the twentieth century (Neat 1996: 65–103).

17. Note the importance of the local press as authoritative recorders of local legends. Legend-tellers often refer to the newspaper they just read: "It was in the paper!"

18. As this adult community expresses its ambiguity concerning supernatural encounters (some may not want to be seen as "superstitious" in public, suspecting that others might see them as ridiculous), they speak permissively about the conventional ritual behavior of the kids. The two educators listened to their pupils' creativity in changing and elaborating the legend, and even encouraged them to write it down for the school paper.

19. A negative version as "incredible" also appears among the "credible" versions of the Bedford redaction of the legend.

20. This transcript was previously in Folklore 1996: 39–40.

21. Another set of Spooklight legends, in Rudinger (1976: 52–63), contains twenty-seven texts.

22. Dégh (1991: 86–95). Photographer Lela Zacharias drove around looking for the two identical bridges at Plainfield and Avon to take pictures for my article, but she was unable to find them. No one could tell where the "Avon Bridge" or the "Plainfield Bridge" was located, but everyone, including anglers, the postmistress, and policemen, knew where the "Haunted Bridge" was (Dégh 1969a: 75–77).

23. Miclot's small, self-published book, written in 1975, combines facts and folklore about Skiles Test's life.

24. I subscribed to an Indiana clipping agency service to collect news on local Halloween events within Indiana from September 15 to November 1 in 1978 and 1982.

25. These seem to be very common names. See Gutowski 1970; Bird and Dow 1972; and Calkins 1989. Also see references to Ghost or Dark Hollow in this chapter in the section "Example 3: Hauntings in Vincennes."

26. I am grateful for the help of Rudolf Schenda, who checked the addresses and phone numbers for the Moosleerau informants.

27. I am indebted to Egle Zygas, who sent me the entire package.

28. As an invited discussant of a legend panel at the 1989 meeting of the American Folklore Society ("Contemporary Legends in Emergence"), Stevens also stressed the importance of the context. From the vantage point of the anthropologist, he made suggestions as to how folklorists should study legends. Folklorists are "successful at studying things, things that can be collected and analyzed," Stephens observed, while charging that "many folklorists today are not well trained in looking for relationships among things. That has often affected their conclusions" (1990: 121). He goes on to explain what anthropologists do: "A premise of anthropology is that understanding aspects of human behavior and belief requires consideration of their cultural context." Furthermore, he informs the members of the American Folklore Society that "another working premise for anthropological analysis of a cultural thing is that nothing develops in isolation. Everything has a history and everything is shaped by certain social and cultural factors that have operated laterally on it throughout its development, and that operate at the time of its observation" (122). This statement of the obvious to any college student who has ever taken a folklore class in the United States is not meant as an encouragement to follow suit. Stephens congratulates legend scholars for what he thinks they do because they do it well: They collect things. And what they should do, he suggests, is to continue to collect things because they can enlighten the masses and comfort the fearful of legendary horrors with their interesting popular books. But what is the difference between the folkloristic and the anthropological context? We employ similar techniques for diverse goals, and occasionally anthropologists would benefit in learning approaches from folklorists (Dundes 1986).

## 4. Legend-Tellers

1. These questions were raised by Lutz Röhrich, in his introduction to the papers presented at the Ninth International Congress for Folk Narrative Research, Budapest, 1989 (1990: 11).

2. To my knowledge, the first legend book published from student collections was by Louis C. Jones, 1959.

3. The Indiana University Folklore Archive that holds the largest classified body of legend collections by graduate and undergraduate students and resident scholars had been closed and boxed and stored in the Archives of Traditional Music for lack of funds to hire a student archivist. In addition, the most notable student legend collections are in the holdings of the University of California, Los Angeles, Center for the Study of Folklore and Mythology; the Folklore Archives of Wayne State University in Detroit; and the Folklore Archives of Indiana State University, Terre Haute. Since the 1970s, legend research was greatly improved by the systematic work of graduate students in the United States. New ground was broken, and new methods and approaches

tested. Ph.D. dissertations by Sylvia Grider, Elizabeth Tucker, Thomas E. Bullard, Louise Russell, Janet Langlois, and Linda Milligan are some of the pioneer works on contemporary legend.

4. John Harden's book on North Carolina ghost legends (1945) is a good example. "A shelf of books could not even list the residential habitats of ghosts," writes the author. "Almost every community has its haunted house" (52). Yet, the stories are compressed into one representative text devoid of all personal, local feature. No actors, no locations are mentioned; "names and places were withheld by request," and only a fictitious "Miss Storyteller" is referred to as an informant (53).

Another author, Fred Morgan (1972) is also impressed by the ghost stories that "permeate the Uwharries," his native region. But Morgan's flowery fantasies make it hard to discern, even for an experienced folklorist, what remains of "the native oldsters' stories."

Unfortunately, the two West Virginia collections by folklorist Ruth Ann Musick (1965, 1977) are not much better. Ninety percent of her texts were written down by her students, who "applied literary rather than folk standards." As Jansen noted, "there are stories here that are too polished. . . . But polished or not, the core is from the oral tradition and each narrative is a recognizable legend" (1977: xiii). Indeed, placed into the context of the given conditions, these texts are useful for scholarly consideration.

5. McClendon, an influential reporter who has covered the White House since 1946, claims that the Roswell crash "has become, to many minds, America's greatest 'cover-up'" (1996). Her 1997 press releases, which discussed the Clinton administration's interest and "many briefings on the subject," were widely circulated on the Internet (1997a, 1997b).

6. This phenomenon, generally known as "telepathy" and "zweites Gesicht" by social scientists (Schmëing 1954; Grober-Glück 1959) and as ESP by parapsychologists (Hansel 1966; Bender 1977), was intensively studied by Virtanen 1990 and Cohn 1998, 1999a, 1999b.

7. *Psi phenomena* is a term used by parapsychologists studying telepathy, clairvoyance, and precognition, also known as ESP (extrasensory perception). Countless occult chapters of local enthusiasts have been generated. PSI, Inc. is one such organization.

8. Misunderstanding from the science fiction film *The Empire Strikes Back*.

9. Mark confided that he had great fear of gorillas, but it became clear in discussion that he meant guerrillas.

10. A 1978 *Blondie* cartoon shows Dagwood Bumstead taking the kids camping and entertaining them with the Headless Horseman and werewolf tales. The cartoon illustrates the camping-out ghost storytelling repertoire — headless horsemen and werewolves — and its effectiveness.

11. For example, the children's section of Monroe County Library in Bloomington published two separate bibliographies, "Shivers and Shrieks: A Selected List of the Pool of the Supernatural and the Mysterious" and "Tales of the Weird and Horrible," for their young readers. In 1990, I copied the titles of twenty-eight horror books for children, from a showcase flanked by appropriate Halloween decorations, in a bookstore in a Chapel Hill, North Carolina, shopping center. In 1998 the two megabookstores of Barnes & Noble and Borders in Bloomington moved the most scary horror storybooks out of their plentiful standard stacks of mystery and horror and up to the front of the store.

12. Baughman mistakenly classifies these as catch tales because they culminate with a punchline. The carefully built suspense of the ghost story climaxes with an unexpected sudden resolution that is screamed or shouted to scare the listeners and relieve the tension (see, for example, Clements 1969).

13. A systematic study of the slumber party is still regrettably missing, although — or perhaps because — it is so common. Of course, it is very difficult to do fieldwork in a situation that strictly prohibits the presence of adults. Even folklorist-friendly girls would hesitate to give away age group secrets. Among the student term papers, I would like to mention Margaret Steiner's (1975) and Julia Oxrieder's (1980) observations of two events. As of this writing, it seems to me that ingenuity and self-reliance in performing this improvised, gendered, and highly dramatized folklore miscellany has lost its earlier appeal. During the 1990s, I happened to be at a dinner party while children were having a slumber party in the family room. We heard the ritual screams and giggles as the guests — both boys and girls — arrived. But about half an hour later, there was complete silence. What had happened? The boys were sent to the video store to bring home some horror movies. Couch-potato passivity has replaced the vibrant creativity of the slumber party.

14. Adolescence is defined as a biologically, psychologically, and sociologically stressful transitional period of life between childhood and adulthood. In general, folklorists accept the psychologist's vague delimitation of this period as approximately between the ages of 12 and 20, and label the legends that deal with the problems, conflicts, and anxieties of growing up, leaving home, adjusting to a new environment, sexual maturation, and socialization as being characteristically adolescent. However, the nine years between 12 and 20 comprise radical transformations and cannot be handled as one category. The convenience of accepting the child psychologist's definition to generalize about adolescent behavioral patterns might backfire for the interpretation of the legends that young people tell. Even if we accept that certain legends deal with certain critical conflicts of adolescent life, the fact that they are not limited to that age group and are told by children and adults as well alerts us to be careful of generalization (*The New Encyclopaedia Britannica*, 1974, I, 96 a, b; XIX 1090–1097).

15. Mark 3:14–15. "And he ordained twelve, that they should be with him, and that he might send them forth to preach, and to have power to heal sicknesses, and to cast out devils" (King James version).

16. A notable exception is the essay of Hans-Werner Blum in the *Neue Zürcher Zeitung*, January 20, 1969, musing over the court trial that followed a deadly exorcism on a mentally sick man.

17. The U.S. newspapers of the day had varying opinions of the film: "elegant occultist claptrap," "a costly carnival of nausea," "best movie of the year," "a real shocker." In Europe, there was even more controversy: The *Frankfurter Allgemeine* (September 21, 1974) asked, "What the heck kind of film is this?" *Die Zeit* (September 26, 1975) writes, "The film *Exorcist* has made the devil fashionable again." The film prompted even further discussions: "Should Satan go?" asked a theologian. "He can't: his milk brother the almighty God would go with him." Author Hansjakob Stehle discusses the theological viewpoint: "Is the Devil a proof of God's existence?"

In the article "Exorcist teaches German moviegoers fear," the *Wochenend* (1974: vol. 45: 17) described the beating death of a possessed Swiss girl. I first heard about the Anneliese Michel exorcism case in a CBS news report by Hal Walker in 1977. And the debate goes on: "No sympathy for the Devil: a Cardinal decries Satanic influence," neatly summarized the situation in *Time*, March 19, 1990.

18. Systematic study of the Michel case was done by two parapsychologists and an anthropologist (Goodman 1980; Mischo and Niemann 1984).

19. Recorded in the presence of Szondi's wife Lilla and Andrew Vázsonyi. Szondi did not mention that his only son, Peter, a professor of comparative literature at the University of Berlin, Germany, had committed suicide by drowning himself in the river Spree.

20. The relationship between science and religion — as viewed by sixty leading scientists who answered questions that concern science, God, origins of the universe, life, and *Homo sapiens* — shows more harmony than conflict, but the two are rather phenomena that belong in two different spheres, complementary of each other. Like Darwin, Einstein, and Planck, most of the scientists considered the existence of God seriously, but more on the basis of their private, personal, culture-specific religious belief than as a part of their scientific convictions (Margenau and Varghese 1992).

Here are some randomly selected quotes: "no contradiction exists whatsoever between faith and the facts of evolution" (45); "a series of miracles could demonstrate to me that forces are at work in the universe that are utterly out of the reach of human comprehension and that is as close as I can come to the proposition of a proof for the existence of a Creator" (45); "I believe that God exists but do not have a personal understanding of what this means" (53); "an unknowable source of divine order and purpose" (53); "science deals with what is, religion with what ought to be" (111); "natural selection is the way God works ... there is a process that has some guidance from above, but the details are correctly described by the Darwinists" (49). Summarily, distinction between the two spheres is made by Nobel Prize–winning physiologist Robert W. Holley:

> Religion deals with the "unknowable," science with the "knowable." Conflicts arise when people think something that has been "unknowable" has become "knowable." (179). I consider the existence of God as "unknowable," and therefore part of one's religious view. There is a great deal to marvel or wonder about in the universe. Whether one wants to attribute the marvelous things to the existence of God depends upon one's nature and experience. Such a belief appeals to some people and not to others. Since it is unknowable, I think it should be a very personal matter. (180)

In an entirely different relationship, the American Anthropological Association chose as its central theme "the known, unknown and unknowable" for 1996–1997. It concerns discussion of the changing face of the discipline through the discovery of new territories, tools, and skills, interdisciplinary collaboration, and globalization. "The process by which the unknown and the (previously) unknowable becomes known," writes Sandra Morgen, "is most indebted to developments in technologies, methodologies or theories that reveal what was once hidden or inaccessible" (1997).

21. See chapter 5 for more of the Koehler letter, and the notes to chapter 5 for more on the Porticos.

22. The Ouija board (combination of the French "oui" and the German "ja") was invented and commercially distributed by the American Elijah Bond in 1892. From social game it soon became a magic device of communication with the dead. For the background and the history of the board, see Eliason (1996). Its broad popularity is indicated by the fact that not only occult bookstores but also supermarkets keep it in stock.

As we will see also in the next example of Val and others, it is used ritually by sectarians, mostly in the practice of spiritualist groups; but it is also lightheartedly played at social gatherings by people who are confronted with a supernatural mystery they cannot resolve, as in the case of Bob P. and the Martinsville circle of friends.

Although many devout Christians view it as a harmless pastime, just like table levitation and New Year's Eve lead-divination, fundamentalist believers see it as an invocation of the devil — that is, the object itself is an incarnation of Satan. As the tabloid *Sun* reports (December 9, 1986), when given as a birthday present to a 6-year-old girl, "a simple ouija board became a passport into Hell for a family that accidentally summoned a demon into their living room." A handout from "Un-chained Ministries" that I picked up at an Ellettsville church contains a legend, told in the first person, of how the demon summoned by "Valerie" destroyed her health so she had to be committed to a mental institution.

One of Dear Abby's correspondents wrote: "My sister's boyfriend died last year and she and I have been talking to his spirit on a Ouija board ever since. We have also talked to two other spirits on the Ouija board. My aunt says that we shouldn't use the Ouija board because it is the work of the devil. Can you give me any information about Ouija boards? Are they bad or not?" And she answered: "The only way one can 'talk' to a spirit is through prayers. And you don't need a Ouija board for that. A Ouija board is all right to use as a 'game,' but don't take it seriously" (*Chicago Tribune*, September 14, 1975).

Evidently, the ambiguous messages sent out by authority figures led to the "Ouija board ritual," in which Hazleton teens spoke to the devil in the then-current satanism scare atmosphere, as the penetrating monographic study of Ellis (1994) suggested.

23. When Jung spoke of the formation of legends about UFOs, he described human thinking in the same sense as Bob: "We on our side want to fly to the moon or to Mars, and on their side the inhabitants of other planets in our system, or even on fixed stars, want to fly to us" (Jung 1958: 27).

24. The group who accompanied BarBara Lee consisted of myself and my husband, Andrew Vázsonyi; three graduate folklore students, Sylvia Grider, Sharon Sherman, and Elizabeth Tucker; and two audio-visual specialists, Martin Heltai and John Bunch.

25. My recording of the Stepp Cemetery ceremony was transcribed by Elizabeth Tucker. She also wrote a very insightful term paper about the event, which she submitted to a summer session class taught by Roger Abrahams at the Folklore Institute of Indiana University, 1975.

26. The legend masterfully contextualized by spiritualist exorcism practice and pertinent spirit belief system resembles the traditional *Sennenpuppe* legend known to cattle herders of the Swiss, Austrian, and German Alps (Isler 1971). The legend concerns the summer pasture lodge, vacated for the winter and occupied by sacrilegious lumbermen, hunters, and other drifters. Because of the invaders' debauchery — drinking, card playing, cursing, and womanizing — the doll constructed of wood and other organic substances that was left to protect the settlement turns into an avenging evil spirit.

BarBara's china doll is the hiding place of a criminal and is probably related to the five Indiana variants of stories in my files about the beautiful china doll that kills the little girl who owns it, her parents, the rest of the family, and is out to destroy the whole world. In one of the texts the doll is a vampire, and kills the family with a neck bite. Elizabeth Tucker informs us about "The China Doll," or "The Purple Doll," a favorite legend monster of adolescent girls; the doll attacks the family members of the little girl, giving a sound "Hrrrunch!" before killing (Tucker 1999: 561). I suspect literary origin of this horror story. According to Linda Spetter's Mexican informants, there was a movie about such a doll and they used it in a legend-telling session one Halloween night.

27. Ann is a Roman Catholic of Italian extraction.

28. I have thoroughly discussed the historic development and scholarly practices of the contextual recording of folklore texts (Dégh 1989, 1995a). Regina Bendix's book (1997) rounds up a decade of deliberations over "authenticity" at meetings of the American Folklore Society.

29. Although West European folk narrative specialists reacted to the call of Anglo-American urban legend collectors to join their forces, so far the collections that popularized the term "urban legend" in Europe, including Ethel Portnoy's *Broodje Aap* (1978 Dutch; 1985 in English); Bengt af Klintberg's *Råattan I Pizzan* (Swedish 1986; in Danish, Norwegian, and German, 1990) and *Den Stulna Njuren* (The stolen kidney, 1994); Leea Virtanen's *Varestettu isoäti* (The runaway grandmother, Finnish, 1987), as well as Rolf Brednich's four paperback volumes (1990–1996) have not followed the principle of contextual verbatim recording. The authors depend heavily on non-oral or secondarily oral materials.

30. Herbert George Wells's famous 1898 science fiction story about a Martian invasion of England was adapted by the then 23-year-old Orson Welles for the broadcast script of *The War of the Worlds*. The hour-long radio drama, which aired from a New York studio on October 30, 1938, caused an unexpected panic among its listeners who believed the broadcast was true. The mass reaction of people running for shelter from monstrous invaders puzzled the experts, but the tremendous success of the make-believe event also informed the entertainment industry of the sales potential of science fiction horrors.

Many similar horror shows have been produced since, but this model has become a classic; it was replayed time after time, and has become a repertory piece for Halloween. H. G. Wells might not rest in peace knowing that his 120th novel has been recontextualized to fit the culture of fear. As have the films *Dracula, Frankenstein, The Wolfman, The Phantom of the Opera, The Omen, Candyman,* and *Jaws,* Wells's fantasy adds to the confusion between science and religion. Supernatural and technological horrors (supernatural and horror legends) connected with lunacy, crime, and extreme violence keep the audience whimpering.

On Halloween of 1998, newspapers celebrated the 60th anniversary of *The War of the Worlds*. Bartholomew (1998) discusses the mass panic in 1938, the story's relevance today, and the increase of mass scares that manifest in unique delusions among an increasingly mass media–indoctrinated population.

31. My translation of the following: "Das Feld in dem wir uns bewegen, ist verwirrender und complexer geworden. Aber die Herausforderung, sich in diesem Felde zu orientieren, ist mindestens ebenso animierend wie die frühere Aufgabe" (Bausinger 1992: 12). "Nie ist es der Folklore besser gegangen als unter der Fahne der Massenkultur . . . Die Folklore-Debatte ist also nicht abgeschlossen. Sie wird im total elektronisierten Jahre zweitausend erst richtig aktuell werden" (Schenda 1992).

32. It is worth mentioning that Procter and Gamble fought the ridiculous accusation of serving satanist causes (through their logo — an anthropomorphical moon, surrounded by 13 stars representing the first 13 states of the Union — which purportedly signified the "sign of the beast" [666]), but eventually succumbed. The attack of funda-

mental Christians achieved high publicity in 1981, and until 1990 lawyers and prosecutors were active in negotiating and settling between the accusers and the accused
behind closed doors. Although authorities and respected religious leaders made statements that the company's leaders were committed Christians, and talk-show hosts
Merv Griffin and Phil Donahue both denied that Procter and Gamble's executives
had claimed satanic associations while on their shows, the rumors solidified into legend; folklore about the mark of the beast (666) continued to spread through photocopies.

To curtail the damage, starting in 1985 the company consented to gradually remove the moon and star marks from most of its products. New logos were presented
to the board of directors on July 9, 1991; according to an Associated Press report, "the
management was developing guidelines on when to use which symbols." The news
that the company had successfully sued independent Amway distributors James H. and
Linda K. Newton of Newton and Associates for spreading false and malicious rumors
that associated P&G with satanism (a $75,000 monetary judgment) probably never
reached the gullible public. Neither did P&G's pamphlet "Rumor Mongers Beware"
(April 30, 1990).

A similar rumor-legend surfaced two weeks before Halloween 1998, in Bloomington, Indiana. In 1968 the clairvoyant in the legend was Sybil Leek or Jeane Dixon who
had predicted on a television show the mass killing of twenty-five coeds in several college dorms (Dégh 1969c: 70–74). The story can be traced to a European legend about
double prophecy (Klintberg 1990a). As reported in the Thursday, October 22, 1998,
*Indiana Daily Student* ("False Rumor Causes Panic"), a psychic's prediction of mass
murder in McNutt or Foster Quad was disclaimed by talk-show host Oprah Winfrey
(or David Letterman?). But the Web site informed the students that this story was an
"urban legend" inspired by the recently released movie with the same title. But since
other schools also heard of the prediction, tight security was suggested because of the
proximity of Halloween. The next day, October 23, reporter Susan Hilbish ("Rumor
Creates Uneasiness at McNutt") expanded the story about the panic at McNutt as the
probable site of the massacre at a Midwestern university predicted several weeks ago
on the Oprah Winfrey show. Informed by several students, teachers, and staff members, the student reporter displayed typical legend ambiguities mixing belief and non-
belief concerning fear of Halloween spooks, the rising of the dead in the nearby cemetery, attack of deranged criminals, and other horrors, such as *The War of the Worlds*
panic which an educator brought up while assuring that extra security would help to
survive the attack of sinister forces during the night of October 31. Halloween, once
again, appeared as the embodiment of the culture of fear. Piecing together from
legend-ingredients of a variety of disparate sources and blending bits and pieces of
media legendry to reinforce the shudder, commentaries in the form of hearsay and
gossip help retextualize the master legend for the season. The current variant of the
legend about the prophecy of a Halloween coed massacre at McNutt is supported by
reference to (1) the talk-show host's warning, (2) the Urban Legend movie, (3) a miscellany of supernatural horrible and dreadful Halloween events, and (4) *The War of
the Worlds*. The readiness of campus police is more oil on the fire than sedative to the
victimized audience.

### 5. The Landscape and the Climate of the Legend

1. The anti-legend is a disclaimer based neither on belief nor in its negative corre-
late. Its message was not conceived in the "legend climate" but rather on the "legend

landscape," both concepts defined by W. E. Peuckert (Peuckert 1965). It is based in facts and knowledge accepted by contemporary society. For example, a tradition might recognize the erratic flame of the foxfire as the revenant of an engineer, who in life cheated people out of their property by making false measurements. When expert scientists verify that the flame is methane swamp gas, this produces a genuine anti-legend, destructive of everything for which legends, positive or negative, stand.

Under the pressures of the majority, or of an opinion-leading minority, the teller of the positive or negative legend will try to find rational and possibly scientific evidence, even if it is based on belief and requires no verification. This means irrational behavior will be presented as rational. Thus, it will be possible that, in the guise of objectivity, a teller narrates a disproving anti-legend by applying unsuperstitious, sober, and seemingly unbiased scientific references; at the same time, he exhibits his own passionate belief, in the form of a legend that only appears to be rational.

What we observe here is then process of rationalization. Often the anti-legend is only a legend in disguise. The science it appeals to is pseudo-science, and its rationality is pseudo-rationality.

2. This may be a restatement of the often argued fact that movie violence generates real violence. However, a brief and factual news item from California, entitled "'Scream' copycat killers convicted," deserves the attention of folklorists, for it illustrates the folklore-generating mass media's callous banalization of the murder of parents.

> Mark Padilla, 17, was found guilty Thursday in the killing of his mother 37-year-old Gina Castillo. A separate jury convicted Samuel Ramirez, 15, earlier this week. That verdict was sealed until Padilla's panel returned its verdict. During the preliminary hearing one of the boys said that the slayings depicted in "Scream" were "cool." And on the way home from one of many viewings, he told a pal: "It was a perfect way to kill somebody." (Bloomington *Herald-Times*, July 2, 1999)

3. The Warren couple's "extraordinary career" is fully documented in the 1980 book *The Demonologist*, written for them by G. Brittle; in it, this self-proclaimed "world famous team of psychic researchers" reveals much about the haunted house phenomenon and the practice of nonclerical exorcism.

A second book that the Warrens co-authored with Robert Curran (*The Haunted, One Family's Nightmare*, 1988) focuses on the "demonic infestation" of a single family house, presenting the case monographically, with almost ethnographic accuracy. Members of the Smurl family narrate "the harrowing true story of demonic attack and intimidation," piecing together conventional episodes of spirit presence stories. (Note that this narrative is remarkably close to the experience of the Littleton family discussed in this chapter; see "That Scared Me Half to Death.") Their personal, first-person experiential encounters are based on a firm belief in revenants. The acts of demons are individually reported by the victims and observing members of their community; the demons are counteracted by a team of exorcists led by the Warrens, who are advised by a priest, Father McKenna, familiar with the formal rite of exorcism. Curran, a news reporter, shapes the events and actions into a genuine horror story with an additional subplot: an anatomy of a collective nightmare.

A worthwhile experiment that only the folklorist could do would be to analyze the personality and the creative fantasy of the members of the victimized family, and examine the influence of the demonologists on the family's mental health.

4. I am depending on the valuable materials in the Folklore Archives of Indiana

University, Bloomington, and Indiana State University, Terre Haute, and on the collections made by students in both of my graduate and undergraduate classes. A collaborative project with my colleagues John William Johnson and John McDowell in 1986 focused on haunted house visits at Halloween. The three of us taught an undergraduate introductory folklore class, a graduate fieldwork class, and a graduate class in legend, respectively, and we looked at different levels of participation in the visit to and performance at haunted places. Another project (1986–1991), which contributed more texts and contexts, was aimed at mapping haunted locations in Indiana. With the help of a news release by the Indiana University News Bureau on March 27, 1986 (editor Rose McIlveen), we asked local newspaper editors, who are possibly the most authentic and knowledgeable people throughout the state, to send us a copy of their previously printed materials on hauntings and to print our appeal for their readers to send us their experiences with haunted sites. My two graduate folklore assistants, Betty Belanus and Sabina Magliocco, gave me invaluable help in the transcription, assessment, and classification of the rich incoming materials from ninety-two Indiana counties, and helped in contacting correspondents in person and re-recording their handwritten or printed accounts.

5. Dee Bruner's 1990 term paper "A Folklore Investigation of the Chain," written for my F391 Indiana Folklore course, explores the facts and fictions about the tombstone and the life and death and family relations of Floyd Pruett. As a lifelong resident of Orange County, Bruner had been to the grave with friends at Halloween in 1982; he "knew" since then that the chain grows a link every year. He was fascinated by the mystery and was determined to go beyond the collection of legend variants; to form an opinion about what has happened, he examined archive records and talked to those who had also visited the tomb, as well as contacting local authorities, relatives, neighbors. This was the conclusion of his report:

> The true reason why the chain and the cross are on the tombstone of Floyd Pruitt's [Pruett] remains a mystery. The stories of why it is there will surely circulate for many, many years to come, and perhaps one day the "fad" of going out to see the tombstone will be "in" once again. Trends come and go as the stories change. Maybe there is something mystical about Floyd's tombstone after all. After visiting Bonds Chapel and taking pictures of Floyd Pruett's tombstone, my brother's-in-law new camera stopped working. Who knows?

6. Motif E721.1 Soul wanders from body in sleep.

7. The prominence of the ideology of *pars pro toto* in the belief system supporting Janet Callahan's legend is well established by Betty's recounting of her experience when she looked over the bunches of clothing and jewelry in the attic prior to the liquidation sale. Betty had never met Alice, but she experienced her presence when she sifted through her belongings.

> All of a sudden, I'll never understand to this day, if I actually heard it . . . but I could hear a voice, it was something like saying, oh, oh, . . . "TAKE IT, TAKE IT, I'M DEAD," over and over, like that. Well, gosh. It's like I wanted to take my ears and clean them out of something. But I looked around and there wasn't anybody in the room talking to me. It was kind of like a woman's voice.

Betty took a few things home and "stuck them beneath my bed." After she had lain down, she had the feeling that something was there, and then that somebody was touching her.

I got out of bed and I went to the bathroom . . . and I wiped off my face and stuff like that, cause my face felt sweaty. . . . I felt somebody was standing on the outside of the door. . . . In my mind I could see a woman who looked like a witch. You know, I mean her hair, the way it was pulled back made her look like the witch in the *Wizard of Oz* show.

She was up the rest of that night, and wondered, "Is there something about them clothes I put under the bed?" Her feeling of presence left her only when she gave the clothing away. Janet Callahan asked her mother to describe what she'd seen:

And the next time I came to your house, you got a picture and you said: "Mom, is this the woman you saw?" I said, "My gosh, yes." And you said, "That's Alice."

8. The constructed legend of The Porticos restaurant in Bloomington is an example. In the 1980s, one of Bloomington's late-nineteenth-century mansions, which previously had housed a furniture store, was converted into an elegant restaurant that appealed not only to the gourmet diner but also to those who like "the moods of the past" and the thrill of the presence of resident spirits. The back page of the menu of The Porticos gave a brief account of both the history of the building and the stories about current apparitions that the owners had observed and "collected." But the thus-disseminated haunted house stories (sounds of running water, breaking glasses, smoke without a fire, noise of moving furniture, and ball-bouncing children upstairs who call out "Mommy, come and play with us") have no venerable history. Folklorists traced the fate of the building, from owner to owner — resident families, business entrepreneurs, and a Greek fraternity — without trapping the ghost. Amateur folklorists had more success: a disc jockey slept upstairs on Halloween night and his tape recorder captured the sound of voices; a spiritualist medium transmitted a scripted message of the spirit children. Talking to waiters and waitresses, the same stories were repeated.

This haunted house is indeed an invented legend that discontinued with the closing of The Porticos restaurant. Although the stories are traditional, well known, and related to the numerous genuine haunted houses of Indiana, they could not persist in that particular building after their promoters (or inventors) had abandoned it.

9. This text is taken from a letter by Maggie Birge, whose husband Jerry worked for *The Herald*, Jasper's daily paper. After Nellie's death, local reporters took an interest in spreading the ghost story, which had been told by first-hand believers to both second-hand believers and skeptics.

As Ms. Birge notes, the quoted informants were not scared of the ghost, a woman they'd known well before her death; she was a strange character in life, but harmless, and they were absolutely convinced that they saw her — not on a dark, hazy, or foggy night but in broad daylight. They were reluctant to come out into the open, because "when they had told their stories to people close to them, there was a lot of disbelief and ridicule." It is little wonder that the original experiencers did not want to be identified by name.

As the story spread throughout the county, second- and third-hand versions took the shape of rumors stressing the controversiality of the legend. Jerry Birge's article "Celestine Ghost Has Skeptics, Believers" (*The Herald*, October 31, 1980) stresses the controversy aspect, predicting that "the sightings of 'The Ghost of Celestine' may eventually come to an end but the arguments and disagreements between the skeptics and believers will continue for many months to come."

## 6. Texts, Contextualized and Processed

1. *Webster's Third New International Dictionary of the English Language* (Merriam Co.), and the *Encyclopedia Britannica*, vol. 3 (Philippines Co.), 1971.

2. According to the *Petit Larousse*, an *acte gratuit* is the only free act "sans aucun motif, dont totalement libre, selon certains philosophes."

3. Seldom indeed, but it might happen. Mr. Steve Csala, my Indiana Harbor joke-teller, had two jokes in his repertoire that did not make sense. I recorded them repeatedly, twice when only Andrew Vázsonyi and I were present, and several times when he told them to others. Both were risqué jokes, and on one occasion Andrew drew Uncle Steve aside for a "man to man" talk to ask, what was the point of these jokes? Uncle Steve was clearly embarrassed, and when Andrew proposed a solution, he was visibly relieved, and exclaimed cheerfully, "Yeah, yeah, exactly! Finally you got it!" I had the feeling that for him, the topic in itself was funny enough (a comparison of the rabbit's copiousness to that of the husband by his oversexed wife), even with the punchline missing. His standard audience rewarded him with funny comments and laughter, so our dissatisfaction did not really matter.

4. Here I am referring to Roman Jacobson's famous model of the six factors inalienably involved in verbal communication (1960: 353).

5. "The model of the set used as the basis for the mathematical analysis of data means that the data is divided into sets or categories and subcategories on the basis of some classification (types of individuals, types of responses of experimental situations, group membership, etc.). Certain logical axioms and propositions about the relationship between sets and subsets are then applied to the observed data and used to test hypotheses about the data." See also "mental set" as "a mental orientation expressing the readiness of an individual to respond in a specified way to his environment . . . on terms of previously learned and organized interests and expectations" (Theodorson and Theodorson 1968).

6. A friend of a friend sent this collection to me, because his grandchildren in Columbus, Ohio, could not read it. They didn't even know what language it was written in!

7. In his *Paradoxe sur le comédien* (written in 1773–1778 and published in 1830), Diderot argued that great actors are insensitive and must remain frivolous puppets.

8. The Aarne-Thompson tale type catalogue is now in the works for revision. In 1998, a committee was formed at the Twelfth Congress of the International Society for Folk Narrative Research in Göttingen, Germany, to launch this long overdue project. Following an intensive period of discussions and exploration of feasibility, the best solution was found. Early in 1999, our hope was realized by Hans-Jörg Uther's proposal for the revision to be undertaken by the scholars publishing the *Enzyklopädie des Märchens*, an independent institution under the aegis of the German Akademie der Wissenschaften. I believe this team of experts under the leadership of Dr. Uther is guaranteed to complete the arduous task, which researchers so urgently need.

9. Attributed to H. Rap Brown.

10. I cannot go into the details of our discussion of ostensive action as means of legend-telling, but this essay clearly defines our position. Since then, Ellis has applied the theory to confirm our sense of danger (Ellis 1989). Fine insightfully defined legend-telling by ostension as translating legend into behavior (1992: 205), and has kindly reminded us that the power of ostension may be benign as well.

11. For my collection of clippings and oral versions I depended on the Indiana Clipping Service and students in my classes at Indiana University and at the University of California at Los Angeles (in 1992), who enjoyed the thrill of search and analysis of constructed prototypes in tabloids.

12. According to Ellis, legends about murder and mutilation "are not just expressions of fictive horror, they are paradigms for making the world more horrifying" (Ellis 1989: 219).

# Bibliography

Aarne, Antti, and Stith Thompson. 1962. *The Types of the Folktale.* Folklore Fellows Communications 184. Helsinki: Academia Scientiarum Fennica.

Abrahams, Roger D. 1976. Genre Theory and Folkloristics. *Studia Fennica* 20: 13–19.

———. 1992. The Past in the Presence: An Overview of Folkloristics in the Late 20th Century. In *Folklore Processed, in Honor of Lauri Honko,* ed. Reimund Kvideland, pp. 32–51. Helsinki: Academia Scientiarum Fennica.

———. 1993. Phantoms of Romantic Nationalism in Folkloristics. *Journal of American Folklore* 106: 3–37.

Abrahamson, David. 1970. *Our Violent Society.* New York: Funk & Wagnalls.

Adams, Linda Kinsey. 1998. "The Interrelationship of Myth and Legend in a Mexican-American Community in Chicago: The 'La Llorona' Legend as an Inversion of the Adam and Eve Sacred Narrative." Ph.D. dissertation, Indiana University.

Allport, G. W., and L. J. Postman. 1947. An Analysis of Rumor. *Public Opinion Quarterly* 10: 501–517.

Alver, Brynjulf. 1967. Category and Function. *Fabula* 9: 63–69.

Ames, Louis Bates. 1966. *Children's Stories.* Gesell Institute of Child Development, Genetic Psychology Monographs 73.

Anderson, Susan M. 1978. City Plans to Raze Famed "House of Blue Lights." *Indianapolis Star,* August 30, p. 6.

Anderson, Walter. 1923. *Kaiser und Abt: Die Geschichte eines Schwanks.* Folklore Fellows Communications 42. Helsinki: Academia Scientiarum Fennica.

———. 1935. *Zu Albert Wesselski's Angriffen auf die finnische folkloristische Forschungsmethode.* Tartu.

———. 1951. *Ein volkskundliches Experiment.* Folklore Fellows Communications 141. Helsinki: Academia Scientiarum Fennica.

———. 1956. *Eine neue Arbeit zur experimentelle Volkskunde.* Folklore Fellows Communications 168. Helsinki: Academia Scientiarum Fennica.

———. 1960. Volkserzählungen in Tageszeitungen und Wochenblättern. In *Humaniora: Essays in Literature, Folklore, Bibliography,* ed. Wayland D. Hand and Gustave O. Arlt, pp. 58–68. New York: J. J. Augustin.

Anson, Jay. 1977. *The Amityville Horror.* Englewood Cliffs, N.J.: Prentice-Hall.

Apo, Satu. 1986. Questions Arising in the Comparative Study of Magic Tales. *Journal of Folklore Research* 23 (2/3): 177–186.

———. 1995. *The Narrative World of Finnish Fairy Tales.* Folklore Fellows Communications 256. Helsinki: Academia Scientiarum Fennica.

Applebee, Arthur N. 1978. *The Child's Concept of Story Ages Two to Seventeen.* Chicago: University of Chicago Press.

Arora, Shirley. 1987. Memorate as Metaphor: Some Mexican Treasure Narratives and Their Narrators. In *Perspectives on Contemporary Legend II,* ed. Gillian Bennett, Paul Smith, and J. D. A. Widdowson, pp. 79–92. Sheffield: Sheffield Academic Press.

Asadowskij, Mark. 1926. *Eine sibirische Märchenerzählerin.* Folklore Fellows Communications 168. Helsinki: Academia Scientiarum Fennica.

Assion, Peter. 1975. Zur Kritik einer parapsychologischen Volkskunde. *Zeitschrift für Volkskunde* 71: 161–180.

———. 1976. *Legitimierte Irrationalität — Zur popularisierten Parapsychologie.* DGV Informationen Münster, 38–39.

Baker, Ronald L. 1969. The Face in the Wall. *Indiana Folklore* 2(2): 29–46.

———. 1970. Legends about Spook Hill. *Indiana Folklore* 3(2): 163–189.

Balassa, Iván. 1963. *Karcsai Mondák.* Budapest: Akadémiai Kiadó.

Baron, Robert and Nicholas R. Spitzer, eds. 1992. *Public Folklore.* Washington, D.C.: Smithsonian Institution Press.

Barth, Edna. 1981. *Witches, Pumpkins and Grinning Ghosts.* New York: Clarion Books.

Bartholomew, Robert E. 1998. The Martian Panic Sixty Years Later: What Have We Learned? *Skeptical Inquirer* 22(6): 40–43.

Bartlett, F. C. 1920. Some Experiments on the Reproduction of Folk Stories. *Folklore* 21: 30–47. Reprinted in *The Study of Folklore* by A. Dundes, pp. 247–258. Englewood Cliffs, N.J.: Prentice-Hall, 1965.

———. 1932. *Remembering.* Cambridge: Cambridge University Press.

Bauer, Eberhard, and Walter von Lucadou. 1983. *Spektrum der Parapsychologie.* Freiburg im Breisgau: Aurum-Verlag.

Baughman, Ernest W. 1966. *Type and Motif Index of the Folktales of England and North America.* Indiana University Folklore Series, no. 20. The Hague: Mouton.

Bauman, Richard. 1980. The Ethnography of Speaking in Folk Narrative Research. *ARV: Scandinavian Yearbook of Folklore* 36: 39–41.

———. 1983. The Field Study of Folklore in Context. In *The Handbook of American Folklore,* ed. Richard M. Dorson, pp. 362–368. Bloomington: Indiana University Press.

———. 1989a. American Folklore Studies and Social Transformation: A Performance-Centered Perspective. *Text and Performance Quarterly* 9(3): 175–184.

———. 1989b. Folklore. In *International Encyclopedia of Communications,* vol. 1, ed. Erik Barnouw, pp. 177–181. New York: Oxford University Press.

———. 1992a. Genre. In *Folklore, Cultural Performances, and Popular Entertainments: A Communications Centered Handbook,* ed. Richard Bauman, pp. 53–59. Oxford: Oxford University Press.

———. 1992b. Performance. In *Folklore, Cultural Performances, and Popular Entertainments: A Communications Centered Handbook,* ed. Richard Bauman, pp. 41–49. Oxford: Oxford University Press.

Bausinger, Hermann. 1958. Strukturen des alltäglichen Erzählens. *Fabula* 1: 239–254.

———. 1961. *Volkskultur in der technischen Welt.* Stuttgart: W. Kohlhammer.

———. 1967. Bemerkungen zum Schwank und seinen Formtypen. *Fabula* 9: 118–136.

———. 1968. *Formen der "Volkspoesie."* Berlin: Erich Schmidt Verlag.

———. 1969. Folklorismus in Europa: Eine Umfrage. *Zeitschrift für Volkskunde* 65: 1–8.

———. 1980. *Formen der "Volkspoesie."* Berlin: Erich Schmidt Verlag. (Revised and expanded edition of Bausinger 1968.)

———. 1985. Einfache Formen. In *Enzyklopädie des Märchens*, ed. Kurt Ranke, pp. 1211–1226. Berlin: Walter de Gruyter.

———. 1992. Tradition und Modernisierung. In *Tradition and Modernisation: Plenary Papers Read at the 4th International Congress of the Société Internationale d'Ethnologie et de Folklore*, ed. Reimund Kvideland, pp. 9–11. Turku: NIF Publications 25.

Bausinger, Hermann, and Wolfgang Brückner, eds. 1969. *Kontinuität? Geschichtlichkeit und Dauer als volkskundliches Problem*. Berlin: Erich Schmidt.

Bellah, Robert N. 1970. *Beyond Belief. Essays in Religion in a Post-Traditional World*. Berkeley: University of California Press.

Ben-Amos, Dan. 1969. Analytical Categories and Ethnic Genres. *Genre* 2: 275–301.

———. 1971. Toward a Definition of Folklore in Context. *Journal of American Folklore* 84: 3–15.

———. 1976. *Folklore Genres*. Austin: University of Texas Press.

———. 1992. *Do We Need Ideal Types (in Folklore)? An Address to Lauri Honko*. NIF Papers 2.

Bender, Hans. 1976. *Parapsychologie: Ihre Ergebnisse und Probleme*. Darmstadt: Fischer Taschenbuch.

———. 1977. *Telepathie, Hellsehen und Psychokinese*, 4th edition. Aufsätze zur Parapsychologie R. Pieper et co.: München.

———. 1984. Spuk — Täuschungen und Tatsachen. In *Psi — was verbirgt sich dahinter?*, ed. Eberhard Bauer and Walter von Lucadou. Freiburg in Breisgau: Herder, Freiburg.

Bendix, Regina. 1987. Marmot, Memet, and Marmoset: Further Research on the Folklore of Dyads. *Western Folklore* 46: 171–191.

———. 1988. The Challenge of a Concept. *International Folklore Review* 6: 5–15.

———. 1989. Tourism and Cultural Displays: Inventing Traditions for Whom? *Journal of American Folklore* 102(404): 131–146.

———. 1997. *In Search of Authenticity: The Formation of Folklore Studies*. Madison: University of Wisconsin Press.

Bennett, Gillian. 1984. The Phantom Hitchhiker: Neither Modern, Urban nor Legend. In *Perspectives on Contemporary Legend*, ed. Paul Smith, pp. 45–63. Sheffield: CECTAL.

———. 1985. What's "Modern" about the Modern Legend? *Fabula* 26: 219–229.

———. 1988. Problems in Collecting and Classifying Urban Legends: A Personal Experience. In *Monsters with Iron Teeth: Perspectives on Contemporary Legend III*, ed. Gillian Bennett, Paul Smith, and J. D. A. Widdowson, pp. 15–30. Sheffield: Sheffield Academic Press.

———. 1988. Legend: Performance and Truth. In *Monsters with Iron Teeth: Perspectives on Contemporary Legend III*, ed. Gillian Bennett and Paul Smith, pp. 13–36. Sheffield: Sheffield Academic Press.

———. 1989a. "Belief Stories": The Forgotten Genre. *Western Folklore* 48: 289–311.

———. 1989b. Playful Chaos: Anatomy of a Storytelling Session. In *The Questing Beast: Perspectives on Contemporary Legend IV*, ed. Gillian Bennett and Paul Smith, pp. 193–211. Sheffield: Sheffield Academic Press.

———. 1991a. Contemporary Legend: An Insider's View. *Folklore* 102: 187–191.

———. 1991b. Sex and Cannibalism in the Service of Satan: A Checklist of Articles about Satanic Abuse in the British Quality Press. February 1989 to October 1990. *Dear Mr. Thoms* 20: 36–44.

Bennett, Gillian, and Anne Rowbottom. 1998. "Born a Lady, Died a Saint": The Deification of Diana in the Press and Popular Opinion in Britain. *Fabula* 39: 197–208.

Bennett, Gillian, and Paul Smith, eds. 1988. *Monsters with Iron Teeth: Perspectives in Contemporary Legend III*. Sheffield: Sheffield Academic Press.

———. 1993. *Contemporary Legend: A Folklore Bibliography*. New York and London: Garland.

Best, Joel. 1990. *Threatened Children: Rhetoric and Concern about Child Victims*. Chicago: University of Chicago Press.

Best, Joel and Gerald T. Horiuchi. 1985. The Razor Blade in the Apple: The Social Construction of Urban Legends. *Social Problems* 32: 488–499.

Bettelheim, Bruno. 1976. *The Uses of Enchantment: The Meaning and Importance of Fairy Tales*. New York: Alfred A. Knopf.

Beutel, M., I. M. Greverus, R. Schanze, E. Speichert, and H. Wahrlich. 1978. *Tourismus: Ein kritisches Bilderbuch*. Bensheim: Päd Extra Buchverlag.

Beyschlag, Siegfried. 1941. Weltbild der Volkssage. *Dichtung und Volkstum* 41: 186–205.

Bihari, Anna. 1980. *A Catalogue of Hungarian Folk Belief Legends*. Budapest: MTA Néprajzi Kutatócsoport.

Bird, Donald Allport. 1979. "Rumor as Folklore: An Interpretation and Inventory." Ph.D. dissertation, Indiana University.

Bird, Donald Allport, and James R. Dow. 1972. Benjamin Kuhn: Life and Narratives of a Hoosier Farmer. *Indiana Folklore* 5(2): 143–263.

Bird, S. Elizabeth. 1994. Playing with Fear: Interpreting the Adolescent Legend Trip. *Western Folklore* 53: 191–210.

Birge, Jerry. 1980. "Celestine Ghost" Has Skeptics, Believers. *The Herald* (Jasper, Ind.), October 31.

Bîrlea, Ovidiu. 1973. Über das sammeln Volkstümlichen Prosaersählgutes in Rumänien. In *Wege der Märchenforschung*, ed. F. Karlinger. Darmstadt: Wissenschaftliche Buchgesellschaft, pp. 445–466.

Blatty, William Peter. 1971. *The Exorcist*. New York: Harper and Row.

Blehr, Otto. 1967. The Analysis of Folk Belief Stories and Its Implications for Research on Folk Belief and Folk Prose. *Fabula* 9: 259–263.

———. 1974. *Folketro og Sagnforskning*. Bergen, Oslo, and Tromsø: Universitetsforlaget.

Bloch, Dorothy. 1978. *"So the Witch Doesn't Eat Me": Fantasy and the Child's Fear of Infanticide*. Boston: Houghton Mifflin.

Bødker, Laurits. 1965. *International Dictionary of Regional European Ethnology and Folklore*, vol. 2. Copenhagen: Rosenkilde and Bagger.

Bolte, Johannes, and Georg Polívka. 1963. *Anmerkungen zu den Kinder und Hausmärchen der Brüder Grimm*, 5 vols. Hildesheim: Georg Olms.

Boratav, Pertev Naili. 1966. Zur Beziehung zwischen Märchen und Sage. *Deutsches Jahrbuch für Volkskunde* 12: 361–365.

Bosiger, Walter. 1986. [Spookhouse To Be Demolished: Whole Village Fears Immured Spirit.] *Blick* (Zürich), October 5.

Bošković-Stulli, Maja. 1966. Beitrag zur Diskussion über die Katalogisierung der Volkssagen. *Fabula* 8: 192–207.

———. 1988. Telling about Life: On Questions of Contemporary Oral Literary Genres. *Narodna Umjetnost*, special issue 2: 11–42.

Boss, Judith. 1991. Is Santa Claus Corrupting Our Children's Morals? *Free Inquiry* 11(4): 24–27.

Boyes, Georgina. 1984. Belief and Disbelief: An Examination of Reactions to the Presentation of Rumor Legends. In *Perspectives on Contemporary Legend*, ed. Paul Smith, pp. 64–78. Sheffield: CECTAL.

Brandes, Stanley. 1980. *Metaphors of Masculinity: Sex and Status in Andalusian Folklore*. Philadelphia: University of Pennsylvania Press.

———. 1998. The Day of the Dead, Halloween, and Mexican National Identity. *Journal of American Folklore* 111: 359–380.

Brednich, Rolf Wilhelm. 1990. *Die Spinne in der Yucca-Palme*. München: C. H. Beck.

———. 1991. *Die Maus im Jumbo-Jet: Neue sagenhafte Geschichten von heute*. München: C. H. Beck.

———. 1993. *Das Huhn mit dem Gipsbein: Neueste sagenhafte Geschichten von heute*. München: C. H. Beck.

———. 1996. *Die Ratte am Strohhalm: Allerneueste sagenhafte Geschichten von heute*. München: C. H. Beck.

Briggs, Charles L., and Richard Bauman. 1992. Genre, Intertextuality, and Social Power. *Journal of Linguistic Anthropology* 2: 131–172.

Briggs, Katharine M. 1971. *A Dictionary of British Folk-Tales*. Part B, 2 vols. Bloomington: Indiana University Press.

Brinkmann, O. 1933. *Das Erzählen in einer Dorfgemeinschaft*. Münster: Aschendorff.

Brittle, Gerald. 1980. *The Demonologist*. New York: Berkley Books.

Bronner, Simon. 1990. *Piled Higher and Deeper: The Folklore of Campus Life*. Little Rock: August House.

Brown, Lee. 1989. "Debunking the Mutilated Boy. A Study of Newspaper Editors and an Inflammatory Rumor." Paper presented to the Newspaper Division, convention of the Association for Education in Journalism and Mass Communication, Washington, D.C. (unpublished manuscript).

Browne, Ray B. 1958. *Popular Beliefs and Practices from Alabama*. Folklore Studies 9. Berkeley: University of California Press.

Bruford, Alan, and D. A. MacDonald, eds. 1994. *Scottish Traditional Tales*. Edinburgh: Polygon.

Brunold-Bigler, Ursula, and Hermann Bausinger, eds. 1995. *Hören, Sagen, Lesen, Lernen. Bausteine zu eine Geschichte der Kommunikativen Kultur*. Festschrift für Rudolf Schenda zum 65 Geburtstag, Berlin/New York: Peter Lang.

Brunvand, Jan Harold. 1963. A Classification for Shaggy Dog Stories. *Journal of American Folklore* 76: 42–68.

———. 1981. *The Vanishing Hitchhiker*. New York: Norton.

———. 1984. *The Choking Doberman*. New York: Norton.

———. 1986. *The Mexican Pet*. New York: Norton.

———. 1987. The Tale of "AIDS Mary" Is (Surely?) Apocryphal. *The Herald-Telephone* (Bloomington, Ind.), March 12, p. C6.

———. 1988. Classic Chain Letter Promotes Love, Adds a Threat. *Sunday Herald-Times* (Bloomington, Ind.), December 18, p. E2.

———. 1990. Some News from the Miscellaneous Legend Files. *Western Folklore* 49: 111–120.

———. 1993. *The Baby Train*. New York: Norton.

———. 1994. *The Big Book of Urban Legends: Adapted from the Works of Jan Harold*

*Brunvand,* ed. Robert Loren Fleming and Robert F. Boyd, Jr. New York: Paradox Press.

———. 1999. "Urban Legends. Introduction." *Skeptical Inquirer* 23, no. 3: 29.

Buch Moses. 1979. *Das sechste und siebente Buch Moses. Einleitung und Bildkommentare by Wolfgang Bauer.* Berlin: Karin Kramer Verlag (reprint).

Buchan, David. 1981. The Modern Legend. In *Language, Culture and Tradition: Papers on Language and Folklore presented at the Annual Conference of the British Sociological Association, April 1978,* ed. A. E. Green and J. D. A. Widdowson, pp. 1–15. Sheffield: CECTAL.

Bullard, Thomas E. 1982. "Mysteries in the Eye of the Beholder: UFOs and Their Correlates as a Folkloric Theme Past and Present." Ph.D. dissertation, Indiana University.

Burkhardt, Heinrich. 1951. *Zur Psychologie der Erlebnissage.* Zürich: Foreign Dissertation.

Calkins, Carolyn. 1989. "The True Legend of Devil's Hollow." Indiana University, Bloomington (unpublished manuscript).

Campbell, John Francis. 1860–1862. *Popular Tales of the West Highlands. Orally collected,* 4 vols. Edinburgh: Edmonston and Douglas.

Campion-Vincent, Véronique. 1988. Les légendes urbaines: Rumeurs du quotidien, objet d'étude pluridisciplinaire. *Cahiers de littérature orale* 24: 75–91.

———. 1989. Complots et avertissements: Légendes urbaines dans la ville. *Revue française de sociologie* 30: 91–105.

———. 1990. The Baby-Parts Story: A New Latin American Legend. *Western Folklore* 49: 9–25.

———. 1993. Demonologies in Contemporary Legends and Panics: Satanism and Baby-Parts Stories. *Fabula* 34: 238–251.

———. 1997. Organ Theft Narratives. *Western Folklore* 56 (winter): 1–37.

Campion-Vincent, Véronique, and Bruno Renard. 1992. *Légendes Urbaines: Rumeurs d'aujord hui.* Paris: Éditions Payot.

Carey, George. 1971. Some Thoughts on the Modern Legend. *Journal of the Folklore Society of Greater Washington* 2: 3–10.

Carpenter, Inta Gale, and Richardas Vidutis, eds. 1984. Culture, Tradition, Identity Conference March 26–28, 1984. *Journal of Folklore Research* 21(2/3), special issue.

Carrington, Hereward, and Fodor Nandor. 1953. *The Story of the Poltergeist Down in Centuries.* London: Rider.

Caughey, John L. 1984. *Imaginary Social Worlds: A Cultural Approach.* Lincoln: University of Nebraska Press.

Cawelti, John G. 1976. *Adventure, Mystery, and Romance: Formula Stories as Art and Popular Culture.* Chicago: University of Chicago Press.

Christiansen, Reidar Th. 1958. *The Migratory Legends.* Folklore Fellows Communications 175. Helsinki: Suomalainen Tiedeakatemia.

Church, Francis. 1896. Yes Virginia, There Is a Santa Claus. *New York Sun.*

Church, George J. 1982. Copycats Are on the Prowl — Emulators of the Tylenol Killer Made This Halloween Truly Scary. *Time,* November 8.

Čistov, K. V. 1967. Das Problem der Kategorien mündlicher Volksprosa nicht-märchenhaften Charakters. *Fabula* 9: 27–40.

Clements, William. 1969a. The Chain. *Indiana Folklore* 11(1): 90–96.

———. 1969b. The Walking Coffin. *Indiana Folklore* 2(2): 3–10.

———. 1973. Unintentional Substitution in Folklore Transmission: A Devolutionary Instance. *New York Folklore Quarterly* 29: 243–253.

Clements, William, and William E. Lightfoot. 1972. The Legend of Stepp Cemetery. *Indiana Folklore* 5(1): 92–141.

Cochrane, Timothy. 1987. The Concept of Ecotypes in American Folklore. *Journal of Folklore Research* 24(1): 33–55.

Cockrum, Col. William Monroe. 1907. *Pioneer History of Indiana, including Stories, Incidents and Customs of the Early Settlers*. Oakland City: Press of Oakland City Journal.

Cohn, Shari A. 1994. A Survey on Scottish Second Sight. *Journal of the Society for Psychical Research*.

———. 1998. Second Sight: Fact or Fiction? *EDIT: The University of Edinburgh Magazine* 14: 28–31.

———. 1999a. A Questionnaire Study on Second Sight Experiences. *Journal of the Society for Psychical Research* 63: 129–157.

———. 1999b. A Historical Review of Second Sight: The Collectors, Their Accounts and Ideas. *Scottish Studies* 33: 146–183.

Cord, Xenia E. 1969. Department Store Snakes. *Indiana Folklore* 2(1): 110–114.

Corliss, Richard. 1999. The X Phones. *Time*, August 9, pp. 64–65.

Cox, Bill G. 1990. Satan's Disciples Demanded Human Sacrifices! In *Cult Killers: Their Secret Rituals Always End in Death*, ed. Rose G. Mandelsberg, pp. 406–438. New York: Windsor.

Curran, Robert, with Jack Smurl, Janet Smurl, Ed Warren, and Lorraine Warren. 1988. *The Haunted: One Family's Nightmare*. New York: St. Martin's Press.

Crowley, Aleister. 1929. *Magick: In Theory and Practice*. New York: Dover, 1976.

Czubala, Dionizjusz. 1993. *Współczesne legendy miejskie*. Katowice: Uniwersytet Slaski, pp. 1–35.

Dale, Rodney. 1978. *The Tumour in the Whale: An Hilarious Collection of Apocryphal Anecdotes*. London: W. H. Allen, Universal Books.

Davies, Christie. 1990. "Nasty" Legends, "Sick" Humour and Ethnic Jokes about Stupidity. In *A Nest of Vipers: Perspectives on Contemporary Legend V*, ed. Gillian Bennett and Paul Smith, pp. 49–68. Sheffield: Sheffield Academic Press.

Daxelmüller, Christoph. 1979. Dämonologie. *Enzyklopädie des Märchens* 3(1): 283–259.

Dégh, Linda. 1963. A Systematic Ordering of the Hungarian Legends. In *Tagung der "International Society for Folk-Narrative Research" in Antwerp*, pp. 66–74. Antwerp: Centrum voor Studie en Documentatie.

———. 1965a. *Folktales of Hungary*. Chicago: University of Chicago Press.

———. 1965b. Processes of Legend Formation. *Laographia* 23: 77–87.

———. 1968a. The Negro in the Concrete. *Indiana Folklore* 1(1): 61–67.

———. 1968b. The Runaway Grandmother. *Indiana Folklore* 1: 68–77.

———. 1969a. The Haunted Bridges near Avon and Danville and Their Role in Legend Formation. *Indiana Folklore* 2(1): 54–89.

———. 1969b. The House of Blue Lights Revisited. *Indiana Folklore* 2(2): 11–28.

———. 1969c. The Roommate's Death and Other Related Dormitory Stories from Indiana. *Indiana Folklore* 2(2): 55–74.

———. 1969d. Two Old World Narrators in Urban Setting. In *Kontakte und Grenzen*, pp. 71–86. Göttingen: Schwartz. Reprinted in *Women's Folklore, Women's Culture*, ed. R. Jordan and S. Kalcik, pp. 3–25. Philadelphia: University of Pennsylvania Press, 1985.

———. 1971. The "Belief Legend" in Modern Society. In *American Folk Legend: A Symposium*, ed. Wayland D. Hand, pp. 55–68. Berkeley: University of California Press.

———. 1972. Folk Narrative. In *Folklore and Folklife*, ed. Richard M. Dorson, pp. 53–84. Chicago: University of Chicago Press.

———. 1975. *People in the Tobacco Belt: Four Lives*. Ottawa: National Museum of Man. Reprint New York: Arno Press, 1980.

———. 1976. Symbiosis of Joke and Legend: A Case of Conversational Folklore. In *Folklore Today: A Festschrift for Richard M. Dorson*, ed. Linda Dégh, Henry Glassie, and Felix J. Oinas, pp. 101–122. Bloomington: Research Center for Language and Semiotic Studies.

———. 1977a. Biologie des Erzählguts. In *Enzyklopädie des Märchens*, pp. 386–406. Berlin: Walter de Gruyter.

———. 1977b. UFO's and How Folklorists Should Look at Them. *Fabula* 18(3–4): 242–248.

———. 1983. Erzählen, Erzähler. In *Enzyklopädie des Märchens*, pp. 315–342. Berlin: Walter de Gruyter.

———. 1985. Der ungarische Müller als Rattenfänger. In *Geschichten und Geschichte: Erzählforschertagung in Hameln, Oktober 1984*, ed. Norbert Humburg, pp. 71–75. Hildesheim: Lax.

———. 1986. The Living Dead and the Living Legend in the Eyes of Bloomington Schoolchildren. *Indiana Folklore and Oral History* 15(2): 127–152.

———. 1989. *Folktales and Society: Story-Telling in a Hungarian Peasant Community*. Rev. ed. Bloomington: Indiana University Press.

———. 1990a. Maybe It Was Somebody . . . Like Acting Like God: A Hitchhiker Memorate from Indiana. *FOAFtale News* 19 (October): 2–4.

———. 1990b. How Storytellers Interpret the Snakeprince Tale. In *The Telling of Stories: Approaches to a Traditional Craft—A Symposium*, ed. Morten Nøjgaard, pp. 47–62. Odense: Odense University Press.

———. 1991. What Is the Legend after All? *Contemporary Legend* 1: 11–38.

———. 1992. The Legend Conduit. In *Creativity and Tradition in Folklore*, ed. Simon J. Bronner, pp. 105–126. Logan: Utah State University Press.

———. 1994a. The Approach to Worldview in Folk Narrative Study. *Western Folklore* 53: 243–252.

———. 1994b. Satanic Child Abuse in a Blue House. *Contemporary Legend* 4: 119–133.

———. 1994c. *American Folklore and the Mass Media*. Bloomington: Indiana University Press.

———. 1995a. *Narratives in Society: A Performer-Centered Study of Narration*. Folklore Fellows Communications 255. Helsinki: Academia Scientiarum Fennica.

———. 1995b. Eine aussergewöhnliche Variante der Sage von der "gestohlenen Grossmutter." In *Medien popularer Kultur. Erzählung, Bild und Objekt in der volkskundlichen. Forschung: Rolf Wilhelm Brednich zum 60. Geburtstag, 1995*, ed. Carola Lipp, pp. 34–47. New York/Frankfurt: Campus.

———. 1996. What Is a Belief Legend? *Folklore* 107: 33–46.

Dégh, Linda, and Andrew Vázsonyi. 1971. Legend and Belief. *Genre* 4(3): 281–304.

———. 1973. *The Dialectics of the Legend*. Folklore Preprint Series 6. Bloomington: Indiana University Folklore Institute.

———. 1974. Memorate and Proto-Memorate. *Journal of American Folklore* 87: 225–239.

———. 1975. Hypothesis of Multi-Conduit Transmission in Folklore. In *Folklore, Performance and Communication*, ed. Dan Ben-Amos and Kenneth S. Goldstein, pp. 207–252. The Hague: Mouton.

———. 1976. Legend and Belief. In *Folklore Genres*, ed. Dan Ben-Amos, pp. 93–123. Austin: University of Texas Press.

———. 1978. The Crack on the Red Goblet, or Truth and Modern Legend. In *Folklore in the Modern World*, ed. Richard M. Dorson, pp. 253–272. The Hague: Mouton.

———. 1979. Magic for Sale: Märchen and Legend in TV Advertising. *Fabula* 20: 47–68.

———. 1983. Does the Word "Dog" Bite? Ostensive Action: A Means of Legend Telling. *Journal of Folklore Research* 20: 5–34.

Dobos, Ilona. 1971. *Tarcal Története a Szóhagyományban*. Budapest: Akadémiai Kiadó.

Dolby, Sandra. 1989. *Literary Folkloristics and the Personal Narrative*. Bloomington: Indiana University Press.

Dorson, Richard M. 1952. *Bloodstoppers and Bearwalkers*. Cambridge, Mass.: Harvard University Press.

———. 1959. *American Folklore*. Chicago: University of Chicago Press.

———. 1968. Defining the Legend. In *Forms upon the Frontier*, ed. Austin Fife, Alta Fife, and Henry Glassie, pp. 163–166. Logan: Utah State University Press.

———. 1981. *Land of the Millrats*. Cambridge, Mass.: Harvard University Press.

Douglas, Sheila. 1987. *The King o the Black Art and Other Folk Tales*. Aberdeen: Aberdeen University Press

Dow, James R., and Hannjost Lixfeld, eds. and trans. 1986. *German Volkskunde: A Decade of Theoretical Confrontation, Debate, and Reorientation (1967–1977)*. Bloomington: Indiana University Press.

Dundes, Alan, ed. 1965. *The Study of Folklore*. Englewood Cliffs, N.J.: Prentice-Hall.

———. 1966. Metafolklore, or Oral Literary Criticism. *The Monist* 50: 505–516.

———. 1969. Thinking Ahead: A Folkloristic Reflection of the Future Orientation in American Worldview. *Anthropological Quarterly* 42: 53–72.

———. 1971. On the Psychology of Legend. In *American Folk Legend: A Symposium*, ed. Wayland D. Hand, pp. 21–36. Berkeley: University of California Press.

———. 1980. *Interpreting Folklore*. Bloomington: Indiana University Press.

———. 1986. The Anthropologist and the Comparative Method in Folklore. *Journal of Folklore Research* 23: 125–146.

———. 1996. Dundes Speaks on Freud, Feminism, and Fieldwork. *Folklore Institute Traditions* 10: 4.

———. 1998. Bloody Mary in the Mirror: A Ritual Reflection of Prepubescent Anxiety. *Western Folklore* 57, nos. 1–2: 119–136.

Dundes, Alan, and Carl R. Pagter. 1975. *Urban Folklore from the Paperwork Empire*. Austin, Texas: American Folklore Society.

Dux, Günter. 1982. *Die Logik der Weltbilder. Sinnstrukturen im Wandel der Geschichte*. Frankfurt a. M. Suhrkamp.

Eco, Umberto. 1979. A *Theory of Semiotics*. Bloomington: Indiana University Press.

Eliason, Eric. 1996. Ouija. In *American Folklore: An Encyclopedia*, ed. J. Brunvand, p. 534. New York/London: Garland.

Ellis, Bill. 1982–83. Legend-Tripping in Ohio: A Behavioral Study. In *Papers in Comparative Studies*, no. 2, ed. Daniel Barnes, Rosemary O. Joyce, and Steven Swann Jones, pp. 61–73. Columbus, Ohio: Center for Comparative Studies in the Humanities.

———. 1983. "De Legendis Urbis": Modern Legends in Ancient Rome. *Journal of American Folklore* 96: 200–208.

———. 1987. Why Are Verbatim Transcripts of Legends Necessary? In *Perspectives on Contemporary Legend II*, ed. Gillian Bennett, Paul Smith, and J. D. A. Widdowson, pp. 31–60. Sheffield: Sheffield Academic Press.

———. 1989. When Is a Legend? An Essay in Legend Morphology. In *The Questing Beast: Perspectives on Contemporary Legend IV*, ed. Gillian Bennett and Paul Smith, pp. 31–53. Sheffield: Sheffield Academic Press.

———. 1989b. Death by Folklore: Ostension, Contemporary Legend, and Murder. *Western Folklore* 48(3): 201–229.

———, ed. 1990a. Contemporary Legends in Emergence. *Western Folklore* 49(1), special issue.

———. 1990b. The Devil-Worshippers at the Prom: Rumor-Panic as Therapeutic Magic. *Western Folklore* 49: 27–49.

———. 1991a. Cattle Mutilation: Contemporary Legends and Contemporary Mythologies. *Contemporary Legend* 1: 39–80.

———. 1991b. Contemporary Legend: Cracks or Breakthroughs. *Folklore* 102: 183–186.

———. 1991c. Contemporary Legend: The Pale Cast of Thought? — An Editorial. *FOAFtale News* 21: 7–8.

———. 1991d. Legend Trips and Satanism: Adolescents' Ostensive Traditions as "Cult" Activity. In *The Satanic Scare*, ed. James T. Richardson, Joel Best, David C. Bromley, pp. 279–296. New York: Aldine and de Gruyter.

———. 1991e. Why "The Hook" Is Not a Contemporary Legend. *Folklore Forum* 24(2): 62–67.

———. 1993. The Highgate Cemetery Vampire Hunt: The Anglo-American Connection in Satanic Cult Lore. *Folklore* 104: 13–39.

———. 1994a. "The Hook" Reconsidered: Problems in Classifying and Interpreting Adolescent Horror Legends. *Folklore* 105: 61–76.

———. 1994b. Speak to the Devil: Ouija Board Rituals among American Adolescents. *Contemporary Legend* 4: 61–90.

———. 1996. Satanic Deja Vu in Northeastern Pennsylvania. *FOAFtale News* 40/41: 4–8.

El-Shamy, Hasan. 1967. "Folkloric Behavior. A Theory for the Study of the Dynamics of Traditional Culture." Ph.D. dissertation, Indiana University, Bloomington.

———. 1976. Behaviorism and the Text. In *Folklore Today: Festschrift for Richard M. Dorson*, ed. L. Dégh, H. Glassie, and F. Oinas, pp. 145–160. Bloomington: Indiana University.

Erixon, Sigurd. 1949. Nyorienteringar inom folklivsforskningen. *Folkliv* 1948–49.

———. 1951a. An Introduction to Folklife Research or Nordic Ethnology. *Folkliv* 1950–51.

———. 1951b. Ethnologie régionale ou folklore. *Laos* 1.

Evans, Charles. 1991. *Teens and Devil Worship*. Lafayette, La.: Huntington House.

Fair, Charles. 1974. *The New Nonsense: The End of the Rational Consensus*. New York: Simon and Schuster.

Faragó, Joseph. 1971. Storytellers with Rich Repertoires. *Acta Ethnographica* 20: 439–443.

Feintuch, Burt, ed. 1995a. Common Ground: Keywords for the Study of Expressive Culture. *Journal of American Folklore* 108, special issue.

———. 1995b. Introduction: Words in Common. *Journal of American Folklore* 108: 391–394.

Festinger, Leon, Henry W. Riecken, and Stanley Schachter. 1956. *When Prophecy Fails: A Social and Psychological Study of a Modern Group That Predicted the Destruction of the World*. Minneapolis: University of Minnesota Press.

Fine, Elizabeth. 1984. *The Folklore Text*. Bloomington: Indiana University Press.

Fine, Gary Alan. 1985. Gerücht. In *Enzyklopädie des Märchens*, ed. Kurt Ranke, pp. 1102–1110. Berlin: Walter de Gruyter.

———. 1987. Welcome to the World of AIDS: Fantasies of Female Revenge. *Western Folklore* 46: 192–197.

———. 1992. *Manufacturing Tales: Sex and Money in Contemporary Legends*. Knoxville: University of Tennessee Press.

Fischer, Helmut. 1978. *Erzählgut der Gegenwart: Mündliche Texte aus dem Siegraum*. Cologne: Rheinland.

———. 1990. Kontinuität oder Transformation: Die mündliche Volksüberlieferung im Zeitalter der Massen-Kultur. *SIEF*: 136–156.

———. 1991. *Der Rattenhund, Sagen der Gegenwart*. Cologne/Bonn: Habelt.

Fish, Lydia M. 1976. Jesus on the Thruway: The Vanishing Hitchhiker Strikes Again. *Indiana Folklore* 9(1): 5–13.

Fix, Ulla. 1994. Moderne Sagen in der DDR. *Fabula* 35: 94–109.

Fohrer, George. 1965. Die Sage in der Bibel. In *Sagen und ihre Deutung*, ed. M. Lüthi, G. Fohrer, and L. Röhrich, pp. 59–80. Göttingen: Vandenhoeck and Ruprecht.

Franklin, Dixie. 1989a. *Haunts of the Upper Great Lakes*. Jarco Holt, Mich.: Thunder Bay Press.

———. 1989b. Heartland Haunts. *Home & Away*, September/October.

Frazier, Kendrick. 1997. World Survives Roswell Hysteria, Aliens Remain Elusive. *Skeptical Inquirer* 21(5): 5–7.

Freedland, Nat. 1972. *The Occult Explosion*. New York: Berkley Medallion.

Frykman, Jonas, and Orvar Löfgren, eds. 1987. *Culture Builders: A Historical Anthropology of Middle-Class Life*. New Brunswick, N.J.: Rutgers University Press.

Fuller, Elizabeth. 1978. *My Search for the Ghost of Flight 401*. New York: Berkley Medallion.

Fuller, John G. 1976. *The Ghost of Flight 401*. New York: Berkley Medallion.

Furlow, Bryant. 1997. Medical School Faith Healing: Report on a Spirituality Conference. *Skeptical Inquirer* (September/October): 49.

Gaál, Károly. 1965. *Angaben zu den abergläubischen Erzählungen aus dem südlichen Burgenland*. Eisenstadt: Burgenländische Landesmuseum.

Gardner, Gerald. 1954. *Witchcraft Today*. New York: Magickal Childe, 1982.

———. 1959. *The Meaning of Witchcraft*. London: Rider.

Gardner, Martin. 1997. Heaven's Gate: The UFO Cult of Bo and Peep. *Skeptical Inquirer* (July/August): 15–17.

Genoni, Thomas C. 1997. Religious Belief among Scientists Stable for Eighty Years. *Skeptical Inquirer* (September/October): 13.

George, Philip Brandt. 1972. The Ghost of Cline Avenue: "La Llorona" in the Calumet Region. *Indiana Folklore* 5(1): 56–91.

Georges, Robert. 1969. Toward an Understanding of Storytelling Events. *Journal of American Folklore* 82: 313–328.

———. 1971. The General Concept of Legend: Some Assumptions to Be Reexamined and Reassessed. In *American Folk Legend: A Symposium*, ed. Wayland D. Hand, pp. 1–20. Berkeley: University of California Press.

———. 1986. The Pervasiveness in Contemporary Folklore Studies of Assumptions, Concepts and Constructs Usually Associated with the Historic-Geographic Method. *Journal of Folklore Research* 23(1/2): 87–103.

Gerndt, Helge. 1983. Zur Frühgeschichte der Sagenforschung. In *Dona Ethnologica Monacensia*, ed. Helge Gerndt, Klaus Roth, and Georg R. Schroubek, pp. 251–266. München: Bayerisches Nationalmuseum, Institut für Deutsche und Vergleichende Volkskunde.

———. 1991. Gedanken zur heutigen Sagenforschung. *Bayerisches Jahrbuch für Volkskunde*, pp. 137–145.

Gilbert, Helen. 1975. The Crack in the Abbey Floor: A Laboratory Analysis of a Legend. *Indiana Folklore* 8: 61–79.

Glassie, Henry. 1984. *Irish Folk History*. Philadelphia: University of Pennsylvania Press.

———. 1995. Tradition. *Journal of American Folklore* 108: 395–412.

Glazer, Mark. 1987. The Cultural Adaptation of a Rumour Legend: The Boyfriend's Death in South Texas. In *Perspectives on Contemporary Legend II*, ed. Gillian Bennett, Paul Smith, and J. D. A. Widdowson, pp. 93–108. Sheffield: Sheffield Academic Press.

Golowin, Sergius. 1964. *Magische Gegenwart*. Bern.

———. 1966. *Berns Stadtgespenster*. Bern und München: Viktoria.

———. 1967. *Götter der Atom-Zeit. Moderne Sagenbildung und Sternenmenschen*. Bern: Francke.

Goodman, Felicitas. 1980. *Anneliese Michel und ihre Dämonen*. Stein Am Rhein, Schweiz: Christiana Verlag.

Goodwin, Joseph P. 1989. *More Man Than You'll Ever Be: Gay Folklore and Acculturation in Middle America*. Bloomington: Indiana University Press.

Goss, Michael. 1984. *The Evidence for the Phantom Hitch-hikers: An Objective Survey of the Phantom Hitch-hiker Phenomenon in All Its Manifestations*. Wellingborough, England: Aquarian Press.

Granberg, Gunnar. 1969. Memorat und Sage, einige methodische Gesichtspunkte. In *Vergleichende Sagenforschung*, ed. Leander Petzoldt, pp. 90–98. Darmstadt: Wissenschaftliche Buchgesellschaft.

Greverus, Ina-Maria. 1965. Thema, Typus und Motiv zur Determination in der Erzählforschung. In IV International Congress for Folk-Narrative Research in Athens, *Laographia* 22: 131–139.

———. 1978. *Kultur und Alltagswelt: Eine Einführung in Fragen der Kulturanthropologie*. München: C. H. Beck.

Grider, Sylvia. 1973. Dormitory Legend-Telling in Progress: Fall 1971–Winter 1973. *Indiana Folklore* 6(1): 1–32.

———. 1976. "The Supernatural Narratives of Children." Ph.D. dissertation, Indiana University, Bloomington.

———. 1984. The Razor Blades in the Apples Syndrome. In *Perspectives on Contemporary Legend*, ed. Paul Smith, pp. 128–140. CECTAL Conference Papers Series, no. 4. Sheffield: University of Sheffield.

Grimm, die Brüder. 1812–1815. *Kinder und Hausmärchen*, 2 vols. Berlin: Realschulbuchhandlung.

———. 1816. *Deutsche Sagen*. Münich: Wilhelm Goldmann.

Grober-Glück, Gerda. 1959. Zur Verbreitung und Deutung des Zweiten Gesichts nach den Sammlungen des Atlas der deutschen Volkskunde. *Zeitschrift für Volkskunde* 55: 227–258.

Gugitz, Gustav. 1952. *Die Sagen und Legenden der Stadt Wien*. Vienna: Brüder Hollinek.

Guinee, William. 1987. Satanism in Yellowood Forest: The Interdependence of Antagonistic Worldviews. *Indiana Folklore and Oral History* 16: 1–30.

Gutowski, John A. 1970. Traditions of the Devil's Hollows: Relationship Between a Place Name and Its Legends. *Indiana Folklore* 3(2): 190–213.

Gwyndaf, Robin. n.d. Memorates, Chronicates and Anecdotes in Action: Some Remarks towards Definition of the Personal Narrative in Context (unpublished manuscript).

———. 1994. The Past in the Present: Folk Beliefs in Welsh Oral Tradition. *Fabula* 35: 226–260.

Haiding, Karl. 1965. *Österreichs Sagenschatz*. Vienna: Verlag Fritz Molden.

Hall, Gary. 1973. The Big Tunnel. *Indiana Folklore* 6: 139–173.

Halpert, Herbert. 1971. Definition and Variation in Folk Legend. In *American Folk Legend: A Symposium*, ed. Wayland D. Hand, pp. 47–54. Berkeley: University of California Press.

Halpert, Herbert, and J. D. A. Widdowson. 1996. *Folktales of Newfoundland*, 2 vols. New York: Garland.

Hand, Wayland D., ed. 1961/1964. Popular Beliefs and Superstitions from North Carolina. In *The Frank C. Brown Collection of North Carolina Folklore*, vols. 6–7. Durham: Duke University Press.

———. 1964. Stabile Funktion und variable dramatis personae in der Volkssage. In *Acta Ethnographica 13 (Tagung der Sagenkommission der International Society for Folk-Narrative Research)*, ed. Gyula Ortutay, pp. 49–54. Budapest: Akadémiai Kiadó.

———. 1965. Status of European and American Legend Study. *Current Anthropology* 6(4): 439–446.

———, ed. 1971. *American Folk Legend: A Symposium*. Berkeley: University of California Press.

Handler, Richard, and Jocelyn Linneken. 1984. Tradition, Genuine or Spurious. *Journal of American Folklore* 97: 273–290.

Handy, Bruce. 1997. Roswell or Bust. A Town Discovers Manna Crashing from Heaven and Becomes the Capital of America's Alien Nation. *Time*, June 23, pp. 62–67.

Hansel, C. E. M. 1966. *ESP: A Scientific Evaluation*. New York: Charles Scribner & Sons.

Harden, John. 1954. *Tar Heel Ghosts*. Chapel Hill: University of North Carolina Press.

Harkort, Fritz. 1966. Volkserzählungstypen und -motive und Vorstellungsberichte. *Fabula* 8: 208–223.

Heilfurth, Gerhard, and Ina-Maria Greverus. 1967. *Bergbau und Bermann in der deutschsprachigen Sagenüberlieferung Mitteleuropas*. Marburg: N. G. Elwert.

Heim, Walter. 1981. Moderne "Straßengeister." *Schweizer Volkskunde* 71: 1–5.

Henssen, Gottfried. 1952. Sammlung und Auswertung volkstümlichen Erzählgutes. *Hessische Blätter für Volkskunde* 43: 5–29.

———. 1954. *Volk erzählt: Münsterländische Sagen, Märchen und Schwänke*. Münster: Aschendorff.

Herdan, G. 1956. *Language as Choice and Chance*. Groningen: P. Noordhoff.

Herranen, Gun. 1984. Aspects of a Blind Storyteller's Repertoire. Auditive Learning: Oral Tradition. In *Le Conte. Pourquoi? Comment? Folktales. How and Why?* ed. Geneviève Calame-Griaule et al. Paris: Centre National de la Recherche et des Enseignements Superieurs (CNS), pp. 511–525.

Hicks, Robert D. 1990. Police Pursuit of Satanic Crime. *Skeptical Inquirer* 14(3): 276–286.

Hiemäe, Mall, and Arvo Krikmann. 1992. On Stability and Variation on Type and Genre Level. In *Folklore Processed: In Honour of Lauri Honko on His 60th Birthday*, pp. 127–140. Studia Fennica Folkloristica 1. Helsinki: Suomalaisen Kirjallisuuden Seura.

Hilferding, A. F. 1873. *Onezhskie byliny* [Onega Epic Songs], 3 vols. St. Petersburg: Academy of Sciences.

Hobbs, Sandy, and David Cornwell. 1990. Vanishing Hitchhiker Survey: A Progress Report. *FOAFtale News* 19: 1–2.

Hobsbawm, Eric, and Terence Ranger, eds. 1983. *The Invention of Tradition*. Cambridge: Cambridge University Press.

Hofer, Tamás. 1984. The Perception of Tradition in European Ethnology. *Journal of Folklore Research* 21(2/3): 133–147.

Hoffman, Bill, and Cathy Burke. 1997. *Heaven's Gate Cult Suicide in San Diego*. New York: HarperCollins.

Hoffman-Krayer, Eduard. 1902. *Die Volkskunde als Wissenschaft*. In Kleine Schriften zur Volkskunde, in Schriften der Schweizerische Gesellschaft für Volkskunde, vol. 30, 1946. Zürich.

Holbek, Bengt. 1987. *Interpretation of Fairy Tales*. Folklore Fellows Communications 239. Helsinki: Academia Scientiarum Fennica.

Holley, Robert W. 1992. I Consider the Existence of God as Unknowable. In *Cosmos, Bios, Theos: Scientists Reflect on Science, God, and the Origins of the Universe, Life, and Homo sapiens*, ed. Henry Margenau and Roy Abraham Varghese, pp. 179–180. LaSalle, Ill.: Open Court.

Holzer, Hans. 1973. *The Witchcraft Report*. New York: Ace Books.

Honko, Lauri. 1962. *Geisterglaube in Ingermanland*. Folklore Fellows Communications 185. Helsinki: Suomalainen Tiedeakatemia.

———. 1965. Memorates and the Study of Folk Beliefs. *Journal of the Folklore Institute* 1(1/2): 5–19.

————. 1968. Genre Analysis in Folkloristics and Comparative Religion. *Temenos* 3: 48–66.

————. 1976. Genre Theory Revisited. *Studia Fennica* 20: 20–25.

————. 1980a. Genre Theory. *ARV* 36: 42–45.

————. 1980b. Empirical Genre Research. In *Congressus Quintus Internationalis Fenno-Ugristarum Turku 20–27. Viii. 1980. Pars IV. Dissertationes symposiorum ad ethnologiam, folklore et mythologiam, archaeologiam et anthropologiam, litteras pertinentium,* ed. O. Ikola, 4 pp. Turku: Suomen Kielen Seura.

————. 1983. Research Traditions in Tradition Research. *Studia Fennica* 27: 13–22.

————. 1984. Empty Texts, Full Meanings. On Transformal Meaning in Folklore. In *The 8th Congress for the International Society for Folk Narrative Research: Papers I,* ed. Reimund Kvideland and Torunn Selberg, pp. 273–282. Bergen, Norway: Forlaget Folkekultur.

————. 1989. Folkloristic Theories of Genre. *Studia Fennica* 33: 13–28.

Honko, Lauri, Chinnappa Gowda, Anneli Honko, and Viveka Rai. 1998. *The Siri Epic as Performed by Gopala Naika. Part II.* Folklore Fellows Communications 265. Helsinki: Academia Scientiatum Fennica.

Hoppál, Mihály. 1969. A magyar lidérc-hiedelemkör szemantikai modellje. *Ethnographia* 80(3): 402–414.

————. 1986. Chain Letters: Contemporary Folklore and the Chain of Tradition. In *Contemporary Folklore and Culture Change,* ed. Irma-Riita Järvinen, pp. 62–80. Finnish Literature Society Editions 431. Helsinki: Suomalaisen Kirjallisuuden Seura.

Hufford, David J. 1982a. *The Terror That Comes in the Night: An Experience-Centered Study of Supernatural Assault Traditions.* Philadelphia: University of Pennsylvania Press.

————. 1982b. Traditions of Disbelief. *New York Folklore Quarterly* 8(3/4): 47–55.

————. 1984. The Comparative Method and the Study of the Empirical Bases of Supernatural Belief (unpublished manuscript).

Hultkrantz, Åke, ed. 1960. *International Dictionary of Regional European Ethnology and Folklore,* vol. 1. Copenhagen: Rosenkilde and Bagger.

Humburg, Norbert, ed. 1985. *Geschichten und Geschichte: Erzählforschertagung in Hameln.* Hildesheim: Lax.

Humes, Edward. 1999. Mean Justice. In *A Town's Terror, A Prosecutor's Power: A Betrayal of Innocence.* New York: Simon and Schuster.

Hyatt, Harry Middleton. 1970. *Hoodoo — Conjuration — Witchcraft — Rootwork.* Quincy, Ill.: Hyatt.

Hymes, Dell. 1972. The Contribution of Folklore to Sociolinguistic Research. In *Toward New Perspectives in Folklore,* ed. Américo Paredes and Richard Bauman, pp. 42–50. Austin: University of Texas Press.

Incollingo, Larry. 1966. Lady in White Is No Ghost. Reporter Can't Find Lady in Black, but, oh, There's Dilly One in White! *The Herald-Telephone* (Bloomington, Ind.), sec. 1, p. 2.

————. 1966. Mystery "Woman in Black" Figures in Incident. Three Youths Charged in Case of Hanged Dogs. *The Herald-Telephone* (Bloomington, Ind.), August 30, p. 1.

————. 1969. Bonds Chapel Tombstone Shrouded by Mystery. *Target,* November 16, pp. 3, 6.

————. 1977. Lovers Beware! Spooks with Hooks Hang around Those Trysting Places. *The Herald-Telephone* (Bloomington, Ind.), September 9.

————. 1979. The Legend of the Logger Dies Hard. *The Herald-Telephone* (Bloomington, Ind.), February 19, pp. 1, 6.

Institoris, Heinrich, and James Sprenger. 1484. *The Malleus Maleficarum of Heinrich Kramer and James Sprenger.* Edited and translated by Montague Summers. Dover, 1971.

Isler, Gotthilf. 1971. *Die Sennenpuppe: Eine Untersuchung über die religiöse Funktion einiger Alpensagen.* Schriften der Schweizerischen Gesellschaft für Volkskunde Band 52. Basel: Verlag G. Krebs.

Jacobs, Melville. 1959. *The Content and Style of an Oral Literature.* Chicago: University of Chicago Press.

————. 1966. A Look Ahead in Oral Literature Research. *Journal of American Folklore* 79: 413–427.

Jakobson, Roman. 1960. Closing Statement. Linguistics and Poetics. In *Style and Language,* ed. Thomas A. Sebeok, pp. 350–377. Cambridge: M.I.T. Press.

Jansen, William Hugh. 1977. Foreword. In *Coffin Hollow and Other Ghost Tales,* by Ruth Ann Musick, pp. ix–xv. Lexington: University of Kentucky Press.

Jaroff, Leon. 1991. "It Happens in the Best Circles." *Time,* September 23.

Jason, Heda. 1971. Concerning the "Historical" and the "Local" Legends and Their Relatives. *Journal of American Folklore* 84: 134–144.

————. 1990. Contemporary Legends: To Be or Not to Be? *Folklore* 101: 221–222.

Jeggle, Utz. 1987. Die Sage und ihre Wahrheit. *Der Deutschunterricht* 6: 37–50.

Jolles, André. 1929. *Einfache Formen.* Tübingen: Max Niemeyer.

Jones, Louis C. 1959. *Things That Go Bump in the Night.* New York: Hill and Wang.

Jones, Michael Owen. 1996. Organizational Folklore. In *American Folklore: An Encyclopedia,* ed. Jan Harold Brunvand, pp. 531–533. New York and London: Garland.

Jordan, Rosan A., and Susan Kalčik. 1985. *Women's Folklore, Women's Culture.* Philadelphia: University of Pennsylvania Press.

Jung, Carl G. 1958. *Flying Saucers: A Modern Myth of Things Seen in the Skies.* New York: Signet, 1969. (Reprint and translation of *Ein moderner Mythus von Dingen, die am Himmel gesehen werden.*)

Kaivola-Bregenhøj, Annikki. 1989. Folklore Narrators. *Studia Fennica* 33: 45–54.

————. 1990. From Dream to Interpretation. *International Folklore Review* 7: 86–96.

————. 1996. *Narrative and Narrating: Variation in Juho Oksanen's Storytelling.* Folklore Fellows Communications 261. Helsinki: Academia Scientiarum Fennica.

Kapferer, Jean-Noël. 1990. *Rumor: Uses, Interpretations, and Images.* New Brunswick, N.J.: Transaction Publishers.

Kapfhammer, Günther. 1984. Sage und Geschichte — Neue Überlegungen zur Erzählforschung am Beispiel der Hamelner Rattenfängersage. In *Geschichten und Geschichte: Erzählforschertagung in Hameln,* ed. Norbert Humburg, pp. 13–18. Hildesheim: Lax.

Katona, Lajos. 1912. *Irodalmi Tanulmányai* [Literary Essays], 2 vols. Budapest: Franklin.

Kelley, Charles Greg. 1991. Three Men, a Baby, and a Boy behind the Curtain: A Tradition in the Making. *Midwestern Folklore* 17(1): 5–13.

———. 1992. Joseph E. Brown Hall: A Case Study of One University Legend. *Contemporary Legend* 2: 137–153.

Kirshenblatt-Gimblett, Barbara. 1983. The Urban Frontier. *Folklore Forum* 16: 175–234.

———. 1988. Mistaken Dichotomies. *Journal of American Folklore* 101(400): 140–155.

Klímová, Dagmar. 1996. Heutige orale Traditionen: Marginalien zur Märchensituation in Böhmen. *Märchenspiegel* 4: 42–45.

Klintberg, Bengt af. 1974. Nordiska Museet, K. U. Questionnaire 199: The Rumours of Our Time. *NIF Newsletter* 4: 10–11.

———. 1985. Legends and Rumors about Spiders and Snakes. *Fabula* 26: 274–287.

———. 1986. *Råttan I Pizzan: Folksägner I Vår Tid*. Stockholm: Norstedts.

———. 1988. "Black Madame, Come Out!" On Schoolchildren and Spirits. *ARV: Scandinavian Yearbook of Folklore* 44: 155–167.

———. 1989. Legends Today. In *Nordic Folklore*, ed. Reimund Kvideland and Henning K. Sehmsdorf, pp. 70–89. Bloomington: Indiana University Press.

———. 1990a. Die doppelte Prophezeiung. In *Dona Folcloristica: Festgabe für Lutz Röhrich zu seiner Emeritierung*, ed. L. Petzoldt and S. Top, pp. 113–125. Beiträge zur Europäischen Ethnologie und Folklore. Reihe A: Texte und Untersuchungen. Frankfurt am Main: Peter Lang.

———. 1990b. *Die Ratte in der Pizza*. Kiel: Wolfgang Butt.

———. 1990c. Do the Legends of Today and Yesterday Belong to the Same Genre? In *Storytelling in Contemporary Societies*, ed. Lutz Röhrich and Sabine Wienker-Piepho, pp. 113–123. Tübingen: Gunter Narr Verlag.

———. 1993. The Types of the Swedish Folk Legend: Report on an Unfinished Catalogue. *ARV* 49: 67–73.

———. 1994. *Den Stulna Njuren: Sägner Och Rykten I Vår Tid*. Stockholm: Norstedts.

Knapp, Mary and Herbert. 1976. *One Potato, Two Potato*. New York: Norton.

Knierim, Volker. 1985. Auto, Fremde, Tod: Automobile und Reisen in zeitgenössischen deutschsprachigen Sensationserzählungen. *Fabula* 26: 230–244.

Krauthamner, Charles. 1996. The Return of the Primitive. *Time*, January 29, p. 82.

Kroeber, A. 1948. *Anthropology*. 2nd ed. New York: Harcourt, Brace.

Künzig, Johannes. 1936. "Typensystem der deutschen Volkssage" (unpublished manuscript).

Kurtz, Paul. 1994. The Growth of Antiscience. *Skeptical Inquirer* 18(3): 255–263.

Kvideland, Reimund. 1990. Storytelling in Modern Society. In *Storytelling in Contemporary Societies*, ed. Lutz Röhrich and Sabine Wienker-Piepho, pp. 15–22. Tübingen: Gunter Narr Verlag.

———, ed. 1992. *Tradition and Modernisation: Plenary Papers Read at the 4th International Congress of the Société Internationale d'Ethnologie et de Folklore*. Turku: NIF Publications, vol. 25.

Laistner, Ludwig. 1879. *Nebelsagan*. Stuttgart: W. Spemann.

———. 1889. Das Rätsel der Sphinx. *Grundzüge einer Mythengeschichte*. Berlin: W. Hertz.

Langlois, Janet L. 1978. "Mary Whales, I Believe in You": Myth and Ritual Subdued. *Indiana Folklore* 11(1): 5–33.

————. 1985. *Belle Gunness: The Lady Bluebeard.* Bloomington: Indiana University Press.

Laurens, Kenneth. 1978. The Incredible True Story That Changed My Life Forever! [Genie in a Bottle]. *The Globe,* June 13, p. 21.

Leach, Maria, ed. 1949. *Funk and Wagnalls Standard Dictionary of Folklore, Mythology and Legend,* 2 vols. New York: Funk and Wagnalls.

Leary, James P. 1973. The Boondocks Monster of Camp Wapehani. *Indiana Folklore* 6(2): 174–190.

Lecocq, J. G. 1973. The Ghost of the Doctor and a Vacant Fraternity House. *Indiana Folklore* 6(2): 191–204.

Legman, Gershon. 1949. Not for Children. In *Love and Death: A Study in Censorship.* New York: Hacker Art Books, 1963. (Reprint of the New York: Breaking Point edition.)

Leonard, Mike. 1990. Demons Trash Indianapolis Home — Believe It or Not. *The Herald-Times* (Bloomington, Ind.), March 2.

Limon, José. 1983. Legendry, Metafolklore, and Performance: A Mexican-American Example. *Western Folklore* 42: 191–208.

Linedecker, Cliff. 1982. War of Witches: Satan's Disciples Killing for Power. *National Examiner,* September 14.

Lixfeld, Hannjost. 1994. *Folklore and Fascism: The Reich Institute for German Volkskunde,* ed. and trans. James R. Dow. Bloomington: Indiana University Press.

Loewith, Karl. 1970. Weber's Interpretation of the Bourgeois-Capitalistic World in Terms of the Guiding Principle of "Rationalisation." In *Max Weber,* ed. Dennis Wrong, pp. 101–122. Englewood Cliffs, N.J.: Prentice-Hall.

Loftus, Elizabeth, and Katherine Ketcham. 1994. *The Myth of Repressed Memory: False Memories and Allegations of Sexual Abuse.* New York: St. Martin's Press.

Luhrmann, T. M. 1989. *Persuasions of the Witch's Craft: Ritual Magic in Contemporary England.* Cambridge, Mass.: Harvard University Press.

Lüthi, Max. 1961. *Volksmärchen und Volkssage.* Bern: Francke.

————. 1970. *Once upon a Time: On the Nature of Fairy Tales.* Bloomington: Indiana University Press.

Lysaght, Patricia. 1986. *The Banshee: The Irish Supernatural Death-Messenger.* Dublin: Glendale Press.

MacDougall, Curtis D. 1983. *Superstition and the Press.* New York: Prometheus Books.

Machač, Alexander. 1972. *Bericht über das geheimnisvolle Kreuz von Eisenberg/Raab.* Vienna: Kreuz Verlag.

Maller, Josef. 1971. *Wunder um Eisenberg. Autentische Pilgerberichte.* Vienna: Maller.

Mandelsberg, Rose G. 1991. *Cult Killers. Their Secret Rituals Always End in Death.* New York: Pinnacle Books.

Margenau, Henry, and Roy Abraham Varghese, eds. 1992. *Cosmos, Bios, Theos: Scientists Reflect on Science, God, and the Origins of the Universe, Life, and Homo sapiens.* LaSalle, Ill.: Open Court.

Marót, Károly. 1940. *Idios et koinoi: Gondolatok Fedics Mihály meséiröl.* Budapest: Egyetemes Philologiai Közlöny.

McCarl, Robert S. 1978. Occupational Folklife: A Theoretical Hypothesis. *Western Folklore* 37: 145–160.

————. 1996. Occupational Folklore. In *American Folklore: An Encyclopedia,* ed. Jan Harold Brunvand, pp. 519–523. New York and London: Garland.

McClendon, Sarah. 1996. Roswell, New Mexico, 1947: America, 1996. In *Mr. President, Mr. President!: My 50 Years of Covering the White House*. Santa Monica, Calif.: General Publishing Group.

———. 1998a. White House Briefed on UFOs. McClendon News Service, March 30. *UFOmind* <http://www.ufomind.com/misc/1998/apr/d02-001.shtml>, page created April 2, 1998.

———. 1998. Pressure Building for Congressional Hearings on UFOs. McClendon News Service, July 1. *UFOmind* <http://www.ufomind.com/misc/1998/jul/d03 001.shtml>, page created July 3, 1998.

McCulloch, Gordon. 1987. Suicidal Sculptors: Scottish Versions of a Migratory Legend. In *Perspectives on Contemporary Legend II*, ed. Gillian Bennett, Paul Smith, and J. D. A. Widdowson, pp. 109–116. Sheffield: Sheffield Academic Press.

McLuhan, Marshall. 1964. *Understanding Media*. New York: Signet Books.

McNeil, William K. 1971. Mrs. F.-Little Joe: The Multiple Personality. *Indiana Folklore* 4(2): 216–245.

Meurger, Michel. 1985. Zur Diskussion des Begriffs "modern legend" am Beispiel der "Airships" von 1896–97. *Fabula* 26: 254–273.

Meves, Christa. 1972. *Wunschtraum und Wirklichkeit: Lernen an Irrwegen und Illusionen*. Freiburg: Herder.

———. 1983. *Erziehen und Erzählen: Über Kinder und Märchen Erweiterte Neuausgabe*. Herstellung: Freiburger Graphische Betriebe.

Miclot, K. J. 1975. *Skiles Test and the House of Blue Lights*. Indianapolis: Kay J. Miclot.

Milligan, Linda. 1988. *The UFO Debate: A Study of a Contemporary Legend*. Ph.D. Ohio State University.

Mischo, Johannes, and Ulrich J. Niemann. 1983. Die Besessenheit der Anneliese Michel (Klingenberg) in interdisziplinärer Sicht. *Zeitschrift für Parapsychologie und Grenzgebiete der Psychologie* 25(3/4): 129–193.

Mitchell, Roger E. 1979. The Press, Rumor, and Legend Formation. *Midwestern Journal of Language and Folklore* 5: 5–61.

Montell, William Lynwood. 1975. *Ghosts along the Cumberland: Deathlore in the Kentucky Foothills*. Knoxville: University of Tennessee Press.

Moore, R. Laurence. 1977. *In Search of White Crows: Spiritualism, Parapsychology, and American Culture*. New York: Oxford University Press.

Morgan, Fred T. 1972. *Ghost Tales of the Uwharries*. Winston-Salem, N.C.: J. F. Blair.

Morgen, Sandra. 1997. Shaping the Constitution of Knowledge — Producing Communities. *Anthropology Newsletter* 38(5): 1, 4–5.

Moser, Hans. 1962. Vom Folklorismus in unserer Zeit. *Zeitschrift fur Volkskunde* 58: 177–209.

Mullarký, Magnús Einarsson. 1968. The House of Blue Lights. *Indiana Folklore* 1(1): 82–91.

Mullen, Patrick B. 1970. Modern Legend and Rumor Theory. *Journal of the Folklore Institute* 9: 95–109.

———. 1971. The Relationship of Legend and Folk Belief. *Journal of American Folklore* 84: 406–413.

Müller, Ingeborg, and Lutz Röhrich. 1967. Der Tod und die Toten. *Deutsches Jahrbuch für Volkskunde* 2: 346–397.

Murray, Margaret A. 1921. *The Witch-Cult in Western Europe*. Oxford: Clarendon.

Musick, Ruth Ann. 1965. *The Telltale Lilac Bush*. Lexington: University of Kentucky Press.

———. 1977. *Coffin Hollow and Other Ghost Tales*. Lexington: University of Kentucky Press.

Narayan, Kirin. 1995. The Practice of Oral Literary Criticism. *Journal of American Folklore* 108: 243–264.

Nathan, Debbie, and Michael Snedeker. 1995. *Satan's Silence: Ritual Abuse and the Making of a Modern American Witch Hunt*. New York: Basic Books.

Naumann, Hans. 1922. *Grundzüge der deutschen Volkskunde*. Leipzig: Quelle and Meyer.

Neat, Timothy. 1996. *The Summer Walkers. Travelling People and Pearl-Fishers in the Highlands of Scotland*. Edinburgh: Canongate Books.

Newall, Venetia J. 1987. The Adaptation of Folklore and Tradition (Folklorismus). *Folklore* 98(ii): 131–151.

Newcomb, Theodore M. 1952. *Social Psychology*. London.

Nickell, Joe. 1997. The Two: A Fantasy-Assessment Biography. *Skeptical Inquirer* (July/August): 18–19.

———. 1999. Incredible Stories: "Fortean Mystery Mongering." *Skeptical Inquirer* 23 (January/February): 53–55.

Nickell, Joe, and John F. Fischer. 1992. The Crop-Circle Phenomenon. An Investigative Report. *Skeptical Inquirer* 16(2): 136–149.

Nicolaisen, W. F. H. 1984. Legends as Narrative Response. In *Perspectives on Contemporary Legend*, ed. Paul Smith, pp. 167–178. Sheffield: CECTAL.

———. 1987. The Linguistic Structure of Legends. In *Perspectives on Contemporary Legend II*, ed. Gillian Bennett, Paul Smith, and J. D. A. Widdowson, pp. 61–76. Sheffield: Sheffield Academic Press.

———. 1988. German Sage and English Legend: Terminology and Conceptual Problems. In *Monsters with Iron Teeth: Perspectives on Contemporary Legend III*, ed. Gillian Bennett and Paul Smith, pp. 79–88. Sheffield: Sheffield Academic Press.

Niles, John. 1989. The Berkeley Contemporary Legend Files. In *The Questing Beast: Perspectives on Contemporary Legend IV*, ed. Gillian Bennett and Paul Smith, pp. 103–111. Sheffield: Sheffield Academic Press.

Opie, Iona, and Peter Opie. 1959. *The Lore and Language of Schoolchildren*. Oxford: Clarendon Press.

Oring, Elliott. 1978. Transmission and Degeneration. *Fabula* 19: 193–210.

———. 1984. Dyadic Traditions. *Journal of Folklore Research* 21(1): 19–28.

———. 1986. *Folk Groups and Folk Genres: An Introduction*. Logan: Utah State University Press.

———. 1990. Legend, Truth and News. *Southern Folklore* 47: 163–177.

Ortner, Sherry B. 1974. Is Female to Male as Nature Is to Culture? In *Woman, Culture, and Society*, eds. Michelle Zimbalist Rosaldo and Louise Lamphere. Stanford: Stanford University Press, pp. 67–88.

Ortutay, Gyula. 1940. *Fedics Mihály meséi. Uj Magyar Népköltési Gyüjtemény 1*. Budapest: Az Egyetemi Magyarságtudományi Intézet kiadása.

———. 1959. Principles of Oral Transmission in Folk Culture. *Acta Ethnographica* 8: 169–189.

———, ed. 1964. Tagung der Sagenkommision der International Society for Folk-Narrative Research. Budapest, 14–16 Oktober 1963. *Acta Ethnographica* 13(1–4).

———. 1966. *Kis Magyar Néprajz*. Budapest: Gondolat.

480

————. 1972. *Hungarian Folklore*. Budapest: Akadémiai Kiadó.

Ostling, Richard N. 1990. No Sympathy for the Devil. A Cardinal Deceives Satanic Influence. *Time* (March 19): 55–56.

Otto, Rudolf. 1958. *The Idea of the Holy: An Inquiry into the Non-rational Factor in the Idea of the Divine and Its Relation to the Rational*. Oxford: Oxford University Press.

Oxreider, Julia Woodbridge. "The Slumber Party Transition into Adolescence." Williamsburg, Va. (unpublished manuscript).

Palmenfelt, Ulf. 1993. On the Understanding of Folk Legends. In *Telling Reality: Folk Studies in Memory of Bengt Holbek*, ed. Michael Chesnutt, pp. 143–168. Copenhagen: NIF Publications.

Panzer, Friedrich. 1905. *Märchen, Sage und Dichtung*. München: Beck.

Paredes, Américo, and Ellen Steckert, eds. 1970. The Urban Experience and Folk Tradition. *Journal of American Folklore* 83(328), special issue.

Peeters, K. C., ed. 1963a. *Tagung der "International Society for Folk-Narrative Research" in Antwerp, September 6–8, 1962*. Antwerp: Centrum voor Studie en Documentatie.

————. 1963b. Theorie et pratique. In *Tagung der "International Society for Folk-Narrative Research" in Antwerp, September 6–8, 1962*, ed. K. C. Peeters, pp. 13–27. Antwerp: Centrum voor Studie en Documentatie.

Pentikäinen, Juha. 1968. Grenzprobleme zwischen Memorat und Sage. *Temenos* 3: 136–167.

————. 1968. *The Nordic Dead-Child Tradition: Nordic Dead Child Beings — A Study in Comparative Religion*. Folklore Fellows Communications 85. Helsinki: Academia Scientiarum Fennica.

————. 1970. Quellenanalytische Probleme der religiösen Überlieferung. *Temenos* 6: 89–118.

————. 1978. *Oral Repertoire and World View. An Anthropological Study of Marina Takalo's Life History*. Folklore Fellows Communications 180. Helsinki: Academia Scientiarum Fennica.

————. 1989. The Structure and the Function of Legend. *Studia Fennica* 33: 176–186.

Perkins, Alden. 1982. *The Santa Claus Book*. Secaucus, N.J.: Lyle Stuart.

Petsch, Robert. 1900. *Formelhafte Schlüsse in Volksmärchen*. Berlin: Weidmann.

Pettit, Thomas, Paul Smith, and Jacqueline Simpson. 1995. Contemporary Legend: The Debate Continues. *Folklore* 106: 96–100.

Petzoldt, Leander. 1989. *Dämonenfurcht und Gottvertrauen*. Zur Geschichte und Erforschung unserer Volkssagen. Darmstadt: Wissenschaftliche Buchgesellschaft.

————. 1990. Phantom Lore. In *Storytelling in Contemporary Societies*, ed. Lutz Röhrich and Sabine Wienker-Piepho, pp. 51–58. ScriptOralia 22. Tübingen: Gunter Narr Verlag.

————. 1999. Folklore Zwischen Globalisierung und Kommerz. *Lares* 65½: 5–18.

Peuckert, Will-Erich. 1965. *Sagen: Geburt und Antwort der mythischen Welt*. Berlin: Erich Schmidt.

Pfander, Margareta. 1986. Please Don't Condemn Us to Hell! *Weekly World News*, October 21.

Phelps, Elizabeth Stewart. 1869. *The Gates Ajar*. New York: HarperCollins, 1997. (First published in Boston by Fields, Osgood.)

Phillips, Phil, and Joan Hake Robie. 1987. *Halloween and Satanism*. Lancaster, Penn.: Starburst Publishers.

Pickard, P. M. 1961. *I Could a Tale Unfold: Violence, Horror and Sensationalism in Stories for Children.* New York: Humanities Press.

Pieper, Joseph. 1963. *Belief and Faith.* New York: Pantheon.

Pinsker, Maria. 1976. *Segen über Eisenberg.* Vienna: Kreuz-Verlag.

Pocius, Gerald. 1995. Art. *Journal of American Folklore* 108: 413–431.

Pomplun, Kurt. 1963. Berlins Alte Sagen. Berlin: Bruno Hessling.

Portnoy, Ethel. 1978. *Broodje Aap: De folklore van de post-industriële samenleving.* Amsterdam: Uitgeverij De Harmonie.

Poulsen, Richard G. 1978. The Ghost Ship: A Legend among Airline Personnel. *Indiana Folklore* 11(1): 63–70.

Preston, Dennis R. 1982. "Ritin" Fowklower Daun 'Rong: Folklorists' Failures in Phonology. *Journal of American Folklore* 95: 304–326.

Prêtre, Marcel G. 1963. *Eine Goldene Tante.* Kerzers, Schweiz: Arnen.

Primiano, Leonard Norman. 1995. Vernacular Religion and the Search for Method in Religious Folklife. *Western Folklore* 54(1): 37–56.

*Progress.* 1955a. Orders of the Day: Children and Young Persons (Harmful Publications) Bill. February 22, pp. 1072–1186.

———. 1955b. Children and Young Persons (Harmful Publications) Bill. March 24, pp. 2298–2419.

———. 1955c. Orders of the Day: Children and Young Persons (Harmful Publications) Bill. March 28, pp. 49–118.

Puckett, Newbell Niles. 1926. *Folk Beliefs of the Southern Negro.* Chapel Hill: University of North Carolina Press.

Purdue University News Service. 1997. News Accounts of UFOs Affect Beliefs, Purdue Researcher Glenn Sparks Finds. *Skeptical Inquirer* 21(5): 8.

Quine, W. V., and J. S. Ulian. 1970. *The Web of Belief.* New York: Random House.

Randle, Kevin D., and Donald R. Schmitt. 1994. *The Truth about the UFO Crash at Roswell.* New York: Avon.

Randolph, Vance. 1947. *Ozark Superstitions.* New York: Columbia University Press.

Ranke, Friedrich. 1925. Grundfragen der Volkssagenforschung. *Niederdeutsche Zeitschrift für Volkskunde* 3: 12–23.

———. 1926a. Sage. In *Deutsche Volkskunde,* ed. John Meier, pp. 193–218. Berlin: Walter de Gruyter.

———. 1926b. Grundsätzliches zur Wiedergabe deutscher Volkssagen. *Niederdeutsche Zeitschrift für Volkskunde* 4: 44–47.

Ranke, Kurt. 1961. Einfache Formen. In *Internationaler Kongress der Volkserzählungsforscher in Kiel und Kopenhagen,* ed. Kurt Ranke, pp. 1–11. Berlin: Walter de Gruyter.

———. 1967. Kategorienprobleme der Volksprosa. *Fabula* 9 (1–3): 4–12.

Ray, Linda McCoy. 1976. The Legend of Bloody Mary's Grave. *Indiana Folklore* 9(2): 175–187.

Redfield, Robert. 1960. *The Little Community: Peasant Society and Culture.* Chicago: University of Chicago Press.

Reich, Wendy. 1971. The Uses of Folklore in Revitalization Movements. *Folklore* 82: 233–244.

Renard, Jean-Bruno. 1991. LSD Tattoo Transfers: Rumor from North America to France. *Folklore Forum* 24(2): 3–26.

———. 1994. Old Contemporary Legends: 19th Century French Folklore Studies Revisited. *FOAFtale News* 32: 1.

———. 1999. Que sais-je? *Rumeurs et légendes urbaines.* Paris: Presses Universitaires de France.

Rhine, Joseph Banks. 1937. *New Frontiers of Mind.* New York: Farrar and Rinehart.

Riemann, Fritz. 1984. *Grundformen der Angst.* Munich: Ernst Reinhardt.

Riesman, David. 1964. *Abundance for What? and Other Essays.* New York: Anchor Books, 1965.

Roberts, Leonard. 1955. *South from Hell-fer-Sartin: Kentucky Mountain Folktales.* Lexington: University of Kentucky Press.

Roemer, Danielle. 1971. Scary Story Legends. *Folklore Annual* 3: 1–15.

Röhrich, Lutz. 1958. Die deutsche Volkssage. *Studium Generale* 11: 664–691.

———. 1966. *Sage.* Stuttgart: J. B. Metzler.

———. 1969a. Die deutsche Volkssage. In *Vergleichende Sagenforschung,* ed. Leander Petzoldt, pp. 217–286. Darmstadt: Wissenschaftliche Buchgesellschaft.

———. 1969b. Das Kontinuitätsproblem bei der Erforschung der Volksprosa. In *Kontinuität? In Geschichtlichkeit und Dauer als volkskundliches Problem,* ed. H. Bausinger and W. Brückner. Berlin: Schmidt, pp. 131–132.

———. 1974. *Märchen und Wirklichkeit.* Wiesbaden: Franz Steiner.

———. 1984. Sage-Märchen-Volksglauben. Kollektive Angst und Ihre Bewältigung. In *Studium Generale der Johannes Gutenberg-Universität,* ed. G. Eifler, O. Saame, and P. Schneider. Mainz: Textgestaltung, Manfred Moser.

———. 1988. The Quest of Meaning in Folk Narrative Research. In *The Brothers Grimm and Folktale,* ed. James M. McGlathery, pp. 1–15. Urbana: University of Illinois Press.

———. 1990. Introduction. In *Storytelling in Contemporary Societies,* ed. Lutz Röhrich and Sabine Wienker-Piepho, pp. 9–13. Tübingen: Gunter Narr Verlag.

———. 1996. Sage und Märchen. *Märchenspiegel* 7(2): 1–4.

Röhrich, Lutz, and Erika Lindig, eds. 1989. *Volksdichtung zwischen Mündlichkeit und Schriftlichkeit.* Tübingen: Gunter Narr Verlag.

Rooth, Anna Birgitta. 1979. *Om Memorat.* Småskriftsserie 16. Uppsala: Ethnologiska Institutionen.

Rosenblatt, Roger. 1997. Ah, Cyberspace! How Do We Want to Live? *Ideas* 5(1): 20–35.

———. 1997. The Year Emotions Ruled. *Time,* December 22: 64–66.

Rosnow, Ralph L., and Gary Alan Fine. 1976. *Rumor and Gossip: The Social Psychology of Hearsay.* New York: Elsevier.

Rothenberg, Jerome. 1969. Total Translation: An Experiment in the Presentation of American Indian Poetry. *Stony Brook* 3/4. Reprinted in *The World of Translation,* ed. George Quasha, pp. 203–222. New York: P.E.N. American Center, 1971.

Rudinger, Joel D. 1976. Folk Ogres of the Firelands: Narrative Variations of a North Central Ohio Community. *Indiana Folklore* 9(1): 41–49.

Rybnikov, P. N. 1861–67. *Songs,* 4 vols. Ed. A. E. Gruzinskii. The Hague: Europe Printing, 1909.

Rumpf, Marianne. 1955. *Ursprung und Entstehung von Warn-und Schreckmärchen.* Folklore Fellows Communications 160. Helsinki: Academia Scientiarum Fennica.

Saler, Benson, Charles A. Ziegler, and Charles B. Moore. 1997. *UFO Crash at Roswell: The Genesis of a Modern Myth.* Washington, D.C.: Smithsonian Institution Press.

Samuelson, Sue. 1981. European and American Adolescent Legends. *ARV* 37: 133–139.

Sanderson, F. Stewart. 1981. The Modern Urban Legend. The Katharine Briggs Lecture, no. 1, delivered November 3, 1981, to the Folklore Society at University College, London. London: The Folklore Society, p. 15.

Santino, Jack. 1999. Editorial. *Journal of American Folklore* 112: 3–5.

Scheible, Johann, and Joseph Ennemoser. 1797. *The Sixth and Seventh Book of Moses.* Kila, Mont.: Kessinger, 1997.

Schenda, Rudolf. 1970. *Volk ohne Buch. Studien zur Serialgeschichte der populären Lesestoffe (1770–1910).* Frankfurt a.M.: Klostermann.

———. 1981. Folkloristik und Sozialgeschichte. In *Erzählung und Erzählforschung im 20. Jahrhundert,* ed. Rolf Kloepfer and Gisela Janetzke-Dillner, pp. 441–448. Stuttgart/Mainz: Kohlhammer Verlag.

———. 1992. Folklore und Massenkultur. In *Tradition and Modernisation,* ed. Reimund Kvideland. Turku: Nordic Institute of Folklore.

Schenda, Rudolf, and Hans ten Doorkaat. 1988. *Sagenerzähler und Sagensammler der Schweiz.* Studien zur Produktion volkstümlicher Geschichte und Geschichten vom 16. bis zum frühen 20. Jarhundert. Stuttgart: Paul Haupt.

Schmëing, Kurt. 1954. *Seher und Seherglaube. Soziologie und Psychologie des Zweiten Gesichts.* Darmstadt: Themis-Verlag.

Schmidt, Friedrich Wilhelm. 1929. Die Volkssage Als Kunstwerk. Eine Untersuchung über Formgesetze der Volkssage. *Niederdeutsche Zeitschrift für Volkskunde* 7: 129–143, 230–244.

Schmidt, Leopold. 1963. *Die Volkserzählung. Märchen. Sage. Legende. Schwank.* Berlin: Erich Schmidt Verlag, pp. 107–112.

———. 1965. Von einer neuen Ära der Sagenforschung. *Österreichische Zeitschrift für Volkskunde* 19: 53–74.

Schneider, Ingo. 1996. Erzählen im Internet: Aspekte kommunikativer Kultur im Zeitalter des Computers. *Fabula* 37: 8–27.

Schneidewind, Gisela. 1960. *Herr und Knecht. Antifeudale Sagen aus Mecklenburg.* Aus der Sammlung Richard Wossidlos. Berlin: Akademie.

Schreiber, Mathias. 1997. Der Diana-Effekt. Magie der Gefühle. Vom Sieg der Emotion über die Vernunft. *Der Spiegel* 39 (September 22): 244–265.

Schwietering, Julius. 1935. Volksmärchen und Volksglaube: Dichtung und Volkstum. In *Neue Folge des Euphorion Zeitschrift für literaturgeschichte* 36: 173–178.

Scot, Reginald. 1584. *The Discoverie of Witchcraft.* New York: Dover, 1989.

Seaman, Barrett. 1988. Good Heavens! An Astrologer Dictating the President's Schedule? *Time,* May 16, pp. 24–25.

Sebold, Hans. 1995. Hexenkinder. Der Mythos der kindlichen Wahrhaftigkeit. *Bayerische Blätter für Volkskunde* 22: 129–143.

Shibutani, Tamotsu. 1966. *Improvised News. A Sociological Study of Rumor.* Indianapolis: Bobbs-Merrill.

Shils, Edward. 1981. *Tradition.* Chicago: University of Chicago Press.

Showalter, Elaine. 1997. *Hystories: Hysterical Epidemics and Modern Culture.* New York: Columbia University Press.

Siegel, Barry. 1992. The Devil & Rupert, Idaho. *Los Angeles Times Magazine,* May 17: 16–22, 42.

Siikala, Anna-Leena. 1990. *Interpreting Oral Narrative.* Folklore Fellows Communications 245. Helsinki: Academia Scientiarum Fennica.

Silberman, Charles. 1978. *Criminal Violence, Criminal Justice.* New York: Random House.

Simonides, Dorota. 1987. Moderne Sagenbildung im polischen Grosstadtmilieu. *Fabula* 28: 269–278.

———. 1990. Contemporary Urban Legends in Poland. In *Storytelling in Contemporary Society*, ed. Lutz Röhrich and Sabine Wienker-Piepho, pp. 45–50. Tübingen: Günter Narr.

Simonsuuri, Lauri. 1961/1987. *Typen und Motivverzeichnis der finnischen mythischen Sagen.* Folklore Fellows Communications 182. Helsinki: Academia Scientiarum Fennica.

———. 1964. Über die Klassifizierung der finnischen Sagentradition. *Acta Ethnographica* 13: 19–26.

Simonsuuri, Lauri, and Pirkko-Liisa Rausmaa. 1968. *Finnische Volkserzählungen.* Berlin: de Gruyter.

Simpson, Jacqueline. 1994. Hecate in the Primrose Wood: The Propagation of a Rumour. *Contemporary Legend* 4: 91–118.

———. 1995. "The Eaten Heart" as Contemporary Legend. *Folklore* 106: 100.

Simtoss, Lynn. 1975. Keeping Tabs on Bo, Peep and Flock. *Los Angeles Times* (December 22): 3–4.

Siporin, Steve. 1994. Halloween Pranks: "Just a Little Inconvenience." In *Halloween and Other Festivals of Death and Life*, ed. Jack Santino. Knoxville: University of Tennessee Press.

Slotkin, Edgar M. 1988. Legend Genre as a Function of Audience. In *Monsters with Iron Teeth: Perspectives in Contemporary Legend III*, ed. Gillian Bennett and Paul Smith, pp. 88–112. Sheffield: Sheffield Academic Press.

Smith, Moira. 1982. "Cars on Rooftops and Tipping Over Outhouses: Symbolic Inversion in Halloween and Legend" (unpublished manuscript, 13 pp.).

Smith, Paul. 1984. On the Receiving End: When Legend Becomes Rumour. In *Perspectives on Contemporary Legend*, pp. 197–215.

———. 1987. Contemporary Legend and the Photocopy Revolution. In *Perspectives on Contemporary Legend, vol. 2*, pp. 177–204.

———. 1995. Contemporary Legends: Prosaic Narratives? *Folklore* 106: 98–99.

Sokolov, Y. M. 1966. *Russian Folklore.* Trans. Catherine Ruth Smith. Hatboro, Penn.: Folklore Associates.

Spamer, Adolf. 1934. *Die Deutsche Volkskunde*, 2 vols. Leipzig and Berlin: Bibliographisches Institut a. g.

Sparks, Glenn G. 1998. Paranormal Depictions in the Media: How Do They Affect What People Believe? *Skeptical Inquirer* 22(4): 35–39.

Spohn, Lawrence. 1997. AIAA Honors Scientist Who Says He Caused Roswell Incident. *Skeptical Inquirer* 21(5): 7.

Stearns, Peter N., and Timothy Hoggerty. 1991. The Role of Fear. Transition in American Emotional Standards for Children 1850–1950. *American Historical Review* 96: 63–94.

Stern, Stephen. 1977. Ethnic Folklore and the Folklore of Ethnicity. *Western Folklore* 36(1): 7–32.

Stevens, Phillips, Jr. 1990. "New" Legends: Some Perspectives from Anthropology. *Western Folklore* 49(1): 121–141.

Stine, Scott Aaron. 1999. The Snuff Film. The Making of an Urban Legend. *Skeptical Inquirer* (May/June): 29–33.

Strobach, Hermann. 1987. Folklore — Folklorepflege-Folklorismus. Jahrbuch für Volkskunde und Kulturgeschichte: 25–40.

———. 1987. ". . . aber wann beginnt der Vorkrieg? Anmerkungen Zum Thema Volkskunde und Faschismus (Vor und um 1933)." In *Volkskunde und Nazionalsozialismus*, ed. Helge Gerndt. München Beiträge zur Volkskunde vol. 7, München, 23–38.

Stukeley, William. 1752. *Memoirs of Sir Isaac Newton's Life by William Stukeley*, ed. A. Hastings White. London: Taylor and Francis, 1936.

Swahn, Jan-Öjvind. 1955. *The Tale of Cupid and Psyche*. Lund: CWK Gleerup.

Sweeney, Margaret. 1967. *Fact, Fiction and Folklore of Southern Indiana*. New York: Vantage Press.

Szalai, Alexander. 1978. *Media Abundance and the Future of Mass Communications*. Unpublished paper presented at the International Media Congress. South Tyrol, Italy.

Szondi, Lipót, Ulrich Moser, and Marvin W. Webb. 1959. *The Szondi Test in Diagnosis, Prognosis, and Treatment*. Philadelphia: Lippincott.

Tangherlini, Timothy R. 1994. *Interpreting Legend: Danish Storytellers and Their Repertoires*. Milman Parry Studies in Oral Tradition. New York and London: Garland.

Tedlock, Dennis. 1977. On the Translation of Style in Oral Narrative. *New Literary History* 8: 507–519.

Theodorson, George A., and Achilles G. Theodorson. 1969. *A Modern Dictionary of Sociology*. New York: Harper and Row.

Thigpen, Kenneth A., Jr. 1972. Adolescent Legends in Brown County: A Survey. *Indiana Folklore* 4(2): 141–215.

Thompson, Stith. 1955. *Narrative Motif Analysis as a Folklore Method*. Folklore Fellows Communications 161. Helsinki: Academia Scientiarum Fennica.

———. 1955–58. *Motif-Index of Folk-Literature*, Rev. ed., 6 vols. Bloomington: Indiana University Press.

Thoms, William. 1846. Folklore. In *The Study of Folklore*, ed. Alan Dundes, pp. 4–6. Englewood Cliffs, N.J.: Prentice-Hall.

Tillhagen, Carl-Herman. 1964. Was ist eine Sage? Eine Definition und ein Vorschlag für ein europäisches Sagensystem. In *Acta Ethnographica* 13 (Tagung der Sagenkommission der International Society for Folk-Narrative Research), ed. Gyula Ortutay, pp. 9–17. Budapest: Akadémiai Kiadó.

Toelken, Barre. 1994. *Ghosts and the Japanese: Cultural Experience in Japanese Death Legends*. Logan: Utah State University Press.

Top, Stefaan. 1990. Modern legends in the Belgian Oral Tradition. *Fabula* 31: 272–278.

Touflexis, Anastasia. 1993. Weird Case, Baby? Uh Huh! *Time*, June 28.

Tribute to Princess Diana. *Time* (commemorative issue), September 15, 1997: 30–77.

Tucker, Elizabeth G. 1977. "Tradition and Creativity in the Storytelling of Pre-Adolescent Girls." Ph.D. dissertation, Indiana University, Bloomington.

———. 1999. Preadolescent Girls' Storytelling. In *Traditional Storytelling Today: An International Sourcebook*, ed. Margaret Read MacDonald, pp. 559–562. Chicago/London: Fitzroy Dearborn Publishers.

Turner, Patricia A. 1987. Church's Fried Chicken and the Klan: A Rhetorical Analysis of Rumor in the Black Community. *Western Folklore* 46: 294–306.

Twitchell, James B. 1985. *An Anatomy of Modern Horror*. New York, Oxford University Press.

Underwood, Peter. 1986. *The Ghost Hunter's Guide*. London, New York: Javelin Books.

Utley, Francis Lee. 1961. Folk Literature: An Operational Definition. *Journal of American Folklore* 74: 193–206.

Vajkai, Aurél. 1947. Az ördöngös molnárlegény. *Ethnographia* 58: 55–69.

Vanden Heuvel, Jon. 1991. *Untapped Sources: America's Newspaper Archives and Histories.* New York: Gannett Foundation Media Center.

Victor, Jeffrey S. 1989. A Rumor-Panic about a Dangerous Satanic Cult in Western New York. *New York Folklore* 15: 23–49.

———. 1990. Satanic Cult Legends as Contemporary Legend. *Western Folklore* 49: 51–81.

———. 1991. The Dynamics of Rumor: Panics about Satanic Cults. In *The Satanism Scare*, ed. James T. Richardson, Joel Best, and David G. Bromley, pp. 221–236. New York: Aldine and de Gruyter.

———. 1993a. *Satanic Panic: Creation of a Contemporary Legend.* Chicago: Open Court.

———. 1993b. The Sociology of Contemporary Legends: A Review of the Use of the Concept by Sociologists. *Contemporary Legend* 3: 63–83.

Virtanen, Leea. 1988. *Varastettu Isoäiti.* Helsinki: Kustannusosakeyhtiö Tammi.

———. 1989. Dream Telling Today. In *Studies in Oral Narrative*, ed. Anna-Leena Siikala, pp. 137–148. Studia Fennica 33. Helsinki: Suomalaisen Kirjallisuuden Seura.

———. 1990. *"That Must Have Been ESP!": An Examination of Psychic Experiences.* Bloomington: Indiana University Press.

———. 1992. Have Ghosts Vanished with Industrialism? In *Folklore Processed, in Honor of Lauri Honko*, ed. Reimund Kvideland, pp. 225–231. Helsinki: Suomalaisen Kirjallisuuden Seura.

Voigt, Vilmos. 1972. *A Folklór Esztétikájához.* Budapest: Kossuth.

———. 1976. Towards a Theory of Theory of Genres in Folklore. In *Folklore Today: A Festschrift for Richard M. Dorson*, ed. Linda Dégh, Henry Glassie, and Felix J. Oinas, pp. 485–496. Bloomington: Research Center for Language and Semiotic Studies.

———. 1990. Modern Storytelling — stricto sensu. In *Storytelling in Contemporary Societies*, ed. Lutz Röhrich and Sabine Wienker-Piepho, pp. 23–32. Tübingen: Gunter Narr Verlag.

von Sydow, Carl Wilhelm. 1934. Kategorien der Prosa-Volksdichtung. In *Volksskundliche Gaben John Meier dargebracht.* Berlin. Reprinted in *Carl Wilhelm von Sydow, Selected Papers on Folklore*, pp. 60–85. Copenhagen: Rosenkilde & Bagger, 1948.

Wachs, Eleanor. 1990. The Mutilated Shopper at the Mall: A Legend of Urban Violence. In *A Nest of Vipers: Perspectives on Contemporary Legend V*, ed. Gillian Bennett and Paul Smith, pp. 143–160. Sheffield: Sheffield Academic Press.

Wagner, Roy. 1981. *The Invention of Culture: Revised and Expanded Edition.* Chicago: University of Chicago Press.

Ward, Donald, trans. and ed. 1981. *The German Legends of the Brothers Grimm*, 2 vols. Philadelphia: Institute for the Study of Human Issues.

———. 1990a. Idionarrating and Social Change. In *Storytelling in Contemporary Societies*, ed. Lutz Röhrich and Sabine Wienker-Piepho, pp. 33–44. Tübingen: Gunter Narr Verlag.

———. 1990b. Supranormale Begegnungen: Memorate und Erlebnissagen aus Kalifornien. In *Dona Folcloristica: Festgabe für Lutz Röhrich zu seiner Emeritierung*, ed.

L. Petzoldt and S. Top, pp. 229–237. Beiträge zur Europäischen Ethnologie und Folklore. Reihe A: Texte und Untersuchungen. Frankfurt am Main: Peter Lang.

———. 1991. On the Genre Morphology of Legendry: Belief Story versus Belief Legend. *Western Folklore* 50: 296–303.

Warner, W. Lloyd. 1953. *American Dreams and Reality*. Chicago: University of Chicago Press.

Warshaver, Gerald E. 1972. "Setting of Boy Scout Camp as Legend Ground" (unpublished manuscript).

Weber, Max. 1905 [1930]. *The Protestant Ethic and the Spirit of Capitalism*. Translated by Talcott Parsons, with a foreword by R. G. Tawney. New York: Scribner.

Weber-Kellerman, Ingeborg. 1955. Berliner Sagenbildung 1952. *Zeitschrift für Volkskunde* 52: 482–488.

Weible, Wayne. 1990. *Miracle at Medjugorje*, 8 pp. Fargo, N.D.: Medjugorje Center.

Weiss, Richard. 1946. *Volkskunde der Schweiz*. Erlenbach-Zürich: Eugen Rentsch Verlag.

Weisser, Herbert. 1968. Zur Entstehung von Sagen in der Gegenwart. In *Volksüberlieferung: Festschrift für Kurt Ranke*, ed. F. Harkort, K. C. Peeters, and R. Wildhaber, pp. 401–414. Göttingen: Schwartz.

Wertham, Frederic. 1954. *Seduction of the Innocent*. London: Museum Press.

Wesselski, Albert. 1931. *Versuch einer Theorie des Märchens*. Reichenberg: Sudetendeutscher Verlag.

———. 1935. Die Formen des volkstümlichen Erzählguts. In *Die deutsche Volkskunde*, vol. I, ed. Adolf Spamer. Leipzig: Bibliographisches Institut, pp. 131–188.

Wickes, Francis G. 1963. *The Inner World of Choice*. New York: Harper and Row.

Widdowson, J. 1971. The Bogeyman. *Folklore* 82: 99–115.

Williams, Noel. 1984. Problems in Defining Contemporary Legends. In *Perspectives on Contemporary Legend*, ed. Paul Smith, pp. 197–228. Sheffield: CECTAL.

Wilson, Sheryl C., and Theodore X. Barber. 1983. The Fantasy-Prone Personality. In *Imagery: Current Theory, Research and Application*, ed. Amnees A. Sheikh. New York: John Wiley and Sons.

Woods, Barbara Allen. 1959. *The Devil in Dog Form: A Partial Type-Index of Devil Legends*. Folklore Studies 11. Berkeley: University of California Press.

Workman, Mark. 1978. "Son of Sam": As Interpreted by Crime Reporters and as Possible Source of Folklore. *Indiana Folklore* 11(2): 151–159.

Wyckoff, Donna. 1993. Why a Legend? Contemporary Legends as Community Ritual. *Contemporary Legend* 3: 1–36.

Zeitlin, Steven J., Amy J. Kotkin, and Holly Cutting Baker. 1982. *A Celebration of American Family Folklore: Tales and Traditions from the Smithsonian Collection*. New York: Pantheon.

Zender, Matthias. 1937. *Sagen und Geschichten aus der Westeifel*. Bonn: Ludwig Röhrscheid, 1966.

# INDEX

*Italicized page numbers refer to illustrations.*

LINDA DÉGH, Distinguished Professor Emerita of Folklore at Indiana University, is a folklorist/ethnologist whose specialty is the analysis of personally observed creative processes of narration in both traditional and modern communities of Europe and North America. Her numerous publications include *Four Lives: People in the Tobacco Belt*; *Folktales and Society* (Indiana University Press); *American Folklore and the Mass Media* (Indiana University Press); and *Narratives in Society*.